World Clean Energy Buyers Guide & Directory 2004 (Book & CD-ROM)

"A Complete Buyers Guide to Clean Energy Products & Services Worldwide"

Published by:
Unisun Technologies (P) Limited
#21, Kamadhenu Annexe, Opp. Taj Residency,
Trinity Circle, M G Road, Bangalore-560 008. India.
Tel: 91-080-25362238, 22282411
Fax: 91-080-22289294
E-mail: unisun@vsnl.com
Web: www.unisun.net

ISBN 81-88234-03-6

Price in India : Rs. 1300.00 (Book & CD)

Price outside India : US $ 80.00 (Book & CD)

Printed at :

W.Q. Judge Press
Bangalore, India

CONTENTS

AFRICA

ASIA

AUSTRALIA

EUROPE

NORTH AMERICA

SOUTH AMERICA

About Us - Unisun Technologies (P) Limited

We are a new company in the field of Clean Sustainable Energy, **UNISUN TECHNOLOGIES (P) LTD.**, a 3-year-old organization put together by professionally qualified people who are in business. We have identified our mission as ***"To Promote Technically and Commercially Viable Products and Services in Clean Sustainable Energy".***

Currently, we are active in the following areas: -

(A) EVENTS: We have organised and conducted two World class events, International Clean Energy Expositions and Seminars in Bangalore, India: -

(i) **Smiles'99** - 27th - 31st October'99 at J.N. Tata Auditorium, Indian Institute of Science, Bangalore

(ii) **Smiles 2000** - 25th - 31st November 2000 at Hotel Ashok, Bangalore.

The events consisted of Exposition, Seminar, Public Events & Personality of the Year Awards, which were judged by an International Jury consisting of our **Patrons,**

Dr. Cesare Silvi, President, International Solar Energy Society (ISES), Italy,

Dr. A. Ramachandran, President, Solar Energy Society of India (SESI), India

Dr. S.C.Bhattacharya, Professor, Asian Institute of Technology (AIT), Bangkok, Thailand.

The events focused on promoting Clean Sustainable Energy Industry. For further information, visit our website on the above events **http://www.smiles2000.net.**

(iii) A third major event, and international exposition of major international players in the Clean Sustainable Energy field, **Clean 2003, 20th - 23rd February 2003**, in Bangalore, in association with Pradeep Deviah & Associates a leading professional group experienced in organising international expos and conferences for specialised industries in the high-technology area.

(B) PUBLICATIONS: We have brought the following publications-

(i) Clean Sustainable Energy World Directory & Buyers' Guide: - World Directory 1999 and World Directory 2000 have already been published.

(ii) The World Clean Energy Buyers Guide & Directory 2001 is currently in your hands. The Directory is marketed worldwide and also has a yellow pages section.

(iii) We take pleasure in announcing the 2nd Edition of the World Clean Energy Buyers Guide & Directory 2001 to be released shortly

(iv) Spinning Sunshine Book - Children's' stories

(v) Sunshine Meals - Solar cooking

(C) INTERNET: We have created the worlds' first Business to Business Portal web site for Clean Sustainable Energy: www.unisun.net . Please visit and register online as a Seller and let us have your feedback.

What is unisun.net?

Unisun.net **is a vertical portal providing complete information on Clean Sustainable Energy and allied industries. It intends to be a neutral, online business encyclopedia for the Sustainable Energy industry around the World.** Unisun.net's **strength lies in its immense data bank. This consequently lays the foundation for a market place wherein buying and selling Sustainable Energy products and services is conducted. Besides this,** unisun.net **also aims at providing intrinsic information on Sustainable Energy & its allied industries to the end users.**

The team at **unisun.net** believes in improving and updating the site constantly. Features are consistently being added to enhance the site as per the requirement of the users, in accordance to the discretion of the management.

Contact Us:
Unisun Technologies (P) Limited
#21, Kamadhenu Annexe, Opp. Taj Residency,
Trinity Circle, M G Road, Bangalore-560 008. India.
Tel: 91-080-25362238, 22282411
Fax: 91-080-22289294
E-mail: unisun@vsnl.com
Web: www.unisun.net

Foreword

It is with great pleasure that we introduce the third edition of our most affordable World Clean Energy Buyers Guide & Directory 2004. The tremendous response received by us to our pioneering, albeit modest, earlier efforts in publishing a comprehensive directory listing manufacturers and service providers in all the different areas of clean sustainable energy, has encouraged us to publish this 4th edition of our directory to serve a wide cross section of users across the spectrum from governmental policy bodies concerned with clean sustainable energy, to manufacturers, suppliers, distributors, funding agencies, traders to actual users at the retail level, and research and development organisations, consultants, universities and students. We are gratified that the need for a comprehensive and yet affordable directory listing all the players in the field of Clean Energy has been attempted to be filled by us.

The need for clean sustainable energy worldwide cannot be over emphasized. This need is even greater in the emerging economies of countries that are struggling to emerge from subsistence levels to catch up with the developed world, without pollution and environmental degradation, to take their rightful place in the world economic order. Conventional energy forms require enormous investments and the use of non-replenishable resources from the earth, which the emerging economies can ill afford. The way out for most emerging economies is to take to clean, sustainable energy forms from the initial stages itself and not to repeat the mistakes made earlier by the developed economies.

Our mission is to promote Technically and Commercially Viable Clean Energy via our products and services, international exhibitions and seminars, our business-to-business web site on the internet, events, and by means of this comprehensive world directory of manufacturers, suppliers, and the trade involved in all forms of clean, sustainable energy. With your active support and encouragement we hope to publish this Directory on an annual ongoing basis.

While every attempt has been made to correctly include all the players in all areas of Clean, Sustainable Energy, worldwide we may have inadvertently overlooked or missed some newer entrants or made some errors. If your organisation's name and details are missing or if they have been incorrectly represented please do write in with your details or corrections which we will include in our next edition which will be brought out in about a month's time.

Editorial Team

World Clean Energy Buyers Guide & Directory 2004

Published by:

Unisun Technologies (P) Limited
#21, Kamadhenu Annexe, Opp. Taj Residency,
Trinity Circle, M G Road, Bangalore-560 008. India.
Tel: 91-080-25362238, 22282411
Fax: 91-080-22289294
E-mail: unisun@vsnl.com
Web: www.unisun.net

The Need for Clean Energy - an Overview

Human development over the centuries has been fueled by Man's discovery of energy in his surroundings and Man's use of this energy to further his growth and development. From the time man first used fire and domesticated cattle and harnessed the power of oxen to the invention of the wheel and the waterwheel, to steam engines to the modern day motor vehicles, Man's need for more and more energy has been insatiable. In spite of the invention and widespread use of electricity to power industry and homes, the use of fossil fuels will continue to be an important part of the overall fuel mix for the production of energy. According to the World Energy Assessment, a report of the United Nations organisations, comprising of the UNDP, the UNDES, and the WEC, one third of the earth's population, or 2 billion people do not have access to electricity. The cooking fire, the world's oldest energy technology, is the most widespread fuel-using technology today.

This over dependence on traditional fuels and technologies, results in energy-linked emissions which pollute and degrade the environment at the local and regional levels and finally at the global level. The local impacts associated with this energy use results in keeping a large proportion of humanity more particularly the women, locked into repeating cycles of poverty, ill-health and deprivation and also results in some 3 million premature deaths per year.

Again as per the World Energy Assessment, energy activities account for about 85 % of anthropogenic emissions of sulphur dioxide, which contributes not only to local air pollution but to regional atmospheric acidification also. Fuel combustion emissions contribute to 78 % of human caused carbon dioxide emissions, which are a major factor in global warming representing an unprecedented threat to the whole of humanity.

With the nature of the economies of the different areas of the Earth, fossil fuel will continue to be a major part of the overall fuel mix. According to UN projections, the fossil resource base is at least 600 times current fossil fuel use. Oil and gas reserves are forecast to last well into the 21st century and coal reserves will last comfortably for centuries to come. Hence scarcity of these fuels will not be the motivation for changes in energy systems worldwide, and petroleum and coal products are expected to supply more than half of energy demand 50 years from now. But if the harmful environmental effects produced by fossil fuels are not countered soon, local and regional pollution will continue and global warming will accelerate causing catastrophic disasters worldwide.

In this bleak scenario, great promise is held out by emerging technologies. However, popular awareness, user-friendliness, commercial viability, affordability of the new technologies, and resultant pressure from the people and governmental policy support will be needed to popularise and encourage widespread development and use of these technologies.

The various ways these new technologies can help are by more efficient use of energy, by increasing energy efficiency, and by harnessing renewable energy including solar, wind, biomass, small hydropower, and geothermal energies. In the short term, advanced nuclear energy technologies as well as advanced fossil fuel technologies, fuel cell technologies in the medium term and in the long term, large scale recapturing and storage of carbon dioxide can be instrumental in removing carbon from the world energy systems and halting global warming.

As overall global energy efficiency is estimated to be 37% more efficient use of energy will yield immediate results. Tremendous potential exists for large gains from increasing energy efficiency at the point of use through more energy efficient vehicles, appliances and buildings. These gains are cost effectively possible, both in the developed countries and to a larger extent in the developing countries provided energy conservation is actively encouraged by effective policy. Harnessing renewable forms of energy are more complicated and capital intensive. However policy initiatives and reduction or elimination of subsidies to fossil energy, can provide a proper stimulation for the renewables market. The needs of 2 billion people, or one third of all humanity, with inadequate access to energy services can be met by localised, decentralised energy solutions including solar and wind power, and biomass systems if governmental policy support initiatives are forthcoming and innovative funding mechanisms are used.

Faster and more visible results can be achieved by advanced nuclear energy technologies if only irrational fears of the people can be properly addressed and public concerns of reactor safety, radiation hazards, and waste disposal can be transparently and adequately satisfied. The use of fuel cells promises to be a major breakthrough and costs can be effectively lowered if research is adequately funded. This is more urgent in developing countries where the new routes can be followed instead of making the same mistakes as the earlier developed countries more so as installed capacity is small and all new investment can be directed to innovative technologies to produce clean energy. Farsighted funding policies would enable developing countries to "leapfrog up the technology curve" and widen access to adequate energy services.

Clearly, long term sustainable development, the health and quality of life, and a prosperous, equitable and environmentally healthy world, requires that energy is produced, distributed and utilised in very different ways in the future. This will be possible with far sighted policy initiatives, and complementary efforts locally, nationally, regionally, and internationally, at all, governmental industrial, local community and individual levels.

Editorial Team

World Clean Energy Buyers Guide & Directory 2004

Published by:

Unisun Technologies (P) Limited
#21, Kamadhenu Annexe, Opp. Taj Residency,
Trinity Circle, M G Road, Bangalore-560 008. India.
Tel: 91-080-25362238, 22282411
Fax: 91-080-22289294
E-mail: unisun@vsnl.com
Web: www.unisun.net

HOW DO I FIND A LISTING?

Classification:

i. The listings have been classified by Continent & Country respectively.

ii. Under each Country the listings have been divided into the categories mentioned below and are indicated by a label accordingly at the beginning of the relevant category in the respective Country;

BUSINESS CATEGORIES

MAIN CATEGORIES

I. Solar Thermal
II. Solar Photvoltaics
III. Wind
IV. Biomass
V. Cogeneration
VI. Hydrogen
VII. Fuel Cells
VIII. Electric Vehicles
IX. Small Hydro
X. Tidal
XI. Geothermal
XII. Waste to Energy
XIII. Energy Efficiency
XIV. Finance / Banking and Funding
XV. Associations
XVI. Government
XVII. Research and Development
XVIII. Universities
XIX. NGO's
XX. Consultants
XXI. Design & Engineering
XXII. Carbon Exchange
XXIII. Hybrid Systems
XXIV. Forests
XXV. Others

SUPPLIER CATEGORIES

A. Batteries/ Inverters/ Tanks
B. Cables/ Wires/
C. Instrumentation
D. Insulation
E. Coatings & Paints
F. Metals
G. Glass
H. Construction Services
I. Others (Suppliers)

Example: To find a listing for Solar Photovoltaic Applications (Lighting, Cells, Films) in United Kingdom

Step I: Go to Continent Europe & find country United Kingdom in the Content.

Step II: In United Kingdom go to the label **SOLAR PHOTOVOLTAIC**

to find the listings which have been arranged alphabetically.

ASSOCIATION

ACTIVE SOLAR THERMAL INDUSTRY GROUP - ASTIG
CONTACT : T P Bokhoven
Rue Abbé Cuypers 3,
1040 Brussels, Belgium
TEL : 32 2 741 24 49
FAX : 32 2 734 79 10
E-MAIL : astig@compuserve.com

ALTERNATIVE TECHNOLOGY ASSOCIATION ATA
PO Box 2001, Lygon Street North,
East Brunswick, Victoria 3057,
Australia
TEL : + 61 3 9388 9311
FAX : + 61 3 9388 9322
E-MAIL : ata@ata.org.au
WEB : http://www.ata.org.au

APERE
Rue Royale 171,
1210 Bruxelles
Belgium
CONTACT : Michel Huart
TEL : + 32 21 218 78 99
FAX : + 32 21 219 21 51
E-MAIL : apere@skynet.be
WEB : http://www.users.
skynet.belapere

ASOCIACIÓN COSTARRICENSE DI ENERGIA SOLAR - ACES
CONTACT : DR SS Nandwani
c/o Departmento de Fisica,
Universidad Nacional, Heredia,
Costa Rica
TEL : + 506 277 3482
FAX : + 506 260 1197
E-MAIL : snandwan@una.acr

AUSTRALIAN AND NEW ZEALAND SOLAR ENERGY SOCIETY
CONTACT : Bill Parker
Solar Progress, Box 322,
Mount Lawley 6929, Australia
TEL : + 61 8 9371 6373
FAX : + 61 8 9471 7945
E-MAIL : renew@iinet.net.au
WEB : http://www.anzses.org

BIOENERGY AUSTRIA
Postfach 208, 1013 Vienna, Austria
TEL : + 43 1 470 12 25
FAX : + 43 1 470 12 25
E-MAIL : info@iec.at
WEB : http://www.bioenergy.at

BRITISH BIOGEN
CONTACT : Nikki Kerrigen
7th Floor, 63-66 Hatton Garden,
London ECIN 8LE, UK
TEL : +44 20 7 831 7223
FAX : +44 20 7 831 7223
E-MAIL : info@britishbiogen.co.uk

CANADIAN SOLAR INDUSTRIES ASSOCIATION - CANSIA
CONTACT : A Pritchard
250-2415 Holly Lane, Ottawa,
Ontario KIV 7P2, Canada
TEL : + 1 613 736 9077
FAX : + 1 613 736 8938
E-MAIL : info@cansia.ca
WEB : http://www.cansia.ca

CANADIAN WIND ENERGY ASSOCIATION
100 3533 31 Street NW, Calgary,
Alberta T2L 2K7, Canada
TEL : + 1 403 289 7713
FAX : + 1 403 282 1238

COGEN EUROPE
CONTACT : Dr Simon Minett
98 Rue Gulledelle, 1200 Brussels,
Belgium
TEL : + 32 2 772 85 90
FAX : + 32 2 772 50 44
E-MAIL : simon.minett@cogen.org

DANISH WIND TURBINE MANUFACTURERS ASSOCIATION
CONTACT ; Soren Krohn
Vester Voldgade 106,
DK-1552 Copenhagen V, Denmark
TEL : + 45 3373 0330
FAX : + 45 3373 0333
E-MAIL : danish@windpower.dk

EUROPEAN BIOMASS ASSOCIATION - AEBIOM
CONTACT : J M Jossart
Place Croix du Sud 2, BP 11,
1348 Louvain la Neuve, Belgium
TEL : + 32 10 473455
FAX : + 32 10 473455
E-MAIL : jossart@ecop.ucl.ac.be

EUROPEAN BIOMASS INDUSTRY ASSOCIATION - EUBIA
CONTACT : Dr. Giuliano Grassi
Square de Meeus 35,
1000 Brussels, Belgium
TEL : + 32 2 5021514
FAX : + 32 2 5022077

EUROPEAN ENERGY-FROM-WASTE COALITION - EEWC
CONTACT : William Seddonb-Brown
146 Boulevard du Soevena,
1160 Brussels, Belgium
TEL : + 32 2 280 19 33
FAX : + 32 2 280 18 83

EUROPEAN PHOTOVOLTAIC INDUSTRY ASSOCIATION - EPIA
CONTACT : Dr Murray Cameron
Avenue Charles-Quint 124,
PO Box 14, 1083 Brussels, Belgium
TEL : + 32 2 465 9162
FAX : + 32 2 46 82430
E-MAIL : epia@epia.org
WEB : http://www.epia.org

EUROPEAN RENEWABLE ENERGY CENTRES AGENCY EEIG-EUREC AGENCY
CONTACT : Karel Derveaux
26 rue du Trône,
3001 Leuven, Belgium
TEL : + 32 2 513 83 10
FAX : + 32 2 502 92 84
E-MAIL : derveaux@eurec.be
WEB : http://www.eurec.be

EUROPEAN SOLAR INDUSTRY FEDERATION - ESIF
CONTACT : Rainer Berkmann
Dieselstr 45, 87437 Kempten,
Germany
TEL : + 49 831 5750070
FAX : + 49 831 5750072
WEB : http://erg.ucd.ie/esif.html

EUROPEAN WIND ENERGY ASSOCIATION
CONTACT : Vicky Pollard
Rue du Trône 26, B-1040 Brussels,
Belgium
TEL : + 32 2 546 1940
FAX : + 32 2 546 1944
E-MAIL : ewea@ewea.org
WEB : http://ewea.org

EUROSOLAR EUROPÄISCHE SONNENENERGIE-VEREINIGUNGEV
CONTACT : Irm Pontenagel
Kaiser-friedrich-straße 11,
53113 Bonn, Germany
TEL : + 49 2 28 362373
FAX : + 49 2 28 361279
E-MAIL : inter-office@eurosolar.org
WEB : http://www.eurosolar.org

GERMAN SOLAR ENERGY INDUSTRIES ASSOCIATION – BSE
CONTACT : Frido Flade
Elisabethstrabe 34,
80796 München, Germany
TEL : + 49 89 27 81 34 24
FAX : + 49 89 27 31 28 91
E-MAIL : info@bse.solarindustries.com
WEB : http://www.bse.solar industries.com

INTERNATIONAL COGENERATION ALLIANCE - ICA
rue Gulledelle 98, 1200 Brussels, Belgium
TEL : + 32 2 772 26 11
FAX : + 32 2 772 25 08
E-MAIL : ica@localpower.org
WEB : http://www.localpower.org

INTERNATIONAL DISTRICT ENERGY ASSOCIATION - IDEA
CONTACT : John Fiegel
1200 19th Stree NW, Suite 300,
Washington DC 20036-2412, USA
TEL : + 1 202 429 5111
FAX : + 1 202 429 5113
E-MAIL : idea@dc.sba.com
WEB : http://www.districtenergy.org

INTERNATIONAL NETWORK ON SMALL HYDROPOWER - INSHP
CONTACT : Tong Jiandong
PO Box 202, 136 Nanshan Road,
Hangzhou 310002, China
TEL : + 86 571 7070070
FAX : + 86 571 7023353
E-MAIL : hic@mail.hx.zj.cn
WEB : http://www.digiserve.com/inshp

NATIONAL HYDROGEN ASSOCIATION
1800 M Street N.W., Suite 300
Washington, DC 20036-5802, U.S.A.
Phone: +1.202.223.5547
Fax: +1.202.223.5537

ÖSTERREICHISCHER ENERGIEK ONSUMENTEN-VERBAND - ÖEKV
CONTACT : Franz Urban
Museumstraße 5, 1070 Wien, Austria
TEL : + 43 1 523 75 11
FAX : + 43 1 526 36 09
E-MAIL : oekv@netway.at

PLANETARY ASSOCIATION FOR CLEAN ENERGY INC
CONTACT : A Michrowski
100 Bronson Avenue, Suite 1001,
Ottawa, Ontario KIR 6GB, Canada
TEL : + 1 613 236 6265
FAX : + 1 613 235 5876

SOLAR ENERGY SOCIETY OF CANADA INC - SESCI
CONTACT : A Michrowski
116 Lisgar Street, Suite 702, Ottawa,
Ontario K2P 0C2, Canada
TEL : + 1 613 234 4151
FAX : + 1 613 234 2988
E-MAIL : sesci@cyberus.ca
WEB : http://www.solarenergy society.ca

SOLAR ENERGY SOCIETY OF INDIA (SESI)
c/o Tata Energy Research Institute
Darbari Seth Block
Habitat Place, Lodhi Road
New Delhi - 110 003
Tel. +91 11 462 2246, 460 1550
Fax +91 11 462 1770, 463 2609
e-mail mailto:sesi@teri.ernet.in

SUSTAINABLE ENERGY INDUSTRY ASSOCIATION (AUSTRALIA) LTD
CONTACT : J David Abba
PO Box 411, Dickson,
ACT 2602, Australia
TEL : + 61 6 230 0271
FAX : + 61 6 230 0273
E-MAIL : seia@seia.com.au
WEB : http://www.seia.com.au

TECHNOLOGY TRANSFER

ASIAN AND PACIFIC CENTRE FOR TRANSFER OF TECHNOLOGY - APCTT
CONTACT : N Srinivasan
Post Box 4575,
Qutab Institutional Area,
New Delhi 110016, India
TEL : + 91 11 6966619
FAX : + 91 11 6856274
E-MAIL : postmaster@apctt.org
WEB : http://www.apctt.org

FOLKE CENTER FOR RENEWABLE ENERGY
CONTACT : Preben Maegaard
Kammersgaardsvej 16,
7760 Hurup Thy, Denmark
TEL : + 45 97 95 66 00
FAX : + 45 97 95 65 65
E-MAIL : energy@folkecenter.dk
WEB : http//www.folkecenter.dk

INTERNATIONAL NETWORK FOR SUSTAINABLE ENERGY - INFORSE
CONTACT : G Olesen
European Division, c/o OVE-Europe,
GL Kirkevej 56, 8530 Hjortshoj,Denmark
TEL : + 45 86 227 000
FAX : + 45 86 227 096
E-MAIL : ove@inforse.dk
WEB : http://www.inforse.dk

GOVERNMENT

COMMONWEALTH SECRETARIAT
CONTACT : Peter de Groot
Commonwealth Science Council,
45 Gaywood Road,
London E17 4QA, UK
TEL : + 44 20 7 747 6213
FAX : + 44 20 7 839 6174
E-MAIL : comsci@gn.apc.org

DEPARTMENT OF NATURAL RESOURCES CANADA
CONTACT : Michel Lamanque
Energy Technology Branch - CADDET
Energy Efficiency Network,
580 Booth Street, 13th Floor, Ottawa,
Ontario KIA 0E4, Canada
TEL : + 1 613 947 3812
FAX : + 1 613 947 1016
E-MAIL : mlamanqu@nrcan.gc.ca
WEB : http://www.caddet-ee.org

INDIAN RENEWABLE ENERGY DEVELOPMENT AGENCY LTD. (IREDA)
CONTACT : Dr. V. Bakthavatsalam
Core-4a, 1st Floor East Court
India Habitat Centre, Lodhi Road
New Delhi - 110003, India
TEL : 91-11-4601344 / 4642367
FAX : 91-11-4602855
E-MAIL: gen@ireda.globemail1.com
WEB : www.ireda.nic.in

MINISTÉRE ENERGIE RESSOURCES QUEBEC
CONTACT : Donald Maltais
5700 - 4E Avenue Ouest,
Charllesbourg, Quebec GIH 6RI, Canada
TEL : + 1 418 643 4561
FAX : + 1 418 643 8337
WEB : http://www.mrn.gouv.qc.ca

MINISTRY OF NON-CONVENTIONAL ENERGY SOURCES
CONTACT : P M Nair
Block-14, CGO Complex, Lodhi Road,
New Delhi - 110 003, India
TEL : 91 11 4361481
FAX : 91 11 4362772
E-MAIL : secymnes@ren02.nic.in
WEB : http://www.mnes.nic.in

INTERNATIONAL BODIES

INTERNATIONAL ENERGY AGENCY - IEA/OECD
CONTACT : Rick Sellers
9 rue de la Fédération,
75739 Paris Cedex 15, France
TEL : + 33 1 40 57 67 50
FAX : + 33 1 40 57 67 59
E-MAIL : koch@iea.org
WEB : http://www.iea.org

INTERNATIONAL SOLAR ENERGY SOCIETY - ISES
CONTACT : Dr Cesare Silvi
International Headquarters, Villa Tannheim, Wiesentalstraße 50,
D-79115 Freiburg, Germany
TEL : + 49 761 459 06-0
FAX : + 49 761 459 06 99
E-MAIL : hq@ises.org
WEB : http://www.ises.org

UNITED NATIONS ECONOMIC & SOCIAL COMMISSION FOR ASIA & THE PACIFIC - ESCAP
CONTACT : Pranesh C Saha
Energy Resources Section,
Environmental and Natural Resources Development Divi,
UN Building, Rajdamnern Ave,
Bangkok 10200, Thailand
TEL : + 66 2 288 1546
FAX : + 66 2 288 1059
E-MAIL : saha.unescap@un.org
WEB : http://www.unescap.org/enrd/energy

UNITED NATIONS ENVIRONMENT PROGRAMME
United Nations Avenue, Gigiri
PO Box 30552, Nairobi, Kenya
Tel: (254-2) 621234
Fax: (254-2) 624489/90
E-mail:eisinfo@unep.org
Web:http://www.unep.org

US-AEP
Asia/Near East Burea
U.S. Agency for International Development 1300 Pennsylvania Avenue, NW, 4th Floor
Washington, DC 20523-4101, USA
Mr. Peter Kimm, Executive Director
Tel: 1-202-712-4156
Fax: 1-202-216-3379
E-mail: pekimm@usaid.gov

WORLD HEALTH ORGANISATION
CONTACT : Micheal Zaffran
Via Appia, 1211 Genève 27, Switzerland
TEL : + 41 22 791 2111
FAX : + 41 22 791 4193
E-MAIL : zaffranm@sho.ch
WEB : http://www.who.ch

WORLD RENEWABLE ENERGY NETWORK - WREN
CONTACT : Prof AAM Sayigh
147, Hilmanton, Lower Earley,
Reading RG6 4HN, UK
TEL : + 44 118 961 1364
FAX : + 44 118 961 1365
E-MAIL : asayigh@netcomuk.co.uk
WEB : http://www.wrenuk.co.uk

UNDP - GLOBAL ENVIRONMENT FACILITY (GEF)
CONTACT : Rafael Asenjo
304 E, 45th 10th Floor
New York, NY 10017, USA
TEL : +212 906 5044
FAX : +212 906 6998
E-MAIL : rafael_asenjo@undp.org
WEB : http://www.undp.org

FINANCE / BANKING

CLEAN ENERGY FUND
CONTACT : Peter Dunev
33 St James Street,
London SWIA IHD, UK
TEL : + 44 20 7930 1030
FAX : + 44 20 7930 1080
E-MAIL : dunev@cleanenergyfund.org
WEB : http://www.cleanenergyfund.org

DANISH INTERNATIONAL DEVELOPMENT ASSISTANCE - DANIDA
CONTACT : Jean Paul Laude
Ministry of Foreign Affairs,
Asiatisk Plads 2,
1448 Copenhagen K, Denmark
TEL : + 45 33 92 00 00
FAX : + 45 33 92 07 90
E-MAIL : jealau@um.dk

WORLD BANK
CONTACT : Karl Jechoutek
F2K-146, 1818 H Street NW,
Washington, DC 20433, USA
TEL : + 1 202 458 2872

RESEARCH & DEVELOPMENT

AUSTRIAN ASSOCIATION FOR AGRICULTURAL RESEARCH - OEVAF
CONTACT : Otto Schutz
Kleine Sperlgasse 1/37,
A-1020 Vienna, Austria
TEL : + 43 1 214 5903 x 78
FAX : + 43 1 214 5903-9
E-MAIL : aevaf-wien@oevaf.at

ASIAN INSTITUTE OF TECHNOLOGY
CONTACT : Prof SC Bhattacharya
Energy Program, PO Box 4,
Klong Luang, Pathumthani 12120, Thailand
TEL : + 66 2 524 5440
FAX : + 66 2 524 5439
E-MAIL : epcoord@ait.ac.th
WEB : http://www/ep.ait.th

CENTRE FOR RENEWABLE ENERGY SYSTEMS TECHNOLOGY - CREST
Angela Marmont Renewable Energy Laboratory, Loughborough University,
Loughborough,
Leicestershire LEII 3TU, UK
TEL : + 44 1509 223466
FAX : + 44 1509 610031
E-MAIL : a.j.whitel@lboro.ac.uk
WEB : http://www.lboro.ac.uk/departments/el/research/crest
CONTACT : Allison White

FRAUNHOFER INSTITUTE FÜR GRENZFLÄCHEN UND BIOVERFAHRENSTECHNIK
Nobelstrabe 12, 70569 Stuttgart, Germany
TEL : + 49 711 970 4000
FAX : + 49 711 970 4200
E-MAIL : info@igb.fhg.de
WEB: http://www.igb.fhg.de
CONTACT : Prof Dr Walter Trosch

NATIONAL RENEWABLE ENERGY LABORATORY
CONTACT : Bob Noun
US Department of Energy,
1617 Cole Blvd., Golden,
Colorado - 80401, USA
TEL : +1 303 275 3000
FAX : +1 303 275 3097
E-MAIL : public_affairs@nrel.gov
WEB : http://www.nrel.gov

THE ENERGY RESEARCH INSTITUTE (TERI)
CONTACT : Dr. R K Pachauri
Darbari Seth Block, Habitat Place,
Lodhi Road, New Delhi 110 003,
India
TEL : +91 11 2462 2246
FAX : +91 11 2462 1770
E-MAIL : mailbox@teri.res.in
WEB : http://www.teriin.org

NGO's

GREENPEACE INTERNATIONAL
CONTACT : Karl Mallon
Energy Solutions Unit,
Keizersgracht 176, 1016 DW
Amsterdam, Netherlands
TEL : + 31 20 523 6222
FAX : + 31 20 523 6200
E-MAIL : karl.mallon@ams.greenpeace.org
WEB : http://www.greenpeace.org

INTERNATIONAL GEOTHERMAL ASSOCIATION-IGA
CONTACT : Ruggero Bertani
C/o Erga Gruppo ENEL,
Via A Pisano 120, 56122 Pisa, Italy
TEL : + 39 50 535891
FAX : + 39 50 535893
E-MAIL : igasel@enel.it
WEB : http://www.demon.co.uk/geosci/igahome.htm

WORLD ENERGY COUNCIL
CONTACT : Gerald Doucet
5th Floor Regency House,
1-4 Warwick Street,
London WIB 5LT, UK
TEL : + 44 20 7734 5926
FAX : + 44 20 7734 5926
E-MAIL : info@worldenergy.org
WEB : http://www.worldenergy.org

WINROCK INTERNATIONAL
CONTACT : Frank Tugwell
38 Winrock Drive, Morrilton,
Arkansas 72110
Tel. 501 727 5435

TRADE ORGANIZATION

BRANCH EFORENINGEN FOR DECANTRAL KRAFTVARME
CONTACT : Henrik Lilja
Handverksradet, Amaliegade 31,
1256 Copenhagen K , Denmark
TEL : + 45 33 93 20 00
FAX : + 45 33 32 01 74
E-MAIL : Lilja@hvr.dk
WEB : http://www.hvr.dk

EC-ASEAN COGEN PROGRAMME
CONTACT : Michael Pennington
Asian Institute of Technology, KM42,
Phaholyothin Highway, Klongluang
Pathumthani 12120, Thailand
TEL : + 66 2 524 5399
FAX : + 66 2 524 5396
E-MAIL : cogenait.ac.th

AFRICA

SOLAR THERMAL

METAL CO (HEATERS) LTD
PO Box 28939, CY-2084 Strovolos, Nicosia, Cyprus
TEL: +357 2 425382
FAX: +357 2 494693
E-MAIL: metalco@spidernet.com.cy
WEB: http://www.metalcoheaters.com

LARISTO LTD
PO Box 8564, CY-2080 Strovolos, Nicosia,Cypus
TEL: +357 2 313411
FAX: +357 2 426107
E-MAIL: laristo@cytanet.com.cy
CONTACT: Dr Loucas Aristodemou

SOLAR PHOTOVOLTAIC

AT MICROSOLAR LTD
31 Lphigenias Str, 4TH Floor, PO Box 28941,2084 Nicosia, Cyprus
TEL: +357 225 12886
FAX: +357 225 12891
E-MAIL: info@atmicrosolar.com

FZE POWERTECH GREEN ENEGY LTD
Marketing PO Box 42109, Larnaca Free Trade Zone, Larnaca 6531, Cyprus
TEL: +357 4 360 764
FAX: +357 4 360 771
WEB: http://www.wodete.com.cy
CONTACT: Mr Takis Christofis

GEREKA ELECTRICAL CONSTRUCTION LTD
G Elkosary 19, Strovolos, Cyprus
TEL : + 357 2 420034
FAX : + 357 2 774817
CONTACT : G T Parpas

SUPPLIES

PROPLAN LTD
Ergates Industrial Estate Phase II, 2643 Ergates, PO Box 5672, 1311 Nicosia, Cyprus
TEL: +357 2 624374
FAX: +357 2 624263
E-MAIL: proplan@spidernet.com.cy
CONTACT: Seamus Collins

We kindly request more listings in this country.

You can submit any additional listings by E-mail: unisun@vsnl.com

Fax: 91 80 22289294

We will include these in the next edition

Kindly inform us of any errors and omissions in the listings by:

E-mail: unisun@vsnl.com

Fax: 91 80 22289294

SOLAR THERMAL

MISR AMERICA GROUP FOR INVESTMENTS
Solar Energy Department, 215 El Hegaz Street, Heliopolis, Cairo, Egypt
TEL : +20 2 452366
FAX : +20 2 406008
CONTACT : Dr Samia Danial

UNITED COMPANY FOR LIGHT INDUSTIES-PILCO
2 suliman Abaza, Mohandessin, Giza, Egypt
TEL : +202 3617060
FAX : +20 2 3367706
E-MAIL : fimco@link.com.eg
CONTACT : Eng Galal Maamoun

SOLAR PHOTOVOLTAIC

ARABIAN SOLAR ENERGY AND TECHNOLOGY CO-ASET
11 Sherif Street, Cairo, Egypt
TEL: +20 2 393 6463
FAX: +20 2 392 9744
WEB: http://www.asetegypt.com
CONTACT: Mustafa Ebeed

BIC FOR ELECTRONICS ENVIRONMENT AND ENERGY
Photovoltaic Division, 9, Marouf Street, Cairo 11522, Egypt
TEL : +20 2 5798334
FAX : +20 2 5795744
E-MAIL : bit@bicegypt.com
WEB : http://www.bicegypt.com
CONTACT : A Elmarsafawy

SOLAR AND SPACE RESEARCH DEPARTMENT
National Research Inst of Astronomy & Geophysics, Helwan,
Cairo, Egypt
TEL : +20 2 556 0046
FAX : +20 2 554 8020
E-MAIL : mamshaltout@frcu.eun.eg
CONTACT : Prof MA Mosalam Shaltant

SOLENCO
Solar& Environment
17 Kasr EL Nil
I I I I I Cairo Egypt
TEL :+20 2 393 7678
FAX :+20 2 393 9362
E-MAIL : w-adel@hotmail.com
CONTACT : Abel Wasfy

WASTE TO ENERGY

DYNEX INTERNATIONAL INC
372, Pyramids Street,
Giza Egypt
TEL : + 20 2 581 8912
FAX : + 20 2 585 9593
CONTACT : A Kafafi

ASSOCIATION

EGYPTIAN SOLAR ENERGY SOCIETY
PO Box 487, Dokki, Egypt
TEL : +20 2 345 2850
FAX : +20 2 345 1236
E-MAIL : eses@soficorn.com.eg
WEB : http://www.soficom.com/eg/eses
CONTACT : M Mahmoud

RESEARCH & DEVELOPMENT

ELECTRONICS RESEARCH INSTITUTE
Photovoltaic Cells Department,
National Research Centre Building,
El Tahrir Street, Dokki,
Cairo 12311, Egypt
TEL : +20 202 3310512
FAX : +20 202 3351631
E-MAIL : pv@ers.sci.eg
CONTACT : Dr Zahran

We kindly request more listings in this country.

You can submit any additional listings by E-mail: unisun@vsnl.com

Fax: 91 80 22289294

We will include these in the next edition

Kindly inform us of any errors and omissions in the listings by:

E-mail: unisun@vsnl.com

Fax: 91 80 22289294

SOLAR PHOTOVOLTAIC

DEING LIMITED
Solar Energy South East Alajo, Off Nsawam Road, PO Box AN 1996
Accra, Ghana
TEL : + 233 21 233779
FAX : + 233 21 233778
E-MAIL : deng@africainvoce.com.gh
CONTACT : A Osae

SOLARWINDS ENGINEERING SERVICES
P O Box TN152 TNE-Accra, Ghana
TEL:+233 21 712473
FAX:+233 21 712713
E-MAIL:solarwinds@dftcc.africaonline.com.gh
CONTACT:Matt Knack-Baiden

SUN SOLAR LTD
Northern Sector Ghana,
P O Box K S 5400, Kumasi, Ghana
TEL: 233 51 36189
E-MAIL : jafriyie@kspo.africaonline.com.gh
CONTACT:John Kwasi Afriyie

SUN SOLAR LTD
PO Box AM 282, Amasaman,
Accra, Ghana
TEL : +233 21 7012422
FAX : +233 21 7012422
E-MAIL : sunsolar@excite.com
CONTACT : Owusu Marfo Charles

GOVERNMENT

MINISTRY OF MINES AND ENERGY
PMB Ministry Post Office,
Accra, Ghana
TEL: +233 21 667151
FAX: +233 21 668262
CONTACT: Joseph Essandoh-Yeddu

UNIVERSITIES

KWAMENKRUMAH UNIVERSITY OF SCIENCE & TECHNOLOGY-KNUST
Mechanical Engineering Department
Kumasi Ghana
TEL: +233 51 60232
FAX: +233 51 60232
E-MAIL: foakuffo@africaonline.com.gh
CONTACT : Prof F O Akuffo

NGO's

GREEN EARTH ORGANIZATION
PO Box AN 16641, Accra-North, Ghana
TEL : + 233 21 232762
FAX : + 233 21 230455
E-MAIL : greeneth@ncs.com.gn
CONTACT : Joshua Awuku Apaw

CONSULTANTS

WADOK VENTURES LTD
PO Box 11877, Accra-North, Ghana
TEL: +233202003534
FAX: +14132157662

We kindly request more listings in this country.

You can submit any additional listings by E-mail: unisun@vsnl.com

Fax: 91 80 22289294

We will include these in the next edition

Kindly inform us of any errors and omissions in the listings by:

E-mail: unisun@vsnl.com

Fax: 91 80 22289294

SOLAR PHOTOVOLTAIC

BP SOLAR EA
PO Box 47796, Nairobi, Kenya
TEL : +254 2 569780
FAX : +254 2 573339
E-MAIL : bpsea@africaonline.com
WEB : http://www.bpsolarex.com
CONTACT : Francis H

KENITAL LTD
Argwings Kodhek Road, PO Box 55517, Nairobi, Kenya
TEL: +254 2 572 384
FAX: +254 2 572 424
E-MAIL: silvio@kenital.com
WEB: htttp://www.kenital.com
CONTACT : S. Borraccino

SOLAGEN LTD
The Mall, Westlands, PO Box .45679
Nairobi, Kenya
TEL:+254 2 441160
FAX:+254 2 444182
E-MAIL:eric@solagen.com
WEB:http://www.solagen.com
CONTACT:Eric Muhanji

TELEVISION SALES & RENTALS LIMITED
PO Box 45525, Nairobi, Kenya
TEL: +254 2 21 3143
FAX: +254 2 745655
CONTACT: Anil N Abdulla

FINANCE & BANKING

PIPAL LTD
PO Box 42777, Nairobi, Kenya
TEL: +254 2 742552
FAX: +254 2 740687

CONSULTANTS

ENERGY ALTERNATIVES AFRICA LTD
PO Box 76406, Nairobi, Kenya
TEL: +254 2 714 623
FAX: +254 2 720 909
E-MAIL: energyaf@iconnect.co.ke
CONTACT : Mark K

OTHERS

KENYA ELECTRICITY GENERATING CO LTD
PO Box 47936, Nairobi, Kenya
TEL: +254 2 751557
FAX: +254 2 337351
CONTACT : Swaleh Imu

NAPSKENYA
PO Bo 19558 Nairobi, Kenya
TEL: +254 2 56 1096
FAX: + 254 2 56 1098
CONTACT: Jan Fanning

SUPPLIERS

INSTRUMENTS

KENITAL (K) LTD
Ngong Road PO Box19764-00202, Nairobi, Kenya
TEL: +254 2 71 5960
FAX: +254 2 71 5960
E-MAIL: silvio@kenital.com
WEB: http://www.kenital.com
CONTACT: Silvio Borraccino

We kindly request more listings in this country.

You can submit any additional listings by E-mail: unisun@vsnl.com

Fax: 91 80 22289294

We will include these in the next edition

Kindly inform us of any errors and omissions in the listings by:

E-mail: unisun@vsnl.com

Fax: 91 80 22289294

RESEARCH & DEVELOPMENT

CENTER FOR SOLAR ENERGY STUDIES
Applied Research, PO Box 12932
Tripoli, Libyan Arab Jamahiriya
TEL : +218 21 3601101
FAX : +218 21 3601108

ASSOCIATION

INTERNATIONAL ENERGY FOUNDATION
P O Box 83617, Tripoli,
Libyan Arab, Jamahiriya
TEL: +218 21 33 31822
FAX: +218 21 33 31832
E-MAIL: iefmuntasser@hotmail.com
CONTACT: Dr MA Muntasser

We kindly request more listings in this country.

You can submit any additional listings by E-mail: unisun@vsnl.com

Fax: 91 80 22289294

We will include these in the next edition

Kindly inform us of any errors and omissions in the listings by:

E-mail: unisun@vsnl.com

Fax: 91 80 22289294

SOLAR PHOTOVOLTAIC

ENERGIE TECHNOLOGIE
Centre Commercial Somacodis,
Antanimena, PO Box8566,
Antananarivo 101, Madagascar
TEL: +261 20 22 62908
FAX: +261 20 22 62908
E-MAIL: enertech@dts.mg
CONTACT: Olivier Rasoldier

We kindly request more listings in this country.

You can submit any additional listings by E-mail: unisun@vsnl.com

Fax: 91 80 22289294

We will include these in the next edition

Kindly inform us of any errors and omissions in the listings by:

E-mail: unisun@vsnl.com

Fax: 91 80 22289294

SOLAR THERMAL

AFRISOL SA
219 Rue Mustapha El Maani,
20000 Casablanca, Morocco
TEL: +212 2 01225
FAX: +212 20 13 30

PHOTOTHERM ELECTRONIQUE
54 Avenue Moulay R'chid,
Gueliz, Marrakech, Morocco
TEL : +212 4 44 6887
FAX : +212 4 43 4007
E-MAIL:
phototherm@cybernet.net.ma
CONTACT: Lahcen Boudad

TROPICAL POWER
Solar Energy, 301 Hay El Menzeh,
Rabat, Morocco
TEL: +212 7 790856
FAX: +212 7 290237
CONTACT: Zour Khadija

SOLAR PHOTOVOLTAIC

GETRADIS
Energles Renouvelables,
50 Avenue de Souissi, Rabat
Sousis, 10000 Rabat, Morocco
TEL : + 212 7 753 814
FAX : + 212 7756864
E-MAIL : getradis@mail.sis.net.ma
CONTACT : Ibriou Chiekh M

SIGMA TECH SA
5 Rue Midelt, Rabat 1000, Morocco
TEL: +212 7 76 89 61
FAX: +212 7 76 89 64
E-MAIL: sigmatech@mail.sis.net.ma
CONTACT: Abdelouhed Derouiche

TAQA SHAMS SA
No 3 Zone Industrielle de Sale,
Tabriquet, Sale, Morocco
TEL : +212 7 85 35 95
FAX : +212 7 85 35 78
CONTACT : Bennouna Youssef

RESEARCH & DEVELOPMENT

GROUP ED'ETUDES ET DE RECHER CHES SURLES ENERGIES RENOUVELABLES ET L'ENVIRONNEMENT- GERER
C/o IAV Hassan II, BP 6202,
10101 Rabat, Morocco
TEL : + 212 7 77 7443
FAX : + 212 7 77 58 45
E-MAIL : senhaji@mtds.com
CONTACT : F Senhaji

THERMAL SOLAR ENERGY AND ENVIRONMENT LABORATORY - LTEE
Physics Department Faculty of
Science, BP 2121, Tefouan,
Morocco
TEL: +212 1 145186
FAX: +212 9 994500
E-MAIL: H-ezbakhe@hotmail.com
CONTACT: Prof Hassan Ezbakhe

WIND

MAROC AERO ENERGIE
24 Bd El Fatouaki, Oujda, Morocco
TEL: +212 6 68 96 88
FAX: +212 6 68 25 59
CONTACT: Messaoudi Boujemaa

We kindly request more listings in this country.

You can submit any additional listings by E-mail: unisun@vsnl.com

Fax: 91 80 22289294

We will include these in the next edition

Kindly inform us of any errors and omissions in the listings by:

E-mail: unisun@vsnl.com

Fax: 91 80 22289294

NAMIBIA

SOLAR THERMAL

NAMBIA ENGINEERING CORPORATION NE CESS(PTY) LTD
PO Box 5052, Windhoek,
Namibia
TEL: +264 61 236720
FAX: +264 64 232805
EMAIL: necess@iafrica.com
WEB:http://www.namencor.com.na
CONTACT: NT Bruckner

SOLAR PHOTOVOLTAIC

SCANSOLAR NAMIBIA
Marketing, PO Box 1316,
Tsumeb, Namibia
TEL: +26467222219
FAX: +26467222251
E-MAIL: ghamutwe@mweb.cim.na
CONTACT: Gottlieb Hamutwe-Jr

SOLAR AGE NAMIBIA(PTY)LTD
PO Box 9987, Windhoek,
Namibia
TEL:+264 61 215 809
FAX:+264 61 215 793
E-MAIL:solarage@iafrica.com.na
WEB:http://www.iafrica.com.na/solar
CONTACT:Conard E Roedern

TERRASOL
PO Box 6036, Windhoek, Namibia
TEL: + 264 61 239454
FAX: + 264 61 239454
E-MAIL: terrasol@iafrica.com.na
CONTACT: Werner Schultz

SMALL HYDRO

NAMPOWE
Generation,
PO Box 2864, Windhoek
Nambia
TEL: +264 61 2054111
FAX: +264 64 232805
CONTACT: Relner Jagau

RESEARCH & DEVELOPMENT

UNIVERSITY OF NAMIBIA
Multidisciplinary Research Centre-Science and Te,
Private Bag 13301,
Windhoek,
Namibia
TEL: +264 61 206 3051
FAX: +264 61 206 3684
E-MAIL: kftjipangandjara@unam.na
CONTACT: Dr. KF Tjipangandjara

CONSULTANTS

EMCON CONSULTING ENGINEERS
PO Box 1900, Windhoek,
Namibia
TEL : +264 61 224725
FAX : +265 61 233207
E-MAIL : volker@emcon.com.na
WEB : http://www. Emcon.com.na
CONTACT : Volker R

HYBRID SYSTEMS

HPS ENG
PO Box 30905,
Windhoek 9000
Namibia
TEL: +264 63 265600
FAX: +264 63 265600
CONTACT: Edward Drotsche

HYBRID POWER SYSTEMS-HPS ENGINEERING
PO Box 30905, Windhoek 9000,
Namibia
TEL: +264 63 265600
FAX: +264 63 265600
E-MAIL: hpseng@mweb.com.na
CONTACT: Eduard Drotsche

We kindly request more listings in this country.

You can submit any additional listings by E-mail: unisun@vsnl.com

Fax: 91 80 22289294

We will include these in the next edition

Kindly inform us of any errors and omissions in the listings by:

E-mail: unisun@vsnl.com

Fax: 91 80 22289294

DESIGN & ENGINEERING

SOLAR ENERGY SYSTEMS AND PRODUCTS COMPANY –SESP
256 Ikorodu Road, PO Box 622,
Surulere, Lagos, Nigeria
TEL: +23414973570
FAX: +23414973643
CONTACT: R Tunji Ajani

SOLAR THERMAL

BUHAN & TEISSEIRE
Hydraulic-Energy,
Place Kernel, BP
119, Dakar, Senegal
TEL : +221 82339 41
FAX : +221 823 71 18
E-MAIL : teisseir@sonatel.senet.net
CONTACT : A Farcot

RESEARCH & DEVELOPMENT

CERER
BP 476, Dakar, Senegal
TEL : +221 21 14 14
FAX : +221 24 63 18
CONTACT : Prof M Kane

FINANCE / BANKING

PERFORMANCES
BP 7935, Dakar, Senegal
TEL : + 221 821 58 11
FAX : +221 821 58 11
E-MAIL: legendre@metissacana.sn
CONTACT : Bruno Legendre

We kindly request more listings in this country.

You can submit any additional listings by E-mail: unisun@vsnl.com

Fax: 91 80 22289294

We will include these in the next edition

Kindly inform us of any errors and omissions in the listings by:

E-mail: unisun@vsnl.com

Fax: 91 80 22289294

SOLAR THERMAL

ELECTRAHOT INDUSTRIAL
PO Box 1135, Germiston,
1400 Gauteng,South Africa
TEL : +27 11 873 6841
FAX : +27 11 873 6690
E-MAIL :hotwater@cis.co.za
CONTACT : P H Weber

HAVOTEX ENGINEERING & MARKETING PTY LTD
Industrial Design Associates - IDA,
14 Killarney Avenue, Lakefield,
Benoni 1501,Gauteng, South Africa
TEL : + 27 11 918 5748
FAX : + 27 11 918 5749
CONTACT : Brian Harmer

SOLAR 2000 CC
PO Box 25852,
East Rand 1462, South Africa
TEL:+27 11 397 453
FAX:+27 11 397 4518
E-MAIL:solar200@jhbmail.co.za
CONTACT:BC Ross

SOLAR PHOTOVOLTAIC

HAVOTEX ENGINEERING & MARKETING PTY LTD
Industrial Design Associates - IDA,
14 Killarney Avenue, Lakefield,
Benoni 1501, Gauteng, South Africa
TEL : + 27 11 918 5748
FAX : + 27 11 918 5749
CONTACT : Brian Harmer

LISELO SOLAR (PTY) LTD
PO Box 52869, Wierda Park 0149,
South Africa
TEL: +27 12 661 6604
FAX: +27 12 661 7165
E-MAIL: david@liselosolar.co.za
CONTACT: David Risk

SOLAR-FABRIK (PTY) LTD
Southren Africa 7,Guild House 239
Bronkhorst Street Pretoria 0181
South Africa
TEL:+27 12 346 7608
FAX:+27 12 346 7609
E-MAIL:sfsa@yebo.co.za
WEB:http://www.solar-fabrik.de
CONTACT:Henning Holm

TENESA (PTY) LTD
PO Box 14524, Kenwyn.
Cape Town 7790, South Africa
TEL: +27 21 73 41 575
FAX: +27 21 73 96 11
E-MAIL: s.jallat@tenesa.co.za
WEB: http://www.tenesa.co.za
CONTACT: Stephane Jallat

COGENERATION

STEAM & TECHNICAL SERVICES PTY LTD
PO Box 15060, Impala Park,
1472, South Africa
TEL: +27 11894 2255
FAX: +27 27 11 894 7930
E-MAIL:steamtek@iafrica.com
WEB:http://www.steamtek.co.za
CONTACT:Dave Hall

RESEARCH & DEVELOPMENT

MINERALS & ENERGY POLICY CENTRE
Energy, PO Box 395,
Wits 2050, South Africa
TEL: +27 11 403 8013
FAX: +27 11 403 8023
E-MAIL: info@mepc.org.za
WEB: http://www.mepc.org.za
CONTACT: Paul M Mathaha

UNIVERSITIES

HAUPTBERATNGSSTELLEFÜR ELEKTRIZITÄSANWENDUNG EV HEA
Am Haupbahnhof 12
60329 Frankfurt am Main,
Germany
TEL : + 49 69 256 19-0
FAX : + 4969 2327 21
E-MAIL : energieberatung@
hea.fi.eunet.de
WEB : www.nex.de
CONTACT : Korin Münch

UNIVERSITY OF PRETORIA
Faculty of Natural and Agricultural
Science,
Pretoria 0002,
South Africa
TEL: +27 124 02478
FAX: +27 124 03890
E-MAIL: dean@Bioagric.up.ac.za
WEB: http://www.up.ac.za/academic
science
CONTACT: Prof Robin M Crewe

UNIVERSITY PRETORIA
School of the Built Environment,
Research & Postgraduate Study,
South Campus,
Bldg 4 East Rm 2-13,
Pretoria 0002,
South Africa
TEL: +27 12 420 3815
FAX: +27 12 420 3837
E-MAIL: dholm@postino.up.ac.za
CONTACT: Dieter Holm

NGO's

DEVELOPMENT ACTION GROUP DAG
101 Lower Main Road
Observatory 7925, South Africa
TEL : + 27 21 448 7886
FAX : + 27 21 447 1987
E-MAIL : dag@wn.apc.org

CONSULTANTS

DUARD BARNARD & ASSOCIATES
PO Box 35453, Menlo Park,
Pretoring 0102, Gauteng,
South Africa
TEL : + 27 12 460 8982
FAX : + 27 12 460 2989
E-MAIL : duard@safrica.com
CONTACT : Duard Barnard

ENERGY & DEVELOPMENT GROUP
PO Box 261, Noordhek 7985,
South Africa
TEL: +27 21 789 2920
FAX: +27 21 789 2954
E-MAIL: admin@edg.co.za
WEB: http://www.edg.co.za
CONTACT : Mark Borchers

STEWART SCOTT INTERNATIONAL
PO Box 784506, Sandton 2146
South Africa
TEL: +27 11 780 0611
FAX: +27 11 883 6789
E-MAIL:sissan@ssi.co.za
WEB:http://www.stewartscott.com

HYBRID SYSTEMS

MINUS 40 (PTY) LTD
PO Box 254,
Eppindust 7475,
South Africa
TEL: +27 21 386 2290
FAX: +27 21 386 2295
E-MAIL: info@minus40.co.za
WEB: http://www.minus40.co.za
CONTACT: Steve Davison

OTHERS

ESKOM
Non-Grid Electrification,
Private Bag 40175,
Celveland 2022, Johannesburg,
South Africa
TEL: +27 11 629 5062
FAX: +27 11 629 5361
E-MAIL : Rodney.Buttle@eskom.co.za
CONTACT : Rodney Buttle

DIVWATT (PTY) LTD
Box 3926, Honeydew 2040,
South Africa
TEL : + 27 11 794 3825
FAX : + 27 11 794 1244
E-MAIL : diwatt@africa.com
WEB : http://www.dirwatt.co.za
CONTACT : Bernd Pichulik

SUPPLIERS

BATTERIES/INVERTERS

FIRST NATIONAL BATTERY CO (PTY) LTD
Liverpool Road, Industrial Sites
Benoni, PO Box 5015,
Benoni South 1502, South Africa
TEL: +27 11 741 3600
FAX: + 27 11 421 2642
E-MAIL: marketing@battery.co.za
CONTACT : Colin Mckay

SOLAR ENGINEERING SERVICES

SOLAR ENGINEERING SERVICES
PO Box 628, Kloof 3640,
South Africa
TEL: +27317646292
FAX: +27317641266
E-MAIL:
soleng@solarengineering.co.za
WEB: http://
www.solarengineering.co.za
CONTACT: Will Cawood

We kindly request more listings in this country.

You can submit any additional listings by E-mail: unisun@vsnl.com

Fax: 91 80 22289294

We will include these in the next edition

Kindly inform us of any errors and omissions in the listings by:

E-mail: unisun@vsnl.com

Fax: 91 80 22289294

SOLAR PHOTOVOLTAIC

NATIONAL COMPANY FOR MANUFACTURING WATER EQUIPME NT LTD, NCMWE
Research & Development
PO Box 15007, Amarat,
Khartoum 122717, Sudan
TEL: +249 11 466671
FAX: +249 11 223451
CONTACT: Abdeen Mustafa Omer

DESIGN & ENGINEERING

NATIONAL COMPANY FOR MANUFACTURING WATER EQUIPMENT LTD-NCMWE
Research & Development,
PO Box 15007, Amarat,
Khartoum 12217, Sudan
TEL: +249 11 466671
FAX: +249 11 223451
CONTACT: Abdeen Mustafa Omer

SOLARMAN CO
PO Box 3844 khartoum, Sudan
TEL:+249 11 473 158
FAX:+249 11 473 138
E-MAIL:solarman29@hotmail.com
CONTACT: Siddiq Awad Hassan

SUPPLIERS

SUDATEL-D AR-EL HATIF
Power Planning, PO Box 11155,
Khartoum, Sudan
TEL: +249 11 77 9099
FAX: +249 11 77 677
E-MAIL: kajallo@sudatel.net
CONTACT: Abdalla Kajallo

We kindly request more listings in this country.

You can submit any additional listings by E-mail: unisun@vsnl.com

Fax: 91 80 22289294

We will include these in the next edition

Kindly inform us of any errors and omissions in the listings by:

E-mail: unisun@vsnl.com

Fax: 91 80 22289294

DESIGN & ENGINEERING

PROGRESSIVE DEVELOPMENT CENTRE
PO Box 4040, Damascus,
Syrian Arab Republic
TEL: +963 11 231 0943
FAX: +963 11 231 2985
CONTACT: Jamal Aswad

SOLAR THERMAL

KARAGWE DEVELOPMENT ASSOCIATION-KARADEA
Solar Training Facility(KSTF) PO Box 299, Karagwe - Kagera, Tanzania
TEL: +255 66 22541
FAX: +255 66 22541
CONTACT : M Musa

SONET
PO Box 12809, Dar es Salaam, Tanzania
TEL: +255 51 600518
E-MAIL: sonex@twiga.com
CONTACT: Kirsten Nohr

NGO's

TANZANIA TRADITIONAL ENERGY DEVELOPEMT AND ENVIRONMENT ORGANISATION-TATEDO
PO Box 32794, Dar es salaam, Tanzania,
TEL : + 255 51 700771
FAX : + 255 51 74400
E-MAIL : tatedo@raha.com
CONTACT : Estomi HN Sawe

DESIGN & ENGINEERING

ORKONEREI SOLAR ENERGY PROJECT-OSEP
PO Box 12785, Arusha, Tanzania
TEL: +255 812 400 246
FAX: +255 57 508 965
E-MAIL: rpdbyrne@yahoo.com
CONTACT: Lukas Kariongi

OTHERS

ULTIMATE ENERGY LTD
PO Box 23005, Dar es Salaam, Tanzania
TEL : +255 51 118145
FAX : +255 811 321321
E-MAIL : hburris@twiga.com
CONTACT : Harold D Burris

We kindly request more listings in this country.

You can submit any additional listings by E-mail: unisun@vsnl.com

Fax: 91 80 22289294

We will include these in the next edition

Kindly inform us of any errors and omissions in the listings by:

E-mail: unisun@vsnl.com

Fax: 91 80 22289294

SOLAR PHOTOVOLTAIC

SOLAR ENERGY FOR AFRICA INC
Operations Department,
Plot 40 Bombo Road,
Nitco House, PO Box 4155,
Kampala, Uganda
TEL:+256 41 250 125
FAX:+256 41 250 131
E-MAIL:solar@swiftuganda.com
CONTACT:Mr Kimbowa S Emmy

SOLAR PROMOTION
PO Box 8061, Kampala Uganda
TEL:+256 41 77408583
E_MAIL:wibrod@avu.org
CONTACT:Ms wilbrod birabwa

CONSULTANTS

INCAFEX SOLAR SYSTEMS LTD
ISSL PO Box 8867,
Kampala, Uganda
TEL: +256 41 250008
FAX: +256 41 250008
E-MAIL: incafexsolar@africaonline.co.ug

We kindly request more listings in this country.

You can submit any additional listings by E-mail: unisun@vsnl.com

Fax: 91 80 22289294

We will include these in the next edition

Kindly inform us of any errors and omissions in the listings by:

E-mail: unisun@vsnl.com

Fax: 91 80 22289294

WIND

TECHNICAL SUPPLIES CENTRE LTD TSC
Head Office, Moh'd Ad-Durra Street, East Of Awqaf Complex, PO Box 7186, Sana'a Yemen
TEL: +9671440430
FAX: +9671440431
E-MAIL: zabarah@y.net.ye
WEB: http://www.tsc.com.ye
CONTACT: Hilal Ghalib

We kindly request more listings in this country.

You can submit any additional listings by E-mail: unisun@vsnl.com

Fax: 91 80 22289294

We will include these in the next edition

Kindly inform us of any errors and omissions in the listings by:

E-mail: unisun@vsnl.com

Fax: 91 80 22289294

ZIMBABWE

SOLAR THERMAL

IMPACT SOLAR SYSTEMS
Box CY 1639, Causeway,
Harare, Zimbabwe
TEL: +263 4 752245
FAX: +263 4 752262
CONTACT: Charm Muchenje

SOLAMATICS (PVT) LTD
31 Edison Crescent,
Graniteside, Harare,
Zimbabwe
TEL: +2634749930
FAX: +2634771212
E-MAIL: mikem@mcdiarmid.co.zw
CONTACT: Mike Mollatt

SUN-TECH SYSTEMS
PO Box St 100,
Southerton, Harrare,
TEL: +263 4 65254/5
FAX: +263 4 61308
CONTACT : Sullivan

SOLAR PHOTOVOLTAIC

BATTERY WORLD-SOLAR WORLD
PO Box CY 793,
Causeway, Harrare, Zimbabwe
TEL : +263 4 757575
FAX : +263 4 770192
CONTACT : Flanagon

IMPACT SOLAR SYSTEMS
Box CY 1639, Causeway,
Harare, Zimbabwe
TEL: +263 4 752245
FAX: +263 4 752262
CONTACT: Charm Muchenje

POWERVISION (PVT) LTD
16 Telford Road, Graniteside,
Box 4533, Harare, Zimbabwe
TEL: +263 4 771581
FAX: +263 4 771580
E-MAIL: renewable@power.co.zw
CONTACT: Duncan Kerridge

SIEMENS (PVT) LTD
PO Box 4680, Harare, Zimbabwe
TEL: +263 4 307050
FAX: +263 4 307067
E-MAIL: siemens@siemens.co.zw
CONTACT: Mr Murandu

SOLAR PRODUCTS(PVT) LTD
PO Box ST628, Southerton,
Harare, Zimbabwe
TEL:+263 4 772677
FAX:+263 4 772677
CONTACT:Peter Nyamadzawo

SOLARBRIGHT ENERGY SYSTEMS (PVT) LTD
Solar Division, 50-5th Cresent,
Warren Park I, Harare, Zimbabwe
TEL:+263 4 70 80 77
FAX:+263 4 756185
E-MAIL:solarbright@zimdev.
africaonline.com
CONTACT : Eric Tokwe

SOLAR POWERED SYSTEMS
P O Box FM215, Famona,
Bulawayo, Zimbabwe
TEL:+263 9 65024

SUPERSONIC
PO Box ST319, Southerton,
Harare, Zimbabwe
TEL: +263 4 669211
FAX: +263 4 669113
E-MAIL:solarcom@primenet.co.zw
CONTACT:Butch Kotze

JEC (PVT) LTD
Fanum House, 57 Samora Machel
Avenue, Harare, Zimbabwe
TEL: +263 4 757644
FAX: +263 4 757645
E-MAIL:jec@harare.iafrica.com
CONTACT : L Stefano

KIEL-ELECTRONICS LTD
PO Box 8251, Belmont,
Bulawayo, Zimbabwe
TEL: +263 9 62304
CONTACT : B Brunaus

WIND

POWERVISION (PVT) LTD
16 Telford Road, Graniteside,
Box 4533, Harare, Zimbabwe
TEL: +263 4 771581
FAX: +263 4 771580
E-MAIL: renewable@power.co.zw
CONTACT: Duncan Kerridge

AFRICAN WINDPOWER
Unit 1 14 Telford Road,
Graniteside, Box
4533, Harare, Zimbabwe
TEL: +263 4 771 581
FAX: +263 4 771580
E-MAIL: power@ecoweb.co.zw
CONTACT: Oloff Smyth

SMALL HYDRO

POWERVISION (PVT) LTD
16 Telford Road, Graniteside,
Box 4533, Harare, Zimbabwe
TEL: +263 4 771581
FAX: +263 4 771580
E-MAIL: renewable@power.co.zw
CONTACT: Duncan Kerridge

RESEARCH & DEVELOPMENT

ENERGY TECHNOLOGY INSTITUTE
Renewable Energy, SIRDC,
PO Box 6640, Harare, Zimbabwe,
TEL : + 263 4 860322
FAX : + 263 4 860351
E-MAIL : mosad@icon.co.zw
WEB : www.srdc.ac.zw

DESIGN & ENGINEERING

ALTERNATIVE TECHNOLOGIES PLC
Renewables Department,
PO Box CH 40, Chisipite, Harare,
Zimbabwe
TEL: +263 4 499451
FAX: + 263 4 499452
E-MAIL: snakes@zambezi.net
CONTACT: Lloyd Searle

OTHERS

JOAMAC (PVT) LIMITED
PO Box 1393, Bulawayo,
Zimbabwe
TEL: +263 9 78238
FAX: +263 9 78053
CONTACT : M N Tshawe

BATTERIES/INVERTERS

BATTERY WORLD-SOLAR WORLD
PO Box CY 793,
Causeway, Harrare,
Zimbabwe
TEL : +263 4 757575
FAX : +263 4 770192
CONTACT : Flanagon

HATHORN TRADING (PVT) LTD
Batteries & Radiators,
PO Box 2431, Harare,
Zimbabwe
TEL : + 263 663388
FAX : + 263 553389
CONTACT : Mr Curruthers

LEWSEY PAUL (PVT) LTD
PO Box A439, Avondale,
Harare, Zimbabwe
TEL: +263 4 755435
FAX: +263 4 755434
CONTACT: Paul Lewsey

POWERVISION (PVT) LTD
16 Telford Road,
Graniteside,
Box 4533, Harare,
Zimbabwe
TEL: +263 4 771581
FAX: +263 4 771580
E-MAIL: renewable@power.co.zw
CONTACT: Duncan Kerridge

CABLES/WIRES

HATHORN TRADING (PVT) LTD
Batteries & Radiators,
PO Box 2431, Harare, Zimbabwe
TEL : + 263 663388
FAX : + 263 553389
CONTACT : Mr Curruthers

INSTRUMENTATION

KIEL-ELECTRONICS LTD
PO Box 8251, Belmont,
Bulawayo, Zimbabwe
TEL: +263 9 62304
CONTACT : B Brunaus

OTHERS (S)

CENTRE FOR RENEWABLE ENERGY AND ENVIRONMENTAL TECHNOLGY -CREET
PO Box CY 295,
Causeway, Harare, Zimbabwe
TEL : +263 4 733669
FAX : +263 4 733669
CONTACT : Dr G Mandishona

ECOLOGICAL DESIGNS
PO Box 6084 Unit 3 Level 2,
Kelvin Courner Building,
Graniteside Harare, Zimbabwe
TEL : + 263 4 756 961
FAX : + 263 4 756 924
CONTACT : W. Makoko

We kindly request more listings in this country.

You can submit any additional listings by E-mail: unisun@vsnl.com

Fax: 91 80 22289294

We will include these In the next edition

Kindly inform us of any errors and omissions in the listings by:

E-mail: unisun@vsnl.com

Fax: 91 80 22289294

NOTES

ASIA

ASSOCIATION

INTERNATIONAL SOLAR ENERGY SOCIETY ISES BANGLADESH
Dhaka University, Physics Department
Dhaka 1000, Bangladesh
TEL: +880 2 815940
FAX: +880 2 8615583
E-MAIL: durmail@du.bangla.net
CONTACT: Prof M Hussain

RAHIMAFROOZ SOLAR
104, Motijheel C.A., Dhaka-1000, Bangladesh
TEL : +880-2-9565238
FAX : +880-2-9554160
E-MAIL : rabl@bangla.net

AMAZ-K TECHNOTRADE
43, Mymensingh Road,
Dhaka, Bangladesh 1000
TEL : 880-2-9663727
WEB : http://www.agni.net/amaz
E-MAIL : amaz@dhaka.agni.com

BORDERLESS WORLD INC - BWI,
Overseas Operation
Nahar Peace Garden,
202/1, Tutpara Main Road,
Khulna Metro 9100, Bangladesh
TEL : +880 41 730 309
FAX : +880 880 41 730 309
CONTACT : Mr Shireen Akhter

MEGATEK ENGINEERING LTD
8 Jasimuddin Avenue Sector
3 Uttara Model Town, DHAKA,
Bangladesh 1230
TEL : 880 2 891556
E-MAIL : mega@citechco.net

TECHNOLINK INTERNATIONAL
120/17/1 Kabi Benazir Bagan,
Shahjahanpur, Dhaka,
Bangladesh 1217
TEL : 880-2-9351548
FAX : 880-2-9351548
E-MAIL : techno@bangla.net

We kindly request more listings in this country.

You can submit any additional listings by E-mail: unisun@vsnl.com

Fax: 91 80 22289294

We will include these in the next edition

Kindly inform us of any errors and omissions in the listings by:

E-mail: unisun@vsnl.com

Fax: 91 80 22289294

CHINA

SOLAR THERMAL

BEIJING T SINGHUA SOLAR LTD
Research and Development,
100084 Beijing, China
TEL : +86 10 6781760
FAX : +86 10 62780198
E-MAIL : yinzag@public.bta.net.cn
CONTACT : Guo Ciqiong

BEIJING TURBOSUN ENERGY TECHNOLOGY DEVELOPMENT CO. LTD
2B, Shaoyaoju, Taiyanggong,
Chaoyang District,
Beijing 100029, China
TEL : +86 10 6497 0926
FAX : +86 10 6429 0828
E-MAIL : sales@turbosun.com
WEB : http://www.turbosun.com
CONTACT : Jinsong Pei

NATIONAL ENGINEERING RESEARCH CENTER FOR RENEWABLE ENERGY
Solar Thermal Utilization-Photovoltaic
Technology, 3 Huayuan Road,
Haidan District,
Beijing 100083, China
TEL: +86 10 62001016
FAX: +86 10 62012880
EMAIL:bseri@public3.bta.net.ca
WEB:http://www.beijingsunpu.com.cn
CONTACT:Li Zhongming

SHANGHAI SONNE TRADE CORPORATION
Flat 2307 No 6 Lane 123,
Yan Ping Road, Shanghai 200042,
China
TEL: +862162461810
FAX: +862162461032
E-MAIL: sunhong@guomai.sh.cn
CONTACT: Sun Hong

WING HING SOLAR ENERGY CO LTD
International Sales Department,
Room, 1804-1805 Friendship
International Building, No 98
Jinsha Mid Road,
Shantou SEZ, Guangdong,
China
TEL: +86 754 8910033
FAX: +86 754 8608799
E-MAIL:winghing@public.shantou.gd.cn
WEB: http://www.winghingsolar.com
CONTACT: Mr Alex Yeh

YANGZHCU HUAYANG SOLAR ENERGY WATER HEATER CO LTD
No 2 Zhenxing Road,
Yangzhou Economic Development
Zone, Jiangsu,
TEL: +86 514 797 1008
FAX: +86 514 787 3263
CONTACT: Huang Yongli

ZHEJIANG MACHINERY & EQUIPMENT IMPORT & EXPORT CORPORATION
99 Jiefang Road,
Hangzhou 310009, China
TEL: +86 571 7828927
FAX: +86 571 7828900
E-MAIL: zmec@public.hz.zj.cn
WEB: http://www.zmec.com
CONTACT: Mr Jiang Xianxiao

SOLAR PHOTOVOLTAIC

NATIONAL ENGINEERING RESEARCH CENTER FOR RENEWABLE ENERGY
Solar Thermal Utilization-Photovoltaic
Technology, 3 Huayuan Road,Haidan
District, Beijing 100083, China
TEL: +86 10 62001016
FAX: +86 10 62012880
EMAIL:bseri@public3.bta.net.ca
WEB:http://www.beijingsunpu.com.cn
CONTACT:Li Zhongming

SHENZHEN TOPWAY SOLAR CO LTD
8-202 Hualian Huayuan, Nanshan
Dadao, Nanshan, Shenzhen, China
TEL: +86 755 6402765
FAX: +86 755 6402722
E-MAIL: sntopway@public.szptt.net.cn
WEB: http://www.suntopway.com
CONTACT: Mr Simon Xu

TIANJIN INSTITUTE OF POWER SOURCES CHINA
18 Lingzhung Road,
Tianjin 300381,
China
TEL: +86 22 2399396
FAX: +86 22 23383783
E-MAIL:xrtong@tips.ac.cn
WEB:http://www.tips.compaql.ac.cn
CONTACT:Fanjian Kong

TRONY SCIENCE & TECHNOLOGY DEVELOPMENT CO LTD
Technology Guide,
8th Floor East,
2nd Block, Shenzhen,
China
TEL: +86 755 2404654
FAX: +86 755 2425344
E-MAIL: sztrony@hotmail.com
WEB: http://www.trony.com
CONTACT: Jeff Chen

WIND

INFRA VEST
C-615 Beijing Lufthansa Centre, 50
Liangnaqiao Road, Chaoyamg,
Beijing, 10006 China
TEL: +86 10 64651908
FAX: +86 10 64622114
E-MAIL: infrvest@public.fhnet.cn.net
WEB: http://www.Infra-Vest.com
CONTACT: Dr Weilin Ma

NORDEX GMBH
C-812A Beijing Lufthansa Center, 50
Liangmagiao Road, Chaoyang
District, Beijing 100016, China
TEL: +86 10 6463 7923
FAX: +86 10 6465 1847
E-MAIL: info@nordex.com.cn
WEB: http://www.nordex-online.com
CONTACT: Dr Karl-Eugen Feifel

GEOTHERMAL

TIANJIN GEOTHERMAL RESEARCH AND TRAINING CENTRE
Tianjin University,
Weijin Road 92, Nankai District,
300072 Tianjin, China
TEL : +86 22 335 8803
FAX : +86 22 335 8329
CONTACT : Dai Chuanshan

FINANCE / BANKING

INFRA VEST
C-615 Beijing Lufthansa Centre, 50
Liangnaqiao Road, Chaoyamg,
Beijing, 10006 China
TEL: +86 10 64651908
FAX: +86 10 64622114
E-MAIL: infrvest@public.fhnet.cn.net
WEB: http://www.Infra-Vest.com
CONTACT: Dr Weilin Ma

ASSOCIATION

INTERNATIONAL NETWORK ON SMALL HYDROPOWER - IN SHP
PO Box 202, 136 Nanshan Road,
Hangzhou 310002, China
TEL: +86 571 7070070
FAX: +86 571 7023353
E-MAIL: hic@mail.hz.zj.cn
WEB: http://www.digiserve.com/inship
CONTACT: Tong Jiandong

INTERNATIONAL TRADE PROMOTION CO LTD
SIF Organizing Committee,
7th Floor Qiao Qiao Mansion,
757 Xi Kang Road,
Shanghai 200040, China
TEL: +86 21 62560 100
FAX: +86 21 62561 068

WEB: http://www.sif-expo.com
CONTACT: Mr Hua Hua

GOVERNMENT

MINISTRY OF AGRICULTURE PEOPLES REPUBLIC OF CHINA
Chengdu Biogas Scientific Research Institute, 4-13 People's South St. Chengdu, 610041 Sichuan,China
TEL: +86 28 5230735
E-MAIL: wulibinbobo@cd.col.com.cn
CONTACT: Wu Libin

RESEARCH & DEVELOPMENT

ASIA PACIFIC REGIONAL BIOGAS RESEARCH AND TRAINING CENTRE-BRTC
4Th Section, Renming South Street, Chengdu, Sichuan 610041 China
TEL: +86 28 5230735
CONTACT: Wu Libin

BEIJING SOLAR ENERGY RESEARCH INSTITUTE - BSERI
Solar Thermal Utilization-Photovoltaic Technology, 3 Huayuan Road, Haidian District, Beijing 100083, China
TEL : +86 10 62028646
FAX : +86 10 62012880
E-MAIL : bseri@public3.bta.net.ca
WEB : http://beijingsunpu.com.cn
CONTACT : Ma Fengwen

BEIJING T SINGHUA SOLAR LTD
Research and Development, 100084 Beijing, China
TEL : +86 10 6781760
FAX : +86 10 62780198
E-MAIL : yinzag@public.bta.net.cn
CONTACT : Guo Ciqiong

MINISTRY OF AGRICULTURE PEOPLES REPUBLIC OF CHINA
Chengdu Biogas Scientific Research Institute, 4-13 People's South St. Chengdu, 610041 Sichuan,China
TEL: +86 28 5230735
E-MAIL: wulibinbobo@cd.col.com.cn
CONTACT: Wu Libin

UNIVERSITY OF SCIENCE AND TECHNOLOGY OF CHINA
Thermal science and energy Engineering Department, Anhui Province, 230026heifi, China
TEL:+86 5513601670
FAX:+86 5513631760
E-MAIL: -xsge@ustc.edu.cn
CONTACT: Xin Shi Ge

UNIVERSITY OF SHANGHAIJIAO TONG
School of Power & Energy, 1954 Huashan Road
200030 Shanghai, China
TEL : +8621647109O
FAX : +8621647695
E-MAIL : jma@mail.sjtu.edu.cn
CONTACT : Jie Ma

CONSULTANTS

CHINA CHENGDU ENERGY ENVIRONMENT INTERNATIONAL CORPORATION - CEEIC
No.13, Section 4, People's South Street, Chengdu 610041, China
TEL : +86 28 523 0735
E-MAIL : wulibinbobo@cd.col.com.in
CONTACT : Wu Libin

HYBRID SYSTEMS

SHANGHAI SOLAR-WATT COMPANY LTD
Sales, Room 515, 680 Guiping Road, Shanghai, China
TEL: +862154261460
FAX: +862154261462
E-Mail: mashusheng@sina.com
WEB: http://www.solar-watt.com
CONTACT: Shusheng Ma

OTHERS

BEIJING SUNPU TECHNICAL COMPANY
No.3, Huayuan Road, Haidian District
Beijing 100083, China
TEL : + 86 10 6202 8646
FAX : +86 10 6201 2880
E-MAIL :Sunpubj@public.east.cn.net
WEB : http:/www.beijingsunpu.com.cn
CONTACT : Ma Fengwen

SUPPLIERS

BATTERIES/INVERTERS

TIANJIN INSTITUTE OF POWER SOURCES CHINA
18 Lingzhung Road, Tianjin 300381, China
TEL: +86 22 2399396
FAX: +86 22 23383783
E-MAIL:xrtong@tips.ac.cn
WEB:http://www.tips.compaql.ac.cn
CONTACT:Fanjian Kong

OTHERS (S)

BEIJING SUNDA SOLAR ENERGY TECHNOLOGY LTD
No. 3, Hyuauan Road, Haidian District,
Beijing 100083, China
TEL : +86 10 6200 1008
FAX : +86 10 6237 4906
E-MAIL : sunda@public3.bta.net.cn
WEB : http://www.beijing sunpu.com.cn
CONTACT : Lin Reimers

SHENZHEN TOPWAY SOLAR CO LTD
10Lwestern Coast Mansion, Nanyou Dadao, Shenzhen, China
TEL: +867556070440
FAX: +867556070222
E-MAIL: sntopway@public.szptt.net.cn
WEB: http://www.suntopway.com
CONTACT: Mr. Henry Hsia

Kindly inform us of any errors and omissions in the listings by:

E-mail: unisun@vsnl.com

Fax: 91 80 22289294

HONG KONG

SOLAR PHOTOVOLTAIC

EVER STEP DEVELOPMENT LTD
15/F Tak King Industrial Building, 27 Lee Chung Street, Chaiwan, Hong Kong.
TEL: +852 896 2471
FAX: +852 897 2365
E-MAIL: everstep@asiansources.com
CONTACT : Jenny Lam

JENXON LIMITED
Marketing Department, Rm 701-4, 341 King 's Road, North Point, Hong Kong
TEL: +852 288 79262
FAX: +852 288 77724
E-MAIL:info@jenxon.com
WEB: http://www.jenxon.com
CONTACT : Paul Chan

REGENT CRAFT SYSTEMS LTD
Flat 10 14/F, Kodak House 2, 39 Healthy Street East, North Point, Hong Kong
TEL : +852 2590 7104
FAX : +852 2811 2300
E-MAIL:101474,2513@ compuserve.com
CONTACT : Mr Mok Siu Cheun

STAR POWER INTERNATIONAL LTD
912 Worldwide Industrial Centre, 43 Shan Mei St, Fotan, Hong Kong
TEL: +852 2688 5555
FAX: +852 2605 6466
E-MAIL:info@starpower.com.hk
CONTACT:Dick Wong

SYNERGY POWER CORPORATION
20/Floor Wilson House, 19-27 Wyndham Street, Central, Hong Kong
TEL : +852 2846 3168
FAX : +852 2810 0478
E-MAIL : spc@synergypowercorp.com
WEB : http:// www.synergypowercorp.com
CONTACT : Michael Elliott

COGENERATION

BUILDING SERVICES DESIGN LTD
B1 16/F 36 Nathan Road, TST, Hong Kong
TEL : +852 2723 1600
FAX : +852 2739 7799
E-MAIL : browne@vol.net
WEB : http://www.bsdltd.com
CONTACT : C T Browne

WASTE TO ENERGY

SWEDISH TRADING COMPANY LIMITED
Unit 204 2nd Floor, New Bright Building, 11 Sheung Yuet Road, Kowloon Bay Kowloon, Hong Kong
TEL: +852 2953 5111
FAX: +852 2798 8262
E-MAIL:stcstih@hk.super.net
CONTACT:Spencer Li

CONSULTANTS

ENVIROSHONGKONG LTD.
Room A 18/F Chun Wo Commercial Centre, 23-29, Wing Wo Street, Central, Hong Kong
TEL : +852 2815 2221
FAX: +852 2815 3377
E-MAIL : norman.dipemo@envirus.com.hk

ERM-HONGKONG LTD
6F Hecny Tower, 9 Chatham road, Tsimshatsui, Kowloon, Hong Kong,
TEL: + 852 2271 3000
FAX: + 852 2723 5670
E-MAIL: daa@ermhk.com
WEB: http://www.ermhk.com
CONTACT : David Arthur

SUPPLIERS

OTHERS

CHINA LIGHT POWER INTERNATIONAL
Engineering Department, 22/F, CMG Asia Tower, The Gateway Harbour City, 15 Canton Road, Kowloon, Hong Kong
TEL: +85231831051
FAX: +85231831033
CONTACT: Albert Li

COASTAL INTERNATIONAL EXHIBITION CO LTD
Room 3808 China Resources Building, 26 Harbour Road, Wanchai, Hong Kong
TEL: +852 28276766
FAX: +852 28276870
E-MAIL: general@coastal.com.hk
WEB: http://www.coastal.com.hk
CONTACT: Kammy Shum

STAR POWER INTERNATIONAL LTD
912 Worldwide Industrial Centre, 43 Shan Mei St, Fotan, Hong Kong
TEL: +85226885555
FAX: +85226056466
E-MAIL: info@starpower.com.hk
CONTACT : Dick Wong

We kindly request more listings in this country.

You can submit any additional listings by E-mail: unisun@vsnl.com

Fax: 91 80 22289294

We will include these in the next edition

Kindly inform us of any errors and omissions in the listings by:

E-mail: unisun@vsnl.com

Fax: 91 80 22289294

SOLAR THERMAL

A.R. SOLAR SYSTEM
A-2, Aradhana Apts.,
Hubli, India
TEL : +91 836 373334
CONTACT: Ms. Asharaj

ADITYA- NEEMA SOLAR SHOP
57, Montieth Road,
Egmore, Chennai- 600 008
TEL: +91 44 28555713/28555716
FAX: +91 44 28555716

ADITYA SOLAR SHOP
519/19, Varuna Bridge Road
Near Taj Gangesh
Nadeshwar, Varanasi
TEL: +01 0542 345063

ADITYA SOLAR SHOP
6 Budha, Bhavanam,
M.C.H Shopping Complex,
Ranigunj, Secunderabad.
TEL: +91 40 7834581
FAX: +91 40 7805438

ADITYA SOLAR SHOP
Alipore (Opposite Zoo)
Kolkata- 700 027
TEL: +91 33 24790406

ADITYA SOLAR SHOP
Arindom Shopping Complex
Christianbasti, G.S. Road
Guwahati-781005
TEL: +91 361 621006
FAX: +91 361 548475

ADITYA SOLAR SHOP
C.G.R. 1,Nehru Place,
Tonk Road, Jaipur
TEL: +91 141 382759
FAX: +91 0141 380928

ADITYA SOLAR SHOP
Kesavadasapuram
Ullur Road (N.H)
Thiruvananthapuram-695004
TEL: +91 0471 440121
FAX: +91 0471 449458

ADITYA SOLAR SHOP
Nachan Road, Distt.
BurdwanDurgapur-4
West Bengal
TEL: +91 0343 569922

ADITYA SOLAR SHOP
Near Zila Parishad
Company Bagh,
Jalandhar
TEL: +91 181 282231

ADITYA SOLAR SHOP
No.247, Thiruvalluvar Salai,
Pillaithottam, Pondicherry- 605013
TEL: +91 413 252834/252820/
253052
FAX: +91 413 251494
E-MAIL: pasic@md2.vsnl.net.in

ADITYA SOLAR SHOP
Shantivan Ashram Of
Brahmakumaris
Abu Road, Rajasthan
TEL: +91 2974 28101 to 28108

ADITYA SOLAR SHOP
No.XL, 1/2319,
Opp. North Square,
Paramara Road, Cochin
TEL: +91 484 555564
FAX: +91 484 532862

ADITYA SOLAR SHOP
Ramkrishna Mission
Narendrapur- 743 508
South 24 Parganas (W.B)
TEL: +91 33 4770975
FAX: +91 33 4772070
E-MAIL: rkmlpndp@Cat.vsnl.net.In

ADITYA SOLAR SHOP
Sanjay Bazar, 355
Kishen Nagar, Dehradun.
TEL: +91 135 758246

ADITYA SOLAR SHOP
Sewak Road, 2nd Mile
WBSB Complex
Siliguri, District Darjeeling
TEL: +91 353 548342

ADITYA SOLAR SHOP
Shivaji Stadium, Bus Terminus
New Delhi – 110 001.
TEL: +91 11 23362750

ADITYA SOLAR SHOP
Shop No.21, Shubham Market
Opposite Ram Mandir
Bhubaneswar –751001
TEL: +91 674 516724
FAX: +91 674 504899
E-MAIL: adityasolar@satyam.net.in

ADITYA SOLAR SHOP
Shop No.23,
Sahakar Vaibhav Building,
Jafagate, Nava Mondha,
Aurangabad, (Maharashtra)
TEL: +91 2432 345744

ADITYA SOLAR SHOP
Shop No.6, Janpath Market, Lucknow
TEL: +91 522 217073
FAX: +91 522 217073

ADITYA SOLAR SHOP
Suresh Plaza Market
First Floor, Behind Vikas
Bhawan, Agra
TEL: +91 562 355937

ADITYA SOLAR SHOP
Surya Complex
Civil Lines, M.G.Marg,
Allahabad.
TEL: +91 532 422437

ADITYA SOLAR SHOP
Upica Handloom House,
Gomti Santhanpur, Kanpur
TEL: +91 512 234007

ADITYA SOLAR SHOP
Urja Bhavan, Kasumpti,
8-A SDA Complex, Shimla - 171009
TEL: +91 177 221783/221430
FAX: +91 177 221783

ADITYA SOLAR SHOP
Urja Bhavan, Main Road, No.2,
Shivajinagar, Bhopal- 461016
TEL: +91 755 556245/553672
FAX: +91 755 556566

ADITYA SOLAR SHOP
Vikas Sadan,
DRDA Office Complex
(Opp. New Court), Gurgaon
TEL: +91 916 632221

ADITYA SOLAR
62-B (2658), 37th Cross,
28th Main Road 9th Block,
Jayanagar,
Bangalore 560069, India
TEL : +91 80 26646990
FAX : +91 80 26613775
CONTACT: Mr. A.R. Srinath

AEGIS ASSOCIATES,
99/20, 20A, Doddanna Indl. Estate,
Near Peenya 2nd Stage,
Bangalore – 560 091
TEL: +91 80 28360847
FAX: +91 80 28361080
E-MAIL: aegis@bplnet.com

AKSHAY URJA PVT. LTD.
5, Sitabagh Colony
Girija, Vitawadi Road
Pune - 411 004, India

ALARCH INDUSTRIES,
15, Bahubali Nagar,
Jallahalli,
Bangalore – 560 013, India
TEL :+91 80 28381609
CONTACT : Mr. K. S. Suresh

BHARAT HEAVY ELECTRICALS LTD
16th Floor, Hindustan Times House,
18-20, Kasturba Gandhi Marg
New-Delhi -110 001
TEL: +91 11 23323199, 23327547
FAX: +91 11 23721680

BIPIN ENGINEERS PVT. LTD.
S.No.143, Vadgoan-Dhayari,
Pune 411 041, India
TEL : +91 20 4392064
FAX : +91 20 5292084
CONTACT : Mr. Revankar

CHAITANYA ENTERPRISES
597, 2nd Block, 1st Main,
Rajajinagar,
Bangalore - 560010, India
TEL : +91 80 23325022
CONTACT: Mr. Anil Arjunagi

CHEMSOLAR ENERGY SYSTEMS PVT LTD.
47, 8 Main, Malleswaram
Bangalore - 560055, India
TEL :+91 80 23341062/23316329
FAX : +91 80 23376302
E-MAIL : mvbppt@giasbgl.vsnl.net.in
CONTACT: Dr. S. N. Joshi

COLLEFF ENGINEERING
Survey No 469, Kapadgoan
Near Godke Mata Londand
Dist. Satara (Maharashtra), India

DECCAN ELECTRO WORKS PANEL DIVISION
G-76, MIDC Gokul Shirgaon,
Taluka Karveer,
Dist Kolhapur – 416 234
TEL: +91 231 672984

DHEEMANTH ENGINEERING
14, Behing Check Post,
1st Main, Kamakshipalya Layout,
Vijayanagar North
Bangalore – 560 079, India
TEL : +91 80 23489377
CONTACT: Mr. Bhaskar Awadhani

DISOL SOLAR SYSTEMS
814, Laggere Main Road,
Chowdeshwari Nagar, Peenya,
Bangalore - 560058, India
TEL :+91 80 28398471/ 28391123
CONTACT: Mr. Prabhanna

DIVYA INDUSTRIES
814, Chowdeshwari Nagar,
Laggeri Main Road,
Laggeri Peenya Post,
Bangalore – 560058
TEL: +91 80 28398471

ECOSOLAR SYSTEMS (INDIA) LTD.
117/A/2 Pune-Sinhgad Road,
Pune-411030, India
TEL : +91 20 4336999/
4330442/4330481
FAX : +91 20 4336412
CONTACT : Mr. Nitant Mate

EMVEE SOLAR SYSTEMS
No.253, 5th Main Road,
10th Cross Vasanthappa Block,
Bangalore – 560 032
TEL: +91 80 23337033, 23331950
FAX: +91 80 23334804
E-MAIL: emmvee@vsnl.com

ENGEE SOLAR LTD.,
435, IMAD, 18th Main,
6th Block, Koramangala,
Bangalore – 560 095, India
TEL : +91 80 25536922
CONTACT: Mr. V. P. Mehta

ENN CEE ENTERPRISES
542, 1 Stage, C.M.H. Road,
Indiranagar,
Bangalore - 560 038, India
TEL : +91 80 25259858
FAX : +91 80 25259858
EMAIL : enncee.chaugule@
mantraonline.com

ENSOLAR SYSTEMS
No.1567, 7th Cross, 2nd Main,
Govinda Raja Nagar,
Bangalore – 560 079 (Karnataka)
TELEFAX: +91 80 23355333, 23385500

ERENA TECHNOLOGIES (INDIA)
No.52, Doddanna Industrial Estate,
Near Peenya 2nd Stage,
Bangalore – 560 091 (Karnataka)
TEL: +91 80 28364014

GADHIA SOLAR ENERGY SYSTEMS PVT LTD
Plot No. 86, Old G.I.D.C. Gundlav,
Valsad-396 035.
Gujarat, India
OFFICE TELEFAX: +91 02632 222423
WORKS TEL: +91 2632-236703/ 237408
FAX: +91 2632 237342
E-MAIL: gadhiasolar@yahoo.co.in
WEB: http://www.gadhiasolar.net

GANGA INDUSTRIES
No.4020/3562, B.M.Shankarappa
Industrial Estate,
Sunkada Katte,
Magadi Main Road,
Vishwaneedam Post,
Bangalore – 560 091
TEL: +91 80 23285031

GARODIA ENERGY SYSTEMS PVT. LTD.
149/156, Garodia Shopping Centre,
Garodia Nagar, Ghatkopar (E),
Mumbai - 400077, India
TEL : +91 22 25110342

GENISES GOLD SOLAR
Heaven Hill, # 72, Further Extn.,
Mahalakshmi Layout,
Bangalore – 560 086, India
TEL : +91 80 23499954
CONTACT: Mr. Allen A. George

HI-TECH SOLAR SYSTEMS
44, Temple Road, Malleswaram,
Bangalore – 560 003, India
TEL : +91 80 23344902
CONTACT: Mr. G. K. Shivalingappa

HONEY HILLS SYNERGY SYSTEMS,
No. 365, IV Phase,
Peenya Industrial Area,
Bangalore – 560 058
TELEFAX: +91 28361282, 28361469

HOT HOLD SYSTEM PVT. LTD.,
474/354, Kottige Palya,Magadi Road,
Bangalore – 560 079, India
TEL : +91 80 3388358
CONTACT: Mr. Prakash Shetty

INDIA SOLAR EQUIPMENTS
#297,8th Main,10th Cross,1st
Block, Jayanagar,
Bangalore - 560011, India
TEL: +91 80 26552099
CONTACT: Mr. Narayan. H.S

INTER SOLAR SYSTEMS (P) LTD.,
Plot No. 39, Industrial Area,
Phase-II, Chandigarh – 160 002
TEL: +91 172 655349, 579002
FAX: +91 172 652319
E-MAIL: intersolar@glide.net.in

J.H. IMPEX PVT. LTD.,
4, "Srikrishna",
Behind Bimajyothi LIC Colony,
West of Chord Road,
Bangalore 560 079, India
TEL : +91 80 23483152

JAIN IRRIGATION SYSTEMS LTD
Solar Division,
PO Box No 72,
Bambhori,
Jalgaon 425001, India
TEL: +91 257 250011
FAX: +91 257 251111
E-MAIL: jains@jains.com
WEB: http://www.jains.com
CONTACT: Sanjeev Phadnis

JYOTHI SOLAR EQUIPMENTS (P) LTD.
1, Tata Nagar, Kodigehalli
Nagashetty Halli Main Road,
Shahkara Nagar Post,
Bangalore - 560 092, India
TEL : +91 80 23417020
E-MAIL :brp_bhat@skybiz.com
CONTACT: Mr. Ravi Prakash

KADUR INDUSTRIES LTD
R.V.V. Post, Mylasandra,
Bangalore - 560 059, India
TEL : +91 80 28601181/28601182
EMAIL : kadursolco@hotmail.com
CONTACT: Mr. S.V. Kadur

KAUSHAL SOLAR EQUIPMENTS PVT. LTD.,
767/7, Neel-Kusum, Near PVC Gym.,
Pune-4, India
TEL : +91 20 5676379 / 0472
FAX : +91 20 5677789
CONTACT: Mr. C.M Kaushal

KAYNES ENERGY SYSTEMS
23-25, Belagola Food
Indl. Estate, Metagalli P.O.
Mysore - 570 016, India
TEL : +91 821 511612
FAX : +91 821 512701
EMAIL : kaynessolar@vsnl.com
CONTACT: Mr. Ramesh Kannan

KHAMBETE AND KHAMBETE
65-66, Audyogik Vasahat,
Ajintha Road, Jalgaon – 425 003
TEL: +91 257 210650, 210206
FAX: +91 257 210948
E-MAIL: khambete@bom6.vsnl.net.in

KOTAK URJA PVT LTD
226, 1st Floor,
Opp. Sai Baba Temple, 14th Cross,
Sampege Road, Malleshwaram,
Bangalore-560 003
TEL: +91 80 23560456/57
FAX: +91 80 23562233

KRAFTWORK SOLAR PRIVATE LTD
Door No. VI/99-A,
Major Industrial Estate,
PO Kalamassery DP
Kochi – 683 109 (Kerala)
TEL: +91 484 542337
FAX: +91 484 370073
E-MAIL: kraftworksolar@usa.net

M. LAXMAN & CO.
15/A/2, PWD Colony, Near Varunraj,
Erandawane, Pune 4, India
TEL : +91 20 340719
FAX : +91 20 338201
CONTACT: Mr. Mahabaleshwarkar

M/S SUNRISE SOLAR PVT LTD
P.B No. 2130, 1190/8,
13th Main Road,
Prakash Nagar
Bangalore – 560021
TEL: +91 80 23328533
E-MAIL: solar@bgl.vsnl.net.in

M/S. MASTER ENGINEERS
Sl.No.139, Warje Malwadi,
Dudhane Estate,
Pune – 411 052
TEL: +91 20 5290499
MOBILE: 98220 62487

M/S. RASHMI INDUSTRIES
No. 60 & 61, Begur Road,
Hongasandra Village,
Bangalore – 560 068
TEL: +91 80 25734115, 25734114
FAX: +91 80- 25732309
E-MAIL: hpngroup@vsnl.net

MACHINOCRAFT
154-A, Pune-Satara Road
Vasudeo Estate,
Pune - 411043, India
TEL : +91 20 571457 / 579529
FAX : +91 20 574623
CONTACT : Mr. A. W. Wagh

MARUT ENERGY EQUIPMENTS PVT. LTD,
D-1/18, MIDC, Ambad,
Nashik – 422 010
TEL: +91 253 804910
FAX: +91 253 384061
E-MAIL:
marketing@solarecindia.com

MERLONI TERMO SANITARI (INDIA) LTD.,
#122, Maruthi Market, Kilari Road,
Bangalore - 560053, India
TEL : +91 80 22262353
FAX : +91 80 22204047
E-MAIL :venky_seshadri@yahoo.com
CONTACT: Mr. S Venkatesh

MYSORE SALES INTERNATIONAL LTD.
"MSIL HOUSE"
36, Cunningham Road,
Bangalore – 560 052, India
TEL : +91 80 22264021
CONTACT: Mr. Rangaswamy

MYTRON SYSTEMS INC.
161, Vidyut Nagar B,
Ajmer Road
Jaipur-302021, India
TEL : +91 141 373682
E-MAIL:yogeshc@jp1.dot.net.in

NAMSI SOLAR PRIVATE LIMITED
No.240, 2nd Floor, 32nd Cross,
7th Block, Jayanagar,
Bangalore – 560 082
TEL: +91 80 26647308
FAX: +91 80 26644429
E-MAIL: info@namsisolar.com

NAVKAR ENGINEERS
Behind Guptanagar Bus Stand
Devas Road, Vasna
Ahmedabad - 380 007, India
TEL:91 79 6632048/6633098/
6633048
FAX :91 79 6632048/6633098/
6633048
EMAIL : navkar@satyam.net.in
CONTACT: Nitin Shah

NAZUMM METTALLICA PVT. LTD.,
36/3, 1 Cross, Pukaraj Layout,
1st Cross, Bannergatta Road,
Adugodi, Bangalore 560 030,
India
TEL : +91 80 22225804
CONTACT: Mr. Husain

NEBULAR POWER EQUIPMENTS PVT. LTD.
Shree, 496/A, Kasba Peth
Pune - 411011, India
TEL : +91 212 456057

NEXUS ENERGYTECH PVT. LTD.
117/A/2, Sinhgad Road,
Parvati,
Pune – 411 030, India
TEL : +91 212 536800
CONTACT : Mr. Aravind Karandikar

NRG TECHNOLOGIES
989/6, G.I.D.C. Makarpura,
Vadodara – 390 010 (Gujarat)
TEL: +91 265 642094
E-MAIL: nrgtechnologists@yahoo.com

NUETECH SYSTEMS SOLAR GEYSER
P.B. No. 9167,
Sunkadakatte,
Vishwaneedam Post,
Bangalore – 560 091, India
TEL : +91 80 23481905
CONTACT: Mr. Surendrakumar

PEENYA ALLOYS PVT. LTD.,
248, 3rd Cross,
3rd Phase,
Peenya Industrial Area,
Bangalore – 560 058,
India
TEL : +91 80 28394259
CONTACT : Mr. George Kutty

PITTIE SOLAR PRIVATE LTD
Pittie Renewable Energy Systems,
Pittie Centre, 37/1b Vadgaon Sheri,
Pune
TEL: +91 20 7033417
FAX: +91 20 7031150
E-MAIL: pittie@vsnl.com
WEB: http://www.pittiesolar.com
CONTACT: Ravi Pittie

PRABHU ENERGY SYSTEMS
2nd Floor, Hameed Complex,
Kuloor Ferry Road, Alake,
Mangalore – 575003
TEL: +91 824 491967
FAX: +91 024 458315
E-MAIL: prbengsy@sancharnet.in

R. C. ENTERPRISES
2, 8th Main,
Between 7th & 8th Cross,
Malleswaram
Bangalore – 560 003, India
TEL : +91 80 23344918
CONTACT : Mr. Rajshekhar

R. K. SOLAR POWER SYSTEMS PVT. LTD.,
6, 6th Cross, Malleswaram,
Bangalore – 560 003, India
TEL : +91 80 23493920
CONTACT: Mr. S. Ramakrishnan

RAVI PRECISION P LTD.
37/1B, Vadgoan Sheri,
Pune - 411 014, India
TEL : +91 20 680792 / 683417
FAX : +91 20 680150
CONTACT:Mr. Ravi Pittie

RAVI SOLAR HOT POTS
62 B, 37th Cross, 28th Main
Jayanagar 9th Block,
Bangalore – 560 069, India
TEL : +91 80 26646990
CONTACT: Mr. Srinath

RENEWABLE ENERGY SYSTEMS LTD.,
779, 13th Main, 1st Cross
H.A.L. 1st Stage,
Bangalore – 560 008, India
TEL : +91 80 25263210
CONTACT: Mr. Srinivas Prasad

SABHA SOLAR ENERGY
Flat No. 1/D, No.5, 9th Main Road,
(Behind Rajmahal Mini Market),
Rajmahal Vilas Extn.
Sadashivnagar,
Bangalore- 560 080
TEL: +91 80 23340245, 23342980
FAX: +91 80 233456221

SAIRAM ENERGY PRODUCTS (INDIA) PVT. LTD.
3-6-369, A/11, Street No.1
Himayatnagar,
Hyderabad - 500 029, India

SAVEMAX SOLAR SYSTEMS PVT. LTD.,
Jayaprabha,
Jadhavnagar,
Vadgaon Bk., Pune – 41.
TEL: +91 20 4358613, 4358781
FAX: +91 20 4358613
E-MAIL: savemax@vsnl.com

SHIMSHON RENEWABLES PVT. LTD.
M-10/1697,
Mtl Board, Yerwada,
Pune – 411 006, India
CONTACT : Mr. Samson I Raymond

SHIVA SOLAR SYSTEMS PVT. LTD.
7378,Prem Nagar, Gali No 5
Subzi Mandi
New Delhi 110 007, India
TEL : +91 11 2925938 / 2930827
CONTACT: Bharat Shetty

SHRINGAR ENGINEERING & ENERGY SYSTEMS PVT. LTD.
C-74, III Stage,
Peenya Industrial Area,
Bangalore – 560 058
TEL: +91 80 28362304
E-MAIL: suryakanthi@vsnl.net.in

SIGMA STEEL & ENGINEERS (P) LTD.
225/11, Bagmari Road,
Kolkata –700054
TEL: +91 33 23515942
E-MAIL: ssepl@cal.vsnl.net.in

SKYLARK THERMAL ENERGY SYSTEMS
37, Aundh Road
Ambedkar Chowk
Pune 411 003, India

SOLAHART INDIA
EPL India Ltd. H4A,
Kalkaji
New Delhi - 110 019, India
TEL : +91 11 26286010 / 26204333
FAX : +91 11 26231993
CONTACT : Mr. Bharat Shetty

SOLAR CATCHER
9/10 Bendrenagar,
Subramanyapur Main Road,
Bangalore – 560 070
TEL: +91 80 26663129, 26660161

SOLAR ENERGY ENTERPRISES
17,Janishram Society
B/H, Sahjanand College Amhawadi
Ahmedabad - 380015, India
TEL : +91 79 446119

SOLAR ENERGY SERVICES
Plot No. 303, Savli GIDC Estate,
Savli, Near Village Manjusar,
Savli Road, Dist Vadodara – 391775
TEL: +91 265 337674, 351703

SOLAR PRODUCT CO.,
II/61, Mukund Nagar,
Pune – 411 037
TEL: +91 212 464182
FAX: +91 212 369815

SOLAR TECH ENTERPRISES
39/68, Mahakavi. G. Road,
Iyyattil Junction,
Cochin - 682 011, India
CONTACT : Mr. George Mathew

SOLAR TECHNOLOGIES &SERVICES INDIA (P) LTD.
39/68 Mahakav G.Rao
Cochin-682011, Kerala, India
TEL : +91 0484 366572
FAX : +91 0484 362483
E-MAIL : solar@giasmd01.vsnl.net.in
CONTACT : Mr. Vinod Anthraper

SOLARTECH INDIA LTD.
B-15A Chomu House, Jaipur,
Rajasthan - 302001, India
TEL : +91 141 377140
E-MAIL :yogesh@jp1.dot.net.in

SOLCHROME SYSTEMS INDIA LTD.
161, Sukhdev Vihar,
New Delhi-11025, India
TEL : +91 11 26838365
FAX : +91 11 26835160

SOLKER INDUSTRIES LTD.
No.436, Sidco Industrial Estate,
Behind Telephone Exchange,
Ambattur,
Chennai – 600 098
TEL: +91 44 28274142, 28271819
FAX: +91 44 28273435
E-MAIL: solker20@hotmail.com,
sales@solker.com

SPACE – AGE ELECTRO TECHNOLOGY (I) PVT. LTD.,
36-B, II Phase,
Peenya Industrial Area, Bangalore,
India
TEL : +91 80 28392445.
CONTACT: Mr. Jayaramu

SRI VAISHNAVI INDUSTRIES
22, Metagalli Extension
Mysore-570016, India
TEL : +91 0821 513595
FAX : +91 0821 521550
CONTACT: Mr. N. Asnnamalai

SRINIVAS SOLAR SYSTEMS
404, 36th Cross, 17th Main,
4th T Block, Jayanagar,
Bangalore – 560 041, India
TEL : +91 80 26653034
CONTACT: Mr. Srinivas Iyer

STANDARD PRODUCTS MFG. CO.
2/14, Marol Coop Indl. Estate,
M. Vassanji Road,
Sakinaka, Andheri (E)
Mumbai – 400 059
TEL: +91 22 2850 0970
FAX: +91 22 2850 6703

STANDARDS ENGINEERING CO.,
131/7B, 'Chandan' Hadapsar
Industrial Estate, Pune – 411 013
TEL: +91 212 670237
FAX: +91 212 670414
E-MAIL: pungaliya@mantramail.com

STEELHACKS INDUSTRIES,
9A/1, GIDC Vithal Udyognagar – 388 121 (Gujarat)
TEL: +91 2692-36156, 35558
FAX: +91 2692-36534
E-MAIL: unisol@icenet.net

SUDARSHAN SAUR SHAKTI PVT. LTD.
35, Bhagya Nagar, Aurangabad
Maharastra - 431001, India
TEL : +91 0240 333491
FAX : +91 0240 356197
CONTACT : Mr. Sanjay Jinturker

SUN BEAM SOLAR WATER HEATER
21/5, Konanakunte Cross,
Kanakapura Road,
Bangalore – 560 062, India
TEL: +91 80 26663328
CONTACT: Mr. Chandrashekhar

SUN SOURCE INDIA LTD.
1st Floor, Ecotech Navrang Centre,
Swastik Char Rasta
Navrangpura
Ahmedabad-380 009, India

SUNBEAM SOLAR THERMAL CO.
1114/11 University Road
Pune – 411016, India
TEL : +91 0212 356097
E-MAIL: sushil@giaspn01.vsnl.net.in

SUNCARE SOLAR SYSTEMS PVT. LTD.
3 & 4, Buddanna Indl. Estate,
Vidyapeetha Road, Kengeri
Bangalore – 560 060
TEL: +91 80 28483044

SUNRISE SOLAR,
P.B. No. 2130,
1191/8, 13th Main Road,
Prakashnagar,
Bangalore – 560 021, India
TEL : +91 80 23328533
CONTACT : Mr. A. Palani

SUNTRAP DEVICES
B-49, N.G.O. "B" Colony,
Tirunelveli – 627007 (Tamilnadu)
TEL: +91 462 553693
E-MAIL: suntrap@md4.vsnl.net.in

SURABHI SOLAR WATER HEATER
121 ITI /
Dyavasandra Indl. Estate,
Whitefield Road,
Bangalore – 560 048, India
TEL : +91 80 26632090
CONTACT: Mr. Shreedhar

SURAJ TECHNO BUILD
311, Chikka Banaswadi
Govt. School Road,
Bangalore – 560 043, India
TEL : +91 80 25450789
CONTACT: Mr. Loganathan

SURVODAYA SOLAR EQUIPMENTS,
43/1, 5th Main Road,
Malleswaram,
Bangalore – 560 003, India
TEL : +91 80 23346185
CONTACT: Mr. S. K. Raghu

SURYA ENTERPRISE
6/80/4, Bijoygarh,
Kolkata -700032, India
TEL : +91 033 24127465
E-MAIL: sumit_roy@hotmail.com

SURYA JYOTI DEVICES (INDIA) PVT. LTD
Village Challon, PO Kurali,
District Ropar, Punjab
TEL: +91 1888 32039, 32340

SURYA SHAKTHI,
2, 1st Floor, Sree Bharathi,
V.H.B.C.S. Layout,
Basaveshwaranagar 1st Stage,
Magadi Main Road,
Bangalore – 560079
TEL: +91 80 23486138, 23487342, 9845053216

SURYA SHAKTI
739, Industrial Area, Phase-II,
Chandigarh
TEL: +91 172 653299, 773214
FAX: +91 172 771576

SURYAKIRAN PVT. LTD.
Development Area,
Binanipuram PO, Edayar,
Kochi – 683 502
TEL: +91 484 559184

SURYODAYA HI -TECH ENGINEERING (P) LTD
1-10-68/4, Chikoti Gardens,
Begumpet, Hyderabad – 500 016
TEL: +91 40 7765831
FAX: +91 40 7767813

SWAMY SOLAR SYSTEMS
"Sapthagiri Nivas",
117/10, Main Channel Road,
Lingahinapalya, Ulsoor,
Bangalore – 560008
TEL: +9180 25545131, 25252731
FAX: +91 80 25561250

SWATHI SOLAR INTERNATIONAL
64, 3rd Cross,
Banasankari 3rd Stage, 1st Block,
Bangalore – 560 085, India
TEL : +91 80 26694638
CONTACT: Mr. A.K.V. Raghu

TATA BP SOLAR INDIA LTD
Marketing, Plot No. 78,
Electronic City, Hosur Road,
Bangalore 561229, India
TEL: +91 80 28520083
FAX: +91 80 28520116
E-MAIL: tatabp@tatabp.com
WEB: http://www.tatabpsolar.com
CONTACT: K Subramanya

TECHNOMAX SOLAR DEVICES,
4 –A, Venkateshwara School
Street, R.M.V. 2nd Stage,
Nagashetty Hally, Bangalore 560094,
TEL : +91 80 23418723
CONTACT: Mr. Santosh Tampi

USHAKIRAN SYSTEMS
56, 3rd Main Road,
Vyalikaval, Bangalore - 560 003
TEL : +91 80 23311639
CONTACT: Mr. M.S. Satish

VIJAYA INDUSTRIES
166/2 Katapady – 574 105
Udupi Dist, Karnataka
TEL: +91 8252 557127, 557327
FAX: +91 8252 557700
E-MAIL: vijaya-vip@zetainfotech.com

VISHAL INDUSTRIES
315,A-31, Deen Building
Compound, N.M. Joshi Marg
Mumbai - 400011, India
TEL : +91 022 23076426

YESHOMA INDUSTRIES
No. 59 (New No.8, 3rd Cross,
Ittamadu Village Extn.
Banashankari 3rd Stage,
Bangalore – 560 085
TEL: +91 80 22235029, 22624991

SOLAR PHOTOVOLTAIC

AMMINI ENERGY SYSTEMS PVT. LTD.
Industrial Estate Pappanamcode,
Trivandrum, Kerala-695019, India
TEL : +91 0471 490508
FAX : +91 0471 490832
E-MAIL : ammini@vsnl.com

BHARAT ELECTRONICS LTD.,
16/2, Race Course Road,
Bangalore – 560 001, India
TEL : +91 80 22259705
CONTACT : Mr. I. S. Isaac

BHARAT HEAVY ELECTRICAL LTD.
BHEL House, Siri fort
New Delhi 110 016, India
TEL : +91 11 26492043 / 26492745
FAX : +91 11 26493021

CENTRAL ELECTRONICS LTD.,
51, CMH Road, Indiranagar,
Bangalore – 560 038, India
TEL : +91 80 25251740
CONTACT: Mr. M. Banerjee

CROMPTON GREAVES LTD.
Electronics Technology Division
Solar Systems Group, 71-72, MIDC,
Satpur, Nashik 422 007, India

ECOSOLAR SYSTEMS (INDIA) LTD.
117/A/2 Pune-Sinhgad Road,
Pune-411030, India
TEL : +91 20 4336999/
4330442/4330481
FAX : +91 20 4336412

GLOBAL SOLAR ENERGY (INDIA) LTD.
2,Ring Road Kilokri,
Opp. Maharani Bagh
New Delhi-110014, India
FAX : +91 11 26823978.

GREEN DOT ELECTRIC LIMITED
G-9 Hemkunt Towers 98
Nehru Place,
New Delhi –110019, India
TEL : +91 11 26222088
E-MAIL:greendot@emails.com

GRUNDFOS PUMPS INDIA PVT LTD.
C-202, Samrat Apts., 39th Cross,
East End, D Main Road,
9th Block, Jayanagar,
Bangalore - 560 069, India
TEL : +91 80 26344788
TEL/FAX: +91 80 26552604
E-MAIL : ranga@grundfos.com
WEB : http://www.grundfos.com
CONTACT: Mr. L. Rangarajan

ISOVOLTA INDIA PVT LTD
78, Victoria Road
Bangalore 560047, India
CONTACT: Mr. H.G. Nagaraj

ITI
45/1, Magrath Road,
Bangalore – 560 025, India
TEL : +91 80 25366116 / 25364618
CONTACT : Mr. Shaukat Ahmed

JELTRON SYSTEMS (I) PVT. LTD.
P.B.No. 49, 6-3-1199/2,
Vaman Naik Lane, Umanaga Colony,
Begumpet,
Hyderabad – 500 016, India
TEL : +91 40 311159 / 3322586
CONTACT: Mr. Sanjay Pajpai

K.J. ELECTRONICS PVT. LTD.
105, Arun Chambers
317, SBS Road, Fort
Mumbai- 400001, India
TEL : +91 22 22617336
CONTACT: Mr. K.J.John

KAUSHAL SOLAR EQUIPMENTS PVT. LTD.,
767/7, Neel-Kusum,
Near PVC Gym.,
Pune-4, India
TEL : +91 20 5676379 / 0472
FAX : +91 20 5677789
CONTACT : Mr. C.M Kaushal

KAYNES ENERGY SYSTEMS
23-25, Belagola Food
Indl. Estate, Metagalli P.O.
Mysore - 570 016, India
TEL : +91 0821 511612
FAX : +91 0821 512701
EMAIL : kaynessolar@vsnl.com
CONTACT: Mr. Ramesh Kannan

KOTAK URJA PVT. LTD.
378, 10th Cross, IV Phase, Peenya
Industrial Estate, Bangalore-560 058
TEL :+91 80 28362136/23560457
FAX : +91 80 28366670
E-MAIL : kotakurja@vsnl.com
WEB : www.kotakurja.com
CONTACT : Mr. Srinivas Kumar

MAHARISHI SOLAR TECHNOLOGY LTD.
A-14, Mohan Co-op. Indl. Estate,
Mathura Road,
New Delhi – 110044, India
TEL :91 11 26959401(O) 26832486 (R)
FAX : +91 11 2683 6682
E-MAIL : abishek@maharishi.net
WEB : http://www.maharishisolar.com
CONTACT: Ajay Prakash Shrivastava

MERIDIAN ENERGY SYSTEMS
2 H.S.G House, Vijay Cross Roads
Navrangpura, Ahmedabad
Gujarat - 380009, India
TEL : merdian@ad1.vsnl.net.in

NEPTUNE ENERGY TECHNOLOGIES (P) LTD.
No. 779, 13th Main, 1st Cross,
H.A.L. II Stage,
Bangalore - 560 008, India
TEL : +91 80 25263210
FAX : +91 80 25263210
E-MAIL : neptun@satyam.net.in

OMEGA ELECTRONICS
Indl Estate, Pappanam Code
Trivandrum - 695 019, India
TEL : +91 0471 490508
FAX : +91 0471 490832
E-MAIL : ammini@vsnl.com
CONTACT : Madhu K G

PENTAFOUR SOLEC TECH LTD.
332-2, Arcot Road, Kodambakkam,
Madras -600 024
TEL : +91 044 24334292
FAX :91 044 24834517
CONTACT:Mr. S. Krishnamurthy

PHOTON ENERGY SYSTEMS LTD
Plot No. 775-K, Road No. 45,
Jubilee Hills, Hyderabad 33, India
TEL: +91 40 3231 698
FAX: +91 40 3231 545
CONTACT: D T Barki

POLYENE GENERAL INDUSTRIES PVT. LTD.
A-11 & 12
Industrial Estate, Guindy
Madras - 660 032, India

PREMIER SOLAR SYSTEM (P) LTD.
41& 42.S.V. Co-op.Indl. Estate
Balanagar, Hyderabad –500037

RANS ELECTRONICS
157, 3rd Cross, Domlur Layout,
Bangalore – 560 071, India
TEL :91 80 25363936
CONTACT: Mr. P.T. Ramjee

RENEWABLE ENERGY SYSTEMS LTD.,
779, 13th Main, 1st Cross
H.A.L. 1st Stage,
Bangalore – 560 008, India
TEL :91 80 25263210
CONTACT: Mr. Srinivas Prasad

REPL SYNERGY POWER SYSTEMS LTD.
Saroosh Building,
2nd Floor, Dr. D N Road, Fort
Bombay - 400001, India
TEL :91 22 2621139
FAX :91 22 2042922

SHELL RENEWABLES INDIA PVT. LTD.
S 907, Manipal Centre,
47, Dickenson Road,
Bangalore – 560 042, India
TEL :91 80 25587850
FAX: +91 80 25585827
CONTACT: Mr Ramesh

SHRI SHAKTI LPG LTD.
Venus Plaza,
Begumpet,
Hyderabad-16, India
TEL :91 40 7899416
CONTACT : Mr. D.V. Sathya Kumar

SIEMENS LIMITED
Component Division
No. 84, Keonics Electronics City
Hosur Road,
Bangalore - 561229, India
TEL :91 08337 8521121
CONTACT: Mr. S.B. Variar

SOLAR TECH ENTERPRISES
39/68, Mahakavi. G. Road,
Iyyattil Junction,
Cochin - 682 011, India
CONTACT: Mr. George Mathew

SOLAR TECHNOLOGIES &SERVICES INDIA (P) LTD.
39/68 Mahakav G.Rao
Cochin-682011, Kerala
TEL :91 0484 366572
FAX :91 0484 362483
E-MAIL : solar@giasmd01.vsnl.net.in
CONTACT : Mr. Vinod Anthraper

SOLKER INDUSTRIES LTD.
436, Sidco Indl. Estate
Behind Telephone Exchange
Ambattur,
Chennai - 600 098, India
TEL :91 44 26257869, 26244878
FAX :91 44 28273435
EMAIL : solker20@hotmail.com
CONTACT : Mr. K. E. Ragunaathan

SUNTIME ENERGY LIMITED
E-3 Lajpat Nagar-II,
New Delhi 110024. India
TEL: +91 11 26834129
FAX: +91 11 26839444
E-MAIL: suntime@del3.vsnl.net.in
WEB: http://www.suryajyoti.com
CONTACT: RS Ahluwalia

SUNWATT ENERGY INDIA
MIG C-20 Dr. AS Rao Nagar,
ECIL PO, Hyderabad 500062, India
TEL: +91 40 7135381
FAX: +91 40 7135381
E-MAIL: a_nair@vsnl.com
WEB: http://www.sunwatt-energy.com
CONTACT : Anil Nair

SUPERTRONIX
23/819, Valiyasalai Street
Trivandrum- 695 036, India

TATA BP SOLAR INDIA LTD.,
78, Electronic City, Hosur Road,
Bangalore – 560 029, India
TEL :91 80 28520082
CONTACT: Mr. A. K. Vora

TITAN ENERGY SYSTEMS LTD.
16, Aruna Enclave,
Trimulgherry,
Secundrabad – 500 015, India
TEL : +91 842085

TITAN INDUSTRIES LTD.,
Tower "A", Golden Enclave,
Airport Road,
Bangalore – 560 017, India
TEL : +91 80 25273180
CONTACT : Mr. Vikram Rajaram

UDHAYA SEMICONDUCTORS LTD.
#1/482, Avanashi Road
Neelambur,Coimbatore - 641014
TEL :91 0422 827003 / 827545
FAX :91 0422 828504 / 572675
EMAIL : udhaya@vsnl.com
CONTACT : U. Ashok

UNITRON ENERGY SYSTEMS PVT. LTD.
12 A1, Bldg, Indira Park,
Nagar Road,
Pune – 411 006, India
TEL :91 20 687006 / 684399
CONTACT:Mr. M. P. Ravindranath

VISTAR ELECTRONICS PVT. LTD.
42 A /1B Nilgiri Apt., Karve Road
Pune - 411030, India
TEL : +91 20 5431207
CONTACT : Mr. H. V. Joshi

WEBEL –SI ENERGY SYSTEMS LTD.
14B, Everest House
46C, Chowringhee Road
Kolkata 700 071, India
TEL :91 33 22428634

WIND

ASIAN WIND TURBINES (PVT.) LTD.
4/262 ,Old Mahabalipuram Road
Kandanchavadi
Chennai-600096, India
TEL: +91 44 2448 0183
FAX: +91 44 2492 56719
CONTACT : Mr. Saibaba Vutukuri

BHARAT HEAVY ELECTRICAL LTD.
BHEL House, Siri fort
New Delhi 110 016, India
TEL :91 11 26492043 / 26492745
FAX :91 11 26493021

CONTROLS & JACOBS WIND ENERGY
22, Okhla Industrial Area
New Delhi 110 020, India
TEL : +91 11 26836020
FAX : +91 11 26847154

DAS LAGERWAY WIND TURBINES LTD.
Wescare Towers Cenatoph Road,
Tynampet Chennai - 600018, India
TEL: +91 44 2436 0581
FAX: +91 44 24360 583
CONTACT : Mr. Raghunathan

ENERCON (INDIA) LTD.
Kolsire House,
Block No.31,
Shah Indl. Estate
Veeradesai Road Andheri(West)
Mumbai-400053, India
E-MAIL: eildir@gnbir.global.net.in
TEL: +91 22 26364848
CONTACT : Mr. Yogesh Mehra

FLOVEL TACKE (P) LTD.
Wind Power Systems,
A-219, Okhla Industrial Area,
Phase I
New Delhi 110 020, India
TEL :91 11 26223274 / 26210019
FAX :91 11 26223075

INDUJ ENERTECH LIMITED
"Avadh" Avadesh Parisar
Shree Ram Mills Premises
G.K.Marg, Worli
Mumbai-400018, India
TEL: +91 22 24965701
CONTACT : Mr. Vikas Kasliwal

INDIA

NEPC MICON
36, Wallajah Road
Chennai-600002, India
TEL: +91 44 25589834
E-MAIL: nepcind@md2.vsnl.net.in
CONTACT : Mr. Rajkumar Khemka

PIONEER WINCON LTD.
16-SP,Developed Plot,Industrial Estate, Guindy,Chennai-600032, India
TEL : +91 44 22334621
FAX : +91 44 22346626
E-MAIL: pwl@md3.vsnl.net.in
CONTACT : A.Sudhkaran

SUZLON ENERGY LTD
Suzlon house 5 Shrimali Society,
nr Shree Krishna Centre,
Navarangpura,
Ahmedabad 380009, India
TEL: +91796449551
FAX: +91796565540
E-MAIL: bnshah@suzlon.com
CONTACT: Jayesh Kajrekar

SUZLON ENERGY
5th Floor, Godrej Millenium,
9 Koregan Park Road,
Pune 411001, India
TEL: +9120 - 4022000
FAX: +9120 - 4022100
E-MAIL: tvivek@suzlon.com
WEB: http://www.suzlon.com
CONTACT: Vivek Taneja

TTG INDUSTRIES
TTG House, 36, College Road
Chennai 600006, India
TEL : +91 44 22651592
FAX : +91 44 26257780
CONTACT : Mr. P. Ashok

VENTIS INDIA PVT. LTD.
4, 3rd Cross, 3rd Main, 3rd Block, Koromangala,Bangalore-560034, India
TEL : +91 80 25534798
CONTACT : Mr. D'souza

VESTAS RRB INDA LIMITED
189 Sukhdev Vihar,
New Delhi 110025 India
TEL: +91 11 26327711
FAX: +91 11 26327733
E-MAIL:
pawanshakthi@vestasrrb.com
WEB: http://www.vestasrrb.com
CONTACT: Rakesh Bakshi

WIND POWER LTD.
Royalpettah, Chennai 600004, India
TEL :91 44 28551466
91 44 28551577
FAX :91 44 2855128

WINDIA POWER LTD.
Vinay Bavya Complex,
A Wing, 159-A, CST Road,
Kalina,
Santa Cruz, Mumbai 400098, India
TEL :91 22 26175188
FAX :91 22 22063272

BIOMASS

ANKUR SCIENTIFIC ENERGY TECHNOLOGIES PVT. LTD.
"Ankur", Near Old Sama Jakat Naka,
Baroda - 390 008, India
TEL :91 265 793098 / 794021
FAX : +91 265 794042
E-MAIL : ascent@wilnetonline.net
WEB : www.ankurscientific.com
CONTACT : Dr. B.C. Jain

CICON BIOENERGY SYSTEMS LTD.
Plot 61-B, Kasturba Nagar
Bhopal – 462024, India
TEL :91 755 789446
CONTACT: Sheeja Vargavan

DECENTRALISED ENERGY SYSTEMS INDIA (P) LTD.
B- 32, TARA Crescent,
Qutab Institutional Area,
New Delhi – 110016, India
CONTACT: Mr. P.K. Bhatnagar

NETPRO RENEWABLE ENERGY (INDIA) LTD.
#139/B, 10th Main,
Rajmahal Vilas Extn.,
Bangalore - 560 080, India
TEL :91 80 23360202
CONTACT: Ms. Anandi Sharan

RADHE ENGINEERING CO.
D-110 Rajdoot Industrial Estate,
4-Umakant Pandit Udyog Nagar,
Near MavadiPlote-
Rajkot,
Gujarat- 360004, India
TEL :91 281 372557 / 67

COGENERATION

THERMAX LIMITED
Cogen Division, Sai Chambers,
15,Bombay Pune Road
Wakdewadi,
Pune 411 003, India
CONTACT: Shri Kirtiraj Jilkar

FUEL CELL

BHARAT HEAVY ELECTRICAL LTD.
BHEL House, Siri fort
New Delhi 110 016, India
TEL :91 11 6492043 / 6492745
FAX :91 11 6493021

SPIC SCIENCE FOUNDATION
111, Mount Road, Guindy,
Chennai-32, India
TEL: +91 44 22352400 / 2235 2342
FAX: +91 44 22351504 / 22352163
CONTACT : Dr. K.S.Dathathreyan

ELECTRIC VEHICLES

BHARAT HEAVY ELECTRICAL LTD.
BHEL House, Siri fort
New Delhi 110 016, India
TEL :91 11 26492043 / 26492745
FAX :91 11 26493021

REVA ELECTRIC CAR COMPANY
122 E Bommasandra Industrial Area
Bangalore – 562158, India
FAX :91 80 232580
91 80 234436
CONTACT: Mr. Jason Alexander

SMALL HYDRO

ASEA BROWN BOVERI LTD.
Vasvani Chambers
264/265, Dr. Annie Besant Road,
Bombay - 400025, India
TEL :91 22 24308231
FAX :91 22 24300143

BATLIBOI FORAS LTD.
99/2,99/3 ,2nd Floor ,N. R. Road
Bangalore-560002, India
TEL: +91 80 22218824
FAX: +91 80 22218825
E-MAIL: bforasin@bgl.vsnl.net.in
CONTACT : Mr. P. Dinesh Kumar

BOVING FOURESS PVT LTD.
Plot No 7,
KIADB Industrial Area,
P B 11 Hosakote
Bangalore - 562114, India
TEL : +91 80 7971263
FAX : +91 80 7971399
CONTACT : Mr. K. Sreenath

JYOTI LTD.
Industrial Area,
P O Chemical Industries,
Vadodra - 390 003, India
TEL : +91 265 321041 / 321038
FAX : +91 265 320766

KIRLOSKAR ELECTRIC CO LTD
PB 5555, Malleswaram West
No.2, 17th Main,
100 Ft Road,
4th B Block,
Bangalore - 560011, India
TEL :91 80 26431229 / 26445469
FAX :91 80 26445471
TEL/FAX : +91 80 25534798

RDF POWER PROJECTS LIMITED
318,Amrutha Ville,
Raj Bhavan Road,
Somajiguda
Hyderabad-500 082, India
CONTACT: M.Venkateshwarlu

STEEL INDUSTRIALS KERALA LTD. (HYDRO ELECTRICITY)
Silk Nagar, Athani P O
Mulamgunnathukavu
Thrissur, Kerala, India
FAX : 91 0487 95532

TECHNOLOGY INFORMATICS DESIGN ENDEAVOUR (TIDE)
19, 9th Cross, 6th Main
Malleshwaram,
Bangalore-560003, India
TEL : 91 80 23315656
CONTACT: Mr. Sampath Kumar

TRIVENI ENGINEERING WORKS LTD (TURBINES DIVISION)
Peenya Industrial Estate
Bangalore - 560 058, India
TEL : 91 80 28394721 / 28394771
FAX : 91 80 28395211

ENERGY EFFICIENCY

BAJAJ ELECTRICALS
Head Office
51, Mahatma Gandhi Road
Mumbai 400023, India
TEL: +91 22 22043780 / 22875135
FAX: +91 22 22828250

CROMPTON GREAVES LTD.
Electronics Technology Division
Solar Systems Group,
71-72, MIDC, Satpur,
Nashik 422 007, India

DCM SHRIRAM CONSOLIDATED LTD. (Energy Business)
5th Floor, Kanchenjunga Building,
18, Barakhamba Road,
New Delhi-110001, India.
TEL: +91 11 23316801-9
FAX: +91 11 23318072
E-MAIL: dscl@dscl.com
CONTACT : Dr. G. C. Duttaroy

GE LIGHTING (INDIA) LTD
H.R. Complex, 310/6,
Indl. Main Road,
5 Block, Koramangala
Bangalore - 560 095, India
TEL : 91 80 25522023
FAX : 91 80 25522021
CONTACT: Mr. Venu Gopal

INTESCO ASIA LTD.
144, Oakland Apartments
Ulsoor Road Cross
Bangalore - 560 042, India
TEL: +91 80 25583726
CONTACT : Mr. R. Kumar

OSRAM INDIA LTD.
Indo Mag House, 81/1 Adchini,
Shri Aurobindo Marg
New Delhi-110017,
India
TEL : 91 11 26566241
FAX : 91 11 26526184
CONTACT: Mr. Raj Sahgal

OMEGA ELECTRONICS
Indl Estate, Pappanam Code
Trivandrum - 695 019, India
TEL : 91 471 490508
FAX : 91 471 490832
E-MAIL : ammini@vsnl.com
CONTACT : Madhu K G

PHILIPS INDIA LTD
P-65, Taratolla Road
Calcutta - 700 088, India
TEL : 91 33 4014637
FAX : 91 33 4014357
EMAIL : sanjay.gupta_2@ philips.com
CONTACT: Sanjay Gupta

FINANCE / BANKING

INDIAN RENEWABLE ENERGY DEVELOPMENT AGENCY LTD
A Government Of India Enterprise, India
Habitat Centre Complex,
Core 4A East Court 1st Floor,
Lodi Road,
New Delhi 110003, India
TEL: +91 11 24682214-21
FAX: +91 11 24682202
E-MAIL: mdireda@rediffmail.com
WEB: http://www.ireda.nic.in
CONTACT: V Bakthavatsalam

THE DANISH INDUSTRIALISATION FUND FOR DEVELOPING COUNTRIES
14-F, Basant Lok, Vasant Vihar,
New Delhi - 110 057,
India
CONTACT: Deepa A. Hingorani

SREI INTERNATIONAL FINANCE LTD
86C, Topsia Road (South)
Calcutta - 700 046
TEL : +91 33 285 0112
FAX : +91 33 285 7542
E-MAIL : corporate@srei.com
WEB : http://www.srei.com
CONTACT : Mr Banerjee

ASSOCIATION

FORUM OF SCIENTISTS, ENGINNERS & TECHNOLOGISTS (FOSET)
15, Lindsay Street
New CMC Buildings (5th Floor)
Kolkata - 700087, India

NON CONVENTIONAL ENERGY EQUIPMENT MANUFACTURERS ASSOCIATION OF INDIA
57, Montieth Road,
Chennai-600008, India
TEL : 91 44 28555713
FAX : 91 44 28555716
CONTACT: Mr. S. Rajendran

PETROLEUM CONSERVATION RESEARCH ASSOCIATION
1014, New Delhi House,
27, Barakhamba Road,
New Delhi - 110 001, India

GOVERNMENT

AGENCY FOR NON – CONVENTIONAL ENERGY & RURAL TECHNOLOGY (ANERT)
Pottam PO No.1094,
Kesavadasapuram
Thiruvananthapuram - 695 004, India
TEL/FAX : +91 471 449854.

AP NON-CONVENTIONAL ENERGY DEVELOPMENT CORPORATION
5-8-207/ Pisgah Complex
Yatrik Compound
Hyderabad - 500 001, India

ARUNACHAL PRADESH INDUSTRIAL & FINANCIAL DEV. CORP. LTD.
Nahariagun, Itanagar - 791 110, India

ASSAM SCIENCE TECHNOLOGY & ENVIRONMENT COUNCIL
Panchawati, Silpukhuri,
Guwahati - 781 003, Assam, India

BIHAR RENEWABLE ENERGY DEVELOPMENT AGENCY (BREDA)
Lal Kothi, Shikarpur House,
Dr. T.N. Banerjee Road,
Patna - 800 001, Bihar, India

BIHAR STATE HYDROELECTRIC POWER CORPORATION LTD.
Sane Bhawan Birchand Paph: Marg,
Patna - 800 001, India

COUNCIL OF SCIENCE, TECHNOLOGY AND ENVIRONMENT
Govt. Of Assam
Panchwati, Silpukhuri
Guwahati - 781 003, Assam, India

DELHI ENERGY DEVELOPMENT AGENCY (DEDA)
37, Tughlakabad Institutional Area,
New Delhi - 110 062,
India

DEPARTMENT OF ELECTRICITY
Andaman & Nicobar Islands,
Port Balair - 744 101
Andaman & Nicobar Islands,
India

DEPT. OF RURAL DEVELOPMENT (ENERGY DIVISION)
Admn. Of Dadra & Nagar Haveli
Civil Division No.1
Silvassa, India

DEPT. OF SCIENCE & TECHNOLOGY
Environment Assam Rifles Complex,
Grakhbasti, Kunjaban Township,
Agartala - 799 001
Tripura, India

DEPT. OF SCIENCE & TECHNOLOGY
Vikas Bhavan, Salt Lake
Govt. Of West Bengal
Calcutta, India

ELECTRICITY DEPARTMENT
(Via) H.P.O. Cochin, Kavaratti,
Lakshadweep, India

ENERGY MANAGEMENT CENTRE,
Dept of Power, Govt. Of Kerala
Karamana, Thiruvananthapuram,
Kerala 695002, India
FAX : 91 471 345587
E-MAIL : emck@vsnl.com

GUJRAT ENERGY DEVELOPMENT AGENCY (GEDA)
Suraj Plaza II, 2nd Floor,
Sayajigunj,
Vadodara - 390 005
Gujrat, India

GUJRAT STATE ELECTRICITY BOARD
Vidyat Bhawan, Race Course,
Vadodara - 390 007, India

H.P. STATE ELECTRICITY BOARD
Vidyut Bhawan, Kumar House,
Simla, India

HARYANA STATE COUNCIL OF SCIENCE & TECHNOLOGY SCIENCE & TECHNOLOGY DEPARTMENT,
S C O No 24, Sector 26,
Madhya Marg,
Chandigarh - 160020
Haryana, India

INDIAN RENEWABLE ENERGY DEVELOPMENT AGENCY LTD.,
(Ireda), Core-4a, 1 Floor East Court,
India Habitat Centre,
Lodhi Road,
New Delhi - 110003, India
TEL : 91 11 24601344 / 24642367
FAX : 91 11 24602855
E-MAIL : gen@iredal.globemail1.com
CONTACT: Dr. V. Bakthavatsalam

INFORMATION & PUBLICITY DIVISION MINISTRY OF NON-CONVENTIONAL ENERGY SOURCES
Block No.14, C.G.O.Complex,
Lodhi Road,
New Delhi-110003, India
CONTACT: Ghattak

J & K ENERGY DEVELOPMENT AGENCY
Govt. Of J&K Civil Secretariate
Science & Technology Dept.
Jammu, Jammu & Kashmir, India

KARNATAKA POWER CORPORATION LTD.,
82, Race Course Road,
Bangalore – 560 001, India
TEL : 91 80 22255606
CONTACT: Mr. Jyothiramalingam

KARNATAKA POWER TRANSMISSION CORPORATION LTD
Cauvery Bhavan,
Bangalore – 560 009, India
TEL : 91 80 22213417
CONTACT: Mr. V.P. Baligar

KARNATAKA RAJYA VIJNAN PARISHAT (KRVP)
IISC Campus,
Bangalore - 560 012, India

KARNATAKA STATE COUNCIL FOR SCIENCE & TECHNOLOGY
Indian Institute of Science
Banglore - 560 012, India

MADHYA PARDESH URJA VIKAS NIGAM LTD. (MPUVN)
B Block,GTB Complex, TT Nagar,
Bhopal - 620003
Madhya Pradesh, India

MAHARASHTRA ENERGY DEVELOPMENT AGENCY (MEDA)
6th Floor, New Kamani Chambers,
Ballard Estate,
Mumbai - 400038
Maharshtra, India

MAHARASHTRA STATE ELECTRICITY BOARD
Prakashgad, 3rd Floor,
Bandra (East)
Mumbai - 400 051, India

MEGHALAYA NON-CONVENTIONAL AND RURAL ENERGY DEVELOPMENT AGENCY
Opposite P&T Dispensary
Lachumiere, Shillong - 793 001
Meghalaya, India

NEW & RENEWABLE SOURCES OF ENERGY DEPARTMENT
Government of Sikkim,
Tashiling, Gangtok - 737 101
Sikkim, India

NON CONVENTIONAL ENERGY DEVELOPMENT AGENCY
Vibhuti Khand, Gomtinagar,
Lucknow - 226 010
Uttar Pradesh, India

ORISSA RENEWABLE ENERGY DEVELOPMENT AGENCY (OREDA)
S-59, Mancheswar Ind. Estate
Bhubaneswar - 751 010
Orissa, India

ORISSA STATE ELECTRICITY BOARD
P.B. No. 52329
Bhubaneshwar - 751 007, India

PUNJAB ENERGY DEVELOPMENT AGENCY
S.C.O. 54-56, Sector 17 A
Chandigarh, India

RAJASTHAN ENERGY DEVELOPMENT AGENCY (REDA)
E-166, Yudhisther Marg "C"
Scheme, Jaipur
Rajasthan, India

STATE COUNCIL FOR SCIENCES, TECHNOLOGY & ENVIRONMENT
Govt. Of Manipur,
Imphal - 795 001, Manipur, India

TAMIL NADU ELECTRICITY BOARD
10th Floor, Eastern Wing
NPICRR Maligai 800, Anna Salai,
Chennai - 600 002, India

TAMIL NADU ENERGY DEVELOPMENT AGENCY (TEDA)
G R. Plaza, 714,
Anna Salai
Pathari Road,
Chennai - 600 006, India

THE MADHYA PRADESH STATE INDUSTRIES CORPN LTD.
Ratlam Alcohol & Carbon Dioxide
Plant Industrial Estate
Ratlam - 457 001, India

TRIPURA INDUSTRIAL DEVELOPMENT CORP. LTD.
Building of Dept. of Industries,
3rd Floor Assam Rifles Complex,
Gurkha Basti
Agartala - 799 001, India

U.P LAGHU JAL VIDYUT NIGAM LTD.
22 Station Road
Lucknow - 226 019, India

UNITED NATIONS EDUCATIONAL SCIENTIFIC AND CULTURAL ORGANISATION
Regional Office,
New Delhi, India
Contact: Mr. Meo Eiadi

W. B. STATE ELECTRICITY BOARD
New Sectt. Bldg., 1KS Roy Road,
7th Floor
Kolkata, India

WEST BENGAL RENEWABLE ENERGY DEVELOPMENT AGENCY (WBREDA)
L A Block B-04, Sector III,
Salt Lake City,
Kolkata - 700 091
West Bengal, India

RESEARCH & DEVELOPMENT

CENTRE FOR SCIENTIFIC RESEARCH
Auroshilpam, Auroville - 605 101
Tamil Nadu, India
CONTACT : Mr. Hamant Lamba

COUNCIL OF SCIENTIFIC AND INDUSTRIAL RESEARCH (CSIR)
New Delhi, India
CONTACT : Dr. R K. Bhandari

ELECTRONICS TEST & DEVELOPMENT CENTRE
Ring Road, Peenya Industrial Estate,
Bangalore - 560 058, India
CONTACT : Mr. G.R. Dayanandan

INDIAN AGRICULTURAL RESEARCH INSTITUTE
Division of Agricultural Engineering,
New Delhi-110 012, India
CONTACT: O.P Singhal

INTERNATIONAL DEVELOPMENT AND RESEARCH CENTRE
South Asia Regional Office,
17 Jor Bagh,
New Delhi-110003, India
CONTACT: Ms Prabha Sethuraman

INTEGRATED RURAL TECHNOLOGYCENTRE- IRTC
Mundur P.O., Palakkad,
Kerala 678 592
TELEFAX: 0491 832324, 832663, 832132
E-MAIL: irtc@vsnl.com

M S SWAMINATHAN RESEARCH FOUNDATION,
3rd Cross Street,
Taramani Institutional Area,
Chennai - 600113, India
CONTACT:Prof. M.S.Swaminathan

STRUCTURAL ENGINEERING RESEARCH CENTRE,
CSIR Campus, Taramani,
Chennai -600 113, India
FAX : 91 44 22350508
CONTACT:Mr. J. Shanmaugasundaram

TATA ENERGY RESEARCH INSTITUTE
DARBARI SETH BLOCK,
India Habitat Centre,
Lodhi Road,
New Delhi - 110 003, India
CONTACT: Dr. V.V.N. Kishore

THAPAR CENTRE FOR INDUSTRIAL RESEARCH & DEVELOPMENT
Thapar Technology Campus,
PO Box 68, Patiala 147001
India
TEL : +91 175 214868
FAX : +91 175 212002
CONTACT: Prof M P Kapoor

WIND ENERGY PROGRAMME
National Aerospace Laboratories
P.B. No-1779
Bangalore -560 017, India
CONTACT:Mr. M.P Ramesh

WIND ENERGY RESEARCH & DEVELOPMENT CENTRE (WERDC),
Kagal,
Kolhapur - 416 001, India

UNIVERSITIES

BIRLA INSTITUTE OF TECHNOLOGY & SCIENCE
Pillani, Rajasthan - 333 031, India
CONTACT : Mr. Hurbert Klapheck

CENTRE FOR ENERGY STUDIES
Indian Institute of Technology,
Haus Khas, New Delhi - 110016, India
CONTACT: Prof. H.P. Garg

DEPT. OF ELECTRONICS & PH:E-COMMUNICATION ENGINEERING,
Jadavpur University,
Kolkata - 700032, India
CONTACT:Dr. Hiranmay Saha

ENERGY SCIENCE & TECHNOLOGY MECHNANICAL ENGINEERING DEPARTMENT
School of Energy Studies,
Jadavpur University
Kolkata -700 032, India
CONTACT: Dr. Subhasis Neogi

INDIAN INSTITUTE OF TECHNOLOGY
Department of Physics,
Madras 600 036, India
TEL : + 91 44 2235 1365 / 3236
FAX : + 91 44 2235 0509
CONTACT: Dr A Subrahmanyam

INDIAN INSTITUTE OF TECHNOLOGY
Powai, Mumbai, India
CONTACT : Prof. S.K. Sukhatme

INSTITUTE OF PUBLIC ENTERPRISES
Osmania University Campus
Hyderbad- 500 007, India

JADAVPUR UNIVERSITY
School of Energy Studies
Kolkata 700 032,
India
TEL : +91 33 473 2853
FAX : +91 33 472 5823
CONTACT: Dr Biswajit Ghosh

PUNJAB TECHNICAL UNIVERSITY
P.O. R.E. C.
Jalandhar - 144011
Punjab, India
CONTACT: Mr. Anup Singh

SARDAR PAPH: RENEWABLE ENERGY RESEARCH INSTITUTE
Post Box No.2
Vallabh Vidyanagar
Gujarat-388 120, India
CONTACT: Shri S.K. Philip

SCHOOL OF ENERGY STUDIES
Jadavpur University
Kolkata -700 032,
India
CONTACT: Dr. Samir Kr. Saha

NGO's

AGA KHAN RURAL SUPPORT PROGRAMME (INDIA)
Choice Premises, Swastik Cross Road,
Navarangpura, Ahmedabad - 380009
Agency for Non-conventional Energy and Rural Technology

AUROVILLE GREENWORK RESOURCE CENTRE (AGRC)
Kottakari,
Auroville - 605 104, India

DEVELOPMENT ALTERNATIVES
B-32 Tara Crescent,
Qutab Institutional Area
New Delhi-110016, India
TEL : 91 11 26851158
FAX : 91 11 26866031
CONTACT: Mr. Ashok Koshla

E.D.S.
Gloria Land Farm,
Sri Arvindo Ashram,
Pondichery - 605 002, India

ENERGY SOCIETY OF INDIA
Pub- Sarania, Rajgarh
Byelane No.11, Guwahati,
Assam-781003, India
CONTACT: Shri P.C. Sarma

HIMACHAL ENVIRONMENT & LANDSCAPE PROTECTION SOCIETY (HELPS)
Village & P.O. Dari, Dharmshala,
Kangra Dt. - 176 057, India

IFREE INDIA INITIATIVE
B-54, Journalist Colony,
Renewable Energy Consultant,
2/210, (Upstairs),
Nawabpet,
Nellore - 524 002,
Andhra Pradesh, India
CONTACT: Dr. A. Jagadeesh - Manager

INTERNATIONAL ENERGY INITIATIVE
25/5, Bore Bank Road,
Benson Town,
Bangalore – 560 046, India
TEL : 91 80 25548426
CONTACT: Dr. Sudhir Chella Rajan

PLANTERS ENERGY NETWORK SCHOOL OF ENERGY, ENVIRONMENT & NATURAL RESOURCES,
Madurai Kamaraj University,
Madurai - 625 021,
India

PONDICHERRY SCIENCE FORUM (PSF)
Pasteur Nagar
Vinoba Nagar Extension,
Pondicherry - 605 008, India

SOCIETY FOR ANDAMAN & NICOBAR ECOLOGY (SANE)
Post Box. 63, Port Blair,
Pin - 744 101, India

SOCIETY FOR CONSERVATION OF FOREST & WILDLIFE
S Amita, Swanand Society,Sahakar
Nagar 1, Parwati, Pune 411 009, India

SOCIETY FOR ENERGY ENVIRONMENT & DEVELOPMENT
Plot No.30, Road-5,Jubilee Hills
Society, Hyderabad - 34, India

SOCIETY FOR RURAL ENVIRONMENTAL CONSERVATION (SREC)
Parigam Chack, Yaripara,
Anantnag - 192 232, India

SOCIETY FOR TECH & ACTION FOR RURAL ADVANCEMENT (TARA)
Tara Crescent, Qutab Institutional Area,
New Delhi - 110 016, India

SRI AUROBINDO ASHRAM
Solar Energy Unit,
Pondicherry – 605 002, India
CONTACT : Mr. C. L. Gupta

WINROCK INTERNATIONAL INDIA
7, Poorvi Marg, Vasanth Vihar
New Delhi-110057, India
Tel : 91 11 26142965
Fax : 91 11 26146004

WORLD WIDE FUND FOR NATURE INDIA
172 - B, lodhi Estate, Max Muller Marg,
New Delhi-110003, India

CONSULTANTS

ADVANCED TECHNOLOGY GROUP ENGINEERING OFFICE COMPLEX
Plot No.A-8, Sector-24,
Post Box N0.13,
Noida,
Uttar Pradesh-201301,
India
CONTACT: N. Qureshi

ARUVI ENGINEERS AND CONULTANTS (INDIA) (P) LTD.
M- Block No.43, Anna Nagar
Chennai -600 102,
India
CONTACT:Mr. Chikobba

BATLIBOI LTD.
Batliboi House SV Road
Jogeshwari West
Mumbai-400102, India
TEL : +91 22 26792111
CONTACT : Mr. N. Bhogilal

ELPRO ENERGY DIMENSIONS PVT. LTD.
#6,7,8 4th N Block, Dr. Sudha
Commercial Complex, Dr. Rajkumar
Road, Rajajinagar Entrance,
Bangalore - 560 010, India
TEL: 91 80 23102676 / 23103238.
CONTACT: Mr. Ramesh Singh

ENGINEERS INDIA LTD.
El Bhawan, 4th Floor, Power
Division, 1, Bhikaiji Cama Place,
New Delhi – 110066, India
CONTACT : Mr. Atul Bhalla

ITCOT LTD.
50-A,Greams Road, Chennai-600 006
TEL : +91 44 28225561, India
CONTACT : Mr. D. Vaidhyanathan

IT POWER INDIA PVT LTD
No. 6 Romain Rolland Street,
Pondicherry 605 001, India
TEL: +91 413 342 488
FAX: +91 413 332 776
E-MAIL: bp@itpi.co.in
WEB: http://www.itpower.co.uk
CONTACT: Binu Parthan

THERMAX
Thermax House,
4 Mumbai Pune Road,
Shivajinagar, Pune 411005, India
TEL: +91 20 5512112
FAX: +91 20 5512242
E-MAIL:
abunglow@thermaxindia.com
WEB: http://www.thermaxindia.com

VSM CONSULTANT
79, South Park Apartments
Kalkaji, New Delhi – 110019, India

OTHERS

ABAN LLOYD CHILES OFFSHORE LTD.
12, 5th Cross Street, CIT Colony,
Mylapore, Chennai - 600004,
India
TEL : 91 44 24992680 / 24990931
FAX : 91 44 24995680

BARON POWER LTD.
Bakthi Towers, 766, Anna Salai
Chennai - 600002, India
TEL : 91 44 28523017 / 28522240
FAX : 91 44 28525748

BEACON NEYRPIC LTD.
39 Industrial Estate (North)
Ambattur, Chennai 600098, India
TEL :91 44 26265539 / 2651541
FAX :91 44 26257059

BELLISS (I) LTD.
18, Community Centre, East of Kailash, New Delhi 110 065, India
TEL :91 11 26431756
FAX :91 11 26468089

BEST & CROMPTON ENG. LTD.
(solar energy division)
39, Industrial Estate North,Ambattur
Madras 600 098, India

BP & T MARKETING
715, Hari Complex, 22nd Cross, K. R. Road, Banasankari 2nd Stage, Bangalore – 560 070, India
TEL :91 80 26644484
CONTACT: Mr. Thomas

BRITTO ENERGY ENG.
At Satpale, P O Agashi Via-Virar (western Rly.) Tal. Bassein,
Thane,
Maharashtra 401301, India

CANON POWER CORPORATION
U & I Centre F-41, South Extension Part I, New Delhi 110 049, India
TEL : +91 11 24621586 / 24699421
FAX : +91 11 24623305

CASE PVT. LTD.
458, Udyog Vihar, Phase V,
Gurgaon, Haryana 122 016,
India
TEL :91 124 340941
E-MAIL:sangal_m@hotmail.com

CII, RENEWABLE ENERGY SUB COMMITTEE
3,6, Institutional Area,
Lodhi Road,
New Delhi - 110 001,
India
CONTACT:Mr. V. Raghuraman

EASTERN OVERSEAS CORPORATION
P O Box No 5572,
Framroz Court
60, D Phalke Road
Bombay - 400 014, India

FLEX ENGINEERING LTD.
M-32,Commercial Complex
Greater Kailash –11
New Delhi - 110048, India
TEL :91 11 26449552
FAX :91 11 26429511
CONTACT: Mr. R.K. Karihaloo

FLEXITRON
114,Kathalipalya, 6th Cross,
VI Block,
Koramangala,
Bangalore 560034, India

NOVAL ENERGY PVT. LTD.
119, DSIDC Shed
Okla Industrial Area, Phase I
New Delhi-110 020, India

PHEMATS INDIA PVT. LTD.
A-3, Chitranjan Park
New Delhi 110 019, India
TEL :91 11 26411309 / 26472995
FAX :91 11 26470174

PRESIDENT NE CHAPTER OF SOLAR
IAG - Green, IAG House, Swantantra Nagar Gali-7, Near Shiv Mandir
Opp. Rly. Stn., Narela
Delhi-110040, India

SCARAB (I) PVT. LTD.,
473/1, Indiranagar 1st Stage,
Bangalore – 560 038, India
Tel :91 80 25582778.
Contact: Mr. Manohar Prabhu

VANGUARD POWER
F5, Burkit Road, T Nagar
Madras - 600017, India
TEL :91 44 24341893 / 24341894
FAX :91 44 24340024

VEEKAY COOLERS
55, Kamannahalli Main Road,
Bangalore – 560 084, India
TEL :91 80 25460646
CONTACT: Mr. Shanmugam

SUPPLIERS

BATTERIES/INVERTERS

ALTECH BATTERIES
5, Malaviya Street
(Opp To Seetharam Hotel)
Ramnagar,
Coimbatore- 641 009
TEL: +91 422 232084
FAX: +91 422 236724
MOBILE: 9843021775, 9842721770

AMARA RAJA BATTERIES LTD
19D, Mysore Deviation Road,
(Near Minerva Mills),
Bangalore-23
TEL: 080-23102140/ 2141/ 3811
FAX: 080-23102142
E-MAIL: banim@amararaja.co.in

AMARAJA BATTERIES LTD.
Renigunta -Cuddapan Road
Karakambadi,
Tirupathi- 517520, India
CONTACT:Mr. Ramachandra Naidu Galla

AMCO BATTERIES LTD.,
Unity Building, J. C. Road,
Bangalore – 560 002, India
TEL: 91 80 25599602
CONTACT:Mr. C. Rajagopalan

BASE MEDIA (P) LTD.,
810, Barton Centre, M. G. Road,
Bangalore - 560 001, India
TEL :91 80 25586502
CONTACT: Mr. G. Ajith Kumar

BPS BANGALORE POWER SUPPLIES & CONTROLS
#126, Coconut Avenue,
Malleshwaram, Bangalore-560003
TEL: 080-23315568, 23342928
FAX: 080-23342928
MOBILE: 9845023509, 9844034295

COLT BATTERIES
36, Netaji Road,
Bangalore – 560 005, India
TEL :91 80 25368812
CONTACT:Mr. M. I. Nehruji

EXIDE AUTOPARK
50, Church Street, Bangalore-560001
TEL: 080-25585464, 25582908, 25582909
TELEFAX: 080-5586842

EXIDE INDUSTRIES LTD.
Exide House, 751, Anna Salai,
Chennai – 600 002,
India
TEL :91 44 28525070
CONTACT:Mr. K. Krishnamoorthy

KIRLOSKAR BATTERIES LTD
Pb # 2231, Yeshwanthpur
Bangalore - 560 022,
India
TEL :91 80 23376935
CONTACT: Ms. Gayathri

POABS BATTERY CONTAINERS PVT. LTD.
Kuttoor (P .O) Thiruvalla,
Kerala-689106, India
TEL :91 0473 603160
E-MAIL : poabs@giasmd01.vsnl.net.in

INDIA

SAKTHI BATTERY INDUSTRIES
H.O: #231, 1st Main, 3rd Cross,
KSRTC Layout,
J.P. Nagar 2nd Phase, Bangalore-78
TELEFAX: 080-26588251,
266587740, 26589739
E-MAIL: sakthibatteries@vsnl.com
WEB: http://www.sakthipower.com

SOUTHERN BATTERIES
30, Kiadb Indl. Area Bommasandra,
Bangalore - 562158, India
TEL: 91 80 28422971/ 28422272
FAX : 91 80 28422631 / 28424446

CABLES/WIRES

CCI CABLES LTD.
7, Central Market,
West Punjabi Bagh, New Delhi-26
TEL: +91 11 25168686
FAX: +91 11 25169696
MOBILE: 9811113305
E-MAIL: cci_cables@yahoo.co.in

FINECAB
2-3-465/7, Minister Road
Secunderabad- 500003
TEL: 040-7818908,7840525
FAX: 040-7221916

FINOLEX CABLES LTD
320 Raheja Chambers
12 Museum Road –1
Bangalore
TEL: 080-25588817

HAVELL'S INDIA LTD
1 Raj Narain Marg, Civil Lines,
Delhi-110054
TEL: +91 11 23935237, 22944469
FAX: +91 11 23921500, 23981100
E-MAIL: marketing@havells.com
WEB: http://www.havells.com

LAPP INDIA PVT. LTD.
LAPP KABEL Plot No.98
J & K, Jigani Industrial Area,
II Phase, Anekal Taluk,
Bangalore 562 106
TEL: 08110-26000 (8lines)
FAX: 08110-25479
E-MAIL: lappind@blr.vsnl.net.in

POLYCAB
1st Floor, Hico House,
North Wing,
771, Pandit Satavalekar Marg,
Mahim (W) Mumbai-400016
TEL: +91 22 24327070/ 74
FAX: +91 22 24327075
E-MAIL: polycab@bom3.vsnl.net.in
WEB: http://www.polycab.com

SKYTONE CABLES
SKYTONE ELECTRICALS (INDIA) LTD.
T-34, Okhla Industrial Area, Phase-II
New Delhi-110020
TEL: +91 11 26313911 Upto 15
FAX: +91 11 26848974
WORKS: 42-43 Industrial Area, N.I.T
Faridabad-121 001
TEL: 0129-5233394, 5232395
FAX: 0129-5232456
E-MAIL: info@skytonecables.com
WEB: www.skytonecables.com

SWADNA CABLES PVT. LTD.,
21, 1st Main, III Stage,
Vinayaka Layout, Vijayanagar,
Bangalore 560040, India
TEL : +91 80 23300704
CONTACT: Mr. Shashikant Singhal

INSTRUMENTATION

A J ELECTRONICS
Prerana, 21 Amar Society
44/2, Erandawane
Pune - 411 046, India

ELTECH ELECTRONICS & COMMUNICATIONS LTD.
3391, 6 Main Road, 3 Cross,
Vijayanagar 2 Stage
Bangalore - 560 040, India
TEL : +91 80 23302423
FAX : +91 80 23302423
CONTACT: M. Venugopal Rao

ENERCON SYSTEMS (PVT.) LTD.
23, KHB Light Industries Area,
Yelhanka,
Bangalore - 560064, India
TEL : +91 80 2846 0666
FAX: +91 80 2846 0667
E-MAIL: enercon@enerconindia.com
CONTACT : Mr. Thomas Abel

EXCEL POWERCONS SERVICES PRIVATE LTD.
19, First Main Road,
Indiranagar, Adyar,
Chennai -600020
Tamil Nadu, India
TEL : +91 44 24417056
FAX : +91 44 24453439

INSTRUMENT RESEARCH ASSOCIATES LTD
P B No 2304, 19, Mysore Deviatur Road,
Near Minerva Mills,
Gopalapuram, Bangalore-560 023,
India
TEL : 23387536
CONTACT : Mr Nagaraj

INTERNATIONAL MARKETING CORPORATION
418, Swastic Chambers
Sion Trombay Road, Chembur,
Mumbai- 400071, India
TEL : +91 22 25228170
CONTACT : Mr. Prashant Shah

MECO INSTRUMENTS PVT. LTD.
P O Box 6388, Sewree
Mumbai- 400015, India
TEL: +91 22 24137423 / 24137253
FAX: +91 22 2414 6234

TOSHNIWAL BROTHERS PVT. LTD.
268,Kilpauk Garden Road
Chennai- 600010, India
TEL : 91 44 6448983
FAX : 91 44 6441820
CONTACT : Mr. A.K.Sait

UNIVERSAL INSTRUMENTS MFG. CO. PVT. LTD.,
#26/A, 2 Phase Peenya Industrial Area,
Bangalore - 560 058, India
TEL : 91 80 28394289
91 80 28394907
CONTACT: Mr. Ashok Toshniwal

YOKOGOWA BLUESTAR
40 / 4, Lavelle Road
Bangalore- 560 001, India
TEL: 22271513
CONTACT : Mr. J. P. Singh

INSULATIONS

LLOYD INSULATIONS (INDIA) LTD.
5 A, Haddows Lane, Chennai-6
TEL: +91 44 28273753
E-MAIL: lloydinsul@vsnl.com
CONTACT : Vineet P Munjal

ROCKWOOL INDIA LTD.
Plot # 32, Flat # 202 Shiva Sai
Sanidhi Apartments. Dwarkapuri Colony,
Pinjatgutta, Hyderabad-82, India
TEL : +91 40 3356129 / 3356152
+91 40 356155
CONTACT: Mr. Neville D'souza

GLASS

ANNAPURNA GLASS WORKS
197 Smg Road Mvm-3
TEL: 3344631

EURO GLASS
48/39, Sarva Bhowma Nagar,
IIMB Post, Bilekahalli,
Bangalore-560076
TEL: +91 80 26584551
FAX: +91 80 26587237
E-MAIL: euroglass@rediffmail.com

GSE TOUGHENED GLASS
C-46, Sector – 57, Noida, India
TEL: 91 11 84581171 / 84581201 / 91 11 84581202
CONTACT : Mr. Sharanjit Singh

IMPACT SAFETY GLASS WORKS (P) LTD.
152, Wheeler Road, Frazer Town
Bangalore-560 005, India
TEL: 91 80 25364254/ 25365593
CONTACT : Mr. R K Dutta

INDO ASAHI GLASS CO. LTD.
3, Hungerford Street
Kolkata – 700 017, India
TEL: 4484341
CONTACT : Mr. K.Ishiyana

SECURIT SAINT GOBAIN LTD.
T-94 /95 MIDC Bhosri
Pune-26, India
TEL: 91 20 7119812
FAX: 91 20 7120777
CONTACT : Mr. Ashok Bidkar

SOUTHERN AUTO PRODUCTS
41/A-1 2nd Phase PIA-58
TEL: 839 5883

VICTORY GLASS & INDUSTRIES LTD.
205, Midford House, M. G. Road,
Bangalore- 560001, India
TEL : 91 80 25581920
CONTACT : Mr. S.N. Dey

CONSTRUCTION SERVICES

LARSEN & TURBRO LTD.
L & T House, Ballard Estate
Bombay 400 001, India
TEL : 91 22 5781401
91 22 5781411
FAX : 91 22 5780618

SUBHASH PROJECTS & MARKETING LTD.
Subhash House, F-27/2,
Okhla Industrial Area, Phase II
New Delhi 110 020, India
TEL : 91 11 26844980 / 2635598
FAX : 91 11 26846003 / 26210832

SOLAR ENERGY EQUIPMENTS

JOLLY ENTERPRISE,
#1A, Akshay Bhawan, R.G. Street,
Tharpakhana,
Ranchi – 834001
JhRkhand,
Ph: 0651-2200979 / 2313647
Fax: 2306279
Email: jollyenterprise@hotmail.com
Contact : Mr. S. Chaudhury

ALUMINIUM

PLAS- MET-CHEM CORPORATION ALUMINIUM ALLOYS & DURALUMIN
No.4, Byrappa Lane,
Post Box No. 7161,
Ranasinghpet,
Bangalore- 560 053
TEL: 080- 26701120, 26701121
TELEFAX: 080-26702121

MARUTI METALS
THE METAL SHOPPEE
1/1, S.P Road, 1st Cross,
Bangalore- 560 002
TEL: 080-22293514, 22242985
TELEFAX: 080-22243247

SHUJA METAL INDUSTRIES
No.57, S.P.Road, Bangalore-2
TEL: 080-22234264,22223340
FAX: 080-22290065
E-MAIL: shujametal@hotmail.com

VICTORY ALUMINIUM
No.14, Mriswamy Mutt Road,
(A.M.Road),
Kalaispalyam Extension,
Bangalore-560 002
TEL: 080-26706060, 26706070
FAX: 080-26703890

COPPER

COPRAL COPPER & ALUMINIUM CONDUCTORS
Plot No.12, SPICOT PhaseII,
Hosur-635 109
Tamil Nadu
TELEFAX: +91 4344 560396, 560796

SAI FORGE PVT. LID.
Puliembedu,
Numbal Village,
P H Road,
Chennai-600 077
TEL: +91 44 226272249, 26272525
FAX: +91 44 26272579
E-MAIL: saiforge@vsnl.com
WEB: http://www.saiforge.com

SHARP METAL INDUSTRIES
114/14, 1st Main Road,
P.P. Industrial Estate,
Deepanjali Nagar,
Mysore Road,
Bangalore-26
TELEFAX: +91 80 22226927, 22276827,26755225
MOBILE: 2795000, 9844053000
E-MAIL: sharpmetal@vsnl.com

STAINLESS STEEL

MILLENIUM STEEL TECH
183/5, Puttappa Compound,
M.D.Pura Bus Stop,
Whitefield Road, Bangalore-48
TEL: 9845217312, 28517575
E-MAIL: mst2000@rediffmail.com

MYSORE STEEL SUPPLIERS
No.7 P.C.Lane, S.P.Road Cross,
Bangalore-560002, India
TEL: +91 80 22213868, 22245777
FAX: +91 80 22217144
E-MAIL: mmi@blr.vsnl.net.in

PAL ENGINEERING CO.
11th K.M Kanakapura Road,
Bangalore-62
TEL: 26321248
TELEFAX: 26586925
MOBILE: 9844056868

RAJASTHAN INDUSTRIAL SUPPLIERS
No.1, Benki Nawab Street,
S.P Road Cross, Bangalore-2
TEL: +91 80 22279218, 22271079, 22294447
FAX: +91 80 2227577
E-MAIL: rajasthanmetals@vsnl.com

RIDDHI SIDDHI METALS
152/1, Kumbarpet Main Road,
S.P. Road Cross, Bangalore-560002
TEL: +91 80 22221597, 22994558
TELEFAX: +91 80 22230781
E-MAIL: riddhisiddhi@vsnl.net

SALEM STEEL SUPPLIES
43, (154/5)
Sadar Patrappa Road,
Bangalore-560 002
TEL: +91 80 22215144, 23372658
FAX: +91 80 22222864,23376591
E-MAIL: salemss@bgl.vsnl.net.in

SANGHVI STEEL SYNDICATE
No.72, MRR Lane,
S.J.P. Road Cross,
Bangalore-560 002
TEL: +91 80 22237767
TELEFAX: +91 80 22294467
MOBILE: 9844030479
E-MAIL: sanghvisteel@vsnl.net

SIDHARTH SALES AGENCIES
155 Sadar Patrappa Road,
Bangalore-560 002
TEL: +91 80 22223477,22292986
FAX: +91 80 22272569
E-MAIL: ssasteel@bgl.vsnl.net.in

PAINTS

ASIAN PAINTS LIMITED
32b 2nd Phase PIE –58
TEL: 8395669

BERGER PAINTS INDIA LTD
1st Cross Bhawani Towers
Hosur Road, Wilson Garden-27
TEL: 080-22291567

JENSON & NICHOLSON (INDIA) LTD
33/1, New Timber Yard Layout,
Mysore Road, Bangalore- 560 026
TEL: 080-26745737, 26745800, 26752739

NEROLAC PAINTS LTD.
TEL: 080-5522970,5525197

TIDAL

MAHARASHTRA RENEWABLE ENERGY LTD
Renewable Energy, B/8,
STC Employees Society,
Prof N S Phadke Marg,
Andheri (East) Mumbai 400069, India
TEL: +91 22 2832 3917
FAX: +91 22 2834 1733
CONTACT: Mr Prafulla S Shirke

OTHERS

BHARAT EARTH MOVERS LTD.,
23/1, 4th Main,
Sampingram Nagar,
Bangalore - 560 027, India
TEL : +91 80 22224141
CONTACT:Shri. K. R. Anantharaman

GREMACH CNC LTD.
1, Club House Road,
Chennai, India
TEL : +91 44 28521839 / 3258
FAX : +91 44 22534355

N.G.E.F LTD.,
P. B. 3876, Byappanahalli,
Bangalore – 560 038, India
TEL : +91 80 25243719.
CONTACT: Dr. A. A. Natarajan

NOBLE ENERGY SOLAR TECHNOLOGIES-NEST
42 Radhaswamy Colony, Sikh Road,
Secunderabad 500009, India
TEL: +91 40 776 9053
FAX: +91 40 776 9054
E-MAIL: dtbarki@usa.net
CONTACT: Dharmappa Barki

INDIA - CANADA ENVIRONMENT FACILITY,
D-1/56,Vasant Vihar,
New Delhi-57, India
CONTACT: Dr. Bhaskar Natrajan

JASH ENGINNEERING LTD.
31, Sector 'C' Industrial Area
Sanwer Road, Indore
Madhya Pradesh-452001, India
TEL : +91 731 420143
FAX : +91 731 420499
E-MAIL : info@jashindia.com

JASH PROJECTS PVT. LTD.
30/384 Phrang Road
Mumbai –400019, India
E-MAIL : manishk@gisa bm01.vsnl.net.in

JAY INDUSTRIES
D 64, MIDC Indl. Area
Miraj 416 410, India
Dist. Sangli
TEL/FAX : +91 0233 344464

PRADEEP DEVIAH & ASSOCIATES PVT LTD
PDA House #32/2 Spencer Road,
Frazer town, Bangalore 560 005, India
TEL: +91 80 25547434
FAX: +91 80 25542258
E-MAIL: pdaexpo@vsnl.com
WEB: http://www.pdatradefairs.com
CONTACT: Mr Yogesh Srinivasan

THERMOCRAFT
B 3-7, Srivatraq Society
Pand Road
Pune-411 029, India

We kindly request more listings in this country.

You can submit any additional listings by E-mail: unisun@vsnl.com

Fax: +91 80 22289294

We will include these in the next edition

Kindly inform us of any errors and omissions in the listings by:

E-mail: unisun@vsnl.com

Fax: 91 80 22289294

SOLAR THERMAL

PT SUNDAYA INDONESIA
Solar Home System,
Pondok Randu No 38, Cengkareng,
Weat Jakarta, Indonesia
TEL: +62 21 541 6103
FAX: +62 21 541 6106
E-MAIL: andi@sundaya.com
WEB: http://www.sundaya.com
CONTACT: Andi Trisno

ASSOCIATION

GET PERTIWI
Urban Division, PO Bos 325,
Solo 57103, Indonesia
TEL : + 62 271 710465
FAX : + 62 271 718756
E-MAIL : gita@slo.merg.net.id

We kindly request more listings in this country.

You can submit any additional listings by E-mail: unisun@vsnl.com

Fax: 91 80 22289294

We will include these in the next edition

Kindly inform us of any errors and omissions in the listings by:

E-mail: unisun@vsnl.com

Fax: 91 80 22289294

WIND

ARMAN ENGINEERING DESIGNING CO
Wind Turbine, PO Box 71955-793,
Shiraz, Iran
TEL: +98 711 6258114
FAX: +98 711 6245945
E-MAIL: arman@farsindustry.org.ir
WEB: http:// arman.7p.com
CONTACT: Abbas Jafari

SADID INDUSTRIAL GROUP
Sadid Saba Niroo Co,
PO Box 13185-473,
14, 2nd St, Ahmad Qasseer Ave,
Tehran 15134, Iran
TEL: +98218753070-8
FAX: +98218732002
E-MAIL: sadidig@sadid.ir
WEB: http://www.sadid.ir
CONTACT: Seyed Nasrolah Ghazimirsaeed

RESEARCH & DEVELOPMENT

RENEWABLE ENERGY ORGANIZATION OF IRAN – SUNA
PO Box 14155-6398,
Shahrak Ghods Poonak,
Bakhtari, Tehran, Iran
TEL: +98218084771
FAX: +98218086970
CONTACT: A Moosavifar

We kindly request more listings in this country.

You can submit any additional listings by E-mail: unisun@vsnl.com

Fax: 91 80 22289294

We will include these in the next edition

Kindly inform us of any errors and omissions in the listings by:

E-mail: unisun@vsnl.com

Fax: 91 80 22289294

SOLAR THERMAL

ACKTAR LIMITED
GAT High Tech Center,
Derech Hata Asia 70/4,
PO Box 720, Kiriat GAT 82000, Israel
TEL: +97286814213
FAX: +98286810198
E-MAIL: acktar@netvision.net.il
WEB: http://www.acktar.com
CONTACT: Ms Dina Katsir

SOLEL SOLAR SYSTEMS LTD
Industrial Zone West
PO Box 811,
Beit Shemesh 99000, Israel
TEL:+972 2 999 6620
FAX:+972 2 999 5521
E-MAIL:solel@netvision.net.il
WEB:http://www.solel.com

SUNTREE ENERGY
Box 2177, Herzliya 46120
TEL: +972 99 505456
FAX: +972 99 505461
E-MAIL: barry.swersky@suntree.co.il
CONTACT: Barry Swersky

TOTEC LTD
PO Box 3311, 47264 Ramat Hasharon, Israel
TEL: +972 3 5493766
FAX: +972 3 5497298
CONTACT : J A Roni

SOLAR PHOTOVOLTAIC

INTERDAN LTD
Astra Tower, Tchernichovsky 35,
Haifa 35709, Israel
TEL: +972 4 833 7997
FAX: +972 4 833 9116
CONTACT: A Nezer

ISRAEL ELECTRIC CORPORATION
Planning Development and Technology Division, PO BOX 10,
31000 Haifa, Israel
TEL: +972 4 8649960
FAX: +972 59 8649770
E-MAIL: dani@iec.co.il
CONTACT : Dan Weiner

SOLMECS (ISRAEL) LTD
Solar Energy, Omer Industrial Park,
PO Box 3026, Omer 84965,Israel
TEL: +972 7 6900950
FAX:+972 7 6900953
E-MAIL:sales@pvsolmecs.com
WEB:http://www.pvsolmecs.com
CONTACT: Uri Ovnat

SOLOR-ENERGY FROM THE SUN
PO Box 16007,
61160 Tel Aviv, Israel
TEL:+972 3 6884668
FAX:+972 3 5248945
E-MAIL:solor@netvision.net.il
CONTACT: Ami Elazzari

GOVERNMENT

MINISTRY OF NAITIONAL INFRASTRUCTURES
Division of Research and Development, PO Box 13106,
91130 Jerusalem, Israel
TEL: +972 2 531 6127
FAX: +972 2 531 6081
E-MAIL: aarbib@mni.gov.il
CONTACT: Dr H A Arbib

RESEARCH & DEVELOPMENT

CTI CREATIVE TECH ISRAEL
49 Dagan Street, Jerusalem 93886, Israel
TEL : +972 2 645 2086
FAX : +972 2 645 2489
CONTACT : Prof Lavie

CONSULTANTS

PIMAT-DEVELOPMENT OF ALTERNATIVE ENERGY SOURCES LTD
Vilorama Building, Industrial Zone,
43000 Raanana, Israel
TEL : + 972 9 448548
FAX : + 972 9 448644
CONTACT : David Ponieman

RMZ TECHNOLOGY LTD
24 Gilad Street, PO Box 81
Kochav-Yair 44864, Israel
TEL: +97 2 9 7494 128
FAX: +97 2 9 7493 682
E-MAIL: rmze@israsrv.net.il
CONTACT: Y Rubinstein

ROTEMINDUSTRIES LTD
PO Box 9046, 84190 Beer Sheva, Israel
TEL: +97257 568 300
FAX: +97257 554 502
CONTACT: Dr Yehuda Boneh

TAHAL CONSULTING ENGINEERING LTD
PO Box 11170,
61111 Tel Aviv, Israel
TEL : +972 3 6924434
FAX : +972 3 269969
CONTACT : Ralph Samson

SAMAR GROUP
Solar Head Energy Systems,
Kibbutz Samar, 88815,
DN Eilot, Israel
TEL: +97286356734
FAX: +97286356758
E-MAIL: bryanmedwed@yahoo.com
CONTACT: Bryan Medwed

DESIGN & ENGINEERING

CHROMAGEN
Export Division,
Sha'ar Ha'amakin 30097, Israel
TEL: +972 4 983 9476
FAX: +972 4 983 9246
WEB: http://www.chromagen.com
CONTACT: Uri Shalev

ENVIRONMENTAL ENGINEERING DESIGN COMPANY LTD
PO Box 58195, Tel-Aviv 61580, Israel
TEL: +972 3 6481250
FAX: +972 3 6481250
E-MAIL:goldsmid@inter.net.il

SOLAR HEAD ENERGY SYSTEMS
Kibbutz Samar, 88815 DN Eilot, Israel
TEL:+972 76 35 67 34
FAX:+972 76 35 67 58
E_MAIL : solarheadenergysystems@yahoo.com
CONTACT : Bryan Medwed

OTHERS

COOLINGTEC INDUSTRIES LTD
PO Box 3311, Ramaz Hasharon 47264, Israel
TEL : +972 9 894 9593
FAX : +972 9 894 6999
CONTACT : B Ephrain

FEEDING STUFF & CHEMICAL LTD
15 Hague, Deniya,
34980 Haifa, Israel
TEL: +972 4 826 2657
FAX: +972 4 826 2339
E-MAIL: efraimg@netvision.net.il
CONTACT : Glaser

MEDITERRANEAN ENERGY AND ECOLOGY CENTER
PO Box 725, Kiryat-Ono 55000, Israel
TEL: +972 3 5346 447
FAX: +972 3 5346 447
E-MAIL: meec@bezeqint.net
CONTACT: Prof St Sinatov

SUPPLIERS

BATTERIES/INVERTERS

ELECTRIC FUEL LTD
POB 23073, 91230 Jerusalem, Israel
TEL : +972 2 589 0890
FAX : +972 2 589 2252
E-MAIL : info@electric-fuel.com
WEB: www.electric.fuel.com
CONTACT : J Whartman

OTHERS (S)

AGS TECHNOLOGIES LTD
PO Box 33498,Tel-Aviv 61334, Israel
TEL: +97237395425
FAX: +97236313480
E-MAIL: info@agsglobalservices.com
WEB: http://www.agsglobalservices.com

INTERNATIONAL UNION OF ARCHITECTS-UIA
Work Programme on Architecture and Energy, PO Box 8543,
91083 Jerusalem, Israel
TEL: +972 2 561 0066
FAX: +972 2 563 8324
E-MAIL: lr-arch@netmedia.net.il
CONTACT : Lahar

IZIEGLER ELECTRICAL ENGINEERING LIMITED
9 Kehilat Saloniki
Street 69513
Tel Aviv, Israel
TEL: +972 3 491140
FAX: +972 3 491145
CONTACT: Shmuel Koch

METEO-TECH METEOROLOGICAL SERVICES LTD
11, Moshe Sneh,
69350 Tel Aviv, Israel
TEL: +972 3 649 2962
FAX: +972 3 647 1443
E-MAIL: meteotec@actcom.co.il
CONTACT: Dr N Wolfson

ORMAT INDUSTRIES LTD
PO Box68, 81100 Yavne, Israel
TEL: +97289433777
FAX: +97289439901
E-MAIL: ormat@ormat.com

We kindly request more listings in this country.

You can submit any additional listings by E-mail: unisun@vsnl.com

Fax: 91 80 22289294

We will include these in the next edition

Kindly inform us of any errors and omissions in the listings by:

E-mail: unisun@vsnl.com

Fax: 91 80 22289294

SOLAR THERMAL

M WATANABE & CO LTD
Nanwa Nihonbashi Building,
2-16 4-Chome,
Nihonbashi-Muromachi chuo-ku,
Tokyo 103-0022, Japan
TEL: +81 3 3241 9141
FAX: +81 3 3241 9170
E-MAIL: n-miyake@m-watanabe.co.jp

NIPPON ELECTRIC GLASS CORPORATION LTD
Solar Systems Division,
1-14 Miyahara 4- Chome,
odogawa-ku, Osaka 532-0003,
Japan
TEL: +81 6 399 2721
FAX: +81 6 399 2731
TELEX: 523-3885 NEGLAS J
CONTACT: Masao Togawa

SHIROKI CORPORATION
Overseas Business Department,
3-7-3 Shin-Yokohama, Kohoku-ku,
Yokohama 222-0033, Japan
TEL: +81 45 473 4691
FAX: +81 45 473 6019
E-MAIL: furuno@shiroki.co.jp
WEB: http://www.shiroki.co.jp
CONTACT: Makoto Furuno

SOLAR PHOTOVOLTAIC

KANEKA CORPORATION
2-4 Nakanoshima 3-chome,
Kita-ku, Osaka 530,
Japan
TEL: +81 66 226 5071
FAX: +81 66 226 5038
CONTACT : Kaneka

KYOCERA CORPORATION, SOLAR ENERGY DIVISION
2F Eisen Karasuma
Building 680,
Karasumadori-Bukkoji-
Sagaru Shimogyo-ku,
Kyoto 600, Japan
TEL : +81 75 344 8241
FAX : +81 75 344 8240
WEB : http://www.kyocera.com
CONTACT : Mr Y Tsuji / Mr H Yagi

KYOCERA CORPORATION
Corporate Solar Energy Division,
6 Takeda Tobadono-Cho,
Fushimi-ku, Kyoto-Shi, Kyocto,
Japan
TEL: +81 75 604 3500
FAX: +81 75 604 3501
CONTACT: Yoshihisa Tsuji

MSK CORPORATION
19F STEC Joho Building,
1-24-1 West Shinjuku, Shinjuku,
Tokyo 160 0023, Japan
TEL: +81 3 3342 3838
FAX: +81 3 3342 6534
E-MAIL: staff@msk.ne.jp
WEB: http://www.msk.ne.jp
CONTACT: James Plastow

RESOURCES TOTAL SYSTEM CO LTD
2-3-11 Shinkawa, Chuo-ku,
Tokyo, Japan
TEL : +81 3 3551 6345
FAX : +81 3 3553 8954
E-MAIL : ikki@rts-pv.com
CONTACT : Osamu Ikki

SHOWA SOLAR ENERGY KK
Daiba Frontier Building 3-2,
Daiba 2 Chome, Minato-ku,
Tokyo 135-8074, Japan
TEL: +81 3 5531 5781
FAX: +81 3 5531 5788
E-MAIL: pv-shell@za2.so-net.ne.jp
CONTACT: Takashi Hasegawa

WACOM ELECTRIC CO LTD
Light Sources Division, 568 Tanaka,
Kawamoto-Machi, Osato-Gun,
Saitama 369-1108, Japan
TEL: +81 485 83 5676
FAX: +81 485 83 5259

WIND

FUJI HEAVY INDUSTRIES LTD
Aerospace Division, 1-1-11 Yonan
Utsunomiya City, Tochigi Pref, Japan
TEL: +81 28 684 7006
FAX: +81 28 684 7006
E-MAIL: wind@uae.subaru-fhi.co.jp
WEB: http://www.fhi.co.jp
CONTACT: Masayoshi Kubota

MITSUBISHI HEAVY INDUSTRIES LTD
Power Systems International
Operations Dept. 5-1 Marunouchi
2-chome, Chiyoda-ku,
Tokyo 100, Japan
TEL: +81 45 224 9547
FAX: +81 45 223 1725
E-MAIL: 15288@hq.mhi.co.jp
CONTACT: Nakamura Hiroaki

BIOMASS

YOSHIDA & CO
5-1-18 Nakagosho, Nagano City,
Nagano Pref, Japan
TEL: +81 26 223 0011
FAX: +81 26 227 8008
E-MAIL: solyoshi@nag.avis.ne.jp
CONTACT: Soichiro Yoshida

SMALL HYDRO

IWANAKA ELECTRIC WORKS LTD
3-5-8 Oyama Sagamihara-shi,
Kanagawa-ken 229-1105,
Japan
TEL: +81 42 772 3606
FAX: +81 42 774 3232
E-MAIL:ydw6124a@msn.com
CONTACT : Mr. Iwanaka

WASTE TO ENERGY

KAWASAKI HEAVY INDUSTRIES LTD
Power Plant Export Sales Dept.
World Trade Centre Building 2-4-1
Hamamatsu-cho,
Minato-ku,
Tokyo 105-6116,
Japan
TEL: +81 3 3435 2265
FAX: +81 3 3435 2099
CONTACT : Michina

ASSOCIATION

JAPAN SOLAR ENERGY SOCIETY
2-44-14 Yoyogi, Shibuya-ku,
Tokyo 151-0053,
Japan
TEL: +81 3 3376 6015
FAX: +81 3 3376 6720
CONTACT : T Yamadu

UNIVERSITIES

MIE UNIVERSITY
Department of Mechanical
Engineering,
1515 Kamihama-cho,
Tsu, Mie 514-8507,
Japan
TEL: +81 59 231 9382
FAX: +81 59 231 1572
E-MAIL: maeda@mach.mie-u.ac.jp
WEB: http://www.fel.mach.mie-u.ac.jp
CONTACT: Takao Maeda

NGO's

JAPAN CENTER FOR A SUSTAINABLE ENVIRONMENT AND SOCIETY-JACSES
2nd Floor, Dai-32 Kowa Building,
5-2-32 Minami Azabu,
Minato-ky
Tokyo 106-0047,
Japan
TEL : +81 3 3447 9515
FAX : 81 3 3447 9383
CONTACT : J Adachi

JAPAN

NEW ENERGY AND INDUSTRIAL TECHNOLOGY DEVELOPMENT ORGANISATION
NEDO Information Centre,
Sunshine 60 30F, 1-13 Chome
Higoshi-Ikebukuro, Toshima-Ku,
Tokyo 170-0013, Japan
TEL: +81 3 3987 9313
FAX: +81 3 3987 8539
E-MAIL: qinf@nedo.go.jp
WEB: http://www.nedo.go.jp
CONTACT: Kiyosasu Yamada

WORLD INFO CENTRE - WIC
1-22-7-107 Takamatscho, Tachikawa
Shi 190 0011, Tokyo, Japan
TEL: +81 425 26 0597
FAX: +81 425 26 0597
CONTACT: Mizanur Rahman

CONSULTANTS

EX CORPORATION
Mejiro Nakano Building 6F,
2-17-22 Takada, Toshima-ku,
Tokyo 171, Japan
TEL: +81 3 5956 7503
FAX: +81 3 5956 7523
E-MAIL: kyo04644@niftyserver.co.jp
CONTACT : K Sakaguchi

OTHERS

TOKYO ELECTRIC POWER COMPANY
4-1 Egasaki-cho, Tsurumi-ku,
Yokohama-shi, Kanagawa 230, Japan
TEL: +81 45 585 8680
FAX: +81 45 585 8693
CONTACT: Kyoichi Machida

SUPPLIERS

OTHERS (S)

CANON INC
E- Business Promotion
Headquarters, 3-30-2 Shimomaruko,
Ohta-ku, Tokyo 146-8501, Japan
TEL: +81 3 3757 6675
FAX: +81 3 3757 7134
CONTACT: Mr Masayuki Miyazaki

KANEKA CORPORATION
PV Business Development Division,
3-2-4 Nakanoshima, Kita-Ku,
Osaka 530-8288 Japan
TEL: +81 6 6226 5315
FAX: +81 6 6226 5144
E-MAIL: JDK01740@nifty.ne.jp
WEB: http://www.kaneka.co.jp
CONTACT: Yoshiki Takeoka

OM ENVIRONMENT PLANNING INC
Nissei Annex 8F,
325-34 Sunayama-Cho,
Hamamatsu-city,
Shizuoka Pref430-0926 Japan
TEL: +81 53 450 0777
FAX: +81 53 458 0225
E-MAIL: take@omplan.co.jp
WEB: http://www.omplan.co.jp
CONTACT: Miwako Takeuchi

We kindly request more listings in this country.

You can submit any additional listings by E-mail: unisun@vsnl.com

Fax: 91 80 22289294

We will include these in the next edition

Kindly inform us of any errors and omissions in the listings by:

E-mail: unisun@vsnl.com

Fax: 91 80 22289294

SOLAR THERMAL

DAYSON ELECTRONICS COMPANY LIMITED
Room 31, Duckwoo Building,
1640 27, Seocho-dong,
Seocho-go-Seoul
Korea Republic
TEL : + 82 2 581 1241
FAX : + 82 2 581 1244

SOLAR PHOTOVOLTAIC

NAM SUNG CO LTD
10-2 Juk Gok-Ri,
Jin Young-Eub, KimHae City,
Keyong Nam 621 -800
Korea Republic
TEL: +82 525 45 2533
FAX: +82 525 45 2541
CONTACT:Kim Byong Hak

ELECTRIC VEHICLE

HYUNDAI MOTOR COMPANY
Research And Development Division,
772-1 Changduk-Don, Whasung-City,
Kyonggi-Do 445-706,
Korea Republic
TEL: +82 31 369 7246
FAX: +82 31 369 6299
E-MAIL: jasonkoo@shinbiro.com
WEB: http://www.hyundai.com

We kindly request more listings in this country.

You can submit any additional listings by E-mail: unisun@vsnl.com

Fax: 91 80 22289294

We will include these in the next edition

Kindly inform us of any errors and omissions in the listings by:

E-mail: unisun@vsnl.com

Fax: 91 80 22289294

RESEARCH & DEVELOPMENT

KUWAIT INSTITUTE FOR SCIENTIFIC RESEARCH –KISR
Building & Energy Technologies Department-BET, PO Box 24885, Safat 13169, Kuwait
TEL: +965 483 6100
FAX: +965 484 5763
E-MAIL: sjandal@safat.kisr.edu.kw
WEB: http://www.safat.kisr.edu.kw
CONTACT: Saad S Al Jandal

SUPPLIERS

BATTERIES/INVERTERS

AL TAFOOQ INTERNATIONAL
P O BOX : 1465, Safat,
Kuwait 13015
TEL :965 4820083 / 7
FAX :965 4820085

We kindly request more listings in this country.

You can submit any additional listings by E-mail: unisun@vsnl.com

Fax: 91 80 22289294

We will include these in the next edition

Kindly inform us of any errors and omissions in the listings by:

E-mail: unisun@vsnl.com

Fax: 91 80 22289294

SOLAR THERMAL

RENEWABLE ENERGY SYSTEMS SDN BHD
97B Jin Gasing,
46000 Petaling Jaya, Malaysia
TEL : +60 3 926 9906
FAX : +60 3 756 5803
E-MAIL : azsolar@tm.net.my
CONTACT : A Zechariah

SOLAR RESEARCH DESIGN SDN BHD
Microsolar water heaters,
2 Jin ss 14/7F, 47500 subang
Jaya selangor, Malaysia
TEL:+60 3 7373735
FAX:+60 3 7334398
E_MAIL:microsolar@hotmail.com
WEB:http://
www.microsolarsystem.com
CONTACT:Josephine Goh

SOLARTECH SDN BHD
26 Medan Setia 2, Bukit Damansara
50490 Kuala Lumpur, Malaysia
TEL:+60 3 255 9222
FAX:+60 3 255 8622
E-MAIL:roy@solartech.com.my
WEB:http://www.solartech.com.my
CONTACT:Roy Chok

SUMMER SALES & SERVICE SDN BHD
10 jin Tsbl, Taman Industri 56
Buloh,
47000 Sungai Buloh, Selangor,
Malaysia
TEL: +60 3 656 0988
FAX: +60 3 657 1889
CONTACT : C S Yap

SOLAR PHOTOVOLTAIC

RENEWABLE ENERGY SYSTEMS SDN BHD
97B Jin Gasing,
46000 Petaling Jaya, Malaysia
TEL : +60 3 926 9906
FAX : +60 3 756 5803
E-MAIL : azsolar@tm.net.my
CONTACT : A Zechariah

SOLAR VOLTAIC SDN BHD
Research Department,
56 Jalan 7 / 152,
Taman Perindustrian 7 / 152,
Batu 6 Jalan Puchong,
58200 Kuala Lumpar, Malaysia
TEL: +60377817668
FAX: +60377820668
E-MAIL: solarcon@tm.net.my
CONTACT: Mr. Paul Millott

COGENERATION

JEBSEN &JESSEN ENGINEERING (M) SDN BHD
S16 Jalan 51A 225,
46100 Petaling Jaya, Malaysia
TEL: +60 3 776 3722
FAX: +60 3 775 9130
CONTACT :Leonard Liew

SMALL HYDRO

SPEC ENGINEERING SDN BHD
No 50 Jalan Bagan Nira 26/8,
Seksyen 26 Kaw,
Perindustrian Hicom, 40400
Shah Alam Selangor, Malaysia
TEL: +60 3 511 6878
FAX: +60 3 511 5451
CONTACT: Chong Fat Leong

ENERGY EFFICIENCY

DPC ENERGY SDN BHD
Gang Angkasaraya Kuala Lumpur
Malaysia
TEL : + 60 3 241 2403
FAX : + 60 3 243 3814
CONTACT : S Halskov

NGO's

CENTRE FOR ENVIRONMENTAL TECHNOLOGY AND DEVELOPMENT MALAYASIA CETDEM
PO Box 382, 46740 Petaling,
Jaya, Malaysia
TEL : +60 3 77 57767
FAX : +60 3 77 540390
E-MAIL : cetdem@po.jaring.my
CONTACT : Gurmit Singh

CONSULTANTS

CRESCENT SYNERGY (M) SDN BHD
Energy Division, 13 Jalan Bunga
Melati 2/2 40000 Shah Alam,
Selangor, Malaysia
TEL: +60 3 55 193870
FAX: +60 3 41 082193
CONTACT: Zakaria Ishak

OTHERS

TUV BAYERN (M) SDN BHT
No 22-3 Jalan USJ 9/5R,
Petaling Jaya Selangor,
47620 UEP Subang Jaya, Malaysia
TEL: +60 3 724 40 16
FAX: +60 3 724 40 19
E-MAIL: tuv@po.jaring.my
CONTACT: Gunther Kuhn

SUPPLIERS

GREEN AGE SOLAR TECHNOLOGY SDN BHD
92 Jalan Kota Permai, Taman Kota
Permai, 14000 Bukit Mertajam,
Penang Malaysia
TEL: +60 4 5082331
FAX: +60 4 5082330
E-MAIL: sales@ga2020.com
WEB: http://www.ga2020.com
CONTACT: Anne Goh

We kindly request more listings in this country.

You can submit any additional listings by E-mail: unisun@vsnl.com

Fax: 91 80 22289294

We will include these in the next edition

Kindly inform us of any errors and omissions in the listings by:

E-mail: unisun@vsnl.com

Fax: 91 80 22289294

SOLAR PHOTOVOLTAIC

SOLENERG LTD
Motorway M3, Riche Terre,
Terre Rouge Mauritius
TEL : +2302481114
FAX : +2302491594
E-MAIL : solenerg@intnet.mu
CONTACT: Mike Ah-Piang

We kindly request more listings in this country.

You can submit any additional listings by E-mail: unisun@vsnl.com

Fax: 91 80 22289294

We will include these in the next edition

Kindly inform us of any errors and omissions in the listings by:

E-mail: unisun@vsnl.com

Fax: 91 80 22289294

SOLAR PHOTOVOLTAIC

ABE PHOTOVOLTAICS LTD
P O Box 591, Ulaanbaatar 13,
Mongolia
TEL : +976 1 53450
FAX : +976 1 321336
E-MAIL : galbatar@magicnet.mn
CONTACT : Dr T Galbaatar

ADRA / MONGOLIA
PO Box 1038,
Ulaan Baatar 210613, Mongolia
TEL : +976 1 323086
FAX : +976 1 323086

NGO's

INSTITUTE FOR RENEWABLE ENERGY
P O Box 52/40
210152, Ulaanbaatar, Mongolia
TEL :976 1 342377
FAX :976 1 342377

We kindly request more listings in this country.

You can submit any additional listings by E-mail: unisun@vsnl.com

Fax: 91 80 22289294

We will include these in the next edition

Kindly inform us of any errors and omissions in the listings by:

E-mail: unisun@vsnl.com

Fax: 91 80 22289294

SOLAR PHOTOVOLTAIC

NEPAL HYDRO & ELECTRIC (P) LTD
PO Box #11728, Kathmandu
Kumaripatti, Lalitpur, Nepal
TEL: +977 1 536750
FAX: +977 1 536751
E-MAIL: marketing@nhe.com.np
CONTACT: Nawa Raj Shrestha

SMALL HYDRO

ENERGY SYSTEMS
PO Box 1571, Kathmandu, Nepal,
TEL : + 977 1 372171
E-MAIL : eystems@info.com.np
CONTACT : Shrestha

NEPAL HYDRO & ELECTRIC (P) LTD
Marketing Department,
PO Box # 11728
Kathmandu, Kumaripati,
Lalitpur, Nepal TEL: +977 1 536750
FAX: +977 1 536751
E-MAIL: marketing@nhe.com.np
WEB: http://www.nhe.com.np
CONTACT: Nawa Raj Shrestha

WISDOM LIGHT GROUP (P) LTD
Module & System Manufacturing,
Ghat 2, 178 Siphal-Kalopul,
PO Box 6921, Nepal
TEL: +977 1 480672
FAX: +977 1 482154
E-MAIL: wisdom@mos.com.np
WEB: http://www.wisdomlight.com.np
CONTACT: Soniya Thapa

DESIGN & ENGINEERING

LOTUS ENERGY PVT LTD
PO Box 9219 Batbhateni Dhunge Dhara, Kathmandu Nepal
TEL: +977 1 418 203
FAX: +977 1 412 924
EMAIL: info@lotusenergy.com
WEB:http://www.lotusenergy.com
CONTACT:Adam Friedensohn

We kindly request more listings in this country.

You can submit any additional listings by E-mail: unisun@vsnl.com

Fax: 91 80 22289294

We will include these in the next edition

Kindly inform us of any errors and omissions in the listings by:

E-mail: unisun@vsnl.com

Fax: 91 80 22289294

SOLAR PHOTOVOLTAIC

MERIN (PVT) LTD,
Agro-tool division
Dada Chambers, M A Jinnah Rd,
Karachi, Pakistan 74000
TEL : +92 21 2411988

SOLAR CORPORATION
Moonshine Apt 3,
Plot 306/1 Ashoka Street,
Gardeneast, Karachi-74550, Pakistan
TEL: +92 21 722 3206
FAX: +92 21 722 3206
CONTACT: Mansoorali Shalwani

NGO's

AFGHAN DEVELOPMENT ASSOCIATION - ADA
House No 342, Old Bara Road,
University Town, UPO Box 922,
Peshawar, Pakistan
TEL : +92 91 45333
FAX : +92 91 42230
CONTACT : Ghulam Jeloni Popal

ENERGY EFFICIENCY

A & COMPILLERS
Dyal Singh Manision
66-The Mall, Lahore, Pakistan
TEL : + 92 42 7551893
E-MAIL : sah@brain.net.pk

CONSULTANTS

TECHNOLOGY TRANSFER INTERNATIONAL
586 A-1 Township, Lahore, Pakistan
TEL: +92425120932
FAX: +92425120932
E-MAIL: tti@nexlinx.net.pk

We kindly request more listings in this country.

You can submit any additional listings by E-mail: unisun@vsnl.com

Fax: 91 80 22289294

We will include these in the next edition

Kindly inform us of any errors and omissions in the listings by:

E-mail: unisun@vsnl.com

Fax: 91 80 22289294

PHILIPPINES

ASSOCIATIONS

RENEWABLE ENERGY ASSOCIATION OF THE PHILIPPINES – REAP
C/O Matec, Tech Center Buencamino Street, Alabang Muntinlupa City, Philippines
TEL: +6328506450
FAX: +6328508801

SOLAR THERMAL

SOLAHART PHILIPPINES
A Division of Gopez Corporation,
4 Kitanlad Street,
Quenzon City
Philippines
TEL:+63 2 731 58 39
FAX:+63 2 731 68 34
E-MAIL:gopezphl@skynet.net
WEB:http://www.gopezcorp.com
CONTACT:Euberto G Lorenzo

BIOMASS

BIO-GAS INCORPORATED
11, Galaxy Street,
GSIS Hts, Matina,
Davao City 8000, Philippines
TEL : +63 299 2298
CONTACT : A Tabin

WASTE TO ENERGY

PHILIPPINE BIO-SCIENCE COMPANY INC
C/o PEI, 10th Floor
Strata 100 Building,
Emerald Avenue Ortigas Centre,
Pasig City 1605,
Philippines
TEL: +63 2 631 2826
FAX: +63 2 632 7097
E-MAIL:philbio@pacific.net.ph
CONTACT:Alberto Pascua

FINANCE / BANKING

PHILIPPINE BIO-SCIENCE COMPANY INC
C/o PEI, 10th Floor
Strata 100 Building,
Emerald Avenue Ortigas Centre,
Pasig City 1605,
Philippines
TEL: +63 2 631 2826
FAX: +63 2 632 7097
E-MAIL:philbio@pacific.net.ph
CONTACT:Alberto Pascua

GOVERNMENT

PHILIPPINES DEPARTMENT OF ENERGY
Energy Utilization Management Bureau / Fuels and Appliance Testing Laboratory,
PNOC-ERDC Compound,
Commonwealth Avenue,
Diliman, Quenzon City,
Philippines
TEL: +63 2 927 7201
FAX: +63 2 929 5474
E-MAIL:deofatl@skyinet.net
CONTACT:Mirna R Campanao

RESEARCH & DEVELOPMENT

DEPARMENT OF ENERGY
PNPC Complex, Merit Road Fort,
Bonifacio, MetroManila,
Philippines
TEL : + 63 818 86 14
FAX : + 63 818 86 14
CONTACT : R Quejas

INSTITUTE FOR SMALL-SCALE INDUSTRIES (ISSI)
University of the Phillipines,
ET Virata Hall, E Jacino Street,
Diliman Quenon City,
Phiippines
TEL: +63 92870 76
FAX: +63 92710 34
E-MAIL: dotsie@upissi.ph.net
WEB: http://www.upissi.ph.net
CONTACT: Fortunato T dela Pena

PHILIPPINES NATIONAL OIL COMPANY - PNOC-ENERGY DEVELOPMENT CORPORATION-EDC
Energy Research & Development Center-ERDC,
PO Box 22,
UP Campus, Diliman,
Quenzon City, Philippines
TEL: + 63 2 929 76 11
FAX: + 63 2 929 34 12
E-MAIL: erdc@info.com.ph
CONTACT : Mr.Rogelio Z Aldover

CONSULTANTS

FLORO INTERNATIONAL CORPORATION
500 C Palanca Street,
San Miguel, Manila 1001,
Philippines
TEL: + 63 2 735 0001
FAX: + 63 2 734 9458
E-MAIL:floro@mni.sequel.net
CONTACT : Victor Floro

PCV CONSULTING AND RESEARCH SERVICES
Lot 2 Block 3,
Pamahay Village,
San Jose,
1860 Rodriguez Rizal,
Philippines
TEL: +63 2 997 9929
E-MAIL:
pcv_consulting@mailcity.com
CONTACT: Pablo C Villasenor

We kindly request more listings in this country.

You can submit any additional listings by E-mail: unisun@vsnl.com

Fax: 91 80 22289294

We will include these in the next edition

Kindly inform us of any errors and omissions in the listings by:

E-mail: unisun@vsnl.com

Fax: 91 80 22289294

SOLAR THERMAL

SAUDI SOLAR HEATERS FACTORY
PO Box 68935, 11537 Riyadh,
Saudi Arabia
TEL: +96612652031
FAX: +96612652331
E-MAIL: info@saudisolar.com
WEB: http://www.saudisolar.com
CONTACT: Mr. Ahmad Zaidan

SUPPLIERS

OTHERS (S)

FLORISSANT CS
PO Box 30530, Al-Khobar,
31952, Saudi Arabia
TEL: +966 53 812 044
FAX: +966 3 893 5551
E-MAIL: glippis@rteksa.com
CONTACT: George Lippis

We kindly request more listings in this country.

You can submit any additional listings by E-mail: unisun@vsnl.com

Fax: 91 80 22289294

We will include these in the next edition

Kindly inform us of any errors and omissions in the listings by:

E-mail: unisun@vsnl.com

Fax: 91 80 22289294

SOLAR PHOTOVOLTAIC

MAXON CORPORATION
Asia Representative Office,
10 Collyer Quay, 11-10 Ocean Building,
049315, Singapore
TEL: +65 538 2616
FAX: +65 538 8316
E-MAIL: maxon@cyberway.com.sg
WEB: http://www.maxoncorp.com
CONTACT: Mr SK Tay

SIEMENS SHOWA SOLAR PTE LTD
166 Kallang Way, 349249,
Singapore
TEL: +65 842 3886
FAX: +65 842 3887
E-MAIL:
ssspv@solar.siemens.com.sg
WEB: http://www.siemenssolar.com
CONTACT: Dr Thomas Reindl

TOTAL ENERGIE
331 North Bridge Road,
#22-04 Odeon Towers,
188720, Singapore
TEL: +65 8792259
FAX: +65 8792207

SUPPLIERS

BATTERIES & INVERTERS

WORLEY ENERGY CELLS
491 B River Valley Rd,
09-01 Valley point, Singapore
TEL: +65 97 92 76 56
FAX: +65 67 35 74 44
E-MAIL: john.grzan@worley.com.sg
WEB: http://www.worley.com.au/wecs
CONTACT: John Grzan

We kindly request more listings in this country.

You can submit any additional listings by E-mail: unisun@vsnl.com

Fax: 91 80 22289294

We will include these in the next edition

Kindly inform us of any errors and omissions in the listings by:

E-mail: unisun@vsnl.com

Fax: 91 80 22289294

ASSOCIATIONS

MAS ENTERPRISES
Renewable Energy, 10/1 Gangadara Mawatha, Mount Lavinia, Sri Lanka
TEL: +94 1 71 8554
FAX: +94 1 71 8554
E-MAIL: mas@lgo.lk
CONTACT: Amara M Peeris

FINANCE / BANKING

DFCC BANK
PO Box 1397, 73/5 Galle Road
Colombo 3, Srilanka
TEL : + 94 1 440366
FAX : + 94 1 440376
E-MAIL : dfccplan@srilanka.net
WEB : http://www.dfcc.com
CONTACT : J Nagendran

We kindly request more listings in this country.

You can submit any additional listings by E-mail: unisun@vsnl.com

Fax: 91 80 22289294

We will include these in the next edition

Kindly inform us of any errors and omissions in the listings by:

E-mail: unisun@vsnl.com

Fax: 91 80 22289294

SOLAR THERMAL

KUPO CO LTD
6F No.4 Lane 609 Sec 5,
Chung Shin Road, San Chung,
Taipei, Taiwan
TEL: +886 2 2999 1906
FAX: +886 2 2999 1955
WEB: http://www.solasia-solarheater.com.tw
CONTACT: Mr Maico Chang

SUNCUE COMPANY LTD
396 Min Sheng Road, Wu Feng,
Taichung, Taiwan
TEL: +886 4 2339 7171
FAX: +886 4 2330 2939
WEB: http://www.suncue.com
CONTACT: Wen-Bao Lee

SUNTECH SOLAR TECHNOLOGY CO LTD
Sales & Marketing,
No 25 Ta-Jin St, Nantun,
Taichung, Taiwan
TEL: +886423385089
FAX: +886423385079
E-MAIL: service@suntek.com.tw
WEB: http://www.suntek.com.tw
CONTACT: Herman Lai

SOLAR PHOTOVOLTAIC

MOTECH INDUSTRIES INCORPORATED
Solar Electricity. No. 3 Da-shun
9th Rd, Hsin-shi,
Tainan 744, Taiwan
TEL:+886 6 5050789
FAX: +886 6 5051789
EMAIL:solar@motechind.com
WEB:http://www.motechind.com
CONTACT : Eugenie Wang

SINONAR CORPORATION
8 Prosperity Road,
1 Science-Based Industrial Park,
Hsinchu, Taiwan
TEL: +886 35 783366
FAX: +886 35 781812
E-MAIL: jameslee@mail.sinonar.com.tw
CONTACT: Dr Yuh-Han Shing

CONSULTANTS

GLOBAL CHANGE CENTER
National Taiwan University
Section 4, Roosvelt Road,
Taipei, Taiwan
TEL : + 886 2 365 5671
FAX : + 886 2 365 9154
E-MAIL : liucm@ccms.utu.edu.tw
CONTACT : Prof Chung Ming Liu

SOLASIA ENERGY DEVELOPMENT CO LTD
6F No 4 Lane 609 Sec 5
Chung Shion Road Taipei,
Taiwan,
TEL : +886 2 2999 1906
FAX : +886 2 2999 1955
E-MAIL : solasia@kupo.com.tw
WEB : http://www.solasia solarheater.com.tw
CONTACT : Wu-hsiung Chang

RESEARCH & DEVELOPMENT

ERL / ITRI
Renewable Energy Research
Division, Bdlg, 32, 195-6 Sec. 4
Chung Hsing Road,
Chutung Hinchu 310, Taiwan
TEL : + 886 35916262
FAX : + 886 35820030
E-MAIL : cschu@itri.org.tw
CONTACT : Ching-Sung Chiu

We kindly request more listings in this country.

You can submit any additional listings by E-mail: unisun@vsnl.com

Fax: 91 80 22289294

We will include these in the next edition

Kindly inform us of any errors and omissions in the listings by:

E-mail: unisun@vsnl.com

Fax: 91 80 22289294

ASSOCIATION

COUNCIL ON RENEWABLE ENERGY IN THE MEKONG REGION - CORE SERT,
Naresuan University,
Phitsanulok, 65000, Thailand
TEL : +66 55 261067
FAX : +66 55 261067
E-MAIL : sert@psnulok.foxinfo.co.th
CONTACT : P Muangnalad

EC ASEAN COGEN PROGRAMME
Asian Institute of Technology
KM42, Phaholythin Highway,
Klonguang, Pathumthani 12120,
Thailand
TEL :+ 66 2 524 5399
FAX : +66 2 524 5395
E-MAIL : cogen@ait.ac.th
CONTACT : M Pennington

REGIONAL WOOD ENERGY DEVELOPMENT PROGRAMME IN ASIA
Maliwan Mansion, Phra Atit Road,
Bangkok 10200, Thailand
TEL : +66 2 280 27 60
FAX : +66 2 280 07 60
E-MAIL : rwedp@fao.org
WEB : http://www.rwedp.org
CONTACT : Dr Wim Hulscher

GOVERNMENT

UNITED NATIONS ECONOMIC & SOCIAL COMMISSION FOR ASIA & THE PACIFIC-ESCAP
Energy Resources Section
Enivronment and Natural Resources
Development Division,
UN Building, Rajdamnern Ave,
Bangkok 10200
Thailand
TEL: +66 2 288 1546
FAX: +66 2 288 1059
E-MAIL: saha.unescap@un.org
WEB: http://www.unescap.org/enrd/energy
CONTACT:Pranesh C Saha

RESEARCH & DEVELOPMENT

SOLAR ENERGY RESEARCH AND TRAINING CENTER-SERT
Naresuan University,
Phitsanulok 65000,
Thailand
TEL : +66 55 261067
FAX : +66 55 261067
E_MAIL : sert@psnulok.loxinfo.co.th
CONTACT : Prof W Rakwichian

SOLARTRON CO LTD
38 2nd Floor Chavanich Building
sukhumvit 69 (Soi Salinimit)
Prakanong Klongtoey, Bangkok
10110
Thailand
TEL:+66 2 392 0224
FAX:+66 2 381 2971
CONTACT:Miss Wandee
Khunchornyakong

ASIAN INSTITUTE OF TECHNOLOGY
Centre for Energy-Environment
Research & Development-CEERD
Klong Luang PO BOX 4,
Pathumthani 12120, Thailand
TEL : +66 2 524 5401
FAX : +66 2 524 5441
E-MAIL : lefevre@ait.ac.th
WEB :http://www.ceerd.ait.ac.th
CONTACT : T Leferre

UNIVERSITIES

ASIAN INSTITUTE OF TECHNOLOGY
Centre for Energy-Environment
Research & Development-CEERD
Klong Luang PO BOX 4,
Pathumthani 12120, Thailand
TEL : +66 2 524 5401
FAX : +66 2 524 5441
E-MAIL : lefevre@ait.ac.th
WEB :http://www.ceerd.ait.ac.th
CONTACT : T Leferre

KING MONGKUT'S INSTITUTE OF TECHNOLOGY
School of Energy and Materials
Division of Energy,
Thonburi 91Suksawat Road,
48 Bangmod Ratburana,
Bangkok 10140, Thailand
TEL: +66 2 427 0162 8
FAX: +66 2 427 9062
E-MAIL: ijonlabh@cc.kmitt.ac.th
CONTACT : Dr J Hirutilabh

CONSULTANTS

THE ENERGY CONSERVATION CENTER OF THAILAND
108 Bangkok Thai Tower 9 Floor,
Rangnam Road, Ratchathevi,
Bangkok 10400, Thailand
TEL: +66 2 642 7090
FAX: +66 2 642 7099
E-MAIL: ecct@moart.inet.co.th

DESIGN & ENGINEERING

LEGO ENGINEERING LTD
99/10 Soi Chalermsuk,
Palonyothin Road,
Bangkean, Bangkok 10900,
Thailand
TEL: +66 2 513 5073
FAX: +66 2 513 5073
CONTACT: Mr C Lilavivat

LEGO ENGINEERING LTD
99/10 Soi Chalermsuk,
Pahonyothin Road, Bangkean,
Bangkok, 10900, Thailand
TEL: +66 2 513 5073
FAX: +66 2 513 5073
CONTACT: Mr C Lilavivat

SUPPLIERS

INSTRUMENTATION

SITHIPORN ASSOCIATES CO LTD
451 Sirinthorn Road,
Bangbumru, Bangplud,
Bangkok 10700, Thailand
TEL: +66 2 4338331
FAX: +66 2 4331679
CONTACT: Mr Vongchinsri

LEO ELECTRONICS CO LTD
119/51 Moo 8. Bagna-Trad Road,
Bagna, Bangkok 10260,
Thailand
TEL: +66 2 7468708
FAX: +66 2 3120911
E-MAIL: global_business@leonics.com
WEB:http://www.leonics.com
CONTACT: Pornlert Laorsuwan

Kindly inform us of any errors and omissions in the listings by:

E-mail: unisun@vsnl.com

Fax: 91 80 22289294

TURKEY

SOLAR THERMAL

ELIT LIMITED
Abidin Daver Sokak 26/8,
TR/06550, Cankaya-Ankara,
Turkey
TEL : +90 312 441 0294
FAX : +90 312 441 7714

SOLAR PHOTOVOLTAIC

PHOTONIC PRODUCTS LTD
4 Adsiz Asker Sokak G Magosa,
Merslin 10, Turkey
TEL :+ 90 392 852 2103
FAX : + 90 392 365 0240
E-MAIL:erzat@eenet.ee.emu.edu.tr
CONTACT: Dr. Erzat G Erdil

RESEARCH & DEVELOPMENT

KOCAELI UNIVERSITY
New and Renewable Energy
Resources and Technologies
Research Unit, Anitpark Yani,
Izmit 41300 Kocaeli, Turkey
TEL: +90 532 7744525
FAX: +90 262 3249909
E-MAIL: tanay@kou.edu.tr
WEB: http://www.iyi.gen.tr
CONTACT : Dr. T S Uyar

KOMBASSAN HOLDING AS
Energy Systems Ar-Ge, Oba Yolu,
Cikcilli Belediyesi, PK 159, 07400
Alanya, Turkey
TEL: +90 242 511 0200
FAX: +90 242 515 0192
E-MAIL: kombassanarge@
superonline.com
WEB: http://www.kombassan.com.tr
CONTACT : Dr I Kubo

CONSULTANTS

BIOSOFT TECHNOLOGY LTD-IMMC
Foreign Business Department,
Oguzlar Mahallesi 52 Sokak
No: 2/9, Balgat, 06520 Ankara,
Turkey
TEL: +90 312 287 81 30
FAX: +90 312 284 32 49
E-MAIL: biosoft@superonline,con
WEB: http://www.immcint.com
CONTACT: Yakup Topal

PHOTONIC PRODUCTS LTD
4 Adsiz Asker Sokak, G Magosa,
Mersin 10, Turkey
TEL: +90 392 630 1449
FAX: +90 392 365 0240
E-MAIL: erzat.erdil@emu.edu.tr
CONTACT: Dr Erzat G Erdil

We kindly request more listings in this country.

You can submit any additional listings by E-mail: unisun@vsnl.com

Fax: 91 80 22289294

We will include these in the next edition

Kindly inform us of any errors and omissions in the listings by:

E-mail: unisun@vsnl.com

Fax: 91 80 22289294

CONSULTANTS

FICHTNER CONSULTING ENGINEERS
P.O.Box. 3657, Abu Dhabi,
United Arab Emirates
TEL: + 971 2 728099
FAX: + 971 2 728900
CONTACT : F Donnachie

We kindly request more listings in this country.

You can submit any additional listings by E-mail: unisun@vsnl.com

Fax: 91 80 22289294

We will include these in the next edition

Kindly inform us of any errors and omissions in the listings by:

E-mail: unisun@vsnl.com

Fax: 91 80 22289294

GOVERNMENT

SUPPORT PROGARM FOR SUSTAINABLE ENERGY DEVELOPMENT
Ministry of Science Technology
& Environment, 39 Tran Hung Dao,
Hanoi, Vietnam
TEL : +84 48 261843
FAX : +84 48 252733
E-MAIL : enconpro@
bdvn.vnmail.vnd.net
CONTACT : Nguyen Thuong
General services consultants

SMALL HYDRO

VIETNAM INSTITUTE FOR WATER RESOURCES RESEARCH
Hydro Power Centre,
299 Tayson Str,
Dongda Dist. Hanoi, Vietnam
TEL : +84 4 8521298
FAX : +84 4 5630667
E-MAIL : hpc@fpt.vn
CONTACT : Nguyen Tung Phong

We kindly request more listings in this country.

You can submit any additional listings by E-mail: unisun@vsnl.com

Fax: 91 80 22289294

We will include these in the next edition

Kindly inform us of any errors and omissions in the listings by:

E-mail: unisun@vsnl.com

Fax: 91 80 22289294

AUSTRALIA

SOLAR THERMAL

BEASLEY INDUSTRIES PTY LTD
PO Box 104, Hindmarsh,
Southern Australia 5007,
Australia
TEL : +61 8 340 2299
FAX : +61 8 340 0829
E-MAIL :hotwater@beasley.com.au
WEB : http://www.beasley.com.au
CONTACT : Michael Wagstaff

DEMAND SOLAR AND DEMAND INSULATION
1 Maclaurin Parade,
Roseville New
South Wales, 2069, Australia
TEL : + 61 2 415 1077
FAX : + 61 2 415 2062
CONTACT : Doug Mill

EDWARDS ENERGY SYSTEMS PTY LTD
Export Department,
PO Box 1415,
Canning Vale,
6970 Perth, Australia
TEL : +61 8 933 44248
FAX : +61 8 933 44200
E-MAIL : edenergy@edwards.com.au
WEB : http://www.edwards.com.au
CONTACT : Varghan Boultwood

SOLAHART INDUSTRIES PTY LTD
112 Pilbara Street,
Welshpool
Western Australia 6106,
Australia
TEL:+61 89458 6211
FAX:+61 89351 8034
E-MAIL:solahart@solahart.com.au
WEB:http://www.solahart.com.au
CONTACT:Rodger Meads

SOLA-KLEEN SMALLS
24 Bassendean Road Bayswater,
Western Australlia 6053,
Australia
TEL:+61 8 9271 5725
FAX:+618 9271 6136
E-MAIL:sola@sola-kleen.com.au
WEB:http://www.sola-kleen.com.au
CONTACT:Doug Sheppard

SOLAR CHARGE PTY LTD
115 Martin Street,
Brighton, Victoria 3186,
Australia
TEL:+61 3 9596 1974
FAX:+61 3 8596 1989
E-MAIL:solarcharge@one.net.ao
WEB:http://www.solarcharge.com.au
CONTACT:Richard Potter

SOLCO INDUSTRIES PTY LTD
126 Sheffield Road,
Welshpool Westren
Australia 6016, Australia
TEL:+61 8 93562844
FAX:+61 8 93518290
E-MAIL:solco@solco.com.au
WEB:http://www.solco.com.au
CONTACT : A Marwick

SUNLIGHTSOLARSYSTEMS AUSTRALIA
5 Kelly Court,
North Geelong,
Victoria 3215, Australia
TEL: +61 352 721 588
FAX: +61 352 77 9493
E-MAIL:sunlight@
northsteelbu.aust.com
WEB:http://
www.sunlightsolar.com.au
CONTACT:David Reid

SOLAR PHOTOVOLTAIC

AUSTRALIAN ENERGY RESEARCH LABORATORIES P/L
MS 660, Lawsons Broad Road,
Proston, Queensland, 4613,
Australia
TEL : +61 7 41 689 308
FAX : +61 7 41 689 197
E-MAIL : aeri@hotkey.net.au
CONTACT : Stuart Watkinson

BP SOLAR AUSTRALIA PTY LTD
2 Australia Avenue,
Homebush Bay,New South Wales,
2127 Australia
TEL : +61 2 8762 5777
FAX : +61 2 8762 5889
E-MAIL : farret@dzl.bp.com
WEB : http://www.bpsolarex.com
CONTACT : Cindy Farrelly

CUMMINS POWER GENERATION AUSTRALIA
11 Manton Street, Hindmarsh,
South Australia 5007, Australia
TEL : +61 8 346 3832
FAX : +61 8 340 3448
CONTACT : Brenton Williams

DANIEL ORANJE PTY LTD
9, Norfolk Street, Moonee Ponds,
Victoria 3039, Australia
TEL : + 61 3 3 9370 6379
FAX : + 61 3 9346 7023
E-MAIL : dooranje@optusnet.com.au/~doranje
WEB : http://www.optusnet.com.au/
~doranje
CONTACT : Daan Oranje

DEMAND SOLAR AND DEMAND INSULATION
1 Maclaurin Parade,
Roseville New
South Wales, 2069, Australia
TEL : + 61 2 415 1077
FAX : + 61 2 415 2062
CONTACT : Doug Mill

GIPPSLAND ENERGY ALTERNATIVE
325 Bellbird Road, Clifton Creek,
Victoria 3875, Australia
TEL : + 61 3 51 57 9304
CONTACT : Noel Bates

GOING SOLAR
320 Victoria Street, North
Meibourne, Victoria 3051, Australia
TEL : + 61 3 9328 4123
FAX : + 61 3 9328 1249
E-MAIL : retail@goingsolar.com.au
Web : http://www.goingsolar.com.au
CONTACT : Stephen Ingrouille

MONOPUMPS (AUSTRALIA) PTY LTD
338-348 Lower Dandenong Road,
PO BOX 123 Mordialloc,
Melbourne 3195, Australia
TEL:+61 3 9580 5211
FAX: +61 3 9580 9036
EMAIL:oz.sales@mono-pumps.com
WEB:http://www.mono-pumps.com
CONTACT:Douglas Darville

PACIFIC SOLAR PTY LIMITED
82-86 Bay Street, Botany,
NSW 2019, Australia
TEL: +61 2 9316 68 11
FAX: +61 2 9666 4079
E-MAIL: info@psolar.com.au
WEB: http://
www.pacificsolar.com.au
CONTACT: Peter Lawley

PECAN ENGINEERING PTY LTD
13 Acorn Road, Dry Creek, Southern
Australia 5094, Australia
TEL: +61 8 83498 332
FAX: +61 8 82606 643
E-MAIL: info@pecansolar.com.au
WEB: http://www.pecansolar.com.au
CONTACT: Richard Mitchell

PLASMATRONICS PTY LTD
42 Bell Streetm, Fitzroy,
Victoria 3065 Australia
TEL: +61 3 9486 9902
FAX:+61 3 9486 9903
E-MAIL : pladmin@vicnet.net.au
WEB:http://
www.plasmotronics.taz.net.au
CONTACT : Mr Brendan English

AUSTRALIA

PLATYPUS POWER
1-57 Churchill Ave, Bright,
Victoria, 3641,
Australia
TEL: +61 3 5755 2383
FAX:+61 3 5750 1777
E-MAIL : plapower@netc.net.au
WEB:http://www.netc.net.au/platypus
CONTACT : Peter Barret

SOLAR CHARGE PTY LTD
115 Martin Street,
Brighton, Victoria 3186,
Australia
TEL:+61 3 9596 1974
FAX:+61 3 8596 1989
E-MAIL:solarcharge@one.net.ao
WEB:http://www.solarcharge.com.au
CONTACT:Richard Potter

SOLAR RESEARCH CORPORATION PTY LTD
6 Luton Lane, Hawthorn,
Victoria 3122,
Australia
TEL:+61 3 9819 9544
FAX:+61 3 9819 9063
E_MAIL:john@solarsystems.com.au
WEB:http://www.solarsystems.co.au
CONTACT:Mr John B Lasich

SOLAR SALES PTY LTD
PO Box 190 Welshpool,
Western Australia 6986,
Australia
TEL : +61 8 9362 2111
FAX : +61 8 9472 1965
E_MAIL : info@solarsales.com.au
WEB:http : //www.solarsales.com.au
CONTACT : John Hall

SUNLIGHTSOLARSYSTEMS AUSTRALIA
5 Kelly Court,
North Geelong,
Victoria 3215, Australia
TEL: +61 352 721 588
FAX: +61 352 77 9493
E-MAIL:sunlight@
northsteelbu.aust.com
WEB:http://
www.sunlightsolar.com.au
CONTACT:David Reid

THE TWELVE VOLT SHOP
U4112 Kewdale Road,
Welshpool, Western Australia 6106,
Australia
TEL: +6 8 947 05949
FAX: +6 8 947 05991
E-MAIL: 12volt@icenet.com.au
WEB: http://www.12volt.com.au
CONTACT: Sue Godfrey

UTILUX PTY LTD
I&E Division,
14 Commercial Road,
Kingsgrove 2208, Australia
TEL: +61 2 95542600
FAX: +61 2 95021753
E-MAIL: phil.timbreil@utilux.com
WEB: http://www.utilux.com
CONTACT: Phil Timbrell

BIOMASS

ARBOR PRODUCTS AND WASTE EQUIPMENTS
2/45, Gilbert Park Drive,
Knoxfield, Victoria 3180,
Australia
TEL : +61 3 976 37699
FAX : +61 3 976 41762
EMAIL : arbor@enternet.com.au
CONTACT : Nicholas Rivett

LYNDON ZIMMERMANN AND ASSOCIATES
24 Waverley Street,Mitcham,
South Australia,Australia
TEL: +61 8 8272 9262
FAX: +61 8 8172 1494
E-MAIL: lyndonz@senet.com.au
WEB: http://users.senet.com.au/-
lyndonz
CONTACT: Lyndon Zimmermann

WIND

GP & HILL PTY LTD
29, Owen Road, Kelmscott, West,
Australia 6111, Australia
TEL : + 61 89 399 5265
FAX : +61 89 497 1335
E-MAIL : venwest@iinet.net.au
WEB : www.venwest.iinet.net.au
CONTACT : Geoft Hill

UNIVERSITY OF NEW CASTLE MECHANICAL ENGINEERING
Callagahan nsw 2308, Australia
TEL: +61249216198
FAX:+61249216 946
EMAIL:medhw@newcastle.edu.au
WEB:http://www.eng.newcastle.edu.au/
me/wind
CONTACT : DAVID WOOD

WASTE TO ENERGY

DUMAG KG VERTRENNUNGS TECHNIK
SchwarzenbergplatzP. 1037, Wien,
Australia
TEL : + 43 1 712 41 05
FAX : + 43 1 712 41 09
E-MAIL : dumag@aon.at

ENERGY EFFICIENCY

BP ARCHITECTS
Environmental Conscious Design,
157 North Road, Langwarrin,
Victoria 3910, Australia
TEL : +61 3 9776 7616
FAX : +61 3 9776 7616
E-MAIL : bridgetpuszka@
hotmail.com
CONTACT : Bridget Puszka

GUNN & SCOTT ARCHITECTS
PO Box 77,South West Rocks,
NSW 2431,Austraila
TEL : + 61 2 6566 7623
FAX : + 61 2 6566 7623
CONTACT : Trevor Scott

INTEGRATED ENERGY MANAGEMENT CENTRE
PO Box 349, Moonah,
Tasmania 7009, Australia
TEL: +61 02 733355
FAX: +61 02 733420
E-MAIL: barrie.brumby@
auroraenergy.com.au
CONTACT: Barrie Brumby

SMALL HYDRO

RESHAPE PTY LTD
I Alternative Way, Nimbin,
New South Wales 2480
TEL : +61 2 6689 1088
FAX : +61 2 6689 1109
E-MAIL : sales@rpc.com.au
WEB : http://www.rps.com.au
CONTACT : Dave Lambert

TYCO FLOW CONTROL PACIFIC
Tamar Designs, 67 Main Road,
Exeter, Tasmania 7275, Australia
TEL : +61 03 6394 3132
FAX : +61 03 6394 3179
E-MAIL : turbines@tama.com.au
WEB : http://www.tamar.com.au
CONTACT : Mike Wellman

FUEL CELL

CERAMIC FUEL CELLS LIMITED
Corporate Development,
170 Browns Road,
Noble Park,
VIC 3174,
Australia,
TEL : +61 3 955 42 300
FAX : +61 3 979 05 600
E-MAIL : rohang@cfcl.com.au
WEB : http://www.cfcl.com.au
CONTACT : Rohan Gillespie

ASSOCIATION

ELECTRICITY SUPPLY ASSOCIATION AUSTRALIA - ESAA
Level 11, 74,
Castleragh Street
Sydney, NSW2000, Australia
TEL : +61 2 9233 7222
FAX : +61 2 9233 7244
WEB : http://www.essa.com.au
CONTACT : Kylie Paterson

ELECTRICITY SUPPLY ASSOCIATION OF AUSTRALIA LIMITED
PO Box A 2492 Sydney South,
New South Wales, 1235,
Australia
TEL : +61 2 9233 7222
FAX : +61 2 9233 7244

SUSTAINABLE ENERGY INDUSTRY
ASSOCIATION (AUSTRALIA) LTD
Po Box 411,
Dickson, ACT 2602,
TEL: +60 6 230 0271
FAX: +61 6 230 0273
E-MAIL : seia@.com.au
WEB : http://www.seia.com.au
CONTACT : J David Abba

RESEARCH & DEVELOPMENT

ACRE LTD
C/O Murdoch University,
South Street, Murdoch,
WA 6150,
Australia
TEL: +61 8 9360 6620
FAX: +61 8 9360 6624
CONTACT: Dr Frank Reid

AUSTRALIAN NATIONAL UNIVERSITY
Solar Thermal Group, Centre for Sustainable Energy,
Department of Engineering,
Canberra,
ACT 0200, Australia
TEL : +61 6249 3976
FAX : +61 6249 0506
E-MAIL : keith@faceng.anu.edu.au
WEB : http://www.engn.anu.edu.au/solar/index.html
CONTACT : Dr. Keith Covegrove

BARDAK SOLAR POWER
Unit 2, 66-70, Railway Road,
Blackburn, Victoria 03130,
Australia
TEL : +61 3 894 2544
FAX : +61 3 894 3370
CONTACT : Susan Saunders

BIOMASS ENERGY SERVICES AND TECHNOLOGY PTY LTD
56, Gindurra Road,
Somersby,
New Soth Wales 2250,
Australia
TEL : +61 243 40 4911
FAX : +61 243 40 4878
E-MAIL : best@biomass.com.au
CONTACT : Rupert Lipscombe

CURTIN UNIVERSITY OF TECHNOLOGY
Centre for Renewable Energy & Sustainable Technologies, Australia
CRESTA, GPO Box U1987,
Perth Western, Australia 6485,
Australia
TEL : +618 9266 7934
FAX : +61 8 9266 3107
E-MAIL : cresta@ece.curtin.edu.au
WEB : http://www.ece.curtin.edu.au/cresta
CONTACT : Prof. Chem V Nayar

FREE HEAT INDUSTRIES
5/7 Oatland Esplanade, Runway Bay, Queensland 4216,
Australia
TEL: +61 7 55 319057
FAX: +61 7 55 377003
E-MAIL:info@freeheat.com.au
CONTACT : Hal Reynolds

MURDOCH UNIVERSITY
Institue for Sustainability and Technology Policy-ISTP,
South Street Murdoch,
Western Australia 6150, Australia
TEL: +61 8 9360 2913
FAX: +61 8 9360 6421
CONTACT: Prof Peter Newman

SOLAR RESEARCH CORPORATION PTY LTD
6 Luton Lane,
Hawthorn,
Victoria 3122,
Australia
TEL:+61 3 9819 9544
FAX:+61 3 9819 9063
E_MAIL:john @solarsystems.com.au
WEB:http://www.solarsystems.co.au
CONTACT:Mr John B Lasich

TELEPOWER AUSTRALIA
2/71 Rushdale Street Knoxfield
Victoria 3180, Australia
TEL: +61 3 9764 2001
FAX: +61 3 9764 2611
E-MAIL: telepower@telepower.com.au
WEB: http://www.telepower.com.au
CONTACT:Mr. Tim Robbins

DESING & ENGINEERING

AUSTRALIASIAN RESEARCH & DEVELOPMENT
Research Department, 2A Victory, Place, Lesmurdie, Perth, Western Australia 6076, Australia
TEL : +61 8 9291 9917
FAX : +61 8 9291 9917
E-MAIL : rhpearce@iinet.net.au
CONTACT : Mr. Robert Pearce

ENERGY DEVELOPMENTS LTD
EDL 848 Boundary Road, Richlands,
Queensland 4077, Australia
TEL: +61 7 3275 5555
FAX: +61 7 3217 0733
E-MAIL: bill.lazarus@edl.com.au
WEB: http://www.edl.com.au
CONTACT : Mr. Bill Lazarus

HEALEY ENGINEERING PTY LTD
PO Box 21, Victoria Park,
WA 6979, Australia
TEL: +61 9470 2122
FAX: +61 8 9470 9189
E MAIL: cngincer@iinet.net.au
CONTACT: John Healey

NOWY MOUNTAINS ENGINEERING CORPORATION LTD
South Wales 2630, Australia.
TEL:+61 64 52 0222
FAX:+61 64 52 0400

NGO'S

AUSTRALIAN CONSERVATION FOUNDATION ACF
340 Gore Street, Fitzroy,
Victoria 3065, Australia
TEL : +61 3 9416 1166
FAX : +61 3 9416 0767
CONTACT : Peter Kinrade

GREENPEACE-AUSTRALIA
GPO Box 337, Sydney NSW 2001,
Australia
TEL : + 61 2 9261 4666
FAX : +61 9261 4588
E-MAIL : greenpeace@au.greenpeace.org
CONTACT : greenpeace.org.au

UNIVERSITIES

BARRIER REEF INSTITUTE OF TAFE PMB
1, Townsville, DC,
Queensland 4810, Australia
TEL : +61 7 47 505211
FAX : +61 7 47 505268
E-MAIL : eter.brock@detir.qld.gov.au
CONTACT : Peter Brock

AUSTRALIA

MURDOCH UNIVERSITY
Australian CRC for Renewable Energy Ltd,
South Street, Murdoch, Perth, WA 6150, Australia
TEL: +61 8 9360 2384
FAX: +61 8 9360 6183
E-MAIL: c.lund@murdoch.edu.au
WEB: http://www.acre.murdoch.edu.au/education
CONTACT: Dr Chris Lund

UNIVERSITY OF MURDOCH
Perth, Western Australia 6150, Australia
TEL: +61 8 9360 2433
FAX: +61 8 9310 1711
E-MAIL: jennings@acre.murdoch.edu.au
WEB: http://www.acre.murdoch.edu.au
CONTACT: Prof Phillip Jennings

UNIVERSITY OF NEW SOUTH WALES
National solar Architecture Research Unit Kensington,
New south wales 2052, Australia
TEL : +61 29385 4868
FAX : +61 293856735
E-MAIL:d.prasad@unsw.edu.au
WEB:http://wwwfbe.unse.edu.edu.au/units/solarch
CONTACT:Prof Deo Prasad

UNIVERSITY OF NEW SOUTH WALES
Centre for Photovoltaic Engineering,
Sydney, NSW 2339, Australia
TEL: +61 2 9385 4018
FAX: +61 2 9662 4240
WEB: http://www.pv.unsw.edu.au

UNIVERSITY OF NEW SOUTH WALES
Electrical Engineering, Sydney 2052, Australia
TEL: +61 2 3855457
FAX: +61 2 6624240
E-MAIL: m.guelden@unsw.edu.au
CONTACT: Hugh Outhred

UNIVERSITY OF SOUTH AUSTRALIA
Sustainable Energy Centre,
The levels Mawson Lakes,
South Australia 5095, Australia
TEL: 6188302 3008
FAX:+61883023380
E-MAIL: wasim.saman@unisa.edu.au
CONTACT :Prof Wasim Saman

UNIVERSITY OF TASMANIA
Centre for Environment studies
GPO Box 252-78 Hobart,
Tasmania 7001, Australia
TEL:+61362262390
FAX: +61362262989
WEB:www.geoi.utas .edu
CONTACT:prof John Todd

CONSULTANTS

ULTRA SYSTEMS TECHNOLOGY PTY LIMITED
PO Box 241,
Indooroopilly,
Queensland 4068, Australia
TEL : +61 7 3876 9222
FAX : +61 7 3876 9333
E-MAIL : juniper@ultrasys.co.au
WEB : http://www.ultrasys.co.au
CONTACT : Peter Cameron

OTHERS

AUSTRALIAN SUN POWER
Unit 4/204,
Balcatta Road, 6021,
Balcatta, West Australia, Australia
TEL : +61 8 924 02 994
FAX : +61 8 924 02 993
E-MAIL : pump@iinet.net.au

INTEGRAL ENVIRONMENTAL ENERGIES
PO Box 6366,
Blacktown 2148,
NSW, Australia
TEL: +61 2 4228 2999
FAX: +61 2 4228 2890
E-MAIL: grimmett@sre.aust.com
CONTACT: Robert Grimmett

MIDSUMMER SPARKS ELECTRICS
Huonbrook Road Lot 7,
Mullumbimby,
New South Wales 2482, Australia
TEL: +612 6684 0051
FAX: +612 6684 0051
E-MAIL: midsum@dingoblue.net.au
WEB: http://www.llinknet.com.au/midsum
CONTACT: Franz Zellner

SUNDIALS AUSTRALIA
3 Bedford Street,
Kensington Park,
South Australia 5019, Australia
TEL: +61 8 8285 4099
FAX: +61 8 8285 4099
CONTACT:Mr John Ward

SUPPLIERS

BATTERIES & INVERTERS

BATTERY ENERGY
Commercial, PO Box 202, Manly NSW 2095, Australia
TEL : +61 407 22 44 56
FAX : +61 2 9632 4622
E-MAIL :horizonsr@aol.com

NORCOAST REFRIGERATION COMPANY
50 Grigor Street, Caloundra,
Queensland, 4551, Australia
TEL: +61 7 5491 1849
FAX: +61 7 5491 7627
E-MAIL: norcoast@norcoast.com.au
WEB: http://www.norcoast.com.au
CONTACT: Margaret Albiez

PLASMATRONICS PTY LTD
42 Bell Streetm, Fitzroy,
Victoria 3065 Australia
TEL: +61 3 9486 9902
FAX: +61 3 9486 9903
E-MAIL : pladmin@vicnet.net.au
WEB:http://www.plasmotronics.taz.net.au
CONTACT: Mr Brendan English

INSTRUMENTATION

ADVANCED ENERGY SYSTEMS
Unit 1 11 Brodie Hall Drive,
Technology Park, Bentley,
Western Australia 6102, Australia
TEL: +61 8 9 470 4644
FAX: +61 8 9 470 4504
E-MAIL: info@aesltd.com.au
WEB: http://www.aesltd.com.au
CONTACT: Stephen Phillips

CHOICE ELECTRIC CO (AUST) PTY LTD
U2/2 Sneyd Street, Bowen Hills,
Queensland, 4006, Australia
TEL: +61 7 3252 4909
FAX: +61 7 3854 1038
E-MAIL:choice@choiceelectri.com.au
WEB: http://www.choiceelectric.com.au
CONTACT: John S Cooper

BRIGHT STAR ENVIRONMENTAL
PO Box 535, 848 Boundary Road,
Richlands Queensland 4077, Australia
TEL: +61 7 3275 5634
FAX: +61 7 3217 0733
E-MAIL: bill.lazarus@brightenv.com
WEB: http:/www.brightstarenvironmental.com
CONTACT: Mr Chris Stapleton

ENVIRONDATA AUSTRALIA PTY LTD
44 Percy Street,
Warwick,
Queensland 4370,
Australia,
TEL : +61 76 61 4699
FAX: +61 76 61 2485
CONTACT : Peter Rodeck

POWERCORP PTY LIMITED
3406 Export Drive,
Trade Development Zone,
Northern Territory 0822,
Australia
TEL: +61 8 8947 0933
FAX: +61 8 8947 0925
E-MAIL: mail@pcorp.com.au
CONTACT: Alan Langworthy

SOLARCH
National Solar Architecture Research Unit, University of New South Wales,
Sydney 2052, Australia
TEL: +61293854868
FAX: +61293856735
E-MAIL: d.prasad@unsw.edu.au
WEB. http://www.fbe.unse.edu.au/units/solarch
CONTACT: Prof Deo Prasad

SOLAR ENERGY AUSTRALIA
1/15 Nicole Close, Bolyswater,
Victoria 3153, Australia
TEL:+61 3 9761 5877
FAX:+61 3 9761 7789
E-MAIL:sales@solaraustralia.com.au
WEB:http://www.solaraustralia.com.au
CONTACT:Lindsay Hart

SUNWIND ENERGY SYSTEMS
5 Little Underwood St, Forbes,
NSW
2871, Australia
TEL: +61268516642
FAX: +61268512977
E-MAIL: sunwind@westserv.net.au
CONTACT: Darren Pascoe

INSULATION

DEMAND SOLAR AND DEMAND INSULATION
1 Maclaurin Parade,
Roseville New
South Wales, 2069, Australia
TEL : + 61 2 415 1077
FAX : + 61 2 415 2062
CONTACT : Doug Mill

OTHERS (S)

MONO PUMPS (AUSTRALIA) PTY LTD
338-348 Lower Dandenong Road,
Mordialloc, Victoria 3195, Australia
TEL: +61 3 9580 5211
FAX: +61 3 9580 6659
E-MAIL: rural@mono-pumps.com
WEB: http://www.mono-pumps.com
CONTACT: Douglas Darville

NOVERA ENERGY LIMITED
PO Box 468, Spit Junction,
NSW 2088, Australia
TEL: +61 2 8969 3400
FAX: +61 2 9969 0128
E-MAIL: mail@noveraenergy.com
WEB: http://www.noveraenergy.com
CONTACT: Mr Perry Toms

ORIGIN ENERGY
Generation, 29 Fernwood Way,
Upper Sturt, South Australia,
Australia
TEL: +61 8 821 75800
FAX: +61 8 821 75855
WEB: http://www.originenergy.com.au
CONTACT: David Ellery

SOLAR THERMAL

NORTHLAND SOLAR LTD
Solar, PO Box 86, Kaeo,
North Land 0471 New Zealand
TEL: +64 9 4051 312
FAX: +64 9 4051 313
E-MAIL: team@hitemp.co.nz
CONTACT: Blue Dorward

SOLA 60 NZ
PO Box 2310, 45 Waihi Road,
Tauranga, New Zealand
TEL:+64 7 578 2754
FAX:+64 7 578 2744
E-MAIL:info@sola60.co.nz
WEB:http://www.sola60.co.nz
CONTACT:Lindsay Richards

SUNPOWER LIMITED
433 Ardmore Quarry Road, Avondale,
Auckland 7, New Zealand
TEL: +6492961158
FAX: +6492961126
E-MAIL: steve@sunpower.co.nz
WEB: http://www.sunpower.co.nz
CONTACT: Steve Bayliss

SUNPOWER POOL HEATERS LIMITED
62 New Windsor Road,
Avondale, Auckland 7, New Zealand
TEL: +64 9 828 7569
FAX: +64 9 827 569
E-MAIL:sunpower@titan.co.nz
WEB:http://www.spectel.co.nz
CONTACT:Bob Gordon

SYNERGEX SYSTEMS NEW ZEALAND LIMITED
Box 35588, Browns Bay,
Auckland 310, New Zealand
TEL: +649 415 7652
FAX: +649 415 7651
CONTACT: Nick Schofield

THERMOCELL LTD
PO Box 12205, Christchurch,
New Zealand
TEL: +6439825000
FAX: +6439825001
E-MAIL: martin@thermocell.co.nz
WEB: http://www.thermocell.co.nz
CONTACT: Martin Fry

SOLAR PHOTOVOLTAIC

GNB TECHNOLOGIES
Industrial, Hutt Park Road,
Gracefield, Wellington, New Zealand
TEL : + 64 4 568 4269
FAX : + 64 4 568 6687
E-MAIL : rbolton.gnbnz@xtra.co.nz
WEB: http://www.gnb.com

INDEPENDENT POWER (NZ) LIMITED
Box 35243, Browns Bay,
Auckland, New Zealand
TEL: +64 9 415 6686
FAX: +64 9 415 6685
E-MAIL: sales@indepower.co.nz
CONTACT: Bruce Page

PCM SOLECTRIC CO LTD
16 Lorne Street, Dunedin NZ,
New Zealand
TEL: +64 3 4550 308
FAX: +64 3 4550 309
E-MAIL: paul@pcmsolectric.co.nz
WEB: http://www.pcmsolectric.co.nz
CONTACT: Paul Mierzejewski

RD ELECTRONICS
11 Selwyn Road,
Rotorua 3201,
New Zealand
TEL : +64 7 3456043
FAX : +64 7 3456043
E-MAIL : rdelectronics@xtra.co.nz
CONTACT : Rob Duthie

SOLAR ELECTRIC SPECIALISTS LTD
Sales, PO Box 6302,
Christchurch,
New Zealand
TEL: +64 25 576527
E-MAIL: john@gosolar.co.nz
WEB: http://www.gosolar.co.nz
CONTACT: John Veix

WIND

FERGUSON MANUFACTURING
835 Old North Road, RD2
Waimauku 1250,
New Zealand
TEL: +64 9 4128655
FAX: + 64 9 4128897
E-MAIL: ferman@windmills.co.nz
WEB: http://www.windmills.co.nz
CONTACT: Ross Ferguson

VORTEC ENERGY LTD
PO Box 90-368, Auckland Mail
Centre, New Zealand
TEL: +64 9 3062710
FAX: +64 9 3062711
E-MAIL: vortec@vortecenergy.com
WEB: http://www.vortecenergy.com
CONTACT: Phillip Wight

WIND TORQUE LTD
12 Scotston Avenue, Papanni
Christchurch 5,
New Zealand
TEL: +64 3 352 2104
FAX: +64 3 352 2104
E-MAIL: geoffh@wtl.co.nz
CONTACT: Geoff Henderson

SMALL HYDRO

POWERFLOW LTD
4/8 Lipman Street, Mt Victoria,
Wellington, New Zealand
TEL: +64 4 384 1988
FAX: +64 4 384 1977
E-MAIL: service@powerflow.co.nz
WEB: http://www.powerflow.co.nz
CONTACT: M Woods

GEOTHERMAL

CENTURY RESOURCES
New Zealand Division, PO Box 341,
Taupo, New Zealand
TEL : +64 7 3748899
FAX : +64 7 3748508
E-MAIL : cdes@centurydrilling.co.nz
WEB : http://
www.centurydrilling.co.nz
CONTACT: Mr. Kevin J Koorey

GOVERNMENT

ENERGY EFFICIENCY AND CONSERVATION AUTHORITY EECA
PO Box 388, Wellington, New Zealand
TEL: +64 4 470 2200
FAX: +64 4 499 5330
WEB: http://www.energywise.co.nz
CONTACT: Fiona Weightman

RESEARCH & DEVELOPMENT

CRL ENERGY LTD
68 Gracefield Road, PO Box 31244
Lower Hutt, New Zealand
TEL : +64 4 570 3700
FAX : +64 4 570 3701
E-MAIL : jkessels@crl.co.nz
WEB : http://www.crl.co.nz

INDUSTRIAL RESEARCH LIMITED
Electotec Group, 5 Sheffield
Crescent, Bishopdale,PO Box 20-028
Christchurch, New Zealand
TEL: +64 3 3589 189
FAX: +64 3 6589 506
E-MAIL: a.gardner@irl.cri.nz
WEB: http://www.irl.cri.nz
CONTACT: Alister Gardiner

NGO's

GREENPEACE NZ INC
113 ValleyRoad, Mount Eden,
Auckland, New Zealand
TEL : + 64 9 630 6317
FAX : + 64 9 630 7121
E-MAIL : greenpeace.new.zerland
@dialb.greenpeace.org
CONTACT: Adam Laildlaw

CONSULTANTS

CRL ENERGY LTD
68 Gracefield Road,
PO Box 31-244,
Lower Hutt, New Zealand
TEL: +64 4 570 3700
FAX: +64 4 570 3701
E-MAIL: j.kessels@crl.co.nz
WEB: http://www.crl.co.nz
CONTACT: John Kessels

EMPOWER CONSULTANTS LTD
Renewable Energy, PO Box 28145
Kelburn, Wellington, New Zealand
TEL: +64 4 47 12525
FAX: +64 4 47 12526
E-MAIL: info@mpwr.co.nz
WEB: http://www.mpwr.co.nz
CONTACT: Ann McLean

SUPPLIERS

BATTERIES/INVERTERS

EBBEITT AUTOMATION LTD
70 72 Victoria Street, Petone
Wellington, Newzealand
TEL : + 64 4 568 6377
FAX : + 64 4 568 2374
E-MAIL : ebbett.automation@clear.net.nz
CONTACT: Graeme A Ebbet

GNB TECHNOLOGIES
Industrial, Hutt Park Road,
Gracefield,
Wellington,
New Zealand
TEL : + 64 4 568 4269
FAX : + 64 4 568 6687
E-MAIL : rbolton.gnbnz@xtra.co.nz
WEB: http://www.gnb.com

We kindly request more listings in this country.

You can submit any additional listings by E-mail: unisun@vsnl.com

Fax: 91 80 22289294

We will include these in the next edition

Kindly inform us of any errors and omissions in the listings by:

E-mail: unisun@vsnl.com

Fax: 91 80 22289294

SOLAR THERMAL

BRIAN BELL & COMPANY PTY LTD
PO Box 1228, Boroka,
Papua New Guinea
TEL : +675 3255411
FAX : +657 3250167

OTHERS

APPROPRIATE TECHNOLOGY DEVELOPMENT INSTITUTE
University Of Technology, Private Mail Bag Lae, Morobe Province,
Papua New Guinea
TEL: +675 4734778
FAX: +675 4734303
CONTACT: GD Gayife

We kindly request more listings in this country.

You can submit any additional listings by E-mail: unisun@vsnl.com

Fax: 91 80 22289294

We will include these in the next edition

Kindly inform us of any errors and omissions in the listings by:

E-mail: unisun@vsnl.com

Fax: 91 80 22289294

GOVERNMENT

SOUTH PACIFIC APPLIED GEOSCIENCE COMMISSION-SOPAC
Energy Unit, Private Mail Bag,
Suva, Fiji
TEL: +679 381377
FAX: +679 370040
E-MAIL: Solomone@sopac.org.fj
CONTACT: Unit Co-ordinator

We kindly request more listings in this country.

You can submit any additional listings by E-mail: unisun@vsnl.com

Fax: 91 80 22289294

We will include these in the next edition

Kindly inform us of any errors and omissions in the listings by:

E-mail: unisun@vsnl.com

Fax: 91 80 22289294

NOTES

EUROPE

SOLAR THERMAL

AST EIS UND SOLAR TECHNIK GMBH & CO KG
Untermarkt 33, A-6600 Reutte, Austria
TEL : +43 5672 607 18
FAX : +43 5672 607 199
E-MAIL :ast@aon.at
WEB : http://www.ast.at
CONTACT : Lechner

AUSTRIA SOLAR INNOVATION CENTER (ASIC)
Durisolastr.7. 4600 Wels, Austria
TEL : + 43 (0) 7242 9396
FAX : + 43 (0) 7242 9396
E-MAIL : leeb.kurt@asic.at
CONTACT : Gerti Sperrer

ECOTHERM GMBH
Heat Transfer Technology
Karlingstrasse B, A-4081, Hartkirtchen, Austria
TEL : +43 7273 6030
FAX : +43 7273 6336
E-MAIL : office@ecotherm.at
WEB : www.ecotherm.at
CONTACT : Herbert B

MEA MASCHINEN UND ENERGIEANLAGEN GESMBH
Enerwitzdorfer StraBe 40, 4210 Gallneukirchen, Austria
TEL: +43 7235 63020
FAX: +43 7235 6302010
E-MAIL: office@mea-solar.at
CONTACT: Franz Plank

SOLKAV SOLARTECHNIK GESMBH
Industriegebiet Nord, 3150 Wilhelmsburg, Austria
TEL: +43 2746 24 300
FAX: +43 2746 24 3043
CONTACT: Parviz Hakim-Elahi

SOLAR PHOTOVOLTAIC

ISOVOLTA AKTIENGESELLSCHAFT
A-8402 Werndorf/Graz, Austria
TEL: +43 3135 54314
FAX: +43 3135 54200
CONTACT : Dr. Albert Plessing

SOLAREX AUSTRIA INC
Business Park Vienna, Wienerbergstrabe II B, Top 4209 A 1810 Vienna, Austria
TEL:+43 1 600 00161
FAX:+43 1 600 00163
E-MAIL:gstangl@solarex.com
WEB:http://www.solarex.com
CONTACT: Gunter Stangl

WIND

C/O ZENTRALANSTALT FUR METEOROLOGIE UND GEODYNAMIK
Climatology, Hohe Warte 38, 1190 Wien, Austria
TEL : +43 1 36026
FAX : +43 1 3691233
E-MAIL : dion@zamg.ac.at
WEB : http://www.zamg.ac.at

PEHR INTERTECH GMBH
Hart 101, 9586 Furtinz,
TEL : +43 4257 3950
FAX : +43 4257 3954
CONTACT : Manfred Pehr

WINDTEC ANLAGENERRICHTUNGS-UND CONSULTING GMBH
Alfred Nobel Strabe 1, 9100 Volkermarkt, Austria
TEL : +43 4232 4460-400
FAX : +43 4232 4460-444
E-MAIL : gerald.hehenberger@mail.windtec.com
WEB : http://www.tlk.co.at/windtec
CONTACT : DI Gerald Hehenberger

BIOMASS

AUSTRIAN BIOFUELS INSTITUTE
Graben, 14/2, PO Box 97, A-1014, Vienna, Austria
TEL : +43 1 53456
FAX : +43 1 53456
E-MAIL : werner-koerbitz@biodiesel.at
WEB : http://www.biodiesel.at
CONTACT : Werner K

BDI ANALANGENBAU GMBH
Bio Diesel International, Eduard-Ast-StraBe 1, 8073 Feldkirchen/Graz, Austria
TEL : +43 316 2402 379
FAX : +43 316 2402 375
E-MAIL : bdi@biodiesel-intl.com
CONTACT : Wilhelm H

ENERGEA UNWELTTECHNOLOGIE GMBH
Wiplinger Str 31, 1010 Wien, Austria
TEL : +43 1 535 31 50
FAX : +43 1 535 31 50 - 10
E-MAIL : mail@energea.at
WEB : http://www.energea.at
CONTACT : Ergun

ENTEC-ENVIRONMENT TECHNOLOGY UMWELTTECHNI GMBH
Schilfweg 1, A-6972 Fussach, Austria
TEL : + 43 5578 7946
FAX: + 43 5578 73638
E-MAIL : enterc@biogas.at
WEB: http:/www.biogas.at
CONTACT : Simon Schulz

INGRA-AUSTRIA
Biomass Engineering,
Perkonigweg 7,
9210 Portschach, Austria
TEL: +43 4272 36800
FAX: +43 4272 36802
E-MAIL: ingra@carinthia.com
WEB: http://www.biomass-engineering.com
CONTACT: Herbert L Graf

KALKGRUBER-PRULLER
Hintstein 69, 4463 Grossbraming, Austria
TEL: +43 7259 5002
FAX: +43 7259 5002
E-MAIL:solarfocus@ris.at
WEB:http://www.ris.at/homes/solar
CONTACT : Kalkgruber

MAWERA HOLZFEUERUNGEN GESMBH & CO KG
NeulandstraBe 30, 6971 Hard, Austria
TEL: +43 5574 743 01
FAX: +43 5574 7430120
CONTACT: Calus Steurer

POLYTECHNIK GMH & CO KG
A-2564 Weissenbach
TEL: +43 2672 890-0
FAX:+43 2672 890-13

WINDHAGER ZENTRALHEIZUNG AG
Anton-Windhager-Str 20, 5201 Seekirchenam Wallersee,
TEL: +43 62 12 23410
FAX: +43 62 124228
E-MAIL: info@windhager-ag.at
WEB: http://www.windhager-ag.at
CONTACT: August Lackner

COGENERATION

CERTUSS GESMBH
Franz-Lechner-StraBe, 6, 3012 Wolfsgraben, Austria
TEL : + 43 22 33 71 48

ENERGIE AG OBERTOSTRREICH
BohmerwaldstraBe 3, 4021 Linz, Austria
TEL : +43 732 6593 3514
FAX : +43 732 6593 3600
CONTACT : Michael S

JENBACHER AG
Energie, A-6200 Jenbach, Austria
TEL: +43 5244 60000
FAX: +43 5244 63255
E-MAIL:contact@jenbacher.com
WEB:http://www.jenbacher.com
CONTACT : Andreas Span

AUSTRIA

OMV COGENERATION GMBH
Gerasdorfer Strasse 1551,
1210 Vienna,
Austria
TEL: +43 1 404 40 30 71
FAX: +43 1 404 40 99 74
E-MAIL: cogeneration@omv.com
WEB: http://www.omv.com
CONTACT: Egon Kubiczek

ELECTRIC VEHICLES

ENERGIE AG OBERTOSTRREICH
BohmerwaldstraBe 3, 4021 Linz,
Austria
TEL : +43 732 6593 3514
FAX : +43 732 6593 3600
CONTACT : Michael S

SMALL HYDRO

GUGLER HYDRO ENERGY GMBH
4085 Niederranna 41,
Austria
TEL: +43 7285 514
FAX: +43 7285 514 20
E-MAIL: info@gugler.com
WEB: http://www.gugler.com
CONTACT: Gerhard Gugler

GUGLER GMBH & CO KG
4085 Niederranna 41,
Austria
TEL : + 43 7285 514
FAX : + 43 7285 514
E-MAIL : gugler@resi.at
CONTACT : Gerhard G

KOSSLER GMBH
Sales Dept, A-3151 St Polten/St Georgen,
Austria
TEL: +43 2742 885272
FAX: +4 2746 2626
E-MAIL: office@koessler.com
WEB: http://www.koessler.com/koessler
CONTACT : Herbert S

WASTE TO ENERGY

ELIN AB ELECTRO TECHNIK GMBH
PenzingerstraBe 76, 1141 Wien,
Austria
TEL : +43 1 89100
FAX : +43 1 89 42 004
CONTACT : Albert W

INTEMANN GMBH
Dammstr 4, 6923 Lautenach,
Austria
TEL: +43 5574 43277
FAX: +43 5574 48058
CONTACT: Dieter Intemann

KANZLER VERFAHRENSTHNIK GMBH-KVT
StiftingtalstraBe 165c,
8010 Graz, Austria
TEL : +43 316 321 404-0
FAX : +43 316 321 404-22
E-MAIL : kvt@sime.com
CONTACT : W Kanzler

ENERGY EFFICIENCY

ELIN AB ELECTRO TECHNIK GMBH
PenzingerstraBe 76, 1141 Wien,
Austria
TEL : +43 1 89100
FAX : +43 1 89 42 004
CONTACT : Albert W

ASSOCIATION

AUSTRIAN ASSOCIATION FOR AGRICULTURAL RESEARCH OEVAF
Kleine Sperlgasse 1/37, A-1020,
Vienna, Austria
TEL : +43 1 214 5903
FAX : +43 1 214 5903
E-MAIL : oevaf-coien@oevaf.at
CONTACT : Otto S

AUSTRIAN BIOMASS ASSOCIATION ABA
Hamerlingg 3, A-8010 Graz Styria,
Austria
TEL : +43 316 8050 1241
CONTACT : Dr Heinz K

BIOENERGY AUSTRIA
Postfach 208, 1013, Vienna,
Austria
TEL : +43 1 470 12 25
FAX : +43 1 470 12 25
E-MAIL : info@iec.at
WEB : http://www.bioenergy.at

GOVERNMENT

LANDESENERGIEVEREIN
Burggasse 9-11, 8010 Garz,
Austria
TEL : +43 316 877 3389
FAX : +43 316 877 3389
CONTACT : Gerhard Ulz.

RESEARCH & DEVELOPMENT

ARSENAL RESEARCH
Renewable Energy, Faradaygasse 3,
1030 Wien, Austria
TEL: +43 1 79747 299
FAX: +43 1 79747 390
E-MAIL: fechner.h@arsenal.ac.at
WEB: http://www.arsenal.ac.at
CONTACT: Hubert Fechner

ENERGIEWERKSTATT GMBH
Heiligenstatt 24, 5211 Friedburg, Austria
TEL: +43 7746 3771
FAX: +43 7746 3771-14
E-MAIL: office@energiewerkstatt.at
WEB: http://www.energiewerkstatt.at
CONTACT: Johann Winkelmeier

IHS KAERNTEN
Institute for Advanced Studies
Domgasses 5, 9010 Klagenfurt,Austria
TEL: +43 463 592150
FAX: +43 463 592150
E-MAIL: info@carinthia.ac.at
WEB: http://www.carinthia.ac.at
CONTACT: Dr Reinhard Madlener

IFZ-INTER UNIVERSITY RESEARCH CENTRE
Schloegelgasse 2, A-8010 Graz,
Austria
TEL: +43 316 813909
FAX: +43 316 810274

JOANNEUM RESEARCH
Institute of Energy Research,
Elisabethstrasse 5, A-8010 Graz,
Austria
TEL: +43 316 876 1338
FAX: +43 316 876 1320
E-MAIL"josef.spitzer@joanneum.ac.at
WEB:http://www.joanneum.ac.at
CONTACT : Josef Spitzer

NGO's

ENERGIEVERWERTUNGSAGENTUR EVA
Linke Wienzeile 18, 1060 Wien,
Austria
TEL: +43 1 586 15 24
FAX: +43 1 586 94 88
E-MAIL: rakos@eva.wsr.ac.at
WEB: www.eva.wsr.ac.at
CONTACT : Christian R

CONSULTANTS

MANAHL SUTTER & PARTNER CONSULTING GMBH-MS&P
PO Box 63, A-6901 Bregenz,
Austria
TEL: +43 5574 73931
FAX: +43 5574 73931
E-MAIL: g.sutter@rsb-roundtech.com
CONTACT: Gerhard Sutter

VERBUNDPLAN GMBH
Am Hof 6A, 1010 Wien, Austria
TEL: +43 1 53605-0
FAX: +43 1 53605 54748
E-MAIL: vpl@verbundplan.at
WEB: http://www.verbundplan.com
CONTACT: Dr Thomas Ubeleis

DESIGN & ENGINEERING

VOGELBUSCH GMBH
Blechturmgasse 11, A-1050 Vienna, Austria
TEL: +43 1 54 661-0
FAX: +43 1 545 29 79
E-MAIL: office@vienna.vogelbusch.com
WEB: http://www.vogelbusch.com
CONTACT: Katharina Harlander

WIND

WINDHAGER ZENTRALHEIZUNG AG
Anton-Windhager-Str 20, 5201 Seekirchen am Wallersee, Austria
TEL: +43621223410
FAX: +4362124228
E-MAIL: info@windhager-ag.at
WEB: http://www.windhager-ag.at
CONTACT: August Lackner

OTHERS

AUSTRIAN ENERGY & ENVIRONMENT SPG/WAAGNER-BIRO GMBH
Siemensstrasse 89, A-1211, Wien, Austria
TEL : +43 1 250 4575
FAX : +43 1 258 4139
E-MAIL :contact@aee.vatech.co.at
WEB : http://www.aee.vatech.co.at
CONTACT : Werner D

MANNESMANN ANLAGENBAU AUSTRIA AG
Oberlaaer Str 331, 1230 Wien, Austria
TEL: +43 1 610 36 0
FAX: +43 1 610 36 287

ISOVOLTA OSTERREISCHISCHE ISOLIERSTOFFWERKE AG
Electrical Instulation Departement. A-2335 Wiener Neudorf, Austria
TEL: +43 2236 605-479
FAX: +43 2236 605-477
E-MAIL: icosolar@isovolta.com
CONTACT : Sandra G

LATERAL TECHNOLOGY
PO Box 674, Moe, Victoria 3825, Australia
TEL: +61 351 681 224
FAX: +61 315 743 301
CONTACT: Geoff Collins

SUPPLIERS

BATTERIES & INVERTERS

FRONIUS INTERNATIONAL GMBH
Solar Electronics,
Gunter Fronius-Strasse 1,
A-4600 Wels-Thalheim, Austria
TEL: +43 7242 241-254
FAX: +43 7242 241-224
E-MAIL: pv@fronius.com
WEB: http://www.fronius.com
CONTACT: Martina Dickinger

OEKOSTROM AG
Mariahilferstrasse 89/30,
1060 Wien, Austria
TEL: +43 1 961 05 61 -0
FAX: +43 1 961 05 61 –25
E-MAIL: office@oekostrom.at
WEB: http://www.oekostrom.at

VA TECH HYDRO GMBH & CO
LH-ST, Lunzenstrabe 78, 4031 Linz Austria
TEL: +437326987-3451
FAX: +437326980-2554
WEB: http://www.vatech-hydro.com
CONTACT: Kurt Wolfartsberger

INSULATIONS

HAARDT & CO GESMBH
Staudgasse 55, A-1180 Vienna,Austria
TEL : + 43 1 4084538
FAX : + 43 1 4083466
CONTACT : William K

KE KELIT KUNSTSTOFFWERK GESMBH
Ignaz-Mayer-StraBe 17, 4017 Linz, Austria
TEL : +43 732 779206-0
FAX : +43 732 779206-18
E-MAIL : ke-kelit@magnet.at
CONTACT : Wolfgang P

PIPELIFE FLEXALEN TRADING GMBH & CO KG
Kaiserstrasse 45,
A-1070 Vienna, Austria
TEL: + 43 1 523 26 25
FAX : +43 1 523 26 25
E-MAIL : office@flexalen.com
CONTACT : Katharina Pachta

TANKS

ECOTHERM GMBH
Heat Transfer Technology
Karlingstrasse B, A-4081, Hartkirtchen, Austria
TEL : +43 7273 6030
FAX : +43 7273 6336
E-MAIL : office@ecotherm.at
WEB : www.ecotherm.at
CONTACT : Herbert B

OTHERS (S)

ENERGEA ENVIRONMENT TECHNOLOGY GMBH
Freudenauer Hafenstrasse 8-10, 1020 Vienna, Austria
TEL: +43 1 729 94 01
FAX: +43 1 729 94 01 560
E-MAIL: mail@energea.at
WEB: http://www.energea.at
CONTACT: Mr Ergun

FLEXALEN TRADING GMBH & CO KG
Kaiserstrasse 45, A-1070 Vienna, Austria
TEL: +43 1 523 26 25-0
FAX: +43 1 523 26 25-24
E-MAIL: office@flexalen.com
WEB: http://www.flexalen.com
CONTACT: Oscar Schmidt

FROLING- HEIZKESSEL-UND BEHALTERBAU GESMBH
Industriestrabe 12, 4710 Grieskirchen Austria
TEL: +43 7248 606
FAX: +43 7248 62387
CONTACT: Mr Monitzer

POLYMARIN BPORRUMWELTTECHNIK GMBH
Kelsenstrasse 7/1 Stock, 1030 Wien
TEL: +43 50626 2012
FAX:+43 50626 2033
E-MAIL : put@porr.at
CONTACT: Georg Pammer

VA TECH ELIN EBG MOTOREN GMBH
Penzinger Strasse 76, A-1141 Wien, Austria
TEL: +43 1 89990-2227
FAX: +43 1 8946280
WEB: http://www.elinebgmotoren.at

BELGIUM

SOLAR THERMAL

BALTIMORE AIRCOIL INTERNATIONAL NV
Industriepark-zone A,
2220 Heist-opden-Bergen, Belgium
TEL : +32 15 257 700
FAX : +32 15 244 779
E-MAIL : infoh@baltaircoil.be
WEB : http://www.baltaircoil.be
CONTACT : Andreas Coumnass

CLAYTON OF BELGIUM NV
Rijksweg 30, 2880 Bornem, Belgium
TEL: +32 3 890 5700
FAX: +32 3 890 5701
CONTACT: Fvan Riet

DAIKIN EUROPE NV
Zandvoordestraat 300, 8400
Oostende Belgium
TEL : + 32 59 558111
FAX : + 32 59 558899
CONTACT : Mr Rashid

EUROBAT NV
Molenveld 30, 1840 Londerzeel,
Belgium
TEL: +32 52 30 01 14

EUROPEAN SOLAR ENGINEERING - ESE
Parc Industrial 39,
B-5580 Rochefort, Belgium
TEL: +32 84 37 80 65
FAX: +32 84 37 73 39
E-MAIL: ese.solar@skynet.be
CONTACT : G Descy

HONEYWELL EUROPE SA
Avenue de Bourget 3,1140 Brussels
Belgium
TEL: +32 2 728 27 50
FAX: +32 2 728 22 45
E-MAIL:
pascal.stijns@belgium.honeywell.com
WEB: http://www.honeywell.com

SOLAR SHOP
Dambruggestraat 48,2060
Antwerpen,Belgium
TEL:+32 3 2264598
FAX:+32 3 2264598
CONTACT:Jordan Matthews

SOLIO BVBA
Oudenaardseweg 73,
9790 Wortegem-Petegem,
Belgium
TEL: +32 56 68 97 84
FAX: +32 56 68 70 83
CONTACT: Jean-Paul Vantomme

STB DUERINCK CVBA
Oudeheerweg Heide 60,
B-9250 Waasmunster, Belgium
TEL: +32 3 7722882
FAX: +32 3 7722065
E-MAIL:info@duerinck.de
CONTACT:Robert Duerinck

VINCENT COURTEJOIE
Rue de la Station de Woluwe 40,
1200 bruxelles, Belgium
TEL : +32 2 762 96 63
FAX : +32 2 762 96 63
CONTACT : Vincent C

SOLAR PHOTOVOLTAIC

ATV BVBA
Solar Technics, Industrieweg 70,
8800 Roeselare, Belgium
TEL : +32 51 20 20 52
FAX : +32 51 24 73 00
E-MAIL : solar.technics@yucom.be
WEB : http://www.solar-technics.be
CONTACT : L Pierloot

BEAUSAERT PVBA GEBR
Arendstraat, 46, 8000 Brugge,
Belgium
TEL : +32 50 33 70 62
CONTACT : M Beausaert

ENE SA - ENERGIES NOUVELLES & ENVIRONNEMENT
Avenue van der Meerschen 188,
1150 Brussels, Belgium
TEL : + 32 2 271 13 28
FAX : +32 2 271 13 28
CONTACT : G Smekens

IMEC
Kapeldreef 75,
3001 Leuven,
Belgium
TEL: +32 16 28 12 11
CONTACT: Robert Mertens

SOLTECH
Kapeldreef 60,
3001 Heverlee,
Belgium
TEL: +32 16 298 442
FAX: +32 16 298 319
E-MAIL: soltech@soltech.be
WEB: http://www.soltech.be
CONTACT: Stefan Dewallef

TURBOWINDS SA
Brusselssesteenweg 340,
3090 Overijse, Belgium
TEL: +32 2 689 22 92
FAX: +32 2 689 22 00
CONTACT: E Timmermans

WIND

HANSEN TRANSMISSIONS INTERNATIONAL
Leonardo da Vincilaan 1,
2650 Edegem / Antwerpen,
Belgium
Tel :+ 32 3 450 12 11
Fax : + 32 3 450 12 20
E-mail : sales@haentramissions.com
WEB : www.hansentramissions.com
CONTACT : Ivan Brems

HYDRO SOIL SERVICES NV
DEME Group,
Haven 1025, Scheldeijjk 30,
2730 Zwijndrecht,
Belgium
TEL: +32 3 250 53 11
FAX: +32 3 250 56 51
E-MAIL: hss@dredging.com
WEB: http://
www.hydrosoilservices.com
CONTACT: Neil Cash

TURBOWINDS NV
Commercial and R&D Centre, Prins
Bisschopsingel 50,
B-3500 Hasselt,
Belgium
TEL: +32 11 280136
FAX: +32 11 284347
E-MAIL: w.vanmelckebeke@skynet.be
WEB: http://www.turbowinds.com
CONTACT: Mr. Van Melckebeke

BIOMASS

BIOMASS DEVELOPMENT EUROPE
31 Ch de Louvain B-1932
St. Stevens Woluwe,
Belgium
TEL : + 32 711 20 30
FAX : +32 720 20 64
CONTACT : W Buhlmann

ERBE AGENCY
Chaussee de Namur 146,
5050 Gembloux,
Belgium
TEL : + 32 81 61 25 01
FAX: + 32 81 61 58 47
E-mail: vanbelle@cragz.fgov.be
CONTACT : J F Van Belle

MTI
Champ D'al Vau 33,
1380 Lasne-Ohain,
Belgium
TEL: +32 2654 1865
FAX: +32 2654 0477
CONTACT: Dr.E Evangelides

OWS NV
Organic Waste Systems,
Dok Noord 4, 9000 Gent,
Belgium
TEL: +32 9 233 02 04
FAX: +32 9 233 28 25
E-MAIL: mail@ows.be
WEB: http://www.ows.be
CONTACT: Winfried Six

VYNCKE NV
Headquarters, Gentsesteenweg 224,
8530 Harelbeke,
Belgium
TEL: +32 56 730 630
FAX: +32 56 70 41 60
E-MAIL: mail@vyncke.be
CONTACT: Mr Hendrick Duyvejonck

COGENERATION

ELEKTROGROEP DE BECKER
Breker 13, 1730 Asse, Belgium
TEL : +32 2 452 91 32
FAX : +32 2 452 87 08

MAXON INTERNATIONAL NV
Luchthavenlaan 16,
1800 Vilvoorde,
Belgium
TEL: +32 2 255 09 09
FAX: +32 2 251 82 41
E-MAIL: dt@maxon.be
WEB: http://www.maxoncorp.com
CONTACT: DFA Teirlinck

SOLAR TURBINES EUROPE
avenue des Etats-Units 1,6041
Gosselies, Belgium
TEL:+32 71 25 30 18
FAX:+32 71 34 47 39
E-MAIL:agolli_sermet@
solarturbines.com
WEB:http://www.solarturbines.com
CONTACT:Sermet Agolli

TRACTBEL ENERGY ENGINEERING
Avenue Ariane 7,
B-1200 Brussels,
Belgium
TEL: +32 2773 9111
FAX: +32 2773 9900
CONTACT: Jean van Dievort

TRECO SA
Energy Systems, Brusselssesteenweg
340, 3090 Overijse,
Belgium
TEL: +32 2 6892211
FAX: +32 2 6860300
E-MAIL: treco@treco.be
WEB: http://www.treco.be
CONTACT: Robert Brys

HYDROGEN

HYDROGEN SYSTEMS NV
Brugstraat 45/1, B-2300 Turnhout
Belgium
TEL: +32 14 41 61 31
FAX: +32 14 41 21 14
CONTACT Dr H Vandenborre

SMALL HYDRO

ECOWATT NV
Koolmijnlaan 351,
3550 Heusden-Zolder,
Belgium
TEL : +32 11 57 95 00
FAX : +32 11 57 95 01
E-MAIL : info@ecowatt.be
WEB : http://www.ecowatt.be
CONTACT : B Bruno

HANSEN TRANSMISSIONS INTERNATIONAL
Leonardo da Vincilaan 1,
2650 Edegem /
Antwerpen, Belgium
Tel :+ 32 3 450 12 11
Fax : + 32 3 450 12 20
E-mail : sales@haentramissions.com
WEB : www.hansentramissions.com
CONTACT : Ivan Brems

WASTE TO ENERGY

MARKETING AND TECHNOLOGY INTERNATIONAL (MTI)
Champ D'al Vau 33,
1380 Lasne-Ohain, Begium
TEL: +32 2 654 1865
FAX: +32 2 654 0477
E-MAIL: mtiservices@compuserve.com
CONTACT: A Ross McKay

UM ENGINEERING SA
Nesa Product Line, 4 rue du,
Bosquet,
1348 Louvain-la-Neuve,
Belgium
TEL : +32 10 47 56 11
FAX : +32 10 45 04 01
E-MAIL : jeanpierre.mauchien@um.be
WEB : http://www.um.be
CONTACT : Jean-Pierre Mauchien

VITO
Boeretang 200,
B-2400 Mol, Belgium
TEL: +32 14 335800
FAX: +32 14 321185
E-MAIL: kretzscj@vito.be
WEB: http://www.vito.be
CONTACT: Luc Pelkmans

FINANCE / BANKING

EURO-CIS CONSULTING SPRL
rue Froissart 119, Box 9,
1040 Brussels, Belgium
TEL : +32 2 230 21 87
FAX : +32 2 230 4207
CONTACT : Ghislain

HOMES INTERNATIONAL SA
rue Froissart 119, Box 5, 1040
Brussels, Belgium
TEL: +32 2 230 21 87
FAX: +32 2 230 4207
CONTACT: Jean Louis Van de Wouwer

ASSOCIATION

EUROPEAN RENEWABLE ENERGY CENTRES AGENCY EEIG-EUREC AGENCY
26 rue du Trone,
3001 Leuven, Belgium
TEL: +32 2 513 83 10
FAX: +32 2 502 92 84
E-MAIL: derveaux@eurec.be
WEB: http://www.eurec.be
CONTACT : Karel Derveaux

EUROPEAN WIND ENERGY ASSOCIATION
Rue du Trone 26,
B-1040 Brussels, Belgium
TEL: +32 2 546 1940
FAX: +32 2 546 1944
E-MAIL: ewea@ewea.org
WEB: http://www.ewea.org
CONTACT : Vicky Pollard

INTERNATIONAL SOLAR ENERGY SOOCIETY - ISES BELGIUM
66 rue Centry, 1390 Grez-
Doiceau, Belgium
TEL: +32 10 84 09 52
FAX: +32 10 24 19 33
CONTACT: AC Gillet

RESEARCH & DEVELOPMENT

ARCHITECTURE ET CLIMAT
Architecture, Batiment Vinci 1 Place
du Levant, B-1348 Louvain, Belgium
TEL: +32 10 47 2142
FAX: + 32 10 47 2150
E-MAIL: deherde@arch.ucl.ac.be
WEB: http://www-climat.arch.ucl.ac.be
CONTACT: Andre De Herde

IMEC
Kapeldreef 75, 3001 Leuven, Belgium
TEL: +32 16 28 12 11
CONTACT: Robert Mertens

BELGIUM

ISSEP
Rue du Chera 200, 4000 Liege,
Belgium
TEL: +32 4 252 71 50
FAX: +32 4 252 46 65
WEB: http://www.issep.be
CONTACT: Claude Michaux

UNIVERSITE CATHOLIQUE DE LOUVAIN
Groupe Energie Biomasse,
2 Place 'du Levant,
1348 Louvain la Neuve,
Belgium
TEL: +32 10 47 22 32
FAX: +32 10 45 26 92
E-MAIL: sintzoff@term.ucl.ac.be
WEB: http://www.meca.ucl.ac.be/term/geb/overview.html

UNIVERSITE LIBRE DE BRUXELLES (CEESE-ULB)
Centre for Economic and Social Studies on the Envi,
44 Avenue Jeanne,
1050 Brussels, Belgium
TEL: +32 2 650 33 77
FAX: +32 2 650 46 91
E-MAIL: whecq@ulb.ac.be
WEB: http://www.ulb.ac.be/ceese
CONTACT: Walter Hecq

VLAAMSE INSTELLING VOOR TEHNOLOGISCH ONDERZOEK - VITO
Boeretang 200,
B-2400 Mol, Belgium
TEL: +32 14 33 58 00
FAX: +32 14 32 11 85
E-MAIL: jan.kretzschmar@vito.be
WEB: http://www.vito.be
CONTACT: JG Kretzschmar

UNIVERSITIES

FONDATION UNVERSITAIRE LUXEMBOUGEOISE-FUL
Environmental Monitoring,
185 Avenue de Longwy,
6700 Arlon, Belgium
TEL : +32 63 23 08 58
FAX : +32 63 23 08 00
E-MAIL : andre@ful.ac.be
WEB : www.ful.ac.be
CONTACT : A Philippe

INSTITUT WALLON ASBL
Boulevard Frere Orban 4,
5000 Namur, Belgium
TEL: +32 81 25 04 80
FAX: +32 81 25 04 90
E-MAIL: iwallon@iwallon.be
WEB: http://www.iwallon.be
CONTACT: Didier Goetghebuer

NGO's

VITO-CADDET
Boeretang 200, B-2400 Mol, Belgium
TEL: +32 14 33 5911
FAX: +32 14 32 1185
WEB: http://www.vito.be
CONTACT: Gilbertvan Bogaert

CONSULTANTS

3E
Verenigingsstraat 39, 1000 Brussels,
Belgium
TEL: +32 2 2175868
FAX: +32 2 2197989
WEB: http://www.3e.be
CONTACT: Mr Geert Palmers

BEL CONSULTING NV
Oude Stationsstraat 114,
8700 Tielt,
Belgium
TEL : +32 51 403 671
FAX : +32 51 404 335
E-MAIL : info@belconsulting.be
CONTACT : F Wauters

CENERGIE CVBA
Centre for Energy Efficiency,
Gitschotellie 138 B-2600 Berchem
Antwerpen, Belgium
TEL : +32 3 271 19 39
FAX : +32 3 271 13 59
E-MAIL : info@cenergie.be
WEB : http://www.cenergie.be
CONTACT : C D Temmerman

COTA-EXCHANGE GROUP FOR APPROPRIATE TECHNOLOGY
Rue de la Revolution 7,
1000 Brussels, Belgium
TEL : +32 2 218 1896
FAX : + 32 2 223 1495
E-MAIL : cota@village.aunet.be
CONTACT : G Cloes

CRA-STATION DE GENIE RURAL
Department of Agricutlural Engineering,
Chaussee de Namur 146,
5030 Gembloux, Belgium
TEL : +32 81 612501
FAX : +32 81 615847
E-MAIL : genie_eural@cragx.fgov.be
WEB : http://www.cragx.fgov.be
CONTACT : Y Schenkel

ENV CONSULTING
Steenhuffelstraat 6,
1840 Londerzeel, Belgium
TEL : + 32 52 337397
FAX: + 32 52 371870
E-MAIL : jwillocx@worldonline.be
CONTACT : J Willocx

TRACTEBEL DEVELOPMENT
Rue de Buruxelles 69,
5000 Namur, Belgium
TEL: +32 81 25 01 11
FAX: +32 81 23 15 49
E-MAIL : jacques.schittekat@tractebel.be
CONTACT: Jaques Schittekat

DESIGN & ENGINEERING

E+I SA
35, Boulevard Frere Ortban 4000
Liege, Belgium
TEL : + 32 4 253 51 05
FAX : + 32 4 253 04 08
E-MAIL : eplusi@euronet.be
CONTACT : M Cappa

ECD ENERGY AND ENVIRONMENT
Brussiels Office, Rue Abbe Cuypers 3,
1040 Brusselles,Belgium
TEL : + 32 2 741 2442
FAX : + 32 2 734 7910
E-MAIL : ecdebru@attglobal.net
CONTACT : S Burton

INGENIE SPRL
avenue du Luxembourg 38,
4020 Leige, Belgium
TEL: +32 4 342 97 47
FAX: +32 4 342 97 47
CONTACT: Pierre Dessaubies

PAUWELS INTERNATIONAL NV
Antwerpsesteenweg 167,
2800 Mechelen, Belgium
TEL: +32 15 283 486
FAX: +32 15 283 392
E-MAIL: sliminfo@pauwels.com
WEB: http://www.pauwels.com
CONTACT: Mario de Smit

OTHERS

EH2O
Energien Water Techniek Strokerjstraat 30, B-2110 Wijnegem, Belgium
TEL : +32 3 353 3916
FAX : +32 3 354 3993
CONTACT : E Jansseune

ELECTRABEL SA
Boulevard du Regent, 8, 1000
Brussels, Belgium
TEL : +32 2 501 26 78
FAX : +32 2 501 24 74
CONTACT : P Lemmens

SUPPLIERS

GLASS

GLAVERBEL SA
Chaussee de la Hulpe 166. 1170
Brussels, Belgum
TEL : + 32 2 674 3111
FAX : + 32 2 672 44 62
E-MAIL : headquarters@glaverbel.com
WEB : www.glaverbel.com

INSTRUMENTATION

HONEYWELL EUROPE SA
I Avenue de Bourget, 1140 Brussels
Belgium
TEL: +32 2 728 27 50
FAX: +32 2 728 22 45
E-MAIL: pascal.stijns@
belgium.honeywell.com
WEB: http://www.honeywell.com

OTHERS (S)

BEKAERT NV
Avenue Van der Meerschen 188,
1150 Brussels, Belgium
TEL : +32 2 771 13 28
FAX : +32 2 771 13 28

BEKAERT ECD SOLAR SYSTEMS EUROPE NV
Karreweg 13, 9870 Zulte, Belgium
TEL: +32 9 338 59 25
FAX: +32 9 338 59 11
E-MAIL: infosolar@bekaert.com
WEB: http://www.uni-solar.com
CONTACT: Paul Lippens

ELECTRABEL SA
Business project Development- BPD,
Boulevard du Regent 8, 1000
Brussels, Belgium
TEL: +32 2 501 57 34
FAX: +32 2 501 26 40
E-MAIL: jan.bens@electrabel.com
WEB: http://www.electrabel.com
CONTACT: Jan Bens

ENSIVAL INDUSTRIE SA
Rue Hodister 44, Wegnez,
4860 Pepinster, Belgium
TEL : +32 87 468111
FAX: +32 87 46 81 00
E-MAIL: info@e-mpumps.com
WEB: http://www.ensival-moret.com
CONTACT : P Plateus

SECHERS BETTER TECHNOLOGY GROUP
Hoofd 1, B-2830 Willebroek, Belgium
TEL: +3238807700
FAX: +3238807799
E-MAIL: info@bettertechnology.com
WEB: http://www.bettertechnology.com
CONTACT: Mr. Robert Seghers

We kindly request more listings in this country.

You can submit any additional listings by E-mail: unisun@vsnl.com

Fax: 91 80 22289294

We will include these in the next edition

Kindly inform us of any errors and omissions in the listings by:

E-mail: unisun@vsnl.com

Fax: 91 80 22289294

RESEARCH & DEVELOPMENT

BULGARIAN ACADEMY OF SCIENCES
Central Laboratory of Solar Energy & New energy Sources,
72, Tzargradsko, Chaussee Boulevard, 1784 Sofia,
Bulgaria
TEL : +359 2 778 448
FAX : +359 2 754 016
E-MAIL : solar@phys.bas.bg
CONTACT : A Nedjalkova

ENERGOPROKT PLC
51 James Bouther Boulevard, 1407 Sofia, Bulgaria
TEL: +359 2 666 102
FAX: +359 2 66 89 51
E-MAIL: ntm@enpro.bg
CONTACT : T Manoylova

RESEARCH INSTITUTE FOR MECHANIZATION AND ELECTRIFICATION OF AGRICULTURE - NIMESS
Energetics and Transport, Chausee Bankia 3, Sofia 1331, Bulgaria
TEL : +359 2 925 02 24
FAX : +359 2 24 78 42
E-MAIL : nimess @biscom.net
CONTACT : Valden Georgiev

ENERGY EFFICIENCY

BULGARIAN FOUNDATION FOR ENERGY EFFICIENCY
1B, Strumitza Street, 1000 Sofia, Bulgaria
TEL : +359 2 981 88 08
FAX : +359 2 981 88 08
E-MAIL : eef@techno-link.com
CONTACT : K Krantov

We kindly request more listings in this country.

You can submit any additional listings by E-mail: unisun@vsnl.com

Fax: 91 80 22289294

We will include these in the next edition

Kindly inform us of any errors and omissions in the listings by:

E-mail: unisun@vsnl.com

Fax: 91 80 22289294

SOLAR PHOTOVOLTAIC

KONCAR SOLAR CELLS LTD
Tezacki put bb, HR-21000 Split, Croatia
TEL : +385 21 374 381
FAX : +385 21 374 111
E-MAIL : koncar-solar@st.tel.hr
CONTACT : Ante Botic

SMALL HYDRO

ELVAL DOO
Engineering, Puzici br 5, 51000 Rijeka, Croatia
TEL : +385 51 630243
FAX : +385 51 630243
E-MAIL : zvalencic@yahoo.com
CONTACT : M Valencic

KONCAR GENERATORS
Fallerovo Setaliste 22,
10000 Zagreb, Croatia
TEL: +385 1 318 818
FAX: +385 1 318 818
CONTACT : V Vrzic

ASSOCIATION

CROATIAN SOLAR ENERGY ASSOCIATION
Vokovarska 58, 51000, Rijeka, Hrvatska, Croatia
TEL : +385 51 675 801
FAX : +385 51 675 801
E-MAIL : huse@rijeka.riteh.hr
CONTACT : B Frankovic

RESEARCH & DEVELOPMENT

LABORATOIRE D'ENERGIE SOLAIRE
UFR SSMT , 22 BP 582,
Abidjan 22, Cote d'Ivoire, Croatia
TEL: +225 22 44 04 12
FAX: +225 22 44 04 12
CONTACT : Prof S Toure

CONSULTANTS

FEDOR KRITOVAC
Sachsova 6, 10000 Zagreb, Croatia
TEL: +385 1 6136 444
FAX: + 385 1 533 045
E-MAIL: fkritovac @ zg.igh.hr
WEB: http://www.igh.hr
CONTACT : F Kritovac

DESIGN & ENGINEERING

SUN ARH DOO
V Nazora 43 B, 10000 Zagreb, Croatia
TEL: +385 1 482 15 01
FAX: +385 1 482 15 01
E-MAIL:sunarh@zg.tel.hr
CONTACT: Ljubomir Miscevic

We kindly request more listings in this country.

You can submit any additional listings by E-mail: unisun@vsnl.com

Fax: 91 80 22289294

We will include these in the next edition

Kindly inform us of any errors and omissions in the listings by:

E-mail: unisun@vsnl.com

Fax: 91 80 22289294

SOLAR PHOTOVOLTAIC

SOLAR TEC SRO
1 maje 1000/M3,
CZ-756 64
Roznov pod Radhostem 3,
Czech Republic
TEL:+42 651 60 33 77
FAX:+42 651 60 33 93
E-MAIL:solartec@solartec.cz
WEB:http://www.solartec.cz
CONTACT:Jiri Bartek

TRIMEX TESLA SRO
PO Box 30, CZ-756 64 Roznov pod Radhostem 3,
Czech Republic
TEL: +42 651 60 32 45
FAX: +42 651 60 21 09
WEB: http://www.trimex-tesla.cz
CONTACT: Carmen Danisova

WIND

SKODA STEEL
Sales Department, Tylova 57,
31600 Plzen, Czech Republic
TEL: +42197734163
FAX: +42197734276
E-MAIL: vsima@skoda-steel.com
WEB: http://www.skoda-steel.com
CONTACT: Mrs. Jitka Matuchova

SMALL HYDRO

HYDROCINK SRO
Konevova 31,
130 00 Praha 3,
Czech Republic
TEL: +42 2 697 1280
FAX: +42 2 697 1277
E-MAIL: cink@jerrytex.anet.cz
WEB: http://ms.anet.cz/-cink
CONTACT: Martin Exner

WASTE TO ENERGY

BRIKLIS
Slapy 39, 391 76Slapy u Tabora,
Czech Republic
TEL : +42 361 318 050
FAX : +42 361 318 050
E-MAIL : briklis@iol.cz
WEB : http://www.briklis.cz
CONTACT : M Smejkal

ENERGY EFFICIENCY

EKOWATT-THE RENEWABLE AND ENERGY SAVINGS CENTRE
Bubenska 6, 170 00 Praha 7,
Czech Republic
TEL : +42 2 667 10 247
FAX : +42 2 667 10 248
E-MAIL :ekowatt@ekowatt.cz
WEB : http://www.ekowatt.cz
CONTACT : J Beranovsky

CONSULTANTS

SLUNICKO
U Cihenly 5, 370 06 Ceske Budejovice, Czech Republic
TEL: +42 38 741 2272
E-MAIL: karelmu@hbu.cas.cz
CONTACT: Karel Murtinger

SRC INTERNATIONAL CS
Pocernicka 96, Praha 10, CZ-108 03
Czech Republic
TEL: +42 2 6702 1842
FAX: +42 2 6702 1520
E-MAIL: srci@srci.cz
WEB: http://www.srci.cz
CONTACT:Roman Cizek

UB KNORRE
kpt Bartsoe 331, CZ_530 09
Pardubice, Czech Repablic
TEL : +24 040 43 550
FAX : +42 40 43 550
E-MAIL : moritzenconsult@t-online.de
CONTACT : Jaromir Knorre

OTHERS

KRALOVOPOLSKA RIAAS
Business Development, Okruzni 17,
63800 Brno, Czech Republic
TEL: +42 5 7125805
FAX: +42 5 7125864
E-MAIL: lenka.kenslova@kpria.cz
WEB: http://www.kpria.cz
CONTACT : V Enenkl

POULEK SOLAR CO LTD
Kastanova 1481,
CZ-250 01 Brandys,
Prague East District, Czech Republic
TEL: +42 603 342 719
FAX:+42 202 804 017
E-MAIL : poulek@telecom.cz
WEB:http://www.traxle.cz
CONTACT: Vladislav Poulek

VITKOVICE AS
Commercial Department, Ruska ul 101, 706 02 Ostrava 6,
Czech Republic
TEL: +42 69 292 2586
FAX: +42 69 292 1406
E-MAIL: trade@vitovice.cz
WEB: http://www.vitovice.cz
CONTACT: Stanislav Olsak

EKOSOLARIS AS
Kotojedska 2381,
76701 Kromeriz,
Czech Republic
TEL : +42 634 330 344
FAX : +42 634 330 343
E-MAIL :info@ekosolaris.cz
WEB : http://www.ekosolaris.cz

SUPPLIERS

INSTRUMENTATION

CALMET SRO
Jana Masaryka 28, 120 00 Praha 2
Czech Republic
TEL : +42 2 6911301
FAX : +42 2 6911301
CONTACT : Dr J Pohanka

ELEA SRO
Velvraska 9, 160 00 Praha 6,
Czech Republic
TEL : +42 2 312 07 01
FAX : +42 2 312 07 01

POULEK SOLAR CO LTD
Kastanova 1481,
CZ-250 01 Brandys n L,
Prague East District, Czech Republic
TEL: +42 603 342 719
FAX: +420 202 804 017
E-MAIL: poulek@telecom.cz
WEB: http://www.traxle.cz
CONTACT: Vladislav Poulek

Kindly inform us of any errors and omissions in the listings by:

E-mail: unisun@vsnl.com

Fax: 91 80 22289294

SOLAR THERMAL

AIDT MILJO A/S
Kongens Brovej, Aidt, 8881 Thorso, Denmark
TEL: +45 86 96 67 00
FAX: +45 86 96 6955
WEB: http://www.aidt.dk
CONTACT: Hans Jorgen Christensen

APV PRODUCTS
Platinvej 8,DK-6000 Kolding, Denmark
TEL: +45 70 27 84 44
FAX: +45 70 27 84 45
E-MAIL: apv.kolding@post6.tele.dk
WEB: http://www.invensys.apv.com
CONTACT: Mr Per Hedegaard

ARCON SOLVARME A/S
Jyttevej 18, 9520 Skorping, Denmark
TEL: +45 98 39 14 77
FAX: +45 98 39 20 05
E-MAIL: arcon@arcon.dk
WEB: http://www.arcon.dk
CONTACT: Svend Andersen

BATEC A/S
Danmarksvej 8, 4681 Herfolge, Denmark
TEL : +45 56 27 50 50
FAX : +45 56 27 67 87

BELMAN PRODUCTION A/S
Malevrej 4, 6710, Esbjerg V, Denmark
TEL : +45 75 15 59 99
FAX : +45 75 15 59 59
E-MAIL :belman@euroconnect.dk
WEB : http://www.belman.dk
CONTACT : Rolf Rasmussen

DANSTOKER A/S
Industrial And District Heating Boilers, Industrivej Nord 13, Birk, 7400 Herning, Denmark
TEL: +45 99 28 71 00
FAX: +45 99 28 71 11
E-MAIL: info@danstoker.dk
WEB: http://www.danstoker.dk
CONTACT: Ole Kragh-Moller

FLS MILJO A/S
Company Headquarters, Ramsingsvej 30, DK-2500 Valby, Copenhagen, Denmark
TEL: +45 36 18 11 00
FAX: +45 36 17 45 99
E-MAIL: info@flsmiljo.com
WEB: http://www.flsmiljo.com
CONTACT: Jette Hocholdt Mikkelsen

HELIOTECH APS
Energy Division, Grusbakken 12, 2820 Gentofte, Denmark
TEL: +45 2087 0092
FAX: +45 4542 4393
E-MAIL: ps@heliotech.dk
WEB: http://www.heliotech.dk
CONTACT: Mr Per Stobbe

MARSTAL DISTRICT HEATING COMPANY
Jagtvej 2, 5960 Marstal, Denmark
TEL: +45 4032 2267
FAX: +45 6253 2664
E-MAIL: niels.aage@mail.dk
CONTACT: Mr Niels Aage Jensen

MASKINFABRIKKEN REKA A/S
Vestvej 7, 9600 Ars, Denmark
TEL: +45 98 62 40 11
FAX: +45 98 62 40 71
E-MAIL: reka@reka.com
WEB: http://www.reka.com
CONTACT: C Larsen

METRO THERM A/S
Business Development, Randinsvej 55, DK-3200 Helsinge, Denmark
TEL: +45 4879 6211
FAX: +45 4879 7333
E-MAIL: metrodk@ibm.net
CONTACT: Mr Flemming Andersen

SOLAHART SCANDINAVIA APS
Grynderupvejen 16,9610 Norager Denmark
TEL : +45 98 55 12 20
FAX : +45 98 55 18 20
CONTACT : Mr Jenz Dangore

SOLKRAFT
Hvidager 54, 2620 Albertslund, Denmark
TEL: +45 63 46 15
FAX: +45 63 46 15
CONTACT: Ole Wedel-Jorgensen

UNITERM SOLVARME APS
Vestre Boulevard 9B, 9600 Ars, Denmark
TEL: +4598623123
FAX: +4598623544
E-MAIL: niterm@vip.cybercity.dk
WEB: http://www.uniterm.dk
CONTACT: Poul Ellerbaek

VESTTHERM A / S – VESTFROST
Hoegevej 9, 6705 Esbjerg OE, Denmark
TEL: +4579142222
FAX: +4575144818
CONTACT: Peter Laugesen

SOLAR PHOTOVOLTAIC

CORDT AND SON A/S
Vesterbrogade 127A 4th, 1620 Copenhagen, V, Denmark
TEL : +45 40 55 88 86
FAX : +45 33 25 88 86
E-MAIL :cordt-as@mail.teledenmark.dk
CONTACT : Cordt Olsen

ELEKTRONIK LAVPRIS
Vesterbrogade 221-29, 8000 Arhus C, Denmark
TEL : +45 86 13 06 55
FAX : +45 86 13 06 29
WEB : http://www.elektroniklavpris.dk
CONTACT : Peter Sorensen

GAIA SOLAR A/S
Hammerholmen 9-13 I, DK 2650 Hvidovre Denmark
TEL: + 45 36 77 79 76
FAX: +45 36 77 79 75
E-MAIL : info@gaisolar.dk
CONTACT : Christian Johansson

KKF ENERGI APS
Hovedgaden 20, 2791 Dragoer, Denmark
TEL: +45 32 53 71 11
FAX: +45 32 53 75 11

MARSTAL DISTRICT HEATING COMPANY
Jagtvej 2, 5960 Marstal, Denmark
TEL: +45 4032 2267
FAX: +45 6253 2664
E-MAIL: niels.aage@mail.dk
CONTACT: Mr Niels Aage Jensen

SOLDATA CONSULTING V FRANK BASON PHD
Linabakken 13 8600 Silkeborg Denmark
TEL:+45 86 84 11 96
FAX:+45 86 84 45 97
E-MAIL:soldata@netscape.net
WEB:http://www.soldata.dk
CONTACT:frank Bason

SOLKRAFT
Hvidager 54, 2620 Albertslund, Denmark
TEL: +45 63 46 15
FAX: +45 63 46 15
CONTACT: Ole Wedel-Jorgensen

DENMARK

OI -ELECTRIC A/S
Horretvej 61,DK-8320 Maarslet,
Denmark
TEL: +45 8737 6400
FAX: +45 8629 4844
E-MAIL: oi@oi-electric.dk
WEB: http://www.oi-electric.dk
CONTACT: Ove Ibsen

WIND

A2SEA A/S
Prinsessegade 46,7000 Fredericia,
Denmark
TEL: +45 75 92 82 11
FAX: +45 75 92 63 75
E-MAIL: a2sea@a2sea.com
WEB: http://www.a2sea.com
CONTACT: Mr Kurt Thomsen

AH BOLTE A/S
Gl Skartved 9,6091 Bjert, Denmark
TEL: +45 7557 7000
FAX: +45 7557 2307
E-MAIL: info@ah-bolte.com
WEB: http://www.ah-bolte.com

BONUS ENERGY A/S
Fabriksvej 4, Box 171,
DK-7330 Brande,
Denmark
TEL : +45 909 42 22 22
FAX : +45 97 18 30 86
E-MAIL :bonus@bonus.dk
WEB : http://www.bonus.dk
CONTACT : Hening Kruse

BTM CONSULT APS
IC Christensens Alle 1,
DK-6950
Ringkobing,
Denmark
TEL: +45 97 32 52 99
FAX: +45 97 32 55 93
CONTACT: Birger T Madsen

CALORIUS
Spaangervej 2, 4200 Slagelse
Denmark
TEL : +45 58268060
FAX : +45 58268060
E-MAIL : calorius@tele7.dk
CONTACT : Hans Henrik Ekner

DANVEST ENERGY
Rudolfgaardsvej 1B,
8260 Viby J, Denmark
TEL: +45 86 72 00 33
FAX: +45 86 29 65 64
E-MAIL: sales@danvest.com
WEB: http://www.danvest.com
CONTACT: Mr Soeren Q Vestesen

ENXCO
Corporate Head Quarters, Vejlsovej
51, DK-8600, Silkeborg, Denmark
TEL: +45 8921 2270
FAX: +45 8921 2271
WEB: http://www.enxco.com

INDUTRANS A/S
Thrigesvej 28, 8600 Silkeborg
Denmark
TEL: +45 86 81 22 88
FAX: +45 86 81 53 88
E-MAIL: it@industrans.dk
WEB: http://www.industrans.dk
CONTACT: Hari Hensberg

LM GLASFIBER A/S
Rolles Mollevej´1, DK-6640
Lunderskov, Denmark
TEL: +45 79 84 00 00
FAX: +45 79 84 00 01
E-MAIL: info@lm.dk
WEB: http://www.lm.dk
CONTACT: Steen Broust Nielsen

MITA - TEKNIK A/S
Haandvaerkervej 1, 8840
Rodkaersbro, Denmark
TEL: +45 8665 8600
FAX: +45 8665 9290
E-MAIL: mail@mita-teknik.com
WEB: http://www.mita-teknik.com
CONTACT: Jesper Andersen

MOLLER & GRONBORG AS
Landscape Architecture,
Beder Landevej 2,
8330 Beder,
Denmark
TEL: +45 8693 6266
FAX: +45 8693 7893
E-MAIL: beder@mgarkitekter.dk
WEB: http://www.mgarkitekter.dk
CONTACT: Susan Jessien

NORDEX GMBH
Svindbaek, 7323 Give,
Denmark
TEL: 45 75 73 44 00
FAX: 45 75 73 41 47
E-MAIL: nordex@nordex.dk
WEB: http://www.nordex.dk
CONTACT: Jens Pedersen

NEG MICON A/S
Alsvej 21, DK-8900 Randers,
Denmark
TEL: +45 8710 5000
FAX: +45 8710 5001
E-MAIL: mail@neg-micon.dk
WEB: http://www.neg-micon.com
CONTACT: Henri Schumann

ORBITAL APS
Trykkerivej5, 6900 Skjern,
Denmark
TEL: 45 97 35 24 22
FAX: 45 97 35 32 85
E-MAIL: orbital@orbital.dk
WEB: http://www.orbital.dk
CONTACT: Wolfgang Meyer

PCH ENGINEERING A/S
Ved Kloedebo 9,DK-2970 Horsholm
Denmark
TEL: 45 45 76 87 76
FAX: 45 45 76 87 02
E-MAIL: pch@pch-engineering.dk
WEB: http://www.pch-engineering.dk

RISO NATIONAL LABORATORY
Wind Energy Department,
PO Box 49,4000 Roskilde, Denmark
TEL: +4546775097
FAX: +4546775970
E-MAIL: wasp@risoe.dk
WEB: http://www.wasp.dk
CONTACT: Rikke Anne Nielsen

SOLKRAFT
Hvidager 54, 2620 Albertslund,
Denmark
TEL: +45 63 46 15
FAX: +45 63 46 15
CONTACT: Ole Wedel-Jorgensen

SVENDBORG BRAKES A/S
Jernbanevej 9, 5882 Vejstrup,
Denmark
TEL: +45 63 255 255
FAX: +45 62 28 10-58
E-MAIL: sb@svendborg-brakes.dk
WEB:http://www.svendborg-brakes.dk
CONTACT:Yvonne Sorensen

TRIPOD WIND ENERGY APS
Gladsaxe Mollevej 21,
2860 Soborg,
Denmark
TEL: +45 39 66 66 22
FAX: +49 39 66 66 99
E-MAIL: tripod@tripod.dk
WEB: http://www.tripod.dk
CONTACT: Geert Bruun

VESTAS WIND SYSTEM A/S
Smed Sorensens Vej 5,
DK-6950 Ringkobing, Denmark
TEL: +45 96 75 25 75
FAX: +45 96 75 24 36
E-MAIL: vestas@vestas.dk
WEB: http://www.vestas.dk
CONTACT: Heidi Ebey Kristensen

VESTKRAFT A M B A
Project Department,Vestkraftgrade 1,
6700 Esbjerg, Denmark
TEL: +45 75 124700
FAX: +45 75 125132
E-MAIL: esl@vestkraft.dk
CONTACT: Erik Slot

WINCON WEST WIND (A / S)
A Division of A / S Vestfrost,
Hedemolle Erhvervsvej 4,
8850 Bjerringbro, Denmark
TEL: +4586681700
FAX: +4586681734
E-MAIL: sale@wincon.dk
WEB: http://www.wincon.dk
CONTACT: Erik Nielsen

BIOMASS

A B C HANSEN A/S
PO Box 73,
DK-8900 Randers,
Denmark
TEL: +45 86 42 64 88
FAX: +45 86 41 36 22
E-MAIL: abc@abchansen.dk
WEB: http://www.abchansen.dk
CONTACT: UweJurgensen

BAXI A/S
Smedevej, 6880 Tarm, Denmark
TEL: +45 97 37 15 11
FAX: +45 97 37 24 34
E-MAIL: baxi@baxi.dk
WEB: http://www.baxi.dk
CONTACT: Michael Winther Jorgensen

BRUNATA HOLDING A/S
Vibevej 26, PO Box 978,
DK-2400 Copenhagen,
NV, Denmark
TEL : +45 38 34 40 44
FAX : + 45 38 33 29 57
E-MAIL :sales@brunata.com

BURMEISTER & WAIN SCANDINAVIAN CONTRACTOR A/S
Gydevang 35, 3450, Allerod,
Denmark
TEL : +45 48 14 00 22
FAX : +45 48 14 01 50
CONTACT : Christian Grundtuig

DANSK BIOGAS A/S
Jegstrupvej 36,DK-8361 Hasselager,
Denmark
TEL: +45 87 38 65 00
FAX: +45 87 38 05 55
E-mail: post@dkbiogas.com
WEB: http://www.dkbiogas.com
CONTACT: Mr George Mathieson

HEDESELSKABET ENVIRONMENT & ENERGY A/S
International, Jens Juuls Vej 18,
8260 Viby Denmark
TEL: +45 87 386166
FAX: +45 87 386199
E-MAIL: me-int@hedeselskabet.dk
WEB: http://www.hedeselskabet.dk
CONTACT: Klaus Eppler

JUSTEN ENERGIETEKNIK A/S
Grimhojvej 11,
820 Brabrand, Denmark
TEL: +45 86 26 05 00
FAX: +45 86 26 02 84
E-MAIL:justen@justen.dk
CONTACT : Lars Justen

LFG CONSULT
Houlkjarshojen 9, 8800 Viborg,
Denmark
TEL: +45 866 73210
FAX: +45 866 73210
E-MAIL: lfg-cons@post5.tele.dk
WEB: http://homes5.inet.tele.dk
CONTACT: Hans Willumsen

MASKINFABRIKKEN REKA A/S
Vestvej 7, 9600 Ars, Denmark
TEL: +45 98 62 40 11
FAX: +45 98 62 40 71
E-MAIL: reka@reka.com
WEB: http://www.reka.com
CONTACT: C Larsen

SPROUT-MATADOR A / S
Glentevej 5-7, 6706 Esbjerg,
Denmark
TEL: +4572160300
FAX: +4572160301
E-MAIL: welcome@sprout-matador.dk
WEB: http://www.sprout-matador.dk
CONTACT: Lars Bloch

COGENERATION

DANSTOKER A/S
Industrivej Nord 13, Birk, 7400
Herning, Denmark
TEL : + 45 97 72 64 44
FAX : + 45 97 21 04 72
E-MAIL : info@dansttocker.dk
WEB : http://www.dantosker
CONTACT : Ole Kragh Moller

MOBIL OIL I/S
Husmandsgyden 4, 5672 Broby,
Denmark
TEL: +45 62 63 33 23
FAX: +45 62 63 33 13
CONTACT: Jesper Knudsan

MOE & BRODSGAARD A/S
Torringvej 7, 2610 Rodovre,
Denmark
TEL: +45 44 57 60 00
FAX: +45 44 57 60 60
E-MAIL: moe@moe.dk
WEB: http://www.moe.dk
CONTACT: Joergen S Madsen

PM ENERGI A/S
Sondergade 4, 9700 Brondersiev,
Denmark
TEL: +45 98 80 18 22
FAX:+45 98 82 43 28
CONTACT: Soren Juhi

GEOTHERMAL

BROEN VALVE GROUP
Skovvej 30, 5610 Assens,
Denmark
TEL : +45 64 71 20 95
FAX : +45 64 71 21 95
E-MAIL : broen@broen.com
WEB : http://www.broen.com
CONTACT : Bjarne Jepsen

WASTE TO ENERGY

FLS MILJ A/S
Virum Office, Teknikerbyen 25,
2830 Virm, Denmark
TEL: +45 45 85 71 00
FAX: +45 45 85 79 33
E-MAIL: s-ind@data.fls.dk
CONTACT : jettecholdt Mikketsen

KARA A/S
Handverkervej 70,
4000 Rosklde,
Denmark
TEL: +45 46 347500
FAX: +45 46 347510
E-MAIL: kara@kara.dk
CONTACT : Henning Henriksen

NIRO INDUSTRIES A/S
Vejlevej 5,
DK-8700 Horsens,
Denmark
TEL: +45 76 26 64 00
FAX: +45 76 26 64 01
E-MAIL: sales@niroindustries.dk
WEB: http://www.niroindustries.dk
CONTACT: Mr Claus Warming

RENO SYD(I/S)
Norgesvej 13,
8660 Skanderborg,
Denmark
TEL : +45 86 52 52 11
FAX : +45 86 52 52 41
CONTACT : Bent Holst

VESTTHERM/A/S VESTFROST
Hoegevej 9, 6705 Esbjerg OE,
Denmark
TEL: +45 75 14 02 44
FAX: +45 75 14 48 18
CONTACT: Kristian Maegaard

FINANCE / BANKING

VIKING WINDFARMS A/S
Gl Stationsvej 5 1,
8900 Randers,
Denmark
TEL: +45 8641 2177
FAX: +45 8643 9263
E-MAIL: viking@ecology.dk
WEB: http://www.ecology.dk
CONTACT: Svend Enevoldsen

ENERGY EFFICIENCY

CENERGIA ENERGY CONSULTANTS
Set Jacobs Vej, 4,
2750 Ballerup,
Denmark
TEL : +45 44 66 00 99
FAX : +45 44 66 01 36
CONTACT : Peder Vejsig Pederson

CENTRE FOR ALTERNATIVE SOCIAL ANALYSIS-CASA
Environmental Department
Linnesgade25-3,
1361 Cophenhagen K. Denmark
TEL : +45 33 32 05 55
FAX : +45 33 33 05 54
E-MAIL : sys@casa-analyse.dk
WEB :
http://www.casa-analyse.dk
CONTACT : Stig Yding Srensen

COWI CONSULTING ENGINEERS AND PLANNERS AS
Parrallevej a15,
DK-2800 Lyngby,
Denmark
TEL : +45 45 97 22 11
FAX : +45 45 97 22 12
E-MAIL : rmh@cowi.dk
WEB : http://www.cowi.dk
CONTACT : Erik Keis

SRC INTERNATIONAL A/S
Hovedgaden 8,
3460 Birkerod,
Denmark
TEL: +45 70 20 45 90
FAX: +45 70 20 45 91
E-MAIL:srci@srci.dk
CONTACT: Thorkild Kristensen

ASSOCIATION

EUROPEAN DISTRICT HEATING PIPE MANUFACTURERS ASSOCIATION
Miljcentrer, 7000 Fredericia,
Denmark,
TEL: +45 75 94 55 44
FAX: +45 75 94 55 45
E-MAIL: 9-pipe@euhp.com
WEB: http://www.euhp.com
CONTACT : Kurt Feldtfos

INTERNATIONAL SOLAR ENERGY SOCIETY - ISES EUROPE
Mollegade 54-56,
6400 Sonderborg,
Denmark
TEL: +45 73 423 100
FAX: +45 73 423 101
E-MAIL: esb.sdb@esbensen.dk
CONTACT: Torben Esbensen

INTERNATIONAL SOLID WASTE ASSOCIATION - ISWA
Overgaden Oven Vandet 48E,
Dk - 1415 Copenhagen K,
Denmark
TEL: +45 32 96 15 88
FAX: +45 32 96 15 84
E-MAIL: iswa@inet.uni2.dk
WEB: http://www.iswa.org

GOVERNMENT

DANISH INTERNATIONAL DEVELOPMENT ASSITANCE DANIDA
Ministry of Foreign Affairs, Asiatisk
Plads 2, 1448 Copenhagen K.
Denmark
TEL : + 45 33 92 00 00
FAX : + 45 33 92 07 90
E-MAIL : jealau@um.dk
CONTACT : Jean Paul Lande

MINISTRY OF FOOD AGRICULTURE AND FISHERIES DIRECTORATE FOR FOOD FISHERIES AND AGRO BUSINESS
Non-Food Secretariat,
Kampmannsgrade 3, 1780
Copenhagen,
V Denmark
TEL: +45 33 95 8000
FAX: +45 33 95 8035
E-MAIL: fr@dffe.dk
WEB: http://www.dffe.dk
CONTACT: Dr Finn Rexen

RESEARCH & DEVELOPMENT

DANISH TECHNOLOGICAL INSTITUTE
Solar Energy Centre Denmark,
PO Box 141, DK-2630 Tastrup,
Denmark
TEL: +45 7220 2460
FAX: +45 7220 2469
E-MAIL: info@solarenergycentre.com
WEB: http://
www.solarenergycentre.com
CONTACT: Erik Scheldon

FOLKECENTER FOR RENEWABLE ENERGY
Kammersgaardsvej 17,
7760 Hurup Thy, Denmark
TEL: +45 97 95 66 00
FAX: +45 97 95 65 65
E-MAIL: energy@folkcenter.dk
WEB : http://www.folkcenter.dk

TECHNICAL UNIVERSITY OF DENMARK
Department of Energy Engineering-
Fluid Mechanics, Building 404
DTU, 2600 Lyng, Denmark
TEL : +45 45 93 27 11
FAX : +456 42 88 24 21
E-MAIL:et@et.dtu.dk
WEB:http://www.et.dtu.dk
CONTACT:Prof B Maribo Pedersen

ULF MEYER HENIUS
Arnevagen 29, DK-2840 Holte,
Denmark
TEL: +45 45 80 38 90
FAX: +45 45 50 50 95
E-MAIL: ulf.meyen@mail.tele.dk
CONTACT: Ulf Meyer Henius

UNIVERSITIES

HERNING TECHNICAL SCHOOL
Lillelundvej 21,
7400 Herning,
Denmark
TEL: +45 97 12 19 11
FAX: +45 97 12 73 69

TECHNICAL UNIVERSITY OF DENMARK
Department of Buildings and
Energy, Building 118, DK-2800
Lyngby, Denmark
TEL : +45 45 93 44 77
FAX : +45 45 93 44 30
E-MAIL:ss@ibe.dtu.dk
WEB:http://www.ibe.dtu.dk
CONTACT:Svend Svendsen

NGO's

DANISH ORGANISATION FOR RENEWABLE ENERGY
OVE - Europe Gl Kirkevej,
56, 8530 Hjjrtsbal,
Denmark
TEL : + 45 86 22 70 00
FAX : + 45 86 22 70 96
E-MAIL : ove@inforse.dk
WEB : http://www. Orgve.dk/
international/europehtm

INTERNATIONAL NETWORK FOR SUSTAINABLE ENERGY-INFORSE
European Division,
c/o OVE-Europe,
GL Kirkevej 56,
8530 Hjortshoj, Denmark
TEL: +45 86 227 000
FAX: +45 86 227 096
E-MAIL: ove@inforse.dk
WEB: http://www.inforse.dk
CONTACT: Gunnar Boye Oesen

SUSTAINABLE ENERGY NEWS
Editorial Office,
Gl Kirkevej 56,
8530 Hjortshoj,
Denmark
TEL: +45 86 22 70 00
FAX: +45 8 22 70 96
E-MAIL: ove@inforse.dk
WEB: http://www.inforse.dk
CONTACT: Gunner Boye Olesen

CONSULTANTS

BIOSCAN A/S
Tagtaekkervej 5,
DK-5230 Odense M,
Denmark
TEL : +45 66 15 70 71
FAX : +45 66 15 77 71
CONTACT : Birger Norddahl

BIRGER LUND A/S
Damhus Boulevard 5,
2610 Roedovre,
Denmark
TEL : +45 36 70 28 29
FAX : +45 36 41 33 62
CONTACT : Birger Lund

BIRCH & KROGBOE A/S
CONSULTANTS & PLANNERS
Teknikerbyen 34, 2830 Virum,
Denmark
TEL: +45 45 95 55 55
FAX: +45 45 95 55 65
WEB: http://www.birch-krogboe.dk
CONTACT: Flemming Andersen

BRUNN & SORENSEN GROUP A/S
Jens Chr. Skous Vej 9,
DK-8000 Arhus, C. Denmark
TEL : +45 87 39 67 00
FAX : +45 87 39 66 60
CONTACT : Flemming Hammer

CIMBRIA BIOPLAN A/S
Nytorv 3, 8800 Viborg, Denmark
TEL: +45 87 25 97 00
FAX: +45 87 25 97 10
E-MAIL: bioplan@cimbria.dk
CONTACT: Per Thostrup

DANAKON A/S
Kegeej, 22, 2620, Tasvrup,
Denmark
TEL : + 45 43 99 22 77
FAX : + 45 43 71 1996

DANISHHYDRAULIC INSTITUTE
Agern Alle, 5, 2907,
Hoersholm, Denmark
TEL : + 45, 45 76955
FAX : + 45 45 762567
E-MAIL : dhi@dhi.dk
WEB : http://www.dhi.dk
CONTACT : Alan Hooper

DK. TEKNIK ENERGY & ENVIRONMENT
Glad saxe Mllevej 15,
2860 Soborg
Denmark
TEL : + 45 39 69 65 11
FAX : + 45 39 69 60 02

ELKRAFT AMBA POWER COMPANY LTD
Lautruphoj 5, 2750 Ballerup,
Denmark
TEL : +45 44 66 00 22
FAX : +45 44 65 61 04
E-MAIL : ksa@elkraft.dk

ESBENSEEN CONSULTING ENGINEERS
Mollegade 54-56,
DK 6400 Snderborg,
Denmark
TEL: +45 73 42 31 00
FAX: + 45 73 42 31 01
E-MAIL : esb.sdb@esbensen.dk
CONTACT : Torben Estensen

LFG CONSULT
Houlkjarshojen 9, 8800 Viborg,
Denmark
TEL: +45 866 73210
FAX: +45 866 73210
E-MAIL: lfg-cons@post5.tele.dk
WEB: http://homes5.inet.tele.dk
CONTACT: Hans Willumsen

LOWENMARK
Blegdamsvej, 4 2200 Kobenhavn,
N Denmark
TEL: +45 35 37 02 11
FAX: + 45 35 37 45 37
EMAIL: Loewenmark@city.dk
CONTACT:Erik Friis Madsen

PA ENERGY LTD
Snovdrupvej 16, 8340 Malling,
Denmark
TEL: +45 86 93 33 33
FAX: +45 86 93 36 05
CONTACT: Peter Ahm

PLANENERGI
Jyllandsgade l,9520 Skrping,
Denmark
TEL : + 45 96 82 04 00
FAX : + 45 98 39 24 98

RAMBOLL
Teknikerbyen 31, DK-2830 Virum
Denmark
TEL: +4545988790
FAX: +4545988515
E-MAIL: sil@ramboll.dk
WEB: http://www.ramboll.com
CONTACT: Sigurd Lauritsen

STEENSEN & VARMING A/S
Gentoftegade 35,
2820 Gentofte, Denmark
TEL: +45 39 75 60 00
FAX: +45 39 75 60 01
E-MAIL : jks@steensenvarming.dk
WEB : http://
www.steensenvarming.dk
CONTACT : Jorgen Schuttz

TECH-WISE A/S
Karftvaerksvej 53, Skaerbaek,
DK-7000 Fredericea,Denmark
TEL : +45 7923 3333
FAX : +45 7556 4477
E-MAIL : tw@techwise.dk
WEB:http://www.techwise.dk
CONTACT : Jorn Christophersen

TORBEN WORMSLEV A/S
Bernhard Bangs Alle 23,
2000 Frederiksberg, Denmark
TEL: +45 31 10 01 01

WISSENBERG CONSULTING ENGINEERS
Valdemarsgade 14,
DK-1665 Copenhagen,
TEL: +45 33 86 34 86
FAX: +45 33 25 23 55
E-MAIL: office@wissenbergas.dk
WEB: http://www.wissenbergas.dk
CONTACT : Peter Fritzel

DENMARK

DESIGN & ENGINEERING

AALBORG ENERGIE TECHNIK A/S
Niels Jernes Vej 10,
Dk-9220 Aalborg O,
Denmark
TEL: +45 96 354466
FAX: +45 96 352070
E-MAIL: aet@aet-biomass.com
CONTACT: Lars Bronden

ARCHIT MOELLER & GRONBORG
Beder Landevej 2, Beder,
Denmark
TEL : +45 8693 6266
FAX : +45 8693 7893
EMAIL : beder@mgarkitekter.dk
CONTACT : Susan Jessein

BABCOCK WILCOX VLUND APS
Falkevej 2,
6705 Esbjerg O,
Denmark
TEL : +45 75 14 11 11
FAX : +45 75 14 14 02

CARL BRO A/S
Energy and Environment,
Granskoven 8,
2600 Glostrup,
Denmark
TEL : +45 43 48 60 60
FAX : +45 43 96 44 14
E-MAIL : jbs@carlbro.dk
WEB : http://www.carlbro.dk
CONTACT : Jens Brandt Sorensen

CARL BRO A/S
Environmental Division,
Nordlandsvej
60, 8240, Risskov,
Denmark
TEL : +45 89 32 66 11
FAX : +45 89 32 66 55
E-MAIL : phk@carlbro.dk
WEB : http://www.carlbro.dk
CONTACT : Peter Heydorn Kristensen

ENVIKRAFT AS
Topstykket 18,
3460 Brikerod,
Denmark
TEL : + 45 45 82 61 61
FAX : + 45 45 82 61 91
CONTACT : Kurt Bjorkvik

FALCKULLA-ARCHITECTS
Buen 3, 2000 Frederiksberg,
Denmark
TEL: +45 38 74 20 04
FAX: +45 38 74 08 53
CONTACT : Ulla Falck

OTHERS

FREDERIKSHAVN TEKNISKE SKOLE
Miljteknikerafdelingen,
Honbaerkvej 50
9900 Frederikshav,
Denmark
TEL: +45 98 42 42 33
FAX: +45 98 43 32 52
E-MAIL: fhavnts@fhavnts.dk
WEB : http://www.fhavnts.dk

GRENAAMARINE SOLAR DEPARTMENT
Siemmingvej I,
Kirial DK-8500
Grenna, Denmark
TEL :+ 45 86 38 75 38
FAX : + 45 86 38 75 32
E-MAIL : gm@grenaa-marine.dk
WEB : http://www/grenaa-marine.dk
CONTACT : Ahm Nidsen

HAMWORTHY KSESVANEHJ A/S
Fabriksparken 6,
PO Box 30,9230
Svenstrup J. Denmark
TEL : + 45 96 37 72 00
FAX : + 45 98 38 31 56
E-MAIL : svanehoj@ham
worthykse.com
WEB : http://www.suanehoj.com

HASLEISOMAX A/S
Langebjerg 23a,
4000 Roskilde, Denmark
Tel : +45 46 75 30 00
Fax : + 45 46 75 38 40

HECON ENERGI A/S
Kantatevej 32, 2730 Herlev,
Denmark
TEL: +45 44 94 88 99

HILDEN (T) DENMARK
Klostergade 20-22,
DK-8000 Aarhus
C.Denmark
TEL: +45 86 198801
E-MAIL: thilden@post6.tele.dk
CONTACT: T Hiden

HYDRO-X A/S
Tylstrupvej 50,
9320 Hjallerup,
Denmark
TEL: +45 98 28 21 11
FAX: +45 98 28 30 21
E-MAIL: hydrox@internet.dk
WEB: http://www.hydro-x-dk
CONTACT: Ole Kristensen

LODAM ENERGI A/S
Grundtvigs Alle 163, 6400
Sonderborg, Denmark
TEL: +45 74 42 11 32
FAX: +45 74 73 09 31
EMAIL: lodam@lodam.dk
WEB:http://www.lodam.dk
CONTACT: Nils Peter Sleov

MILJ-KEMIDANISH ENVIRONMENTAL CENTER A/S
Swedeskovvej 38, 8464 Galten,
Denmark
TEL: +45 70 22 42 66
FAX: +45 70 22 42 55
E-MAIL:miljo-kemi@meljo-kemi.dk
WEB: http://www.miljo-kemi.com
CONTACT: Jens Vang

M & J INDUSTRIES A/S
Vejlevej 5,8700 Horsens, Denmark
TEL: +45 76 26 64 00
FAX: +45 76 26 64 01
E-MAIL: sales@mj-as.com
WEB: http://www.mj-as.com
CONTACT: Mr Claus Warming

SK POWER COMPANY
Strandvejen 102,
2900 Hallerup, Denmark
TEL: +45 39 47 39 47
FAX: +45 39 47 35 29
E-MAIL: gsc@skpower.dk
WEB: http://www.skpower.dk
CONTACT: Gert Schultz

SOLARVENT
Valby Kirkevej 5 DK-250V\alby
Denmark
TEL:+45 40327882
FAX:+45 3644 3030
E-MAIL:solarvent@image.dk

STARPIPE A/S
Dansk Rorindustri, 7000 Fredericia,
Denmark
TEL: +45 75 92 32 66
FAX: +45 75 93 37 48

TARCO ENTERPRISE A/S
Slipshavnsvej 12,
5800 Nyborg, Denmark
TEL : +45 65 31 00 66
FAX : +45 65 30 13 66
CONTACT : Mr Modens

UNITERM SOLVARME APS
Stenildhojvej 30, 9600 Ars,Denmark
TEL: +45 98 62 31 23
FAX: +45 98 62 35 44
E-MAIL: uniterm@vip.cybercity.dk
CONTACT: Pul Ellerback

WAVEPLANE INTERNATIONAL A/S
Tagesmindevej 1, DK-2820
Gentofte,
Denmark
TEL: +45 3975 1213
FAX: +45 3975 1214
E-MAIL: info@waveplane.com
WEB: http://www.waveplane.com
CONTACT: Erik Skaarup

WINDPOWER MONTHLY
PO Box 100, 8420 Knebel,
Denmark
TE: +4586365900
FAX: +4586365626
E-MAIL: mail@windpower-monthly.com
WEB: http://www.windpower-monthly.com
CONTACT: Lyn Harrison

WINDSTATS NEWSLETTER
Havvej 32, Vrinners Hoved,
8420 Knebel
TEL: +45 86 36 59 00
FAX: +45 86 3656 26
E-MAIL: windstats@forlaget-vistoft.dk
WEB: http://www.gridwise.com/windstats
CONTACT: Bill Canter

SUPPLIERS

COATINGS & PAINTS

HEMPEL'S MARINE PAINTS A/S
Protective Coatins,
Lundtoftevej 150,
2800 Lyngby, Denmark
TEL: +45 45 93 38 00
FAX: +45 45 88 55 18
E-MAIL: protective@dk.hempel.com
WEB: http://www.hempel.com
CONTACT: Morten Lauritzen

METALS

DANISH STEEL WORKS LTD
DK - 3300 Frederiksvaerk, Denmark
TEL : + 45 47 77 03 33
FAX : + 45 47 72 46 66
E-MAIL : marketing@dansteel.dk
WEB : http://www.dansteel.dk

HYBRID SYSTEMS

GRENAAMARINE SOLAR DEPARTMENT
Siemmingvej I, Kirial DK-8500
Grenna, Denmark
TEL :+ 45 86 38 75 38
FAX : + 45 86 38 75 32
E-MAIL : gm@grenaa-marine.dk
WEB : http://www/grenaa-marine.dk
CONTACT : Ahm Nidsen

INSTRUMENTATION

BRUEL & KJAER VIBRO A/S
Lind Alle 5A, 2850 Naerum,
Denmark
TEL: +45 45800500
FAX: +45 45802937
E-MAIL: info@bkvibro.com
WEB: http://www.bkvibro.com
CONTACT: Ellen Nielsen

DIAB APS
Torvet 3, DK-3400 Hillerod,
Denmark
TEL: +45 48 22 04 70
FAX: +45 48 24 40 01
WEB: http://www.diabgroup.com

ELETECO A/S
Gavnoevej 2D,
7400 Herning,
Denmark
TEL : +45 70251845
FAX : +45 70251855
E-MAIL : info@elteco.dk
WEB : http://www.elteco.dk
CONTACT : Bruno Christensen

RACELL
Frederiksberg Alle 28, 1820
Frederiksberg C,
Copenhagen,
Denmark
TEL: +4533259645
FAX: +4533219645
CONTACT: Yakov Safir

SOLDATA CONSULTING V
FRANK BASON PHD
Linabakken 13 8600 Silkeborg,
Denmark
TEL : +45 86 84 11 96
FAX : +45 86 84 45 97
E-MAIL : soldata@netscape.net
WEB : http://www.soldata.dk
CONTACT : Frank Bason

CONSTRUCTION

HEDESELSKABET ENVIRONMENT AND ENERGY A/S
Sofiendalsvej 7, 9200 Aalborg SV,
Denmark
WEB: http://www.hedeselskabet-me.dk
CONTACT: Lone Andersen

OTHERS (S)

ENERGI-OG MILJDATA
Neils Jernesvej 10,
DK-9220
Aalborg o,
Denmark
TEL : +45 9635 4444
FAX : +45 9635 4446
E-MAIL : emd@emd.dk
WEB : http://www.emd.dk
CONTACT : P Nielsen

EXHAUSTO A/S
Odensevej 76,
5550 Langeskov, Denmark
TEL: +45 65 66 12 34
FAX: +45 65 66 11 10
E-MAIL: exhausto@exhausto.dk
WEB: http://www.exhausto.com
CONTACT : Kjeld Jakobsen

LR ENERGI A/S
Sofiendalsvej 7, 9200 Aalborg SV Denmark
TEL: +45 99 35 16 00
FAX: +45 87 60 12 99
EMAIL : lre@renergi.com
WEB : http://www.lronorgi.com
CONTACT : Lone Andersen

BTM CONSULTANTS APS
IC Christensens Allé 1, DK -6950
Ringkbing, Denmark
TEL : +45 97 32 52 99
FAX : +45 97 32 55 93
E-MAIL : btmcvand@post4.tele.dk
CONTACT : Birger T Madsen

DANISH INSTITUTE OF AGRICULTURAL SCIENCES
Department of Crop Prology & Soil
Science, P.O. Box 50, DK 8830,
Tjele, Denmark
TEL : + 45 89 99 1900
FAX : + 45 89 991619
E-MAIL : uffeijorgensen@agrsci.dk
WEB : http://www.agrsci.dk
CONTACT : Uffe Jorgensen

DANSK SOLTEC
R & D Department, Roesaagade 523
2300, Copenhagen, Denmark,
TEL : + 45 32 57 64 76
FAX : + 45 32 57 64 74
E-MAIL : post@danksolte.dk
WEB : http://www.danksoltec.com

DAN TRIM A/S
Island Svej 2,
DK 7480 Vildbjerg, Denmark
TEL : + 45 97 13 3400
FAX : + 45 97 13 34 66
E-MAIL : dantrim#dantri.dk
WEB : http://www.dantrim.com
CONTACT : Ole Soeborg

DENMARK

DARUP ASSOCIATES APS
C/o CAT, PO Box 30,
4000 Rosklde, Denmark
TEL : + 45 46 77 59 25
FAX : + 45 46 32 19 19
E-MAIL : per.lundager@
causcience.dk
WEB : http://www.catscience.dk/
compani
CONTACT : Per Lundsoger

ENERGI CENTERS ELLAND
Engtoften 7, 4593
Eskebjerg, Denmark
TEL : +45 5929 1327
FAX : +45 5929 1347
E-MAIL :energicenter@energicenter
WEB : http://www.energicenter.dk
CONTACT : Frantz Von Müllen

ENVIRONMENT AND ECOLOGY SYSTEMS AS-ENVECOS
International Projects,
Fruebjergvej 3
Compehangen 0, Denmark,
TEL : +45 39 17 96 66
FAX : + 45 39 17 96 67
E-MAIL : envecos@email.dk
CONTACT : Patrick Grimand

GENVIND PRODUCTION A/S
Box 42, 9520 Skrping, Denmark
TEL : + 45 70 20 80 04
FAX : + 45 70 20 80 05
CONTACT : Toni Jensen

GENVIND PRODUCTION A/S
Box 42, 9520 Skrping, Denmark
TEL : + 45 70 20 80 04
FAX : + 45 70 20 80 05
CONTACT : Toni Jensen

GOTFRED BUSINESS DEVELOPMENT
Stenrosevej 69,8330 Beder, Denmark
TEL : + 45 86 93 79 11
FAX : + 45 86 93 79 11
E-MAIL : gotfred@post7.bole.dk
CONTACT : Soren Tomsen

GRUNDFOS A/S
Poul Due Jensens Vej 7, DK-8850
Bjerringbro, Denmark
TEL : + 45 86 68 14 00
FAX : + 45 86 6804 68
CONTACT : Jan Heegaard

KAMSTRUP A/S
Industrivej 28, Stilling, 8660
Skanderborg, Denmark
TEL : +45 89 93 1000
FAX : +45 89 93 1001
E-MAIL : kamstrup@kamstrup.com
WEB : http://www.iswa.org
CONTACT : Knud Bonde

LOGSTOR ROR A/S
Danmarksvej 11,
9670 Logstor, Denmark
TEL: +45 99 66 10 00
FAX: +45 99 66 11 80
CONTACT: Leif Amby

SKUDE & JACOBSEN A/S
Naestvedvej 1, 4760 Vor;
Dingborg, Denmark
TEL: +45 5 371600
FAX: +45 55 341600
E-MAIL: nt@skude-jacobsen-v.dk
WEB: http://www.skude-jacobsen.dk
CONTACT: Niels Thorsen

Kindly inform us of any errors and omissions in the listings by:

E-mail: unisun@vsnl.com

Fax: 91 80 22289294

GOVERNMENT

MINISTRY OF ECONOMIC AFFAIRS OF THE REPUBLIC OF ESTONIA
Energy Sector, Harju 11, 15072
Tallinn, Estonia
TEL: +372 6 210 900
FAX: +372 6 313 051
CONTACT: Arvi Hamburg

CONSULTANTS

ESTIVO LTD
Lastekodu Str 43, Tallinn 10144,
Estonia
TEL: +372 605 3150
FAX: +372 6613655
E-MAIL: estivo@online.ee
CONTACT : U Mets

RENEWABLE ENERGY CENTRE TAASEN
3 Toostuse, 10413 Tallinn,
Estonia
TEL : +372 6 726 690
FAX : +372 6 726 690
E-MAIL : tlausmaa@teleport.ee
CONTACT : Tonu Lausmaa

UNIVERSITIES

TALLINN TECHNICAL UNIVERSITY
Ehitajek tes 5, 19086 Tallinn,
Estonia
TEL : +372 6 202798
FAX : +372 6 202798
CONTACT : Enn Mellikov

We kindly request more listings in this country.

You can submit any additional listings by E-mail: unisun@vsnl.com

Fax: 91 80 22289294

We will include these in the next edition

Kindly inform us of any errors and omissions in the listings by:

E-mail: unisun@vsnl.com

Fax: 91 80 22289294

FINLAND

SOLAR THERMAL

SUNFIN TECHNOLOGIES OY
Koivumaentie 14,FIN-00680 Helsinki
TEL: +358 208 366 000
FAX: +358 40 7801283
E-MAIL:sales@sunfin.com
WEB:http://www.sunfin.com
CONTACT:Roland Hanslin

SOLAR PHOTOVOLTAIC

NAPS SYSTEMS OY (FORTUM GROUP COMPANY)
Customer and Sales Service Center,
Sahkotie, 8 FIN-0510 Vantaa, Finland
TEL: +358 10 4525547
FAX: +358 10 4525744
WEB: http://www.neste.com
CONTACT: Heikki Tikkanen

WIND

ABB INDUSTRY OY
Machines Group/Induction Machine Division, PO Box 186,
00381 Helsinki, Finland
TEL: +358 10 22 23520
FAX: +358 10 22 23565
E-MAIL: timo.heinonen@fi.abb.com
WEB:http://www.abb.com/motor&drives
CONTACT: Mr Timo Heinonen

ABB MOTORS
Business Area Marketing Communication,
PO Box 633, 65101 Vaasa, Finland
TEL: +358 10 22 4000
FAX: +358 10 22 41030
CONTACT: Peter Skeppar

HAFMEX WINDFORCE OY
Hannuksentie 1, Box 35,
02271 Espoo, Finland
TEL: +358 201 980333
FAX: +358 201 980340
E-MAIL: juhani.jokinen@hafmex.fi
WEB: http://www.hafmex.fi
CONTACT: Juhani Jokinen

METSO DRIVES OY
PO Box 158, 40101 Jyvaskyla, Finland
TEL: +358 20 484 7889
FAX: +358 20 484 7933
CONTACT: Erkki Tarvainen

SHIELD LTD
Engelinauko 19B6,
00150 Helsinki, Finland
TEL: +358 9 666 807
FAX: +358 9 622 75777
WEB: http://www.shield.fi
CONTACT: Risto Kilpo

SYNOPTIA OY AB
Vainuddsvagen 5/19, 01150
Söderkulla, Finland
TEL: +358 9 877 1085
FAX: +358 9 877 9593
CONTACT: Gustav Tallquist

VTT ENERGY
Kojvurannantie 1, PO Box 1603,
FIN-40101 Jyvaskyla, Finland
TEL: +358 14 672 611
FAX: +358 14 672 597
E-MAIL: satu.helynen@vtt.fi
WEB: http://www.vtt.fi/ene/enehone.htm
CONTACT: Ms Satu Helynen

WINDSIDE PRODUCTION LTD
Niemenharjuntie 85,
44800 Pihtipudas, Finland
TEL : +358208350700
FAX : +358208350701
E-MAIL : finland@windside.com
WEB : http://www.windside.com
CONTACT : Leila Joutsiniemi

BIOMASS

FORTUM ENGINEERING
POB 10, FIN- 00048 Fortum,
Finland
TEL: +358 10 4511
FAX: +358 10 45 34094
E-MAIL: virpi.lauri@fortum.com
WEB: http://www.fortumengineering.com

HÖGFORS LÄMPÖ OY
PO Box 43, 03601 Karkkila,
Finland
TEL: +358 0 225 0251
FAX: +358 0 225 9422
CONTACT: Ari Hyvonen

HT ENGINEERING LTD
PO Box 120, 42701 keuruu,
Finland
TEL: +358 40 5147 468
FAX: +358 14 7745 215
E-MAIL: engineering@htlaser.fi
WEB: http://www.htlaser.fi
CONTACT: Mr Mika Antitila

VTT ENERGY
Kojvurannantie 1, PO Box 1603,
FIN-40101 Jyvaskyla,
Finland
TEL: +358 14 672 611
FAX: +358 14 672 597
E-MAIL: satu.helynen@vtt.fi
WEB: http://www.vtt.fi/ene/enehone.htm
CONTACT: Ms Satu Helynen

COGENERATION

FOSTER WHEELER ENERGIA OY
PO Box 15, Lautakunnankatn 6,
FIN-20781, Kaarina,
Finland
TEL: +358 10 39311
FAX: +358 10 393 6199
CONTACT: M Mas Kuniitty

WÄRTSILÄNSD CORPORATION
PL 252, 65101 Vassa,
Finland
TEL: +358 9 709 5650
FAX: +358 9 773 3060
WEB: http://www.wartsila-nsd.com
CONTACT: Jussi Heikkinen

WASTE TO ENERGY

CROSS WRAP LTD
Teollisuustie 6, FIN-71800 Siilinjarvi,
Finland
TEL : +358 17 287 0270
FAX : +358 17 287 0271
E-MAIL : info@crosswrap.fi
WEB : http://www.crosswrap.fi

ECO TECHNOLOGY W OY
Valkjarventie 2, RN 02130 Espoo,
Finland
TEL : + 358 9 4357 7477
FAX : + 358 9 4357 7488
E-MAIL : entry@ecotechnology.fi
CONTACT : Per Kock

KVAERNER PULPING OY
PO Box 109,
FIN-33101 Tampere,
Finland
TEL: +358 20 14121
FAX: +358 20 1412210
E-MAIL: info.kpoy@kvaerner.com
WEB: http://www.kvaerner.com

VTT ENERGY
New Energy Technologies,
PO Box 1601,
FIN-02044 VTT,
Finland
TEL: +35814672520
FAX: +35814672597
WEB: http://www.vtt.fi/ene
CONTACT: Lassi Hietanen

SMALL HYDRO

ATA GEARS LTD
PO Box 120, FIN-33101, Tampere, Finland
TEL : +358 3 2870 141
FAX : +358 3 2870 249
E-MAIL :postmaster@ata-gears.fi
WEB : http://www.ata-gears.fi
CONTACT : M Sevia

ENERGY EFFICIENCY

JP-BUILDING ENGINEERING LTD
PO Box 2, 02151 Espoo,
Finland
TEL: +358 9 46811
FAX: +358 9 469 1311
CONTACT: Mr M Kaskimies

MOTIVA OY
PO Box 489, 00101 Helsinki,
Finland
TEL: +358 9 8565 3100
FAX: +358 9 8565 3199
WEB: http://www.motiva.fi

PLANCENTER LTD
Opastinsilta 6, 00520 Helsinki,
Finland
TEL: +358 9 15 641
FAX : + 358 9 15 64445
CONTACT: Timo Vuori

FINANCE / BANKING

ABB TRANSMIT OY
Transmission and Distribution
Projects, PO Box 614, FIN-65101
Vassa, Finland
TEL: +358 10 22 41758
FAX: +358 10 22 41297
CONTACT: Ralf Granholm

NEFCO-NORDIC ENVIRONMENT FINANCE CORPORATION
PL 249, 00171 Helsinki,
Finland
TEL: +358 9 1800341
FAX: +358 9 630 976
E-MAIL: info.nefco@nib.fi
WEB: http://www.nefco.fi
CONTACT: Ms Tua Reinas

ASSOCIATION

ASSOCIATION OF FINNISH PEAT INDUSTRIES
Kuokkalantie 4,
40520 Jyavaskyia,
Finland
TEL : +358 14 677 399
FAX : +358 14 677 405
E-MAIL : raimo.sopo@furvelitto.fi
CONTACT : Raimo Sopo

FINNISH SOLAR ENERGY SOCIETY (AURINKOTEKNILLINENYHDISTYS)
PO Box 3 FIN-06151 Porvoo,
Finland
TEL: +358 400 458790
FAX: +358 19 543209
E-MAIL: aurinko.yhdistys@avenet.fi
WEB: http:/www.avenet.fi/aty
CONTACT : C. Nyman

RESEARCH & DEVELOPMENT

ABO AKADEMI UNIVERSITY
Combustion Chemistry Research
Group, Lemminkainengatan 14-18B,
20500 Abo/Turku, Finland
TEL: +358 2 215 4722
FAX: +358 2 215 4780
E-MAIL: mhupa@abo.fi
WEB: http://rost.abo.fi.org
CONTACT: Prof Mikko Hupa

ARKKITEHTITSTOJARKKO KOSKIKY
Kaskenkatu 8A, 20700 Turku,
Finland
TEL : +358 2 233 3573
FAX : +358 2233 3543
E-MAIL : Jarkko.koski@pp.inet.fi
CONTACT : Jarkko Koski

TECHNICAL RESEARCH CENTRE OF FINLAND , VTT
PO Box 1403,fin-02044 VTT,Finland
TEL : +358 9 456 1
FAX : +358 9 456 7000
E-MAIL:kari.larjava@vtt.fi
WEB :http://www.vtt.fi
CONTACT: Kari Larjava

UNIVERSITIES

HELSINKI UNIVERSITY OF TECHNOLOGY
Advanced Energy Technologies and
Systems, 02150 Espoo, Finland
TEL: +358 9 451 3218
FAX: +358 9 451 3195
E-MAIL: peter.lund@hut.fi
WEB: http://www.hut.fi/hut/nemo/
CONTACT: Peter Lund

NGO's

INTERNATIONAL PEAT SOCIETY
Kuokkalantie 4,
40520 Jyvaskyla,
Finland
TEL: +358 14 674 042
FAX: +358 14 677 405
E-MAIL: ips@peatsociety.fi
WEB: http://www.peatsociety.fi
CONTACT: Raimo Sopo

VINDKRAFTFORENINGENRF (THE FINNISH WIND ENERGY ASSOCIATION)
PO Box 124, 65101 Vasa,
Finland
TEL: +358 6 862886
FAX: +358 6 312 8882
E-MAIL: hbyholm@pp.qnet.fi
CONTACT: Herbert Byholm

CONSULTANTS

CITEC INTERNATIONAL LTD OY
Cirkelvagen 2, PO Box 109,
FIN-65101 Vaasa, Finland
TEL: +358 6 324 0700
FAX: +358 6 324 0800
E-MAIL: jte@citec.fi
WEB: http://www.citec.fi
CONTACT: Jan Teir

ELECTROWATT - EKONO OY
PO Box 93, 02151 Espoo,
Finland
TEL : +358 9 469 11
FAX : +358 9 4691981
E-MAIL :electrowatt-ekono@poyry.fi
WEB : http://www.ekonoenergy.fi
CONTACT : Esa Halttinen

GAIA GROUP
Lonnrotinkatu 19B, FIN-00120
Helsinki, Finland
TEL: + 358 9 6866 6230
FAX: +358 9 6866 6210
E-MAIL : juha, vanhanen @ gaia.fi
WEB: http://www.gaia.fi
CONTACT: J Van hanen

JAAKKO POYRY OY
PO Box 4, 01621 Vantaa,
Finland
TEL: +358 9 89471
FAX: +358 9 8782933
CONTACT: Y Orispaa

PI-CONSULTING OYJ Energy,
Liesikuja 5, PO Box 31,
01601 Vantaa,
Finland
TEL: +358 9 53091
FAX: +358 9 530 9323
E-MAIL: kari.harsunen@pigroup.fi
WEB: http://www.pigroup.fi
CONTACT: Kari Harsunen

SOIL & WATER LTD
Itälahdenkatu , 00210 Helsinki,
Finland
TEL: +358 9 6 32 661
FAX: +358 9 682 6600
E-MAIL: sw@sw.poyry.fi
CONTACT: Harri Leppanen

SOLPROS AY
Ottermannintie 13 A4,
FIN-00620 Helsinki, Finland
TEL: +358405306380
FAX: +35897774958
E-MAIL: solpros@kolumbus.fi
WEB: http://www.kolumbus.fi/solpros
CONTACT: Dr. Heidrun Faninger-Lund

FINLAND

SOLECO LTD
Londbölev 27 FIN-06 100 Poevo,
Finland
TEL: +358 400 458 790
FAX: +358 19 543209
E-MAIL: christer.nyman@avenet.fi
WEB: http://www.avenet.fi/soleco
CONTACT: Christer Nyman

SOLPROS AY
Oltermannintie 13 A4, FIN 00620
Helsinki, Finland
TEL: +358 9 777 4957
FAX: +358 9 777 4958
E-MAIL: solpros@kolumbus.fi
WEB: http://www.kolumbus.fi/solpros
CONTACT: Dr Heidrun Faninger-Lund

DESIGN & ENGINEERING

ABB INSTALLAATIOT OY
International Operations, PO Box 7,
FIN-21531 Paimio, Finland
TEL: +358 10 22 3010
FAX: +358 10 22 31446
E-MAIL: pekka.frantti@fi.abb.com
WEB:http://www.abb.fi/installaatiot
CONTACT: PekkaFrantti

EKOSOLAR OY
Villa Linnais, Kilorinne, 1, 02160
Espo, Finland
TEL : +358 9 513 200
FAX : +358 9 513 288
E-MAIL : info@erat.com
CONTACT L Kari Ristolainen

STUDIO SUONTO
Oravannahkatori I,
02120 Espoo,
Finland
TEL: +358 9 455 4722
FAX: +358 9 460 798
CONTACT: Yrjo Suonto

OTHERS

ENERGENT OY
Varikontie 1,
60800 Ilmajoki,
Finland
TEL : +358 6 424 0300
FAX : +358 6 424 7303
E-MAIL : energent@eg.inet.fi
CONTACT : K Saarenpaa

FINCOIL-TEOLLISUUS OY
Ansatie 3. 01740 Vantaa,
Finland
TEL: +358 9 89 441
FAX: + 358 9 894 4318
WEB:http://www.fincoil.fi
CONTACT : R Syrjanen

FORTUM CORPORATION
Corporate Planning and Development
PO Box 1, 00048 Fortum, Finland
TEL: +358 10 45 29244
FAX: +358 10 45 24858
E-MAIL: seppo.lk.aho@fortum.com
WEB: http://www.fortum.com

FORTUM POWER AND HEAT OY
Fortum Technology, PO Box 20,
00048 Fortum, Finland
TEL: +358 10 453 3304
FAX: +358 9 563 6823
E-MAIL: markko.rajatora@fortum.com
WEB: http://www.fortum.com/quicks.un

HYXO OY
POP Box 16, FIN-04261 Kerava,Finland
TEL: +358 9 417 4500
FAX: +358 9 4174 5100

KESLA OYJ
PO Box 282, Kuurnankatu 24,
80101 Joensuu, Finland
TEL: +358 13 682 841
FAX: +358 13 8300
CONTACT: Issakainen

BATTERIES/INVERTERS

WINDSIDE PRODUCTION LTD
Niemenharjuntie 85, 44800
Pihtipudas, Finland
TEL: +358 20 8350 700
FAX: +358 20 7350 700
E-MAIL: finland@windside.come
WEB: http://www.windside.com
CONTACT: Leila Joutsiniemi

TANKS

VAAHTO GROUP
Keskikankaantie 11,
15860 Hollola 2, Finland
TEL: +358 3 880 511
FAX: +358 3 880 5501
CONTACT: Antii Vaahto

INSTRUMENTATION

ENDEAS OY
Heimolantie 6, 02330 Espoo, Finland
TEL: +358 9 81 960110
FAX: +358 9 81 960111
WEB: http://www.endeas.fi
CONTACT: Mr Jaakko Hyvarinen

FORTUM CORPORATION
Corporate EHS, PO Box 1,
00048 Fortum, Finland
TEL: +358 10 45 32330
FAX: +358 10 45 24781
E-MAIL: kari.t.kankaanpaa@fortum.com
WEB: http://www.fortum.com
CONTACT: Kari Kankaanpaa

VAISALA OYJ
PO Box 26,
FIN-00421 Helsinki,
Finland
TEL: +358 9 894 91
FAX: +358 9 894 9227
E-MAIL: mmk@vaisala.com
WEB: http://www.vaisala.com
CONTACT: Hannu Kokko

CONSTRUCTION SERVICES

PPTH NORDEN OY
Sales, Koskipuhdontie 177,
84100 Ylivieska,
Finland
TEL: +358 8 4113111
FAX: +358 8 4113112
E-MAIL: rauno.isokoski@ppth.fi
WEB: http://www.ppth.fi
CONTACT: Rauno Isokoski

HYBRID SYSTEMS

FORTUM
Head Office,
PO Box 3, 02151 Espoo,
Finland
TEL: +358 204 50 5752
FAX: +358 204 50 5797
E-MAIL:naps.solar@neste.com
WEB: http://www.neste.com

OTHERS (S)

KONECRANES COMPONENTS CORPORATION
PO Box 662,
FIN-05801 Hyvinkaa,
Finland
TEL: +358 20 427 11
FAX:+385 20 427 2289
WEB:http://www.konecranes.com

LPM GROUP
PO Box 19
79101 Leppavirta,
Finland
TEL: +358 17 3665 500
FAX: +358 17 3665 555
EMAIL: sales@lpm.fi; www.lpm.fi
CONTACT: Juhani Suhonen

NELES CONTROLS
PO Box 6,
00881 Helsinki,
Finland
TEL: +358 24 80 150
FAX: +358 204 80 151
E-MAIL:info@nelescontrrols.com
WEB: http://www.nelescontrols.com

VAPO OY
PO Box 22, 40101 Jyvaskyla, Finland
TEL: +358 14 623 623
FAX: +358 14 623 5622
E-MAIL: kari.sankiaho@vapo.fi
CONTACT: Kari Sankiaho

ELOMATIC
Kangasvuorentie 10,
40320 Jysvaskyla, Finland
TEL : +358 14 4467111
FAX : +358 14 4467123
E-MAIL : asko.ojaniremi@elomatic.com
CONTACT : A Ojaniemi

We kindly request more listings in this country.

You can submit any additional listings by E-mail: unisun@vsnl.com

Fax: 91 80 22289294

We will include these in the next edition

Kindly inform us of any errors and omissions in the listings by:

E-mail: unisun@vsnl.com

Fax: 91 80 22289294

SOLAR THERMAL

CHASSAGNEUX ARCHITECT
20 rue du Vorlat, BP 24, 69290 St. Genis les Ollieres, France
TEL : +33 4 78 44 84 28
FAX : +33 4 78 44 86 63
CONTACT: Bernard Chaisagneax

ECONERGIE SARL
Quartier Colmar, 83720 Trans.en. Provence, France
TEL : + 33 4 94 67 74 23
FAX : + 33 4 94 67 70 17
CONTACT: Helene Blanc

ENERGIES NOUVELLS SOLAIRIES
34, Boulevard de Penthievre, 22380 Saint Cast le Guildo, France
TEL: +33 2 96 41 83 11
FAX: +33 2 96 41 60 75
CONTACT: Rene Baullau

ESPACE SOLAIRE
Rue Saint Eloi, 71300 Montceau les Mines, France
TEL: +33 3 85 78 08 97
FAX: +33 3 85 67 50 99
CONTACT: M Bagnato

ETN BAZIFLOR
7 Vieux Chemin de Seillons, 83470 Seillons Source D'Argens, France
TEL: +33 4 94 72 18 91
CONTACT: Ghiringelli

ETUDES ETRECHERCHESDES ENERGIES NOUVELLES-EREN
Bureau d'Etudes, 25 Impassee du Bouillargues, 30000 Nimes, France
TEL: +33 4 66 29 22 88
FAX: +33 4 66 29 22 67
CONTACT: Gabriel Lapierre

GALLAN SOLAIRE
413 Chemin Vicinal, Saint Antoine St Joseph 13015 Marseille, France
TEL: +33 4 91 65 42 36
FAX: +33 4 91 65 42 36
CONTACT: Mr. Gallan

GIORDANO (JACQUES) INDUSTRIES
ZI des Paluds, 529 avenue de la Fleuride, 13685 Aubagne, France
TEL: +33 4 42 84 58 00
FAX: +33 4 42 70 08 70
WEB: http://www.giordano.fr
CONTACT: Pascale Giordano

GODIN SA
532 RUE Sadi Carnot, BP21, 02120 Guise, France
Tel : + 33 3 23 05 70 00
Fax : + 33 3 23 60 41 05
WEB: http://www.godin.fr
CONTACT: Mr. J. Hubert

HABITAT 31
56 rue duCommandant Prat, 81 100 Castres, France
Tel : + 33 5 63 59 53 68
Fax : + 33 5 6372 43 65

INGENIERIE TOUS FLUIDES- ITF
87 Av de Chambery, 73230 St Alban Leysse, France
TEL: +33 4 79 75 00 29
FAX: +33 4 79 85 21 22
E-MAIL: bruno.georges@itf-b-georges.fr
CONTACT: M Bruno Georges

MISSIVE ENERGIE NOUVELLE
4 rue Georges Boisseau, 92110 Clichy, France
TEL: +33 1 42 70 70 94
FAX: +33 1 42 70 59 31
CONTACT: Mr Oucheik

SOFATH/THERMATIS TECHNOLOGIES
BP 100, ZI, 26800 Portes Les Valence, France
TEL: +33 475 57 30 30
FAX: +33 475 57 24 00
WEB: http://www.sofath.com
CONTACT: Pierre Sabatier

SOLAIR AZUR
140 Chermin du Castellas, 83700 Saint Raphael, France
TEL:+ 33 4 94 95 75 59
FAX:+ 33 4 94 19 21 36
CONTACT:C Conings

SOLAIR SOCIETE D'ARCHITECTUREET D'INGENIERIE
47 Boulevaard de la Republique, 13100 Aix-en-Provence, France
TEL:+33 42 26 41 17
FAX:+33 42 26 42 12
E-MAIL:solair@wanadoo.fr
CONTACT:Denis Jacob

SOLARGO
219 avenue du Muret, 31300 Toulouse, France
TEL:+33 5 61 59 56 16
FAX:+33 5 61 59 98 41
E-MAIL:solargo@solargo.asso.fr
CONTACT:Madeleine Charru

SOL-CO
50/52 rue de le Creche, 77100 Meaux, France
TEL:+33 1 60 41 03 03
FAX:+33 1 60 41 04 04
E-MAIL:solcoenergy@aol.com
CONTACT:Corinne Hakim-Elahi

SOLECO-RSU
Valrose, 20290 Borgo, Corse, France
TEL:+33 95 30 72 14
FAX:+49 95 30 73 09
CONTACT: Jean-Pierre Navari

SOLEIL VERSTOIT
LaMartelle 34 10 Cesseras, France
TEL:+33 4 68 91 16 83
FAX:+33 4 68 91 19 20
CONTACT : Phillippe Nivogin

SORELEC SA
10 rue de la Bionne, BP 20011, 45801 Saint Jean de Braye Cedex, France
TEL: +33 2 38 75 29 00
FAX: +33 2 38 75 27 45
CONTACT: Salah Djelouah

TECHNIQUES SOLARES APPLIQUEES-TSA
BP 18, Avenue Georges Coupois, 26340 Saillans, France
TEL: +33 4 75 21 52 27
FAX: +33 4 75 21 58 00
CONTACT: M Maurau

SOLAR PHOTOVOLTAIC

ADVANTAGE SOLAIRE
Chaiteau de Montgermont, 77310 Pringy, France
TEL : +33 1 64 09 92 11
FAX : +33 1 64 09 92 11
E-MAIL : cheminaisf@minitel.net

CENTRE SCIENTIFIQUE ET TECHNIQUE DU BATIMENT (SOPHIA ANTIPOLIS)-CSTB
BP 209, 06904, Sophia Antipolis, Cedex, France
TEL : +33 4 93 95 67 00
FAX : +33 4 93 95 67 33
CONTACT: Lue Bourdeau

DEFI
19, Chemin Des Pouylats 65400 Prechac Chemin, France
TEL : + 33 5 62 87 90 90
FAX : + 33 5 62 97 28 69
CONTACT : Dominique Billot

ENERGIES NOUVELLES ENTERPRISES
Le Mas d Eole D703,Saint Come,
30730 Saint Mamert,
France
TEL: +33 4 66 81 12 36
FAX: +33 4 66 63 21 31
E-MAIL: energies.nouvelles.ent@wanadoo.fr
WEB: http://perso.wanadoo.fr/energiesnouvelles-enterprises
CONTACT: Mr. Champ

ENERGIFRANCE
Les Broc, Teyssieres,
26220 Dieulefit,
France
TEL: +33 4 75 46 86 43
FAX: +33 4 75 46 99 60
E-MAIL: Yvon Tilloy@aol.com
CONTACT: Yvon Tilloy

FORTUM NAPS FRANCE
Le Luzard 3-35, allee du Fevrier 1913
Noisiel 77437 Marne Vallee Cedisi 2,
France
TEL: +331 60 37 35 68
FAX: +331 60 37 84 11
E-MAIL: denis.parenti@fortum.com
WEB: www.fortum.com
CONTACT: Denis Parenti

FREE ENERGY EUROPE SA
Z1 Nord 2 rue Leon Droux,
PO Box 66,
F-62302 Lens, France
TEL: +33 3 21 79 30 60
FAX: +33 3 21 43 65 88
E-MAIL: lens@free-energy.net
WEB: www.free-energy.net
CONTACT : Dominique Guillardeau

JOANNES
Parc d'activites Logis Neuf,
70 chemin Neuf,
BP 74, 69780 Toussieu,
France
TEL: +33 4 72 48 03 03
FAX: +33 4 72 48 03 01
CONTACT: Mr. Pohu

MISSIVE ENERGIE NOUVELLE
4 rue Georges Boisseau,
92110 Clichy, France
TEL: +33 1 42 70 70 94
FAX: +33 1 42 70 59 31
CONTACT: Mr Oucheik

MULTI CONACT FRANCE SA
4 rue del'Industrie,
Zone Industrielle
68220 Hesingue, France
TEL: +33 3 89 67 65 70
FAX: +33 3 89 69 27 96

NAPS FRANCE SA
35Allee du 12 Fevrier 1934,
F-77437 Marnela Valley Cedex 2, France
TEL: +331 60373560
FAX: +33 1 60378411
CONTACT: Denis Parenti

PHOTOWATT INTERNATIONAL
33 rue Saint Honore,
ZI Champfleuri,
38300 Bourgoin-Jallieu,
TEL : +33 4 74 93 80 20
FAX : +33 4 74 93 80 40
E-MAIL:c.bischoff@photowatt.com
WEB: http://www.photowatt.com
CONTACT: Russell Schmit

SOLAIRE ENERGIE TELEDIFFUSION
240 avenue des Gresillons,
92600 Asnieres,
France
TEL:+33 1 47 33 78 91
FAX:+33 1 47 33 84 89

SOLAR ENERGY SYSTEMS
L'Ilot Soleil, ZI Les Cousacs,
83170 Brignoles,
France
TEL:+33 4 98 05 13 13
FAX:+33 4 98 05 13 12
E-MAIL:solensys@karatel.fr
WEB:http://www.karatel.fr/solar
CONTACT:Christian Meric

SOLARCORE ENERGY GROUP SA
3rue Paillet, 75005 Paris,
France
TEL:+33 1 43 29 52 74
FAX:+33 1 43 29 52 74
CONTACT:Jean Marc Aractingi

SORELEC SA
10 rue de la Bionne, BP 20011,
45801 Saint Jean de Braye Cedex,
France
TEL: +33 2 38 75 29 00
FAX: +33 2 38 75 27 45
CONTACT: Salah Djelouah

SUNWATT FRANCE
Energie solaire, 18 rue Rene Cassin
F-74240 Gaillard, France
TEL: +33 450 31 35 85
FAX: +33 450 31 36 85
E-MAIL: sunwatt@wanadoo.fr
CONTACT: Mr. Coqueugniot

TEKFR-UNOVERSITEST JEROME
Lab de Photo-Electr, 13397
Marseilles Cedex 20, France
TEL: +33 4 91 28 83 49
FAX: +33 4 91 28 88 52
CONTACT: Dr M Pasquinelli

TOTAL ENERGIE
7 Chemin du plateau,
69570 Dardilly, France
TEL: +33 4 7252 1320
FAX: +33 4 7864 9100
CONTACT : H. Bonneviot

VERGNET SA
6 rue Henri Dunant,
45140 Ingre (Orleans),
France
TEL: +33 2 38 22 75 00
FAX: +33 2 38 22 75 22
E-MAIL: vergnet@wanadoo.fr
CONTACT: Marc Vergnet

YVES CELLIER
20 rue des Ecoles, 63720 Les
Martres sur Morge, France
TEL : +33 4 73 97 01 63
FAX : +33 4 73 97 01 63
CONTACT : Yves Cellier

WIND

ABIES
Borde Haute,
31290 Gardouch,
France
TEL: +33 561 816 900
FAX: +33 561 816 896
E-MAIL: abies@compuserve.com

ATV ENTERPRISE
Actipole St. Charles,
13710 Fuveau,
France
TEL : +33 4 42 29 14 62
FAX : +33 4 42 29 14 61
CONTACT: Thierry Marechal

CABINET GERBER
14 rue de Thionville,
75019 Paris, France
TEL : +33 1 42 03 18 91
FAX : +33 1 42 41 60 06

DBS
Cost Cessou, La Martyre 29800
Landerneau, France
TEL : + 33 2 98 25 11 18
CONTACT: Jean Pierre Tromelin

DEFONTAINE SA
Rollix Department, 3rue Louis
Renault, BP329, 44803 St Herblain
Cedex, France
TEL: +33 2 40 67 8989
FAX: +33 2 40 67 8903
E-MAIL: info@rollix-defontaine.com
WEB: http://www.rollix-defontaine.com
CONTACT: Didier Borowski

FRANCE

EBRA
Aeroturbine, BP 915,
49009 Anger Cedex 01,
France
TEL : + 33 2 99 69 45 08
FAX : + 33 2 99 69 45 08
CONTACT : Xavier Franque

EOLE INDUSTRIES
46 Quai Francois
Mitterand, BP 72,
13702 La Ciotat Cedex, France
TEL : +33 4 42 08 14 66
FAX : +33 4 42 08 16 56
E-MAIL : eole@topnet.fr
CONTACT: Jean-Marc Armitano

EOLE TECHNOLOGIE
Zd' En Cros. BP 102,
07700 Bourg
Sain Andeol, France
TEL : +33 4 75 54 71 15
FAX : + 33 4 75 54 84 04
E-MAIL : eole.tech@wandoo.fr
CONTACT: Jean-Marc Armitano

HELIULM
46140 Cambayrac,
France
TEL: +33 5 65 36 92 90

JEUMONT SA
27 rue de l'Industrie, Boite Postale
189, 59573, Jeumont Cedex, France
TEL: +33 3 27 69 9109
FAX: +33 3 27 69 9150

LABEL SA
18 Allee de Montreal,
74108 Ville-La-Grand, France
TEL: +33 450 87 72 50
FAX: +33 450 37 67 51
E-MAIL: info@label.fr
WEB: http://www.label.fr
CONTACT: Lionel Janin

LA COMPAGNIE DU VENT
650 rue Louis Lepine, 34000
Montpellier, France
TEL: +33 4 99 52 64 70
FAX: +33 4 99 52 64 71
E-MAIL: cabinet.germa@wanadoo.fr
WEB:http://perso.wanadoo.fr
cabinet.germa
CONTACT: J M Germa

PONCELETET CIE (ETS)
CONSTRUCTIONS MECANIQUES
Place de la Victoire,
10380 Plancy l'Abbaye
TEL: +33 25 37 40 15
FAX:+33 3 25 37 43 72
CONTACT: Anne Lesieur

SIME-STROMAG SAS
13 rue de la Perdrix, BP 40004,
95911 Roissy CDG Cedex, France
TEL: +33149903220
FAX: +33148632338
E-MAIL: sales@sime-stromag.com
WEB:http://www.sime-industrie.com
CONTACT: Bernard Valdenaire

SOCIETE DE CONCEPT INGENIERIE TRAVAUX EXPLOITATION-SCITE
ZI Actipole, 136 avenue Joseph
Kessel, 78961 Voisins
Bretonneux Cedex,
France
TEL: +33 1 34 52 35 10
FAX: +33 1 34 52 35 19

SOCIETE FRANCAISE D'ENERGIES RENOUVELABLES SFER
408 rue du General de Gaulle,
57320 Tromborn, France
TEL: +33 3 87 35 97 45
FAX: +33 3 87 35 91 50

TRAVERE EROGENERATEURS
341, Avenue Ste Marguerite,
06200 Nice, France
TEL: +33 4 93 83 78 97
FAX: +33 4 93 83 78 97

VALOREM
180 Avenue du Marechal Leclerc,
33130 Begles, France
TEL: +33 5 56 49 48 92
FAX: +33 5 56 49 24 56

BIOMASS

BIOMASSE NORMANDIE
42, Avenue du 6 Juin,
14300 Caen,
France
TEL : +33 2 31 34 24 88
FAX : +33 2 31 52 24 91
E-MAIL : biomnor@aol.com
CONTACT: Dominique Plumail

CENTRED' ANIMATION DU BOIS
Filiere Bois, Deffi-Bois
Thinereilles 42560 Saint-Jean-
Soleymieux, France
TEL : +33 4 77 76 76 76
FAX : +33 4 77 76 53 25
CONTACT: Bernard Jullien

ENERGIE 79
ZI rotlte de Niort 79160
Coulonges surl Autize,
France
TEL : +33 49 06 06 60
FAX : +33 49 06 00 60
CONTACT: Philippe Barret

MARTEZO
237 route de Paris,
BP 419, F-86010 Poitiers Cedex,
France
TEL: +33 5 49 37 02 03
FAX: +33 5 49 37 39 79
E-MAIL: martezo@martezo.fr
WEB: http://www.martezo.fr
CONTACT: Marielle Touillet

TECHNIQUES-BOIS-MATERIELS-TDB
6 avenue Valparc,
68440 Habshein, France
TEL: +33 89 64 33 63
FAX: +33 89 64 37 64
E-MAIL: t.b.m@wanadoo.fr
CONTACT: P Meyer

TURBOMECA
64511 Bordes Cedex, France
TEL: +33 559 12 53 19
FAX: +33 559 12 51 70
CONTACT: Bernard Watier

COGENERATION

DALKIA
Quartier Valmy-Espace 21,
33 Place Ronde, 92981 Paris La
Defense Cedex 81 France
TEL: +33 1 71 00 71 00
FAX: +33 1 71 00 71 70
E-MAIL: frabut@dalkia.com
WEB: http://
www.vivendiuniversal.com
CONTACT: Didier Roux-Dessarps

FUEL CELL

ISITEM
Rue Christian Paul, 88 90604,
44306 Nantes Cedex 3, France
TEL: +33 2 40 68 31 00
FAX: +33 2 40 68 31 99
E-MAIL: donald@isitem-univ-nantes.fr
CONTACT: Mr. Schleich

SMALL HYDRO

BOUVIER HYDRO
49/51 Boulevard Paul Langevin,
BP 7 F-38601 Fontaine,
Cedex, France
TEL : +33 4 76 85 95 23
FAX : +33 4 76 26 16 20
E-MAIL : hydro@alpes-net.fr
CONTACT: Dominique Leleux

CENTRALE DE LA VEZE
15160 Veze Allanche, France
TEL : +33 1 64 94 21 39
FAX : +33 1 69 92 72 59
CONTACT: Mme Zelem

CENTRALE DE PAILHAS
Route De Toulouse, 81990 Albi, France
TEL : +33 05 63 54 65 06
FAX : +33 05 63 54 65 06
CONTACT: Jean Alibert

ECOWATT
Atelier de Pressenas,
04250 Clamensane, France
TEL: +33 4 92 68 34 54
FAX: +33 4 92 68 36 76
E-MAIL: ecowatt@wanadoo.fr
CONTACT: Thierry Maillardet

EREMA
Le Pragart, 38320 Herbeys, France
TEL: + 33 4 76 72 03 76
FAX: +33 4 76 72 07 34
CONTACT: Jean Marie Dyon

ESAC ENERGIE SA
BP No.8, Rue Francois Slakta,
70800 Saint-Loup-sur-Semouse,
France
TEL: +33 3 84 93 31 19
FAX: + 33 3 84 94 16 02
CONTACT: Claude Boursiquot

FORCES MOTRICES DU FORON
Rue du Martinet, BP 82, 74950
Scionzier, France
TEL: +33 4 50 96 36 42
FAX: +33 4 50 96 11 01
CONTACT: M Dumont

FORCES MOTRICES DU GEL ON
Place Saint Jean,
73110 La Rochette,
France
TEL: +33 4 79 25 52 40
FAX: +33 4 79 25 50 80
CONTACT: Christophe Convert

GAUDRIOT SA,
33 Rue Cremieux, 75012 Paris, France
TEL: + 33 1 56 95 08 80
FAX: + 33 1 56 95 08 81
E-MAIL:christian.boissavy@gaudriot.fr
WEB: http://ww.gaudriot.com
CONTACT: Christian Boiesavvy

HYDRO-ELECTRICITE PHILIPPE
Rue de Moulin, 82250 Laguepie,France
TEL: +33 5 63 30 28 08
FAX: +33 5 63 30 21 22
CONTACT: Andre Philippe

ISL CONSULTING ENGINEERS
75 Boulevard McDonald,
75019 Paris, France
TEL: +33 1 40 34 50 50
FAX: +33 1 40 34 68 36
E-MAIL: isambert@isl-ingenierie.fr
CONTACT: Freddy Isambert

MCHC - MICRO CENTRALES HYDRAULIQUES CASSING
L'Outre, 05330 Saint Chaffrey,France
TEL: +33 4 92 241 605
FAX: +33 4 92 241 605
CONTACT: Mr F Cassing

MOULIN DE LUCY
02240 Ribemont France
TEL: + 33 3 23 63 78 22
FAX: +33 3 23 63 78 13
E-MAIL: hubert.debruyn@wanadoo.fr
CONTACT: Hubert de Bruyn

SERVICES HYDRO ENERGIE-SHYNERGIE
1 Rue Moliere 92400, Courbevoie,
Paris la Defense, France
TEL: +33147685678
FAX: +33147685678
E-MAIL: hynerg@club-internet.fr
CONTACT: Francois Calando

SHYNERGIE - SERVICES HYDRO ENERGIE
1 Rue Moliere 92400,
Courbevoie,
Paris la Defense, France
TEL: +33 1 47 68 56 78
FAX: +33 1 47 68 56 78
E-MAIL: shynerg@europost.org
CONTACT: Francois Calando

SPIE ENERTRANS
Park Saint Christophe,
Pole Edison 2,
95861 Cergy Pontoise cedex,
France
TEL: +33 1 34 22 56 55
FAX: +33 1 34 22 61 97
CONTACT: Philippe Darragon

THEE
Rue Bois LA Ville,
54200 Toul, France
TEL: +33 3 83 43 29 82
FAX: +33 3 83 03 10 98
CONTACT: JF Bansard

USINE HYDRO ELECTRIQUE DE LA CRONCE
43300 Chastel, France
TEL: +33 471 77 40 37
CONTACT: O Baudin de la Valette

GEOTHERMAL

BRGM
3 Avenue Claude Guillemin,
BP 6009 45060 Orleans,
Cedex, 02, France
TEL : +33 2 3864 34 34
FAX : +33 2 38 64 35 18
CONTACT: Florence Jaudin

SPIE ENERTRANS
Electricity Branch Powerplant
Department, Parc Saint Christophe,
Pole Edison 4, 95861 Cergy
Pontoise cedex, France
TEL : +33134225655
FAX : +33134226254
E-MAIL :
philippe_darragon@spieenertrans.fr
WEB : http://www.spie.fr
CONTACT : Plilippe Darragon

WASTE TO ENERGY

BABCOCK ENTERPRISE
80 Rue Emile-Zola, BP 95, 93123
La Courneuve, Cedex, France
TEL : +33 1 49 37 31 31
FAX : +33 1 43 52 27 70
E-MAIL : babcock-lco@wanadoo.fr
CONTACT: Michel Soquet

BECK-CRESPEL
BP 69, 59427 Amentieres, France
TEL : +33 320 77 78 88
FAX : +33 320 35 52 65
E-MAIL :hcharbonnier@beckcrespel.fr
CONTACT: Hugues Charbonnier

CARAT ENVIRONMENT
49 rue Lamartine,
78000 Versailles, France
TEL : +33 1 39 07 27 15
FAX : +33 1 39 67 04 88
E-MAIL : carat@worldnet.fr
CONTACT: Valery Bonnet

DEFONTAINE SA
183, Avenue duo 18 juin 1940,
92508 Rueil Malmaison Cedex,
France
TEL : + 33 1 46 25 60 00
FAX : + 33 1 42 04 16 99
E-MAIL : froult@dgt.m.fr
WEB : http://www.degrenont.fr

ELYO
235 Avenue George Clemen Leau
92000 Nanterre Cedex, France
TEL : +33 1 41 20 10 00
FAX : +33 1 41 20 10 10
E-MAIL: webmaster@elyo.fr
WEB: http://www.eylo.fr
CONTACT : Gilles Alligner

SITA
132 rue des, Trois Fontanot,
92758 Nanterre Cedex,
France
TEL: +33 1 42 91 63 63
FAX: +33 1 42 91 68 50
WEB: http://www.sita.fr
CONTACT: Marc Blusztejn

FRANCE

STEINMULLER VALORGA SARL
1300 avenue A Einstein, BP 51,
34935 Montpellier Cedex 9, France
TEL: +33 4 67 99 41 00
FAX: +33 4 67 99 41 01
E-MAIL:contact@steinmuller-valorga.fr
CONTACT: Claude Saint-Joly

TIRU SA
134 Boulevard Haussmann, 75378
Paris, France
TEL: +33 1 40 76 38 00
FAX: +33 1 45 61 46 12
CONTACT: Alain Guyader

ENERGY EFFICIENCY

ECOWATT
Atelier de Pressenas,
04250 Clamensane, France
TEL : +33 4 92 68 34 54
FAX : +33 4 92 68 36 76
E-MAIL :ecowatt@wanadoo.fr
CONTACT: Thierry Maillardet

FINANCE / BANKING

GAZDE FRANCE
Expert gaz, 22 rue Marius Aufan,
92300 Levallois - Perret, France
TEL: +33 1 47 54 24 68
FAX: +33 1 47 54 39 10
E-MAIL: claude.mennella@gazdefrance.com
WEB: http://www.gdf.fr
CONTACT : Claude Menella

ASSOCIATION

ASSOCIATION GRENOBLOISE POUR L'ETUDEET LE DEVELOPMENT DES ENERGIES NOUVELLES AGEDEN
MNEI - 5, Place Bir-Hakeim,
38000 Grenoble, France
TEL : + 334 7651 6229
FAX : + 334 7644 1875
E-MAIL : ageden@club-internet.fr
WEB :http://www.ageden.citeweb.net
CONTACT : Etienne Masson

ASSOCIATION JURASSIENNE POUR LA DIFUSSION DES ENERGIES ALTERNATIVES AJENA
BP 149, 28 Boulevard
Gambetta, F-39004 Lons-le-Saunier
Cedex, France
TEL : +33 3 84 47 81 10
FAX : +33 3 84 47 81 19
E-MAIL : ajena@wanadoo.fr
WEB :http://www.perso.wanadoo.fr/ajena
CONTACT: Thierry Bataille

CREATIVITEET HABITAT SOLAIRE
07460 Saint Andre de
Cruzieres, France
TEL : +33 4 75 39 01 60
FAX : +33 4 75 39 37 96
CONTACT : Albro Deraprahamian

DÉTENTE
29 rue Henri Prou.,
78340 Les. Clayes / Bois,
France,
TEL : + 33 1 30 54 69 64
FAX : + 33 1 30 54 59 64
E-MAIL : adorange@wanadoo.fr
WEB :http:/www.altern.orgassdetente
CONTACT: Mr Alain Doranje

GEFOSAT
Maison de la mer. Quai
Baptiste Guitard, 34140 Meze,
France
TEL: + 33 4 67 18 77 02
FAX: + 33 4 67 43 01 24
E-MAIL: gefosat@imaginet.fr
WEB: http://www.imaginet.fr
CONTACT: Thierry Salomon

HELIANTHE
20 rue Littre,
0 1000 Bourg-eu-Bresse,
France
TEL: +33 4 74 45 16 46
FAX: +33 4 74 24 73 56
CONTACT: Christine Devillers

INTERNATIONAL ENERGY AGENCY - IEA/OECD
9 rue de la Federation,
75739 Paris Cedex 15, France
TEL: +33 1 40 57 67 50
FAX: +33 1 40 57 67 59
E-MAIL: koch@iea.org
WEB: http://www.iea.org
CONTACT: Rick Sellers

PHEBUS
1 rue de l 'Oiseliere,
69009 Lyon, France
TEL: +33 4 78 47 29 47
FAX: +33 4 78 47 29 47
E-MAIL:phebus@wanadoo.fr
WEB:http://perso.wanadoo.fr/phebus
CONTACT:Marc Jedliczka

SOCIETE HYDROTECHNIQUE DE FRANCE
25 Rue des Favorites,
75015 Paris, France
TEL: +33 1 42 50 91 03
FAX: +33 1 42 50 59 83
E-MAIL: shf@club-internet.fr
WEB: http://www.shf.asso.fr
CONTACT: Max J Perrin

SEPELCOM
Renewable Energy Exhibition,
Avenue Louis Bleriot, BP 87,
69683 Chassieu Cedex, France
TEL: +33472223260
FAX: +33472223258
E-MAIL: cguillem@sepelcom.com
WEB: http://www.energie-ren.com
CONTACT: Mr. Christophe Guillemet

SYNDICAT DES ENERGIES RENOUVABLES
16 reu Saint Paul,
92200 Neuilly Sur Seine, France
TEL: +33 1 41 49 55 01
FAX: +33 1 41 49 55 29
CONTACT: Erik Guignard

TECHNOSOLAR
Colonne-F, F-39800 Poligny, France
TEL: +33 3 84 37 57 00
FAX: +33 3 84 37 59 73
CONTACT: JP Bresson

THE RENEWABLE ENERGY FOUNDATION - BUREAU EUROPEEN
Le Domaine du Prieure,
106 Route des Courmettes,
06140 Tourettes-sur-Loup
TEL : +33 493 24 18 77
FAX : +33 493 59 36 39
CONTACT : John H Miller

GOVERNMENT

ECOPOLE
Energy Department, 17 rue,
de Bouille 4400, Nantes, France
TEL : + 33 2 40 48 54 54
FAX : + 33 2 40 48 54 55
E-MAIL : info@ecopole.com
CONTACT: Philippe Burban

STRATEGIE ENERGIE ENVIRON-NMENT DEVELOPEMENT - SEED
130 Bd Camelinot,
92240 Malakoff, France
TEL: + 33 1 55 580 500
FAX: + 33 1 55 580 505
E-MAIL:100627.2215@compuserve.com
CONTACT: Bernard Meunier

RESEARCH & DEVELOPMENT

COSTIC
Rue Lavoisier, Zone Industrielle
St. Christophe, 0400 Digne-Les-Bains, France
TEL : +33 4 92 31 19 30
FAX : +33 4 92 32 45 71
E-MAIL : costic.digne@wanadoo.fr
CONTACT: Eric Michel

CREED-VIVENDI GROUP
291 avenue Dreyfous Ducas,
Zone Portzuaire de Limay,
78520 Limay, France
TEL : +33 1 30 98 54 54
FAX : +33 1 30 98 54 10
E-MAIL : creed@creed-vivendi.net
CONTACT: Nasri Chami

ECOLEDES MINES DE PARIS/ARMINES
Centre d Energique - CENERG,
60 Bd St. Michel, 75272 Paris,
Cedex 06, France
TEL : + 33 1 40 51 91 51
FAX : + 33 1 46 34 24 91
E-MAIL : peuportier@cenerg.ensump.fr
WEB : http://www.cenerg.can.fr/welcomeng.html
CONTACT: Bruno Peuportier

ESPACEDE RECHERCHES ET D'APPLICATIONS EN MAITRISE L'ENERGIE ERASME
Centre Scientifique at Technique de Vignola, Route des Sanguinaries,
20000, Ajaccio, France.
TEL: +33 4 95 52 41 41
FAX: +33 4 95 52 10 69
E-MAIL: louche@vignola.univ-corse.fr
CONTACT: Alain Louche

GAZDEFRANCE INTERNATIONAL RELATIONS
Courcellor1, 2 rue Curnonsky,
75017 Paris, France.
TEL: +33 1 47 54 28 87
FAX: +33 1 42 70 33 44

GENEC
CEA Cadarache, 13108 Saint Paul Les Durances, France
TEL : + 33 4 42 25 66 02
FAX : + 33 4 42 25 73 65
E-MAIL : genec@mecadam.cea.fr
WEB: http://www.cad.cla.fr
CONTACT : Philippe Malbranche

INESTENE
5 Rue Bout 75013 Paris, France
TEL: + 45 65 08 08
FAX: + 45 89 73 57
E-MAIL: inestene@wanadoo.fr
CONTACT: Antonie Bonouelle

INSTITUT NATIONALDES SCIENCES APPLIQUEES
Laboratoire de Physique de la Matiere, UMR No 5511 Batiment 502, 20 Avenue Albert Einstein,
69621 Villeurbanne Cedex, France
TEL: +33 47 24 38 161
FAX: +33 47 24 38 531
E-MAIL: guillot@insa-lyon.fr
CONTACT: Mr Laugier

LABORATOIRE DE PHYSIQUE DES INTERFACES ET DES COUCHES MINCES
Ecole Polytechnique, 91128
Palaiseau Cedex, France
TEL: +33 1 69 33 40 09
FAX: +33 1 69 33 30 06
E-MAIL:equer@poly.poltechnique.fr
CONTACT : Prof. P le Goff

LABORATTOIRE DES SCIENCES DU GENIE CHIMIQUE
1 rue de Grandville BP 451, 54001
Nancy, Cedex, France
TEL : +33 3 83 17 50 65
FAX : +33 3 83 32 29 75
CONTACT : Prof P le Goff

SYNOPSIS
Route d'Olmet,34700 Lodeve, France
TEL; +33 4 67 44 04 10
FAX: +33 4 67 44 06 01
E-MAIL:synopsis@wanadoo.fr
WEB:htpp://www.synopsis.org
CONTACT:Dr Michael Grupp

UNIVERSITE DE MONTPELLIER II
Centre d'Electronique et de Micro optoetectronique, Place, E Bataillon,
34095 Montpellier Cedex 05, France
TEL: +33 4 67 14 32 32
FAX: +33 4 67 54 71 34
E-MAIL: duchemin@cem2.univ.montp2.fr
WEB: http://www.cem2.univ-montp2.fr
CONTACT: Dr. S Duchemin

UNIVERSITIES

CENTRE INTERNATIONAL DES ENERGIES NOUVELLES-CIEN
ZA Bastillac Nord, 65000 Tarbes, France
TEL : +33 5 62 93 93 13
FAX : + 33 5 62 93 10 39
CONTACT: Phillippe Tournier

INSA
Laboratoire de Physique de la Matiere, Batiment 502, 20 avenue Albert Einstein, 69621 Villeurbanne Cedex, France
TEL: +33 4 72 43 82 33
FAX: +33 4 72 43 85 31
CONTACT: Prof Laugier

INSTITUT TECHNIQUE EUROPEEN DU BOIS ENERGIE-ITEBE
28 boulevard Gambetta, BP 149,
F-39004 Lons le Saunier Cedex, France
TEL: +33 3 84 47 81 00
FAX: +33 3 84 47 81 19
E-MAIL: info@itebe.org
WEB: http://www.itebe.org
CONTACT: Frederic Douard

LPSE EQUIPE COUCHES MINCESETMATERIAUX NOVEAUX
FSTN 2, rue de la Houssiniere BP 92008, 44322 Nantes Cedex, 3
France
TEL: +33 2 51 12 55 30
FAX: +33 2 51 12 55 28
EMAIL: jean-christian.bernede@physique-univ-nantes.fr
CONTACT: J C Bernede

UNIVERSITE DE MONTPELLIER II
Centre d'Electronique et de Micro optoetectronique, Place, E Bataillon,
34095 Montpellier Cedex 05, France
TEL: +33 4 67 14 32 32
FAX: +33 4 67 54 71 34
E-MAIL: duchemin@cem2.univ.montp2.fr
WEB: http://www.cem2.univ-montp2.fr
CONTACT: Dr. S Duchemin

CONSULTANTS

ANDRE POUGET
6 BIS RUE Baudelique,75018 Paris.
TEL: +33 1 42 59 53 64
FAX:+33 1 42 52 83 47
E-MAIL : etude.thermique.pouget@wanadoo.fr
CONTACT: Andre Pouget

BEST ENERGETIQUE
Les Vignes de la Croze,
71260 La Salle, France
TEL : +33 3 85 37 50 01
FAX : +33 3 85 37 54 75
CONTACT : Jean-Paul Depardon

BERTRAND HERVE
5 Place du Palet,
16000 Angouleme,
France
TEL: +33 5 45 25 33 78
FAX: +33 5 45 25 33 79
CONTACT: Bertrand Herve

CABINET GERMA
Horizon 21,
650 rue Louis Lepine, 34000
Montpellier, France
TEL: +33 4 99 52 64 70
FAX: +33 4 99 52 64 71
E-MAIL: info@cabinet.germa.com
WEB: http://www.cabinetgerma.com
CONTACT: Jean-Michel Germa

ECOSYSTEMES
I rue, de la Chapelle,
64210 Bidarte, France
TEL : + 33 5 59 97 08
FAX : + 33 5 59 54 75 56
E-MAIL : schoolle@intbay.univ.pau.fr
CONTACT: Jen Claude Scholle

FRANCE

ELECTRICITE DE FRANCE
Research and Development Division, Avenue du General du Gaulle, 92141 Clamart Cedex, France
TEL : +33 147 65 31 53
FAX : +33 147 65 32 18
E-MAIL : christophe.nappex@edf.fr
WEB : http://www.edf.fr
CONTACT: Christophe Nappez

ENERGY CONSULTING
La Romaine, 1260 Chemin De Bibemus, F-13100 Aix en Provence, France
TEL: +33 4 42 96 50 21
FAX: +33 4 42 96 50 89
E-MAIL: negro@energy-consulting.com
WEB: http://www.energy-consulting.com
CONTACT: E Negro

ERDYN CONSULTANTS
168 Boulevard Camelinat, 92240 Malakoff, France
TEL: +33 1 47 35 78 47
FAX: + 33 1 47 35 81 83
CONTACT: Louis Drout

ERIC BOISSEL
Les Manim, Saint-sa Embrun, France
TEL : +33 4 92 43 28 22
FAX : +33 4 92 34 53 58

ERFA
7 Boulevard Generaux Forestier, 73100 Aix-Les-Bains, France
TEL: +33 4 79 35 01 05
FAX: +33 4 79 35 01 05
CONTACT: Robert Lecocq

ETUDESETREALISATIONS MONTAGES SOLAIRES
8, rue Christine, 95 160 Montmorency, France
TEL: +33 1 39 64 88 66
CONTACT: Andre Deslandes

FONDS
BP 9, 68801 Thann Cedex, France
TEL: +33 3 89 37 55 00
FAX: +33 3 89 37 75 89

GEOPRODUCTION CONSULTANTS - GPC
Paris-Nord II, 14 rue dela peiduix, Lot 109 BP 50030, 95946 Roissy CDG Cedex, France
TEL : + 33 1 48 63 08 08
FAX : + 33 1 48 63 08 09
E-MAIL : pu_gpc@club-internet.fr
WEB: http://www.gpc.fr
CONTACT: Pierre Ungemach

HELAIR ENERGIE
22 rue de l'Hotel de Ville, 69550 Cublize, France
TEL: +33 4 74 89 53 72
FAX: +33 4 74 89 54 40

HUBERT PENICAUD
13 Rue Bausset, 75015 Paris, France
TEL: +33 145 32 41 58
FAX : +33 1 45 32 40 79
E-MAIL:hubert-penicaud@wanadoo.fr
CONTACT: Hubert Penicaud

INNOVATION TECHNOLOGIE SOLAIRE - ITS
Chalet Helios 73590 Flumet, France
TEL: +33 4 79 31 62 42
FAX: +33 4 79 31 62 42
CONTACT: Pierre Bouchex

JEAN-PIERE BATTEUX
144, ruede Mercey, 80090 Amiens, France
TEL : +33 3 22 46 28 20
FAX : +33 3 22 53 96 71
E-MAIL : jean-pierre.batteau@wanadoo.fr

JURA ENERGIE SOLAIRE
39800 Colonne, France
TEL: +33 3 84 37 57 00
FAX: +33 3 84 37 59 73
E-MAIL:jes@wanadoo.fr
CONTACT: Jean-Pierre Bresson

MORANGE JB
La Caussade, 38 chemin de Cavernes, 33450 Saint Loubes, France
TEL: +33 5 56 78 9679

RHONALPENERGIE ENVIRONNEMENT
10 rue des Archers, 69002 Lyon, France
TEL : +33 4 78 37 29 14
FAX : +33 4 78 37 64 91
E-MAIL : raee@imaginet.fr
WEB : http://www.rhonalpenergie-environnement.asso.fr
CONTACT : Jean Paul Goy

SOFRESID NORD
17 Place de la Gare, 59140 Dunkerque, France
TEL:+33 3 28 63 59 92
FAX:+33 3 28 66 87 25
E-MAIL: contact@ingenord.fr
WEB: http://ingenord.fr
CONTACT: Mr Marc Odul

TECSOL
Tecnosud, BP 434, 66004 Perpignam Cedex, France
TEL: +33 4 68 68 16 40
FAX: +33 4 68 68 16 41
E-MAIL: info@tecsol.fr
WEB: http://www.tecsol.fr
CONTACT: Jean-Yves Quinette

TICO
10 rue Louis Lumiere,31300 Toulouse, France
TEL: +33 5 61 31 98 09
FAX: +33 5 61 31 98 73
CONTACT: Philippe Tico

TRANSENERGIE
3D Allee Claude Debussy, 69130 Ecully, France
TEL: +33 4 72 86 04 04
FAX: +33 4 72 86 04 00
E-MAIL: sun@transenergie.fr

TRIVALOR
367 Avenue Grand Arietaz, Bissy, 73000 Chambery, France
TEL: +33 4 79 69 89 69
FAX: +33 4 79 69 06 00
WEB:http://www.trivalor.fr
CONTACT: Christophe Berard

DESIGN & ENGINEERING

AINELEC
Rue Ernest Mabille, ZI la Boitardiere 37400 Amboise, France
TEL: +33 2 47 23 67 67
FAX: + 33 2 47 23 67 60
E-MAIL: ainelec@ainelec.com
WEB: http://www.ainelec.com
CONTACT: Mr David Heulot

ARCHITECTURE VIVANTE
Velieux, 34220 Saint Pons De Thomieres, France
TEL : +33 4 67 97 19 70
FAX : +33 4 67 97 19 70

ATELIER ARCHITECTURE ET SOLEIL
5 rue du Hahwald, 67000 Straasbourg, France
TEL : +33 3 88 22 06 46
FAX : +33 3 88 32 90 26
E-MAIL :bruno.mosser@wanadoo.fr
CONTACT: Brunno Mosser

ATELIER D'ARCHITECTUREET D'URBANISME JEAN LOUP MSIKA
65 Bouievard Arago, 75013 Paris, France
TEL : +33 1 47 07 40 42
FAX : + 33 1 45 35 87 75
CONTACT : Albine Vermer Msika

BOUILLOT (JEAN) ARCHITECTE
44 rue des Bles,
F-21700 Nuits St Georges,
France
TEL : +33 3 806138 29
FAX : +33 3 80 61 38 30

CABINET D'ARCHITECTURE ORSET
11 Rue Brizeux,
29300 Arzano, France
TEL : +33 2 98 71 75 56
FAX : +33 2 98 71 76 22
CONTACT: Michel Orset

CABINET SIDLER
26160 Felines / Rimandoule,
France
TEL : +33 4 75 90 18 54
FAX : +33 4 75 90 18 54
E-MAIL : sidler@club-internet.fr
CONTACT: Olivier Sidler

DANIEL ALASSEUR
25 rue de Coulmiers,
44000 Nantes, France
TEL : + 33 2 40 37 07 44
FAX : + 33 2 40 37 51 71
WEB : http://www.architectes.net
CONTACT: Daniel Alasseur

DANIEL MASSON
27 rue de la Saulne,
74230 Thones, France
TEL: +33 4 50 02 08 08
FAX: +33 4 50 02 09 82
CONTACT: Daniel Masson

DOMINIQUE MOLARD
2 Que du Repos, 42600
Montbrison, France,
TEL: +33 4 77 96 30 60
FAX: + 33 4 477 58 57 56
EMAIL:archipente@wanadoo.fr
CONTACT:Dominique Molard

ECOSOL. SARL
Z1, Des Vernedes, F-83 480
Puget sur Argens,
France
TEL : + 33 494 199 474
FAX : + 33 494 199 472
E-MAIL : ecosol@wanadoo.fr
WEB : http://www.ecosol.fr
CONTACT: Olivier Dulot

ENERGIE & ARCHITECTURE
27 Rue Jules Ferry, 95880
Eughen Raine,
France
TEL : +33 1 34 12 62 09
FAX : +33 1 34 12 53 29
E-MAIL : pierre.pedregal@wanadoo
CONTACT: Dr. Pierre Diaz Pedregal

ENERPOL INGENIERIE
149 rue Alexander Berrard,
F-01500 Amberieu en Bugey, France
TEL: + 33 4 74 34 59 59
FAX: 33 4 74 38 29 78
CONTACT: Joel Guerry

GROUND COOPERATIVE ARCHITECTURE URBANISME-GCAU
33 rue Brauhauban, BP546, 65005
Tarbes cedex, France
TEL : + 33 5 62 93 04 06
FAX : + 33 5 62 34 46 73
CONTACT: Jean Paul Pagnouse

GROUPEERSOL - ARCHITECTS
23 Rule du Colonel Moil,
33400 Talence, France
TEL : + 33 5 56 0420 23
FAX : + 33 5 56 84 04 10
CONTACT: Dominique Gorse

HABITAT 31
14 avenue des coteaux,
31400 Toulouse, France
TEL : + 33 5 61 52 83 16
FAX : + 33 5 61 52 17 69

INGENIERIE TOUS FLUIDES - ITF
87 Av de Chambery,
73230 St Alban Leysse, France
TEL: +33 4 79 75 00 29
FAX: +33 4 79 85 21 22
E-MAIL: itfbrunogeorges@csi.com
CONTACT: M Bruno Georges

INNOVATION ENERGIE ET DEVELOPMENT
46 rue de Provence, 75009 Paris, France
TEL: +33 1 48 74 62 15
FAX: +33 1 48 74 50 52
CONTACT: Denis Rambaud-Measson

JM JACQUIER
I rue Lacuzon, BP 39, 39171 Saint
Lupicin Cedex, France
TEL: +33 3 84 42 85 94
FAX: +33 84 42 13 62
E-MAIL:jmjacquier@europost.com
CONTACT : J M Jacquier

LELU JEAN-CLAUDE
Architecte,6rue Duhamel, 35000
Rennes, France
TEL: +44 2 99 35 04 10
FAX: +44 2 99 30 77 46

LEYRISSOUX CHRISTIAN
28 rue Paul Brousse, 34000
Montpellier, France
TEL: +33 4 67 92 19 79
FAX: +33 4 67 92 45 30
CONTACT: Christian Leyrissoux

MARIE-FREDERIQUE PERRIN
17 rue Gabriel Peri,26220 Dieulefit
TEL:+33 4 75 46 84 27

ROMUALD MARLIN
Les Guerins, 05130 Sigoyer,France
TEL: +33 4 92 57 87 43
FAX: +33 4 92 57 90 74
CONTACT: Romuald Marlin

SOLUTIONS ALTERNATIVES DU BATIMENT - SAB
11220 Mayronnes, 11220 Aude, France
TEL: +33 468 431 773
FAX: +33 468 431 776
E-MAIL: contact@sab-global.com
WEB:http://www.sab-global.com
CONTACT: Mr Manuel Moineau

OTHERS

ATLAS COPCO CREPELLE
2 Place Guy de Dampierre,
BP 29 59008, Lille Cedex, France
TEL : +33 3 20 52 47 11
FAX : +33 3 20 53 76 51
E-MAIL: :thomecrep@tho
mecrepelle.com
CONTACT: Thierry Denis

CAMIF GROUP
Habitat, Trevins de Chavray, 79045
Mort Cedex 09, France
TEL : +33 5 49 34 5775
FAX : +33 5 49 34 6888
CONTACT: Patrice Bordier

CUMMINS WARTSILA
Power Generation PO Box 1210, 1
rue de la Fonderie, 68054
Mulhouse Cedex, France
TEL : +33 89 66 69 28
FAX : +33 89 66 68 40
CONTACT: Matti Tulkki

ENERGIES ENVIRONMENT 74 NNE
9 avenue du Pont de Tasset,
74960
Meythet, France
TEL: +33 4 50 67 17 54
FAX: +33 4 50 57 79 84
E-MAIL: energies.environnement
74@wanadoo.fr
CONTACT: Mr. Magnier

ETSJIM CLARK
Patinges, 18320 Torteron,
France
TEL: +33 2 48 76 02 95
FAX: +33 2 48 76 13 83
E-MAIL: es@atsat.com
WEB: http://www.jim.clark.com
CONTACT: Jim Clark

GEOCLEAN
5 rure Pascal, BP 170, 69686
Chassieu Cedex, France
TEL : + 33 4 72 9494
FAX : + 33 4 72 47 06 78
E-MAIL : fleclrec@sita.fr
WEB: www.geoclean.com
CONTACT: Franck Leclrec

GROUPE ENERGIES RENOUVABLESET ENVIRONNEMENT - GERES
2 Court Marechal Foch,
13400 Aubagne, France
TEL : + 33 4 42 18 55 88
FAX : + 33 4 42 03 01 56
E-MAIL : geres@worldnet.net/geres_fr
CONTACT: Alain Guinebault

HIBON SA
38 Boulevard de Renims,
59058 Roubaix Cedex 1,
France
TEL: +33 3 20 45 39 40
FAX: +33 3 20 45 39 97
CONTACT: Roland Berroyer

HTS BIO
Bionergies, 59-100 Rue des Quatre Termes, BP 1009, 13781 Aubagne Cedex, France
TEL: +33 4 42 84 30 07
FAX: +33 4 42 84 23 33
E-MAIL: htsbioro@ms24.hinet.net
CONTACT: Jacques Faudin

INSTITUT FRANCAISDE L'ENVIRONNEMENT
61 Boulevard Alexandra Martin,
45058 Orleans, France
TEL: +33 238 79 78 78
FAX: +33 238 79 78 70
E-MAIL: lfen@ifen.fr
WEB: http://www.ifen.fr

LAB SA
129 rue Servient, F-69003 Lyon,France
TEL: +33 4 78 63 70 90
FAX: +33 4 78 60 94 87
CONTACT: Christian Bessy

PASCAL BRON
8 Voie Espagne,
13127 Vitrolles, France
TEL : +33 4 42 79 63 33

SUPPLIERS

BATTERIES/INVERTERS

EXIDE CORPORATION
Standby GBU, 5 a 7 allee des Pierres Mayettes,
92636 Gennevilliers Cedex,
France,
TEL: +33 1 41 21 27 55
FAX: +31 1 41 21 23 12
E-MAIL: koechlinn@exide.fr
CONTACT: Dr. Nicolas Koechlin

GENOIS SA
Les Jardins d'entreprise Bart 1,
213 rue de Gerland,
69366 Lyon cedex 07, France
TEL : + 33 4 72 71 13 46
FAX : + 33 4 72 71 30 53
E-MAIL : info@genois.fr
WEB: www.genois.fr.
CONTACT: Gilles Charmelant

SAFT INDUSTRTIAL BATTERY GROUP
12 rue Sadi Carnot,
93170 Bagnolet, France
TEL: +33149931918
FAX: +33149931950
WEB: http://www.saftbatteries.com

INSTRUMENTATION

ABB CONTROL
Current And Voltage Sensors,
10 rue Ampere,
69685 Chassieu,
France
TEL: +33 4 72 22 17 22
FAX: +33 4 72 22 19 69
E-MAIL: sensors.sales@fr.abb.com
WEB: http:// www.abb.com
CONTACT: Guillaume Rey

ALSTOM POWER CONVERSION
9 rue Ampere,
91345 Massy Cedex,
France
TEL: +33 1 60 13 20 00
FAX: +33 1 60 13 23 66
CONTACT: Alain Peral

CEGELEC
Head quarters,
2, quai Michelet,
923099 Levallois-Perret Cedex,
France
TEL : +33 1 41 49 20 00
FAX : +33 1 41 49 24 85
WEB : http://www.cegelec.fr

CENTRALP
21 rue Marcel Pagnol,
69694 Vennissieux,
Cedex, France
TEL : +33 4 78 75 92 30
FAX : +33 4 78 76 11 23

ENVIRONNEMENT SA
III Boulevard Robespierre,
78300 Poissy,
France
TEL: +33 1 39 22 38 00
FAX: + 33 1 39 65 38 08
E-MAIL : info@environnement-sa.com
WEB : http://www.environnement-sa.com

ESPACE EOLIEN DEVELOPPEMENT SARL FRANCE
16 Rue Faidherebe,
59000 Lille,
France
TEL: +33 3 20 74 04 00
FAX: +33 3 20 74 04 07
E-MAIL: eed@espace-eolien.fr
WEB: http://www.espace-eolien.fr
CONTACT: Philippe Bruyerre

KOHLER POWER SYSTEMS
Generator Division, 60 Avenue Gabriel Peri,
93100 Montreuil Sous Bois,
France
TEL: +33 1 48 18 76 37
FAX: +33 1 48 18 74 57
E-MAIL:
powersystems.emea@kohler.com
WEB: http://
www.kohlerpowersystems.com
CONTACT: Jim Welsh

LABORATOIRE CENTRAL DES INDUSTRIES ELECTRIQUES-LCIE
33 avenue du General Leclerc,
F-92260 Fontenay-aux-Roses
Cedex 08,
France
TEL: +33 1 40 95 60 60
FAX: +33 1 40 95 56 56
CONTACT: Veronique Gielec

MATEX SARL
360 ch du Recredoz,
F-01220 Divonne les Bains,
France
TEL: +33 450 20 00 82
FAX: +33 450 20 35 78
E-MAIL: info@belval.com
WEB: http://www.belval.com
CONTACT: M Petri

NAPAC
Les Chevrons 33 Boulevard du General Martial Valin,
75015 Paris,
France
TEL: +33 1 44 25 20 40
FAX: +33 1 44 25 20 50
EMAIL:napac@napac.fr
WEB:http://www.napac.fr
CONTACT:Robert Bonfils

PROSIM SA
Stratege Batiment A, BP2738.
F-31312 Labege Cedex, France
TEL: +33 5 62 88 24 30
FAX: +33 5 62 88 24 39
E-MAIL: info-sup@prosim.net
WEB: http://www.prosim.net
CONTACT: Vincent Mauries

REMTECH SA
2-4 avenue de l'Europe, BP 101,
78143 Velizy Cedex,
France
TEL : +33 1 39 46 59 58
FAX : +33 1 39 46 63 10
E-MAIL : sales@remtechnic.com
WEB : http://www.remtechnic.com
CONTACT : Christellie Hauet

CONSTRUCTION

CABINET D' ARCHITECTURE R PERNET
2 Rue la Desiree,
17000 La Rochelle, France
TEL : +33 5 46 45 43 44
FAX : +33 5 46 45 43 54
CONTACT: Renaud Pernet

CABINET GERMA
Horizon 21, 650 rue Louis Lepine 34000 Montpellier, France
TEL : +33 1 42 41 07 82
FAX : +31 1 42 41 33 47
E-MAIL : cabinet.germa@wanadoo.fr
WEB : http:// www.perso.wanadoo.fr/ cabinet.germa/index.htm
CONTACT: J T Germa

OTHERS (S)

SIME INDUSTRIE
13 rue de la Perdrix,
BP 40004, 95911 Roissy CDG Cedex, France
TEL: +33 1 49 90 32 20
FAX: +33 1 48 63 23 33
E-MAIL: sales@sime-industrie.com
WEB: http://www.sime-industrie.com
CONTACT: Bernard Valdenaire

SPIE-TRINDEL
70 Chemin de Payssat, 31029
Toulouse Cedex 4, France
TEL : +33561367777
FAX : +33561367556
CONTACT : Frederic Laporte-Fauret

TECHNIQUES MICHEL BROCHIER
ZI route des Chartinieres,
01120 Dagneu, France
TEL: +33 4 78 06 32 22
FAX: +33 4 72 25 98 25

Kindly inform us of any errors and omissions in the listings by:

E-mail: unisun@vsnl.com

Fax: 91 80 22289294

SOLAR THERMAL

AEROLINE TUBESYSTEMS BAUMANN GMBH
Lm Lehrer Feld 30, 89081 Ulm, Germany
TEL: +49 731 932 92 50
FAX: +49 731 932 92 55
E-MAIL: info@aeroline-tubesystems.de
WEB: http://www.aeroline-tubesystems.de
CONTACT: Roland Baumann

ALLIGATOR SUNSHINE TECHNOLOGIES GMBH
Volmerstrabe 9,
D-12489 Berlin, Germany
TEL: +49 30 677984-0
FAX: +49 30 677984-11
WEB: http://www.alligator-sunshine.de
CONTACT: Mr Voight

BLACKE- DUERR SERVICE GMBH
Hans-Joachim-Balcke-Strasse,
D-46049 Oberhausen, Germany
TEL: +49 208 83370
FAX: +49 208 8337 819
E-MAIL: wilfried_koester@balckeduerr.de
WEB: http:// www.bdtengineering.com
CONTACT: Wilfried Koester

BARAL SANITÄR HEIZUNG GMBH
Gewerbestraβe 63, 79194 Gundelfingen, Germany
TEL : +49 761 59259-0
FAX : +49 761 59259-60

BAUMANN ENERGIESYSTEME GMBH
Magirusstraβe 17,
89077 Ulm Germany
TEL : +49 731 932 92 97
FAX : +49 731 932 92 99
CONTACT : Roland Boumann

BAYER SOLAR GMBH
Brthelsdorfer Strabe 113, D-09599 Freiberg/Sachsen, Germany
TEL: +49 3731 301220
FAX: +49 3731 301230
CONTACT: Dr I Schwirtlich

BOMIN SOLAR GMBH
Industriestraβe, 79541 Lrach Germany
TEL : +49 7621 95960
FAX : +49 7621 54368
E-MAIL : info@bormin.de
WEB : http://www.solar.de
CONTACT : Hans Georg Stainmann

CONUS SOLARTECHNIK GMBH
Defreggrestraβe 3, 12435 Berlin, Germany
TEL : +49 30 5348468
FAX : +49 30 5348467
E-MAIL :conus.solartechnik@online.de
CONTACT : Mr Von der Heydt

DURA THERM GMBH
Lindenhohe 10, 8747, Durach Germany
TEL : + 49 831 63955
FAX : + 49 832 61659
CONTACT: Robert Frisch

ENEGIE-BERATUNGS-SERVICE SCHWAB & WILMS
Knaüfstraβe 11,
97424 Schweinfurt, Germany
TEL: +49 9721 86529
CONTACT : Roland Schevab

ENERGIE BERATUNGS-SERVICE EBS
Tiroler Straβe 61,
60596 Frankfurt/M, Germany
TEL: +49 69 636 192
CONTACT : Alfred Wilms

ENERGIETE CHNIK SILZ
Waldstrabe 90,
57080 Siegen.
Germany
TEL: +49 271 352830
FAX: +49 271 352855
CONTACT : Herr Silz

EUROSUN SOLARTECHNIK AG
Ostendstrabe 25, 12459 Berlin, Germany
TEL: +49 30 5304 1033
FAX: +49 30 5304 1030
E-MAIL: zenit@eurosun-solar.de
WEB: http://www.eurosun-solar.de
CONTACT: Dr Klaus Kalberlah

FACHHOCHSCHULE LUBECK LABOR FUR SOLARTECHNIK
Stephensostraβe 3,
23562 Lubeck, Germany
TEL: +49 451 500 51 67
FAX: +49 451 500 51 00
E-MAIL: kreussler@fh-luebck.de
CONTACT: Dr. Siegfried Kreussler

FLABEG SOLAR INTERNATIONAL GMBH
Muhlengasse 7,
D-50667 Köln, Germany
TEL: +49 221 92 59 70-0
FAX: + 49 221 258 11 17
E-MAIL: sales@pilksolar.de
CONTACT: Joachim Benemann

GENKINGER WASSER-WÄRME GMBH
HeimatstraBe 11-13, 72285 Pfalzgrafenweiler, Germany
TEL : + 49 7445 85 310
FAX : + 49 7445 85 3131
CONTACT: Helmut Gen Kinger

GRAMMERKG SOLAR-LUFT TECHNIK
Wernher-von-Braun-Straβe 6,
92224 Amberg, Germany
TEL : + 49 9621 601152
FAX : + 49 9621 601260
E-MAIL : solar.info@grammer.de
WEB: www.bs.grammer.de
CONTACT: Sieg fried Schroepf

GRUPPE ULOG
Solar Cooking Erstelweg 18,
79594 Inlingen, Germany
TEL :+ 497621 140724
FAX : + 49 7621 140724
WEB: www.globsol.in
CONTACT: Christine Lippold

GWU SOLAR GMBH
Hans-Vogel-Straβe 22,
90765 Fürth,
Germany
TEL : + 49911 791019-25
FAX : + 49 911 79019-15
E-MAIL : gwu_solar@solartechnik.de
CONTACT: Wolfgang Wismeth

HERWI-SOLAR GMBH
Industriegebeit 11,
D-63911 Klingenberg,
Germany
TEL: +49 9372 15 54
FAX: +49 9732 1695
CONTACT: Mr Barta

HIGH SOLAR
Prittwitzstrabe 100, 89075 Ulm, Germany
TEL: +49 731 140 45 0
FAX: +49 731 140 45 20
E-MAIL: info@highsolar.de
WEB: http://www.highsolar.de
CONTACT: Harald Haupt

HOCHSCHULE ZITTAU/GÖRLITZ
Institute für Energie und Regionalokonomie, Postfach 1455
02754 Zittau,
Germany
TEL: +49 3583 611676
FAX: +49 3583 611627
E-MAIL: m.schmidt@hs-zigr.de
WEB: http://www.htw-zittau.de/bauwesen/bau
CONTACT: Dr Manfred Schmidt

HOHMANN-KLOSE GMBH (NATÜRLICHE HEIZ SYSTEME)
DorfstraBe 121,
77767 Appenweier-Nesselried,
Germany
TEL: +49 7805 20 77
FAX: +49 7805 20 78
CONTACT: Karl-Heinz Werner Klose

HYDRA ENERGY SPACE HEATING SYSTEMS GMBH
Sachsenweg 9,
59073 Hamm Germany
TEL: +49 1805 24 98 31
FAX: +49 1805 24 98 32
CONTACT: Dr Olaf Haase

IBC HEIZTECHNIK
Heiztechnik, Gudrunstrabe 26,
90459 Nurnberg, Germany
TEL: +49 911 431 39 - 33
FAX: +49 911 431 39 – 30
E-MAIL: wladimir.krawtschuk@ibc-heiztechnik.de
WEB: http://www.ibc-heiztechnik.com
CONTACT: Wladimirk Krawtschuk

INPRO SOLAR SYSTEM
Miesberg 2,
85235 Odelzhausen bei Munchen,
Germany
TEL: +49 8134 6024
FAX: +49 8134 6402
E-MAIL: inprosoar@t-online.de
CONTACT: Georg Huber

LANGBEIN & ENGELBRACHT GMBH
Hattinger Straβe 951,
44879 Bochurm,
Germany
TEL: +49 234 4173-0
FAX: +49 234 4173-100
E-MAIL: le-bochum@t-online.de
CONTACT: Mr Scheider

MITRA SOLARTECHNIK GMBH
Im Geisbaum 13,
63329 Egelsbach, Germany
TEL: +49 6103 45415
FAX: +49 6103 1729
CONTACT: Maria Hakim-Elahi

MÖLLER SOLAR & ELEKTROTECHNIK
Halenseeweg 1,
33619 Bielefeld
Germany
TEL : +49 521 104211
FAX : +49 521 109988
EMAIL : m.&.r.moeller@t-online.de
WEB : http://www.mr-solar.de
CONTACT : Mr. Ricarda Möller

PETKUS WUTHA GMBH
Forschungsgruppe Leipzig,
Adolf-Menzel Str 1,
99848 Wutha-Farnroda, Germany
TEL: +49 341 5666 2424
FAX: +49 341 5666 2442

PRO SOLAR ENERGIETECHNIK GMBH
Deisenfangstrabe 47-51,
D-88121 Ravensburg, Germany
TEL: +49 751 3610-0
FAX: +49 751 3610-10
E-MAIL: post@pro-solar.de
WEB: http://www.pro-solar.de
CONTACT: Mr Raimon Dorr

REINHARD SOLAR TECHNIK GMBH
Brückenstraβe 2,
28857 Syke Barrien, Germany
TEL : +49 4242 80106
FAX : +49 4242 80079
E-MAIL : solar@reinhard- solartechnik.de
WEB : http://www.reinhard-solartechnik.de
CONTACT : Kurt Reinhard

REINHARD POLTE
Schwertfegerstraβe 1 3,
23556 Lübeck, Germany
TEL: +49 451 89090-208
FAX:+49 451 89090-130
CONTACT: Herr Polte

SOLAR STROM + WÄRME
Flacht - Rosenweg 14,
71287 Weissach, Germany
TEL : +49 7044 32147
CONTACT : Helmut Engelhardt

SOLAR-KW
Reimerdingerstrabe 42a,
29640 Schneverdingen,
OT Reimerdingen, Germany
TEL: +4951999911
FAX: +4951999912
E-MAIL: info@solar-kw.de
WEB: http://www.solar.kw.de
CONTACT: Klaus Weber

SOLTRONIC GMBH
Sälzerstrabe 3b, 34587 Felsberg, Germany
TEL: +49 5662 1502
FAX: +49 5662 949749
CONTACT: Michael Heinze

SOWICO ENERGITECHNIC GMBH
Beekebreite 7A, D-4912 GM Hütti
Germany
TEL: +49 5401 870 400
FAX: +49 5401 870 401
E-MAIL: sowico@t-online.de
WEB:http://www.home.t-online.de/home/sowico

STIEBEL ELTRON GMBH & CO KG
Dr Stiebel Straβe, 37601
Holzminden, Germany
TEL: +49 5531 702563
FAX: +49 5531 702606
E-MAIL:briel.marc@stiebel_eltron.com
WEB:http://www.stiebel_eltron.de
CONTACT:Roland Hoehn

SUNSET ENERGIETECHNIK GMBH
Dept Solarenergy, Sunset Building,
Industriestraβe 8-22,
D91325 Adelsdorf
TEL: +49 9195 9494 0
FAX: +49 9195 9494 290
EMAIL:info@sunset-solar.com
CONTACT: Klaus Waldera

SUNTECH REGENERATIVE ENERGIESYSTEME
Hechinger Straβe 203,
72072 Tübingen, Germany
TEL: +49 7071 760 647
FAX: +49 7071 78261
E-MAIL: suntech@suntech.tue.eunet.de
WEB: http://pweb.de.uu.net/suntech.tue
CONTACT: Dr. Thomas Leuthner

SVE SOLAR ENERGY MARKETING AND DEVELOPMENT CO
Hanauer Landstraβe 551,
60386 Frankfurt / Main, Germany
TEL: +49 69 4192145
FAX: +49 69 419247
CONTACT:Heinz Hortrich

TEKON GMBH
Midlicherstraβe 70,
48720 Rosendahl, Germany
TEL: +49 2547 311
FAX: +49 2547 314
E-MAIL: dk@tekon.de
WEB:http://www.tekon.de
CONTACT: Dieter König

THERMISCHE SOLARTECHNIK-TST
Baron Riederer Str 23,
84337 Schonau, Germany
TEL: +49 8726 910 037
FAX: +49 8726 910 039
CONTACT: Thom Setzemann

THERMOLUX GMBH
Sales and Marketing,
Unterwanger Str 3,
87439 Kempten, Germany
TEL: +49 1580 99-0
FAX: +49 1580 99-90
E-MAIL:miranda@thermolux.de
WEB:http://www.thermolux.de
CONTACT: Mrs Miranda Stender

TRICON GMBH
Oltmannsstrabe 3,
D-79100 Freiburg, Germany
TEL: +49 761 400 689-0
FAX: +49 761 400 689-90
E-MAIL: tricontec@t-online.de
CONTACT: Paulas Straub

TYFOROP CHEMIE GMBH
Hellbrookstraβe 5a,
22305 Hamburg, Germany
TEL : +49 40 612 169
FAX : +49 40 615 299
E-MAIL : info@tyfo.de
WEB : http://www.tyfo.de

UFE SOLAR GMBH
Alfred-Nobel Straβe 1, 16255
Eberswalde, Germany
TEL : +49 3334 5257-11
FAX : +49 3334 5257-551
CONTACT : Reinhold Weiser

WACH GMBH
Ingenieurbüro, Ingelsberger Weg 3.
85598 Baldham, Germany
TEL: +49 8106 386-0
FAX: +49 8106 386-51
E-MAIL: info@wach.de
WEB: http://www.wach.de
CONTACT: Wolfgang Wach

WAGNER & CO SOLARTECHNIK GMBH
Zimmermannstrasse 12,
35091 Cölbe, Germany
TEL: +49 6421 8007-0
FAX: +49 6421 8007-187
CONTACT: Andreas Wagner

VITERRA ENERGY SERVCES AG
Grugaplatz 4, 45131 Essen,
Germany
TEL: +492014593410
FAX: +492014593408
WEB: http://www.viterra-es.com

SOLAR PHOTOVOLTAIC

ACR GMBH
Johann- Liesenberger- Str 7,78078
Niedereschach, Germany
TEL: +49 7728 9260-0
FAX: +49 7728 9260-60
E-MAIL: info@acr.de
WEB: http:// www.acr.de
CONTACT: Dr Michael Junger

AKKU GESELLSCHAFT HARNISCH KG
Albert-Schweitzer-Strabe 30,D-02689
Taubenheim, Germany
TEL: +49 35936 34377
FAX: +49 35936 34397
E-MAIL: akkusolar@t-online.de
WEB: http:// www.akkusolar.de
CONTACT: Peter Harnisch

ALANOD ALUMINIUN-VEREDLUNG GMPH CO KG
Egerstrabe 12,D-58256 Ennepetal,
Germany
TEL: +49 2333 986-500
FAX: +49 2333 986-555
E-MAIL: alanod@alanod.de
WEB: http:// www.alanod.de

ALFASOLAR VERTRIEBSGESELLSCHAFT MBH
PV Modules, Calenberger Str, 28,
D-30169 Hannover, Germany
TEL: +49 511 1317190
FAX: +49 511 1317192
E-MAIL: mail@alfasolar.de
WEB: http:// www.alfasolar.de
CONTACT: Martin Denz

ARBEITSGEMEINSCHAFT MOSKO + PARTNER
Schenkelstraβe 36,
52349 Duren, Germany
TEL : +49 2421 13345
FAX : +49 2421 17899
CONTACT : Norbert Mosko

ARES ENERGIESSYSTEME GMBH
Raiffeisenring 5.,
68789 St. Leon-Rot, Germany
TEL : +49 6227 523 55
FAX : +49 6227 522 46
E-MAIL : ebr.ares@t-online.de
WEB : http://www.aresenergy.com
CONTACT : Eberhard Rössler

ARGUS GESSELESCHAFT FOR UMWEL TMETECHNIK MBH
Bollmannsweb 8,
D-26125 Oldenburg, Germany
TEL : +49 441 93503 83
FAX : +49 441 93503 90
E-MAIL : info@argusnet.de
WEB : http://www.argusnet.de
CONTACT : J R Gutkuhn

AUTOMATION IN CLEAN ROOM GMBH
Villinger Strasse 4,
78078 Niedereschach, Germany
TEL : +49 7728 9260-24
FAX : +49 7728 9260-40
E-MAIL : reinhardt@acr.de
CONTACT : Erik Reinhardt

BECK-SOLAR TECHNIK GMBH SOLARSTROMANLAGEN UND ZUBEHOR
Gutleuthofweg 42, 69118,
Heidelberg, Germany
TEL : +49 6221 800830
FAX : +49 6221 809653
E-MAIL : beck_solar@t-online.de
CONTACT : Norbert Beck

BMC SOLAR INDUSTRIE GMBH
Industrie Straβe 29,
42929 Wermelkirchen, Germany
TEL : +49 2196 6075
FAX : +49 2196 3391
CONTACT : Bernd Melchior

CENTRO THERM
Grenzstraβe 28,
01109 Dresden, Germany
TEL : +49 351 885625
FAX : +49 351 889054
E-MAIL : moeller@centrotherm.de
CONTACT : Dr Möller

CHE ELEKTRONIK
Untere Hainberg Straβe 3,
D-35466 Rabenau, Germany
TEL : +49 6407 7058
FAX : +49 6407 8846
CONTACT : Arno Eichmann

CONERGY AG
Photovoltaics, Anckelmannsplatz 1,
20537 Hamburg, Germany
TEL: +49 40 23 71 02 -0
FAX: +49 40 23 71 02 –148
E-MAIL: info@conergy.de
WEB: http:// www.conergy.com
CONTACT: Nikolaus Krane

DOMUS SOLARHAUS GMBH
Buschkoppel 24, 24145,
Kiel, Germany
TEL : + 49 431 712253
FAX : + 49 431 714353
CONTACT: Gerhard W P Bemdt

DORNIER SATELLITEN SYSTEME GMBH
Daimler Benz Aerospace,
88039 Friedrichschafen, Germany
TEL : + 49 7545 89248
FAX : + 49 7545 85589

DRESSEL TECHNIK
Dorfbachweg 10,
96279, Weidhausen, Germany
TEL : + 49 9562 7128
FAX : + 49 9562 5293
CONTACT: Mr. Dressel

ENERGIE BAU KOLN SOLAR TECHNIK UND OKOLOGISCH BAUEN GMBH
Madausstraβe 1,
51109 Köln, Germany
TEL : +49 221 890 2023
FAX : +49 221 890 2011
E-MAIL :energiebau@tillnet.de
WEB : http://www.energiebau.de
CONTACT : Michael Schäfer

ENGCOTEC GMBH
Kronprinstraβe 12, D-70173
Struttgart, Germany
TEL : 49 711 222 967 6
FAX : + 49 711 222 967 77
E-MAIL : engcotec@engoctec.de
WEB: http://www.engocotec.de
CONTACT : Manfred Munzert

ERSOL SOLARSTROM GMBH & CO KG
Wilhelm-Wolff-Strabe23,
99099 Erfurt, Germany
TEL: +49 361 4 42 46 0
FAX: +49 361 4 42 46 25
E-MAIL: info@ersol.de
WEB: http:// www.ersol.de
CONTACT: Dr Claus Beneking

FLABEG SOLAR INTERNATIONAL GMBH
Muhlengasse 7,
D-50667 Köln, Germany
TEL: +49 221 92 59 70-0
FAX: + 49 221 258 11 17
E-MAIL: sales@pilksolar.de
CONTACT: Joachim Benemann

GAIL-INAXAG
Export, Erdkauter Weg 40-50,
Postfach 55, 10,
35392, GieBen, Germany
TEL : +49 641 70 30
FAX : +49 641 70 3509
E-MAIL: bgi.market@t.online.de
WEB: www.gail.de
CONTACT: Mr. Kunert

GARCHING INNOVATION GMBH
Königinstraβe 19,
80539 München, Germany
TEL: +49 89 288279
FAX: +49 89 21081593
E-MAIL: garching_innovation@
compuserve.com
CONTACT: Maria Pasecky

GWU SOLAR GMBH
Hans-Vogel-Straβe 22,
90765 Fürth, Germany
TEL : + 49911 791019-25
FAX : + 49 911 79019-15
E-MAIL :
gwu_solar@solartechnik.de
CONTACT: Wolfgang Wismeth

HERWI-SOLAR GMBH
Industriegebeit 11,
D-63911 Klingenberg,
Germany
TEL: +49 9372 15 54
FAX: +49 9732 1695
CONTACT: Mr Barta

HIGH SOLAR
Prittwitzstrabe 100,
89075 Uim, Germany
TEL: +49 731 960 8484
FAX: +49 731 960 8486
E-MAIL: info@highsolar.de
WEB: http://www.highsolar.de
CONTACT: Harad Haupt

HOTEX GMBH
Leopoldstraβe 6 und 11,
72488 Sigmaringen, Germany
TEL: +49 7511 5732
FAX: +49 7571 3270
E-MAIL: solar4you@aol.com
CONTACT: Hartmut Raus

ING-BUERO MAYER
Kossenerstrasse 6b,
D-81373 Munchen, Germany
TEL: +49 89 743712-13
FAX: +49 89 743712-14
E-MAIL: mayer@ibom.de
WEB: http://www.ibom.de
CONTACT: Dr Oliver Mayer

INPRO SOLAR SYSTEM
Miesberg 2,
85235 Odelzhausen bei Munchen,
Germany
TEL: +49 8134 6024
FAX: +49 8134 6402
E-MAIL: inprosoar@t-online.de
CONTACT: Georg Huber

INSTITUT FOR APPLIED RESEARCH/ENERGY CONVERSION IN SOLAR SYSTEMS
Brauneggerstraβe 55,
78462 Konstanz,
Germany
TEL: +49 7531 206-406
FAX: +49 7531 206-400
E-MAIL: iaf-ewis@fh-konstanz.de
CONTACT: Prof C Schaffrin

KASTNER ELECTRONIC INH DORISKASTNER
Im Neufeld 25,
76359 Marxzell,
Germany
TEL: + 49 7248 5811
FAX: + 49 7248 5820
E-MAIL:kastner.electronic@t-online.de
CONTACT: Peter A Kastner

LAFARGE BRAAS ROOFING ACCESSORIES GMBH & CO KG
Frankfurter Land Strasse 2-4,
D-61437 Oberursel, Germany
TEL: +49 6171 61 2590
FAX: +49 6171 61 2912

LEYBOLD SYSTEMS GMBH
Postfach 15 55,
Wilhelm-Rohn-Straβe 25,
63450 Hanau,
Germany
TEL: +49 6181 34 1728
FAX: +49 6181 34 1270
CONTACT: Dr Klaus Michael

M + W ZANDER FACILITY ENGINEERING
Lotterbergstr 30,
70499 Stuttgart Germany
TEL: +49 711 8804 1259
FAX: +49 711 8804 1950
E-MAIL: photovoltaics@mw-zander.com
WEB: http:// www.mw-zander.com
CONTACT: Dr Klaus Eberhardt

MICHEL SOLAR ELECTRONICS-MSE
Waldstrabe 1, 66287 Quierschield 4,
Germany
TEL: +49 6825 7501
FAX: +49 6825 7501
CONTACT: Mr Michel

MULTI-CONTACT DEUTSCHLAND GMBH
Hegenheimer Strasse 19,
Postfach 1606,
79551 Weil am Rhein, Germany
TEL: + 49 7621 667 0
FAX: +49 7621 667 100

PHOTOTRONICS SOLARTECHNIK GMBH
Hermann-Oberth-Straβe 11,
85640 Putzbrunn, Germany
TEL :+ 49 89 46264-0
FAX: + 49 89 46264
E-MAIL :
106475.3005@compuserve.com
CONTACT: Markus Schmid

PV SILICON GMBH
Wilhelm-Wolff-Strasse 27,
99099 Erfurt,
Germany
TEL: +49 361 417 2026
FAX: +49 361 417 2027
E-MAIL: Hubert.Aulich@pvsilicon.com
WEB: http://www.pvsilicon.com
CONTACT: Hubert A Aulich

RWE SOLAR GMBH
Industriestrabe 13, 63755 Alzenau,
Germany
TEL: +496023911712
FAX: +496023911700
E-MAIL: ase_sales@ase.tessag.com
WEB: http://www.rwesolar.com
CONTACT: Dr. Martin Gorn

SAINT GOBAIN / VEGLA
Julicher Strabe 495,
52070 Aachen, Germany
TEL: +492419667240
FAX: +492419667241

SHELL SOLAR DEUTSCHLAND VERTRIEB GMBH
Schillstr 9, 10795 Berlin Germany
TEL: +4930263916-0
E-MAIL: gerhard.gkleiss@opc.shell.com
CONTACT: Dr. Gerhard Kleiss

SIEMENS UND SHELL SOLAR GMBH
Photovoltaics, Frankfurter Ring 152,
80807 Munich, Germany
TEL: +498963659129
FAX: +498963659173
CONTACT: Bernhard Bein

SOLAR ENERGIE-TECHNIK GMBH
Industriestrasse 1-3,D-68801
AlfluBheim,Germany
TEL:+49 6205 820 6601
FAX:+49 6205 820 3160
E-MAIL:setsolar@t-online.de
CONTACT: Helmut Engelhorn

SOLAR STROM + WÄRME
Flacht - Rosenweg 14,
71287 Weissach, Germany
TEL : +49 7044 32147
CONTACT : Helmut Engelhardt

SOLAR STROM STRAASS
Lindenstraβe 5,
86949 Windach am Ammersee,
Germany
TEL:+49 8193 5024
FAX:+49 8193 8480
CONTACT:Mr Straass

SOLAR SYSTEME SCHUTT GMBH
Am Hang 3,
D-61476 Kronberg,
Germany
TEL: +496173323338
FAX: +496173323337

SOLAR UND REGELTECHNIK
Frankenstraβe 15,
55278 Weinolsheim, Germany
TEL:+49 6249 9051 03
FAX:+49 6249 9051 05
CONTACT:Benno Bantel

SOLAR WERK GMBH
Iserstr, 8-10, D-14513 Teltow
Germany
TEL:+49 33289 448 300
FAX:+49 3328 448 301
E-MAIL:info@solarwerk.de

SOLARA AG
Energy from Sun and Wind
Borselstraβe 3-7, 22765 Hamburg,
Germany
TEL:+49 40 391 065-0
FAX:+49 40 391 065-99
E-MAIL:info@solara.de
WEB:http://www.solara.de
CONTACT:Thomas Rudolph

SOLARC GMBH INNOVATIVE SOLARPRODUKTE
Gustav-Meyer Allee 25,
13355 Berlin, Germany
TEL:+49 30 46 307 165
FAX:+49 30 46 307 167
E-MAIL:service@solarc.de
WEB:http://www.solarc.de
CONTACT:A Frauenrath

SOLAR-FABRIK GMBH
Munzinger Straβe 2 D-79111
Freiburg Germany
TEL:+49 761 4000 0
FAX:+49 761 4000 199
E-MAIL:info@solar-fabrik.de
WEB:http://www.solar-fabrik.de
CONTACT:George Salvamoser

SOLAR SYSTEMS STENHORST
Reichsprasident-Ebert-Straβe
3 D-31832 Springe,
Germany
TEL:+49 5041 62 856
FAX:+49 5041 63 839
EMAIL:113136.2627@compuserve.com
CONTACT:Peter Stenhorst

SONNENENERGIE OPPACH GMBH
Strabe der Freundschaft 8,
02736 Oppach,
Germany
TEL: +49 35872 45283
FAX: +49 35872 32337
CONTACT: K Michaelsen-Fatz

SOTECH REGENERATIVE ENERGIESYSTEME GMBH
Postftch 104511,
40036 Dusseldorf,
Germany
TEL: +49 211 355 9290
FAX: +49 211 355 92920
E-MAIL: sotech.d@t-online.de
CONTACT: Karsten Mosch

STROBL-SOLAR
An der Stangemühle 4, 83471
Schonau am Konigssee,
Germany
TEL: +49 8652 63964
FAX: +49 8652 63587
CONTACT:Georg Strobl

STEINBACH GMBH
Westerfeldstrasse 13,
32758 Detmold, Germany
TEL: +4952319607-0
FAX: +4952319607-50
E-MAIL: d.schroeter@steinbach-tech.de

SUNSET ENERGIETECHNIK GMBH
Dept Solarenergy, Sunset Building,
Industriestraβe 8-22,
D91325 Adelsdorf, Germany
TEL: +49 9195 9494 0
FAX: +49 9195 9494 290
EMAIL:info@sunset-solar.com
CONTACT: Klaus Waldera

SUNTECH REGENERATIVE ENERGIESYSTEME
Hechinger Straβe 203,
72072 Tübingen, Germany
TEL: +49 7071 760 647
FAX: +49 7071 78261
E-MAIL: suntech@
suntech.tue.eunet.de
WEB: http://pweb.de.uu.net/suntech.tue
CONTACT: Dr. Thomas Leuthner

SUNTECHNICS GMBH
Gotenstraβe 10, 20097,
Hamburg, Germany
TEL: +49 40 23 62 08-0
FAX: +49 40 23 62 08-22
WEB: http://www.suntechnics.de

SUNWARESOLARTECHNIK GMBH & CO KG
Dusseldorfer Straβe 80,
47239 Duisburg-Rumein, Germany
TEL: +49 2151 406045
FAX: +49 2151 406208
E-MAIL: info@sunware.de
WEB: http://www.sunware.de
CONTACT: Frank van Buhl

SUNWAYS AG PHOTOVOLTAICS
Macairrestraβe 5,
78467 Konstanz, Germany
TEL: +49 7531 996 77-0
FAX: +49 7531 996 77-10
E-MAIL: info@sunways.de
WEB: http://www.sunways.de
CONTACT: Uwe Rosentreter

THYSSEN BAUSYSTEME GMBH
Willy-Brandt-Str 2,
46535 Dinslaken, Germany
TEL: +49 2064 688 607
FAX: +49 2064 688 555
E-MAIL:info@thyssen-bausysteme.com
WEB:http://www.thyssen-
bausysteme.com
CONTACT:Gordon Brede

UNIVERSITY OF ERLANGEN
Institute of Applied Physics,
Staudstr 7, Bau A3,
D-91058 Ernangen,
Germany
TEL: +49 9131 8528421
FAX: +49 9131 8528423
E-MAIL: max.schulz@physik.uni-erlangen.de
WEB: http://www.physik.uni-erlangen.de
CONTACT: Max Schulz

WAGNER & CO SOLARTECHNIK GMBH
Zimmermannstrasse 12,
35091 Cölbe,
Germany
TEL: +49 6421 8007-0
FAX: +49 6421 8007-187
CONTACT: Andreas Wagner

WURTH SOLAR GMBH & CO KG
Wurth Solergy, Lutwigsburger Strabe 100, 71672 Marbach am Neckar,
Germany
TEL: +49 7144 94 14-26
FAX: +49 7144 94 14-29
E-MAIL: ws.vk@we-online.de
WEB: http://www.we-online.de
CONTACT: Reinhard Eckert

WÜRTH ELECTRONIK GMBH & COKG
Wurth Solergy, Ludwigsburger Straβe
100, 71672 Marbach am Neckar,
TEL: +49 7144 94 14-20
FAX: +49 7144 94 14-19
E-MAIL: ws.vk@we-online.de
WEB: http://www.wuerth-solergy.de
CONTACT: Reinhard Eckert

WIND

ABB NEW VENTURES GMBH
Postfach 10 03 51,
68 128 Mannheim, Germany,
TEL: +49 621 386 29 58
FAX: +49 621 386 39 99
E-MAIL:
volker.biewendt@de.abb.com
WEB: http://www.abb.com
CONTACT: Volker Biewendt

ABB COMPETENCE CENTRE OF WIND POWER
Department DS 1,
Kafertalerstrasse 250,
68167Mannheim, Germany
TEL: +49 621 386 2824
WEB: http://www.abb.com/de
CONTACT: Nils Immerkjaer

ABEKING & RASMUSSEN ROTEC GMBH
an der Fahre 2,
27809 Lemwerder, Germany
TEL: +49 421 67 33-0
FAX: +49 421 67 33-709
CONTACT: Hanno Pfitzer

AEG KODENSATOREN UND WANDLAR GMBH
Sickingenstrabe 71,D-10553 Berlin,
Germany
TEL: +49 30 3 46 92-252
FAX: +49 30 3 46 92-255
E-MAIL: office@aeg-kuw.de
WEB: http://www.aeg-kuw.de

AEROCRAFT ENERGIETECHNIK GMBH
Am Bahnhof 12,27356 Rotenburg
Germany
TEL: +49 4261 960034
FAX: +49 4261 960035
E-MAIL: goedeck.servo@t-online.de
CONTACT: Hans Sturmer

AERODYN ENERGIESYSTEME GMBH
Provianthausstrabe 9,D-24768
Rendsburg, Germany
TEL: +49 43 31 12 75-0
FAX: +49 43 31 12 75-55
E-MAIL: info@aerodyn.de
WEB: http://www.aerodyn.de
CONTACT: Soenke Siegfriedsen

ALSTOM ENERGIETECHNIK GMBH
Decentralized Power Supply, Lyoner Strasse 44-48, D-60528 Frankfurt,
Germany
TEL: +49 69 6632-1213
FAX: +49 69 6632-2245
E-MAIL: ralf.schlosser@tde.alstom.com
WEB: http://www.alstom.com
CONTACT: Ralf Schlosser

BALCKE-DUERR
Muhlenwinkelsweb 13,
47239 Duisburg, Germany
TEL : +49 2102 855 354
FAX : +49 2102 855 218
CONTACT : Dr. Horrighs

BUREAU VERITAS (QUALITY SERVICES)
Huyssenalle 5, 45128 Essen, Germany
TEL : +49 201 81076-18
FAX : +49 201 231234
CONTACT : Herr Gatermann

DEWIND TECHNIK GMBH
Seelandstrasse 1,
D-23569 Lubeck, Germany
TEL : + 49 451 390 9771
FAX : + 49 451 390 9778
E-MAIL : dewind@dewind.de
WEB : http://www. dewind.de
CONTACT: Mr. J D Mayer

DEUBLIN GMBH
Nassaustr 10, D-65719 Hofheim-Wallau, Germany
TEL: +49 6122 8002-0
FAX: +49 6122 15888
E-MAIL: info@deublin.de
WEB: http://www.deublin.de

ENERCON INTERNATIONAL GMBH
Schwachhauser Heerstraβe 299,
28211 Bremen, Germany
TEL : +49 421 2499 20
FAX : +49 421 2499 60
E-MAIL :
sales.international@enercon.de
WEB : http://www.enercon.de
CONTACT : Juanita Fromme

ENRON WIND GMBH
Holsterfeld 5a, 48499 Salzbergen,
Germany
TEL: + 49 5971 980-0
FAX: +49 5971 980-1090
E-MAIL: wind@enron.com
WEB: http://www.wind.enron.com
CONTACT : Herbert C Peels

ENERGIEKONTORAG
Mary Somerville Str 5, 28359
Bremen, Germany
TEL: +49 421 33 04 - 0
FAX: +49 412 33 04 - 444
E-MAIL: info@energiekontor.de
WEB: http://www.energiekontor.de

EUROS ENTWICKLUNGSGESELLSCHAFT FÜR WINDKRAFTANLAGEN MBH
Falkenberger Straβe 146a,
13088 Berlin, Germany
TEL: +49 301 39 87 80 60
FAX: +49 301 39 87 80 62
E-MAIL: stoer@euros.de
WEB: http://www.euros.de
CONTACT: Dr. Roland Stoer

EUROVORTEX GMBH
Bahnhofstrasse 378,
15907 Lubben,
Germany
TEL: +49 3546 7327
FAX: +49 3546 7327
CONTACT: Herr Scherf

EWENATURWATTGWBH
MoslestraBe 3,
26122 Oldenburg,
Germany
TEL: +49 441 350910-0
FAX: +49 441 350910-95
E-MAIL: info@ewe-naturwatt.de
WEB: http://www.ewe-naturwatt.de
CONTACT: Oliver Heitmann

FLENDER AG
Alfred-Flender.Strasse 77,
D-46395 Bocholt,
Germany
TEL: + 49 2871 92-0
FAX: +49 2871 92-2080
WEB: http://www.flender.com
CONTACT: Paul Bollwerk

FORDERGESELLSCHAFT WINDENERGIE EV-FGW
Flotowstrasse 41-43,
22083 Hamburg,
Germany
TEL: +49 40 27 80 91-82
FAX: +49 40 27 80 91 76
E-MAIL: fgw-hh@t-online.de
WEB: wind-fgw.de
CONTACT: Andreas Wagner

FUCHS LUBRITECH GMBH
Hans-Reiner-Strabe 7-13, 67685
Weilerbach, Germany
TEL: +49 63 74 924-5
FAX: +49 63 74 924-940
E-MAIL: info@fuchs-lubritech.de
WEB: http://www.fuchs-lubritech.de

FUHRLANDER AG
Windturbines, Auf der Hohe 4,
56477 Waigandshain, Germany
TEL: +49 2664 99 66-0
FAX: +49 2664 99 66-33
E-MAIL: mail@fuhrlaender.de
WEB: http://www.fuhrlaender.de
CONTACT: Joachim Fuhrlander

GESELLSCHAFT FÜR ÖKOLOGISCHE FORSCHUNG EV
Frohschammerstraβe 14,
8000 Müchen 40, Germany
TEL : + 49 89359 8586
CONTACT: Ekkehar Scheider

GE WIND ENERGY GMBH
Holsterfeld 16,
48499 Salzbergen
Germany
TEL: +49 5971 980 0
FAX: +49 5971 980 1999
E-MAIL: windenergy.germany@ps.ge.com
WEB: http://www.gewindenergy.com
CONTACT: Mercedes Guinales

GETPROJECT GMBH & CO KG
Quinckestraβe 18,
24106 Kiel,
Germany
TEL : + 49 431 38960-0
FAX : + 49 431 38960-16
E-MAIL : getpro@getproject.de
WEB: www.getproject.de

GREVENBROICH GMBH
Energiestraβe D-41517
Grevenbroich, Germany
TEL : + 492181 28 06 70
FAX : + 49 2181 28 06 69
E-MAIL : company.gre@wintest.de

GWU UMWELTTECHNIK
Talstrabe3, 50374 Erftstadt
Friesheim, Germany
TEL: +49 2235 95 52 20
FAX: +49 2235 75 632
E-MAIL: info@gwu-group.de
WEB: http://www.gwu-group.de

HAMBURG MESSE UND CONGRESS GMBH
St Petersburger Str 1,
20355 Hamburg, Germany
TEL: +49 40 3569 2123
WEB: http://www.windenergy-hamburg.de

HARBARTH SELBSTABAU-BEDARF FÜR WINDKRAFTANLAGEN
Hechelner Straβe 32,
78357 Mühlingen, Germany
TEL : + 49 7775 1215
FAX : + 49 7775 920080
CONTACT: Armin Harbarth

HESSEN ENERGIE GMBH
Mainzer straβe 98-102,
65189 Wiesbaden, Germany
TEL: +49 611 74623-0
FAX: +49 611 718224
E-MAIL: kontakt@hesssenenergie.de
WEB: http://www.hessenenergie.de
CONTACT: Dr Erik Siefart

INA WALZLAGER SCHAEFFLER OHG
91072 Herzogenaurach, Germany
TEL: +49 913 282 4457
E-MAIL: info@ina.com
WEB: http://www.ina.com

INGENIEURBURO SCHODER GBRMBH
Graf- Reisach-Strasse 6, D-86688
Graisbach, Germany
TEL: +49 9097 1818
FAX: +49 9097 1819
E-MAIL: info@schoder.de
WEB: http://www.schoder.de
CONTACT: Erwin Schoder

INGENIEURBÜRO FRIES DIPL-ING DIETER
Dompfaffenweg 25F,
22145 Hamburg, Germany
TEL: +49 40 38 606 90
FAX: +49 40 38 606 910
E-MAIL: ingenieurbuero_fries@t-online.de
CONTACT: Dieter Fries

INSTITUT FÜR UMWELTMEBUNG UND PLANUNG GMBH - UMP
Böckerstraβe 6,
30659 Hannover,
Germany
TEL: +49 511 5477-515
FAX: +49 511 6477-516
CONTACT: Stephan Konig

JACOBS ENERGIE GMBH
Rodemis Hallig, D-25813 Husum,
Germany
TEL: +49 4841 662 800
FAX: +49 4841 662 888
E-MAIL: info@jacobs-energie.com
WEB: http://www.jacobs-energie.com
CONTACT: Hans-Henning Jacobs

L&L ROTORSERVICE GMBH
Am Löh 17,27432,Hipstedt, Germany
TEL: +49 47 68 284
FAX: +49 47 68 800
E-MAIL: rotorservice-ll@t-online.de

LOHER AG
Berlin Sales Center Egellsstraβe 21,
13507 Berlin, Germany
TEL:+49 30 4301 2876
FAX: +49 304301 2846
EMAIL:loher.zwick@t-online.de
WEB:http://www.loher.de
CONTACT:Joachim Zwick

LOHMANN + STOLTERFOHT GMBH
Postfach 1860, D-58408 Witten, Germany
TEL: +49 23 02 87 7-2 45
FAX: +49 23 02 87 73 35
E-MAIL: info@lus.de
WEB: http://www.rexroth.com/lohmannstolterfoht
CONTACT: U Vieth

METALL-UND ANGLAGENBAU GMBH
Dorfstrabe 142, 15910 Krausnik,
Germany
TEL: +49 35472 213
FAX: +49 35472 464
CONTACT: Mr Markwik

MICROWIND GMBH
Bonnstrasse 18,
50321 Bruehl, Germany
TEL: +49 2232 411120
FAX: +49 2232 411122
E-MAIL: wenuswind@aol.com
CONTACT: Klaus Krieger

MOLZAN WINDKRAFTANLAGEN
Bleiche 3 Gewerbegebeit,
48366 Laer, Germany
TEL: +49 2554 1341
FAX:+49 25541078
CONTACT: G Molzan

NEG MICON
Osterport 2, 25872 Ostenfeld
Germany
TEL: +49 4845 700-0
FAX: +49 4845 700-17
CONTACT: Freidrich Prei Bler-J-be

NEPTUNI TECHNOPRODUCT GMBH
Lübecker Straβe 30,
Building 206,
18057 Rostock, Germany
TEL: +49 381 86 507-0
FAX: +49 381 86 507-19
CONTACT: Dr Horst Hannemann

NET NATÜRLICHE ENERGIETECHNIK GMBH
Altnegammer Hausdeich 36,
21039 Hamburg, Germany
TEL: +49 40 723-5000
FAX: +49 40 794 17465
CONTACT: Klaus Soltau

NORDEX AG
Bornbarch 2, 22848 Norderstedt,
Germany
TEL: +49 40 500 98 100
FAX: +49 40 500 98 101
WEB: http://www.nordex.de

OSTWIND-GROUP
Danzergasse 8, D-93047
Regensburg, Germany
TEL: +49 941 555 16
FAX: +49 941 555 26
E-MAIL: ostwind@donau.de
WEB: http://www.ostwind.de

PFLEIDERER WIND ENERGY GMBH
Ingolstadter Strabe 51,
92318 Neumarkt, Germany
TEL: +49 9181 28 –8420
FAX: +49 9181 28 – 607
E-MAIL: windenergy@pfleiderer.com
WEB: http://www.pfleiderer-wind.com

RED PROJECT MANAGEMENT GMBH
Hohenstaufenstrasse 1-3, D-60327
Frankfurt Am Main, Germany
TEL: +4969768063600
FAX: +4969768063601
E-MAIL: red@red-project.de
WEB: http://www.red-project.de
CONTACT: Dietrich Mayer

RENNERT ENERGIEPROJEKTE GMBH
Schmiedekamp 15,
D-38536 Meinersen, Germany
TEL : +49 5372 8210
FAX : +49 5372 6195
E-MAIL : renergie@t-online.de
CONTACT : Walter Fett

REPOWER SYSTEMS AG
Flughafenstrabe 54,
D-22335 Hamburg, Germany
TEL: +4940539307-0
FAX: +4940539307-77
E-MAIL: info@repower.de
CONTACT: Jurgen Millhoff

SEEBA ENERGIESYSTEME GMBH
Tielger Allee 60,
32351 Stemwede,
Germany
TEL: +4957738508
FAX: +4957738518
E-Mail: mail@seeba-online.de
WEB: http://www.seeba-online.de/eng/right.htm
CONTACT: Ewald Seebode

SOLARTECHNIK GEIGER
Windener Strabe 14,
85051 Ingolstradt, Germany
TEL:+49 8450 7390
FAX:+49 8450 7390
CONTACT: K Geiger

SUNSET ENERGIETECHNIK GMBH
Dept Solarenergy,
Sunset Building,
Industriestraβe 8-22,
D91325 Adelsdorf, Germany
TEL: +49 9195 9494 0
FAX: +49 9195 9494 290
EMAIL:info@sunset-solar.com
CONTACT: Klaus Waldera

THYSSEN RHEINSTAHL TECHNIK GMBH
Hans-Günther-Sohl-Straβe I,
D-40235 Düsseldorf,
Germany
TEL: +49 211 967-0
FAX: +49 211 967-9219
E-MAIL:heidkamp@ttc.thyssen.de
CONTACT:H B Ripkens

VESTAS DEUTSCHLAND GMBH
Otto-Hahn-Straβe 2,
25813 Husum,
Germany
TEL: +49 4841 971-0
FAX: +49 4841 971-41
CONTACT: Volker Friedrichsen

WALTER KRAUS GMBH
Postfach 410049,
86067 Augsburg,
Germany
TEL: +4982179609-0
FAX: +4982179609-26
E-MAIL: zentrale@kraus.de
WEB: http://www.kraus.de
CONTACT: S Haling

WINDTEST KAISER-WILHELM-KOOG GMBH
Sommerdeich 14b,
25709 Kaiser-Wilhelm-Koog,
TEL: +49 4856 901-0
FAX: +49 4856 901-49
E-MAIL: company.kwk@windtest.de
WEB: http://www.windtest.de
CONTACT: Volker Köhne

WIND TURBINEN SERVICE – WTS
Rudolf-Diesel-Strasse 7, 49479
Ibbenburen, Germany
TEL: +4954515936-0
FAX: +4954515936-22
WEB: http://www.wts-wind.de

WINERGY AG
Generators, Hauptstr 38,
13507 Berlin, Germany
TEL: +493305573496
FAX: +493305570980
E-MAIL: joachim.zwick@winergy-ag.com
WEB: http://www.winergy-ag.com
CONTACT: Joachim Zwick

WKT-WINDKRAFTANLANGEN
Hippolytusstraβe 11, 53840
Troisdorf, Germany
TEL: +49 2241 805488
FAX: +49 2241 805488

BIOMASS

BIOGAS-GRUPPEIM BUNDSCHUH EV
Schillerstraβe 34, 80336,
München,
Germany
TEL : +49 89 595393
FAX : +49 89 598147
CONTACT : Ekkehard Schneider

BIO-SYSTEM GMBH
Lohnerhofstraβe 7,
D-78467
Konstanz, Germany
TEL : +49 7531 690650
FAX : +49 7531 690660
E-MAIL :bio-system@t-online.de
WEB : http://www.bio-system.de
CONTACT : Michael Schuster

BTA GMBH & CO KG BIOTECHNISCHE ABFALL VERWERTUNG
Rottmanstraβe 18,
D-80333 Munchen,
Germany
TEL : +49 89 52 20 14
FAX : +49 89 523 23 29
E-MAIL : btatec@aol.com
CONTACT : Harry Wiljim

GERMANY

ECB ENVIRO BERLIN AG
Buhringstraβe 6,
13086 Berlin, Germany
TEL : + 49 30 47797 0
FAX : + 49 30 47757-101
E-MAIL : info@ecbag.de
WEB : http://www.ecbag.de
CONTACT : Martin Richter

ENERGIE-VERSORGUNG SCHWABEN AG-EVS
Postfach 1255,
88396 Biberach, Germany
TEL: +49 7351 531
FAX: +49 7351 532 150

FACHAGENTUR NACHWACHSENDE ROHSTOFFE EV-FNR
Public Relations, Hofplatz 1,
18276 Gulzow, Germany
TEL: +49 3843 6930-0
FAX: +49 3843 693 01 02
E-MAIL: info@fnr.de
WEB: http://www.fnr.de
CONTACT: Birger Kerckow

FUCHS GAS- UND WASSERTECHNIK GMBH
Stocktal 2, 56727 Mayen,
Germany
TEL: +49 2651 80 04-0
FAX: +49 2651 80 04-135
E-MAIL: info@fuchs-germany.com
CONTACT: Martin Fuchs

HOHMANN-KLOSE GMBH (NATÜRLICHE HEIZ SYSTEME)
DorfstraBe 121,
77767 Appenweier-Nesselried,
Germany
TEL: +49 7805 20 77
FAX: +49 7805 20 78
CONTACT: Karl-Heinz Werner Klose

LIGNASOL HOLZ-SOLAR-SYSTEME
Alberct-Wirt-Straβe 1, 72108
Rpttenburg-Ergenzingen.
Germany
TEL: +49 7457 69 77 15
FAX: +49 7457 69 77 16
E-MAIL: lignasol@bluewin.de
WEB: http://ww.lignasol.de

LINDE-KCA-DRESDEN GMBH
Environmental Protection Processes,
Badenbacher Str 80,
Postfach 210353
01265 Dresden, Germany
TEL : +49 351 4560-255
FAX : +49 351 4560-272
E-MAIL : lkca-dd@lkca.de
WEB : http://www.linde.de
CONTACT : Dr Hubert

KOHLER AND ZIEGLER
Anlagentechnik, Auweg 10c,
35457 Lollar, Germany
TEL: +49 6406 9103-0
FAX: +49 6406 9103-30
E-MAIL: info@koehler-ziegler.de
WEB: http://www.koehler-ziegler.de
CONTACT: Norbert Nordmeyer

LIPP GMBH
Plant Construction + Environment
Technology, Industriestrasse 36,
D-73497 Tannhausen, Germany
TEL: +49 7694 9003-0
FAX: +49 7694 9003-27
E-MAIL: vertrieb@lipp-system.de
WEB: http://www.lipp-system.de
CONTACT: Birgit Haas

MOCO MASCHINEN-UND APPARATEBAU GMBH
Grobe Stellweg 19,
68506 Viernheim, Germany
TEL: +49 6204 9685-0
FAX: +49 6204 751 58
E-MAIL: mocovhm@aol.com
WEB: http://members.aol.com/
mocovhm.index.html
CONTACT: Helmut Boll

MUCHEANLAGENBAU GMBH
Grosser Schratweg 19,
32657 Lemgo, Germany
TEL:+49 5261 97800-0
FAX: 49 5261 97800-50
CONTACT: Achim Sprick

SCHMACK BIOGAS GMBH
Schwandorfer Str 12,
93059 Regensburg, Germany
TEL: +4994183023-13
FAX: +4994183023-25
E-MAIL: Schmack.Biogas@t-online.de
WEB: http://www.Schmack-Biogas
Contact: Markus Ott

SPILLINGWERK GMBH
Werftstasse 5, D-20457 Hamburg
Germany
TEL: +49 40 78 91 75-0
FAX: +49 40 78 92 836
E-MAIL: info@spilling.de
WEB: http://www.spilling.de
CONTACT: Hartmut Kiehne

UWAS UMWELTTECHNIKUND ANLAGENBAU GMBH
BodenseestraBe 228,
81243 Munchen, Germany
TEL: +49 89 871 40 83
FAX: +49 89 871 11 10
CONTACT: Anselm J Gleixner

UMWEL TKONTOR RENEWABLE ENERGY AKTIENGESELLSCHAFT
Brusseler Allee 23, 41812 Erkelenz,
Germany
TEL: +4924319452-456
FAX: +4924319452-199
E-MAIL:
projekte@umweltkontor.com
WEB: http://www.Umweltkontor.com
CONTACT: Henry Lohmann

WALTER KRAUS GMBH
Postfach 410049,
86067 Augsburg, Germany
TEL: +49 82 17 96 09-0
FAX: +49 82 17 96 09 –26
E-MAIL: zentrale@kraus.de
WEB: http://www.kraus.de
CONTACT: S Haling

COGENERATION

BABCOCK BORSIG
Egellsstraβe 21, 13507,
Berlin, Germany
TEL : +49 30 4301 2468
FAX : +49 30 4301 2476
CONTACT : Dr. Malewski

ENCO ENERGIE-CONSULTING GMBH
Harleshauser Straβe, 20,
34130 Kassel, Germany
TEL : +49 561 60 08 02
FAX : +49 561 60 08 55

HENSCHEL RECYCLING TECHNIK GMBH
Henschelplatz 1,
34112 Kassel,
Germany
TEL: +49 561 801-6893
FAX: +49 561 801-6971
E-MAIL: wicht@hen
schel.thyssen.com
CONTACT: Wilfried Parlaska

HERWI-SOLAR GMBH
Industriegebeit 11,
D-63911 Klingenberg,
Germany
TEL: +49 9372 15 54
FAX: +49 9732 1695
CONTACT: Mr Barta

HÖFLER BLOCKHEIZKRAFT WERKE
LadestraBe 26, 88131 Lindau,
Germany
TEL: +49 8382 25057
FAX: +49 8382 23773
E-MAIL: info@hoefler-bhkw.de
WEB: http://www.hoefler-bhkw.de
CONTACT: Lothar Höfler

INCO INGENIEURBÜRO
Alexanderstraβe 69-71,
52062 Aachen, Germany
TEL: +49 241 474670
FAX: +49 241 404161
CONTACT: Martin Klima

INGENIEURBÜRO ENGLMANN GMBH
Meisenweg 6,
84160 Frontenhausen, Germany
TEL: +49 8732 23 06
FAX: +49 8732 66 10
CONTACT: Walter Englmann

INGENIEURBÜRO DR SCHIWEK
Lindenring 40,
79189 Bad Krozingen, Germany
TEL: +49 7633 14016
FAX: +49 7633 14015
CONTACT: Dr Peter Schiwek

KRUPP-UHDE GMBH
Friedrich-Uhde Straβe 15, 44141
Dortmund, Germany
TEL: +49 231 547 2335
FAX: +49 231 547 3032
CONTACT: Jochen Keller

MÜLLER (KARL FRIEDRICH) BERATENDER INGENIEUR
Felkestraβe 1, 55562 Bad
Sobernheim, Germany
TEL: +49 6751 6686
FAX:+49 6751 6676
CONTACT: Karl Friedrich Müller

SOKRATHERM GMBH ENERGIE- UND WÄRMETECHNIK
Milchstraβe 12,
32120 Hiddenhausen, Germany
TEL: +49 5221 96210
FAX: +49 5221 66063
E-MAIL: sokratherm@aol.com
WEB: http://www.sokratherm.de
CONTACT: Mr Pollmeier

UMAG TECHNOLOGIE GMBH
Siemenstrabe 10-12m 25813
Husum, Germany
TEL: +49484196500
FAX: +494841965050
E-MAIL: sales@umag.com
WEB: http://www.umag.de
CONTACT: Hartwig Cardell

WEIER ELECTRIC GMBH
Otto-Hahn-Strabe 7, 23701 Eutin,
Germany
TEL: +49 4521 8040
FAX: +49 4521 80444
E-MAIL: info@weier-electric.de
WEB: http://www.weier-electric.de
CONTACT: Jost Wendt

HYDGROGEN

DEUTSCHER WASSERSTOFF VERBAND EV. DWR
Under den. Eichen 87,
12205 Berlin, Germany
TEL : + 49 700 49376 835
FAX : + 49 700 49375 339
E-MAIL : h2@dwv.info.de
WEB : http://www.dwv.info.de
CONTACT : Ulrich Schmidtchen

H-TEC
Lindenstrabe 48A, 23558 Lubeck,
Germany
TEL: +49 451 498950
FAX: +49 451 4989515
CONTACT: Uwe Kueter

MOOSMANN(JOSEF) ENTWICKLUNG UND FERTIGUNG VON ENERGIESPARSYSTEMEN
Affentale 2a,78144 Tennenbronn,
Germany
TEL: +49 7729 1761
FAX: +49 7729 615
CONTACT:JosesfMoosmann

WA-TECINGENIEURBURO MARTINS STRIPPEL
Fasanenweg 1,
D-64291 Darmstadt, Germany
TEL: +49 6151 351780
FAX: +49 6151 351780
WEB: http://www.members.aol.com/strippel
CONTACT: Martin Strippel

ELECTRIC VEHICLES

SOLARMOBIL-SOLARPOLIS (R)
Graefestraβe 18,
10967 Berlin / Kreuzbergh, Germany
TEL:+49 30 69 508 501
FAX:+49 30 69 508 503
E-MAIL: solar@berlin.snafu.de
WEB: http://www.solarpolis.de
CONTACT: Arno Paulus

SMALL HYDGRO

ARNO EICHMANN CHE ELECTRONIK
Untere HainbergstraBe 3,
35466 Rabenau, Germany
TEL : +49 6407 7058
FAX : +49 6407 8846
CONTACT : Arno Eichmann

BEGA WASSERKRAFT ANLAGEN GMBH
Herderallee 30, 44791, Bochum, Germany
TEL : +49 234 584270
FAX : +49 234 584370
CONTACT : Thomas Guenther

GESELLSCHAFT FÜR PLANUNG MASCHINEN UND MUHLENBAU ERHARD MUHR MBH
Grafenstraβe 27,
83098 Brannenburg, Germany
TEL : + 49 8034 9072-0-
FAX : + 49 8034 9072-24
E-MAIL : muhr@hypernet.de
WEB: www.muhr.com
CONTACT: Roland Muhr

HYDROWATT GMBH
Am Hafen 5, D-76189 Karlsruhe,
Germany
TEL: +49 721 832 860
FAX: +49 721 831 860
E-MAIL: soko@hydrowatt.de
WEB: http://www.hydrowatt.de
CONTACT: Klaus Sommerkorn

INGENIEURBÜRO FLOECKSMÜHLE
Bachstraβe 62-64,
52066 Aachen, Germany
TEL: +49 241 949860
FAX: +49 241 94986-13
WEB: http://
www.floecksmuehle.com
CONTACT: U Dumont

KOPPERN GMBH
Königseiner Straβe 2-12, 45506
Hattingen, Germany
TEL: +49 2324 207 0
FAX: 49 2324 207 207
E-MAIL: info@koeppern.com
WEB: http://www.koeppern.com

OSSBERGER GMBH + CO
Power Generation, Otto-Rieder-Str 7,
91781 Weissenburg Bavaria, Germany
TEL: +49 9141 977-0
FAX: +49 9141 97720
E-MAIL: ossberger@ossberger.de
WEB: http://www.ossberger.de
CONTACT: Helmut Erdmannsdorfer

REITTER (DIPLING ELMAR) WASSERKRAFTANLAGEN
Braunselweg 1,
D-89611 Rechtenstein, Germany
TEL : + 49 7375 212
FAX : + 49 7375 7347
E-MAIL : elmar.reitter@t-online.de
CONTACT : Elmar Reitter

SIEMENS A G
KWU H Ref G, PO Box 3220,
91050 Erlangen, Germany
TEL: +49 9131 18 7605
FAX: +49 9131 18 7714
EMAIL: Dieter.Fromm@erlll.siemens.de
WEB: http://www.siemens.de
CONTACT: D Fromm

GERMANY

VOITH SIEMENS HYDRO POWER GENERATION GMBH & CO KG
Advertising / Marketing Research,
PO Box 2010,
89510 Heidenheim,
Germany
TEL: +49 7321 37 6848
FAX: +49 7321 37 7828
E-MAIL: barbara.fischer.aup perle@voith.de
WEB: http:// www.voithsiemenshydropower.com
CONTACT: Barbara Fischer-Aupperle

WALCHER ELEKTRONIK STEUERUNGSTECHNIK TRANSFORMATOREN
Industriepark Rhon,
36124 Eichenzell, Germany
TEL: +49 6659 1877
FAX: +49 6659 4372
WEB: http://www.walcher.com
CONTACT: Thomas Pruessner

WASSERKRAFT VOLK AG - WKV
Am Stollen 13, D-79261 Bleibach,
Germany
TEL: +49 7685 9106-0
FAX: +49 7985 9106-10
E-MAIL: wkv.ag@t-online.de
CONTACT: Manfred Volk

TIDAL / OCEAN

INGENIEURBÜRO PERNER & WENDT
Badstraβe 46,
93059 Regensburg,
Germany
TEL: +49 7231 358646
FAX: +49 40 3603385017
E-MAIL: rolandwendt@aol.com
CONTACT: R Wendt

GEOTHERMAL

DEUTSCHEMONTAN TECHNOLOGIE GMBH
GeoTec Division,
Am Technologie Park
1, D-45307 Essen, Germany
TEL : + 49 201 172 1970
FAX : + 49 201 172 1971
E-MAIL : gt.info@dmt.de
WEB : http://www.dmt.de
CONTACT : Bernd Hildebrandt

ERDWARME-SOLARENERGIE
Zum Eichholz 2,
57399 Brachthausen, Germany
TEL : +49 2723 2437
FAX: + 49 2723 4669
CONTACT : Georg Haase

GEOTHERMIE NEUBRANDENBURG (GTN) GMBH
Lindenstraβe 39, 17033
Neubrandenburg, Germany
TEL : + 49 395 367 7412
FAX : + 49 395 367 7411
E-MAIL : gtn@nbnet.de
CONTACT: Dr. Hebert Scheider

GEOTHERMISCHE VEREINIGUNG EV
Gartenstraβe 36,
49744 Geeste, Germany
TEL : + 49 5907 545
FAX : + 49 5907 7379
E-MAIL : geothermische-vereinigung@t-online.de
WEB: www.geothermie.de

JUSTUS-LIEBIG-UNIVERSITÄT
Institut für Angewandte
Geowissenschaften, Diezstrasse 15,
D-35390 Giessen, Germany
TEL: +49 641 99 36124
FAX: +49 641 99 36109
CONTACT: Dr Burthard Sanner

MESY-GEOMEB SYSTEME GMBH
Meesmannstraβe 49,
44807 Bochum, Germany
TEL: +49 234 54531
FAX: +49 234 54533
E-MAIL: mesy.bochum@t-online.de
CONTACT: Prof F Rummel

RHEINISCH-WESTFÄLISCHE TECH HSCHULE AACHEN
Lehrstuhi fur Geologie
Geochemie und Lagerstatten,
Lochnerstraβe 4-20,
5100 Aachen, Germany
TEL : +49 241 80 57 48
FAX : +49 241 8888-152
E-MAIL : lek@lek.rwth_aachen.de
CONTACT : Prof R Littke

WASTE TO ENERGY

ABR GMBH
Nickeputz 27, S2349 Duren,
Germany
TEL: +49 2421 610 10
FAX: +49 2421 665 44
CONTACT: Norbert Hettmer

BABCOCK BORSIG POWER
Environment, Fabrikstrabe 1,
D-51643 Gummersback,
Germany
TEL : +49 2261 85-0
FAX : +49 2261 85-2999
WEB : http:// www.babcockborsigpower.de
CONTACT : Mr. Thome

BIG ENTSORGUNGSTECHNOLOGIEN GMBH
Im Farchet, 13,
83646 Bad Tolz,
Germany
TEL : +49 8041 78 77-0
FAX : +49 8041 18 22
CONTACT : Dr Primus

BLOOM ENGINEERING
PVT Division Buttgenbachstraβe 14,
40549 Dusseldorf,
Germany
TEL : +49 211 50 09 10
FAX : +49 211 50 13 97
E-MAIL : biomgmbh@compuserve.com
CONTACT : Joset Domagala

BORSIG ENERGY
GVP, Homberger Strasse 2,
40882 Ratingen,
Germany
TEL : +49 2102 855 72
FAX : +49 2102 855 868
E-MAIL : gerd_koenig@balcke-duerr.de
WEB : http://www.balcke-duerr.de
CONTACT : Mr. Koenig

DOPPSTADT DV GMBH
Steinbrink 4,
D-42555 Velbert,
Germany
TEL : + 49 2052 889 0
FAX : + 49 2052 889 160

FARMATIC ANLAGENBAU GMBH
Kolberger Straβe 13,
24589 Nortorf,
Germany
TEL: +49 43 92 91 77-0
FAX: +49 43 92 58 64

GAS ENERGIETECHINIK GMBH
Hessenstraβe 57,
47809 Krefeld,
Germany
TEL: +49 2151 5255-0
FAX: + 49 2151 5255-55
E-mail : w.weskamp@gas-energie.de
WEB: http://www.gas-energie.de
CONTACT: Walter Wes Kamp

HAASE ENERGIETECHNIK GMBH
Gadelander Straβe 172,
24531 Neumunster,
Germany
TEL : + 49 4321 8780
FAX : + 49 4321 8789
E-MAIL : haase-energietechnik@t-online.de
CONTACT: Oliver Martens

HAMMEL RECYCLINGTECHNIK GMBH
Leimbacher Straβe 103,
36433 Bad Salzungen,
Germany
TEL : + 49 36 95 69 91-0
FAX : + 49 36 95 69 91-23
E-MAIL : info@hammel.de
WEB: www.hammel.de

HEINRICH HÖLTER TER GMBH
BeisensstraBe 39-41,
45964 Gladbeck,
Germany
TEL: +49 2043 9780
FAX: +49 2043 978140
E-MAIL: hhoelter@t-online.de

INGENIEURBÜRO SUTTOR
Steinbach 2,
D-84152 Mengkofen,
Germany
TEL: +49 8774 1342
FAX: +49 8774 424
E-MAIL: suttor@t-online.de
CONTACT: Wolfgang Suttor

MARTIN GMBH FÜR UMWELT- UND ENERGIETECHNIK
Leopoldstraβe 248,
D-80807 Munchen,
Germany
TEL: +49 89 356 17-0
FAX: +49 89 356 17-299
E-MAIL: mail@martingmbh.de
WEB: http://www.martingmbh.de
CONTACT: D Kreuch

SPILLINGWERK GMBH
Werftstasse 5, D-20457 Hamburg
Germany
TEL: +49 40 78 91 75-0
FAX: +49 40 78 92 836
E-MAIL: info@spilling.de
WEB: http://www.spilling.de
CONTACT: Hartmut Kiehne

STEAG AG
STEAG Power International,
Ruttenscheider Straβe 1-3,
45128 Essen, Germany
TEL: +49 201 801 1215
FAX: +49 201 801 6167
E-MAIL:100322.1523@compuserve.com
WEB:http://www.steag.de

STEINMULLER GMBH
Fabrikstrasse I,
51641 Gummersbach,
Germany
TEL: +49 2261 85-4030
FAX: +49 2261 85-4015
CONTACT:Mrs Amrai Schlichter

UET GMBH
Grafinger Straβe 2,
81671 München, Germany
TEL : +49 89 41 86 01-0
FAX : +49 41 86 01-180
E-MAIL : uet@uet.de
WEB : http://www.uet.de
CONTACT : Kartheinz Maurath

ENERGY EFFICIENCY

DEUTSCHE ENERGIE-CONSULT INGENIEURGSELLSCHAFT MBH DECON
Norsk Data Straβe 1, D-61352 Bad. Hamburg, Germany
TEL : + 49 6172 945040
FAX : + 49 6172 9450-20
E-MAIL : decon@decon.de
WEB : http://www.decon.de

EBÖK INGENEURBURO FÜR ENERGIEBERATUNG HAUSTECHNIK UNID OKOLOGISCHE KONZEPTE GBR
Reutlinger Straβe, 16,
72072 Tübingen, Germany
TEL : + 49 7071 9399 - 0
FAX : + 49 7071 9394 99
E-MAIL : mail@eboek.de
WEB : http://www.eboek.de
CONTACT : C Kahlert

ENDRICH (HORST) INGENIEURBÜRO FÜR ENERGIE UND UMWELTTECHNIK
Billinghauser, Straβe 51,
97225 Zellingen,Germany
TEL : +49 9364 93 19
FAX : +49 9364 63 97
CONTACT : Horst Endrich

INGENIEURBÜRO SIEGISMUND+ PARTNER BERATENDE INGENIEURE VBI
Masurenweg I,
61118 Bad Vilbel, Heilsberg,
Germany
TEL: +49 6101 830 33
FAX: +49 6101 887 59
E-MAIL: info@siegismund.de
WEB: http://www.siegismund.de
CONTACT: Reinhard Siegismund

INSTALLA-TOPTHERM GMBH
Bau und Haustechnik,
Lindenau 8-1047661 Issum,
Germany
TEL: +49 2835 3883
FAX: +49 2835 3884
E-MAIL: info@trisolar.de
WEB: http://www.trisolar.de
CONTACT: Rolf-Diether Weiblen

INSTITUT WOHNEN UND UMEWLT GMBH - IWU
AnnastraBe 15,
64285 Darmstadt, Germany
TEL: +49 6151 2904-0
FAX: +49 6151 2904-97
E-MAIL: info@iwu.de
WEB: http://www.iwu.de
CONTACT: Tobias Loga

IST ENERGIECOM GMBH
Stadtjägerstraβe 11, D-86152
Augsburg, Germany
TEL: +49 821 3 46 66 0
FAX: +49 821 3 46 66 11
E-MAIL: info@ist-energiecom.de
WEB: http://www.ist-energiecom.de

JENS TIMAEUS ENERGIE MANAGEMENT GMBH
Bilenbarg 27a. 22397 Hamburg,
Germany
TEL: +49 40 608 25363
FAX: +49 40 608 2821
CONTACT: Jens Timaeus

KELLER LUFTTTECHNIK GMBH
Neue Weilheimer Straβe 30, 73230
Kircheim/Tech, Germany
TEL: +49 70 21 5 74-0
FAX: +49 70 21 5 24 30
E-MAIL: info@kl-direkt.de
WEB: http://www.kl-direkt.de

KROTZ KONZEPT-INTERDISCIPLINARY DEVELOPING
Neckarhalde 33, 72700 Tübingen,
Germany
TEL: +49 7071 410838
FAX: +49 7071 410938
E-MAIL: solararchitektur@addcom.de
CONTACT: Thomas Krötz

NESTRO LUFTTECHNIK GMBH
Odenwaldring 9,
63934 Röllbach,
Germany
TEL: +49 9372 137-0
FAX: +49 9372 137-260
E-MAIL:nestro.roelibach@t-online.de
WEB: http://www.nestro.de
CONTACT: Paulus Nettelnstroth

PLANUNGSGRUPPE ENERGIE UND TECHNIK - PLANET
Humboldt Straβe 38, D-26121
Oldenburg, Germany
TEL: +49 441 85051
FAX:+49 441 88057
E-MAIL : planet.oldenburg@t-online.de
WEB:http://
www.planungsgemeinschaft.de/planet
CONTACT: Robert Steinberger

GERMANY

RENORGA BERATUNGS-GESELLSCHAFT FÜR RATIONELLE ENERGIEVERWENDUNG ORGANISATION UND INNOVATION MBH & CO
Käkenflur 14A,
D-22419 Hamburg, Germany
TEL : +49 40 527 3091
FAX : +49 40 527 3092
CONTACT : Lothar Schedereit

UNABHÄNGIGES INSTITUT FÜR UMWELTFRAGEN EV
Greifswalder Str 4,
10405 Berlin, Germany
TEL : +49 30 428 49930
FAX : +49 30 2428 00485
E-MAIL : energie@ufu.de
WEB : http://www.ufu.de
CONTACT : Malte Schmidthals

VEW ENERGY AG
Hauptverwaltung, Sonnenenergie-Forum, Rheinlanddamm 24, 44139 Dortmund, Germany
TEL: +49 231 438 4965
FAX: +49 231 438 4967
E-MAIl: sonnenergie-firyn@vew.de
WEB: http://www.vew.de
CONTACT: G Schulte

VOLQUARDSEN (JENS) VOLLWÄRMESCHUTZ GMBH
Fährblick 52, 24790 Schacht-Audorf, Germany
TEL: +49 4331 92736
FAX: +49 4331 93410
CONTACT: Jens-Peter Volquardsen

VSK ENERGIE INNOVATION GMBH
Freienberger Weg 15,
D-53639 Königswinter, Germany
TEL: +49 2223 911 236
FAX: +49 2223 911 237
E-MAIL: w-j_schmidt-kuester@t-online.de
CONTACT: Dr Schmidt-Kuster

WÄRMEBÜRO KLAFT GMBH
Untere Konigsstrabe 78-82,
34117 Kassel, Germany
TEL: +49 561 77 30 82
FAX: +49 561 144 67
CONTACT: Herbert Klaft

FINANCE / BANKING

DEUTSCHE STRUCTURED FINANCE
Westendstrabe 24,
D-60325 Frankfurt, Germany
TEL: +49 69 97 1497-22
FAX: +49 69 97 1497-25
E-MAIL: M.Kittelmann@dsf-fra.de
WEB: http://www.DSF-FRA.de
CONTACT: Manfred Kittelmann

ENERGYNATICS GMBH
Mühlstraβe 51, 63225 Langen, Germany
TEL : + 49 177 829077
FAX : + 49 8 7674152
E-MAIL: thoma.ackermann@icec.org
WEB: http://www.energynactics.com
CONTACT : Thomas Ackermann

INGENIEURBÜRO SOLAR ENERGIE INFORMATION
Buchenstraβe 38, 82054 Sauerlach, Germany
TEL: +49 8104 669903
FAX: +49 8104 669905
E-MAIL:
a.horn@amazonas.comlink.apc.org
WEB: http://members.aol.com/axelhorn/homepage.htm
CONTACT: Axel Horn

PLAMBECK NEUE ENERGIEN AG
Peter-Henlein-Strabe 2-4, 27472 Cuxhaven, Germany
TEL: +49 47 21 718-06
FAX: +49 47 21 718-200
E-MAIL: info@plambeck.de
WEB: http://www.plambeck.de

THE HUPPMANN GROUP
PO Box 220,
D-97305 Kitzingen, Germany
TEL: +49 9321 303-0
FAX: +49 9321 303119
E-MAIL: sales@huppmann.com
WEB: http://www.huppmann.com
CONTACT: Thomas Hackensellner

UMWELTKONTOR
Planning / Project Management, Rheinstraβe 7,
41836 Huckelhoven, Germany
TEL : +49 2433 970385
FAX : +49 2433 970137
E-MAIL : zirbes@umweltkontor.com
WEB : http://www.umweltkontor.com
CONTACT : Gerald Zirbes

UNIT ENERGY EUROPE AG
Ober-Eschbacher Strasse 109,
613528 Bad Homburg,Germany
TEL: +49 6172 9245-0
FAX: +49 6172 9245-99
E-MAIL: admin@unit-energy.com
WEB: http:// www.unit-energy.com

VEREIN SONNENKRAFT FREISING EV
Bahnhofstrasse 1,
85354 Freising, Germany
TEL: +49 8161 12256
FAX: +49 8161 12256
CONTACT: Dr E Schrimpff

VERSICHERUNGSBÜROFÜR UNWELTPROJEKTE GMBH
PO Box 1203, 25443 Quikborn, Germany
TEL: +49 4106 6361-0
FAX: +49 4106 636130
E-MAIL: vfu.quickborn@t-online.de
WEB: http://home.t-online.de/home/vfu.quickborn
CONTACT: Peter Paulowski

WINDWÄRTS ENERGIE GMBH
Wind Energy Bruderstraβe 4B,
30159 Hannover, Germany
TEL: +49 511 13323
FAX: +49 511 15217
E-MAIL: 101534.1566@compuserve.com
WEB: http://www.windwrts.de
CONTACT: Roger Lutjen

ASSOCIATION

ASEW
Volksgartenstraβe 22,
50677 Koln, Germany
TEL : +49 221 93 18 19 0
FAX : + 49 221 93 18 19 9
E-MAIL : info@asew.de
WEB : http://asew.de
CONTACT : Rosa Hemmers

BUND DER ENERGIEVERBRAUCHER EV
Grabenstr 17, 53619, Rheinbreitbach, Germany
TEL : +49 2224 92270
FAX : +49 2224 10321
E-MAIL : bde.ev@t-online.de
WEB : http://www.energieverbraucher.de
CONTACT : Dr Aribert Peters

BUNDESVERBAND SOLAR ENERGIE EV-BSE
Elisabethstraβe 34,
80796 Munchen, Germany
TEL : +49 89 278 134 24
FAX : +49 89 278 128 91
CONTACT : Frido Flade

BUNDESVERBAND WINDENERGIE-BWE
Herrrenteichstrasse 1,
49074 Osnabrück, Germany
TEL : +49 541 35060 0
FAX : +49 541 3506030
E-MAIL : bwe-os@t-online.de
WEB : http://www.wind-energie.de
CONTACT : Heinrich Barbett

CARMEN EV
Schulgasse 18, 94315,
Straubing, Germany
TEL : +49 9421 960 300
FAX : +49 9421 960 333
E-MAIL : c.a.r.m.n.@t-online.de
WEB : http://www.carmen-ev.de
CONTACT : Dr. Werner Döller

CARSTEN ARNDT
Tiegartenstraβe 66,
01219 Dresden, Germany
TEL : +49 351 471 3111

DEUTSCHERFACHVERBAND SOLAR ENERGIE - DFS
German Solar Energy Association
Bertoldstraβe 45,
79098, Freiburg, Germany
TEL : + 49 761 29620 90
FAX : + 49 761 29620 99
E-MAIL : dfs.freiburg@t.online.de
WEB : http://
www.dfs.solarframes.de

ENERGIE KOMMUNAL SCHLESWIG-HOLSTEIN EV. EKSH
Hohenwestedter Straβe 6,
24589 Nortorf, Germany
TEL: +49 4392 3153
FAX: +49 4392 2563
E-MAIL: kdiehlmann@t-online.de
CONTACT : Klaus Diehlmann

FACHVERBAND DAMPFKESSEL BEHÄLTER UND ROHRLEITUNGSBAU EV-FDBR
Sternstraβe 36,
40479 Dusseldorf, Germany
TEL: +49 211 498700
FAX: +49 211 498736
E-MAIL: info@fdbr.de
WEB: http://www.fdbr.de
CONTACT: Dr. Maass

FORSHUNGSVERBUND SONNENENERGIE
c/o DLR, 51170 Köln, Germany
TEL: +49 2203 601-3625
FAX: +49 2203 601-4740
E-MAIL:fvs@dlr.de
CONTACT: Dr. H P Hertlein

INGENIEURBÜRO SOLAR ENERGIE INFORMATION
Buchenstraβe 38,
82054 Sauerlach,Germany
TEL: +49 8104 669903
FAX: +49 8104 669905
EMAIL: a.horn@amazonas.comlink.apc.org
WEB: http://members.aol.com/
axelhorn/homepage.htm
CONTACT: Axel Horn

INITIATIVE FUER REGENERATIVE ENERGIEN IN SACHSEN EV
Heinrich-Heine-Str 1,
D-09599 Freiberg, Germany
TEL: +49 3731 21 2920
FAX: +49 3731 21 2920
E-MAIL: info@ires-ev.de
WEB: http://www.ires-ev.de
CONTACT: Stephen Riedel

INTERNATIONAL SOLAR ENERGY SOCIETY-ISES
International Headquarters, Villa Tannheim, Wesentalstraβe 50,
D-79115 Freiburg, Germany
TEL: +49 761 459 06-0
FAX: +49 761 459 06 99
E-MAIL: hq@ises.org
WEB:http://www.ises.org

LAND WIRTSCHAFTLICHE ARBEITSGRUPPE BIOKRAFTSTOFFE
Godesberger Allee 142-148,
53175 Bonn, Germany
TEL: +49 228 8198-232
FAX: +49 228 8198-233
CONTACT: Dietrich Klein

VERBAND KOMMUNALE ABFALL WIRTSCHAFT UND STADTREINIGUNGEV - VKS
Lindenalle 11-17, 50968 Koln
(Marienburg), Germany
TEL: +49 221 3771-135
FAX: +49 221 372 527
CONTACT: Dr. Achim W Schroter

GOVERNMENT

INGENIEURBÜRO HÖGNER
Gaymuhle 10,
54673 Rodershausen, Germany
TEL: +49 6524 93020
FAX: +49 6524 93021
CONTACT: Georg Högner

RESEARCH & DEVELOPMENT

ABEKING & RASMUSSEN ROTEC GMBH
An Der Fahre 2, 27809 Lemwerder
Germany
TEL: +49 421 67 33-0
FAX: + 49 421 67 33-709
CONTACT: Hanno Pfitzer

ARBEITSGEMEINSCHAFT SOLAR
Karl-Heinz-Beckurts Straβe 13,
52428 Julich, Germany
TEL : +49 2461 690-601
FAX : +49 2461 690-890
Email : info@ag-solar.de
WEB : http://ww.ag-solar.de

BREMEN OVERSEAS RESEARCH AND DEVELOPMENT ASSOCIATION EV-BORDA
Breitenweg 55, 28195,
Bremen, Germany
TEL : +49 421 1 37 18

BREMER ENERGIE-INSTITUT
Fahrenheitstraβe ,
28359, Bremen
Germany
TEL : +49 421 201 43-0
FAX : +49 421 29 9986
E-MAIL : bremer-energie-institut@t-online.de
WEB : http://www.t-online.de/home/
bremer-energe-institut
CONTACT : Dr Karin John

BUNDESFORSCHUNGSANSTALT FUR FORST-UND HOLZWIRTSCHAFT
Institu für Forstgenetik und
Forstpflanzenzüchtung,
Sieker Landstraβe 2, 22927,
Brobhansdorf, Germany
TEL : +49 4102 696-0
FAX : +49 696-200
E-MAIL :inst2g@aixh0001holz.uni-hamburg.de
WEB : http://www.dainet.de/bfh
CONTACT : Dr. J Muns

BUNDESFORSCHUNGSANSTALT FUR LANDWIRTSCHAFT
FAL-Institut Für Technologie
Bundasallee 50, 38116
Braunschweig, Germany
TEL : +49 531 596-508
FAX : +49 531 596-363
E-MAIL : peter.weiland@fal.de
WEB : http://www.fal.de
CONTACT : Dr P Weiland

BUREAU VERITAS
Sachsenfeld 4 Haus 5,
Hansa Carree 20006,
Hamburg, Germany
TEL : +49 40 23 62 5-0
FAX : +49 40 23 62 5-100

CENTRE FOR SOLAR ENERGY AND HYDROGEN RESEARCH
HeBbruhlstraβe 21c,
D-70565 Stuttgart,
Germany
TEL : +49 711 787 0219
FAX : +49 711 787 0230
E-MAIL : bandi@tsocstgt.e-technik.uni-stuttgart.de
WEB : http://www.zsoc-etecnk.unisttutgart.de
CONTACT : Dr. Andrees Bandk

DEUTSCHESZENTRUM FÜR LUFT - UND RAUMFAHRT EV DLR
Solare Energietechnik, Linder Höhe
511747, Köln, Germany
TEL : + 49 2203 601 2479
FAX : + 49 2203 66900
E-MAIL : solare-energietechnick@dlr.de
WEB : http://www.dlr.deet.htm
CONTACT: Dr. Manfred Becker

DEWI - GERMAN WIND ENERGY INSTITUTE
Ebertstraβe 96, 26382,
Wilheimsnaven, Germany
TEL : + 49 4421 4808-0
FAX : + 49 4421 4808-43
WEB : http://www. dewi.de
CONTACT: Dr. Knud Rehfeldt

EWFE BRENNWERT HEIZTECHNIK GWBH
Haferwende 23,
28357 Bremen, Germany
TEL: + 49 421 2079-0
FAX: +49 421 2079-997
E-MAIL: ewfe.bremen@t-online.de
CONTACT: T Gaux

FACHHOCHSCHULE FRANKFURT AMMAIN
Technology Transfer,
Nibelungenplatz 1,
60318 Frankfurt
Am Main, Germany
TEL: +49 69 1533 2160
FAX: +49 69 1533 2165
E-MAIL: tib@wt.fh-frankfurt.de
WEB: http://www.fh.frankfurt.de
CONTACT: P Sulzbach

FACHHOCHSCHULE GIEEN FRIEDBERG
Zentrum für Umwelttechnologie.
Labor for anaerobe
Verfahrenstechnik,
WiesenstraBe 14,
35390 Gieben, Germany
TEL: +49 641 385 80
FAX: +49 641 385 80
E-MAIL: thomas.luthardtbehle
@bau.fh-giessen.de
WEB: http://www.fh-gissen.de/
web_wis/gosch.htm
CONTACT: Thomas Luthardt

FACHHOCHSCHULE OSTFRIESLAND FACHBEREICH MASCHINENBAU
Constantiaplatz 4,
26723 Emden, Germany
TEL: +49 4921 807-315
FAX: +49 4921 807-311
CONTACT: Prof. Klaus Kehl

FACHHOCHSCHULE WIESBADEN
Technology and Knowledge Transfer
Kurt-Schumacher-Ring 18,
65197 Wiesbaden, Germany
TEL: +49 611 9495-123
FAX: +49 611 44 46 96
CONTACT: Christoph Rinneberg

FACHHOCHSCHULEKOLN
FB Elektrische Energietechnik
Forschungsschwerpunk,
Betzdorfer StraBe 2,
50679 Koln, Germany
TEL: +49 221 8275-2763
FAX: +49 221 9275-2836
E-MAIL: heinen@server.et-fh-koeln.de
CONTACT: Prof. K U Heinen

FACHOCHSCHULEKONSTANZ
IAF/EWIS,
Postfach 100 543,
78405 Konstanz, Germany
TEL: +49 7531 206 406
FAX: +49 7531 206 400
E-MAIL: iaf-ewis@fh-konstanz.de
WEB: http://ewis.fh-konstanz.de
CONTACT: Prof. Christian Schaffrin

FEDERAL INSTITUTE FOR MATERIALS RESEARCH AND TESTING-BAM
Unter den Eichen 87,
12205 Berlin,
Germany
TEL: +49 30 8104-0
FAX: +49 30 8112029
E-MAIL:info@bam.de
WEB:http://www.bam.de
CONTACT: Dr. Jürgen Lexow

FERNWARME-FORSCHUNGSINSTITUTIN HANNOVER EV
Max-von-Laue Straβe 23,
30966 Hemmingen 1,
Germany
TEL: + 49 511 943 700
FAX: + 49 511 943 7070
E-MAIL:ffi@fernwaerme.de
WEB:http://www.fernwaerme.de
CONTACT: Claus Dieter Kruse

FORSCHUNGINSTITUT FÜR KERNTECHNIK UND ENGERGIEWANDLUNG EV
Pfaffenwaldring 31,
70550 Struttgart,
Germany
TEL: +49 711 685-2137
FAX: +49 711 685-2010
E-MAIL: ike@ike.uni-sttruttgart.de

FORSCHUNGS INTSITUT FOR WÄRMESCHUTZ
Postfach 1525,
82157 Grafelfing,
Germany
TEL: +49 89 85800-0
CONTACT: Peter Hefter

FRAUNHOFER INSTITUT FÜR CHEMISCHE TECHNOLOGIE-ICT
Applied Electrochemistry,
Joseph-von Fraunhofer-Straβe,
76318 Pfinztal, (Berghausen),
Germany
TEL: +49 721 4640-444
FAX: +49 721 4640-526
E-MAIL:Kra@ict.fhg.de
WEB: www.igb.fhg.de
CONTACT: Dr. Michael Krausa

FRAUNHOFER INSTITUT FÜR GREENZFLACHEN UND BLOVERFAHRENSTECHNIK
Nobelstraβe 12,
70569 Stuttgart,
Germany
TEL: +49 711 970-4000
FAX: +49 711 970 4200
E-MAIL:info@igb.fhg.de
CONTACT: Dr. Walter Trösch

FRAUNHOFER-INSITUT FÜR BAUPHYSIK
Postfach 80 04 69,
Miesbacher Straβe 10,
83607 Holzkirchen,
Germany
TEL: +49 8024 643-0
FAX: +49 9024 643-66
CONTACT: Karl A Gertis

FRAUNHOFER-INSTITUT FÜR HOLZFORSCHUNG WILLHELM-KLAUDITZ-INSTITUT
Bienroder Weg 54E,
38108 Braunschweig,
Germany
TEL: +49 531 2155-0
FAX: +49 531 2155-200
E-MAIL: info@wki.fhg.de
WEB: www.wki.fhg.de
CONTACT: Dr. Rainer Marutzky

FRAUNHOFER INSTITUT FUR SOLARE ENERGIESYSTEME – ISE
Oltmannsstrabe 5,
79100 Freiburg,
Germany
TEL: +49 761 4588-0
FAX: + 49 761 4588-100
E-MAIL: info@ise.fhg.de
WEB: http://www.ise.fhg.de
CONTACT: Karin Schneider

GERHARD-MERCATOR-UNIVERSITÄ TDUISBURG
FB Maschinenbau FG
Energietechnik/Prof Sperlich,
Lotharstrabe 1,
47048 Duisburg, Germany
TEL : + 49 203 379 3792921
FAX : + 49 203 379 3085
E-MAIL : verheyen@uni-duisburg.de
WEB: www.uni-duisburg.de
CONTACT: Othmar Verheyen

GERMAN AEROSPACE CENTER DLR
Program Directorate Energy,
Linder Höhe, Köln D-51147, Germany
TEL: + 49 2203 601-3630
FAX : + 49 2203 6014712
E-MAIL : energietechnik@dir.de
WEB: www.germanlloyd.org
CONTACT: Christian Nath

GESELLSCHAFT FÜR UMWELT PLANUNG STUTTGART EV - GUS
Johannesstraβe 71, 70176 Stuttgart, Germany
TEL : + 49 711 6360 901
FAX : + 49 711 6360990
E-MAIL : anadere.gus@t-online.de
CONTACT: C. Anadere

GET-JULICH GESELLSCHAFT FUR ENTWICKLUNGSTECHNOLOGIE MBH
ustriepark Emlndil Mayrisch,
52457 Aldenhoven, Germany
TEL : + 49 2461 690-760
FAX : + 492461 690-769
CONTACT: Ms Jakobs

GKSSFORSCHUNGSZENTRUM GEESTHACHT GMBH
Institutfür Atmosphären-Physik,
Max-Plank-Straβe
21502 Geesthacht, Germany
TEL : + 49 4152 87 1533
FAX : + 49 4152 87 2020
E-MAIL : raschke@gkss.de\
WEB: www.gkss.de

HAHN MEITNER INSTITUT BERLIN GMBH
Glienicker Straβe 100,
14109 Berlin, Germany
TEL : + 49 30 8062 2442
FAX : + 49 30 8062 3199
CONTACT: Prof Tributsch

HAHN-MELTNER-INSTITUT
Section SE2, Glienicker Straβe 100,
14109 Berlin,Germany
TEL : + 49 30 8062 2624
FAX : + 49 8062 3199
E-MAIL : meyer@hmi.de
CONTACT: Prof W Fuhs

HAYDN ENERGIE CONSULT GMBH
Heininger Straβe 60,
8390 Passau,
Germany
TEL: +49 851 989190
FAX: +49 851 8460
E-MAIL: hec@haydn.de
WEB: http://www.haydn.de
CONTACT: Lothar Schramm

HEIDE UND EBERHARD STADT UND REGIONAL PLANER
Prinz Albert Straβe 24,
53113 Bonn, Germany
TEL: +49 228 2237 73
FAX: +49 228 2237 73
CONTACT: Jost Eberhard

HHS PLANER + ARCHITEKTEN BDA - HEGGER HEGGER SCHLEIFF
Habichtswader Straβe 19,
34119 Kassel, Germany
TEL: +49 561 930 940
FAX: +49 561 930 9421
E-MAIL: hhs-ks@t-online.de
CONTACT: Manfred Hegger

HULLMANN WILLKOMM & PARTNER - HWP
Quantel Hotz 24B,
30405 Hannover, Germany
TEL: +49 511 271 2722
FAX: +49 511 271 2723
CONTACT: Prof Heinz Hullimann

ILB. INSTITUT FÜR LICHT - UND BAUTECHNIK ANDER FACHHOCHSCHULEKÖLN
Gremberger Strasse 15la,
51105 Koln, Germany
TEL: +49 22 83 10 96
FAX: +49 22 83 55 13
E-MAIL: gregorhgauss@fo.fh-koeln.de
CONTACT: Arch G Hellenthal

IMR - GMBH MEB UND REGELSYSTEME
Wannenäckerstraβe 25,
74078 Heilbronn, Germany
TEL: +49 7131 2875-0
FAX: +49 7131 227 30
E-MAIL: imr-germany@t-online.de
WEB: http://home.wte.net/imr
CONTACT: Jasmin Bubas

INGENIEURBÜRO DR KRETZSCHMAR - IBK
Steinstraβe 21,
90419 Nürnberg, Germany
TEL +49 911 393 560
FAX: +49 911 3728 299
E-MAIL: ibk-nbg@t-online.de
CONTACT: Johann Krier

INSTITUT FÜR INDUSTRIALISIERUNGDES BAUENS-IB GMBH
Postafch 21 05 60,
30405 Hannover, Germany
TEL: +49 511 796088
FAX: +49 511 756227
CONTACT: Prof H C Helmut Weber

INSTITUT FÜR TECHNISCHE THERMODYNAMIK - DLR
Postfach 800320,
D-70503 Stuttgart, Germany
TEL: +49 711 6862 509
FAX: +49 711 6862-712
E-MAIL: itt@dlr.de
WEB: http://www.st.dlr.de/en/tt
CONTACT: Claus Voigt

INSTITUT FÜRLUFT-UND KÄLTETECHNIK GMBH
Bertolt-Brecht-Allee 20,
01309 Dresden, Germany
TEL: +49 351 408 1510
FAX: +49 351 408 1515
E-MAIL: ILKDresden.PR@t-online.de
WEB: http://www.ilkdresden.de
CONTACT: Siegfried Richter

KTB BERATUNGS-UND PLANUNGS-GESELLSCHAFT MBH
Havensteinstraβe 50, 46045
Oberhausen, Germany
TEL: +49 208 20 95 20
FAX: +49 208 85766-0
CONTACT: Dr H F Hinrichs

LOGID GRÜNE SOLARARCHITEKTUR
Sindelfinger Straβe 85,
72070 Tübingen,
Germany
TEL: + 49 7071 9483 0
FAX: +49 7071 9483 50
EMAIL:agsn@agsn.de/logid
CONTACT:Prof. Dieter Schempp

MAX-PLANCK-INSTITUT FÜR KOHLENFORSCHÜNG
Kaiser-Wilheim-Platz 1, 45470
Mulheim an der Ruhr, Germany
TEL: +49 208 306-1
FAX: +49 208 306-2980
CONTACT: Prof B Bogdanovic

NEVAG
Rheingaustrabe 184,
65203 Wiesbaden, Germany
TEL: +49 611 6098 270
FAX: + 49 611 6098 222
E-MAIL: info@nevag.de
WEB: http://www.nevag.de
CONTACT: Dr Ing Olaf Goebel

PHOTOTRONICS SOLARTECHNIK GMBH
Hermann-Oberth-Straβe 11,
85640 Putzbrunn, Germany
TEL :+ 49 89 46264-0
FAX: + 49 89 46264
E-MAIL : 106475.3005@compuserve.com
CONTACT: Markus Schmid

PHYSIKALISCH-TECHNISCHE BUNDESANSTALT BRAUNSCHWEIGUND BERLIN
Abbestraβe 2-12, 10587 Berlin, Germany
TEL: + 49 30 3481-270
FAX : + 49 30 3481-490
CONTACT : Dr. D Stuck

PHYSIKALISCH-TECHNISCHE BUNDESANSTALT
Light and Radiation,
Potfach 33 45, 38023
Braunschweig, Germany
TEL : + 49 531 592-4100
FAX : + 49 531 592-4105
E-MAIL : juergen.metzdorf@ptb.de
CONTACT : Dr J Metzdorf

PRAAST CONSULTING ENGINEERS
Sonnenberg 27,
67316 Carlsberg Pfalz, Germany
TEL: +49 6356 8593
FAX: +49 6356 5027
CONTACT: Siegfried Praast

RESOL-ELEKTRONISCHE REGELUNGEN GMBH
Export, Heiskampstrabe 10,
D-45527 Hattingen, Germany
TEL: +4923249648-30
FAX: +4923249648-55
E-MAIL: nicole.beinhoff@resol.de
WEB: http://www.resol.de
CONTACT: Nicole Beinhoff

RHEINISCH-WESTFALISCHE TECH HSCHULE AACHEN INSTITUT FÜR VERFAHRENSTECHNIK
Turmstraβe 46,
52056 Aachen, Germany
TEL : +49 241 80 54 70
FAX : +49 241 8888-252
E-MAIL : secretary@ivt.rwth-aachen.de
WEB : http://www.ivt.rwth-aachen.de
CONTACT : Prof Thomas Melin

SOLLNER INSTITUT
WaldmullerstraBe 22,
81479 Munchen, Germany
TEL: +49 89 79 2057
FAX: +49 89 79 16110
E-MAIL: j.Benecke@lrzuni-muenchen.de
CONTACT: Prof Jochen Benecke

TECHNISCHE UNIVERSITÄT BERLIN
Institut für Mikrolektronik and
Festköperelektronik-IMF, Sekr 10,
Jebensstraβe 1,
D-10626 Berlin, Germany
TEL: +49 30 314 26803
FAX: +49 30 314 26804
E-MAIL: neil@imf.ee.tu-berlin.de
WEB: http://mikro.ee.tu-tu-berlin.de/imffe
CONTACT: Dr Matthias E Neli

TECHNISCHE UNIVERSITÄT DARMSTADT
Institut für Wasser bau and Wasseer Wirtschaft,
Rundeturmstrabe1,
64283 Darmstadt, Germany
TEL: +49 6151 162523
FAX: +49 6151 163223
E-MAIL: wabau@hrzpub.tu-darmstadt.de
WEB: http://www.tu-darmstadt.de/fb/bi/wb
CONTACT: Dr F Christoph

TECHNISCHE UNIVERSITÄT DRESDEN
Institut fuer Physikalische Chemie und Elektrochemie,
Mommsenstraβe 13,
01062 Dresden, Germany
TEL: +49 351 463 4907
FAX: +49 351 463 7164
E-MAIL: wplieth@cech04.chm.tu-dresden.de
WEB: http://www.tu.tu-dresden.de
CONTACT: Prof Dr Waldfried Plieth

TECHNISCHE UNIVERSITÄT MÜNCHEN
Landtechnik Weihenstephan
Vöttinger Straβe 36,
85354 Freising, Germany
TEL : +49 8161 71 33 03
FAX : +49 8161 71 35 27
E-MAIL : strsek@tec.agar.tu-muenchen
WEB : http://www.tec.agrar.tu-muenchen
CONTACT : Dr Arno Strehler

TECHNISCHE UNVERSITAT CLAUSTHAL
Institut für Energieverfahernstechnik and Bernnsto, AgricolastraBe 4 (Feldgraben),
38678 Clausthal-Zellerfeld, Germany
TEL: +49 5323 722033
FAX: +49 5323 723155
E-MAIL: bosse@ievv.tv-clausthal.de
WEB: http://www.ievd.tv-clausthal.de
CONTACT: Prof Rainhard Scholz

UNIVERSITÄTSTUTTGART ITW
Institut für Thermodynamlk ünd Warmetechnik, Pfaffenwaldring 6,
70550 Stuttgart, Germany
TEL : +49 711 685-3536
FAX : +49 711 685-3503
E-MAIL : pm@itw.uni-stuttgart.de
WEB : http://www.itw.uni-stuttgart.de
CONTACT : Dr W Heidemann

UNIVERSITY OF ERLANGEN
Institute of Applied Physics,
Staudstr 7, Bau A3,
D-91058 Ernangen, Germany
TEL: +49 9131 8528421
FAX: +49 9131 8528423
E-MAIL: max.schulz@physik.uni-erlangen.de
WEB: http://www.physik.uni-erlangen.de
CONTACT: Max Schulz

UNIVERSITY OF WUPPERTAL
Department of Electrical Engineering,
Institute of Power System Engineering, Fuhlrottstraβe 10,
42097 Wuppertal, Germany
TEL: +49 202 439 2976
FAX: +49 202 439 2977
E-MAIL: verstege@eev.uni-wuppertal.de
WEB: http://www.eev.uni-wuppertal.de
CONTACT: Prof J Verstege

UNIVERSITÄT OLDENBURG
Department of Energy and Semiconductor Research F,
D-26111 Oldenberg, Germany
TEL : +49 441 798 3402
FAX : +49 441 798 3326
E-MAIL : dehe@ehf.uni-oldenburg.de
WEB : http://www.physik.uni-oldenburg.de/ehf
CONTACT : Dr D Heinemann

VERSUCHS-UNDLEHRANSTALT FÜRSPIRITUSFABRIKATION UND FERMENTATIONSTECHNOLGIE IN BERLIN - VLSF
Seestrabe 13, 13353 Berlin, Germany
TEL: +49 30 45080-0
FAX: +49 30 4536-067
CONTACT: Dr Peter Fischer

VIESSMANN WERKE GMBH & CO
Postfach 10, 35108 Allendorf (Eder), Germany
TEL: +496452702698
FAX: +496452702780
CONTACT: Has Schneider

WTZ FÜR MOTOREN UND MASCHINENFORSCHUNG ROBLAU GMBH
Karl-Liebknecht-Straβe 38,
06862 Ro Blau, Germany
TEL: +49 34 901 883 235
FAX: +49 34 901 883 121
E-MAIL: bouche@wtx.de
WEB: http://www.wtz.de
CONTACT: Dr Thomas Bouche

ZEO-TECH ZEOLITH-TECHNOLOGIE GMBH
Max-Planck-Strasse 3, D-85716
Unterschleibheim, Germany
TEL: +49 89 310 44 84
FAX: +49 89 310 44 85
E-MAIL: info@zeo-tech.de
WEB: http://www.zeo-tech.de
CONTACT: Dr Ralf Schmidt

UNIVERSITIES

FACHHOCHSCHULE KEMPTEN FACHBEREICH MASCHINENBAU
Bahnhofstraβe, 87435 Kempten,
Germany
TEL: +49 8395 2986
FAX: +49 8331 2523 229
CONTACT: Prof. Walter Karz

FREE UNIVERSITAT BERLIN FFV
Ihnestraβe 22,
14195 Berlin,
Germany
TEL: +49 30 838 50 98
FAX: +49 30 831 63 51
CONTACT: Dr Lutz Mez

IKU INSTITUT FÜR KOMMUNALE WIRTSCHAFT UND UMWELTPLANUNG
Unter den Eichen 7,
65195 Wiesbaden, Germany
TEL: +49 611 180 870
FAX: +49 611 180 8722
E-MAIL: info@iku.fh-darmstadt.de
WEB: http://www.iku.fh-darmstadt.de
CONTACT: Dr Dieter Wittmann

INSTITUTE FOR ENERGY ECONONOMICS AND THE RATIONAL USE OF ENERGY-UNIVERSITY OF STUTTGART
University of Stuttgart,
Hessbruhlstraβe 49a, 70565
Stuttgart, Germany
TEL: +49 711 780-6116
FAX: +49 711 780-6177
E-MAIL: mk@ier.uni-stuttgart.de
WEB: http://www.biomass-info.net
CONTACT: Dr Martin Kaltschmitt

SOLAR INSTITUTE JÜLICH
Ginsterweg I, 52428 jülich,
Germany
TEL:+49 2461 99 3128
FAX:+49 2461 99 3235
E-MAIL:infosij@fh_aachen.de
WEB:http://www.sij.fh_aachen.de

TECHNICAL UNIVERSITY OF CLAUSTHAL
IEE, Leibnitzstraβe 28,
38678 Clausthal-Zellerfeld,
Germany
TEL: +49 5323 72 2570
FAX: +49 5323 72 2104
CONTACT: Prof HP Beck

TECHNISCHE UNIVERSITÄT MÜNCHEN
Chair for Energy and Environmental Technologies,
Weihenstephaner Steig 22,
85350 Freising,
Germany
TEL : +49 8161 713436
FAX : +49 8161 714415
E-MAIL : mp@elu.blm.tu-muenchen.de
WEB : http://www.edv.agrar.tu-muenchen.de
CONTACT : Dr-Ing W Russ

TECHNISCHE UNVERSITÄT BERLIN
Institut für Lichttechnik,
Ensteinufer 19,
10587 Berlin,
Germany
TEL: +49 30 314 22401
FAX: +49 30 314 22161
CONTACT: Prof H Kaase

UNIVERSITÄT DORTMUND
Lehrstuhl für Thermodynamik FB Chemietechnik,
44221 Dortmund,
Germany
TEL : +49 231 755-2674
FAX : +49 231 755-2572
E-MAIL : kuehl@ct.uni-dortmund.de
WEB : http://www.chemietechnik.uni-dortmund.de
CONTACT : Dr HD Kuhl

UNIVERSITÄT HAMBURG
Institut für Technische and Makromolekulare Chemie,
BundesstraBe 45,
20146 Hamburg,
Germany
TEL : +49 40 4123-3162
FAX : +49 40 4123-6008
CONTACT : Prof Walter Kaminsky

UNIVERSITÄT HANNOVER
Institut für Technik in Gartenbau and Landwirtscha, Herrenhauser StraBe 2, 30419 Hannover, Germany
TEL : +49 511 762 2646
FAX : +49 511 762 2649
E-MAIL : itg@itg.uni-hannover.de
WEB : http://www.itgb.uni-hannover.de/extern/itg/welcome.htm
CONTACT : Prof HJ Tantau

UNIVERSITÄT HOHENHEIM
Institut für Agrütechnik in den Tropen und Subtro,GarbestraBe 9,
70559 Stuttgart, Germany
TEL : +49 711 459 3464
FAX : +49 711 459 3298
E-MAIL : muelbauer@ats.uni-hohenheim.de
CONTACT : Prof W Mühlbauer

UNIVERSITÄT STUTTGART
Institute für Flugzeugbau - Bereich Windenergie, Pfaffenwaldring 31,
70550 Stuttgart, Germany
TEL: +49 711 685 2404
FAX: +49 711 685 2449
E-MAIL: doerner@ifb.uni stuttgart.dc
WEB: http://www.ifb.uni-stuttgart.de/~doerner/doerner.html
CONTACT: Heiner Dörner

UNIVERSITÄT STUTTGART
Institute für Thermodynamik and Warmtechnik - ITW, Pfaffenwaldring 6, D-70550 Stuttgart, Germany
TEL: +49 711 685 3535
FAX: +49 711 685 3503
E-MAIL: hahne@itw.uni-stuttgart.de
WEB: http://www.itw.uni-stuttgart.de
CONTACT: Prof E Hahne

UNIVERSITÄT STUTTGART
Lehrstuhl Konstruktive Bauphysik,
Postfach 80 11 40, Pfaffenwaldring 7, 70511 Stuttgart, Germany
TEL: +49 711 685-6578
E-MAIL: ingrid.schweiker@po.uni-stuttgart.de
WEB:http://www.uni-stuttgart.de/ikb
CONTACT: Prof Karl A Gertis

UNIVERSITÄT WÜRZBURG
Institut für Theoretische Physik,
Am Hubland,
97074 Würzburg, Germany
TEL: +49 931 888 5888
FAX: +49 931 888 5141
E-MAIL: kuemmel@physik.uni-wuerzburg.de
WEB: http://theorie.physik.uni-wuerzburg.de/TPI/kuemmel/profile..html
CONTACT: Prof R Kummel

GERMANY

UNIVERSITÄT ZUKÖLN
Energiewirts Chaftches Institu,
Albertus Magnus Platz 1,
50931 Köln, Germany
TEL: +49 221 470-2258
FAX: +49 221 44 65 37
WEB: http://www.uni-koelu.de/wiso-fak/energie
CONTACT: Frau Schmid

UNIVERSITY OF APPLIED SCIENCES
Department of Building Sciences,
Economics and Social Sciences,
Postfach 1455,
Theodor-Korner-Allee 16,
02754 Zittau, Germany
TEL: +49 3583 611 676
FAX: +49 3583 611 627
E-MAIL: m.schmidt@hs-zigr.de
WEB: http://www.htw-zittau.de
CONTACT: Dr. Manfred Schmidt

UNIVERSITY OF FLENSBURG
Energy and Environmental
Management Studies, Kanzleistr 41-43, 24943 Flensburg, Germany
TEL: +49 461 805 574
FAX: +49 461 805 970
E-MAIL: hohmeyer@uni.flensburg.de
WEB: http://www.uni.flensburg.de/inetbbm/eum/index.htm
CONTACT: Prof Olav Hohmeyer

UNIVERSITY OF OLDENBURG
Department of Physics,
Postgraduate Program Renewable Energy,
PO Box 2503, 26111 Oldenburg
Germany
TEL: + 49 441 798 3544
FAX: +49 441 798 3990
E-MAIL: edu@uni-oldemburg.de
CONTACT :EDU KNAGGE

UNIVERSITY OF STUTTGART
Institute of Physical Electronics
Pfaffenwaldring 47,
70569 stuttgart, Germany
TEL:+497116857140
FAX:+497116857143
E-MAIL:juergen.werner@ipe.uni-stuttgart.de
WEB:www.uni-stuttgart.de/ipe
CONTACT: Prof J H Werner

NGO'S

ENERGIE UND UMWELTZENTRUM AM DEISTER
31832 Springe, Germany
TEL: +49 5044 975-0
FAX: +49 5044 075-66
CONTACT : Franz H Möbius

SOLAR EBRÜCKE EV
Fraf Von Werbenberg Str 6,
89344 Aislingen,
Germany
TEL:+49 8025 7192
FAX:+49 8025 7195
E-MAIL:solarebruecke@t-online.de
CONTACT:Wolfgang Scheffler

CONSULTANTS

BAUMEISTER PETER PLANUNGSBURO
Garbenstrabe, 17, 97295,
Waldbrunn, Germany
TEL : +49 93 06 83 44
FAX : +49 93 06 27 44
CONTACT : Hans Peter Baumeister

BERGISCHE UNIVERSITAT GH WUPPERTAL-BUGHW
Fachbereich 11 - Civil Engineering,
Pauluskirchstrabe, 7,
42285 Wuppertal, Germany
TEL : +49 202 439 4135
FAX : +49 202 439 4196
E-MAIL :dosp@uni-wuppertal.de
WEB : http://www.uni-wuppertal.de
CONTACT : J Dase

CENET - CENTRUM NEUE TECHNOLOGIEN
Engelhardstraβe 12, D-81369
Munchen, Germany
TEL : +49 89 72012-73
FAX : +49 89 72012-40
CONTACT : H P Grimon

DR DIETSCHMANN CONSULTING DDC
Olbrichstr 50, D-60488,
Frankfurt, Germany
TEL : + 49 69 764239
FAX : + 49 69 7681630
E-MAIL : dietschmann@t-online.de

ENERGIE CONSULT
Im Kleinen Grund 16, 65779
Kelkheim, Germany
TEL : +49 6174 964 770
FAX : +49 6174 964 774
E-MAIL : mail@energieeffizienz.de
WEB : http://
www.energieeffizienz.de
CONTACT : Klaus Hoars

ENERGY & UMWELT CONSULT GMBH-EUC
Bilsteinstrasse II,
D-58313 Herdecke, Germany
TEL: +49 2330 129135
FAX: +49 2330 129165
E-MAIL: prof.hafner@t-online.de
CONTACT : Prof Edzard Hafner

ENERKOGMBH,
Gensellschaft Fur \
Energiewritschaftund
Umwelttechn.Landstraβe 20,
52457, Aldenhoven,
Germany,
TEL : + 49 2464 9713
FAX : + 49 2464 7062
E-MAIL: enerko@t-online.de
CONTACT : Rolf Bergedieck

FICHTNER GMBH & CO KG
Sarweystraβe 3,
70191 Stuttgart, Germany
TEL: +49 711 89 95-0
FAX: +49 711 89 95-459
E-MAIL:v@fichtner.de
WEB:http://www.ficht.ner.de
CONTACT: Heike Wahle

FR-FRANKENSOLAR GMBH
Hessestrarnbe 4
90442 Nümberg,
Germany
TEL: +49 911 26 04 66
FAX: +49 911 28 42 20
CONTACT: Helmut Zeltner

GERISCHER ARCHITEKTUR
Climbernstraβe 14,
40545 Düsseldorf-Oberkassel,
Germany
TEL : + 49 211 551449
FAX : +49 211 579672
CONTACT: Prof. Wolf Gerischer

GERLING CONSULTING GRUPPE GMBH
Frankfurter Strabe 720-726,
51145 Koln, Germany
TEL: +49 221 144-7091
FAX: +49 221 144-5604
E-MAIL: Thomas.Meschede@gerling.de
CONTACT: Dr Thomas Meschede

GERTEC INGENIEURGESELLSCHAFT
Viehofer Straβe 11, 45127, Essen
Germany
TEL : + 49 201 24564-0
FAX : + 49201 24564-20
E-MAIL : gertec@t-online.de
CONTACT: Andreas Hübner

GESELLSCHAFT FUR DIE AUFBEREITUNG UND VERWERUNG VON RESTSTOFFEN MBH-GFR
Postfach5629,
97006 Würzgurg,
Germany
TEL : + 49931 90080-0
FAX : + 49 931 90080-30
E-MAIL : gfr@gfr.mbh.com
CONTACT: J Schlichtmann

GESELLSCHAFT FUR ENERGIESYS TEMTECHNIK MBH-EST
Friedrichstraβe 12,
45128 Essen,
Germany
TEL : + 49 201 82032-0
FAX : + 49 201 82032-32
CONTACT: Michael List

GESELLSCHAFT FÜR UNWELTFREUNDLICHE TECHNOLOGIE EV - GUT
Schwengebergstraβe 9.
D - 34132 Kassel,
Germany
TEL : + 49 561 142 93
FAX : + 49 561 103 114
E-MAIL : gb.energie@t-online.de
CONTACT: Gunter Brandt

GET-PLANUNGSGESSELL - SCHAFT ENERGIE - TECHNIK MBH
Berner Straβe 40,
60437 Frankfurt am Main 56,
Germany
TEL : + 49 69 507 6000
FAX : + 49 69 507 6001
CONTACT: U. Kusche

GROABNEHMERVERBAND ENERGIE BADEN-WÜRTTEMBERG EV
Breitlingstraβe 35,
70184 Stuttgart,
Germany
TEL :+ 49 711 237250
FAX : + 49 711 2372599
CONTACT: Jng Rudolf

HLS-ENERGIETECHNIK INGENIEURBURO HOFBAU GMBH
Schanzenweg 27,
94469 Deggendorf,
Germany
TEL: +49 991 371 030
FAX: +49 991 339 36
CONTACT: Anton Hofbauer

HOCHSCHULE BREMERHAVEN
Chemistry, An der Karlstadt 8,
27568 Bremerhaven,
Germany
TEL: +49 471 4823 283
FAX: +49 471 4823 115
CONTACT: Prof Bernd Stephan

HORST WOLL MERATH
Wollbergsreddrer 188,
D-24113 Molfsee,
Germany
TEL: +49 431 658264
FAX: +49 431 658264
CONTACT: Horst Wollmerath

HUBER PETER CURT SOLAR KLEINANLAGEN
Fontanestraβe 33,
50169 Kerpen,
Germany
TEL: +49 2273 68266
CONTACT: Peter Curt Huber

HÜCKSTADT HEIZUNGS-U SANITÄR GMBH
Behler Weg 17,
24306 Plon,
Germany
TEL: +49 4522 50990
FAX: +49 4522 509977
CONTACT: Jürgen Hückstädt

HYDROPLAN INGENIEUR GESELLSCHAFT MBH
Prinz-Carl-Anlage 25,
67547 Worms,
Germany
TEL: +49 62 41 91 03 0
FAX: +49 62 41 91 03 10
E-MAIL: hydroplan@t-online.de
WEB: http://www.hydroplan.de
CONTACT: Sabine Lieth

ICE GMBH - INTERNATIONAL CENTRE FOR ENERGY AND ENVIRONMENTAL TECHNOLOGY
Auenstrasse 25,
D-04105 Leipzig,
Germany
TEL: +49 641 980 49 69
FAX: +49 341 980 34 86
E-MAIL: iceu@iceu.manner.de
WEB: http://www.iceu.net
CONTACT: Dr Jörg Matthies

INFORMATIONSZENTRALE DER ELECTRIZITATSWIRTSCHAFT EV-IZE
Stresemannallec 23,
60596 Frankfurtam Main,
Germany
TEL: +49 69 630 4372
FAX: +49 69 630 4387
E-MAIL: hugo-jung@ize.de
WEB: http://www.strom.de
CONTACT: Hugo Jung

INGAN GMBH INGENIEURBETRIEB FÜR INDUSRIEANLAGEN ZU BERLIN
Rosenthaler Strasse 71,
10119 Berlin,
Germany
TEL: ı 49 30 283 96 6
FAX: +49 30 283 968 85-88
E-MAIL: info@ingan.de
WEB: http://www.ingan.de
CONTACT: Benno Schlickeiser

INGENIEÜRBURO FÜR NEUE ENERGIETECHNIK UND LÄRMSCHUTZ DIPL - ING JURGEN MICHALK
Kichdorfer Straβe 26,
26603 Aurich,
Germany
TEL: +49 4941 955810
FAX: +49 4941 955811
E-MAIL: mail@iel-michalk.de
CONTACT: Jürgen Michalk

INGENIEURBÜRO FÜR UMWELTSCHUTZ UND TECHNIK
Reepschlägerbahn 9,
24937 Flensburg,
Germany
TEL: +49 461 20712
FAX: +49 461 13343
E-MAIL: iut.de@t-online.de
CONTACT: Hans-Peter Zwoch

INGENIEURBÜRO HENNING HOLST
Ludwig-Nissen Staβe 39,
D-25813 Husum,
Germany
TEL: +49 4841 6044
FAX: +49 4841 5044
E-MAIL: info@ing-holst.de
WEB: http://www.ing-holst.de
CONTACT: Henning Holst

INGENIEURBÜRO HOFFMANN-IBH
Batbarastrasse 41,
01129 Dresden,
Germany
TEL: +49 351 801 1853
FAX: +49 351 801 1855
E-MAIL: ibh@ibhoffamann.de
WEB: http://www.ibhoffmann.de
CONTACT: Thomas Hoffmann

INGENIEURBURO JURGEN LENSCHOW
Hessenring 9,
64560 Riedstadt,
Germany
TEL: +49 6158 915076
FAX: +49 6158 915078
E-MAIL: lenschow@t-online.de
CONTACT: Jürgen Lenschow

INGENIEURBÜRO MICHAEL BRÄHLER
Heidkopfweg 4,
36124 Eichenzell-Zillbach,
Germany
TEL: +49 6656 96120
FAX: +49 6656 961212
CONTACT: Michael Brähler

INGENIEURBÜRO PETER LORENTZEN
Königslacher Straβe 15-21,
60528 Frankfurt,
Germany
TEL: +49 69 67 80 92-0
FAX: +49 69 670 86 10
E-MAIL: ipl.lorentzen@t-online.de
CONTACT: Peter Lorentzen

INNOTECSYSTEMANALYSE GMBH
Kurfürstendamm 199,
D-10719 Berlin,
Germany
TEL: +49 30 882 3432
FAX: +49 30 885 4433
E-MAIL: behnke@euweb.de
WEB: http://www.euweb.de/innotec
CONTACT: Rainer Behnke

IST ENERGIETECHNIK GMBH
Ritterweg 1, 79400
Kandern-Wollbach,
Germany
TEL: +49 7626 915417
FAX: +49 7626 915430
E-MAIL: energietechnik@istnet.de
WEB: http://www.istnet.de
CONTACT: Ulrich Laboschik

LAHMEYER INTERNATIONAL GMBH
Energy Division, Friedberger Strabe
173, D-61118 Bad Vilbel, Germany
TEL: +49 6101 55 1460
FAX: +49 6101 55 2101
E-MAIL: geKas@lif.de
WEB: http://www.lif.de
CONTACT: Harald Kaschube

JOACHIM EBLE ARCHITEKTUR
Berliner Ring 47a, 72076 Tubingen,
Germany
TEL: +49 7071 9694-0
FAX: +49 7071 60 09 12
E-MAIL: eble@nepustil.net
CONTACT: Stephan Keppler

KAB-KRAFTWERKS-UND ANLAGENBAU GMBH
Möllendorffstraβe 52, 10367 Berlin,
Germany
TEL: +49 30 54 65-0
FAX: +49 30 54 65-29 99
WEB:http://www.kab-berlin.com
WEB: Eckar Netzmann

KÖHLER & ZIEGLER GMBH ANLAGENT
Augweg 10, 35457 Lollar,
Germany
TEL: +49 6406 9103-0
FAX: +49 6406 9103-30
CONTACT: Harald Köhler

LANDMARK ALTERNATIVE ENERGIEN & CONSULTING
An der Witschke 27,
06118 Halle/Saale,
Germany
TEL : +49 345 2900591
FAX : +49 345 2900592
E-MAIL : landmark@t-online.de
WEB : http://www.landmark-halle.de
CONTACT : Mr Thomas Steinke

MAINGAS AKTIENGESELLSCHAFT
Solmsstraβe 38,
60486 Frankfurt am Main,
Germany
TEL: +49 69 7911-0
FAX: +49 69 7911-1122
CONTACT: Dr Heinrich Stiens

MLINGENIEURBÜRO FÜR TECHNISCHEAÜSRUSTUNG
Kleinottweilerstraβe 8a, 66450
Bexbach, Germany
TEL: +49 6826 4900
FAX: +49 6826 4039
CONTACT: Manfred Loos

MVV CONSULTANTS & ENGINEERS GMBH RENEE,
Kurfurstendamm 199, D-10719
Berlin, Germany
TEL: +49 30 882 3432
FAX: +49 30 885 4433
E-MAIL:
r.behnke@consultants.mvv.de
WEB: http://www.euweb.de/mvv-consultants
CONTACT: Rainer Behnke

PFLEIDERER CONSULTING GMBH
Ingolstadter Straβe 51,
92318 Neumarkt, Germany
TEL: +49 9181 28-0
FAX: +49 9181 22291
WEB:http://www.pfleiderer.com

PLANUNGSBÜRO ROSSOW LTD
Erzgang 3,
17036 Neubrandenburg, Germany
TEL: +49 395 7782125
FAX:+49 395 7782138
E-MAIL : nr@rossow.de
WEB:http://www.rossow.de
CONTACT: Dr Norbert Rossow

PLANUNGSGRUPPE M + M AG
Postfach 1667, 71006 Boblingen,
Germany
TEL: +49 7031 646-0
FAX: +49 7031 646-111
E-MAIL: info@pgmm.com
WEB: http://www.pgmm.com
CONTACT: Mr Frank JJ Ruthsatz

PLANUNGSGRUPPE M + MAG INGEN EURGESELLSCHAFTFUR GEBAUDETECHNIK- BUILDING SERVICES CONSULTANTS
Hanns-Klemm-Straβe 1, 71034
Boblingen, Germany
TEL: +49 7031 646-0
FAX:+49 7031 646-111
E-MAIL : info@pgmm.com
WEB:http://www.pgmm.com
CONTACT: Mr Frank JJ Ruthsatz

POLYPLAN GMBH ENERGIETECHNIK
Vahrenwalder Straβe 7,
30165 Hannover, Germany
TEL: +49 511 9357-180
FAX:+49 511 9357-189
CONTACT: Dieter Bugling

SIEMPELKAMP NUKLEAR-UND UMWELTTECHNIK GMBH & CO
Siempelkampstraβe 45,
47725 Krefeld,
Germany
TEL: +49 2151 894 0
FAX: +49 2151 8948 455
E-MAIL: siempelkamp@t-online.de
CONTACT: Dr Manfred Sappok

SOLAR ANLANGEN LANGE GMBH
Am Jägerhaus 6 48291 Telgte,
Germany
TEL:+49 2504 2169
FAX:+49 2504 72490
CONTACT: K H Lange

SOLAR ENERGY WORLD
Immenweg 41,
42279 Wuppertal,
Germany
TEL:+49 202 522834
FAX:+49 202 522835
CONTACT: Holger Quambusch

SOLAR UND ENERGIEBERATUNGSZENTRUM BERGSTRAbE
Am groBen Markt 8,
64646 Heppenheim,
Germany
TEL:+49 6252 913 460
FAX:+49 6252 913 462
E-MAIL:pegue@hrzl.hrz.
tudarmstadt.de
CONTACT:Peter Gunther

STADATWERKE HANNOVER AG
Ihmeplatz 2, 30449 Hannover
Germany
TEL: +49 4511 430-1
FAX: +49 4511 430-2650
CONTACT:PeterStellmacher

STEINBEIS-TRANSFERZENTRUM ENERGIE-GEBÄUDE-UND SOLARTECHNIK
Hebruhistraβe 15,
70565 Stuttgart, Germany
TEL: +49 711 99 0075
FAX: +49 711 99 007-99
E-MAIL:info@stz-egs.de
WEB:http://www.stz-egs.de
CONTACT:Boris Mahler

STIFTUNG ÖKOLOGIE & LANDBAU
Weinstraβe Süd 51,
67098 Bad Dorkheim, Germany
TEL: +49 6322 8666
FAX: +49 6322 989701
E-MAIL:info@soel.de
WEB:http://www.soel.de
CONTACT: Immo Lünzer

STIFTUNGNATURSCHUTZ BERLIN
Die ökolaube, Potsdamer Straβe 68,
10785 Berlin, Germany
TEL: +49 30 262 60 01
FAX: +49 30 261 52 77
E-MAIL:snb@mail.blinx.de
WEB:http://snb.blinx.de

SÜDSOLAR
Friedhofstraβe 15, 95346
Stadtsteinach, Germany
TEL: +49 9225 1838
FAX: +49 9225 1838
CONTACT:Wolfgang Martin

SVE SOLAR ENERGY MARKETING AND DEVELOPMENT CO
Hanauer Landstraβe 551,
60386 Frankfurt / Main,
Germany
TEL: +49 69 4192145
FAX: +49 69 419247
CONTACT:Heinz Hortrich

TEP
Mutzerheide 23,
51467 Bergisch Gladbach,
Germany
TEL : +49 2022 58620
FAX : +49 2022 58656
CONTACT : K Lorenz

TRANSATLANTIC RENEWABLE ENERGY TECHNOLOGY
Winkel 14, 88090 Immenstaad
Germany
TEL: +49 7545 911102
FAX: +49 7545 911144
E-MAIL: trebt@swol.se
WEB: http://www.trent-consulting.com
CONTACT: Klaus J Lindemann

TRANSSOLAR ENERGIETECHNIK GMBH
Nobel straβe 15,
70569 Stuttgart,
Germany
TEL: +49 711 67976-0
FAX: +49 711 67976-11
E-MAIL: voit@transsolar.com
CONTACT: Peter Voit

TÜV ENERGIE UND UMWELT
TÜV Immissionsschutz und
Energiesysteme,
Am Grauen Stein
51105 Köln,
Germany
TEL: +49 221 806 27 11
FAX: +49 221 806 13 50
E-MAIL: enertest@de.tuv.com
WEB: http://www.eco-tuv.de
CONTACT: Dr. W Wiesner

ULOGFREIBURG
Hauptstraβe 27,
79400 Kandern,
Germany
TEL : +41 61 301 66 22
FAX : +41 61 301 49 59
E-MAIL : ulogbasel@swissonline.ch
WEB : http://www.ulog.ch

UMWELT-UND ENERGIE-CONSULT GMBH-UECBERLIN
Reuchlinstraβe 10-11,
10553 Berlin,
Germany
TEL : +49 30 344 80 39
FAX : +49 30 344 96 74
E-MAIL : uec@snafu.de
WEB : http://www.snafu.de/~uec
CONTACT : Mr Oetjen-Dehne

UT ENGINEERING AND CONSULTING GMBH
Advanced Technologies
Environmental and Energy,
PO Box 2435,
79514 Lorrach,
Germany
TEL: +49 7621 165 333
FAX: +49 7621 165 334
CONACT: Ulrich Tscheuschler

VERBAND UNABHÄNGIG BERATENDER INGENIEURFIRMEN EV - VUBI
Winston Churchill Straβe 1,
53046 Bonn,
Germany
TEL: +49 228 20155-0
FAX: +49 228 20155-55
E-MAIL: info@rubi.com
CONTACT: De Joergen Assmann

WIND-CONSULT INGENIEURGESELLSCHAFT FÜR UMWELTSCHONENDE ENERGIEWANDLUNG GMBH
Reuterstraβe 9, 18211 Bargeshagen,
Germany
TEL: +49 38203 507 25
FAX: +49 38203 507 23
E-MAIL: company@wind-counsult.de
WEB: http://www.wind-consult.de
CONTACT: Joachim Schwabe

WIP-MUNICH
Renewable Energies Division,
Sylvensteinstrabe 2,
D-81369 Munchen, Germany
TEL: +49897201235
FAX: +49897201291
E-MAIL: wip@wip-munich.de
WEB: http://www.wip-munich.de
CONTACT: Peter Helm

DESIGN & ENGINEERING

ARCHITEKTURBÜRO HAGEMANN
Annuntiatenbach 43,
52062 Aachen, Germany
TEL : +49 241 34530
FAX : +49 241 30547
EMAIL : ingo.hagemann@rwth.aachen.de
CONTACT : Ingo Hagemann

ENERGIEBURO FROHNER
GauBstraβe 39, 70193 Stuttgart,
Germany
TEL: +49 711 6363 585
FAX: +49 711 6363 585
E-MAIL: energiebuerofroehner@t-online.de
CONTACT : Ulrich Fröhner

EPROPLAN GMBH
Schottlestraβe 34A, 70597
Strubgart, Germany
TEL : +49 711 769 88-0
FAX: + 49 711 769 88-51
E-MAIL: info@ eproplan.de
WEB: http: //www.eproplan.de
CONTACT : Horst Schlumberger

FACHINFORMATIONSZENTRUM KARLSRUHE GESELLSCHAFT FUR WISSENCHAFTLICH TECHNISCHE INFORMATION
Energy and Environment Information
Services, Hetrmann,
Von-Hemholtz Platz 1, 76344
Eggenstein-Leopoldshafen, Germany
TEL: +49 7247 808 351
FAX: +49 7247 808 134
E-MAIL: kb@fiz-karlsruhe.de
WEB: http://www.fiz-karlsruhe.delpun
CONTACT: Dr. Kurt Bürk

GERMANISCHER LLOYD WINDENERGIE GMBH
Windenergy Department,
Johnnisbollwerk 6-8, 20459,
Hamburg, Germany
TEL: +49 40 31 106 480
FAX: +49 40 31 106 1720
E-MAIL:
WindEnergie@germanlloyd.org
WEB: http://www.gl-wind.org
CONTACT: Christian Nath

HYDROPLAN INGENIEUR SCHAFT GESELL MBH
Scheidtsrasse 28,
67547 Worms, Germany
TEL: +49 6241 91030
FAX: +49 6241 910310
E-MAIL: hydroplan@t-online.de
WEB: http://www.hydroplan.de
CONTACT: Michael Spitz

HYDROPROJEKT INGENIEURGESELLSCHAFT MBH
Dittelsledter Grenze 3,
D-99099 Erfurt, Germany
TEL: +49 361 4376 400
FAX: +49 361 4376 405
E-MAIL: hydroprojekt@
compuserve.com
WEB: http://www.hydroprojekt.de
CONTACT: Bernd Buff

IBC SOLARTECHNIK
Am Hochgericht 10,
96231 Staffelstein,
Germany
TEL: +49 9573 9224-0
FAX: +49 9573 9224-24
E-MAIL: eport@ibc-solar.de
WEB: http://www.ibc-solar.de
CONTACT: Udo Mohrstedt

IBL-UMWELTPLANUNG
Unterm Berg 39,
26123 Oldenburg, Germany
TEL: +49 441 381133
FAX: +49 441 31954
E-MAIL: ibl-umweltplanung@t-online.de
WEB: http://www.ibl-umweltplanung.de
CONTACT: H Brux

INGENIEURBÜRO MENCKE & TEGTMEYER
Laubbreite 21,
D-31789 Hameln, Germany
TEL: +49 5151 96338
FAX: +49 5151 96339
E-MAIL: menckeundtegtmeyer@t-online.de

INSTITUT FÜR SOLARENERGIEFORSCHUNG GMBH - ISFH
Am Ohberg 1,
31860 Emmerthal,
Germany
TEL: +49 5151 999-0
FAX: +49 5151 999 400
CONTACT: Dr Konrad Schreitmuller

JOINT GEOSCIENTIFIC RESEARCH INSTITUTE(GGA)
Geothermics and Groundwater
Dynamics Division, Stilleweg 2, D-30655 Hannover, Germany
TEL: +49 511 643 3496
FAX: +49 511 843 3665
WEB:http://www.bgr.de/n114/
n114gage.html

LELY WELGER RECYLING ENGINEERING GMBH
Gebr-Welger-Straβe 3,
38304 Wolfenbuettrel,
Germany
TEL: +49 5331 404 254
FAX: +49 5331 404 242
E-MAIL: lely.welger_recycling@t-online.de
WEB: http://www.lely.com
CONTACT: Tobias Breichler

MARKERT SOLARPUMPENING BÜRO
Händelstraβe 8,
97456 Dittelbrunn,
Germany
TEL: +49 9725 9862
FAX: +49 9725 9862
CONTACT: Walter Markert

POET INGENIEURGESELLSCHAFT MBH-ENGINEERING CONSULTANTS
Rosentraβe 6,
73466 Lauchheim, Germany
TEL: +49 7363 96690
FAX:+49 7363 9669-39
CONTACT: Hermann Laistner

REA GMBH
Rottmannstraβe 18, 80333
München,
Germany
TEL : +49 89 52 20 17
FAX : +49 89 5 42 07 40
CONTACT : Mathias Ketteler

REINHARD INDERFURTH
Friedrich-Ebert-Straβe, 23,
47877 Willich,
Germany
TEL: +49 2156 60042
FAX: +49 2156 5048
CONTACT: Rheinhard Inderfurth

SOLARMARKT GMBH
Deutschland, Lorracher Straβe 45
79115 Freiburg, Germany.
TEL:+49 761 4738 47
FAX:+49 761 443069
E-MAIL:solarmarkt@yahoo.com
WEB:http://www.solarmarkt.com
CONTACT: Florian Gerber

STÜRMER+SCHÜLEGMBH
Wilhelmstraβe 24a,
79098 Freiburg, Germany
TEL: +49 761 32881
FAX: +49 761 280513
E-MAIL:s-und-s@u-archiv.de
WEB:http://www.u-archiv.de/s-und-s
CONTACT:Mr Sturmer

SWS SOLAR-SOLARSTROM/ WINDENERGIE / SOLARHEIZUNG
Brunnenstraβe 18,
86938 Schondorf, Germany
TEL: +49 8192 7606
FAX: +49 8192 7709
E-MAIL:sws-solar@t-online.de
CONTACT:Wolfgang Gschwender

THERMOWAVE GESELLSCHAFT FUER WAERMETECHNIK MBH
Eichenweg 4, D-06536 Berga,
Germany
TEL: +49 34651 4180
FAX: +49 34651 41813
E-MAIL:thermowave@t-online.de
CONTACT:F Schenker

WINDENERGIE KUKATE
Eystruper Straβe 13,
28325 Bremen, Germany
TEL: +49 421 421115
FAX: +49 421 421115
CONTACT: Prof Horst Crome

OTHERS

ARGE SOLAR EV
Altenkesseler Straβe 17, 0651
Saarbrucken, Germany
TEL : +49 681 97 62 470
FAX : +49 681 97 62 471
CONTACT : Günter Sengelaub

ATW AUTOTECHNIK WALTHER GMBH
RaiffeisenstraBe 10, 74906,
Bad Rappenau, Germany
TEL : +49 7264 91870
FAX : +49 7264 918727
CONTACT : Horst Walther

BACCINI GMBH
Ertenbergweb I. D-75392
Decenpfronn, Germany
TEL : +49 7056 9292-0
FAX : +49 7056 9292 50

BEB ERDOL & ERDGAS GMBH
Reithorst 12,
30659 Hannover,
Germany
TEL : +49 511 2541
FAX : +49 511 2266
E-MAIL : armin.stoltz@beb.de
CONTACT : Dr. Arwin Stottz

BENZING VENTILA ATOREN GMBH
Werastrabe 62, 78056 Villingen
Schwenningen,
Germany
TEL : 49 7720 620 41
FAX : 490 7720 664 68
CONTACT : Angelika Heizmann

BETONBAU GMBH
Schwetzinger Straβe 22-26,
68753 Waghäusei,
Germany
TEL : +49 7254 980-0
FAX : 49 7254 980 419
CONTACT : Dr. Primus

BIELEFELDER VERLAGSANSTALT GMBH
Ravensberger Straβe 10F,
33602 Brelefeld, Germany
TEL : +49 521 595514
FAX : +49 521 595531
E-MAIL : sonnenergie@bvg-bielefield.de
CONTACT : Dr Detlef Koenemann

BINE-INFORMATIONSDIENST
Fachinformationzentrum Karlsruhe,
Gesellschaft für Wissenschaftlich
technische, Infromation mbH
Mechenstraβe 57,
D-53129 Bonn, Germany
TEL : +49 228 923 79-0
FAX : +49 228 923 79-29
E-MAIL :bine@fiz-karlsruhe.de
WEB : http://bine-fiz-karlruhe.de
CONTACT : Jutta Perl-Mai

BORGER GMBH
Benningsweg 24,
D-46325 borken Weseke,
Germany
TEL : +49 2862 91 03-0
FAX : +49 2862 91 03-46
E-MAIL : info@boerger.de

BUNDESTANSTALFÜR GEOWISSENSCHAFTEN UND ROHSTOFFE-BGR
Department B 1.25, Stilleweg 2,
D-30655 Hannover, Germany
TEL : +49 511 643 2820
FAX : +49 511 643 2304
E-MAIL : r.jung@bgr.de
CONTACT : Dr. Reinhard Jung

BUNDESVERBAND BURGERINITIA TIVEN UMWELTSCHUTZEV
Prinz-Albert-Straβe 43, 53113,
Bonn, Germany
TEL : +49 228 214032
FAX : +49 228 214033
E-MAIL : bbu-bonn@t-online.de
CONTACT : Christine Eller Maton

BUSCHJOST IMI NORGREN GMBH+CO KG
Postfach 10 02 52-53,
Detmolder Straβe 256,
32945 Bad Oeynhausen,
Germany
TEL : +49 5731 7 91-0
FAX : +49 5731 791179
E-MAIL : mail@buschjost.de
WEB : http://www.buschjost.de

DAMPKESSELABAU DRESDEN ÜBIGAUGMBH
Wertstrabe BE 5,
D-01139 Dresden,
Germany
TEL : + 49 351 843450
FAX : + 49 351 8454561
CONTACT : Mr. Poister

DEGUSSA HÜLLSAG
Webfrauenustraβe 9, D-60287
Frankfurt Main, Germany
TEL : + 49 69 218 2604
FAX : + 49 69 218 2191
E-MAIL : unit@degussa.de

DEUTZ ENERGY GMBH
Carl. Benz Straβe 5,
D-681167 Mannheim,
Germany
TEL : + 49 621 384 8610
FAX : + 49 621 384 8602
WEB : http://www.deutz.de

DEUTSCHE GESELLSCHAFT FÜR SONNENENERGIE EV - DGS
Augustenstraβe 79,
80333, München,
Germany
TEL : + 49 89 52 40 71
FAX : + 49 89 52 16 68
E-MAIL : info,.@dgs.solar.org
WEB : http://www.dgs-solar.org
CONTACT : Ludwig Klehr

DEUTSCHE VANRIETS CHOTEN & HOUWENSG MBH
Junkersstraβe 12,
30179, Hannover,
Germany
TEL : + 49 511 372070
FAX : + 49 511 637421
CONTACT : Rainer Jordan

DEUTZ ENERGY GMBH
Carl-Benz Straβe 5, D-68167
Mannaheim, Germany
TEL : + 49 621 384 8610
FAX : + 49 621 384 8602
WEB : http://www.deutz.de

DEUTZ AG
Deutz-Mülheimmer Straβe 147-149
DS1057 Köln, Germany
TEL : + 49 221 822-0
FAX : + 49 221 822 5850
CONTACT : Mr. Gipp

DREIZLER (WALTER) GMBH WARMETECHNIK
Max-Planck Straβe 5,
78459 Spaichingen, Germany
TEL : + 49 7424 7009-0
FAX : + 49 7424 7009-90
E-MAIL : info@dreizler.com
WEB : http://www.dreizler.com
CONTACT : Roland Dreizler

DSE ENERGIE UND KÄLTETECHNIK MBH
Am Schlobpark 111 65203
Wiesbaden, Germany
TEL : + 49 611 608838
FAX : + 49 611 65740
WEB : http://www.hessenweb.de/
energie+kaeltetechnik
CONTACT: Mr. Dieter Scherf

DÜRR SYSTEMS GMBH
Otto Dürrstraβe. 18,
70435, Stuttgart, Germany
TEL : + 49 711 136-0
FAX : + 49 711 361716
WEB : http://www. durr.com

EAB ENERGIE ANLAGEN BERLIN GMBH
Flot wellstraβe 4-5, 10785,
Berlin, Germany
TEL : + 49 30 25496-0
FAX : + 49 30 25496-100
CONTACT: Dr.Bernhard Voigt

EBERT-INGENIEURE NUERNBERG
Marientergstrasse 84 90411
Nuernberg, Germany
TEL : + 49 911 9522-0
FAX : + 49 911 9522-100
E-MAIL : ebert@ebert-ingenieure.de
WEB : http://www.ebert-ingenieure.de
Contact : Thomas Gleissner

ESSO LUBRICANTS
Lubricants Technical Service Centre,
Moorburger Bogen 12,
21079 Hamburg, Germany
TEL: +49 40 7671 1202
FAX: +49 40 7671 1389
E-MAIL: thomas.thomsen@eci.exxon.sprint.com
CONTACT: Dr. Thomas Thomsen

FACHINFORMATIONS ZENTRUM
BINE Informationsolienst.
MechenstraBe 57,
D-53129 Bonn, Germany
TEL: +49 228 92379 0
FAX: +49 228 92379 29
E-MAIL: bine@fz-karlsruhe.de
WEB: http://bine.fz-karlsruhe.de
CONTACT: J P Mai

FAG OEM UND HANDLE AG
Georg-Schafer-Straβe
30.97421 Schweinfurt, Germany
TEL: +49 9721 91 33 88-1608
FAX: +49 9721 91 38 32
E-MAIL: zeidlhack_r@fag.de
WEB: http://www.fag.de
CONTACT: Rudolph Zeidlhack

FÖRDERGEMEINSCHAFT BLOCKHEIZKRAFTWERKE
Bismarckstrasse 63,
12163 Berlin Germany
TEL: +49 30 79 47 36 70
FAX: +49 30 79 47 36 60
E-MAIL: fg-bhkw@t-online.de
CONTACT: Adi Golbach

FORUM FÜR ZUKUNFTSENERGIEN
Godesberger Allee 90,
53175 Bonn,
Germany
TEL: +49 228 95 955 0
FAX: +49 228 95 955 50
E-MAIL: info@zukunftsenergien.de
WEB: wwwzukunftsenergien.de
CONTACT: Mr Mathias Ruchser

FRAUNHOFER INFORMATION ZENTRUM RAUM UND BAU - IRB
Postfach 800469, 70504 Stuttgart,
Germany
TEL: +49 711 970 2500
FAX: +49 711 970 2508
E-MAIL:irb@irb.fhg.de
WEB: www.irb.fhg.de
CONTACT: Dr. Ing W Wissmann

FRIEDRICH-ALEXANDER UNIVERSITÄT-LEHRSTUHL FÜRSTRÖMUNGSMECHANIK-LSTM
Cauerstrabe 4,
91058 Erlangen,
Germany
TEL: +49 9131 8529500
FAX: 49 9131 9529503
WEB: http://ww.istm.uni-erlangen.de
CONTACT: Prof. Franz Durst

GEA AHLBORON GMBH
Voss-Straβe 11-13,
31157 Sarstedt, Germany
TEL: +49 5066 990-0

GEA HAPPEL KLIMATECHNIK GMBH
Südstraβe 48,
44625 Hene,
Germany,
TEL: +49 2325 468 0
FAX: + 49 2325 468 222
CONTACT: Karl Herman Fischer

GEBRMÜLLER APPARATEBAU GMBH + COKG-GEMÜ GMBH + COKG - GEMU
Postfach 30,
74665 Ingelfingen,
Germany
TEL: +49 7940 123-0
FAX: +49 7940 123-192
CONTACT: Mr. Braunberger

GE ENERGY PRODUCTS
Bottroper Strasse 398,
45356 Essen, Germany
TEL: + 49 201 8667-0
FAX:+ 49 201 8667 542
CONTACT: Juergen Vinker Fluegel

GHHBORSIG TURBOMASCHINEN GMBH
Egellstraβe 21,
13507 Berlin, Germany
TEL : + 49 30 430 103
FAX : + 49 30 430 12841
WEB: www.ghh-bursig.de

KÖRTING HANNOVERAG
Bereich U, Badenstedter Straβe 56,
Postfach 91 13 63, 3000 Hannover 91, Germany
TEL: +49 511 21 29-0
FAX: +49 511 2129-233
E-MAIL:utk@koerting-hanover-ag.com
WEB:http://www.koertinghannover-ag.com

KRAFTWÄRME TECHNIK KRAFTWERK WÜRMTAL
Würmtalstrabe 11, 75181 Pforzheim,
Germany
TEL: +49 7231 62697
FAX: +49 7231 680311
E-MAIL: kwt-pf@t-online.de
CONTACT: Uwe Makowitz

LEHRSTUHL FÜR ENERGIE-UND UMWELTTECHNIK DER LEBENSMITTELINDUSTRIE TU-MUNCHEN I Weihenstephan,
85350, Freising,Germany
TEL: +49 8161 714362
FAX: +49 8161 714415
E-MAIL: mp@eul.blm.tu-muenchen.de
WEB: http://www.edu.agrar.tu-muerchen.de/blm/leu
CONTACT: Dipl-ing-Martin Gerpmier

LIUJIA SOLAR CORPORATION
Klaragasse 24, 90402 Nuernberg,
Germany
TEL: +49 911 226698
FAX: +49 911 22098
E-MAIL: liuxu@aol.com
WEB: http//www.liujia.com
CONTACT: Gm Liu

LUFTTECHNIK BAYREUTH RÜSKAMP GMPH
Pottensteiner Straβe 6 95447
Bayreuth, Germany
TEL:+49 921 7549 0
FAX:+49 921 7549-11
EMAIL:info@ltb.de
WEB:http://www.ltb.de
CONTACT:Dina Woldert

MAIN KRAFTWERKE AG
Supply of Energy,
Postfach 80 05 2, Bruningstrabe 1,
65929 Frankfurt am Main, Germany
TEL: +49 69 3107-0
FAX: +49 69 3107-2686
CONTACT: Klaus-Peter Kress

MAKROTHERM
Geltinger Strabe 44,
85652 Pliening, Germany
TEL: +49 8121 78800
FAX: +49 8121 81000
E-MAIL: info@makrotherm.de
WEB: http://www.makrotherm.com
CONTACT: Max Widmann

MINISTERIUM FÜR UMWELT UND FORSTEN RHEINLAND-PFALZ
Abteilung 108, Kaiser Friedrich
Strasse 7, 55116 Mainz, Germany
TEL: +49 6131 162343
FAX: +49 6131 164643
CONTACT: Dr Wolfgang Thune

PETERS & THIEDING HOCHSPANNUNGSTECHNIK GMBH
Sudring 40,D-21456 Wentorf.
TEL: +49 40 7292-30
FAX: +49 40 7292-3159
E-MAIL:info@peters-thieding.de
WEB : http://www.peters-thieding.com
CONTACT:Heinz-Dieter Juette
Transmission sub-stations for windfarms and grid connection

PHOENIX SOLAR GMBH
Grabenstr 17, 53619
Rheinbreitbach, Germany
TEL : + 49 2224 92270
FAX : + 49 2224 10321
E-MAIL:bde.ev@t-online.de
WEB:http://www.phoenixsolar.de
CONTACT:Dr A Peters

PLENUM ENERGY GMBH
Tannenweg 11,
25813 Husum
Germany
TEL: +49 4841 9677-0
FAX:+49 4841 9677-15
E-MAIL : plenum.energy@t.online.de
CONTACT: Mr Jorg Beland

RECHTSANWALTSSOZIETÄT KÖNIGSTRÄSSER UND PARTNER - UBERÖRTLICHE SOCIETAT
Munster/Wittenberg/Eilenberg,
Bült 4, 48143 Munster, Germany
TEL : +49 251 427 05
FAX : +49 251 446 22
CONTACT : Hans-Georg Konig

SMA REGEL SYSTEME GMBH
Hannoversche straβe I-5,
34266 Niestetal,
Germany
TEL: +49 561 95 22-0
FAX: +49 561 95 22-100
E-MAIL: info@sma.de
WEB: http://www.sma.de
CONTACT: Marko Werner

SOLARTHEMEN
Guido Bröer & Andreas Witt GbR
Bültestraβe 85,
32545, Bad Oeynhausen,
Germany
TEL:+49 5731 83460
FAX:+49 5731 83469
E-MAIL:redaktion@solarthemen.de
WEB:http://www.
solarthemen.de
CONTACT:Guido Broer

SOLID GMBH SOLAR INFORMATION AND DEMONSTRATION CENTRE
Heinrich-Stranka-Straβe 3-5,
90765 Furth,
Germany
TEL: +49 911 792035
FAX: +49 911 792412
E-MAIL: world@solid.de
WEB: http://www.solid.de
CONTACT: Matthias Huettmann

SOWLWAS GMBH
Eressener Straβe 8,
D-38173 Erkerode,
Germany
TEL: +49 5305 9019222
FAX: +49 5305 9019220
E-MAIL: info@sowlwas.de
CONTACT: Andres Stamer

STADTWERKESAARBRÜCKEN AG
Public Relations,
Hohenzollernstraβe
104-106, 66117
Saarbrückenn Germany
TEL: +49 681 587 2482
FAX: +49 681 587 2056
E-MAIL:info@saarbruecker-stadtwerke.de
WEB:http://www.saarbruecker-stadtwerke.de
CONTACT:Barbel Pfersdorff

UNION ZUR FOERDERUNG VON OEL-UND PROTEINPFLANZEN-UFOP
Godesberger Allee 145-148,
53175 Bonn
Germany
TEL: +49 228 81 198226
FAX: +49 228 8198203
E-MAIL: d.bockey@bauernverband.de
WEB: http://www.UFOP.de
CONTACT: Dieter Bockey

WK WÄRMETECHNISCHE ANLAGEN KESSEL-UND APPARATEBAU GMBH & CO KG
Product & Sales,
Industriestraβe 8-10,
Postfach 17 00 32,
35580 Wetzlar, Germany
TEL: +49 641 92238-0
FAX: +49 641 92238-88
E-MAIL: info@wk-gmbh.xom
WEB: http://www.wk-gmbh.com

HYBRID SYSTEMS

SOLAVENT
Zasiusstraβe 62 79102 Freiburg
Germany
TEL:+49 761 71950
FAX:+49 761 709647
CONTACT:Dr Theo Bracke

SOLON AGFUR SOLARTECHNIK
Schlesische Staβe 27,
10997 Berlin,
Germany
TEL:+49 30 610709-0
E-MAIL:p.rusch@solonag.com
WEB:http://www.solonag.com

SUNSET ENERGIETECHNIK GMBH
Dept Solarenergy,
Sunset Building,
Industriestraβe 8-22,
D91325 Adelsdorf, Germany
TEL: +49 9195 9494 0
FAX: +49 9195 9494 290
E-MAIL:info@sunset-solar.com
CONTACT: Klaus Waldera

TECHNICAL UNIVERSITY OF CLAUSTHAL
IEE, Leibnitzstraβe 28,
38678 Clausthal-Zellerfeld,
Germany
TEL: +49 5323 72 2570
FAX: +49 5323 72 2104
CONTACT: Prof HP Beck

WUSEL TRONIK GBR
Paul-Lincke-Ufer 41, 10999 Berlin,
Germany
TEL: +49 30 61850-71
FAX: +49 30 61850-75
E-MAIL: info@wuseltronik.com
WEB: http://www.wuseltronik.com
CONTACT: Martin Sauter

Kindly inform us of any errors and omissions in the listings by:

E-mail: unisun@vsnl.com

Fax: 91 80 2289294

SUPPLIERS

BATTERIES/INVERTERS

AUTOMATISIERUNG COMPUTER ENERGIE-ACE
Ingenieur-Team GbR,
Am Sandberg, 16, D-51643,
Gummersbach, Germany
TEL : +49 2261 24109
FAX : +49 2261 24112
CONTACT : Achim Kempe

DEUTSCHE EXIDE STANDBY GMBH
Marketing Im Thiergarten, 63654
Budingen, Germany
TEL: +49 60 42 81-70
FAX: +49 60 42 8 15 38
E-MAIL: networkpower@exideworld.com
WEB: http://www.exide.de
CONTACT: Susanne Kraul

HAGEN BATTERIE AG
Coesterweg 45, 59494 Soest,
Germany
TEL : + 49 2921 703-0
FAX : + 49 2921 703-277
CONTACT: Herr Koch

HOPPECKE BATTERIEN - CARL ZÖLLNER UND SOHN GMBH & CO KG
Bontkirchener Straβe,
59929 Brilon, Germany
TEL: +49 2963 61-1
FAX: +49 2963 61-270
E-MAIL: hoppecke.io@t-online.de
CONTACT: Reinhard Niggemeier

INGENIEUBÜRO R GRÜB
Olbergweg 8,
79283 Bollschwell, Germany
TEL: +49 7633 7025
FAX: +49 7633 82129
CONTACT: Dipl-Ing R Grub

KLEIN GUSTAV ELEKROGERATEBAU
Postfach 1248, 86952 Schogau,
Germany
TEL: +49 8861 2090
FAX: +49 8861 209180

MAGNETRONIC GMBH
Kreuzhofstraβe 10,
81476 Munchen, Germany
TEL: +49 89 755 36 70
FAX: +49 89 755 60 59
CONTACT: Mr Seifat

MICHEL SOLAR ELECTRONICS-MSE
Waldstrabe 1, 66287 Quierschield 4,
Germany
TEL: +49 6825 7501
FAX: +49 6825 7501
CONTACT: Mr Michel

Q-CELLS AG
Schlesirche Str 27, 10997 Berlin,
Germany
TEL: +49 30 610 7090
FAX: +49 30 610 70999
WEB: http://www.q-cells.com

ROSENDAHL INDUSTRIEVERTRETUNGEN
Adolf-Dembach-Strabe1,
47829 Krefeld, Germany
TEL: +49 2151 456789-0
FAX: +49 2151 456789-9
E-MAIL: info@rosendahl-energietechnik.de
WEB: http://www.SMA.de
CONTACT: Reiner Rosendahl

SANYO ENERGY (EUROPE) CORPORATE GMBH
Headquarters Stahlgruberring 4,
81829 Munich, Germany
TEL: +49 89 4600 95-0
FAX: +49 89 4600 95-190
E-MAIL: info.Europe@sanyo-energy.com
CONTACT: Josef Zankl

SIEMENS AG / ZN BRAUNSCHWEIG
I&S IS, Frankfurter Strabe 3d, 38122
Braunschweig, Germany
TEL: +495312712-204
FAX: +495312712-323
E-MAIL: siemens-photovoltaik@bwgtd.siemens.de
WEB: http://www.siemens-photovoltaik.de

SOLARA AG
Energy from Sun and Wind
Borselstraβe 3-7, 22765 Hamburg,
Germany
TEL:+49 40 391 065-0
FAX:+49 40 391 065-99
E-MAIL:info@solara.de
WEB:http://www.solara.de
CONTACT:Thomas Rudolph

SOLAR-FABRIK GMBH
Munzinger Straβe 2 D-79111
Freiburg Germany
TEL:+49 761 4000 0
FAX:+49 761 4000 199
E-MAIL:info@solar-fabrik.de
WEB:http://www.solar-fabrik.de
CONTACT:George Salvamoser

SONNENSCHEIN GMBH
Thiergarten, 63654 Budingen,Germany
TEL: +49 60 42 81 -0
FAX: +49 60 42 81 538

SUN POWER SOLAR TECHNIK GMBH
Marktplatz2-4, D-61118,
Bad Vilbel, Germany
TEL: +49 6101 5845 50
FAX: +49 6101 5845 60
E-MAIL:sales@sunpower.de
WEB:http://www.sunpower.de
CONTACT:Hans Oppermann

SUNWARESOLARTECHNIK GMBH & CO KG
Dusseldorfer Straβe 80,
47239 Duisburg-Rumein, Germany
TEL: +49 2151 406045
FAX: +49 2151 406208
E-MAIL: info@sunware.de
WEB: http://www.sunware.de
CONTACT: Frank van Buhl

UMWELTFREUNDLICHE ENERGIEANLAGEN GMBH-UFE
Dorfstraβe 16,
39615 Wanzer, Germany
TEL : +49 3939581-442
FAX : +49 3939581-914

WÜRTH ELECTRONIK GMBH & COKG
Wurth Solergy, Ludwigsburger Straβe
100, 71672 Marbach am Neckar,
TEL: +49 7144 94 14-20
FAX: +49 7144 94 14-19
E-MAIL: ws.vk@we-online.de
WEB: http://www.wuerth-solergy.de
CONTACT: Reinhard Eckert

WUSEL TRONIK GBR
Paul-Lincke-Ufer 41, 10999 Berlin,
TEL: +49 30 61850-71
FAX: +49 30 61850-75
E-MAIL: info@wuseltronik.com
WEB: http://www.wuseltronik.com
CONTACT: Martin Sauter

INSTRUMENTS

ADOLF THIES GMBH & CO KG
Box 3536+3541,
D-37025 Gottingen, Germany
TEL: +49 551 7 90 01-0
FAX: +49 551 7 90 01-65
E-MAIL: info@thiesclima.com
WEB: http:// www.thiesclima.com
CONTACT: Peter Krause

AMMONIT GESELLSCHAFT FUR MESSTECHNIK MBH
Paul-Lincke-Ufer 41,10999 Berlin,
Germany
TEL: +49 30 612 79 54
FAX: +49 30 618 30 60
E-MAIL: ammonit@ammonit.de
WEB: http://www.ammonit.de
CONTACT: Christian Melzer

ANEMOS
Sattlerstrabe 1,21365 Adendorf, Germany
TEL: +49 4131 1895 77
FAX: +49 4131 1826 2
E-MAIL: anemos@t-online.de
CONTACT: Dr Heinz-Theo Mengelkamp

ATEC ELECTRONIC VERTRIEBS GMBH
MulhaustraBe 29, 86938 Schondorf, Germany
TEL : +49 81 92 10 41
FAX : +49 81 92 10 42
CONTACT : Frau Monika Rechberger

DEGERENERGIE
Hochbergstrasse 60,
D-72160 Horb aN,
Germany
TEL: +49 7482 91195
FAX: +49 7482 91194
E-MAIL: info@DEGERRenergie.de
WEB: http://www.DEGERRenergie.de

DEWIND AG
Seelandstrasse 1,
D-23569 Lubeck, Germany
TEL: +49 451 3073 0
FAX: +49 451 3073 730
E-MAIL: export@dewind.de
WEB: http://www.dewind.de
CONTACT: JD Mayer

DOMUS-SOLARHAUS GMBH
Buschkoppel 24, 24145 Kiel, Germany
TEL: +49 431 712253
FAX: +49 431 714353
CONTACT: Gerhard WP Bemdt

DOPPSTAD- DVG MBH
Steinbrink 4, D-42555 Velbert, Germany
TEL: +49 2052 889 0
FAX: +49 2052 889 160

DOW DEUTSCHLAND INC
Postfach 20,
77834 Rheinmunster,
Germany
TEL: +49 72 2791-3395
FAX: +49 72 2791-3608
WEB: http://www.derakane.com
CONTACT: Andrew Miller

DRIESSEN & KERN GMBH
Postfach 1424,
24572 Bad Bramstedt, Germany
TEL : + 49 41 92 9814
FAX : + 49 41 92 7321
CONTACT: Mr H H Driesen

ECÖTECH GMBH UMWELT-MEB SYSTEMS
Siemnsstraβe 8, 53121,
Bonn Germany
TEL : + 49 229 61 47 99
FAX : + 49 229 61 48 86

EGIS GMBH
Flutstrabe 34-38, 63071 Offenbach, Germany
TEL: +49 69 858327
FAX: +49 69 857863
E-MAIL: solar@EGIS.org
WEB: http://www.EGIS.org
CONTACT: Eng Dieter Meixner

ENNOSGMBH
Merzhauserstraβe 110,
D-79100 Freiburg, Germany
TEL : + 49 761 407744
FAX : + 49 761 407605
E-MAIL: sonne@ennos.de
WEB: http://www.ennos.de
CONTACT : Klaus V Dohlen

GRAEFFDE ING RW-RKBE
Domagkweg 7,
D-78126 Koenigsfeld,
Germany
TEL : + 49 7725 91191
FAX : + 49 8825 1620
CONTACT: G Hoffman

HÖRMANN GMBH
Environmental Monotoring,
Haupstraβe 45-47,
85614 Kirchseeon,
Germany
TEL: +49 8091 52262
FAX: +49 8091 1275
E-MAIL: ems@hoermann-gmbh.de
WEB: http://www.hoermann-gmbh.de
CONTACT: Claus Holzheimer

HYDROWATT GMBH
Nordliche Uferstraβe 4-6,
D-76189 Karlsruhe,
Germany
TEL: +49 721 55 72 53
FAX: +49 721 59 36 70
WEB: http://www.hydrowatt.de
CONTACT: Klaus Sommerkorn

ING-BUERO MAYER
Kossenerstrasse 6b,
D-81373 Munchen, Germany
TEL: +49 89 7437 12-13
FAX: +49 89 7437 12 -14
E-MAIL: mayer@ibom.de
WEB: http://www.ibom.de
CONTACT: Dr Oliver Mayer

INGENIEURBURO SCHODER GBRMBH
Graf-Reisach-Strasse 6, D-86688
Graisbach, Germany
TEL: +49 9097 1818
FAX: +49 9097 1819
E-MAIL: info@schoder.de
WEB: http://www.schoder.de
CONTACT: Erwin Schoder

KLUBER LUBRICATION MUNCHEN KG
Geisenhausenstr 7, 81379
Munchen, Germany
TEL: +49 89 7876-0
FAX: +49 89 7876-333
E-MAIL: e-sales@klueber.com
CONTACT: Thomas Kamprath

LANDIS GYR & STAEFA GMBH
Postfach 60 05 29,
Friesstrabe 20-24,
60335 Frankfurt am Main, Germany
TEL : +49 69 4002-0
FAX : +49 69 4002-1590
CONTACT : Herr Stelzer

MAYWIND
Alte Bahnhofstrasse 19,
77933 Lahr, Germany
TEL: +49 7821 983720
FAX: +49 7821 983721
E-MAIL: services@maywind.com
WEB: http://www.maywind.com

MESA SYSTEM TECHNIK GMBH
August-Borsig-Str 20,
78467 Konstanz,
Germany
TEL: +49 75 31 93 71-0
FAX: +49 75 31 93 71-71
E-MAIL: info@mesa-systemtechnik.de
WEB: http://www.mesasystemtechnick.de
CONTACT: Heinrich Bercher

METEOROLOGISCHE MESSTECHNIK GMBH - METEK
Fritz-StraBmann-Straβe 4,
25337 Elmshorn,
Germany
TEL: +49 4121 4359-0
FAX: +49 4121 4359-20
E-MAIL: info@metek.de
CONTACT: H-J Kirtzel

NESSMESS-UND MELDESYSTEME
Langstraβe 40,
D-63526 Eriensee,
Germany
TEL: +49 61 83 90 17 82
FAX: +49 61 83 90 17 83
E-MAIL: nes-viel@t-online.de

GERMANY

NEW ENERGY AND MEASURING SYSTEMS- NES
Langstrabe 40, D-63526 Erlensse
Germany
TEL: +49 61 83 90 17-82
FAX: +49 61 83 90 17-83
E-MAIL: nes-viel@t-online.de
CONTACT: Dr Falk Auer

NOVA SOLAR GMBH
PO Box 1149, 68805 Neulussheim, Germany
TEL: +49 620 539 2847
FAX: +49 620 539 2848
CONTACT: Christian Engelhorn

PHYSICS INSTITUT
Kanzleistraβe 91,
24943 Flensburg,
Germany
TEL : + 49 461 805269
FAX : + 49 461 805300
CONTACT : Prof U Roose

PINTSCH BAMAG GMBH
Hunxer Straβe 149, 46537
Dinslaken, Germany
TEL : + 49 2064 602-0
FAX : + 49 2064 602-266
CONTACT : G Hovermann

RAAB KARCHER ENERGY SERVICE GMBH
Rudolf-von-Bennigsen-Forder-Platz 3,
45131 Essen, Germany.
TEL: +4920145902
FAX: +492014593178
WEB: http://www.rkes.com
CONTACT: Karl-Hans Waldeyer

RESOL-ELEKTRONISCHE REGELUNGEN GMBH
Heiskampstraβe 10,
D-45527 Hattingen,
Germany
TEL : +49 2324 9648-0
FAX : +49 2324 9648-55
E-MAIL : info@resol.de
WEB : http://www.resol.de
CONTACT : Nicole Beinhoff

SHW-SCHWABISCHE HUITTENWERKE GMBH
Materials Handling and Process
Division Wilhelmstrabe 67,
Postfach
32 80, 73433 Aalen,
Germany
TEL : +49 7361 502-430
FAX : +49 7361 502-288
E-MAIL : wa-vt@shw.de
CONTACT : Karsten Bartnicki

SOLON AG FUR SOLARTECHNIK
Schlesische Strabe 27, 10997 Berlin
Germany
TEL: +4930610709-0
E-MAIL: p.rusch@solonag.com
WEB: http://www.solonag.com

SOLAR SYSTEMS SCHUTT GMBH
Am Hang 3, D-61476 Kronberg,
Germany
TEL:+49 6173 323338
FAX:+49 6173 323337
E-MAIL:company@solar-systemeschutt.de

STECA GMBH
Mammostrasse 1,
D-87700 Memmingen, Germany
TEL: +4983318558-0
FAX: +4983318558-11
E-MAIL: info@stecasolar.com
WEB: http://www.stecasolar.com
CONTACT: Jurgen Raach

SUN POWER SOLAR TECHNIK GMBH
Marktplatz2-4, D-61118,
Bad Vilbel, Germany
TEL: +49 6101 5845 50
FAX: +49 6101 5845 60
E-MAIL:sales@sunpower.de
WEB:http://www.sunpower.de
CONTACT:Hans Oppermann

WILMERS MEBTECHNIK GBR
Hirschgraben 24,
D-22089 Hamburg,
Germany
TEL: +494075660898
FAX: +494075660899
E-MAIL: info@wilmers.com
WEB: http://www.wilmers.com
CONTACT: Walter Wilmers

COATING & PAINTS

DOW DEUTSCHLAND INC
Postfach 20,
77834 Rheinmunster,
Germany
TEL : + 49 722791 3395
FAX : + 49 72 2791 3608
WEB : http://www.derakane.com
CONTACT: Mr. Andrew Miller

TRICON GMBH
Oltmannsstraβe 3,
D-79100 Freiburg,
Germany
TEL: +49 761 400 689-0
FAX: +49 761 400 689-90
E-MAIL: tricontec@t-online.de
CONTACT: Paulas Straub

TINOX GMBH
Schwere-Reiter-StraBe 35/2b,
D-80797 Munchen, Germany
TEL: +49 89 3000 72-0
FAX: +49 89 3000 7272
WEB:http://www.tinox.de
CONTACT:Dr M Lazarov

UMWELTKONTOR RENEWABLE ENERGY AKTIENGESELLSCHAFT
Rheinstr 7,
41836 Huckelhoven, Germany
TEL : +49 2433 970385
FAX : +49 2433 970137
E-MAIL : zentrale@umweltkontor.com
WEB : http://www.umweltkontor.com
CONTACT : Henry Lohmann

UP GMBH
Am Technologiepark 1,
03099 Kolkwitz, Germany
TEL: +49 355 7841 430
FAX: +49 355 7841 435
E-MAIL: up.cb@t-online.de
WEB: http://ourworld.compuserve.com/homepages/up_gmbh
CONTACT: Gerhard Kast

VITERRA ENERGY SERVICES AG
Grugaplatz 4, 45131 Essen, Germany
TEL: +49 201 459 02
FAX: +49 201 459 3258
WEB: http://www.viterra-es.com

VOSS ELECTRONIC GMBH
Baaderstrabe 84, D-80469
Munchen, Germany
TEL; +49892011177
FAX: +49892012877
E-MAIL: info@vosselectronic.de
WEB: http://www.vosselectronic.de
CONTACT: Robert Wolf

INSULATIONS

VOLQUARDSEN (JENS) VOLLWÄRMESCHUTZ GMBH
Fährblick 52, 24790 Schacht-Audorf,
Germany
TEL: +49 4331 92736
FAX: +49 4331 93410
CONTACT: Jens-Peter Volquardsen

GLASS

VEGLA VEREINIGTE GLASWERKE GMBH
Kinon Sicherheitsglas GmbH,
Julicher Straβe 495,
D-52070 Aachen, Germany
TEL: +49 241 9667 2-40
FAX: +49 241 9667 2-41
CONTACT: N Luling

CONSTRUCTION SERVICES

DYCKERHOFF & WIDMANN AG
Erdigner Landstraβe 1,
81902 Munchen,
Germany
TEL : + 49 89 92 551
FAX : +, 49 89 55 21 27
E-MAIL : ma.hv@dywidag.de

GAS ENERGIETECHNOLOGIE GMBH
Landfill Gas Biogas and Coal Mine Gas Utilisation,
Hessenstrabe 57,
47809 Krefeld,
Germany
TEL: +49 2151 5255-0
FAX: +49 2151 5255-55
E-MAIL: info@g-a-s-energy.com
WEB: http://www.g-a-s-energy.com
CONTACT: Mr Jurgen Brux

WINKRA ENERGIE GMBH
Leisewitzstraβe 37b,
30175 Hannover,
Germany
TEL: +49 511 288 32 0
FAX: +49 511 288 32-90
E-MAIL: info@winkra.de
WEB: http://www.winkra.de
CONTACT: Martin Lawrenz

FUEL CELLS

ELECTRO-FARMING GMBH
Grottenweg 4, 85253
Grossberghofen,
Germany
TEL: +49 8138 92950
FAX: +49 8138 8935
E-MAIL: info@electro-farming.de
WEB: http://www.electro-farming.de
CONTACT: Christine Angerer

OTHERS

AM SONNENRAIN 80,
79539 Lorrach,
Germany
TEL: +49 7621 44248
FAX: +49 7621 44248
CONTACT: Dipl-Ing.F.Seeger

AQUASOLAR AG
Oberreit 2,
83620 Feldkirchen,
Germany
TEL: +49 8063 809673
FAX: +49 8063 809674
E-MAIL: info@aquasolar.com
WEB: http:// www.aquasolar.com
CONTACT: Oliver Jahnel

ARGUS GESSELLSCHAFT FUR UMWEL TMEBTECHNIK MBH
Goethestrasse 35, D-27721
Ritterhude Germany
TEL: +49 4292 9923 35
FAX: +49 4292 9923 65
E-MAIL: info@argusnet.de
WEB: http:// www.argusnet.de
CONTACT: Joerg R Gutkuhn

BERGISCHE UNIVERSTAT GESAMTHOCHSCHULE WUPPERTAL
Institute für Automatisierungstechnik and Technisch, Fuhlrott Straβe 10,
42097, Wuppertal, Germany
TEL : +49 202 439-2952/3
CONTACT : Prof. Nour Eldin

BOSS PRO-TEC
Renewable Energy,
Im Anwandel 12, 22459 Albstadt.
Germany
TEL : +49 7432 9838-0
FAX : +49 7432 1719 70
E-MAIL : info@boss-pro-tec.de
WEB : http://www.boss-pro-tec.de
CONTACT : Gerd Klaus

BUNDESVERBAND DER AGRARNGENIEUREEV -BAI
Albrecht Durer Strasse 126,
97204 Hochberg, Germany
TEL : +49 931 404 2591
FAX : +49 931 404 2591
CONTACT : Dieter Wittmer

CUBE ENGINEERING GMBH
Tannenweg 11, D-25813 Husum,
Germany
TEL: +49 4841 9677-0
FAX: +49 4841 9677-15
E-MAIL: info@cube-engineering.com
CONTACT: Mr Jorg Beland

DARMSTADT UNIVERSITY OF TECHNOLOGY
Center for Inter disciplinary Studies in Technology, Hochschulstrasse I.D.
64289 Darmstdt, Germany
TEL : + 49 6151 164113
FAX : + 49 6151 166752
E-MAIL : scholand@zit.tu-darmstadt.de
WEB : http://www.zit.tu-darmstadt.de
CONTACT : Markus Scholand

DÄTWYLER INTER AG & CO
Allerfeldstraβe Be 5,
31833 Springe, Germany
TEL : + 49 5045 9109-0
FAX : + 49 5045 9109-11
CONTACT : Mr Speery

DR KNIEHL CONSULTING AND ENGINEERING SERVICES - CES
Ingenieurburo Renet Kniehl
Kleinschmidstraβe, 35, 69115
Heidelberg, Germany
TEL : + 49 6221 16 1686
FAX : + 49 6221 182030
E-MAIL :
106010.327@compuserve.com
CONTACT: Mr Rainer Kniehl

DEUTZ ENERGY GMBH
Carl-Benz-Strabe 5,
D-68167 Mannheim,
Germany
TEL: +49 621 384 8601
FAX: +49 621 384 8602
WEB: http://www.deutz.com

ECOS GESSELLS CHAFT FÜR ENTWICKLING UND CONSULTING OSNABRÜCK MBH
Westerbreite, 7,
49084, Osanadbrück,
Germany
TEL : + 49 541 9776 200
FAX : + 49 541 97778 202
E-MAIL : info@eco.consult.com
WEB : http://www.
Ecos.consult.com
CONTACT : Peter Beck

ECOS GESSELLS CHAFT FOR ENTWICKLING UND CONSULTING OSNABUCK MBH
Westerbrete, 7, 49084,
Osaudbrack,
Germany
TEL : + 49 541 9776 200
FAX : + 49 541 97778 202
E-MAIL : info@eco.consult.com
WEB : http://www.
Ecos.consult.com

EKRA GERMANY GMBH
Zeppelinstrabe 16,
74357 Bonnigheim, Germany
TEL: +49 7143 8844-0
FAX: +49 7143 884422
E-MAIL: sales@ekra.com
CONTACT: Paul Kasulke

ELEKTROHAUSSTAEDLER
Markstraβe 11,
16792 Zehdenick,
Germany
TEL : +49 3307 2618
FAX : +49 3307 2618

ELMAR BOLLIN
Im Hubhof 8, 794, Germany
TEL : +49 7664 58 48
FAX : +49 7664 58 48

ELSITRON REGELSYSTEME GMBH
Oskar-Meyrer-Straβe 15,
65719 Hofheim Ts, Germany
TEL : +49 6192 287160
FAX : +49 6192 287161
E-MAIL : elsitron@t-online.de
WEB : http://www.elstron.de
CONTACT : Ewald Michael

ENERGIEKONTOR WINDKRAFT GMBH
Stresemannstraβe 46,
27570 Bremerhaven, Germany
TEL: +49 471 14072
FAX: +49 471 140209
E-MAIL: info@energiekontor.de
WEB: http:/'/www.energiekontor.de
CONTACT : Dr. B Wilkens

ENVIRONMENTAL PROTECTION ENCOURAGEMENT AGENCY EPEA
Feldstraβe 36, 20357 Hamburg, Germany
TEL : +49 40 43 13 49-0
FAX : +49 40 43 13 40-49
E-MAIL: epea@epea.com
WEB: http://www.epea.com
CONTACT : Dr Michael Braungart

EPCOS AG
PO Box 80 17 09,
D-81617 Munich, Germany
TEL: +49 89 6 36 – 2 38 17
FAX: +49 89 6 36 – 2 27 48
CONTACT: Rudolf Muller

EUPEC GMBH + CO KG
Max-Planck-Strabe5, 59581
Warstein, Germany
TEL: +49 2902 7641-144
FAX: +49 2902 7647-1144
E-MAIL:
norbert.dittmann@eupec.com
WEB: http://www.eupec.com
CONTACT: Norbert Dittman

EURO FUR ENERGIE GERECHTES BAUEN
Architecture Research and Development, MeerfeldstraBe
I.A. D. 50737 Koln, Germany
TEL : +49 221 599 6047
FAX : +49 221 599 6048
E-MAIL : alexlohr@beb-koeln.de

EURO FUR ENERGIE WIRTSCHAFT UND TECHNISCHE PLANUNG GMBH-BET
Theatre Straβe 54-56, 52062,
Aachen, Germany
TEL : +49 241 470 62-0
FAX : +49 241 47062-60
E-MAIL :bet-aachen@t-online.de

FACHVERBAND ELEKTROLEUCHTEN IM ZENTRALVERBAND DER ELEKTROTECHNIK UND ELEKTRONIK INSTUSTRIES EV
Gutes Licht,
Postfach 70 12 61,
Stresemannallee 19,
60596 Frankfurt am Main, Germany
TEL: +49 69 6302 353
FAX: +49 69 6302 400
E-MAIL: licht@zvej.org
WEB: http://www.zvei.de
CONTACT: Dr Ulrich Merker

FÖHS (DIPL-ING) GMBH
Niederkircher Straβe 6, 67146
Deidesheim Weinstr, Germany
TEL: +49 6326 6575/76
FAX: +49 6326 7561
E-MAIL: fohs.gmbh@aol.com
CONTACT: Adi Golbach

FÜR ANGEWAND TE FORSCHUNG GMBH
Postfach 105145,
40042 Dusseldorf, Germany
TEL : +49 211 6707-200
FAX : +49 211 6707-310

GEHRLICHER UMWELTZHOHENDE ENERGISYS TEME GMBH
Guerickestrabe 35, 80805 München.
Germany
TEL : + 49 89 36 1000 80
FAX: + 49 89 36 1000 90
E-MAIL : info@gehrlicher.com
WEB: www.gehrlicher.com

GKOKTEK GMBH
Gwinnerstraβe 46, 60388 Frankfurt,
Germany
TEL : + 49 694011-339
FAX : + 49 69 4011-660

HANS BIEBERSTEIN
Steinlein 9a, 97078 Wurzburg,
Germany
TEL : +49 931 2800 17
FAX : +49 931 24284

HSM PRESSEN GMBH & CO KG
Postfach 1163,
D-88678 Salem, Germany
TEL: +49 7553 822-0
FAX: +49 7553 822-160
E-MAIL: info@hsm-online.de
WEB: http://www.hsm-online.de

INDUSTRIES ASSOCIATION-BSE
Elisabethstraβe 34,
80796 Munchen, Germany
TEL : + 49 89 27 81 34 24
FAX : + 49 89 27 31 28 91
E-MAIL : nfo@bse.solarindustrie.com

KLUBER LUBRICATION
Marketing And Application, Postfach
70 1047, 81310 Munchen,
Germany
TEL: +49 89 7876680
FAX: +49 89 7876573
E-MAIL: thomas.kamprath@klueber.com
WEB: http://www.klueber.com
CONTACT: Thomas Kamprath

KGW SCHWERINER MASCHINENBAU GMBH
Wismarsche Str 380, 19055
Schwerin,
Germany
TEL: +49 385 57310
FAX: +49 385 5731322
E-MAIL: KGW-Schwerin@t-online.de
CONTACT: Mr Helmit Welle

KH ELECTROTECHNIK GMBH
Gederner Straβe 16, 63688 Gedern/
Ober-Seemen, Germany
TEL: +49 6045 961818
FAX: +49 6045 961832
CONTACT: Karl Heinz Henning

LOOS INTERNATIONAL EISENWERK THEDDORLOOS GMBH
PO Box, D-91709 Gunzenhausen,
Germany
TEL: + 49 9831 56 253
FAX: + 49 9831 56274
E-MAIL:sales@loos-int.com
WEB:http://www.loos-int.com
CONTACT:Rudolf Hofmann

MANFRED THUMLER
Hans-Traut-Straβe 25,
90455 Nurnberg, Germany
TEL: +49 9122 78711
FAX: +49 9122 73127
CONTACT:Manfred Thumler

MAX RHODIUS GMBH
Treuchtlinger Straβe 23, 91781
WeiBenburg / Bayern, Germany
TEL: +49 9141 919 0
FAX: +49 9141 919 45
E-MAIL: rhodius@wugnet.baynet.de
WEB: http://www.weissenburg-online.de/rhodius
CONTACT: Andreas Hambach

MEGATEC SYSTEMS - ASEQUA COMPANY
VOC - Control Division,
Honeywellstraβe 18,
D-63477 Maintal, Germany
TEL: +49 6181 9404-0
FAX: +49 6181 466 46
E-MAIL: ruk@megtec.com
CONTACT: R Krueger

MOLLBAUÖKOLOGISCHE PRODUKTE GMBH
Rheintalstraβe 35-43, 68723
Schwetzingen, Germany
TEL: +49 6202 2782-0
FAX: +49 6202 2782-81
EMAIL:moll.proclima@t-online.de
CONTACT: Lothar Moll

PFLEIDERER AG
Infrastruktechnik, Ingolstädter
Strabe 51, D-92318 Neumarkt,
TEL: +49 9181 28-237
FAX: +49 9181 28-514
E-MAIL:hinzmann@pfleiderer.com
WEB:htte/www.pfleiderer.com
CONTACT:Norbert Hinzmann

PLAMBECK CONTRACON BAU UND UMWELTTECHNIK GMBH
Peter-Henlein- Strabe 2-4, 27472
Cuxhaven, Germany
TEL: +49 47 21 718 03
FAX: +49 47 21 718 200
CONTACT: Martin Schmidt

PROLITE GESELLSCHAFT FUR LICHTTECHNIK GMBH
Drost-Huelshoff-Weg 21, D-88709
Meersburg, Germany
TEL: +49 7532 4358 35
FAX: +49 7532 4358 50

RENK AG
Werk Rheine,
Rodder Damm 170,
D-48432 Rheine,
Germany
TEL : +49 5971 790 314
FAX : +49 5971 790 208
CONTACT : Mr Hake

ROTORBLADE COMPOSITE MEGA WATT TECHNOLOGY GMBH
Hildegardstr 16, 10715, Berlin,
Germany
TEL: +49 30 26 484575
FAX: +49 30 26 484576
E-MAIL: wolfgang@holstein.st
WEB: http://www.holstein.st
CONTACT: Dr Wolfgang Holstein

RWE ENERGIE AG
Gesellschaft fur
Kommunikationstechnik und
Mediena,
Montebruch Str 2,
45219 Essen,
Germany
TEL: +492011223906
FAX: +492011222704
WEB: http://www.rweenergie.de
CONTACT: Barbara Exkrich

SOLARMOBIL VEREIN ERLANGEN EV
Schillerstraβe 54,
91054 Ertangen,
Germany
TEL:+49 9131 501 663
FAX:+49 9131 501 663
E-MAIL:solarmobil@fen-net.de
WEB:http://www.fen-net.desolarmobil
CONTACT:Christian Duerschner

SOLOR PROJECT ENERGIES\YSTEMS GMBH
AMbLASIBERG 13_18 88250
Weingarten,
Germany
TEL : +49 751 560 33_0
FAX : +49 751 560 3377
CONTACT : Reiner Niedermann

SOLOR WORLD
Ingenieuburo fur Industrieanlagen
Karl Legien Straβe 190,
D-53117 Bonn, Germany
TEL:+49 228 55920-0
FAX:+49 228 55920-99
E-MAIL:service@solarworld.de
WEB:http://www.solarworld.de
CONTACT: Peter Westermayr

TECHNISCHE UNVERSITÄT BERLIN
Fachgebiet Energie und
Rohstoffwirtschaft.
Müller-Breslau-
StraBe 12, 10623 Berlin,
Germany
TEL: +49 30 314 23214
FAX: +49 30 614 25582
E-MAIL: c.nabe@ww.tu-berlin.de
WEB: http://
www.energiewirtschaft.tu-berlin.de
CONTACT: Charistian Nabe

TRIBOL GMBH
A Burmah Castrol Company,
PO Box 500 210,
41172 Mönchengladbach,
Germany
TEL: +49 2161 909 30
FAX: +49 2161 909 400
WEB: http://www.tribol.de
CONTACT: Ms Willie Manke

TUV NORD EV
Anlangentechnik,
Bei den Drei Pfählen 41,
28205 Bremen,
Germany
TEL: +49 421 4498 111
FAX: +49 421 4498 188
E-MAIL: bremen@tuev-nord.de
WEB: http://www.tuev.nord.de
CONTACT: Helmut Varchmin

TÜVSÜDDEUTSCHLAND BAUUND BETRIEB GMBH
Fachbereich Gebäudetechnik,
Westendstraβe 199,
80686 München, Germany
TEL: +49 89 5791 3313
FAX: +49 89 5791 3355
E-MAIL: ralf.szamer@tuevsued.de
CONTACT: Ralf Szamer

UHLMANNSOLARELECTRONIC GMBH
Tullastr 5, 79331 Tungen, Germany
TEL : +49 7641 8291
FAX : +49 7641 6816
E-MAIL : uhfmann-solar@tgonline.de
WEB : http://www.uhlmann-solar.de
CONTACT : Arno Uhlmann

UNIT ENERGY EUROPE AG
Ober-Eschbacher Strasse 109,
613528 Bad Homburg, Germany
TEL: +4961729245-0
FAX: +4961729245-99
WEB: http://www.unit-energy.com

VALENTIN ENERGY SOFTWARE
Kopenicker Strabe 9,
D-10997 Berlin, Germany
TEL: +49 30 61 79 17 80
FAX: +49 30 61 79 17 88
E-MAIL: info@valentin.de
WEB: http:///www.valentin.de
CONTACT: Denise Dawes

VEWRLAG SOLAR EZUKUNFT
Anna Rosenthal Weg 21,
D-91052 Erlangen, Germany
TEL: +49 9131 303222
FAX: +49 9131 303566
CONTACT: Christian Durschner

Kindly inform us of any errors and omissions in the listings by:

E-mail: unisun@vsnl.com

Fax: 91 80 22289294

GREECE

SOLAR THERMAL

CALPAK-CICERO HELLAS INDUSTRIES LTD
9 Syngrou Avenue, 117-43,
Athens, Greece
TEL : +30 1 924 7250
FAX : +30 1 923 1616
CONTACT: Andreas Constantinedes

EGG PROMOTEUR
Co Konstanidis, GR-37010 Afetes, Greece
TEL : +30 93 29 70 69
FAX : +30 421 59043
CONTACT: Erwin Egg

FOCO SA
Marketing, 108 Karamanli Ave,
13671 Athens, Greece
TEL: +30 1 2406 248
FAX: +30 1 2466 155
E-MAIL: ct@foco.gr
CONTACT: Costas Travassaros

FYROGENIS SA
Development Projects,
20th km National Road
No.1 145 65 Ekali, Athens, Greece
TEL: +30 1 8136 301
FAX: +30 1 8135 301
E-MAIL: fyrogenis@hol.gr
WEB: http://chr.fyrogenis
CONTACT: Michael P Kourtzis

HELIOAKMI LTD
Nea Zoi, 10300 Aspropyrgos,
Attiki, Greece
TEL: +30 1 5595624/5/6
FAX: +30 1 5595723
E-MAIL: ilioakmi@asda.gr
WEB: http://united-hellas.com/industry/helioakmi
CONTACT: Christos Papadopoulos

INTERSOLAR SA
Dimosthenousstr 267, 17674
Kallithea, Greece
TEL: + 30 1 9401596
FAX: +30 1 9409119
E-MAIL: solar@hellois.net.gr
WEB: http://www.intersolar.gr
CONTACT: I Paradissiadis

MABLEKOS A TAXIARCHIS
Iasonos St 22, 38333 Volos, Greece
TEL : +30 421 31736
FAX : +30 421 31736
CONTACT : Mablekos A Taxiarchis

MALTEZOS SA
Thessalonikis 58, 18345 Moschato-Athens, Greece
TEL: +30 1 9430629
FAX: +30 1 9424732
CONTACT: Costas Vrellis

MINOS SA
Thessaloniki Industrial Area (Sindos)
570 22 Thessalonik, Greece
TEL: +30 31 799 502
FAX: +30 31 799 571
E-MAIL : minos@hyper.gr
CONTACT: Yannis Verginis

SILEN
Silen Factory, 11 Ethnikis Antistasis
Street, Rahona Pellas, Greece
TEL: +30 391 53296
FAX: +30 391 53729

SOLE SA
19G Papandreou Street 144 52
Meteamorfosis, Athens, Greece
TEL:+30 1 281 9200
FAX:+30 1 282 5690
E-MAIL:export @sole.gr
WEB:http://www.sole.gr
CONTACT:Chris Nikitak

SOLAR PHOTOVOLTAIC

DISSIOS SA
10, Kariti Square 10561
Athens, Greece
TEL : + 30 1 3220301
FAX : + 30 1 3252453
E-MAIL : mdissios@mail.otenet.gr
CONTACT: Spiras Dissios

MABLEKOS A TAXIARCHIS
Iasonos St 22, 38333 Volos, Greece
TEL : +30 421 31736
FAX : +30 421 31736
CONTACT : Mablekos A Taxiarchis

PHOTOVOLTAIC
12 Polemokratous,
116 35 Athens, Greece
TEL: + 30 1 72 25 471
FAX : + 30 1 72 20 637
E-MAIL : photovol@acci.gr
WEB:http://www.photovoltaic.gr
CONTACT:Marios Sigalas

SILEN
Silen Factory,
11 Ethnikis Antistasis
Street, Rahona Pellas, Greece
TEL: +30 391 53296
FAX: +30 391 53729

TELEPAN COMMERCIAL - TECHNICAL
Solar Electric Systems,
Sorovits 5,112 52 Athens,
Greece
TEL: +30 1 8613 650
FAX: +30 1 8649 010
CONTACT: George Panellis

WIND

FLASH P & P
81st Km Athens, Korinthos Nat Road,
201 00 Korinthos, Greece
TEL: + 30 741 72776
FAX: + 30 1 991 6328
E-MAIL: jpapa@leon.nrcps.ariadne-t.gr
CONTACT: John Pappas

POLITIS PAPPAS CO
81st Athens, Korinthos Nat Rd.
20100 Korinthos, Greece
TEL: +30 741 72776
FAX:+30 741 33403
E-MAIL :jpappa@leon.nrcps.ariadnet.gt
CONTACT: John Pappas

CINAR SA
4 Hadjiyianni Mexi Street,
11528 Athens, Greece
TEL: +30 1725 0360
FAX: +30 1725 0361
E-MAIL: cinar@hol.gr
WEB: http://www.cinar.gr
CONTACT: Dr G Papachristos

BIOMASS

BEK SA
34-36, Orminiou Street,
Ilisia, 115 28 Athens, Greece
TEL : +30- 1 724 8828/724 3865
FAX : +30 1 721 3814
E-MAIL :beksa@otenet.gr
CONTACT: Spiropaulos

DELTA TECHNIKI - K KATSAROS SA
51, Poseidonos Avenue, 183 44
Moschato, Athem, Greece
TEL : + 301 930 0720
FAX : + 30 1 930 3394
CONTACT: Evagelos Papageorgiou

MOUMTZIS KONSTANTINOS
12 Ioustinianou Street 546 31
Thessaloniki, Greece,
TEL: +30 31 277 273
FAX: +33 31 285 152
CONTACT: Aristomenis Mumtzis

POLITIS SHINAS CO
14 Gallias Street, 382 21 Volos, Greece
TEL: +30 421 36190
FAX:+30 421 20846
CONTACT: Michael Roula

SMALL HYDRO

HORIZON SA
I Strimonos Street 621 23 Serres, Greece
TEL: +30 321 20351
FAX: +30 321 57400
CONTACT: Savas Hatzigabriel

ENERGY EFFICIENCY

PERIVALLONTIKI-ENERGIAKI LTD
106b Lontou Street,
Patras 26224, Greece
TEL: +30 61 341 367
FAX : +30 61 324 587
CONTACT : John Athanasopouls

WASTE TO ENERGY

PANAGIOTIS KOLLIAS
Naxu 21, 11256 Athens, Greece
TEL: +30 1 864 8346
CONTACT: Panagiotis S Kollias

ASSOCIATION

CENTRE FOR RENEWABLE ENERGY SOURCES - CRES
19th Km Marathonos Avenue ,
1900 Pikermi, Athens, Greece
TEL : +30 1 60 39 900
FAX : +30 1 60 39 904
E-MAIL :
ktigas@cresdb.cress.ariadne-t.gr
WEB : http://www.cress.ariadne-t.gr.cress.html
CONTACT: Martha Simantoni

GOVERNMENT

GREEK POWDER & CARTRIDGE COMPANY
Illioupoleos Avenue,
172 36 Hymettus, Greece
TEL : + 30 97 53011
FAX : + 30 97 05009
E-MAIL : pyrsales@hol.gr
CONTACT: Athanasios Voyadzis

RESEARCH & DEVELOPMENT

ARISTOTLE UNIVERSITY OF THESSALONIKI
Laboratory of Building Construction and Physics,Department of Civil Engineering, School of Technology, 54006 Thessaloniki, Greece
TEL : +30 31 995777
FAX : +30 31 995603
E-MAIL : niobe@civil.auth.gr
CONTACT : Dr. Niobe Chryssohalidoce

MICRONICS LTD
46 Kritis Street,
Argyroupolis, 16451,
Athens, Greece
TEL: +30 1 996 2948
FAX: +30 1 995 1814
E-MAIL: micronix@otenet.gr
CONTACT : Les Thorley

NATIONAL OBSERVATORY OF ATHENS
P O Box 20048,
GR-11810 Athens,
Greece
TEL: +30 1 3490104
FAX: +30 1 3490120
WEB: http://www.noa.gr
CONTACT: Dr C Papadopoulos

NATIONAL TECHNICAL UNIVERSITY ATHENS-NTUA / BTU
Chemical Engineering Department
Division IV Proce, Zografou
Campus, 15700 Athens
Greece
TEL: +30 1 22 2 3191
FAX: +30 1 22 2 3192
E-MAIL: koukios@orfeas.chem eng.ntua.gr
WEB: http://www.chemeng.ntua.gr
CONTACT: Prof Emmanuel G Koukios

RESPECT ENGINEERING
77 28th October Street,
262 23 Patras,
Greece
TEL : +30 61 431862
FAX : +30 61 435083
CONTACT : Dr Stravros A Pressas

CONSULTANTS

ASPROFOS ENGINEERING SA
Business Development Division,
284El Venizelou Avenue,
176 75 Kallithea, Athens,
Greece
TEL: +30 10 949 1505
FAX: +30 10 949 1610
E-MAIL: asprofos@asprofos.gr
WEB: http://www.asprofos.gr
CONTACT: Loannis Simitzis

ATLANTIS CONSULTING SA
Atlantis Research Organisation,51
Polytechniou Street, 54625
Thessaloniki Greece
TEL : +30 31 524854
FAX : +30 31 552265
E-MAIL : papegeorgiou@ atlantisresearch.gr
WEB : http://www.atlantisresearch.gr
CONTACT: Dimitris Papageorgiou

HELIO DYNAMI LTD
224, Syngrou Avenue,
Kallithea Athens,
Greece
TEL: + 30 1 9592 32 3/9571
FAX: + 30 1 9592 322
CONTACT: Stefanos Gatyfalakis

KANTOR SA
Energy and Utilities, 4 Vas Sofias Street, 106 74 Athens, Greece
TEL: +30 1 7297500
FAX: +30 1 7249528
E-MAIL: central@kantor.gr
WEB:http://www.kantor.gr
CONTACT: Thyrsos Hadjicostas

METOPI CONSULTING
50 Thiras Str, 112 52 Athens,Greece
TEL: +30 1 8658094
FAX: +30 1 8619606
E-MAIL: metopi@tee.gr
CONTACT: Thanassis Angelopoulos

NETWORK CONSULTING GROUP LTD
Energy and Environment,
Arapaki 56 GA 176 76 Kallithea,
Athens, Greece
TEL: +30 1 9574462
FAX: +30 1 9510800
E-MAIL: netcons@otenet.gr
WEB: http://www.otenet.gr/network
CONTACT: Nicholas P Vassilakos

PHAOS LTD
19-21 Dimocharous St,
GR-11521, Athens, Greece
TEL: +30 1 7228746
FAX: +30 1 7293451
E-MAIL:kperr@otenet.gr
CONTACT:Dr Kostis Perrakis

STATEGIC PLANNING EFFECTIVE ENGINEERING & DEVELOPMENT LTD.SPEED
30 Averof Street,
104 33 Athens, Greece
TEL: +30 1 8214407
FAX: +30 1 8225755
E-MAIL:speed@hol.gr
CONTACT:Petros Catsis

DESIGN & ENGINEERING

DEMOCRITOS UNIVERSITY OF THRACE
Electrical Machines Laboratory
Energy Systems Section, School of Engineering, Vassilisis Sofias 1, 67,100 Xanthi, Greece
TEL : + 30 541 79721
FAX : + 30 541 27955
E-MAIL : papadnop/@xanthi.cc.duth.gr
WEB : http://www.duth.grece/enc/emlab.html
CONTACT: Demetrios Papadopoulos

EN + A
National Road, Rodos-Lindos 232,
Rhodes, 85100, Greece
TEL : +30 241 68614
FAX : +30 241 68613
E-MAIL : dpara@tee.gr
CONTACT: Dimitris Parasos

ENERGOTECHSA
602A Vouliagmenis Avenue, 164 52
Argyroupoli, Greece
TEL: +30 1 9959021
FAX: +30 1 9959022
E-MAIL: energogr@otenet.gr

LDK CONSULTANTS ENGINEERS AND PLANNERS
7sp Triantafyllou Str, 113 61 Athens, Greece
TEL: +30 1 861 9660
FAX: +30 1 861 7681
E-MAIL: main@ldk.hol.gr
WEB: http://www.ldk.gr
CONTACT: Leonidas Damianidis

MELETITIKI SEMH LTD
237 Patission,
112 54 Athens, Greece
TEL: +30 1 86 16 107
FAX: +30 1 86 18 942
E-MAIL: minos@compulink.gr
CONTACT: AD Maistros

MELETITIKI – ALEXANDROS N TOMBAZIS AND ASSOCIATES ARCHITECTS LTD
27 Monemvasias Street, GR-151 25
Polydroso Athens, Greece
TEL: +30 10 68 00 690
FAX: +30 10 68 01 005
E-MAIL: meletitiki@mail.hol.gr
CONTACT: Alexandros N Tombazis

METRIXX SYSTEMS SA
10 Ag Ioannou,
GR-166 74 Glyfada,
Athens, Greece
TEL: +30 1 898 3580
FAX: +30 1 898 3520
E-MAIL: pelasgos@compulink.gr
CONTACT: Evan S Kehagias

TOMBAZIS (AN) AND ASSOCIATES ARCHITECTS-MELETITIKI LTD
27 Monevasias Street, GR-151 25
Polydroso Athens, Greece
TEL: +30 1 68 00 690
FAX: +30 1 68 01 005
E-MAIL:meletitiki@mail.hol.gr
CONTACT:Alexandros N Tombazis

FINANCE & BANKING

DAEDALUS INFORMATICS LTD
Renewables Karias 22, 16675
Glyfada, Greece
TEL : + 30 1 9643355
FAX : + 30 1 9627444
E-MAIL : daedalushg@
mail.daedaus.gr
WEB : http://www.daedalus.gr
CONTACT: Evagelos M Mylonas

NATIONAL BANK OF GREECE
Corporate Banking Division,
17 Solomou Street,
Athens 164 51, Greece
TEL: +30 10 9935816

SUPPLIERS

BATTERIES/INVERTERS

ILPRA SA
Industrial Area Thermi, PO Box
355 Theme 570 01, Greece
TEL: +30 3 464 021
FAX: +30 3 464 607
CONTACT: George Sergiadis

INSTRUMENTATION

GEOBIOLOGIKI SA
62 Thrakomakedonon Str. 136 71
Aharnes, Greece
TEL : + 30 1 2405020
FAX : + 30 1 2405026
E-MAIL : info@angelopouos.gr
WEB: www.angelopoulos.grl

SOLE SA
Lefktron & Agonon, 13671 Aharnes,
Athens, Greece
TEL: +30102314246
FAX: +30102825690
E-MAIL: expoet@sole.gr
WEB: http://www.sole.gr
CONTACT: Natali Myrmigelis

METALS

EVIESK SA
49-51 Sof. Venizelou St. 141 23
Likovrisi, Greece
TEL: + 30 1 289 8301
FAX: + 30 1 289 8488
CONTACT: Mr. P Lagoudakis

Kindly inform us of any errors and omissions in the listings by:

E-mail: unisun@vsnl.com

Fax: 91 80 22289294

OTHERS (S)

FEROR PLASTICS SA
Industrial Area of Kilkis,
611 00 Kilkis, Greece
TEL: +30 341 71313
FAX: + 30 341 71693
E-MAIL-feror@spark.net.gr
CONTACT: Vasilis Matskos

DIRAKSA
Export Department Leoforos
Kalohorious, P.O. Box 36, 57009
Kalohori, Thessalonmiki, Macedonia
Greece
TEL : + 30 31 752652
FAX : + 30 31 751419
E-MAIL : dorai@oternet.gr

FOCO LTD
447 Acharnon Street,
111 43 Athens, Greece
TEL: +30 1 2531115
FAX: +30 1 2532873

OLYMPIC SUN
Moyzoyras, Chania-Crete, GR-73100,
Greece
TEL: +30 8210 63131
FAX: +30 8210 63053
E-MAIL: olympic-
sun@cha.forthnet.gr
WEB: http://www.olympicsun.gr
CONTACT: Perakis Alexandros

PUBLIC POWER CORPORATION-PPC
Alternative Energy Forms
Department-DEME,
10 Navarinou Street, GR-106 80
Athens, Greece
TEL: +30 1 364 4811
FAX: +30 1 361 4709
CONTACT: D Kanellopoulos

SOLAR THERMAL

FIORENTINI HUNGARY LTD
Fiosolar Division, Gergely u 83,
H-1103 Budapest, Hungary
TEL: +36 1 431-8884
FAX: + 36 1 431 8861
E-MAIL:fiosolar@mail.datanet.hu
CONTACT : E Kaboldy

SOLAR PHOTOVOLTAIC

DUNASOLAR PHOTOVOLTAICS INC
Export Sales And Marketing,
Kozma u 7, H-1108 Budapest, Hungary
TEL: +36 1 431 9620
FAX: +36 1 264 2637
E-MAIL: sales@dunasolar.hu
CONTACT: Tamas Veghely

FM MUSZAK INTEZET - HIAE
Agro-Energetics, 2100 Godolo
Tessedik, S.u.4, Hungary
TEL: +36 28 420644
FAX: +36 28 420960
E-MAIL: fmmi@mail.pipenet.hu
CONTACT : Dr J Hajdu

HELIO TECH
7624, Pess Aklotmany u.34, Hungary
TEL: +36 72 314 741
FAX: +36 72 313 122
CONTACT: L Patartics

SOLART-SYSTEM LTD
20 Gulyas Street 1112 Budapest,Hungary
TEL:+36 1 246 1783
FAX:+36 1 246 1783
E-MAIL : solartsy@elender.hu
WEB: http://www.elender.hu/~solartsy
CONTACT : Miklos Palfy

WIND

DARCOMEX LTD
Torokvesz 55 III B,1025 Budapest,
Hungary
TEL : + 361 325 51 47
FAX : + 361 325 51 47
CONTACT : Michail Shafit

TEMPO-SPEED LTD
PO Box 2340, Daru Street I,Hungary
TEL: +36 24 430 300
FAX: +36 24 430 583
CONTACT: Mr Zoltan

BIOMASS

FM MUSZAK INTEZET - HIAE
Agro-Energetics, 2100 Godolo
Tessedik, S.u.4, Hungary
TEL: +36 28 420644
FAX: +36 28 420960
E-MAIL: fmmi@mail.pipenet.hu
CONTACT : Dr J Hajdu

ENERGY EFFICIENCY

ECOLOGICAL INSTITUTE FOR SUSTAINABLE DEVELOPMENT
Kossuth U 13, 3525, Miskoic,
Hungary
TEL : + 36 46 352 010
FAX : + 36 46 352 010
CONTACT : Tamas Visnyouslky

RESEARCH & DEVELOPMENT

HIAE HUNGARY
FVM Muszakilntezet Godouo,
Tessedik 5 U4, Hungary
TEL: +36 28 420 644
FAX: +36 28 420 960
E-MAIL: tmmi@mail.eiener.hu
CONTACT: Paul Pecznik

HUNGARAIAN ACADEMY OF SCIENCES
Chemical Research Center Research
Laboratory of Material and
Environment, Pusztaszeri ut 59-67,
1025 Budapest, Hungary
TEL: +36 1 325 5992
FAX: +36 1 325 7892
E-MAIL: minik@chemres.hu
WEB: http://www.chemres.hu
CONTACT: Gyorgy Mink

HUNGARIAN SOLAR ENERGY SOCIETY - HSES
Technical University Budapest,
Muegyetem, Rkp 3, 1111 Budapest,
Hungary
TEL: +36 1 463 3272
FAX: +36 1 463 3272
E-MAIL: imre@eta.enrg.bme.hu
CONTACT: Dr L Imre

THERMAL DESORPTION TECHNOLOGY GROUP LLC OF NORTH AMERICA
Central European Branch, Office,
Szechenyi u 59,
H-1222 Budapest, Hungary
TEL: +36 20 9806996
FAX: +36 1 4240466
E-MAIL: edward@tdt-3r.com
WEB: http://www.tdt-3r.com
CONTACT: Edward Someus

UNIVERSITIES

BUDAPEST UNIVERSITY OF TECHNOLOGY
Department of Building Energetics,
Faculty of Architectural Engineering,
H-1521 Budapest, Hungary
TEL : +36 1 463 1331
FAX : +36 1 463 3547
E-MAIL : zold@egt.bme.hu
WEB : http://www.egt.bme.hu
CONTACT : Prof A Zöld

TECHNICAL UNIVERSITY OF BUDAPEST
Department of Energy, Muegyetem
Rkp 3, 1111 Budapest, Hungary
TEL : +36 1 463 3272
FAX : +36 1 463 3272
E-MAIL : energy@eta.enrg.bme.hu
CONTACT : Dr L Imre

UNIVERSITY MISKOLC
Department of Fluid and Heat
Engineering, H-3515 Miskolc-
Egyetemvaros, Hungary
TEL: +36 46 565 154
FAX: +36 46 360 134
E-MAIL: aramlk@gold.uni-miskolc.hu
CONTACT: Dr. Karoly Lakatos

NGO's

INDEPENDENT ECOLOGICAL CENTER
Miklos Ter 1, 1035 Budapest,
Hungary
TEL: +36 1 368 6229
FAX: +36 1 250 1546
E-MAIL: office@foek.hu
WEB: http://www.foek.hu
CONTACT: Dr P Medgrasszay

CONSULTANTS

BIOX CO
Portyazo u 6, H-1221 Budapest,
Hungary
TEL: +36 1 226 4026
FAX: +36 1 226 4026
E-MAIL:
l.zsuffa@co.energy.datanet.hu
CONTACT: Mr L Zsuffa

ERBE POWER ENGINEERING & CONSULTING LTD
Budafoki ut 95,
1117 Budapest, Hungary
TEL: +36 1 20 44 200
FAX: +36 1 20 44 198
E-MAIL : erbe.energetika@mail.datanet.hu
CONTACT : Eva Maria Vineze

ERM HUNGARIAKFT
Fehervari ut 44, 1119 Budapest,
Hungary
TEL: +36 1 204 3966
FAX: +36 1 204 3966
E-MAIL: ermhun@euroweb.hu
CONTACT : J Egerszegi

SUPPLIERS

BATTERIES/INVERTERS

ACCUSEALED LTD
Kesmerk u, 14,
PO Box 1158
Budapest,
Hungary
TEL: +36 1 417 3469
FAX: +36 1 417 3449
CONTACT: Gabriella Feher

CONSTRUCTION SERVICES

VEGYEPSZER RT - CHEMICAL WORKS BUILDING AND ASSEMBLING CO LTD
Mogyorod u 42, PO Box 17, 1601
Budapest, Hungary
TEL: +36 1 305 1131
FAX: +36 1 305 1194
E-MAIL: bakos_ivan@vegyepszer.hu
WEB: http://www.vegyepszer.hu
CONTACT: Ivan Bakos

We kindly request more listings in this country.

You can submit any additional listings by E-mail: unisun@vsnl.com

Fax: 91 80 22289294

We will include these in the next edition

Kindly inform us of any errors and omissions in the listings by:

E-mail: unisun@vsnl.com

Fax: 91 80 22289294

GEOTHERMAL ENERGY

ORKUVEITA REYKJAVIKUR
Sudurlandsbraut 34 IS108 Reykjavik, Iceland
TEL: +354 585 6000
FAX: +354 585 6190
E-MAIL: thorleifur.finnsson@or.is
WEB: http://www.or.is
CONTACT: Thorleifur Finnsson

We kindly request more listings in this country.

You can submit any additional listings by E-mail: unisun@vsnl.com

Fax: 91 80 2289294

We will include these in the next edition

Kindly inform us of any errors and omissions in the listings by:

E-mail: unisun@vsnl.com

Fax: 91 80 2289294

WIND

DJN
Ballyfair, Curragh, Co Kidare Ireland
TEL : + 353 45 41775
FAX : + 353 45 41775
CONTACT : Joe O' Mahony

EF ENERGY (DEVELOPMENTS) LTD
Antares house, Carrignavar,
CoCork, Ireland
TEL : +353 21 307490
FAX : +353 21 4880341
E-MAIL :efenergy@iol.ie
CONTACT : P J Healy

JENNINGS O'DONOVON & PARTNERS
Finisklin, Sligo, Ireland
TEL: +353 71 61416
FAX: +353 71 61080
E-MAIL:jodirt@iol.ie
CONTACT : D Kiely

COGENERATION

BORD GAIS-COGEN
Business Development- Assets,
Sir John Rogersons Quay,
Dublin 2, Ireland
TEL: +353 1 602 12 84
FAX: +353 1 602 64 68
CONTACT: Rory O' Grady

GEOTHERMAL

BRIAN P CONNOR AND ASSOCIATES LTD
1 Richmond, Priests Road, Tramore,
Co Waterford, Ireland
TEL : +353 51 390650
FAX : +353 51 381932
E-MAIL :bpcassoc@iol.ie
CONTACT : B P Connor

ENERGY EFFICIENCY

HYPERION ENERGY SYSTEMS LTD
Main Street Watergrasshill,
County Cork, Ireland
TEL: +353 21 4889461
FAX: +353 21 4889465
E-MAIL: hyperion.energy@indigo.ie
WEB: http://www.hyperion.ie
CONTACT: Dr Sean Mc Carthy

KERRY ENERGY AGENCY
30 Castle Street, Tralee,
County Kerry, Ireland
TEL: +353 66 21822
FAX: +353 66 21843
E-MAIL: kerryeng@iol.ie
CONTACT : O O'Connor

SYSTEMS OPTIMISATION LTD
Auriga, Islandkeane, Fenor, County
Waterford, Ireland
TEL: +353 51 386869
FAX: +353 51 386844
E-MAIL:gmcnultyiol.ie
CONTACT : Mr Gerard McNulty

FINANCE / BANKING

ENERGY CONTROL SYSTEMS LIMITED - ECS
3 Cranford Hall, Montrose,
Dublin 4, Ireland
TEL: +353 1 283 9182
FAX: +353 1 269 5967
CONTACT : John Brazil

ASSOCIATION

IRISH HYDRO POWER ASSOCIATION
13 Marlboro Road, Dublin 4, Ireland
TEL: +353 1 6680043
FAX:+353 1 6680043
CONTACT : L Staudt

IRISH WIND ENERGY ASSOCIATION
Kellystown, Slane, County Meath, Ireland
TEL: +353 78 46229
FAX:+353 78 46016
E-MAIL:iwea@indigo.ie
CONTACT : L Staudt

SOLAR 2000
Solar House, Kinnard West
Ballinskelligs, Co Kerry, Ireland
TEL:+353 66 79420
FAX:+353 66 79167
CONTACT:James Kenny

RESEARCH & DEVELOPMENT

ENERGY RESEARCH GROUP UNVIERSITY COLLEGE DUBLIN
School of Architecture, Richview,
Clonskeagh, Dublin 14, Ireland,
TEL : + 353 1 269 2750
FAX : + 353 1 283 8908
E-MAIL : lewis @erg.ucd.ie
CONTACT : J O Lewis

CONSULTANTS

ESB INTERNATIONAL
Stephen Court, 18-21 St Stephens
Green, Dublin 2, Ireland
TEL: +353 1 703 8000
FAX: +353 1 661 6600
CONTACT : D More

FINGLETON WHITE & CO LTD
Bride Street Centre,
Portlaoise. Co Laois, Ireland
TEL: +353 502 2 10 10
FAX: + 353 502 2 23 82
E-MAIL: fingleton@ iol.ie
CONTACT : J M Fingleton

TRINITY COLLEGE DUBLIN
Department of Civil Structural and
Environmental, Dublin 2, Ireland
TEL: +353 1 608 2343
FAX: +353 1 677 3072
E-MAIL: pbuckley@tcd.ie
CONTACT: Pearse Buckley

DESIGN & ENGINEERING

ENERGY INNVOTATION LTD.
26, Glenside, Pinercroft, Grange,
Douglas Cork, Ireland
TEL : + 353 86 8286861
FAX : + 353 86 9286861
E-MAIL : donal.kissane@energi.com
WEB: http://www.energi.com
CONTACT : D Kissane

OTHERS

EARTH WATCH MAGAZINE
Dromore, Bantry, Co Cork Ireland
TEL : + 353 28 31853
FAX : + 353 27 50545
E-MAIL : ewmag@eircom.net
CONTACT : L Lüken

ESP POWER GENERATION
27 Lower Fitzwilliam Street,
Dublin 2, Ireland
TEL: + 353 1 702 62 44
FAX: + 353 1 662 12 54
E-MAIL: brian.ryan@mail.esb.ie
CONTACT : B Ryan

MAYO ENERGY AGENCY
Unit 1 The Quay Ballina,
County Mayo, Ireland
TEL: +353 96 74034
FAX: +353 96 70711
E-MAIL: mayonrg@eircom.net
WEB: http://hompage.eircom.net/-mayonrg
CONTACT: Roger Adair

CONSTRUCTION SERVICES

FINGLETON WHITE & CO LTD
Bride Street Centre,
Portlaoise. Co Laois, Ireland
TEL: +353 502 2 10 10
FAX: + 353 502 2 23 82
E-MAIL: fingleton@ iol.ie
CONTACT : J M Fingleton

IRISH ENERGY CENTRE
Renewable Energy Information
Office, Shingh House, Bandon,
Co Cork, Ireland
TEL:+353 23 42193
FAX:+353 23 41304
E-MAIL:carmel@reio.ie
WEB:http://www.Irish-energy.ie/reio.htm
CONTACT : Nyhan

SUPPLIERS

OTHERS (S)

SOLARIS SOLAR ENERGY SYSTEMS
Kilnarovanagh, Toames,
Macroom, Co Cork, Ireland
TEL: +3532646312
E-Mail: solaris@eircom.net
WEB: http://www.solaris-energy.com
CONTACT: Fritz Raake

We kindly request more listings in this country.

You can submit any additional listings by E-mail: unisun@vsnl.com

Fax: 91 80 2289294

We will include these in the next edition

Kindly inform us of any errors and omissions in the listings by:

E-mail: unisun@vsnl.com

Fax: 91 80 2289294

SOLAR THERMAL

ACCOMANDITA TECHNOLOGIE SPECIALI ENERGIA SRL
Strada S Guiseppe 19, 43039
Salsomaggioret Terme(PR), Italy
TEL: +39 524 523668
FAX: +39 524 522145
E-MAIL: accomandita@polaris.it
WEB: http://www.accomandita.com
CONTACT: Alberto Croci

ATDI MARIANI & C SNC
Via E Mattei 461,
47023 Cesena (Fo),Italy
TEL : +39 547 334134
FAX : +39 547 600200
E-MAIL : mmariani@linknet.it
CONTACT : Marco Mariani

CARIVAL SPA
Via Per Azzano San Paolo 26, 24050
Grassobbio (BG), Italy
TEL : +39 35 525 069

CASINGHINI HEATEX SRL
25036 Palazzolo Sull'Oglio,
Brescia, Italy
TEL: +39 30 7402831
FAX: +39 30 7407574
E-MAIL: macasing@tin.it
CONTACT: Marco Casinghini

COOPSETTE SCRL
VIA San Biagio 75, 42024,
Castelnovo de Scotto (RE), Italy
TEL : + 39 522 682741
FAX : + 39 522 683401
CONTACT : Donato Fontanesi

FIORINI SNC
Via Copernico 81/85,
47100 Forli, Italy
TEL: +39 543 723197
FAX: +39 543 720413
CONTACT : Mr. Fabbri

NUOVA THERMOSOLAR SRL
Via Aldo Moro 16/A, 41043
Formigine (MO), Italy
TEL: +39 59 570 907
FAX: +39 59 556 369
E-MAIL: mescoli@thermosolar.it
WEB: http://www.thermosolar.it
CONTACT: Pier Paolo Mescoli

SILE SPA
Via Principale 41,
31030 Casier (TV), Italy
TEL: +39 422 670070
FAX: +39 422 340 425
CONTACT: Mr S Secco

STEFANI SRL(SCAMBIATORI DI CALORE)
Via Roma S/n, 36020 Castegnero
(vi), Italy
TEL: +45 39 75 60 00
FAX: +45 39 75 60 01
E-MAIL:stefani@netbusiness.it
WEB:http://
www.stefani.netbusiness.it
CONTACT:Giovanni Stefani

TECNOCLIMA SPA
Viale de'll Industria 19, 38057 Pergine
Valsugana (Trento), Italy
TEL: +39 461 531676
FAX: +39 461 512432
CONTACT: Mr Roberto Grandi

TELITSRL
via B Marcello N60,
25123 Bresica, Italy
TEL: +39 30 364731
FAX: +39 30 364731
CONTACT: Ing E Tronca

TERRE COOP
Via L M Perpetuo 19,
00174 Rome, Italy
TEL: +3968273542
FAX: +3968273542
E-MAIL: terrecoop@tiscalinet.it
CONTACT: Livia Aromatario

SOLAR PHOTOVOLTAIC

ASTEL SOLAR ENERGY SRL
Via Valtellina 18/20,
20159 Milano, Italy
TEL : +39 2 66 80 2330
FAX : +39 2 68 80 802
CONTACT : Stefano Renditor

AUREL SPA
Automation, Via Foro Dei Tigli-4,
47015, Modigliana (Fo),Italy
TEL : +39 546 941124
FAX : +39 546 941660
E-MAIL : aurel@aurel.it
WEB : http://www.aurel.it
CONTACT : Nerio Samori

BONETTI GIORGIO SRL
Via Cavedine 10, 38070,
Cavedine Trento, Italy
TEL : +39 461 564 668
FAX : +39 461 563 236
CONTACT : Bonetti Giorgio

ECOSOLUZIONI
Via dell'Amorino 2, Cortona,
AR 52044, Italy
TEL: +39 575 630485
FAX: +39 575 630485
E-MAIL: dguidi@vol.it
CONTACT: Mr Daniele Guidi

ELETTORORAVA SPA
Via Don Sapino 176,
10040 Savonera,
Torino, Italy
TEL : +39 011 42402737
FAX : +39 011 4240364
E-MAIL : paulo@elettrorava.com
WEB : http://www.elettrorava.com
CONTACT : Paolo Rava

ENEA-CENTRO RICERCHE PORTI
Via del Vecchio,
Macello, 80055,
Portici, Italy
TEL : +39 81 7723207
FAX : +39 81 7723345
E-MAIL : terzini@portici.enea.it
WEB : http://
www.axpenea.portici.enea.it
CONTACT : Ezio Terzini

ENERGSOL SAS
Via Palermo 7,
39100 Bolzano, Italy
TEL: +39 471 250 177
FAX: +39 471 911 236
CONTACT : Franco Mottironi

ESCOITALIANA SPA
Viale Casiraghi 355,
20009 Sesto San Giovanni (M1)
Italy
TEL: +39 2 2409251
FAX: + 39 2 2409255
CONTACT : Aurelio Busani

EUROSOLARE SPA
Via Augusto d'Andrea 6,
00048 Nettuno (RM),
Italy
TEL: +39 6 985601
FAX: +39 6 9850267
E-MAIL: eurosolare@mondoweb.it
WEB: http://www.eurosolare.it
CONTACT : Daniele Margadonna

FEA (FRATELLI) SN
Via Saluzzo 49/55,
12030 Scarnafigi (CN),
Italy
TEL: +39 175 74134
FAX: +39 175 74639

GECHELIN GROUP SISTEMI FOTOVOLTAICI
Via Ticino 16,
36016 Thiene (VI)
Italy
TEL: + 39 445 380050
FAX: + 39 445 381020
E-MAIL : gechelin@gechelin.com
WEB: http://www.gechelin.com
CONTACT : Vania Scandian

HELIOS TECHNOLOGY SRL
Head Office, Via Postumia 11,
35010 Carmigano di Brenta(PD), Italy
TEL: +34 49 9430288
FAX: +34 49 9430323
E-MAIL: info@helios technology.com
WEB: http://www.helios technology.com
CONTACT: Laura Campagnolo

SISTEMIENERGETICI INTEGRATISRL - SEI
Via S Jacopo 32,
50047 Prato, Italy
TEL: +39 574 605415
FAX: +39 574 39601
E-MAIL: info@sei-sist.it
CONTACT: Massimo Corsi

SOLARES
Via F Lattanzio 53,
70126 Bari, Italy
TEL:+39 80 554 2267
FAX:+39 80 558 9323
E-MAIL:l.laspada@agora.stm.it
WEB:http://www.solares.it
CONTACT:Luigi la Spada

SOLAREX ITALIA SRL
Centro Direzionale Colleoni,
Palazzo Liocorno 2,
20041 Agrae Brianza
(MI), Italy
TEL:+61 2 727 4455
FAX:+61 2 727 7447
CONTACT : F A Fratarelli

SUNERG SOLAR ENERGY
Citta Castello, 06010 Promano, Italy
TEL: +39 75 854327
FAX: +39 75 854327
E-MAIL :sunerg@lineanet.net
WEB:http://www.avt.Krenet.it/sunerg
CONTACT:Lucian Lauri

UFLEX TRADE SRL
Divisone Energia, Via Milte ignoto Ba,
16012 Busalla (GE), Italy
TEL : +39 10 9620 203
FAX : +39 10 9620 333
E-MAIL : ute@ultraflexgroup.It
WEB : http://www.ultr aflexgoup.it/ute
CONTACT : Mr Sergio Cazzulini

WAREX SRL
Via Crescenzio 82, 00193 Rome,
Italy
TEL: +39 6 689 6358
FAX: +39 6 689 6391
E-MAIL: wapexcom@mbox.vol.it
CONTACT: Giovanni Tirabassi

BIOMASS

BIOELETTRICA SPA
Via Cesare Battisti 47,
56125 Pisa, Italy
TEL : +39 50 535479
FAX : +39 50 535477
E-MAIL :delange@bioelectrica.it
CONTACT : Henk de Lange

CALDAIE PELUC CHISRL
Via Montesanto 20,
Monza (Milano), Italy
TEL : +39 2000 990
FAX : +39 2000 240
CONTACT : Giambathista Pelucchi

ESTERECO SRL
Zona Industrialedi Pian D'Assino.
0G019 Umbertice PG, Italy
TEL: +39 75 9413097
FAX: +39 75 9413192
E-MAIL: estereco@retein.net
CONTACT : Ing Ermanno Scalmbra

COGENERATION

ASTER ASSOCIATE TERMOIMPIANTI SPA
Building Services - Energy & Environment
Installation, Viale Fulvio Testi 136,
2002 Cinisello Balsamo, MI Italy
TEL : +39 2 262 501
FAX : +39 2 262 252 50
E-MAIL :info@aster-spa.it
WEB : http://www.aster-spa.it
CONTACT : Mr. Fernando Sola

BONO ENERGIA SPA
Via Resistenza 12, 20068 Peschiera
Borromeo (MI), Italy
TEL: +39 02 5530 2848
FAX: +39 02 547 1955
E-MAIL: sales.bono.en@bono.it
WEB: http://www.bono.it
CONTACT: F Abba

FRANCONI POWER SYSTEM SRL
Via Nomentana Km 15, 00012
Torlupara di Guidonia, Roma, Italy
TEL: +39 774 570052
FAX: +39 774 571021
E-MAIL : Franconi Antonio

NUOVO PIGNONE SPA
Turbotechnica Division, Via F
Matteucci2, 50127 Firenze, Italy
TEL: +39 55 42 32 11
FAX: +39 55 42 33 933
E-MAIL: guelfo.gheri@np.ge.com
WEB: http://www.ge.com/ nuovo.pignone
CONTACT: Guelfo Gheri

SOGES ORGANIZZAZIONEE GESTIONESPA
Energy and Environment, Corso
Turati 49, 10128 Torino,
Italy
TEL: +39 11 319 0833
FAX: +39 11 319 0292
E-MAIL: sogint@tin.it
CONTACT: Fernando Garzello

STC COLENCO SPA
Via Andrea Dragoni 59,
47100 Forli, Italy
TEL: +39 543 411 411
FAX: +39 543 55 06 29
CONTACT:Pietro M Stella

TE TECNOLOGIE PER L'ENERGIA SRL
Via Montanaro 24,
10154 Torino, Italy
TEL : +39 11 2485166
FAX : +39 11 2485139
CONTACT: Elio Tessitore

TECHNAIR SRL
C/o CPL Via Grandi 39,
Concordia Sulia Secchio,
41040 Modena, Italy
TEL : +39 59 28 27 00
FAX : +39 59 28 28 05

FUEL CELL

DE NORA FUEL CELLS SPA
Via Bistofi, 35, 20134, Milano, Italy
TEL : + 39 2 21291
FAX : + 39 2 2129 2403
TELEX : 310552 - 32223 1
ODENOR 1
E-MAIL : fuelCell@denoraic
WEB : http://www. denora.com

SMALL HYDRO

IREM SPA
Micro Hydroelectric Power Plants,
Via Abegg 75,
10050 Borgone di Susa (TO),
Italy
TEL: +39 11 964 6213
FAX: +39 11 964 6385
E-MAIL:irem@irem.it
WEB:http://www.irem.it
CONTACT : Ceuido Usseglio Prinsi

SIEMENS SPA
Viale Piapo Alberto
Pianclli 10, 20126 Milano,
Italy
TEL: +39 2 66 76 1
FAX: +39 2 66 76 4933
WEB: http://www.siemens.it
CONTACT: Vigliamo Vitale

ITALY

SOCIETA NAZIONALE DELLE OFFICINE DI SAVIGLIANO
Corso Mortara 4, 10149 Torino, Italy
TEL: +39 11 2298 111
FAX: +39 11 259077

SOGECO HYDROENERGIE
Route de Romeyer, 26150 Die, France
TEL: +33 4 75 22 12 15
FAX: +33 4 75 22 10 26
CONTACT: Dominique Schmerber

GEOTHERMAL

MEPECO SRL
Via Kennedy 32, 20097 San Donato Milanese (MI), Italy
TEL: +39 2 55700685
FAX: +39 2 55700355
E-MAIL: mepeco@tin.it
CONTACT: Dario Balistrieri

WASTE TO ENERGY

ASJA AMBIENTE ITAIA SPA
Corso Stati Uniti 39, 10129 Torino, Italy
TEL : +39 11 9635570
FAX : +39 11 9635571
E-MAIL : writeitalia@asjai nternational.com
WEB : http://www.asja international.com
CONTACT : Dr. Laco Bergonzoli

GEM SRL ENVIRONMENTAL / IU MACHINERY TECHNOLOGIHEED ECOLOGICHEED ENERGETHIC
Via Zanussi Ziu - Udine 331, Italy
TEL : + 39 432 524374
FAX : + 39 432 529977
E-MAIL : gem@xnet.it/gen
WEB : www.xnet.it/gen

MG MAGNABOSCO SPA
Via Roma 14-19, Zugliano (Vicenza), Italy
TEL: +39 4445 330 111
FAX: +39 445 330 110
E-MAIL: magnabosco@pn.itnet.it
WEB: http://www.tradenet.it/ magnabosco
CONTACT: Luisa Signorini

ASSOCIATION

INTERNATIONAL SOLAR ENERGY SOCIETY-ISES ITALY
Piazza Bologna 22, 00162 Roma, Italy
TEL: +39 6 4424 9241
FAX: +39 6 4424 9243
E-MAIL: info@isesitalia.it
WEB: http://www.isesitalia.it
CONTACT : Leonardo Berlen

ITALIAN BIOMASS ASSOCIATION-ITABIA
Via C Colombo 185, 00147 Roma, Italy
TEL: +39 6 5122 792
FAX: +39 6 5160 1202
E-MAIL:itabia@mclink.it
WEB:http://energ.polimi.it/ITABIA

RENAGRI
Via T, Grossi 6, 00184 Roma, Italy
TEL : +39 6 7008896
FAX : +39 6 7009380
E-MAIL : mc9898@mclink.it

UNAPACE
Via Ombrone 2/G,00198 Roma, Italy
TEL : +39 6 8537281
FAX : +39 6 85346431
E-MAIL : francesco.de.luca@unapae.it
WEB : http://www.unapace.it
CONTACT : Francesco de Luca

RESEARCH & DEVELOPMENT

CESI SPA
Via Rubattino 54, 20134 Milano, Italy
TEL : +39 2 7224 5220
FAX : +39 2 7224 5253
E-MAIL : panzani@pal.enel.it
WEB : http://www.solemio.pal.enel.it
CONTACT : Dr. Lostantino Panzani

CESI SPA
SFR, Via Rubattino 54, 20134, Milano, Italy
TEL : +39 2 21251
FAX : +39 2 21255626
E-MAIL : info@cesi.it
WEB : http://www.ces.it
CONTACT : Dr. Alberto Iliceto

CESI SPA
Via Rubattino 54, 20134 Milano, Italy
TEL : +39 2 2125340
FAX : +39 2 2125481
CONTACT : Nicoleta Boattini

ENEA
CRE Cassacia, Via Anguillarese 301 00060 S Maria di Galeria (Roma), Italy
TEL : +39 6 30483372
FAX : +39 6 30486449
CONTACT : Dr. Dario Malosti

EUROPEAN SOLAR TEST INSTALLATION - ESTI
European Commission joint Research Centre Institute, Via Enrico Fermi 21020 Ispra (Va), Italy
TEL: +39 322 785 885
FAX: +39 332 789 268
E-MAIL: jennifer.rundle@jre.it
CONTACT : Jennifer Rundle

GIANNONI
Via Milano 49/51, 20079 Castirage Vidardo (Lodi) Italy
TEL :+39371 2151
FAX : + 39 371 934 436
E-MAIL : fmele@giannonit.it
WEB : www.giannovi.it

ISTITUTO COOPERATIVOPER L'INNOVZIONE-ICIE
Building Energy Environment, Via Velletri 35, 00198 Roma, Italy
TEL: +39 6 8411819
FAX: +39 6 8550250
E-MAIL: icie.rm@rm.icie.it
WEB: htttp://www.icie.it
CONTACT : Alessandro Busca

POLITECNICO DITORINO
Industrial Electrical Engineering, Corso Duca, Degli Abruzzi 24, 10129 Torino
TEL: +39 11 5647105
FAX:+39 11 5647199
E-MAIL : spertino@athena.polito.it
WEB:http://www.polito.it
CONTACT: Fillippo Spertino

SOLARCONVERT SRLPROCESSIE SISTEMIENERGETICI
Via F Marucelli 8/R, 50134 Firenze, Italy
TEL:+39 55 499678
FAX:+39 55 499669
E-MAIL:solarcon.fi@agora.stim.it
WEB:http://www.
CONTACT:Dr.Paolo Puccetti

UNIVERSITY OF CAGLIARI
Department of Mechanical Engineering, Piazza d'Armi, 09123 Cagliari, Italy
TEL: +39 70 2000 355
FAX: +39 70 2000 362
E-MAIL: picasso@zot.unica.it
WEB: http://www.unica.it
CONTACT: Prof Bruno Picasso

WINSOL ENERGY SYSTEMS
Wind and Solar Energy Systems Research and Development, Via Enrico Fermi 23, 72100 Brindisi, Italy
TEL: +39 831 456 878
FAX: +39 831 546 879
E-MAIL: calcagno@iqsnet.it
WEB: http://www.winsol.com
CONTACT: Dr Pietro Calcagno

UNIVERSITIES

INTERNATIONAL SCHOOL OF GEOTHERMICS
Piazza Solferino 2,
56126 Pisa, Italy
TEL: +39 50 41503
FAX: +39 50 47055
CONTACT: Mrs Mary H Dickson

CONSULTANTS

CESEN SPA
Piazza della Vittoria 11A-8,
16121 Genova, Italy
TEL : +39 10 5759011
FAX : +39 10 541054
E-MAIL : cesen@cesen.it
CONTACT : Dr. Claudio Maccio

ECOSOLUZIONI
Colombais,
Montebenichi,
AR 52000, Italy
TEL : + 39 55 9910092
FAX : + 39 55 99 10092
E-MAIL : dguidi@val.it
CONTACT : Daneile Guidi

MANENS INTERTECNICA SRL
Via Campofiore 21,
37129 Verona,
Italy
TEL: +39 45 8036100
FAX: +39 45 8033954
E-MAIL: manens@manens.com
CONTACT: Gaetano Viero

SILVA
Via Accademia Albertina 29,
10123 Turin, Italy
TEL: +39 11 837871
FAX: +39 11 837871
E-MAIL: rsilva@satnet.it

DESIGN & ENGINEERING

CREA-COOPERATIVA ROMANA ENERGIA E AMBIENTE
Via dei Cessati Spiriti 12,
00179, Roma,
Italy
TEL : +39 6 788 6046
FAX : +39 6 787 453

ERGA
Enel Group, Via
Andrea Pisano 120
56122 Pisa, Italy
TEL: +39 050 535822
E-MAIL: vigotti.roberto@enel.it
CONTACT: Roberto Vigotti

FINCANTIERI CANTIERI NAVALI ITALIANI SPA
Mechanical Products,
Via Cipro 11, 16129 Genoa, Italy
TEL: +39 10 59951
FAX: +39 10 5995352
E-MAIL: mmcme@fincantieri.it
CONTACT: P Pelle

FISIA ITALIMPIANTI SPA
Commercial Division,
Via de Marini 16,
16149 Genova, Italy
TEL: + 39 010 6069 111
FAX: +39 010 6096410
E-MAIL: vend@fisiait.com
WEB:http://www.fisiait.com
CONTACT : Paolo Romiti

FRANCO TOSI MECCANICA SPA
Piazza Monumento 12,
20025 Legnano (Mi), Italy
TEL: +39 331 52 26 56
FAX: +39 331 52 20 02
E-MAIL:
luigi.oldrini@francotosimeccanica.it
CONTACT: Luigi Oldrini

NUOVO PIGNONE SPA
Pumps Valves And Systems Division,
Strada Provinciale Per Modugno 10,
70123 Bari, Italy
TEL: +39 80 5051 111
FAX: +39 80 5051 219
E-MAIL:
lorenzo.bergamini@np.ge.com
CONTACT: Matteo Stero

RIZZI ENERGY SPA
Head Office, Via Nespolo 6,
25030 Adro (Brescia), Italy
TEL: +39 030 73 56 336
FAX: +39 030 74 50 547
E-MAIL: rizzi@rizzienergy.com
WEB: http://www.rizzienergy.com
CONTACT: Dr Italo Rizzi

SOFTECH SRL
Via Cernaia I, 10121 Torino, Italy
TEL: +39 11 5622289
FAX: +39 11 540219
E-MAIL: softech@tin.it
CONTACT: Antonella Marucco

STUDIO ING OLIARO PAOLO
Via Boston 21,
1-10137 Torlno, Italy
TEL: +39 11 329 2527
FAX: +39 11 329 2527
E-MAIL:paolo.oliaro@tin.it
CONTACT:Paolo Oliaro

OTHERS

ARTECH PUBLISHING SRL
Via Gramsci 63, 20032 Cormano,
Milano, Italy
TEL : +39 2 66302904
FAX : +39 2 66302914
E-MAIL: marco.pinetti@fotovoltaici.com
WEB : http://www.fotovoltaici.com
CONTACT : Dr. Marco Pinneti

BABCOCK WANSONITALIANA SPA
Via Roma 147,
20040 Cavenago
Brianza (Milano) Italy
TEL : +39 2 959121
FAX : +39 2 95019252
E-MAIL : bwi.dir@bwl.it
CONTACT : Alessandro Marianelli

BARON TERMODINAMICA SPA
Fraz Olmo, Strada Statale
11n 106 36051, Creazzo (VI), Italy
TEL : +39 444 520 511
FAX : +39 444 523 333
CONTACT : Giuseppc Baron

CAMPI SRL
Via Diamantina 15, 44100,
Ferrara, Italy
TEL : +39 532 770048
FAX : +39 532 55518
E-MAIL :campisrl@mail.asianet.it
CONTACT : Dr. Ugo Penzo

CASINGHINI HEATER SRL
25036, Palazzolo Sull'Oglio,
Brescia, Italy
TEL : +39 30 7401802
FAX : +39 30 7300761
CONTACT : Marco Casinghini

CEMB SPA
Measuring System,
Via Risorgimento 9, 23826,
Mandello del Lario, Lecco, Italy
TEL : +39 0341 706111
FAX : +39 0341 735678
E-MAIL : coti.enrico@cemb.com
WEB : http://www.cemb.com
CONTACT : Enrico Coti Zelati

ENEA MATTEISPA (ING)
Strada Padana Superiore 307,
20090 Vimbodrone (MI), Italy
TEL : +39 2 25305-1
FAX : +39 2 253905-243
CONTACT : Mr. Policastri

FAVRA INTERNATIONAL SRL
Via Guerrazzi 9,
20145 Milano, Italy
TEL: + 39 2 2495151
FAX: 39 2 33104884
CONTACT : Jaques Meystar

FIC SPA
Via Trivulzia 54,
23030 Mese
(Sondrio), Italy
TEL: +39 343 41051
FAX: +39 343 41304
E-MAIL:fic@clavis.it
WEB:http://www.fic.com
CONTACT : Simona Caldera

HIROSS SPA
Via Leonardo da Vinci 8, 35028
Piove di Sacco (PD), Italy
TEL: +39 49 97 19 111
FAX: +39 49 584 1257

HRS ENGINEERING SRL
Via de Gasperi,
Zona Industriale
21010 Ferno, Italy
TEL: +39 331 726111
FAX: +39 331 726104
E-MAIL: hrseng@tin.it
CONTACT: Ernesto Bardelli

JANUS ENERGY SRL
V le A Merloni 1 60044 Fabriano
(AN), Italy
TEL: +39 0732 625 722
FAX: +39 0732 628 680
E-MAIL:janus.energy@pasadena.it

MACCHI SPA
Via per Busto 70,
Fagnano Olona, VA 21054,
Italy
TEL: +39 331 333 111
FAX: +39 331 611 377
E-MAIL: macchi@macchiboiler.it
WEB: http://www.macchiboiler.it

MAPRO INTERNATIONAL SRL
Via Enrico Fermi 3, 20054 Nova
Milanese (Milano), Italy
TEL: +39 0362 366356
FAX: +39 0362 450342
E-MAIL: mapro@mapro.it
CONTACT: C Frisinghelli

MILTRONIK SRL
Via Ranzato 12,
20128 Milano, Italy
TEL: +39 2 27002838
FAX: +39 2 27003262
E-MAIL: miltronik@tin.it
CONTACT: Rainero Manini

RECUTERM & CO SNC
Via Principale 30,
39025 Naturno (BZ), Italy
TEL : +39 473 667128
FAX : +39 473 668398
CONTACT : Elmar Schnarf

SIRE SRL
Via Toti 36/A,
20052 Monza (Milano), Italy
TEL: +39 362668
FAX: +39 2301857
E-MAIL: sire_saving@hotmail.com
WEB: http://yellow.technet.it/sire
CONTACT: R Beltracchini

SOCIETA ITALIANADI TELERISCALDAMENTO-SITEL SRL
Viale Edison 50, 20099 Sesto San
Giovanni (MI), Italy
TEL: +39 2 2623 2028
FAX: +39 2 2623 2029
CONTACT: Giovanni Salvini

TENAX SPA
Geosynthetics Division, Via Industria
3, Vigano Brianza 23897, Italy
TEL: +39 39 921 9307
FAX: +39 39 92 19 200
E-MAIL: geo.div@temax.net
WEB : http://www.tenax.com
CONTACT : Pietro Romoldi

VANESSA SRL
Via Piacenza 1, 29018 Lugagnano
Val D'Arda PC, Italy
TEL: +39 523 890201
FAX: +39 523 890290
CONTACT: Luciano Vertova

SUPPLIERS

INSTRUMENTATION

CAZZANIGA SP
Via Parco SNC,
20046 Biassoni (MI)
Italy
TEL : +39 39 49861
FAX : +39 4986222
WEB : http://www.anima-it.
com/ca zaaniga
CONTACT : A Cazzaniga

HI-TEC SRL
Via Agrigento 9,
20148 Milano, Italy
TEL: +39 2 3271914
FAX: +39 2 39260434
CONTACT: A Ciminaghi

LOMBARD & MAROZZINI SRL
Via A Albricci 9,
00194 Rome,
Italy
TEL: +39 6 36301456
FAX: +39 63293698
EMAIL:lemrm@micane.it
WEB:http://www.micanet.it/lem
CONTACT:Giorgio Marozzini

NUVERA FUEL CELLS EUROPE SRL
Via Bistolfi 35,
20134 Milano,
Italy
TEL: +39 2 21 291
FAX: +39 2 2129 2403
TELEX: 310552-32223 1 ODENORI
E-MAIL: nuvera.eu@nuvera.it
WEB: http://www.nuvera.com
CONTACT: Alessandro Delfrate

RIVA WIND TURBINES SRL
Via Emilia Ponente 72,
40133, Bologna,
Italy
TEL: +39 51 413 0641
FAX: +39 51 413 0654
CONTACT: Christof Stork

STC COLENCO ENGINEERING SRL
Via Bazzane 71,
40012 Calderara
Di Reno, Bologna,
Italy
TEL: +39516462211
FAX: +39516462242
E-MAIL: sce@stcgroup.com
WEB: http://www.stcgroup.com

STF SPA
Via Robecco 20,
20013 Magenta (MI)
Italy
TEL: +392972091
FAX: +3929794977
E-MAIL: stf@stf.it
WEB: http://www.stf.it
CONTACT: Dr. R Trifone

VOLTASPA
Via del Vigenetto 23,
39100 Bolzano,
Italy
TEL: +39 471 561000
FAX: +39 471 561100
E-MAIL: info@volta.it
WEB: http://www.volta.it
CONTACT: Heinrich Kubicek

BATTERIES & INVERTERS

ELETTRONICA SANTERNO SPA
Via G Di Vittorio 3,
40020 Casalifiumanese Bo,
Italy
TEL: +39 0542 668611
FAX: +39 0542 687722
E-MAIL:
salesntd@elettronicasanterno.it
WEB: http://
www.elettronicasanterno.it

FIAMM SPA
Viale Europa 63,
36075 Montecchio
Maggiore (VI) Italy
TEL: +39 444 709636
FAX: +39 444 694178
CONTACT: A Maturo

TANKS

CSC SPA
Via Lago Maggnire 7,
36015 Scho (VI),
Italy
TEL : +39 445 575989
FAX : +39 445 575750
E-MAIL : info@csc-schin.com
WEB : http://www.csc-schio.com

ICI CALDAIE SPA
Sales Via Pascoli 15,
S Maria di Zevio (Verona),
Italy
TEL: +39 45 8730060
FAX: +39 45 8731148
E-MAIL: ici@ifinet.it
CONTACT: Lucchini Simone

OTHERS (S)

CENTRO PER UN APP ROPRIATO SVILPPO TECHNOLOGICO-CAST
Viale dei Tigli 32k 21014
Laveno, Millo (Varese),
Italy
TEL : +39 332 667082
FAX : +39 332 667082
E-MAIL : ascast@tin.it
CONTACT : Stoppa Adriana

CESI SPA
Via Rubattino 54,
20134 Milano,
Italy
TEL: +39 221 255204
FAX: +39 221 255481
E-MAIL: sales@cesi.it
WEB: http://www.cesi.it
CONTACT: Nicoletta Boattini

COLDER ITALIA SRL
Via C Leone 34/A,
10090 Rivoli, Torino, Italy
TEL: +39 011 9588231
FAX: +39 011 9588232
E-MAIL: colder@colder.it
WEB: http://www.colderitalia.com
CONTACT: Andrea Lusena

EMMETI SPA
Via Brigata Osoppo 166,
33070 vignovo (PN) Italy
TEL : +39 434 567911
FAX : +39 434 567902
E-MAIL : info@emmeti.com
WEB : http://www.emmeti.com
CONTACT : L Maschietto

ETA
Renewable Energies, Piazza
Savonarola 10, 40132 Firenze, Italy
TEL: +39 55 500 2174
FAX: +39 55 573 425
E-MAIL: eta@etaflorence.it

FLAMMSPA
Vale Europa 63,
36075 Montecchio
Maggiore (VI) Italy
TEL: + 39 444 709636
FAX: + 39 444 694178

FLUXINOSITALIA SRL
Via Genova 10,
58100 Grosseto, Italy
TEL: +39 564 451 272
FAX: +39 564 454 237

FOCCHISPA
Via Circonvallazione Ovest 9,
Caselia, Postale 19,
47900 Rimini, Italy
TEL: +39 541 740055
FAX: +39 541 742167

GEMMO IMPIANT SPA
Viale dell'Industria 2, 36057
Arcugnano (VI), Italy
TEL : + 39 444 963990
FAX : + 39 444 961551
E-MAIL : commerciale@gemmon.com
WEB : www.gemmo.com

ITALKERO SRL
Via Lumumba 2,
Zona Industriale
Torrazi, 41100 Modena,
Italy
TEL: +39 59 2550711
FAX: +39 59 250126
E-MAIL:italkero@tin.it
WEB:http://www.italkero.it
CONTACT : Lucian Tosetti

ITALPERFO SRL
Via Casana 47, 10139 Torinao, Italy
TEL: +39 11 4343528
FAX: 39 11 4343528
E-MAIL:italperfo@alpcom.it

ITAS SPA
Via Metauro 5, 20052
Monza(Milano), Italy
TEL: +39 039 27 33 18
FAX: +39 039 745 077
E-MAIL: info@itas.com
WEB : http://www.itas.com
CONTACT : Antonio Pozzoli

JANUS ENERGY SRL
V le A Merloni 1,
60044 Fabriano (AN) Italy
TEL: +39 07 32 625 722
FAX: +39 07 32 628 680
E-MAIL: janus.energy@sunnyday.it

O CO
IA s Paolo 25,
20041 Agrate, Italy
TEL:+39 39 650635
FAX:+39 39 650959
E-MAIL:soco@soco.it
WEB:http://www.soco.it
CONTACT:Franco Porta

Kindly inform us of any errors and omissions in the listings by:

E-mail: unisun@vsnl.com

Fax: 91 80 22289294

ENERGY EFFICIENCY

LATVIAN ENERGY EFFICIENCY AGENCY LTD-LEEA
Aizlraukles Str 21,
LV -1006 Riga Latvia
TEL: +371 7013277
FAX: +371 7013266
E-MAIL: shiplovs@edi.iv
CONTACT: Peteris Shipkovs

SUSTAINABLE ENERGY LTD
Information Office (SPARS)
Akademijas Lavk I, Room 447,
Riga LV 1050, Latvia
TEL: +371 721 3566
FAX: +371 721 3566
E-MAIL:spars@bkc.lv
CONTACT:Paul Barons

VAK GREEN CENTRE
Leila Str. 14-116,
Liepaja LV3401, Latvia
TEL: +371 34 27487
FAX: +371 34 24223
E-MAIL: green-c@cs.lpu.lv
CONTACT: Ines Eistere

RESEARCH & DEVELOPMENT

LATVIANACADEMY OF SCIENCES-LAS
Institute of Physical Energetics,
Aizkraukles Str 21,
LV-1006 Riga, Latvia
TEL: +371 7552011
FAX: +371 7550839
E-MAIL: fei@di.iv
WEB: http://www.inniovation.lv/fei
CONTACT: Prof Furis Ekmams

BIOMASS

ENERGI-R LTD
Aizkraukles Str 21,LV-1006 Riga, Latvia
TEL: +371 7553537
FAX: +371 7553537
E-MAIL: shipkovs@edi.lv
CONTACT: Peteris Shipkovs

OTHERS (S)

ENERGI-R LTD
55/2-602 Brivilas Street,
LV-1010 Riga, Latvia
TEL : +371 7013255
FAX : +371 7013256
E-MAIL : shipkovs@edi.kv
CONTACT : Peteris Shipkovs

We kindly request more listings in this country.

You can submit any additional listings by E-mail: unisun@vsnl.com

Fax: 91 80 2289294

We will include these in the next edition

Kindly inform us of any errors and omissions in the listings by:

E-mail: unisun@vsnl.com

Fax: 91 80 22289294

SOLAR THERMAL

LITHUANIAN ENERGY INSTITUTE
Information, 3 Breslaujos,
3035 Kaunas, Lithuania
TEL: +370 7 350 279
FAX: +370 7 351 271
E-MAIL: bartus@isag.lei.it
WEB: http//www.let.it
CONTACT: Sibitas Bartkus

TERMA LTD
Bakanausko 20, 3018 Kaunas,
Lithuania
TEL: +370 7 763 751
FAX: +370 7 757 496
E-MAIL: vyklis@isag.lei.it
WEB: http://www.terma.it
CONTACT: Vylintas Suksteris

UAB TERMA
J Bakanausko 20, 3018 Kaunas,
Lithuania
TEL : +370 7 39 23 11
FAX : +370 7 39 20 96
E-MAIL : terma@takas.lt
WEB : http://www.terma.lt
CONTACT : Vykintas Sukstekis

CONSULTANTS

TERMA LTD
Bakanausko 20, LT-3018 Kaunas,
Lithuania
TEL: +37037392311
FAX: +37037392096
E-MAIL: info@terma.lt
WEB: http://www.terma.lt
CONTACT: Vykintas Suksteris

We kindly request more listings in this country.

You can submit any additional listings by E-mail: unisun@vsnl.com

Fax: 91 80 2289294

We will include these in the next edition

Kindly inform us of any errors and omissions in the listings by:

E-mail: unisun@vsnl.com

Fax: 91 80 2289294

DESIGN & ENGINEERING

ENERGIE ET ENVIRONMENT INGENIEURS-CONSEITSSA
21 Alie Scheffer,
2520 Luxembourg,
Luxembourg
TEL: + 352 22 46 23
FAX: +352 22 46 25

OTHERS

LUXCONTROL SA
Service Energie,
1 Avenue des Terres Rouges,
4330 Esch-sur-Alzette,
Luxembourg
TEL: +352 54 77 11 1
FAX: +352 54 77 11 266
E-MAIL: info@luxcontrol.com
WEB: http://www.luxcontrol.com
CONTACT: Guy Spenner

SOCIETE ELECTRIQUE DE L'OUR SA
2 rue Pierre d'Aspelt,
BP 37, L-2010 Luxembourg,
Luxembourg
TEL: +352 44 9021
FAX:+352 45 1368
E-MAIL:seolux@tcp.ip.lu
CONTACT:Nicolas Glaesener

We kindly request more listings in this country.

You can submit any additional listings by E-mail: unisun@vsnl.com

Fax: 91 80 2289294

We will include these in the next edition

Kindly inform us of any errors and omissions in the listings by:

E-mail: unisun@vsnl.com

Fax: 91 80 2289294

SUPPLIERS

GLASS

MIRYA LTD
A5a Industrial Estate, Marsa, Malta
TEL: +356 242599
FAX: +356 233740
CONTACT: Gaspar Battistino

UNIVERSITIES

ACADEMY OF SCIENCES OF MOLDOVIA
Institute of Applied Physics, 5
Academia Street, MD-2028
Kishinau, Moldovia
TEL : +373 2 72 71 57
FAX : +373 2 73 81 49
E-MAIL : xray@cc.acad.mn
CONTACT : Alexel Simnakench

We kindly request more listings in this country.

You can submit any additional listings by E-mail: unisun@vsnl.com

Fax: 91 80 2289294

We will include these in the next edition

Kindly inform us of any errors and omissions in the listings by:

E-mail: unisun@vsnl.com

Fax: 91 80 2289294

SOLAR THERMAL

AGPO BV
Konijnenberg 24, 4825 BD Breda,
Netherlands
TEL: +31 765725725
FAX: +31 765725770
WEB: http://www.agpo.nl
CONTACT: JJ Feenstra

ATAG VERWARMING BV
Galileistraat 27, 7131 PE
Lichtenvoorde, Netherlands
TEL : +31 544 391 777
FAX : +31 544 391 703
E-MAIL : info@atagverwarming.com
WEB : http://www.atagerwarming.com

AWB CV-KETELS
Postbus 7, 5740 AA Beek en Donk
Netherlands
TEL : +31 493 461 731
FAX : +31 492 461 945
E-MAIL :info@awb.nl.
WEB : http://www.awb.nl

B + E TECHNIEK BV
Atoomweg 498, 3542 AB Utrecht,
Netherlands
TEL: +31 30 2414444
FAX: +31 30 2412453
E-MAIL: info@betechniek.nl
WEB: http://www.betechniek.nl
CONTACT: AJ Smits

DAALDEROP BV
Postbus 7, 4000 AA, Tiel. Netherlands
TEL : + 31 3446 36550
FAX : + 31 3446 20901
E-MAIL : info@daalderop.nl
WEB : http://www.daalderop.nl

DE BEYER RTB BV
Hazenkamp, 24, 6836, BA Anahem
Netherlands
TEL : + 31 26 322 9103
FAX : + 31 26 321 6186
CONTACT : HA de Beyer

EMERGIEBEDRIJF MIDDEN HOLLAND NV
PO Box 26, 2800 AA Gowda,Netherlands
TEL: +31 182 589 610
FAX: +31 182 522 822
E-MAIL: info@emhgouda.nl

ENERGIE NOORD WEST
PO Box 23451, 1100 DZ Amsterdam,
Netherlands
TEL: +31 203 122 666
FAX: +31 203 122 697
E-MAIL: enw@enw.nl
WEB : http://www.enw.nl

INALFA- ARES ENERGY SYSTEMS BV
Nieuwhuisweg 3, 5804 AN Venray,
Netherlands
TEL: +31 478 555 480
FAX: +31 478 555 489
E-MAIL: inalfa-ares@inalfa.nl
WEB: http://www.inalfa-ares.nl
CONTACT: Mr HA de Beyer

JIRLUMAR BV
PO Box 3068, 5930 AB Tegelen,
Netherlands
TEL: +31 77 373 0555
FAX: +31 77 373 0322
CONTACT : JFE Van Eijk

KWADRANT BV
Heunpark 2515, 5261 WC Vught
Netherlands
TEL: +31 73 656 3803
FAX: +31 73 656 1694
CONTACT : JW Van Eijndhoven

LUIGJES ZONNE ENERGIE BV
Gildeweg 15, 3771 NB Barneveld
Netherlands
TEL: +31 342 404040
FAX: +31 342 404049
CONTACT: Mr. Goossens

NEFIT FASTO BV
PO Box 3, 7400 AA Deventer,
Netherlands
TEL: +31 570 67 85 85
FAX: +31 570 67 85 86

POOLTECHNICS BV
Sluisweg 30a,5145 PE Waalwijik
Netherlands
TEL: +31 416 331549
FAX:+31 416 337298
CONTACT : L de Long

RENSA/SOLAHART BV
PO Box 84, 6940 BB Didam,
Netherlands
TEL : +31 316 29 29 72

SOLAHART INDUSTRIES PTY LTD
Europe and Africa,
Vlamoven Weg 12,
5708 JV Helmond, Netherlands
TEL: +31492579696
FAX: +31492579694
E-MAIL: info@solarhart-europe.com
WEB: http://www.solahart.com.au
CONTACT: R Meesters

SOLISTOR BV
Postbus 275, 5500 AG Veldhoven,
Netherlands
TEL: +31 40 254 9499
FAX: 31 40 254 5085
CONTACT: Marc Gebbink

STIEBEL ELTRON NEDERLAND BV
Daviottenweg 36,
5222 BH Den Bosch,
Netherlands
TEL: +31736230000
FAX: +31736231141
E-MAIL: stiebel@stiebel-eltron.nl
WEB: http://www.stiebel-eltron.nl
CONTACT: G Coenen

TRANSSOLAR
Industrial Estate De Oude Werf De
Wagenmaker 2,
1851 PX Heiloo,
Netherlands
TEL: +31 72 533 6540
FAX: +31 72 533 9393
CONTACT: Klaas Schimmel

VAILLANT BV
PO Box 23250,
1100 DT Amsterdam,
Netherlands
TEL: +31 20 565 9200
FAX: +31 20 696 9366
CONTACT: JH ter Hennepe

VICTRON ENERGIE
PO Box 50016,
1305 AA Almere-Haven,
Netherlands
TEL: +31365313333
FAX: +31365311666
WEB: http://www.victronenergie.com
CONTACT: T Bos

ZEN-INTERNATIONAL BV
Lage Gouwe 198, 2801 LM Gouda,
Netherlands
TEL: +31 182 599899
FAX: +31 182 599127
E-MAIL:
101520.1004@compuserve.com
CONTACT: T P Bokhoven

ZONNE ENERGIE NEDERLAND BV
De Run 5421,
5504 DG Veldhoven,
Netherlands
TEL: +31 40 230 7200
FAX: +31 40 230 7210
E-MAIL: info@zen.nl
CONTACT: J Van Dam

SOLAR PHOTOVOLTAIC

ATAG VERWARMING BV
Galileistraat 27, 7131 PE
Lichtenvoorde, Netherlands
TEL : +31 544 391 777
FAX : +31 544 391 703
E-MAIL : info@atagverwarming.com
WEB : http://www.atagerwarming.com

BENELUX SOLAR & TECHNICAL SYSTEMS BV
Gaglveld 7A, PO Box 120,
4844 ZJ Terhejden, Netherlands
TEL : +31 76 393 4143
FAX : + 31 76 593 4138
E-MAIL :wvanbeek@bstgroup.nl
WEB : http://www.bstgroup.nl

EKOMATION SOLAR ENERGY CONSULTANCY
Postbus 29112, 3001 G C Rotterdam
Netherlands
TEL : +31 10 280 72 64
FAX : +31 10 280 72 65
E-MAIL :info@ekomation.nl
WEB : http://www.ekomation.nl

EMERGIEBEDRIJF MIDDEN HOLLAND NV
PO Box 26, 2800 AA Gowda,
Netherlands
TEL: +31 182 589 610
FAX: +31 182 522 822
E-MAIL: info@emhgouda.nl

ENERGIE NOORD WEST
PO Box 23451,
1100 DZ Amsterdam, Netherlands
TEL: +31 203 122 666
FAX: +31 203 122 697
E-MAIL: enw@enw.nl
WEB : http://www.enw.nl

ERES
Nyenstein 10, 3328 ZH Dordrecht.
Netherlands
TEL: 31 78 6180223
FAX: 31 78 6181428
CONTACT : HE Huijnink

FREE ENERGY EUROPE BV
Marketing, PO Box 9564,
5602 LN Eindhoven,
Netherlands
TEL: +31 40 290 1245
FAX: +31 40 290 1249
E-MAIL:info@free-energy.net
WEB: http://www.free-energy.net
CONTACT: Frank Vander Vleuten

HANWEL BV
PO Box 123, 7570 AC Oldenzaal,
Netherlands
TEL : + 31 541 858685
FAX : + 31 541 858687
E-MAIL : verkoop@codinox.com

JIRLUMAR BV
PO Box 3068, 5930 AB Tegelen,
Netherlands
TEL: +31 77 373 0555
FAX: +31 77 373 0322
CONTACT : JFE Van Eijk

LOGIC GREEN ENERGY BV
Nyverheidsweg 9,
3771 ME Barneveld
Netherlands
TEL: +31 342 423738
FAX: +31 342 423383
EMAIL: sales@le.nl
WEB:http://www.le.nl
CONTACT:Jan Nijland

MASTERVOLT SOLAR
Snijdersbergweg 93, 1105 AN
Amsterdam, Netherlands
TEL: +31 20 3422180
FAX: +31 20 3422188
E-MAIL: solar@mastervolt.com
WEB: http://www.mastervoltsolar.com
CONTACT: Ir H Marsman

REMU NV
Atoomweg 50,
3504 AA Utrecht
Netherlands
TEL : +31 35 609 4419
FAX : +31 35 609 4563

SHELL SOLAR BV
Shell Renewables,
PO Box 38000, 1030 BN
Amsterdam, Netherlands
TEL: +31206303000
FAX: +31206302211
E-MAIL: solarinfo@si.shell.com
WEB: http://www.shellsolar.com
CONTACT: Mrs. Ine Hoevenaars

SIEMENS NEDERLAND NV
PO Box 16068, 2500 BB Den Haag,
Netherlands
TEL: +31 703 33 32 11
FAX: +31 703 33 33 82

SOLARNED
PV-solar systems, PO BOx 74791,NL-1070 BT Amsterdam, Netherlands
TEL:+31 20 463 8787
FAX:+31 20 463 8768
E-MAIL:solarned@wxs.net
CONTACT:L K Tan

STORK MARINE SOLAIR BV
PO Box 498, 5600 AL Eindhoven,
Netherlands
TEL: +31 4028 29911
FAX: +31 4028 29915

STROOMWERK ENERGY BV
PO Box 388, 7400 Aj Deventer,
Netherlands
TEL: +31 570 655055
FAX: +31 570 653829
E-MAIL:energy@stroomwerk.nl
WEB:http://www.stroomwerk.com
CONTACT: DP Elzinga

TEMANNING VOF
Schoener 50, 1771 ED Wieringerwerf
Netherlands
TEL : +31 227 60 41 28
FAX : +31 227 60 41 28
E-MAIL:pumps@flowman.nl
WEB :http://www.flowman.nl
CONTACT:Terry Manning

TRANSSOLAR
Industrial Estate De Oude Werf De Wagenmaker 2, 1851 PX Heiloo,
Netherlands
TEL: +31 72 533 6540
FAX: +31 72 533 9393
CONTACT: Klaas Schimmel

VANDEN BERG DUURZAME
ENERGIE AP
PO Box 68,
8445 PK Heerenveen,
Netherlands
TEL: +31 513 63 13 55
FAX: +31 513 63 12 12
E-MAIL: apb@apvdberg.nl

VOLTANOVA BV
Amperelaan I - L, NL-9207 Drachten
Netherlands
TEL: +31 512 589873
FAX: +31 512 589874
WEB: http://www.voltanova.nl
CONTACT: SA Schoustra

WIND

DHV MILIEU & INFRASTRUCTUURE BV
Postbus 1076,
3800 BB Amersfoort,
Netherlands
TEL : + 31 33 468 9111
FAX : + 31 33 468 2801
CONTACT : Jan Van Geest

ENERGIE NOORD WEST
PO Box 23451,
1100 DZ Amsterdam,
Netherlands
TEL: +31 203 122 666
FAX: +31 203 122 697
E-MAIL: enw@enw.nl
WEB : http://www.enw.nl

ENGLISH WORKS
Wim Sonneveldstraat 50,
7558 LW Hengelo,
Netherlands
TEL : + 31 74 2783115
FAX : + 31 74 2783149
E-mail : stacey@dds.nl
CONTACT : Dr Giles Stracey

FORTIS WINDENERGY
Botanicuslann 14,
NL-9751 AC Haren, Netherlands
TEL: +31 50 534 01 04
FAX: +31 50 534 01 04
E-MAIL: fortis-windenergy@wxs.nl
CONTACT: Johan Kuikman

LAGERWEY WIND TURBINE BV
Hanzweg 31, 3771 NG Barneveld,
Netherlands
TEL: +31 342 422 724
FAX: +31 342 422 961
E-MAIL: sales@lagerwey.nl
WEB: http://www.lagerwey.nl
CONTACT: T R Boersma

LMW RENEWABLES BV
Nassaulaan 27, 1213 ba Hilversum
Netherlands
TEL: +31 35 6231908
FAX: +31 35 6284878
CONTACT: PC Hensing

NEG MICON HOLLAND BV
PO Box 118, 3901 AC Rhenen,
Netherlands
TEL: +31 317 619004
FAX: +31 317 612129
WEB: http://www.nedwind.nl
CONTACT: AC Burgers-Kommeroh

PROWIN PROFESSIONAL WINDMILLS
PO Box 217, 6660 AE Elst,
Netherlands
TEL: +31 481 361 362
FAX: +31 481 361 378
E-MAIL: info@prowin.nl
WEB: http://www.prowin.nl

STROOMWERK ENERGY BV
PO Box 388, 7400 Aj Deventer,
Netherlands
TEL: +31 570 655055
FAX: +31 570 653829
E-MAIL:energy@stroomwerk.nl
WEB:http://www.stroomwerk.com
CONTACT: DP Elzinga

TOCARDO BV
De Weel 20, 1736 KB Zijdewind,
Netherlands
TEL: +31 226 423411
FAX: +31 226 423433
CONTACT : JW van Breugel

VESTAS - NEDERLAND WINDTECHNOLOGIE BV
Dr Langemeijerweg 1 A, Postbus 63,
6990 AB Rheden, Netherlands
TEL: +31 26 49 71 500
FAX: +31 26 49 71 555

WINDMASTER NEDERLAND BV
Zuiveringweg 26, 8243 PZ Lelystad,
TEL: +31 320 254940
FAX: +31 320 254576
CONTACT : A Jochems

BIOMASS

BIOFUEL BY
Rendorpark 30, 1963 AM
Heemskerk, Netherlands
TEL : +31 25124601
FAX : +31 25123741
E-MAIL :naber@biofuel.com

CIRMAC INTERNATIONAL BV
PO Box 995, 7301 BE Apeldoorn,
Netherlands
TEL: +31 55 534 0110
FAX: +31 55 534 0050

ENERGIE NOORD WEST
PO Box 23451,
1100 DZ Amsterdam,
Netherlands
TEL: +31 203 122 666
FAX: +31 203 122 697
E-MAIL: enw@enw.nl
WEB : http://www.enw.nl

ESSENT DUURZAAM
PO Box 1856, Room 317,
5200 BW Den Bosch,
Netherlands
TEL: +31 73 615 4500
FAX: +31 73 615 4599
WEB: http://www.pnem.nl
CONTACT: K Krikke

GASTEC NV
Postbus 137,
7300 AC Apeldoorn,
Netherlands
TEL: +31 55 5393 393
FAX: + 31 55 5393 494
E-Mail : post@ gastec.nl
WEB: http://www.gastec.nl
CONTACT: RA Webrans

GROENE WARMT BV
PO Box 200,
3253 ZK Ouddorp.
Netherlands
TEL : + 31 1874 93366
FAX : + 31 1874 93320
E-MAIL : info@groene-warmte.in

HANWEL BV
PO Box 123,
7570 AC Oldenzaal,
Netherlands
TEL : + 31 541 858685
FAX : + 31 541 858687
E-MAIL : verkoop@codinox.com

HOST EFFICIENCY IN ENERGY
Postbus 920,
7550 AX Hengelo,
Netherlands
TEL: +31 74 240 18 01
FAX: +31 74 240 18 10
E-MAIL: info@host.nl
CONTACT: Dr H Klein Teeselink

IMAG
PO Box 43,
6700 AA Wageningen,
Netherlands
TEL: +31 317 47 63 00
FAX: +31 317 42 56 70
WEB: http://www.imag.wageningen-ur.nl
CONTACT: M van den Top

INFORMATION CENTRE OF BIOMASS - ICB
PO Box 342,
7300 AH Apeldoorn
Netherlands
TEL: +31 555 49 33 44
FAX: +31 555 49 32 87
E-MAIL: cb@mep.tno.nl

LABEE GROEP MOERDIJK
PO Box 71,
4780 AB Moerdijk,
Netherlands
TEL: +31 1683 82110
FAX: +31 1683 82015

LANG ENERGY SYSTEMS BV
Dy Kgraafweg 40, Postbus 231,
7300 AE Apeldoorn, Netherlands
TEL: +31 555419333
FAX: +31 555331691
E-MAIL: les@xs4all.nl
CONTACT: A W Karel

STICHTING CPV - CENTRU VOOR PLANTAARDIGE VEZELS - INSTITUTE FOR PLANT FIBRE RESEARCH
PO Box 598,
6700 AN Wageningen,
Netherlands
TEL: +31 317 42 64 59
FAX: +31 317 41 86 45
E-MAIL:mail@cpv.nl
WEB:http://www.biomasster.nl
CONTACT:Dr AM Heineman

STORK THERMEQ BV
PO Box 33,
7550 AA Hengelo
Netherlands
TEL: +31 7424 01060
FAX: +31 7424 24790
E-MAIL:office@thermeq.storkgroup.com
WEB:http://www.colibri-stork.nl

NETHERLANDS

VANDENBROEK INTERNATIONAL BV
Industrial Drying Technology, Nijendal 30, 3972 KC Driebergen, Netherlands
TEL: +31 343 53 09 30
FAX: +31 343 51 37 54
E-MAIL: info@vadeb.nl
WEB: http://www.vadeb.nl
CONTACT: Pobert A Ponsen

COGENERATION

DYNAF SPRUYT GROUP
PO Box 8349 3503,
RH Utrecht, Netherlands
TEL : + 31 30 662 93 02
FAX : + 31 30 662 12 13
E-MAIL : info@sprvyt.com
CONTACT : Jacques Bouwman

EPON INTERNATIONAL
PO Box 10087, 8000 GB Zwolle, Nertherlands
TEL: +31 38 427 29 30
FAX: + 31 38 427 29 06
E-MAIL : huub. Paes@epon.nl
CONTACT : Ir HFM Paes

LANDRE RUHAAK BV
Lange Dreef 10, 4131 NH Vianen, Netherlands
TEL : +31 347 329 372
FAX : +31 347 329 290
E-MAIL : info@landre-ruhaak.nl
CONTACT : S Hall

MTM TECHNISCH BUREAU BV
Houbeneindstraat 5, 6151 CP Munstergeleen, Netherlands
TEL : + 31 4645 81995
FAX : +31 4645 80650
EMAIL : mtm@tbmtm.demon.nl
CONTACT : B G J Ruiters

NEDALO BV
Rendementsweg 4, 3641 SK Mijdrecht, Netherlands
TEL: +31 297 293 200
FAX: +31 297 285 930
E-MAIL: sales@nedalo.nl
WEB: http://www.nedalo.nl
CONTACT: J Zwart

STANDARD FASEL-LENTJESBV
Tractieweg 41, 3534 AP Utrecht, Netherlands
TEL: +31 30 244 9211
FAX: +31 30 244 2596

STORK ENERGY
Postbus 20, 7550 GB Hengelo(OV), Netherlands
TEL: +74 240 1363
FAX: +74 242 0361
CONTACT : Lucas Schoemakers

VAN DER BEYL BV
Postbus 9522, 3007 AM Rotterdam. Netherlands
TEL: +31 10 432 22 22
FAX: +31 10 419 90 36
E-MAIL: info@vanderbeyl.nl
WEB: http://www.vanderbeyl.nl
CONTACT: E Kops]'

FUEL CELL

NEDSTACK BV
Fuel Cell Technology,
Cattepoelseweg 237,
6815 CC Arnhem,
Netherlands
TEL: +31 26 3510119
FAX: +31 26 4423151
E-MAIL:nedstack@nedstack.com
WEB: http://www.nedstack.com
CONTACT: Erik Middleman

TIDAL / OCEAN

TEAMWORK TECHNOLOGY BV
De Weel 20, 1736 KB Zijdewind,Netherlands
TEL : +31 226 423411
Fax : +31 226 423433
E-MAIL : teamwork@multiweb.nl
CONTACT : J W van Breugel

TOCARDO BV
De Weel 20, 1736 KB Zijdewind, Netherlands
TEL: +31 226 423411
FAX: +31 226 423433
CONTACT : J W van Breugel

WASTE TO ENERGY

BOA MACHINEFABRIEK BV
PO Box 212, 7500 AE Erschede Netherlands
TEL : +31 534 300 300
FAX : +31 534 301 425
E-MAIL : info@boanl.nt

CPM EUROPE BV
Distelweg 89, 1031 HD Amsterdam Netherlands
TEL : +31 20 494 6111
FAX : +31 20 636 4294
E-MAIL : info@nl.cpm.net
CONTACT : Steve van den Berg

DEUTZBY
PO Box 59036, 3008 PA Rotterdam Netherlands
TEL : + 31 10 299 26 39
FAX : + 31 10 299 27 81
E-MAIL : deutznl@deytz.de
CONTACT : U Ing RH Koster

DHV MILIEU & INFRASTRUCTUURE BV
Postbus 1076,
3800 BB Amersfoort,
Netherlands
TEL : + 31 33 468 9111
FAX : + 31 33 468 2801
CONTACT : Jan Van Geest

ELTACON
Fokkerstraat 12,
2722 NJ Zoetermeer,
Netherlands
TEL : +31 7934 19711
FAX : +31 7934 19901
E-MAIL : eltacon.eng@wxs.nl

ENERGIE EN MILIEUTECHNIEK BV
Op de Bies 17,
6333 Bv Schimmert,
Netherlands
TEL : +31 45 404 1617
FAX : +31 45 404 9261
CONTACT : W. P. Willems

GIBROS PEC BV
Industriestraat 8, PO Box 7324, 3280 AC Numansdorp, Netherlands
TEL : + 31 186 65 00 00
FAX : + 31 186 65 43 80
E-MAIL : jacco@cad.gibro.nl

GICOM BV COMPOSTING SYSTEMS
Plein 11-13. 8256 AZ Biddinghuizen, Netherlands
TEL : + 31 321 33 26 82
FAX : + 31 321 33 27 84
E-MAIL : sales@gicom.nl
WEB : http://www.gicom.nl

HABOBV
Po Box 92, Spanjeweg 6,2410 AB Bodegraven, Netherlands
TEL : + 31 172 61 93 42
FAX : + 31 172 61 70 79
E-MAIL : habo.bv@wxs.nl
CONTACT : Th JN Lek

ICOVA/ICOPOWER
PO Box 59372, Amsterdam 1040KJ Netherlands
TEL: +31 20 611 40 11
FAX: +31 20 613 90 34
CONTACT: BC de Pijer

TEBODIN BV
Energy and Environmental Technology, PO Box 16029, 2500 BA DenHaag, Netherlands
TEL : +31 70 348 09 11
FAX : +31 70 348 05 91
E-MAIL : c.nijhof@tebodin.nl
WEB : http://www.tebodin.com
CONTACT : C Nijhof

VAN GANSEWINKEL GROEP BV
Recycling, Cranendonck 4, PO Box
Netherlands
TEL: +31 49 591010
FAX: +31 49 592250
CONTACT: T de Jong

VERENIGING VAN AFVAL VERWERKERS - VVAV
Catharijnesingel 55V, 3501 GD
Utrecht, Netherlands
TEL: +31 30 23 23030
FAX: +31 30 233 21 22
E-MAIL: info@vvav.nl
WEB: http://www.vvav.nl
CONTACT: All van de Laar

VORTEX ECP TECHNOLOGY
Energy & Waste, Waterweg 86, 3731
HN De Bilt, Netherlands
TEL: +31 30 220 3141
FAX: +31 30 220 3141
E-MAIL: clh@vortexcw.nl
WEB: http://www.glidarc.com
CONTACT: CLH Winkelman

ENERGY EFFICIENCY

ECONCERN
PO Box 8408,
NL-3503 RK Utrecht,
Netherlands
TEL: +31 30 280 83 55
FAX: +31 30 280 83 01
E-MAIL: info@e-concern.com
CONTACT: Maaike Fernhout

IPC TRAINING CENTRE
PO Box 32, 6710 BA Ede,
Netherlands
TEL: +31 3186 97111
FAX: +31 3186 34472
E-MAIL:pdu@ede.ipcagro.nl
WEB:http://www.agro.stoas.nl/ipcplant

MEGA LIMBURG NV - MAATSCHAPPIJ VOOR ELEKTRICITEIT EN GAS LIMBURG
Postbus 3920,
6202 NX Maastricht,
Netherlands
TEL: +31 433 85 55 25
FAX: +31 433 85 54 78
E-MAIL: megal@ibp.nl

PHILIPS LIGHTING BV
Building EC2,
Po Box 80020,
5600 JM Eindhoven,
Netherlands
TEL: +31 40 275 5893
FAX : + 31 40 275 6038
WEB :http://www.lighting-philips.com
CONTACT : Mrs.Anissa Abbou

VANHEUGTEN BV CONSULTING ENGINEERS
PO Box 305, 6500 AH Nijmegen,
Netherlands
TEL: +31 24 322 8317
FAX: +31 24 323 5016
E-MAIL: luscuere@V-Heugten-bv.nl
CONTACT: Prof PG Luscuere'

FINANCE / BANKING

ASN BANK
PO Box 30502, 2500 GM Den Haag,
Netherlands
TEL : +31 703 569 333
FAX : +31 703 617 948

EKOMATION SOLAR ENERGY CONSULTANCY
Postbus 29112,
3001 G C Rotterdam
Netherlands
TEL : +31 10 280 72 64
FAX : +31 10 280 72 65
E-MAIL :info@ekomation.nl
WEB : http://www.ekomation.nl

ING BANK NEDERLAND
PO Box 1800,
Bijlmerplein 888, 1000
BV Amsterdam, Netherlands
TEL: +31 20 652 39 54
FAX: +31 20 652 39 73
E-MAIL: corporate.investments
@mail.ing.nl

NIB CAPITAL BANK
Carnegieplein 4, PO Box 380,
2501 The Hague, Netherlands
TEL: +31 70 342 54 25
FAX: +31 70 342 55 77
E-MAIL: thehague@nibcapital.com
WEB: http://www.nibcapital.com
CONTACT: Maud Van Buchem

TRIODOS BANK NV
Postbus 55, 3700 AB Zeist,
Netherlands
TEL: +31 30 693 6500
FAX: +31 30 693 6555
E-MAIL: triodos@tridos.nl
WEB:http://www.triodos.com
CONTACT: JF Schut

ASSOCIATION

BELANGENVERENIGING VOOR VERWERKINGS-BEDRIJVEN VAN ORGANISCHE RESTOFFEN-BVOR
PO Box 901,
7301 BD Apeldoorn, Netherlands
TEL : +31 5554 93731
FAX : +31 5554 93784

HOLLAND SOLAR
Korte Elisabethstraat 6, 3511 JG
Utrecht, Netherlands
TEL: +31 30 232 8008
FAX: +31 30 234 1176
E-MAIl: hollandsolar@tref.nl
WEB: http://www.hollandsolar.nl
CONTACT: Mrs Coby Renzen

NETHERLANDS BIO-ENERGY ASSOCIATION-NL-BEA
PO Box 85096, 3508 AB Utrecht
Netherland
TEL: +31 30 2191342
FAX: +31 30 2195115
E-MAIL: pbe@xs4all.nl
WEB: http://www.xs4all.nl/-pbe

VERENIGING ORGANISATIE VOORDUURZAME ENERGIE-ODE
Postbus 750, 3500 AT Utrecht,
Netherlands
TEL: +31 30 276 9224
FAX: +31 30 272 0624
E-MAIL: ode@knoware.nl

WASTE PROCESSING ASSOCIATION VVAV
Post Box 19300, 3501 DH Utrecht-
Netherlands
TEL: +31 30 2323030
FAX: +31 30 2332122
E-MAIL: info@vvav.nl
WEB: http://www.vvav.nl
CONTACT: A van de Haus

RESEARCH & DEVELOPMENT

EUROPEAN TRANING CENTRE FOR MACHINE TECHNOLOGY ETM
PO Box 35, 9930 AA Delfzijl,
Netherlands
TEL: +31 596 63357
FAX: +31 596 633577
E-MAIL: ETM@castel.nl
WEB: http://move.to/etm
CONTACT : Kuiken C

EXENDIS NV
Energy Systems Solar Inverters,
Keesomstraat 4, 6710 AB Ede,
Netherlands
TEL: +31 318676111
FAX: +31 318624615
E-MAIL: r.tiedink@dde.nl
WEB: http://www.exendis.com
CONTACT: Ron Tiedink

GEN BV
Rhijnspoor 221, 2901 LB Capelle a/d
Ijssel, Rotterdam, Netherlands
TEL: +31 10 7980 980
FAX: +31 10 7980 970
E-MAIL: info@gen.nl
WEB: http://www.gen.nl

NETHERLANDS

IVAM ENVIRONMENTAL RESEARCH UNIVERSITY OF AMSTERDAM
Renewable Energy and Energy Efficiency, PO Box 18180,
1001 ZB Amsterdam,
Netherlands
TEL: +31 20 525 5185
FAX: +31 20 525 5850
E-MAIL: office@ivambv.uva.nl
WEB:http://www.ivambv.uva.nl
CONTACT : J Uiteinger

KEMA NEDERLAND BV
Kema Power Generation and Sustainables,
Utrechtseweg 310,
6812 AR Arnhem,
Netherlands
TEL: +31 26 356 60 72
FAX: +31 26 445 82 79
E-MAIL: r.devries@kema.nl
WEB: http://www.kema.nl
CONTACT : Mark L Beekes

KLIMAATBOUW BV
de la Reylaan 17,
2806 DA Gouda,
Netherlands
TEL: ++31 182 516572
FAX: +31 182 528911
E-MAIL: everthkb@wxs.nl
CONTACT : E Hasselaar

NEM BV
Kanaalpark 159, 2300 AD Leiden,
Netherland
TEL: +31 71 579 2444
FAX: +31 71 579 2759
E-MAIL: mgooy@nem.hbg.nl
CONTACT: Mr Karel van Buuren

NETHERLANDS ENERGY RESEARCH FOUNDATION-ECN
PO Box1, NL-1755 ZG Petten,
Netherlands
TEL: +31 224 564949
FAX: +31 224 564480
WEB: http://www.ecn.nl
CONTACT: Hans Bais

PLANTRESEARCH INTERNATIONAL BV
Agricultural Research Department
DLO NL, PO Box 16, 6700 AA
Wageningen, Netherlands
TEL: +31 317 47 70 01
FAX:+31 317 41 80 94
E-MAIL : info@plant.wag-ur.nl
WEB:http://
www.plant.wageningentur.nl
CONTACT: Dr NG Hogenboom

TNO-NETHERLANDS ORGANIZATION FOR APPLIED SCIENTIFIC RESEARCH
Building and Construction Research,
PO Box 49, 2600 AA Delft,
Netherlands
TEL: +31 15 260 8468
FAX: +31 15 260 8432
E-MAIL:a.degeus@bouw.tno.nl
CONTACT: AC de Geus

TUDELFT-DELFT UNIVERSITY OF TECHNOLOGY
Institute for Wind Energy Faculty of Civil Engineering,
Stevinweg 1,
2628 CN Delft, Netherlands
TEL: +31 15 278 5170
FAX: +31 15 278 5347
E-MAIL: windenergie@ct.tudelft.nl
WEB: http://www.ct-tudelft.nl/
windenergy/ivwhome.htm
CONTACT: W A Timmer

UNIVERSITY OF TECHNOLOGY
Institute for wind Energy,
Stevinwegl,
2629CN elft, Netherlands
TEL:+31152785495
FAX:+31152781855
E-MAIL:joka.boshoff@bu.tudelft.nl

UTRECHT UNIVERSITY
Debye Institute,
PO Box 80000,
3508 TA Utrecht,
Netherlands
TEL: +31 30 253 3170
FAX: +31 30 253 3165
E-MAIL: r.e.l.schropp@fys.ruu.nl
CONTACT: Dr REL Schropp

W/E CONSULTANTS SUSTAINABLE BUILDING
Crabethstraat 38j PO Box 733,
NL-2800 AS Gouda,
Netherlands
TEL: +31 182 68 34 34
FAX: +31 182 51 12 96
E-MAIL: w-e@w-e.nl
WEB: htttp://www.w-e.nl
CONTACT: Geurt Donze

UNIVERSITIES

INSTITUUT REINAANDE
Schiedamseweg 74,
3121 JK Schiedam,
Netherlands
TEL: +31 10 4702863
FAX: +31 10 4702688
CONTACT: Chris Zydeveld

INTERNATIONAL INSTITUTE FOR AEROSPACE SURVEY AND EARTH SCIENCES - ITC
Rural Energy and Development, PO Box 420, 7500 Enschede
Netherlands
TEL: +31 20 870 88
FAX: +31 20 870 88
E-MAIL: Klunne@ic.nl
WEB: http://www.itc.nl/ha2/energy
CONTACT: WE Klunne

INTERNATIONAL INSTITUTE OF ENERGY LAW
Faculty of Law, PO Box 9520, 2300 RA Leiden, Netherlands
TEL: +31 71 527 7723
FAX: +31 71 5277509
E-MAIL: e.d.cross@law.leidenuniv.nl
CONTACT: Eugene D Cross

NGO's

GREEN PEACE INTERNATIONAL
Energy Solutions Unit, Keizersgacht 176, 1016 DW Amsterdam,
Netherlands
TEL : + 31 20 523 6222
FAX : + 31 20 523 6200
E-MAIL : karl.mallon@
ams.greenpeace.org
WEB : http://www.greenpeace.org
CONTACT : Karll Mallon

CONSULTANTS

ARRAKIS-RED
Wilhelmina Str 26,
5141 HK Waalwijk
Netherlands
TEL : +31 40 2819 454
FAX : +31 40 2819 602
E-MAIL : info@arrakis.nl
WEB : http://www.arrakis.nl
CONTACT : GC De Jongh

BIOMASS TECHNOLOGY GROUP BV-BTG
PO Box 217, 7500 AE enschede,
Netherlands
TEL : +31 53 489 28 92
FAX : +31 53 489 31 16
E-MAIL : vos@btg.ct.utwente.nl
WEB : http://www.btgworld.com

BROUWSE ENERGIE CONSULT BV
Vijveriann 316 DE Apeldoorn,
Netherlands
TEL : +3 88 322 0200
FAX : +3 88 321 1348
E-MAIL :info@solarbec.nl
WEB : http://www.solarbec.nl

BURO A+
Kelperheide 50, 6037 SZ Kelpen-Ole
Netherlands
TEL : +31 495 652380
FAX : +31 495 65 2336
E-MAIL :info@aples.nl

CE-CENTRE FOR ENERGY CONSERVATION AND ENVIRONEMENTAL TECHNOLOGY
Oude Delft 180, 2611 HH Delft
Netherlands
TEL : +31 15 215 0150
FAX : +31 15 215 0151
E-MAIL : ce@antenna.nl

CORE INTERNATIONAL BV
Heuvelenweg 18, 7241 HZ Lochem,
Netherlands
TEL : +31 573 256358
FAX : +31 573 254420
EMAIL : info@core-international.nl
WEB : http://www.core-international.nl

DEERNS CONSULTING ENGINEERS
Post Box1211, 2280 CE Rijswijk
Netherlands
TEL : + 31 7039 57620
FAX : + 31 7029 57621
E-MAIL : s&o@deerns.nl

ECOFYS
Kanaalweg 16G, NL-3526 KL Utrecht,
Netherlands
TEL: +31 30 2808 300
FAX: +31 30 2808 301
E-MAIL: info@ecofys.com
WEB: http://www.ecofys.com

GASUNIE NV NEDERLANDS
Postbus 19, 9700 MA Groningen,
Netherlands
TEL: +31 505212272
FAX: +31 505211921
E-MAIL: h.j.sachakel@gasunie.nl

GRAMSBERGEN PROJECTBURO VOOR ENERGIEBEHEER
Tus 7, 5507 MG Velhoven.
Netherlands
TEL : + 31 40 2301500
FAX : + 31 40 2301499
E-MAIL : gramsbergen.solar@iae.in

INGENIEURBURO INNOGAS BV
Arkelse Onderweg 4, PO Box 404
4200 AK Gorinchem,Netherlands
TEL: +31 183 625757
FAX: +31 183 621480
E-MAIL:
v.kampschoer@innovaholding.nl
WEB: http://www.innogas.nl
CONTACT: JC van Bemmel

INTERNATIONAL INSTITUTE OF ENERGY LAW
Faculty of Law, PO Box 9520, 2300
RA Leiden, Netherlands
TEL: +31 71 527 7723
FAX: +31 71 5277509
E-MAIL: e.d.cross@law.leidenuniv.nl
CONTACT: Eugene D Cross

POWERPARTNER LTD
Falkejacht 27, 9254 EJ Hardegaryp,
Netherlands
TEL: +31 511 472171
FAX: +31 511 472482
E-MAIL: a.zomers@inter.nl.net
CONTACT: AN Zomers

TEBODIN
PO Box 233, 7550 AE Hengelo,
Netherlands
TEL: +31742496496
FAX: +31742425712
WEB: http://www.tebodin.com

TECHNECO BV
Kleveringweg 9, 2616 LZ Delft,
Netherlands
TEL : +31 70 3272613
FAX : +31 70 3272941
E-MAIl:techneco@techneco.nl
WEB : http://www.techneco.nl
CONTACT : PR Van Alphen

VERHOEF SOLAR ENERGY CONSULTANCY
Gerald Noodstraat 29, 3515 VV
Utrecht, Netherlands
TEL: +31 30 276 2750
FAX: +31 30 276 2751
E-MAIL: l.verhoef@tip.nl
WEB: http://www.vsec.club.tip.nl
CONTACT: Leendert Verhoef

W/E CONSULTANTS SUSTAINABLE BUILDING
Crabethstraat 38j PO Box 733, NL-
2800 AS Gouda, Netherlands
TEL: +31 182 68 34 34
FAX: +31 182 51 12 96
E-MAIL: w-e@w-e.nl
WEB: htttp://www.w-e.nl
CONTACT: Geurt Donze

DESIGN & ENGINEERING

ARCHITECTEN-EN INGENIEURS BUREAU KRISTINSSON
Noordenbergsingel 10,
7411 SE
Deventer, Netherlands
TEL : +31 570 615035
FAX : +31 570 611606
CONTACT : Prof. Kristinsson

BEAR ARCHITECTEN BV
PO Box 349, 2800 AH Gouda,
Netherlands
TEL : +31 182 529899
FAX : +31 182 582599
E-MAIL : office@bear.nl

DACE ENERGY SYSTEMS BV
Poortweg 2, PO Box 5062, 2600 GB
Delft, Netherlands
TEL : + 31 15 256 93 81
FAX : + 31 15 261 63 92
E-MAIL : info@dace.nl
WEB : http://www.dace.nl
CONTACT : Mf Penning

DUOS ENGINEERS & CONTRACTORS
PO Box 561, NL - 1940 AN Beverwijk
Netherlands
TEL : + 31 251 278 181
FAX : + 31 251 278 191
E-MAIL : info@duos.nl
WEB : http://www. duos.nl
CONTACT : CGS Duijn

EGM ARCHITECTS & ENGINEERS
PO Box 298, 3300 AG Dordrecht,
Netherlands
TEL : +31 78 633 0750
FAX : +31 78 614 0071

ELECTEICITE IT SBEDRIJF ZUID HOLLAND - EZH NV
PO B ox 909, 2270 AX Voorburg,
Netherland
TEL : +31 70 382 00 28
FAX : +31 70 383 39 21
WEB : http://ezh.nl.com

HCG INDUSTRIESERVICE BV
Engineering and Technology,
Cobbenhagenstret 7, 2288 ET
Rijswijk, Netherlands
TEL: +31 70 372 29 60
FAX: +31 70 3722 20 09
E-MAIL: hcgrwk@hcg.hbg.nl
CONTACT: Dr JS Dhillon

HMA POWER SYSTEMS BV
Postbus 3007, 2980 DA Ridder
Netherlands
TEL: +31 180 44 52 00
FAX: +31 180 44 52 42
E-MAIL: m.mayer@hma.nl
CONTACT: JM Mayer

JACOBS COMPRIMO NEDERLAND
Radarweg 60, PO Box 58026, 1040
HA Amsterdam, Netherlands
TEL: +31 20 580 7400
FAX: +31 20 580 7050
E-MAIL:
tammo.beishuizen@jacobs.com
CONTACT : Jammo Beishuieen

NETHERLANDS

KAW ARCHTECTEN BV
Hofstraat 8a, 9712 JB Groningen, Netherlands
TEL: +31 50369 5870
FAX: +31 50369 5871
E-MAIL:kaw@kaw.nl
WEB : www.kaw.nl

KRAGTEN DESIGN
Populierenlaan 51, 5492 SG Sint-Oedenrode, Netherlands
TEL: +31 413 475770
FAX: +31 413 475770
CONTACT : Adriaan Kragten

MECAL APPLIED MECHANICS BV
Product Group Windturbines,
P O Box 286,
7500 AG Enschede, Netherlands
TEL: 931 53 433 4300
FAX: +31 53 433 80 80
E-MAIL: f.brughuis.@mecal.nl
WEB: http://www.mecal.nl
CONTACT: Mr Frans Brughuis

MEIJSEN ONDERGRONDSE INFRASTRUCTUREN
't Zand 4,
3544 NC Utrecht,
Netherlands
TEL: +31 30 699 15 15
FAX: +31 30 666 40 92
E-MAIL: meijsen.bbm@wxs.nl
WEB: http://www.meijsen.com
CONTACT: Fj van der Tol

POLYMARIN BV
Nijverheidsweg 7 PO Box 151,
1670 AD Medemblik,
Netherlands
TEL: +31 227 543044
FAX: +31 227 543860
WEB: http://www.polymarin.com
CONTACT: Mr J Berkhout

STORK PRODUCT ENGINEERING BV
Czaar Peterstraat 229, 018 PL
Amsterdam,
Netherlands
TEL: +31 20 556 3444
FAX: +31 20 556 3556
E-MAIL:gjanssen@spe.stork.nl
CONTACT:P Kortbeek

VANHEUGTEN BV CONSULTING ENGINEERS
PO Box 305,
6500 AH Nijmegen,
Netherlands
TEL: +31 24 322 8317
FAX: +31 24 323 5016
E-MAIL: luscuere@V-Heugten-bv.nl
CONTACT: Prof PG Luscuere

OTHERS

ARN BV
Postbus 7006, 6503 GM Nijmegen, Netherland
TEL : +31 24 378 1766
FAX : +31 24 377 97 69
CONTACT : AP de Weijer

BIOSTAR DEVELOPMENT CV
de Boerstraat 24, PO Box 52, 8560 AB Balk, Netherlands
TEL : +31 14 608 650
FAX : +31 14 603 342
E-MAIL : biostar@paques.nl

D.P. PUPMS
Kalkovenoweg 13, 2401,
LJ Alphen aanden Rijn,
Netherlands
TEL : + 31 172 488325
FAX : + 31 172 468930
E-MAIL : dp@dp.pumps.com
WEB : http://www. dp.pumps.com

DE KLEINE AARDE
Sustainable Building, Postbus 151,
5280 AD Boxtel, Netherlands
TEL : + 31 411 684921
FAX : + 31 411 683407
E-MAIL : ineaarde@pznl
WEB : http://www.dekleinaarde

ECOLOGIC ENVIRONMENTAL COMMUNICATIONS
Van Osingaweg. 36, 8744 EW Schettens, Netherlands
TEL : + 31 517 531171
FAX : + 31 517 531167
E-MAIL : ecologic@tref.nl
CONTACT : T Seard Zoethout

EDON DUURZAAM SUSTAINABLE
PO Box 519, 8000 AM Zwolle,
Netherlands
TEL : +31 388 518 540
FAX : +31 388 524 900
E-MAIL :dick.honne@edon.nl
WEB : http://www.edon.nl

ELEKTROADVIES BUREAU BALTUS
Valkkogerweg 29, 1744 GB Valkkoog
Netherlands
TEL : +31 224 296531
E-MAIL :kbaltus@freeler.nl
CONTACT : CWA Baltus

ENECO NV
Rochussenstraat PO Box 2499, 3000 CL Rotterdam, Netherlands
TEL : +31 10 4576295
FAX : +31 10 4577754
E-MAIL : r.c.b.deromph@eneco.nl
CONTACT : RCB de Romph

ENERGIE DELFLAND NV
PO Box 516, 2600 AM Delft
Netherlands
TEL : +31 15 251 42 99
FAX : +31 15 262 19 85
E-MAIL : CJ.Remijnse@energie-delfland.nl
CONTACT : CJ Remijnse

ESSENT ENTERGY TRADING BV
PO box 51, 5580 AB Waalre,
Netherlands
TEL: +31 40 250 33 03
FAX: +31 40 228 56 90
E-MAIL : simon.fris@essentrading.com
WEB: http://www.essent.nl
CONTACT : Simon A Fris

GAIA AKKUMULATOREN WERKEN GMBH
Postbus 111, 2300 AC Leiden,
Netherlands
TEL: +31 71 525 22 45
FAX: +31 71 522 63 64

GRONTMIJ - BRP BV
Water and Waste Management
P O Box 14, 3730 Aa De Bilt,
Netherlands
TEL : + 31 30 6943210
FAX : + 31 30 6993006
WEB : http://www.grontmij.nl
CONTACT : Laam Van Arendont

HERMANS TECHNIEK BV
Schutweg 27, 5145 NP Waalwijk,
Netherlands
TEL: +31 416 651165
FAX: +31 416 650565
E-MAIL: verkoop@hermanstechniek.nl
WEB: http://www.hermanstechniek.nl
CONTACT: Mr H Hermans

HOEKLOOS BV
Business Development,
Havenstraat I,
Postbus 78,
3100 AB Schiedam
Netherlands
TEL: +31 10 246 16 16
FAX: +31 10 246 16 00
E-MAIL: pvangerwen@hoekloos.nl
CONTACT: PF Van Gerwen

IEA HEAT PUMP CENTRE
PO Box 17,
6130 AA Sittard,
Netherlands
TEL: +31 46 4202 236
FAX: +31 46 4510 389
E-MAIL: hpc@heatpumpcentre.org
WEB: http://www.heatpumpcentre.org
CONTACT: Jos Bouma

MESCO
PO Box 242, 9600 AE Hoogezand, Netherlands
TEL: +31 598 394 840
FAX: +31 598 398 729
E-MAIL: msn@noord.bart.nl
CONTACT: N Veenstra

PNEM ENERGIEVERKOOP BV
Postbus 222,
5201 HA Den Bosch,
Netherlands
TEL: +31 73 68 04 804
FAX:+31 73 68 90 900
WEB:http://www.pnem.nl
CONTACT: J Van Gestel

PNEM ENERGY SYSTEMS BV
PO Box 218, 5550 AE Valkenswaard
Netherlands
TEL: +31 73 615 4500
FAX:+31 73 615 4599
WEB:http://www.pnem.nl
CONTACT: K Krikke

UNA NV
PO Box 8475, 3503 RL Utrecht
Netherlands
TEL : +31 30 247 22 11
FAX : +31 30 247 22 55
E-MAIL : unapower@una.nl
WEB : http://www.una.nl
CONTACT : Hl Nieuwland

VATTENFALL NEDERLAND
Kruisweg 803A,2131 Hoofddorp,
Netherlands
TEL : +31 23 557 01 50
FAX : +31 23 557 01 51
E-MAIL : info@vattenfall.nl
WEB : http://www.vattenfall.se
CONTACT : B Hesseling

SUPPLIERS

BATTERIES/INVERTERS

NKF ELECTRONICS
PO Box 415, 2800 AK Gouda,
Netherlands
TEL: +31 182 592 333
FAX: +31 182 592 123
E-MAIL: electronics@nkf.nl
WEB: http://www.nkfelectronics.com
CONTACT: Huub Luijcks

MASTERVOLT SOLAR
Snijdersbergweg 93,
1105 AN Amsterdam,
Netherlands
TEL: +31 20 3422180
FAX: +31 20 3422188
E-MAIL: masstervolt@mastervolt.com
WEB: http://www.mastervolt.com
CONTACT: Ir H Marsman

PHILIPS LIGHTING BV
BU Lighting Electronics And Gear,
PO Box 1, 5340 AA Oss,
Netherlands
TEL: +31 412682378
FAX: +31 412635990
E-MAIL: pvsolar.info@philips.com
WEB: http://www.solar-philips.om
CONTACT: Steven JE Pleging

TANKS

MONOSTORE BV
Postbus 406,
8260 AK Kampen,
Netherlands
TEL: +31 38 33 70700
FAX: + 31 38 33 70708
EMAIL:info@monostore.com
WEB:http://www.monostore.com
CONTACT:Ing AAA Oussoren

INSULATIONS

TONZON BV
Po Box 1375, 7500 BJ Enschede,
Netherlands
TEL: +31534332391
FAX: 31534337405
E-MAIL: tonzon@tonzon.nl
WEB: http://www.tonzon.nl
CONTACT: AJM Wilemsen

COATINGS & PAINTS

SIGMA COATINGS GROUP
Protective Coatings,
Business Unit,
Amsterdamseweg 14,
1422 AD Uithoorn, Netherlands
TEL: +31 297 541557
FAX: +31 297 564086
E-MAIL: jandirk.ruizendaal@si gmacoatings.com
CONTACT: Jan-Dirk Ruizendaal

PUMPS

GRUNDFOS NEDERLAND BV
Pampuslaan 190,
1382 Js Weesp, Netherlands
TEL : + 31 294 4922 22
FAX : + 31 294 49 22 44
E-MAIL : info_gnl@grundfos.nl
WEB : http://www.grundfos.com
CONTACT : Pam Kok

CONSTRUCTION SERVICES

GTICONTRACTONDERHOUD BV
Willingestraat 8, 3087 AN Rotterdam,
Netherlands
TEL : + 31 10 294 29 80
FAX : +31 10 294 29 70
E-MAIL : gco@gco.gti.nl
WEB : http://www.gti.nl
CONTACT : JFM Mass

JACOBS COMPRIMO NEDERLAND
Radarweg 60, PO Box 58026, 1040
HA Amsterdam, Netherlands
TEL: +31 20 580 7400
FAX: +31 20 580 7050
E-MAIL: tammo.beishuizen@jacobs.com
CONTACT : Jammo Beishuieen

INSTRUMENTATION

CALDIC TECHNIEK BV
Energie Techniek,
Postbus 660, 3000
AR Rotterdam,
Netherlands
TEL : +31 10 415 6622
FAX : +31 10 437 2235
E-MAIL : techniek@caldic.nl

DRC BV
Heuvel 21,
4901 KB Oosterhout,
Netherlands
TEL : + 31 162 461010
FAX : + 31 162 461919
E-MAIL : info@drcmedical.com
WEB : http://www.drcmedical.com
CONTACT : GJ van der Ende

EKO POWER
PO Box 4904, NL-5604 CC
Eindhoven,
Netherlands
TEL : +31 40 281 4458
FAX : +31 40 281 4119
E-MAIL :info@ekopower.nl
WEB : http://www.ekopower.nl
CONTACT : Peter Hvan Emden

ITO
Nlc Barnhoornweg 38,
2202 JB
Noordwljk, Netherlands
TEL: +31 71 361 1987
FAX: +31 71 361 4219
CONTACT : AC de Ruiter

KIPP EN ZONEN BV
Rontgenweg 1, 2624 BC Delft,
Netherlands
TEL: +31 15 269 8000
FAX: +31 15 262 0351
E-MAIL: info.holland@kippzonen.com
WEB: http://www.kippzonen.com
CONTACT : CJ Van den Bos

LEIDERDORP INSTRUMENTS
PO Box 319, 2350 AG Leiderdorp,
Netherlands
TEL: +31 71 541 5514
FAX: +31 71 541 8980
E-MAIL: 101756.3506@compuserve.com
WEB: http://ourworld.compuserve.com/homepages/leiderdorpinstruments
CONTACT : J H Liefting

VOLTANOVA BV
Amperelaan I - L,
NL-9207 Drachten
Netherlands
TEL: +31 512 589873
FAX: +31 512 589874
WEB: http://www.voltanova.nl
CONTACT: SA Schoustra

OTHERS (S)

AENEAS TECHNICAL PUBLISHERS
Postbus 101,
5280 AC Boxtel,
Netherlands
TEL: +31 411 650085
FAX: +31 411 650080
E-MAIL: mail@aeneas.nl
WEB: http://www.aeneas.nl
CONTACT: Dr W Koetsenruyter

AKZO NOBEL ENERGY BV
PO Box247,
3800 Ae Amersfoort,
Netherlands
TEL: +31 33 467 63 98
FAX: +31 33 467 61 79
E-MAIL: hans.davidse@akzonobel.com
CONTACT: Ir J Davidsc

ARTIN BV
C Ritsemastraat 7,
3443 HB Woerden,
Netherland
TEL : +31 348 43 47 46
FAX : +31 348 43 47 46

FREE ENERGY EUROPE BV
Marketing, PO Box 9564,
5602 LN Eindhoven,
Netherlands
TEL: +31 40 290 1245
FAX: +31 40 290 1249
E-MAIL: info@free-energy.net
WEB: http://www.free-energy.net
CONTACT: Frank van der Vleuten

GEN BV
Lopikerplein 2A, 2871
Anschoonhoven,
Netherlands
TEL : + 31 18 2389 090
FAX : + 31 18 2389 080
WEB: http://www.gen.nl/turbine

HASKONING CONSULTING ENGINEERS AND ARCHITECTS
Waste Management are Energy
Technology 1151,
Barbarosstraat 35
P.O. Box 151, 6500 AD
Nimtgen, Netherlands
TEL : + 31 24 328 42 84
FAX : + 31 24 360 47 37
E-MAIL : evh@haskoning.hl
CONTACT : A van der

H-ENERGYSYSTEMEN BV
Industrieweg 14-40, 8255 PB
Swifterbant, Netherlands
TEL : + 31 321 322599
FAX : + 31 321 322599

HOROS KLIMAA TTECHNIEK BV
PO Box 516, 3760 AM Soest
Netherlands
TEL: +31 35 6032324
FAX: +31 35 6032384
E-MAIL: info@horos.nl

IMTECH MARINE & INDUSTRY BV
Sluisjesdijk 155,
3087 AG Rotterdam
Netherlands
TEL: +31 10 4871 911
FAX: +31 10 4871 702
E-MAIL: info@renhs.nl
CONTACT: Inge Boseman

IMTECH PROJECTS
PO Box 8584,
3009 AN Rotterdam,
Netherands
TEL: +31 10 44 77 400
FAX: +31 10 44 77 474
E-MAIL: swaa@rhzuid-west.nl
CONTACT: PAGM Willems

JENBACHER ENERGIESYSTEME BV
Stationspark 709,
3364 DA sliedercht,
Netherlands
TEL: +31 184 495 210
FAX: +31 184 415 440
E-MAIL:info@jenbacher.nl
WEB:http://www.jenbacher.nl
CONTACT : Frank K Bouwmeester

KUWAIT PETROLEUM RESEARCH & TECHNOLOGY BV
Lubricants,
PO Box 545, 3190 AL
Hoogvliet, Netherlands
TEL: +31 181285203
FAX: +31 181285327
E-MAIL : ws@kprt.q8.nl

MAN ROLLO BV
PO Box 595, 2700 AN Zoetemeer,
Netherlands
TEL: +31 79 36 836 83
FAX: +31 79 36 149 02
E-MAIL: sales@manrollo.nl
WEB: http://www.manrollo.nl
CONTACT: WCA Ligtvoet

MHI EQUIPMENT EUROPE BV
Dmasluisweg 2, 1332 EC Almere,
Netherlands
TEL: +31 36 538 83 11
FAX: +31 36 532 42 20
CONTACT: GG de Wit

NEDERLANDSE GASUNIE
PO Box 19, 9700 MA Groningen
Netherlands
TEL: +31 50 521 21 62
FAX: +31 50 521 19 42
E-MAIL: w.j.t.van.gemert@gasunie.nl
CONTACT : E Freese

NEM BV
Kanaalpark 159, 2300 AD Leiden,
Netherlands
TEL: +31 71 5792444
FAX: +31 71 5792499
E-MAIL: sales@nem.nl
CONTACT: Mr Karel van Buuren

NUON RENEWABLE ENERGY BUSINESS UNIT
Postbus 9039, 6800 EZ Arnhem,
Netherlands
TEL: +31 26 377 2143
FAX: +31 26 377 2186
WEB: http://www.nuon.nl
CONTACT: Dr Annemarie Goedmakers

STIEBEL ELTRON NEDERLAND BV
Daviottenweg 36,
5222 BH Den Bosch,
Netherlands
TEL: +31 73 623 0000
FAX: +31 73 623 1141
E-MAIL:stiebel@stiebel-eltron.nl
WEB:http://www.stiebel-eltron.nl
CONTACT: G Coenen

TRANSMATE BV
Avelingen West 26,
4202 MS Gorinchem,
Netherlands
TEL: +31 183 65 33 33
FAX: +31 183 63 29 29
CONTACT: E Reijnders

TE MANNING VOF
Schoener 50,
1771 ED Wieringerwerf,
Netherlands
TEL: +31227604128
FAX: +31227604128
E-MAIL: pumps@flowman.nl
WEB: http://www.flowman.nl
CONTACT: Terry Manning

THILOT HOLLAND BV
Hoofdstraat 11-17, 5973 ND Lottum, Netherlands
TEL: +31 77 463 1774
FAX: +31 77 463 2648
E-MAIL:sales@thilot.nl
WEB:http://www.thilot.nl
CONTACT:Mr R Thielen

TNO ENVIRONMENT ENERGY AND PROCESS INNOVATION
Thermal Conversion Technology,
PO Box 342, 7300 AH Apeldoon, Netherlands
TEL: +31 55 5493 493
FAX: +31 55 5493 201
E-MAIL:b.a.heide@mep.tno.nl
WEB:http://www.mep.tno.nl
CONTACT: S Van Loo

VORTEX TECHNOLOGY
Energy & Waste, PO Box 158,
3720 AC Bithoven, Netherlands
TEL; +31302210349
FAX: +31302203141
E-MAIL: eng@vortex.demon.nl
WEB: http://www.glidarc.com
CONTACT: CLH Winkelman

VULKA BV
PO Box 297, 3900 AG Veenendaal, Netherlands
TEL: +31 318 50 09 44
FAX: +31 318 50 09 43

We kindly request more listings in this country.

You can submit any additional listings by E-mail: unisun@vsnl.com

Fax: 91 80 22289294

We will include these in the next edition

Kindly inform us of any errors and omissions in the listings by:
E-mail: unisun@vsnl.com
Fax: 91 80 22289294

NORWAY

SOLAR THERMAL

SIGMA ELEKTROTEKNISK AS
PO Box 58, 1550 Holen,
Norway
TEL: +47 649 82400
FAX: +47 649 82401
E-MAIL: svein@sigma-el.com

SOLBASSENG A/S
Markalleen 64
1320 Stabekk,Norway
TEL:+47 67 58 37 22
FAX:+47 67 58 37 25

SOLAR PHOTOVOLTAIC

ELKEM ASA
Silicon Division, PO Box 5211,
Majorstua, N-0303 Oslo, Norway
TEL : +47 22 45 0100
FAX : +47 22 45 0155
E-MAIL : cyrus.zahedi@elkem.no
CONTACT : Dr. Cyrus Zahedi

METALLKRAFT AS
PO Box 5595 Voiebyen, N-4677
Kristiansand, Norway
TEL: +47 38 08 60 74
FAX: +47 38 08 79 96
E-MAIL:
knut.henriksen@metallkraft.no
CONTACT: Dr Knut Henriksen

MLLER ENERGI A/S
Bergermoen,
3520 Jevnaker, Norway
TEL: +47 61 31 52 00
FAX: +47 61 31 28 46
EMAIL: post@moller-energi.no
CONTACT: Pal Teppan

NAPS NORWAY AS
Strandveien 50 n-1366 Lysaker
Norway
TEL: +47 67 112550
FAX: +47 67 112545
CONTACT: Magne G Vegel

WIND

AS LINJEBYGG
Fannestrandsvn 54,
6400 Molde, Norway
TEL : +47 712 43 000
FAX : +47 712 43 100
E-MAIL : nils.vegsund@
linjebygg.no
CONTACT : Nils Petter Vegsund

BIOMASS

BIOGAS A/S
PO Box2001, 3202 Sandefjord,
Norway
TEL: +47 33 48 21 60
FAX: +47 33 48 21 51
E-MAIL: roar@biogas.no
WEB: http://www.biogas.no
CONTACT: Roar Karlsen

HEIDENREICH A/S
Postboks3457, Bgoelsen 0406
Oslo 4, Norway
TEL: +47 22 23 29 80
FAX: +47 22 23 95 82
CONTACT: Ola Walstad

MOVAR
PO Box 113, 1581 Rygge, Norway
TEL: +47 69 26 21 10
FAX: +47 69 26 21 11
CONTACT: Sverre Gulbrandsen

COGENERATION

COGEN ASA
Nedre Nottveit 62, 5238 Radal,
Bergen, Norway
TEL: +47 55 91 65 16
FAX: +47 55 91 65 17
E-MAIL: loekland@online.no
CONTACT: Lars Egil Okland

ROLLS-ROYCE MARINE AS
Engines Bergen, PO Box 924, 5808
Bergen, Norway
TEL: +47 55 536 000
FAX: +47 55 536 104
E-MAIL: bergen.sales@rolls-
royce.com
WEB: http://www.rolls-royce.com
CONTACT: Tone Lundekvam

ULSTEIN BERGEN AS
P O Box 924, 5808 Bergen,
Norway
TEL : +47 55 536 000
FAX : +47 55 536 104
E-MAIL :sales.ube@
vickersmarine.com
WEB : http://www.vicker
smarine.com
CONTACT : Knut ErikFrederiksen

HYDROGEN

UNIVERSITY OF OSLO
Department of Physics, P O Box 1048
Blindern0316 Oslo, Norway
TEL : +4722856428
FAX : +4722856422
CONTACT : Prof John Rekstad

FUEL CELL

ENERGY DEVELOPMENT AS
Fred Olsensgt 1.0152 Oslo,
Norway
TEL: +47 2241 4333
FAX: +47 2241 4334
E-MAIL:jan.sorensen
@oslo.mail.telia.com
CONTACT : Jan Sorensen

WASTE TO ENERGY

BERGENSOMRADETS INTERKOMMUNALE RENOVASJONSSELKAP- BIR
BiR Avafallsenergie (Bir Waste to
Energy) Jekteviken 5,
5010 Bergen, Norway
TEL : +47 55 56 79 00
FAX : +47 55 23 01 55
E-MAIL :asbjorn.ravnanger
@bir.hl.no.
WEB : http://www.bir.hl.no

ENERGISYSTEMERAS
Aslyveien 9,
3215 Sandefjord, Norway
TEL: +47 33 46 94 91
FAX: +47 33 46 00 08
E-MAIL: birkelan@online.no
CONTACT : Knut H Birkcland

ENERGOSASA
Lokkeveien 99,
4008 Stavanger, Norway
TEL: +47 518 449 07
FAX: +47 518 449 01
E-MAIL: firmapost@energos.no
WEB: http://www.energos.com

FREVAR
Postboks III, 1631 Gamle
Fredrikstad, Norway
TEL: +47 69 32 29 20
FAX: +47 69 32 34 33
E-MAIL:frevar@online.no
WEB : www.frewor.com

KRISTIANSAND KOMMUNE INGENIRVESENET
Waste Management,
Tollbodgaten 22, Postuttak,
466004 Kristiansand, Norway
TEL: +47 38 07 68
FAX: +47 38 07 56 16
E-MAIL: tdi@krkom.no
CONTACT : Mr. Tore Diesen

RESEARCH & DEVELOPMENT

ELKEM ASA RESEARCH
P O Box 8040, Vaagsbygd,
N-4675 Kristiansand, Norway
TEL : +47 38 01 70 00
FAX : +47 38 01 74 94
E-MAIL : eric.ydstie@elkem.no
WEB : http://www.elkem.no
CONTACT : Dr Knut Henriksen

UNIVERSITIES

INSTTUTE FOR ENERGY TECHNOLOGY
Energy Systems, Instituttveien 18,
P O Box 40, N-2007, Norway
TEL: +47 63 80 61 00
FAX: +47 63 80 29 05
E-MAIL: per.finden@ife.no
WEB: http://www.ife.no
CONTACT: Mr Oystein Ulleberg

CONSULTANTS

ENERGY SAVING INTERNATIONAL AS. ENSI
Hasleveien 38,
N-0571 Oslo, Norway
TEL : + 47 22 04 06 20
FAX : + 47 22 04 06 50
E-MAIL : ensi@ensi.no
WEB: http://www.ensi.no
CONTACT : Trond Dahlsueen

INTERCONSULT ASA
Waste Department, PO Box 6412,
Etterstad, N-0605 Olso, Norway
TEL: +47 21 00 92 60
FAX: +47 21 00 92 01
E-MAIL: tmh@interconsult.com
WEB: http://www.interconsult.com
CONTACT: Eigil Bockmann

KANENERGI AS
Baerumsvelen 473,
N-1351 Rud,
Norway
TEL: +47 67 15 38 50
FAX: +47 67 15 02 50
E-MAIL:kanenergie@kanenergie.no
WEB:http://www.kanenergie.com
CONTACT : Christain Grorud

DESIGN & ENGINEERING

DETNORSKE VERITAS AS
Veritasveien 1,
1322 Hövik
Norway
TEL : + 47 67 57 99 00
FAX : + 47 67 57 74 74
E-MAIL : sbj@dnv.com
CONTACT : Elisabeth Harstad

SUN LAB
Alexander Kiellandsgt 2, 4009
Stavanger, Norway
TEL: +47 51 53 34 42
FAX: +47 51 52 40 62
E-MAIL:sunlab@rl.telia.no
CONTACT: Harald N Rostvik

HYBRID SYSTEMS

SOLARNOR AS
Erling Skjalgssons GATE 19B,
N-0267 Oslo,
Norway
TEL:+47 22 12 90 80
FAX:+47 22 12 90 89
E-MAIL:john.rekstad@solarnor.com
WEB:http://www.solarnorr.com
CONTACT:John Rekstad

OTHERS

DRESSER-RAND AS
PO Box 1010, Kirkegaardsveien 45,
3601 Kongsberg, Norway
TEL : + 47 32 28 70 70
FAX : + 47 32 28 70 80
E-MAIL : finn-landgraff@
dresser-rand.no
WEB : www.dresser-rand.no
CONTACT : Finn Landgraff

GATEOPPVARMING A/S
Postboks 55, Kaldebakken,
0901 Osto 9 Norway,
TEL: + 47 22 91 74 00
CONTACT : Ernst Eriksen

JTUL A/S
PO Box 135, 1601Fredrikstad, Norway
TEL: +47 69 35 90 00
FAX: +47 69 34 26 07

KVARENER EUREKA
Joseph Kelers vei 20, 3401, Norway
TEL: +47 32 85 90 00
FAX: +47 32 85 94 40
E-MAIL: process.eureka@
kevt.kvaerner.com
WEB : http://www.kvaerner.com/
oilgas/eureka
CONTACT : Rolf Birketvedt

SMART MOTORS AS
Leiveiriksson Center,
PB 1260 Pirsenter,
7462 Trondheim, Norway
TEL: +47 73 54 63 50
FAX: +47 73 54 63 55
E-MAIL: smartmotor@
smartmotor.no
WEB: http://www.smartmotor.no
CONTACT: Ulf R Aakenes

SUPPLIERS

TANKS

ENERGIEFAKTAAS
P O Box 63,
1719 Greaker, Norway
TEL: +47 69 129509
FAX: +47 69 254578
E-MAIL: steffen.westgaard@
kvaerner.com

INSTRUMENTATION

AANDERAA INSTRUMENTS A/S
Nesttunbrekken97, 5852 Bergen,
Norway
TEL: +47 55 10 99 00
FAX: +47 55 10 99 10
CONTACT: Rune Fjellheim

INSTRUMENT TJENESTEN A/S-ITAS
1432, Aas, Norway
TEL: +47 64 94 98 40
FAX: +47 64 94 20 33
E-MAIL: itas@it-as.no
WEB: http://www.itas.no
CONTACT: Oddvar Haga

NORWAVE AS
Jotunveien 38,
N-1412 Sofiemyr, Norway
TEL: +47 6680 64 10
FAX: +47 6680 46 30
CONTACT: Per Anderssen

SOLARNOR AS
Postboks 352, N-1323 Hovik,
Norway
TEL: +4767815390
FAX: +4767815385
E-MAIL: knut.styrvold@solarnor.com
WEB: http://www.solarnor.com
CONTACT: Knut Styrvold

OTHERS (S)

ENER-PRODUKT AS
P O Box 80, 3800 Bo, Norway
TEL : +47 35 95 11 00
FAX : +47 35 95 16 55

NORWEGIAN BUILDING RESEARCH INSTITUTE
PO Box123 Blindern,
0314 Oslo, Norway
TEL: +47 22 96 55 41
FAX: +47 22 96 57 25
E-MAIL: sb02registration@plus-
convention.no
WEB: http://www.sb02.com
CONTACT: Trine Drystad Pettersen

ORGANIC POWER ASA
Klingenberggt 7a,
PB 1237 Vika, 0110 Oslo,
Norway
TEL: +47 23 11 59 00
FAX: +47 23 11 59 01
E-MAIL:
harald.kleiven@organicpower.com
WEB: http://www.organicpower.com
CONTACT: Harald Kleiven

SMART MOTOR AS
Stiklestadveien 1, 7041 Trondheim,
Norway
TEL: +4773982500
FAX: +4773982501
E-MAIL: ulfaa@smartmotor.no
WEB: http://www.smartmotor.no
CONTACT: Ulf R Aakenes

SONDERE VESTFOLD AVFALLSSELSKAPDA
Grinda, 3271 Larvik, Norway
TEL: +47 3313 5440
FAX: +47 3313 5450
CONTACT : Mr t Aspenes

SVEIN HATVIK A/S
Postboks 4117.
Dreggen. 5023
Bergen, Norway
TEL: +47 55 31 46 50

We kindly request more listings in this country.

You can submit any additional listings by E-mail: unisun@vsnl.com

Fax: 91 80 22289294

We will include these in the next edition

Kindly inform us of any errors and omissions in the listings by:

E-mail: unisun@vsnl.com

Fax: 91 80 22289294

SOLAR THERMAL

RAFAKO BOILER ENGINEERING COMPANY SA
Boiler Plant Division,
ul Lakowa 33, PO Box 112,
47-400 Raciborz,
Poland
TE L: +48324101000
FAX: +48324153427
E-MAIL: info@rafako.com.pl
WEB: http://www.rafako.com.pl
CONTACT: Kizysztof Burek

SOLAR PHOTOVOLTAIC

POLISH ACADEMY OF SCIENCES
Institue of Metallurgy
and Materials Science, Photovoltaic Laboratory
Krakowska 22, 43-340 Kozy,
Poland
TEL: +48 33 174 249
FAX:+48 33 174 231
E-MAIL : solpan@pb.bielsko.pl
CONTACT: Dr Marek Lipinskigtv

WIND

EPA LTD
Al Wozska Polskiego 154,
71-324 Szczecin,
Poland
TEL: +48 91 4874 885
FAX: +48 91 4875 014
E-MAIL: epa@epa.com.pl
WEB: http://www.epa.com.pl
CONTACT: Mr K Prahatek

SMALL HYDRO

HYDRO PROJEKT-WARSZAWA LTD
9 Dubois Street,
00-182 Warszawa,
Poland
TEL: +48 22 6355708
FAX: +48 22 6350020
E-MAIL: rlewandowski@
hydroprojekt.com.pl
CONTACT: Ryszard Lewandowski

COGENERATION

EN ERGOMONTAZPWSA
UlKatowicka 47,
41-5200 Chorzow,
Poland
TEL: I 48 32 411 281
FAX: +48 32 414 911
CONTACT : Z Sutkowski

RESEARCH & DEVELOPMENT

INSTITUTE FOR BUILDING MECHANIZATION AND ELECTRIFICATION OF AGRICULTURE
EC Baltic Renewable Energy Centre-
EC BREC, Rakowiecka 32,
02 532 Warsaw, Poland
TEL: +48 22 484832
FAX: +48 22 491737
E-MAIL: grewis@ibmer.waw.pl
WEB: http://www.ecbrec.waw.pl
CONTACT: Grzegorz Wisniewski

WARSAW UNIVERSITY OF TECHNOLOGY
Institute of Micro & Optoelectronics,
IMIO PW, Koszykowa 75, 00-662
Warsaw, Poland
TEL: +48 22 660 7782
FAX: +48 22 628 8740
E-MAIL: pietruszko@imio.pw.edu.pl
WEB: http://www.imio.pw.edu.pl/
wwwzmite/pietruszko/index.html
CONTACT: Dr Stanislaw M Pietruszko

CONSULTANTS

AJPOS FIRMA KONSULTINGOWO HANDLOWA
Renewable Energy,
Ul Zgr Zmiya 1/33,01-875 Warsaw,
Poland
TEL: +48 22 866 8584
FAX: +48 22 866 8585
E-MAIL: ajpos@wp.pl
CONTACT: Jan Pogorzelski

CENTRE FOR CLEAN ENERGY CCE
Powstancow Sl 164/S, 53-139
Warsaw, Poland
TEL : +48 71 732138
FAX : +48 71 732138
CONTACT : Dr W Kowalczyk

DESIGN & ENGINEERING

BOREN ENERGIA NOVA
Plac Czerwony 1/3/5, 53-661
Warsaw Poland
TEL : +48 71 556790
FAX : +48 71 555148
E-MAIL :borenaborne.com.pl
CONTACT : K Smereczynski

ENERGOPROJEKT WARSAW SA
Consulting, 6-14 Krucza Street,
PO BOX 184,
00-950 Warsaw, Poland
TEL: +48 22 628 3699
FAX: +48 22 628 2766
E-MAIL: epconsul@epconsul.com.pl
WEB: http://www.epconsul.com.pl
CONTACT : Z Radomski

EUROS POLSKA SPZOO
Ul y Kreta 2, 43-450 Ustron,
Poland
TEL: +48 33 854 3694
FAX: +48 33 854 3894
CONTACT : Dr Roland Steer

NGO's

EC BREC / IBMER Res-Opet
Poland Ul Reduta Zbik 5
80-761, Gdansk, Poland
TEL : + 48 58 30 166 36
FAX : + 48 58 30 157 88
E-MAIL : ecbrec@me.tech.gda.pl
WEB : http://www.ibner.wew.pl/ecrec
CONTACT : K Gierulski

KLUB GAJA
PO Box 261, 43-301 Bielsko-Biala
1,Poland
TEL: +48 33 12 36 94
FAX: +48 33 12 36 94

OTHERS

VERDAJ BRIGADOJ
Green Brigades Publishing House,
Szawkowska 12/24, 31-014 Krakow,
Poland
TEL: +48 12 4222147
FAX: +48 12 4222147
E-MAIL: zb@zb.most.org.pl
WEB: http://www.most.org.pl/zb
CONTACT: Andrzej Zwawa

Kindly inform us of any errors and omissions in the listings by:

E-mail: unlsun@vsnl.com

Fax: 91 80 22289294

PORTUGAL

SOLAR THERMAL

FALCONER LDA
Avenida Duque de Loule, 47 - 3 DTO, 1050-086 Lisbon, Portugal
TEL: +351 1 527058
FAX: + 351 529136
CONTACT: Mr. Falconer

SOLAR PHOTOVOLTAIC

MATERIAIS DE CONSTRUCAO CUNHA GOMES SA - MAGON
Rua da Constituicao 2309,
4200 Porto, Portugal
TEL: +351 2 813158
FAX: +351 2 8302376
CONTACT: Armando Matos

TELEXTRONICA
Avenda do Colegro Militar 153-B,
1500-182 Lisboa, Portugal
TEL: +351 1 715 2123
FAX: +351 1 715 5684
E-MAIL: telextronica@mail.telpac.pt
CONTACT: MC Pinheiro

COGENERATION

HAFFNER LDA
Rua Martins Barata 5 R/L.
1400 Lisbon, Portugal
TEL : + 351 1 301 7550
FAX : + 351 1 301 7366
E-MAIL : haffnere@aol.com
CONTACT: Darian Haffner

SMALL HYDRO

ESPLAN LDA
Rua Martins Barata 5 r/c, 1400 Lisboa, Portugal
TEL : +351 1 301 8588
FAX: + 351 1 301 6472
CONTACT: Eric Haffner

HIDROERG-PROJECTORS ENERGETICOS LDA
Rua dos Lusiadas no 9-4° Dto,
1300-365 Lisboa, Portugal
TEL: +351 1 3540122
FAX: +351 1 3540072
E-MAIL: hidroerg@mail.telepac.pt
CONTACT: Antonio Eira Leitao

HIDROQUATRO-CONSULTORES DE HIBRAULICA RECURSOS HIDRICOSE AMBIENTE LDA
Rua Dr Antonio Loureiro
Borges 9-4° Arquiparque-Miraflores,
1495 Alges, Portugal
TEL: +351 1 7934747
FAX: +351 1 7932656
CONTACT: Antonio Sa da Costa

TIDAL / OCEAN

ABOLASPERSAO E BOMBAGEM LDA
Rua Boavista 76/78,
1200 Lisboa, Portugal
TEL: +351 1 346 6051
FAX: +351 1 346 8533
CONTACT: Crespo de Carvalho

FINANCE / BANKING

SOCIEDADE TERMICA PORTUGESA SA
Renewable Energies,
Av Fontes Pereira de Me No 29 3°,
1050-117 Lisboa, Portugal
TEL: +351 1 3192530
FAX: +351 1 3192539
E-MAIL: tpsa@teleweb.pt
CONTACT: Alvaro Brandao Pinto

ASSOCIATION

CENTRO DE ENERGIA E TECHNOLOGIA LDA-CENERTEC
Rua Gago Coutinho 185-187,
4435 Rio Tinto, Portugal
TEL : +351 2 973 4624
FAX : +351 2 9730746
E-MAIL :albino.reis@mail.telepac.pt
CONTACT: Prof. Albino Reis

INDUMA MAQUINAS INDUSTRIAS LIMITADA
Rua Cova de Moura No 2-1°,
1350-117 Lisboa, Portugal
TEL: +351 1 392 86 80
FAX: +351 1 395 02 99
CONTACT: Joao Abrantes

GOVERNMENT

CENTRO PARA A CONSERVA CAO DE ENERGIA
Estrada de Alfragide, Praceta 1,
2720-537 Amadora, Porgugal
TEL : +351 1 471 8235
FAX : +351 1 471 1316
E-MAIL : dmre.cce@mail.telepac.pt
CONTACT: Luis Silra

RESEARCH & DEVELOPMENT

INSTITUTO NACIONAL DE ENGENHARIA E TECHNOLOGIA INDUSTRIAL - INETI
Department of Renewable Energy,
Estrada do Paco do Lumiar,
1699 Lisboa Codex, Portugal
TEL: +351 1 7162712
FAX: +351 1 7163797
E-MAIL: teresa.pontes@ite.ineti.pt
CONTACT: Maria Teresa Pontes

LNEC LABORATORIO NACIONAL DE ENGENHARIA CIVIL
Av do Brasil 101,
1799 Lisboa Codex,
Portugal
TEL: +351 1 848 21 31
FAX: +351 1 847 47 59
CONTACT: Luis Faceira

NATIONAL INSTITUTE FOR INDUSTRIAL ENGINEERING AND TECHNOLOGY –INETI
Renewable Energies Department,
Estrada Paco Do Lumiar,
1649 038 Lisboa,
Portugal
TEL: +351 21 712 7237
FAX: +351 21 712 7195
E-MAIL: sec.der@ineti.pt
WEB: http://www.ineti.pt

NGO's

AS-SOCIEDADA PORTUGUESA DE GAS NATURAL SA
Estrada Nacional 116,
Bila De Rei,
2674-505 Bucelas,
Portugal
TEL : +351 21 968 82 00
FAX : +351 21 968 82 84
E-MAIL : commercial@transgas.pt

CONSULTANTS

ENERPRO-PROJECTOSDE ENERGIAS RENOVANEIS LDA
Taguspark - Edificio
Inovacao 1-211,
Estrada Nacional 249-Km3,
2780 Oeiras,
Portugal,
TEL : + 351 1 4228900
FAX : + 351 1 R228901
CONTACT : A Poenca

MELO QUEIROZ LDA
Praca des Paolo 19-2° Dt,
Apartado 2356,
1109 Lisboa Codex,
Portugal
TEL: +351 1 347 3747
FAX: +351 1 347 2637
CONTACT: Antonio Melo Queiroz

TECNOVERITAS LTD
Rua do Moinho Velho No 18,
3655-101 Ericeira, Portugal
TEL: +351261869251
FAX: +351261869252
WEB: http://www.tecnoveritas.net
CONTACT: Jorge Antunes

OTHERS

AS-SOCIEDADA PORTUGUESA DE GAS NATURAL SA
Estrada Nacional 116,
Bila De Rei,
2674-505 Bucelas,
Portugal
TEL : +351 21 968 82 00
FAX : +351 21 968 82 84
E-MAIL : commercial@transgas.pt

INSTITUTO DE ENGENHARIA MECNICA E GESTO INDUSTRIAL - INEGI
CETERM, Rua do Barroco 174,
4465 S Mamede de Infesta,
Portugal
TEL: +351 2 957 8711
FAX: +351 2 953 7352
E-MAIL: mjlvf@crazy.fe.up.pt
WEB: http://www.fe.up.pt/-inegi
CONTACT: Miguel Ferreira

SUPPLIERS

BATTERIES/INVERTERS

SOCIEDADE PORTUGUESA DO ACUMULADORTUDORSA
Rua Actor Tasso I,
1050 Lisboa,
Portugal
TEL:-351 1 3165 200
FAX:-351 1 3165 295
CONTACT: Garcia Passarinho

INSTRUMENTATION

VORTICE EQUIP MENTOS CIENTIFICOSLDA
Ceutro Empressarial Tejo,
Rua de Xabregas,
1900 Lisboa,
Portugal
TEL: +351 1 8583559
FAX: +351 1 8582946
E-MAIL: vortice@esoteria.pt
CONTACT: Jose Manuel Silveira

OTHERS (S)

CAMA-EQUIPMENTOS TERMICOSLDA
Vale de Acores,
3450 Mortagua,
Portugal
TEL : +351 31 922574
FAX : +351 31 921716

FF-SISTEMAS DEENERGIAS ALTERNATIVAS
Sitio do palheirinho,
8670 Aljezur, Portugal
TEL: + 351 82 998745
FAX: + 351 82 998746
EMAIL:ffsolar. wind@mail.telepac.pi
WEB:http://www.ffsolar.com

FOGO MONTANHA
Coca Maravilhas 26,
8500 Portimae, Portugal
TEL: +351 476001
FAX: +351 82 475369

INETI DER,
Estrada do Paco do Lumiar,
1649038 Lisboa, Portugal
TEL: +351 1 7165141
FAX: +351 1 7164305
CONTACT: Antonio Rego Teixeira

SITEL - SOC INSTALADORA DE TUBAGENS EQUIPAMENTOS LDA
Av Fontes Pereira de Melo 15,
1050 Lisbon, Portugal
TEL: +351 1 3563281/2/3
FAX: +351 1 3150129
E-MAIL: sitel.lda@mail.telepac.pt
CONTACT: Mario Franchi

We kindly request more listings in this country.

You can submit any additional listings by E-mail: unisun@vsnl.com

Fax: 91 80 22289294

We will include these in the next edition

Kindly inform us of any errors and omissions in the listings by:

E-mail: unisun@vsnl.com

Fax: 91 80 22289294

ROMANIA

SOLAR PHOTOVOLTAIC

RESEARCH INSTITUTE FOR ELECTRICAL ENGINEERING-ICPE
New Energy Sources Laboratory,
Splaiul Unirill No 313, 74204
Bucharest,
TEL : +40 1 321 7230
FAX : +40 1 321 7247
E-MAIL : danteo@icpe.ro
CONTACT : Dr Dan I Teodoreanu

SMALL HYDRO

INSTITUTE OF HYDROELCETRIC STUDIES AND DESIGN
5-7 Galati Street Sector 2,
79669 Bucharest, Romania
TEL: +40 1 6147270
FAX: +40 1 3 12 09 25
CONTACT: Nicolae Dascalesu

ENERGY EFFICIENCY

ENERGOBIT SRL
Str Donath Nr 182,
3400 Cluj Napoca, Romania
TEL: +40 64 420450
FAX: +40 64 420451
E-MAIL: ebit@energobit.com
WEB: http://www.energobit.com
CONTACT : Peter Pal

WASTE TO ENERGY

RESEARCH AND ENGINEERING INSTITUTE FOR ENVIRONMENT-ICIM
Waste Department,
Spl Independentei 294, sector 6,
77703 Bucharest 78, Romania
TEL : +40 1 637 3020
FAX : +40 1 312 1393
E-MAIL : icim@sunu.rnc.ro
CONTACT : Luminita Stafanescu

RESEARCH & DEVELOPMENT

ICEMENERG SA
8 Energeticienilor Blvd,
74568 Bucharest 3, Romania
TEL: +40 1 322 0917
FAX: +40 1 322 2790
E-MAIL: crit@icemenerg.vsat.ro
CONTACT: Gheorhe Voicu

CONSULTANTS

NATIONAL AGENCY FOR RENEWABLE ENERGY-NARE
Physics Department,
Bucharest Polytechnic University,
313 Splaiul Independentei,
Sesctior 7, RO -77206 Bucharest
Romania,
TEL: +40 1 4119603
FAX: +40 1 4119962
EMAIL : anesr@nare.renerg.pub.ro
WEB:http://www.nare.renerg.pub.ro
CONTACT: Prof Laurentin Fara

DESIGN & ENGINEERING

HIDROTIM SA
Str Calea Martirilor 1989 n1,
1900 Timisoara, Romania
TEL: +40 56 162865
FAX: +40 56 220987
E-MAIL: hidrotim@hidrotim.dnttm.ro
CONTACT: Jacob Voia

OTHERS

IPA SA AUTOMATION ENGINEERING
RES Department, 71295 Bd Mircea
Eliade No 18, Bucharest, Romania
TEL: +40 1 230 2293
FAX: +40 1 230 7862
E-MAIL: +40 1 230 7862
E-MAIL:sfara@kronos.ipsaro.ro
WEB:http://www.ipa.ro
CONTACT : S Fara

SUPPLIERS

UNIVERSITIES

TECHNICAL UNIVERSITY OF IASI
Department of Pulp Paper and
Fibers, Faculty of industrial
Chemistry,
Dimitrie Manreron No 71A,
Lasi 6600, Romania
TEL: +40 32 278683
FAX :+40 32 211150
E-MAIL:vipopa@ch.tulasi.ro
CONTACT:Prof Valentia 1 Popa

Kindly inform us of any errors and omissions in the listings by:

E-mail: unisun@vsnl.com

Fax: 91 80 2289294

SOLAR THERMAL

INSOLAR-INVEST
B Filevskaya 32-2, 121433
Moscow,
Russian Federation
TEL: +7 95 144 06 67
FAX: +7 95 144 01 75
E-MAIL: insolar-invest@mtu-net.ru
WEB: http://www.insolar.ru
CONTACT: Grigori Vasiliev

SOLAR PHOTOVOLTAIC

AF IOFFE PHYSICAL-TECHNICAL INSTITUTE
Russian Academy Of Sciences,
Politechnicheskaya 26,
194021 St Petersburg,
Russian Federation
TEL: +7812 247 9394
FAX: +7812 247 1017
E-MAIL: andreev@
scell.ioffe.rssi.ru
CONTACT: Vyacheslav Andreev

INTERTECHNOLOGY
Bolshoi Volokolamsky proezd 16,
Post Box#12, 123060 Moscow,
Russian Federation
TEL: +7 95 194 73 22
FAX: +7 95 192 80 40
E-MAIL:intertechnology@usa.net
CONTACT : S Khotinsky

MUSSON
Tamanskaya 180,
350040 Krasnodar
Russian Federation
TEL: +7 8612 33 85 48
FAX: +7 8612 33 85 48
CONTACT: Aleksey Ivanchenko

SOLAR WIND
Krasnodar Bazovskay 69,
Russian Federation
TEL: +78612552286
FAX: +678612552286
E-MAIL: solwind@krasnodar.ru
WEB: http://solwind.da.ru
CONTACT: Marat Zaks

TELECOM-STV COMPANY LTD
1 Solnechnaya Alleya,
Zelenograd,
Moscow 103527,
Russian Federation
TEL: +7955318351
FAX: +7955318354
E-MAIL: akam@dataforce.net
WEB: http://www.telstv.ru
CONTACT: Dr. Andrew Kaminski

VIESH
1st Veshnjakovskij Street 2,
109456 Moscow,
Russian Federation
TEL: +7 095 1711920
FAX: +7 095 1705101
E-MAIL: viesh@dol.ru
CONTACT: Prof Dmitry Strebkov

WIND

ASSOCIATION FOR WIND ENERGY UTILIZATION
P O Box 10,
109147 Moscow,
Russian Federation
TEL : +7 95 160 14 41
FAX : +7 95 160 14 12
CONTACT : N Sviridov

KVARK
Gimnazicheskaya 65,
Off 5, 350000
Krasnodar,
Russian Federation
TEL: +7 861 215 28 74
FAX: +7 861 215 62 89
CONTACT : Marat Z

KYZNETSOV MICHAIL
ul Gzatskaja 21,
195220 St Petersburg,
Russian Federation
TEL: +7 812 5355445
FAX: +7 812 535 6720
CONTACT: Kyznetsov Michail

LMW WIND ENERGY COMPANY
26, Pavlovich Str,
Khabarovsk 680030
Russian Federation
TEL: +7 21 73 52
FAX: +7 22 13 84
CONTACT: Lev G Ovis

BIOMASS

CENTER ECOROS
Lininski pr 33-2-1 117192,
Moscow,
Russian Federation
TEL : +7 95 147 36 69
FAX : +7 95 147 36 69
CONTACT : E Pantskhava

ENERGO TECHNOLGOY
Kalinina 13,
198099 St. Petersburg,
Russian Federation
TEL: +7 812 186 98 55
FAX: +7 812 552 18 12
E-MAIL: root@entech.spb.ru

SMALL HYDRO

INSET
Gorohovaya 20,
191186 St Petersburg,
Russian Federation
TEL: +7 812 312 68 04
FAX: +7 812 311 67 42
E-MAIL: jib@inset.spb.ru
CONTACT: Iakov Blyashko

GEOTHERMAL

TSNIIEP OF UTILITIES
Profsojusnaja Street 93a,
117853 Moskva,
Russian Federation
TEL: +7 95 330 4166
FAX: +7 95 336 4255
E-MAIL: director@engsoft.msk.ru
CONTACT: Roald Perel

ENERGY EFFICIENCY

INSOLAR-INVEST
B Filevskaya 32-2,
121433 Moscow,
Russian Federation
TEL: +7 95 144 01 75
FAX: +7 95 144 99 47
E-MAIL: insolar@glasnet.ru
CONTACT: Grigori Vasiliev

MOSCOW POWER ENGINEERING INSTITUTE
Scientific and
Technical Innovation Center for
Energy,
Krasnokazarmennaya 14,
11250 Moscow,
Russian Federation
TEL : + 7 95 273 5071
FAX : +7 95 362 7103
EMAIL : admin@stic-eett.ru
WEB : http://www.stic-eett.ru
CONTACT : Dr Manchkha Sergey

ASSOCIATION

INTERNATIONAL SOLAR ENERGY SOCIETY - ISES RUSSIA
Viesh, 1-st
Veshnjakovsky pr. 2.
Moscow 109456,
Russian Federation
TEL: +7 95 171 1920
FAX: +7 95 170 5101
E-MAIL:energy@viesh.msk.ru
WEB: http://
www.openweb.ru/ises/
CONTACT : Prof. Strebkev

RESEARCH & DEVELOPMENT

INSTITUTE FOR HIGH TEMPERATURES OF THE RUSSIAN ACADEMY OF SCIENCES - IVTAN
Izhorskaya 13/19,
127412 Moscow, Russian Federation
TEL: +7 95 485 93 90
FAX: +7 95 485 7936
E-MAIL: andy@glasnet.ru
CONTACT: Evald Shpilrain

CONSULTANTS

GEOPOLIS CONSULTING ENGINEERS
Shipilovskaya Street 64-1-290,
115682 Moscow,
Russian Federation
TEL : + 7 95 396 0222
FAX : + 7 95 396 0222
E-MAIL : ekolog@mail.cntru
CONTACT : Vladamir

DESIGN & ENGINEERING

CENTRAL RESEARCH AND EXPERIMENTAL DESIGN INSTITUTE
Profsojuzhaja 93a, 117853 Moskva,
Russian Federation
TEL : +7 095 330 7933
FAX : +7 095 336 4255
E-MAIL : engutil@aha.ru
CONTACT : R Perel

ELECTRONIC RADIO AUTOMATION-ERA
Profsouznya 78, 117420 Moscow,
Russian Federation
TEL: +7 95 3306 222
FAX: +7 95 3306 222
E-MAIL: vpribylov@hotmail.com
CONTACT: Valery Pribylov

OTHERS

SMALL ENERGETICS
Tkatskaya 1,
105058 Moscow,
Russian Federartion
TEL: +7 95 962 94 40
FAX: +7 95 964 19 00
CONTACT: Alexander Polushkin

SUPPLIERS

OTHERS (S)

JSC
Energy, Prospect Stroitelei 25,
630055
Novosibirsk, Russian Federation
TEL: +7 3832 32 11 52
FAX: +7 3832 32 11 52
CONTACT : Y Petin

PODOLSKY CHEMICALS & METALLURGICAL PLANT
Roschinskaya Str 3. Podolsk,
142100, Russian Federation
TEL: +7 95 137 92 98
FAX:+7 967 54 89 17
E-MAIL : pcmp@podolsk.ru
CONTACT: Evgeni A Joukovski

We kindly request more listings in this country.

You can submit any additional listings by E-mail: unisun@vsnl.com

Fax: 91 80 2289294

We will include these in the next edition

Kindly inform us of any errors and omissions in the listings by:

E-mail: unisun@vsnl.com

Fax: 91 80 2289294

SOLAR THERMAL

ENERGETIKA LJUBLJANA DOO
Verovskova 70, SI-1000 Ljubljana, Slovenia
TEL: +386 1 5889 000
FAX: +386 1 5889 609
E-MAIL: energetika@energetika-lj.si
WEB: http://www.energetika-lj.si

THERMO-SOLAR LTD
Na-Varticke, PO Box 45,
96503 Ziarnad Hronom,
Slovakia
TEL: +42 1 857 6016080
FAX: +42 1 857 6722844
E-MAIL:mnovak_tsz@zsnp.sk
CONTACT:Novakovia Pavla

SOLAR PHOTOVOLTAIC

SLOVAK UNIVERSITY OF TECHNOLOGY BRATISLAVA
Faculty of Electrical Engineering and Information Technology,
likovicova 3,
SK-81219 Bratislava, Slovakia
TEL: +421 7 60291 724
FAX: +421 7 65420 415
E-MAIL: ruzinskm@elf.stuba.sk
CONTACT: Dr Michal Ruzinsky

ENERGY EFFICIENCY

RFC
Trieda SNP 2, 97401 Banska Bystrica, Slovakia
TEL : +42 88 42858
FAX : +42 88 745702
CONTACT : Marian Rutsek

RESEARCH & DEVELOPMENT

FACULTY OF CHEMICAL TECHNOLOGY
Chemical and Biochemical Engineering Radlinskeho 9,
812 37 Bratislava, Slovakia
TEL: +42 1 7 396920
FAX: +42 1 7 396743
E-MAIL: bales@cvt.stuba.sk
WEB: http://www.cvt.stuba.sk
CONTACT : Prof. V. Bales

TECHNICAL UNIVERSITY OF ZVOLEN
Faculta envoronmentalnej a vyrobnej techniky, T G Masaryka 24,
96053 Zvolen, Slovakia
TEL: +42 1 855 5310 148
FAX: +42 1 588 5333 562
E-MAIL: viglasky@vsld.tuzvo.sk
CONTACT: Jozef Viglasky

CONSULTANTS

ENERGOTECH
Pod Kostanji 8, 1000 Ljubljana, Slovenia
TEL: +386 1 429 20 30
FAX: +386 1 429 20 35
E-MAIL: peter.novak@energotech.si
CONTACT: Dr Peter Novak

SLOVAK ENERGY INSPECTION ENERGY AGENCY
Rudlovska cesta 53, 974 28 Banski Bystrica, Slovakia
TEL: +42 88 742 352
FAX: +42 88 742 351
CONTACT: Josef Slavkovsky

SMALL HYDRO

LITOSTROJ EI
Litostrojska 40,1000 Ljubljana, Slovenia
TEL: +386 15824 108
FAX: +386 15824 171
E-MAIL: franc.klemenc@litostroj-ei.si
WEB: http://www.litostroj-ei.si
CONTACT: Franc Klemenc

OTHERS (S)

FOUNDATION FOR ALTERNATIVE ENERGY - SZOPK
PO Box 35,
850 07 Bratislava
Slovakia
TEL: +421 7 63 836984
FAX: +421 7 63 836964
E-MAIL:bedi@ba.telecom.sk
WEB : http://www.fae.s.k
CONTACT : Emil Bedi

SUPPLIES

BATTERIES & INVERTERS

KON TIKI SOLAR DOO
Ljubljanska 21K, 1241 Kamnik, Slovenia
TEL: +386 1 83 10 380
FAX: +386 1 83 10 380
E-MAIL: kon.tiki.solar@siol.net
WEB: http://www.kontiki-solar.si
CONTACT: Gasper Skarja

CONSTRUCTION SERVICES

KIV ENGINEERING DOO
Vransko66, 3305 Vransko, Slovenia
TEL: +386 3 70 34 100
FAX: +386 3 70 34 150
E-MAIL: info@kiv.si
WEB: http://www.kiv.si
CONTACT: Ivo Kreca

We kindly request more listings in this country.

You can submit any additional listings by E-mail: unisun@vsnl.com

Fax: 91 80 22289294

We will include these in the next edition

Kindly inform us of any errors and omissions in the listings by:

E-mail: unisun@vsnl.com

Fax: 91 80 22289294

SOLAR THERMAL

ARESOL
San Prudencio 13-15,
26004 Logrono, Spain
TEL : +34 941 25 58 68
FAX : +34 941 25 58 68
CONTACT: Pedro Garcia Maliner

COMERCIAL SACLIMA SL
Poligono Industrial 'Els Mollons',
Calle Torners 21, 46970 Alaquas
(Valencia), Spain
TEL: +34 6 151 6162
FAX: +34 6 151 2288
E-MAIL: info@saclima.com
WEB: http://www.saclima.com
CONTACT: Juan Amador Climent Barbera

ENERCLISA
AvdAlcalde Luis Urunuela 6,
Edificio Congresos 301,
41020, Sevilla, Spain
TEL : +34 95 425 53 15
FAX : +34 95 425 54 28
CONTACT: Antonio Rodriguez Garcia

ESAK SA
Callee Gran Via 62-10° dcha,
28013 Madrid, Spain,
TEL:+ 34 915 41 11809
FAX: +34 915 482340
CONTACT: Chris Avramov

IBERSUN
Oms 3, 07003 Palms de
Mallorca, Spain
TEL: +34 71 723476
FAX: +34 71 710271

INSTALACIONES TECHNICAS CURIEL - KLIMA CENTER
C/Chueca 11-Bajos,
18004 Granada, Spain
TEL: +34 958 46 52 51
FAX: +34 958 46 64 65
CONTACT: Luis Francisco Curiel Arostegui

ISOFOTON SA
Headquarters, C/Montalban 9,
2° Izda, 28014 Madrid, Spain
TEL: +34 91 531 26 25
FAX: +34 91 531 10 07
E-MAIL:isofoton@isofoton.es
CONTACT: Juan Fernandez

JOCA INGENIERIA Y CONSTRUCCIONES SA
Sinforiano Madronero 24,26,
06011 Badaioz, Spain
TEL: +34 924 207 200
CONTACT: Andres Gulindo Prieto

RAYOSOL SA
Ctra de Cadiz,
km 238 - Carril de Cutara,
29004 Malaga, Spain
TEL : +34 95 223 84 23
FAX : +34 95 224 05 65
E-MAIL : info@rayosol.es
WEB : http://www.rayosol.es
CONTACT : Mark Wikholm

SOLAR JIENNE NSE SL
Carretera de La Guardia,
4 Acceso, 23002, Jaen,
Spain
TEL:+34 953 23 94 20
FAX:+34 953 23 94 25
E_MAIL:solarjiennense@worldonline.es
CONTACT:Juan Ramon Eyras

TÉCNICASE DE ENERGIA AMBIENTAL SA
Carretera de la Playa 11,
297187 Maro,
Malaga, Spain
TEL: +34 52 529538
FAX: +34 52 529538
E-MAIL: teasa@centerboot.com
CONTACT: Asger Noes Mundbjerg

TFM-ENERGIA SOLAR FOTOVOLTAICA SA

Pol Ind Pla d'em Coll C/Gaia 5,
08110 Montcada I Reixac,
Barcelona,
Spain
TEL: +3435753666
FAX: +3435650057
E-MAIL: info@tfm.es
WEB: http://www.tfm.es
CONTACT: Luis Gordo

TEULA DESIFACANES MULTIFUNCIONALS SA-TFM
Pol Ind Pta den Coll C/Gaie 5.
08110 Montcadai,
Reixach,
Spain
TEL: +34 3 575 3666
FAX: +34 3 575 3442
E-MAIL: tfm@tfm.es
WEB: http://www.tfm.es
CONTACT: Oscar Aceves

VITREX SA
Poligono Malpica Calle F,
Parcela 90-91,
50016-Zaragoza,
Spain
TEL: +34 976 57 11 76
FAX: +34 976 57 42 49
CONTACT: Sr. Palomera

SOLAR PHOTOVOLTAIC

ARDOZ INGENIEROS
C/ Hilados 122-1-9,
Torrejon de Ardoz, 28850 Madrid,
Spain
TEL : +34 91 677 3845
FAX : +34 91 66 9244
E-MAIL : ardoz@mx2.redestb.es
CONTACT: Damaso Campana

ASTRA SOLAR
Cami del Bony 16,
Poligono Industrial 46470,
Catarroja, Valencia,
Spain
TEL : +34 961 278 150
FAX : +34 961 278 151
E-MAIL : astrasolar@astrasolar.com
WEB : http://www.astrasolar.com
CONTACT: Robert Muhn

ATERSA
Comercial, Fernando Poo 6,
28045 Madrid, Spain
TEL: +34 915 178 580
FAX: +34 914 747 467
E-MAIL: atersa@atersa.com
WEB: http://www.atersa.com
CONTACT: Alfredo Gonzalez

BIO-SOL
Juan de Mena 29 bajos 3a,
08035 Barcelona, Spain
TEL : +34 3 4281280
FAX : +34 3 4285277
CONTACT: Pedro Puigpiqud Armengol

BP SOLAR ESPANA SA
Poligono Industrial de Valportillo
Calle Primera 5,
28100 Alcobendas,
Madrid, Spain
TEL : +34 1 657 2660
FAX : +34 1 657 2661
CONTACT: Luis Gordo

IBERSUN
Oms 3,
07003 Palms de Mallorca,
Spain
TEL: +34 71 723476
FAX: +34 71 710271

INGENIERIA DE EQUIPOS DE CONTROL SL
Montasterio de Rueda 9,
50007 Zaragoza,
Spain
TEL: +34 76 27 70 88
FAX: +34 76 27 49 37
CONTACT: Carlos Yubero Fernandez

INSTALACIONES TECHNICAS CURIEL - KLIMA CENTER
C/Chueca 11-Bajos,
18004 Granada, Spain
TEL: +34 958 46 52 51
FAX: +34 958 46 64 65
CONTACT: Luis Francisco Curiel Arostegui

ISOFOTON SA
Headquarters, C/Montalban 9,
2° Izda, 28014 Madrid, Spain
TEL: +34 91 531 26 25
FAX: +34 91 531 10 07
E-MAIL:isofoton@isofoton.es
CONTACT: Juan Fernandez

SOLAR JIENNE NSE SL
Carretera de La Guardia,
4 Acceso, 23002, Jaen, Spain
TEL:+34 953 23 94 20
FAX:+34 953 23 94 25
E_MAIL:solarjiennense@worldonline.es
CONTACT:Juan Ramon Eyras

SOLUCIONES ENERGETICAS SA
Batalla del Salado 2,
28045 Madrid, Spain
TEL: +34 1 530 6743
FAX: +34 1 539 2700
CONTACT: Jose Maria Vela Vico

TEULA DESIFACANES MULTIFUNCIONALS SA-TFM
Pol Ind Pta den Coll C/Gaie 5.
08110 Montcadai,
Reixach, Spain
TEL: +34 3 575 3666
FAX: +34 3 575 3442
E-MAIL: tfm@tfm.es
WEB: http://www.tfm.es
CONTACT: Oscar Aceves

WIND

AEROGENERADORES CANARIOS SA-ACSA
Dr Apolinario Macias,
35/Bajo, 35011 Las Palmas de Gran Canaria, Spain
TEL: +34 28 257 701
FAX: +34 28 250 588
E-MAIL: acsa@iies.es
CONTACT: Pedro M Marrero O'Shanahan

ARDOZ INGENIEROS
C/ Hilados 122-1-9, Torrejon de Ardoz, 28850 Madrid, Spain
TEL : +34 91 677 3845
FAX : +34 91 66 9244
E-MAIL : ardoz@mx2.redestb.es
CONTACT: Damaso Campana

ARESOL
San Prudencio 13-15,
26004 Logrono, Spain
TEL : +34 941 25 58 68
FAX : +34 941 25 58 68
CONTACT: Pedro Garcia Maliner

BORNAY (J) AEROGENERADORES
PO Box 116,
03420 Castali
(Alicante),
Spain
TEL : +34 965 560 025
FAX : +34 965 560 752
E-MAIL : bornay@bornay.com
WEB : http://www.bornay.com
CONTACT: Juan de Dios Bornay

DESARROLLO SEOLICOS SA
Avenda Buhaira No.2,
41018 Sevilla,
Spain
TEL : + 34 5 493 7000
FAX : + 34 5 493 7017
E-MAIL : blora@d_eolicos.abeugo.com
CONTACT: Begona Lora

ECOTECNIA SCOOP
Amistat. 23 1 08005 Barcelona,
Spain
TEL : + 34 93 225 76 00
FAX : + 34 93 223 09 39
E-MAIL : ecotechnia@ecotechnia.com
WEB : http://www.ecotechnia.com
CONTACT: Antonio Martinez

EN BAZAN SA
Turbine Factory, Paseo de la Casteliana 55,
28046 Madrid, Spain
TEL : +34 1 3358474
FAX : +34 1 3358638
WEB : http://www.enbazan.es
CONTACT: J Diaz Carro

IZAR
Aptd Postal 440,
15480 Ferrol, La Coruna, Spain
TEL: +34 981 35215
FAX: +34 981 354900
E-MAIL: turbinasferrol@izar.es
WEB: http://www.izar.es

IZAR PROPULSION Y ENERGIA
Turbine Factory,
Paseo de la Castellana 55,
28046 Madrid,
Spain
TEL: +34 1 3358474
FAX: +34 1 3358638
E-MAIL: jdiazcarro@izar.es
WEB: http://www.izar.es
CONTACT: J Diaz Carro

MADE TECNOLOGIAS RENOVABLES SA
Paseo de Castellana 95,
Planta 29, Torre Europa,
28046 Madrid, Spain
TEL: +34 91 598 37 28
FAX: +34 91 597 48 93
E-MAIL: ibrihuega@made.es
WEB: http://www.made.es
CONTACT: Mr Sureda

MOLINS DEVENT TARRAGO
Raval Sta Anna 30-32,
43400 Montblanc, Spain
TEL: + 34 977 86 20 14
FAX: + 34 977 86 09 08
EMAIL : uenu@xz.uni.karlsruhe.de
CONTACT : Rosa Tarrago

SOLAR JIENNE NSE SL
Carretera de La Guardia,
4 Acceso, 23002, Jaen, Spain
TEL:+34 953 23 94 20
FAX:+34 953 23 94 25
E-MAIL:solarjiennense@worldonline.es
CONTACT:Juan Ramon Eyras

TERRANOVA ENERGY CORPORATION SA
Diagonal 652, Edificio D,
7A Planta, 08034 Barcelona, Spain
TEL: +34 93 206 17 20
FAX: +34 93 206 17 30
CONTACT: Michael Stenderup

BIOMASS

EN BAZAN SA
Turbine Factory, Paseo de la Casteliana 55, 28046 Madrid, Spain
TEL : +34 1 3358474
FAX : +34 1 3358638
WEB : http://www.enbazan.es
CONTACT: J Diaz Carro

GASIFICACION DEBIOMASA SL,
Calle Fuenterbia 35- 3,
20005 San Sebastian, Spain
TEL : + 34 43 46 92 46
FAX : + 34 43 47 26 74
CONTACT: Manuel Michelena

GHESA INGENIERIAY TECHONOLOGIA SA
Magallanes 37, 28015 Madrid, Spain
TEL : + 34 1 3098119
FAX : + 34 1 5942428
CONTACT: Angel Sancho Ros

GUASCOR SA
Barrio de Olkia 44,
20759 Zumaia, Gipuzkoa, Spain
TEL : + 34 943 86 52 00
FAX : + 34 943 86 52 10
E-MAIL : guasor@guasor.com
CONTACT: Holdo Mendizabal

SENER GRUPO DE INGENIERIA SA
Environment & Energy Area,
c/Severo Ochoa 4, Parque
Tecnologico de Madrid, 28760
Tres Cantos, Madrid, Spain
TEL: +3418077161
FAX: +3418077212
E-MAIL: dep.ambiente@sener.es
WEB: http://www.sener.es
CONTACT: Jeronimo Angulo

COGENERATION

EN BAZAN SA
Turbine Factory, Paseo de la
Casteliana 55, 28046 Madrid,
Spain
TEL : +34 1 3358474
FAX : +34 1 3358638
WEB : http://www.enbazan.es
CONTACT: J Diaz Carro

GHESA INGENIERIAY TECHONOLOGIA SA
Magallanes 37, 28015 Madrid,
Spain
TEL : + 34 1 3098119
FAX : + 34 1 5942428
CONTACT: Angel Sancho Ros

NEXTEC SL
Walden 4-71,
08960 Sant Just Desvern,
Spain
TEL: +34 93 473 8146
FAX: +34 93 473 5173
CONTACT: Francesc Bonvehi

RECURSOS ENERGETICOS LOCALES - RELSA
Av Parallel 51 - la planta,
08004 Barcelona,
TEL : +34 93 404 18 60
FAX : +34 93 404 17 12
E-MAIL : jepueyo@enher.es
WEB : http://www.readysoft.es/relsa
CONTACT : Jose E Pueyo Vergara

TERRANOVA ENERGY CORPORATION SA
Diagonal 652, Edificio D,
7A Planta, 08034 Barcelona,
Spain
TEL: +34 93 206 17 20
FAX: +34 93 206 17 30
CONTACT: Michael Stenderup

SMALL HYDRO

AVERLY SA
Paseo Maria Agustin 59,
50004, Zaragoza, Spain
TEL : +34 76 43 46 22
FAX : +34 76 44 50 72
CONTACT: Guillermo Hauke Beo

ENERGY RESOURCES SA
Major de Sarria, 185-187,
Atico 080 17 Barcelona, Spain,
TEL : + 34 3 252 38 40
FAX : + 34 3 252 38 45
E-MAIL : hydroner@lix.intercome.es
CONTACT: Maria Jose Monfort

GUASCOR SA
Barrio de Olkia 44, 20759 Zumaia,
Gipuzkoa, Spain
TEL: +34 943 86 52 00
FAX: +34 943 86 52 10
E-MAIL: guascor@guascor.com
WEB: http://www.guascor.com
CONTACT: Koldo Mendizabal

HIDROENER SA
Calle Ribadeo 2 entlo, 27002 Lugo, Spain
TEL: +34 82 227889
FAX: +34 82 243411
E-MAIL: pfcastro@gecoisa.com
CONTACT: Pablo Fernandez Castro

INGEHYDRO SL
Parque Techologica 106,
48170 Zamudio, Vizcaya, Spain
TEL: +34 94 4039836
FAX: +34 94 4039837
E-MAIL: ingehydro@ingeteam.es
CONTACT: Ignacio Romero

INGELECTRIC TEAM SA
Parque Technologico,
Edif 106, 48170 Zamudio, Spain
TEL: +34 87 720 9699
FAX: +34 97 720 9680
CONTACT: Alberto Belaustegui

MECANICA DE LA PENA SA
Calle Aita Gotzon 37,
48610 Urduliz Vizcaya, Spain
TEL: +34 4 676 50 00
FAX: +34 4 676 5577
CONTACT: Pedro Almandoz

PEQ CENTRALES HIDROLECTRICALS
Padilla 40, 28006 Madrid,
TEL: +34 91 575 6600
FAX : +34 91 575 3970
E-MAIL: km-proyectos@jet.es
CONTACT: Birgit Martin

RECURSOS ENERGETICOS LOCALES - REL SA
Av Parallel 51 - la planta,
08004 Barcelona,
Spain
TEL : +34 93 404 18 60
FAX : +34 93 404 17 12
E-MAIL : jepueyo@enher.es
WEB : http://www.readysoft.es/relsa
CONTACT : Jose E Pueyo Vergara

WASTE TO ENERGY

EUROCOMER SA
Environmental Division,
C/Cervanters No.6, 33004 Oviedo, Spain
TEL: +34 98 596 62 42
FAX: +34 98 596 62 41
E-MAIL:proyectors@eurocomercial.com
CONTACT: Adrian Beyebach

LURGIES PANOLA SA
Avenida General
Peron 29-9, 28020 Madir, Spain
TEL: +34 1 598 1519
FAX: +34 1 556 4277
CONTACT: A Garcia Moreno

SUGIMAT SL
Colada d'Arago s/n, 46930 Quart de
Poblet Valencia, Spain
TEL: +34 96 1597230
FAX: +34 96 1920026
E-MAIL:sugimat@arrakis.es
CONTACT: Alejandro Montesirro

TECNICAS REUNIDAS ECOLOGIA SA
Enivronmental Division,
Arapiles 14, 28015 Madrid, Spain
TEL: +341 592 03 00
FAX: +34 1 592 0420
E-MAIL: ecol@mail.tecnicaserunidas.se
CONTACT: Jose S Padilla

ENERGY EFFICIENCY

IDAE
P de la Castellana 95, Planta 21,
E- 28046 Madrid Spain
TEL: +34 91 456 4900
FAX: +34 91 555 1389
WEB: http://www.idea.es
CONTACT: A Luis Iglesias

FINANCE / BANKING

INSTITUTO PARALA DIVERSIFICACION Y AHORRO DE LA ENERGIA - IDEA
Paseo De La Castellana 95,
21st Floor, 28046 Madrid, Spain
TEL: +34 91 456 49 60
FAX: +34 91 555 1389
E-MAIL: jgaran@idea.es
WEB: http://www.idea.es
CONTACT: Jose Luis Garcia Angulo

TERRANOVA ENERGY CORPORATION SA
Diagonal 652, Edificio D,
7A Planta, 08034 Barcelona,
Spain
TEL: +34 93 206 17 20
FAX: +34 93 206 17 30
CONTACT: Michael Stenderup

ASSOCIATION

SOLVENT ASSOCIACIO PERALA DIFUSIO DE LOSENERGIES RENOVABLES
Europa Av174-176
L'hospitalet 08907, Spain
TEL:+34 3 93 586 45 59
E-MAIL:solvent@inicla.es
WEB:http//www.inicia.es/de/solavent
CONTACT:Candido Garcia

GOVERNMENT

SOCIEDAD PAR AEL DESARROLLO ENTERGETI CODE ANDALUCIA SA (SODEAN)
C/Isaac Newton S/N,
Pabellon de Portugal,
Isla de la Cartuja,
41092 Sevilla, Spain
TEL: +34 5 4626001
FAX: +34 5 4626301
E-MAIL: sodean@lander.es
CONTACT: Maria Luisa Borra Marcos

RESEARCH & DEVELOPMENT

ASTRO SOLAR
Cami Del Bony 16,
Poligono Industrial,
46470 Catarroja,
Valencia, Spain
TEL: +34 961 278 150
FAX: +34 961 278 151
E-MAIL: astrasolar@astrasolar.com
WEB: http//www.astrasolar.com
CONTACT: Robert Muhn

SOCIEDAD GADITANA DE ENERGIAS ALTERNATIVAS
Esc UP, Calle Ramon Pujol s/n
11202 Algeciras, Cadiz,
Spain
TEL: +34 56 662112
FAX: +34 56 662385
E-MAIL: gabriel.ramiro@uca.es
CONTACT:Mr. JGG Ramiro

UNIVERSITIES

CENTRO DE ESTUDIOS DE LA ENERGIA SOLAR-CENSOLAR
Parque Industrial Pisa,
C/Comercio 12, 41927,
Mairena del Aljarafe,
Sevilla Spain
TEL : + 34 954 186200
FAX: + 34 954 186111
WEB : http://www.censolar.org
E-MAIL: censolar@censolar.org
CONTACT: Raimundo Gonzalez

INTIAM RUAI SL
Joan Miro S/N,
Edifici Rubi+D,
08191 Rubi,
Spain
TEL: 34 93 581 39 02
FAX: +34 93 588 61 95
EMAIL:consultas@intiam.com
WEB:http://www.intiam.com
CONTACT: Mr Pere Soria

UNIVERSITAT POLITECHNICA CATALUNYA
Enginyeria Electronica Department,
Jordi Girona 1-3 Modul c-4,
E-08034 Barcelona, Spain
TEL : +34 93 401 1002
FAX : +34 93 401 6756
E-MAIL : jpuigd@cel.upc.es
WEB : http://www.upc.es

UNIVERSITY OF BARCELONA
Department Chemical Engineering,
Marti I Franques I Pta 6,
08028 Barcelona,
Spain
TEL: +34 93 402 1305
FAX: +34 93 402 1291
E-MAIL: jmata@medicina.ub.es
CONTACT: Prof J Mata-Alvarez

UNIVERSITY OF OVIEDO
Energy Department,C /
Independencia
13, 33004 OVIEDO, SPAIN
TEL: +34 98 5104327
FAX: +34 985104322
E-MAIL: pcen5@etsimo.uniovi.es
CONTACT: Jorge Xiberta Bernat

UNVERSIDAD DE ZARAGOZA
Grupo de Biomasa,
Maria de Luna 3,
50015 Zaragoza,
Spain
TEL : +34 976 761880
FAX : +34 976 761879
E-MAIL : bacaicoa@posta.unizar.es
CONTACT : Dr Pedro Garcia-Bacaicoa

NGO's

INSTITUT CERDA
Energy and Environment Area,
Numanca 185,
08034 Barcelona,
Spain
TEL: +34 93 280 23 23
FAX: +34 93 280 11 66
E-MAIL: institut.cerda@icerda.es
WEB: http://www.icerda.es
CONTACT: Jose Luis Rovira

CONSULTANTS

BESEL SA
RET, Po General Martinez Campos
11, 28101 Madrid, Spain
TEL: +34 91 4445901
FAX: +34 91 4477527
WEB: http://www.vasertel.es/~besel
CONTACT: Guillermo Jose Escobar

ENERGIES NATURALS CB
Placa Toni Mus 74,
07500 Manacor, Mallorca, Spain
TEL: +34 971 84 43 62
FAX: +34 971 84 56 83
CONTACT: Rolf Uhle

ENERSOFT SL
Calle Caspe 46, 5G,
08010 Barcelona, Spain,
TEL : + 34 3 3171827
FAX: + 34 3 3171635
CONTACT: Victor Almagro

ENTE VASCO DELA ENERGIA EVE
San Vicenete 8, Edificio Albial -
Planta 14, 48001 Bilbao, Spain,
TEL : + 34 4 4235050
FAX : + 34 4 4249733
CONTACT: D Javier Marques

GECOISA CONSULTORDE INGENIERIA SA
Engineering, Ribadeo 2 entlo
27002, Lugo, Spain.
TEL: +34 82 22 78 89
FAX: +34 82 24 34 11
CONTACT: Marta Fernandez Castro

GEO HABITAT
Pl Iglesia 12, 04738 Vicar, Spain
TEL : + 34 50 553366
FAX : + 34 50 55332
CONTACT: Alfanso Sevilla

RECUPERACION DE ENERGIA SA - RESA
Gran Via de las Corts Catalanes
184 5-1, 08038 Barcelona, Spain
TEL : +34 93 431 83 11
FAX : +34 93 432 35 95
E-MAIL : resa@bcn.servicom.es
CONTACT : Fernando Sanchez

SOLSULET SL
Cr Major 93 3, PO Box 140,
E-08759 Vallirana, Spain
TEL: +34936834230
FAX: +34936835075
EMAIL: solar@solsulet.com
WEB: http://www.solsulet.com
CONTACT: Jordi Vea I Aguirrezabal

SPAIN

TRAMA TECNOAMBIENTAL SL
Ripolles 46, E-08026 Barcelona, Spain
TEL : +34934463234
FAX : +34934566948
E-MAIL : info@tramatecnoambiental.es
WEB : http://www.tramatecnoambiental.es
CONTACT : Jens Merten

DESIGN & ENGINEERING

ABB TRAFOSA (ESTFO)
DDT, Ctra de Madrid Km 314,
50012 Zaragoza, Spain
TEL: +34 976 76 93 00
FAX: +34 976 76 93 06
E-MAIL: alfredo.parres@es.abb.com
WEB: http://www.abb.com/es
CONTACT: Mr Alfredo Parres

ABENER ENERGIA SA
Avda de la Buhaira 2,
41018 Sevilla, Spain
TEL: +34 5 493 71 11
FAX: +34 5 493 70 10
E-MAIL: abener@abengoa.com
WEB:http://www.abengoa.com
CONTACT: Francisco Morillo Leon

ARIES INGENIERIAY SISTEMAS SA
P* de la Castellana 163,
28046 Madrid, Spain
TEL : +34 91 570 2737
FAX : +34 91 570 2766
E-MAIL : aries@iies.es
WEB : http://www.ariesing.com
CONTACT: Mr. Jorge Fernandez

ASESORIA ENERGITICA SA-AE SA
Avda Diagonal 445 1 2a,
08036 Barcelona, Spain
TEL : + 34 93 444 93 00
FAX : + 34 93 444 93 01
E-MAIL : aesa@aesa.net
WEB : http://www.aesa.net
CONTACT: J M Roqueta Matias

BCN CAMBRA LOGICA PROJECTES SL
Sant Joan 8, 08629 Torrelles de Llobregat, Barcelona, Spain
TEL : +34 3 689 01 36
FAX : +34 3 689 05 45
E-MAIL :bcn@bcnprojectes.es
WEB : http://www.bcnprojectes.es
CONTACT: Xavier Traver

BIU ARQUITECTURA (BONFILL URBANO & ASSOCIATES)
PJE Bonfill3 (LA floresta), 08190 SantCugatdel, Valles, Barcelona, Spain
TEL : +34 3 6741727
FAX : +34 3 6741727
E-MAIL :biu@coac.es
WEB : http://www.coac.es
CONTACT: Josep Bonfill

GEONICA SA
Alejandro Rodriguez,
Madrid, Spain
TEL : + 34 1 450 5118
FAX : + 34 1 459 4614
CONTACT: Carlos Gomez Carrio

IMOGEP SA
C/ Darrerra Sant Marti 15-1,
25004 Lleida, Spain
TEL: +34 73 248631
FAX: +34 73 248417
E-MAIL: imogep@paeria.es
CONTACT: Josep M Juvilla Aige

TRAMA TECNOAMBIENTAL SL
Ripolles 46, 08026 Barcelona, Spain
TEL: +34 93 4504091
FAX: +34 93 4566948
E-MAIL : tta@mx3.redestb.es
CONTACT: Xavier Vallve

OTHERS

ACANDER SL
Avenida Sta Lucia, Urbanizacion Sta Lucia 55,
41500 Alcal de Guadaira,
Sevilla, Spain
TEL: +34 5 5682600
FAX: +34 5 5680948
E-MAIL: acander@ibm.net
CONTACT: Carlos Cardenoso

EGUZKI INDAR SL
Usabal 37, 20440, Tolosa, Spain
TEL : +34 943 67 42 56
FAX : +34 943 67 42 56
E-MAIL : eguikind@eniac.eniac.es
WEB : http://
www.eniac.es/eguzkind
CONTACT: Aldazabal Jokin

ENERGY WORKS
Rodriguez Arias
15-6" 48008 Bilbao,
Spain
TEL: + 34 94 470 20 34
FAX : + 34 94 470 25 10
E-MAIL: jfgetino@energyworks.es
CONTACT: Jose Luis Fernandez Getino

GAS NATURAL SDG SA
C/ Corcega 373,
6a Planta 08307
Barecelona,
Spain
TEL: + 34 93 402 50 41
FAX: + 34 93 402 53 71
EMAIL: joaquim.lloret.rodriguez@gasnatural.es
WEB: http://www.gasnaturals.es
CONTACT: Joaquim Lloret Rodriguez

TECHNO SUN SL
Perez Galdos 27, 46018 Valencia, Spain
TEL : +34 963 826565
FAX : +34 963 842721
E-MAIL : solosol@ctv.cs
CONTACT : Antoni Ramos

We kindly request more listings in this country.

You can submit any additional listings by E-mail: unisun@vsnl.com

Fax: 91 80 22289294

We will include these in the next edition

SUPPLIERS

BATTERIES/INVERTERS

BIO-SOL
Juan de Mena 29 bajos 3a,
08035 Barcelona, Spain
TEL : +34 3 4281280
FAX : +34 3 4285277
CONTACT: Pedro Puigpiqud Armengol

ENERTRON SA
Calle Amsterdam s/n,
Poligono Industrial de torres de Alameda, 28813 Madrid, Spain
TEL: + 34 1 885 8634
FAX: + 34 1 886 8077
E-MAIL: enertron@releline.es
CONTACT: Manuel Visters Guinot

INSTRUMENTATION

FULLTRON SA
Playa De Ribeira3, 28290 Las Matas, Madrid, Spain
TEL: +34 916 305 628
FAX: ı 34 916 305 508
E-MAIL: info@fulltron.es
WEB: http://www.fulltron.es
CONTACT: Rafael Aguilar

INDAR SA
Avda Navarra 20,
20.200 Bealsain Guipuzcoa, Spain
TEL: +34 943 882800
FAX: +34 943 887541
E-MAIL: indar@indar.net
CONTACT: Gorka Bilbao

SIEMSA
18 Ingeniero Torres Quevedo,
28022 Madrid, Spain
TEL: +34 1 3294228
FAX: +34 1 3194235
CONTACT: Pedro Parbole

SONDER REGULACION SA
Avda La Lana 93, P1 La Liana,
08191 Rubi Barcelona, Spain
TEL: +34 93 5884211
FAX: +34 93 5884994
E-MAIL:info@sonder-regulacion.com
WEB: http://www.sonder-regulacion.com
CONTACT: Albert Gaju Raventos

TALLERES MARTINEZ SA
Poligono Ind, La Cerrada No 14,
Apartado No 9, 39600 Maliano,
Cantabria, Spain
TEL : +34 422 51450
FAX : +34 422 52411

TERMOMETROS WEC SA
Roger 15, 08028 Barcelona,
Spain
TEL: +34 93 339 38 50
FAX: +34 93 339 52 71
E-MAIL: twec@mx3.redestb.es

COATINGS & PAINTS

GRES DE NULES & KERABEN
Ctra Nacional 340 km 44 3,
12250 Nules (Castellan), Spain
TEL :+ 34 64 67 2752
FAX :+ 34 64 67 26 09
E-MAIL : c.arrebola@keraben.com
CONTACT: Cristobal Adrebola Jimenenz

CONSTRUCTION SERVICES

FOSTER WHEELER IBERIA SA
Parque Empresarial Madrid
Las Rozas, Gabriel Garcia
Marquez 2, 28230 Las Rozas
(Madrid), Spain
TEL: +34 1 336 25 00
FAX: +34 1 336 25 55
CONTACT: Jose Sanchez Garcia

INTERNACIONAL DE INGENIERIA Y ESTUDIOS TECHNICOS SA - INTECSA
C/ Orense 70-6,
28020 Madrid, Spain
TEL: +34 91 567 39 08
FAX: +34 91 567 38 04
CONTACT: Jose Ruiz Girela

OTHER (S)

DRAGADOS INDUSTRIAL SA
Avenue Tenerife 4-6,
28700n San Sebastion de Los Reyes Spain
TEL : + 34 91 583 35 37
FAX : + 34 91 583 78 91
E-MAIL : rff-dragadosgruppo@dragados.com
CONTACT: Rafael Fernandez

ENERGIAS RENOVABLES
Avda Colmenar Viejo11-2 B,
28700 San Sebastian De Los Reyes,
Madrid, Spain
TEL: +34 91 653 1553
FAX: +34 91 653 1553
E-MAIL: lmerino@energias-renovables.com
WEB: http://www.energias-renovables.com
CONTACT: Luis Merino

INGENIERIA ESPANOLA SA-INGESPA
Ctra Cassellon,
Pgno La Cartuja c/a 50720 La Cartuja Baja (Zaragoza),
Spain
TEL: +34 76 500 246
FAX: +34 76 500 385
CONTACT: Juan I Gomez Diaz-Bravo

INTECSA-UHDE INDUSTRIAL SA
Rostario Pino-14,
28020 Madrid,
Spain
TEL: +34 91 7497000
FAX: +34 91 7497001
E-MAIL: inteuhde@mad.servicom.es
WEB: http://www.inteuhde.com
CONTACT: Fernando Pollastrini

LEGRAND ESPANOLA SA
Canada, 49 Pol,
Ind Torrejon Ardoz,
Spain
TEL: +34 1 656 18 12
FAX: +34 1 656 67 88
CONTACT: Luis de la Campa

SOLAR TECH CO
PO Box 265, 29620 Torremolinos,
Malaga, Spain
TEL: +34952389370
E-MAIL: solartechnology@usa.net
CONTACT: Forouhar Aghili

Kindly inform us of any errors and omissions in the listings by:

E-mail: unisun@vsnl.com

Fax: 91 80 22289294

SWEDEN

SOLAR THERMAL

BLEKING E EXERGI O MILJÖ HB
Vieryds agen 30, 372 33,
Ronneby, Sweden
TEL : +46 457 278 78
FAX : +46 457 278 78
E-MAIL : blekinge.exergi@
swiopnet.se
WEB : http://www.solgruppen.se
CONTACT : Nils-Erik Mattsson

BO FERM ENERGI & TEKNIK
Stuveröd 4528,
450 34 Fiskebäckskil,
Sweden
TEL : +46 523 22866
FAX : +46 523 22866
CONTACT : B O Ferm

ENERGIVERKSTATI
Dalarna AB, Sparbanksgatan2,
793 31 Leksand, Sweden
TEL: +46 247 109 88
FAX: +46 247 153 55
CONTACT : Göran Svärdstrom

SOLSAM SUNERGY AB
Box 12870,
112 98 Stockholm, Sweden
TEL: +46 8 6518384
FAX: +46 8 6527980
E-MAIL: info@sunergy.se
WEB: http://www.sunergy.se
CONTACT: Goran Bolin

SYDKRAFT AB
Carl Gustafs Väg 1,
205 09 Malmo, Sweden
TEL: +46 40 255000
FAX: +46 40 976069
CONTACT : Bertil Strandh

TEXSUN ENERGY AB
Lagergatan 3, SE,
931 36 Skelleftea, Sweden
TEL: +46 910 717880
FAX: +46 910 717889
E-MAIL: info@texsun.se
WEB: http://www.texsun.se
CONTACT: Hans Lindquist

SOLAR PHOTOVOLTAIC

BO FERM ENERGI & TEKNIK
Stuveröd 4528,
450 34 Fiskebäckskil,
Sweden
TEL : +46 523 22866
FAX : +46 523 22866
CONTACT : B O Ferm

GALLIVARE PHOTOVOLTAIC AB-GPV AB
Foretagscentrum, Box 840 Hus 60,
S-982 28 Gallivare, Sweden
TEL: +46 970 158 30
FAX: +46 970 158 98
E-MAIL: contact@gpv-solar.com
WEB: http://www.gpv-solar.com
CONTACT: Andreas Hinzer

MOLLER UNDENAS TURBIN AB
Bruksvagen 2,
54673 Forsvik, Sweden
TEL: +46 505 41400
FAX: 46 505 41450
EMAIL:leif@undenas.se
WEB:http://www.undenas.se
CONTACT : Leif Chressman

NAPS SWEDEN AB
PO Box 26, 5-127 21
Skärholmen, Sweden
TEL: +46 8 4495930
FAX: +46 8 7405001
CONTACT: Leif Selhagen

SOLSAM SUNERGY AB
Hornsbruksgatan 28,
117 34 Stockholm, Sweden
TEL: +4686523041
FAX: +4686527980
E-MAIL: info@sunergy.se
WEB: http://www.sunergy.se
CONTACT: Goran Bolin

SYDKRAFT AB
Carl Gustafs Väg 1,
205 09 Malmo, Sweden
TEL: +46 40 255000
FAX: +46 40 976069
CONTACT : Bertil Strandh

WIND

NORDIC WINDPOWER AB
Box 520, S-183 25 Taby, Sweden
TEL: +46 8 544 408 50
FAX: +46 8 732 84 30
CONTACT: Staffan Engstrom

PITCHWIND SYSTEMS AB
PO Box 89, 44322 Lerum, Sweden
TEL: +46 708 23 72 19
FAX: +46 302 159 04
E-MAIL: info@pitchwind.se
WEB: http://www.pitchwind.se

RA-INNOVACO
Stackvagen 4, 43254 Varberg,
Sweden
TEL: +46340670878
FAX: +46340670878
CONTACT: Runne Adolfsson

TRELLEBORG INDUSTRIALAVS
Trelleborg Industrial AVS Sweden,
SE-231 81 Trelleborg, Sweden
TEL: +46 410 510 00
FAX: +46 410 193 70
E-MAIL: novibra@trelleborg.com
WEB: http://www.trelleborg.com/
novibra
CONTACT: Poul Gustavsson

VATTENFALLENERGISYSTEM AB
PO Box 528, 16215 Stockholm,
Sweden
TEL: +46 8 739 60 00
FAX: +46 8 739 62 26
E-MAIL: sven.nordin@
energisystem.vattanfall.se

BIOMASS

BIO ENERGY INTERNATIONAL
Postbus 716, 8440 AS Heerenveen,
Sweden
TEL: + 46 513 61 02 70
FAX: +46 513 61 04 49
CONTACT: Patrick Storm

BIOALCOHOL FUEL FOUNDATION
Box 826, 89118,
Oernskoeldsvik, Sweden
TEL : +46 660 78722
FAX : +46 660 54903
E-MAIL : info@baff.nu
WEB : http://www.baff.nu
CONTACT : Jan Lindstedt

BRUKS MEKANISKA AB
PO Box 46, 820 10 Arbra, Sweden
TEL : +46 278 642500
FAX : +46 278 642520
E-MAIL : info@bruks.com
WEB : http://www.bruks.com
CONTACT : John Eriksson

ENERGIPROJEKT AB
Dämmvagen 7.571 75 Nässjö, Sweden
TEL: +46 380 260 65
FAX: +46 380 260 26
E-MAIL: cadmen.konstru
ktion@savsjo.com
WEB: http://mail.telia.com
CONTACT : Martin Bernaas

FUEL CELL

CATELLA GENERICS AB
Veddestavägen 7,
175 62 Järfälla, Sweden
TEL : +46 8 445 79 60
FAX : +46 8 445 79 99
E-MAIL : cgr@cgr.se
WEB : http://www.cgr.se
CONTACT : BO Andersson

ECO TRAFFIC ERD AB
Karlayagen 18, PO Box 5671,
S-11486, Stockholm, Sweden
TEL : +46 8614 5008
E-MAIL :eco@ecotraffic.se
WEB : http://www.ecotraffic.se
CONTACT : Bengt Sävbark

SMALL HYDRO

ITT FLYGT AB
PO Box 1309, 17125 Solna,
Sweden
TEL: +46 8 4756500
FAX: +46 8 4756500
E-MAIL: monica.spendilow@flygt.com
WEB: http://www.flygt.com
CONTACT: Roman Gabryjonczyk

TURAB TURBIN & REGULATORSERVICE AB
Förradsgatan 2,
571 39 Nässjö, Sweden
TEL: +46 380 15510
FAX: +46 380 15530
E-MAIL:turab@turab.se
WEB:http://www.turab.com
CONTACT: Christer Abrahamsson

TURBEC AB
Box 21512, Regnvatteng 1,
SE-20021 Malmo, Sweden
TEL: +46 40 680 00 00
FAX: +46 40 680 00 01
E-MAIL: info@turbec.com
WEB: http://www.turbec.com
CONTACT: Lars Malmrup

WAPLANS MEKANISKA VERKSTADS AB
SE-830 44 Nälden, Sweden
TEL: +46 640 177 00
FAX: +46 640 177 80
E-MAIL: waplans@waplans.se
WEB: http://www.waplans.se
CONTACT: Lars Eric Kilian

WASTE TO ENERGY

HEDEMORA DIESEL AB
Box 206, 776 28 Hedemora,
Sweden
TEL: +46 225 15540
FAX: +46 225 15440
E-MAIL: diesel@hedemoradiesel.se
WEB: http://www.hedemoradiesel.se
CONTACT: Gerhard Lindholm

INGVAR INGRIDS AB
Sorvik, 77192 Ludvika, Sweden
TEL: +46 240 39225
FAX: +46 240 39568
CONTACT: Ingvar Ingrids

MVM KONSULT AB
Terminalvägen 16, 861,
Timrä, Sweden
TEL : +46 60 57 33 20
FAX: + 46 60 57 33 29
EMAIL:mvm.timra@mvm.se
WEB:http://www.mvm.se
CONTACT: Mr. Jan Olofsson

SOLID WASTE COMPANY OF SOUTH WEST SCANIA THE-SYSAV
Östergata 30,
211 22 Maml, Sweden
TEL: +46 40 680 1800
FAX: +46 40 680 18 10
E-MAIL: rylander.hk@sysav.com
WEB: http://www.sysav.se
CONTACT: Hakan Rylander

SYSAV-THE SOLID WASTE COMPANY OF SOUTH WEST SCANIA
PO Box 50344, SE-202 13 Malmo,
Sweden
TEL: +46406801800
FAX: +46406801810
E-MAIL: epost@sysav.se
WEB: http://www.sysav.se
CONTACT: Mr. Hakan Rylander

TEKNISKA VERKENI LINKÖPING AB
Energy PO Box 1500,
SE-581 15, Linköping, Sweden
TEL: +46 13 20 80 00
FAX: +46 13 20 80 06
E-MAIL: ingcar@teknis
kaverken.linkoping.se
CONTACT: Ingvar Carlsson

THOREN AB
VEDA 1067, 87015 Utansjo, Sweden
TEL: +46 612 42500
FAX: +46 612 42320
E-MAIL:thomas@thoren.nu

ENERGY EFFICIENCY

EB VÄRMEINREGLERING AB
Box 119, 275 23 Sjöbo, Sweden
TEL : + 46 416 511 606
FAX : + 46 416 511 774
E-MAIL : eb-metoden@ebv.se
Web : www.ebmetoden.com

GOVERNMENT

SWEDISH NATIONAL ENERGY ADMINISTRATION ENERGIMYNDIGHETEN
Box 310, 631 04 Eskilstuna, Sweden
TEL: +46 16 5442000
FAX: +46 16 5442261
CONTACT:Stefan Jakelius

RESEARCH & DEVELOPMENT

LUND INSTITUTE OF TECHNOLOGY
Department of Environmental &
Energy Systems Studi,
Gerdagatan 13,
SE-223 62 Lund, Sweden
TEL: +46 46 222 86 41
FAX: +46 46 10 86 44
E-MAIL: Leif.gustavsson@miljo.ith.se
CONTACT: Dr Leif Gustavsson

TPS TERMISKA PROCESSER AB
S-611 82 Nyköping, Sweden
TEL: +46 155 22 13 00
FAX: +46 155 26 30 52
E-MAIL:info@tps.se
WEB : http://www.tps.se
CONTACT : Lars Waldheim

UNIVERSITIES

CHALMERS UNIVERSITY OF TECHNOLOGY
Department of Building
Physics 41296 Göteborg, Sweden
TEL : +46 31 7721000
FAX : +46 31 7721132
CONTACT : Jan-Olof Dalenbäck

NGO's

SVENSKA SOLGRUPPEN
Björneröd Pl 6215,
452 93 Strömstad, Sweden
TEL: +46 526 32320
Fax: +46 526 32320
WEB: http://www.solgruppen.se
CONTACT:Anders Jernelius

CONSULTANTS

BENGT DAHLGREN AB
Energy & Environmental Analysis
Victor Hasselblads gata 16,
421 31 V Frolunda,
Sweden
TEL : +46 31 7202500
FAX : +46 31 7202501
E-MAIL : anders.nilson@
bengtdahlgren.se
WEB : http://
www.bengtrdablgren.se
CONTACT : Anders Nilson

BRA VVS-KONSULT AB
Erik Dahlbergs Vag 9,
392 35 Kalmar, Sweden
TEL : +46 480 478590
FAX : +46 480 51579
E-MAIL : bravvs@bravvs.se
WEB : http://www.bravvs.se
CONTACT : Bengt Persson

KANENERGI SWEDEN AB
Box 41, Jarnvagsg 10,
SE-532 21 Skara, Sweden
TEL: +46 511 347 664
FAX: +46 511 347 665
E-MAIL: mats.rydehell@kanenergi.se
WEB:http://www.kanenergi.com
CONTACT : Mats Rydehell

MVM KONSULT AB
Timra Office, Terminalvagen 16,
861 36 Timra, Sweden
TEL: +46 60 57 33 20
FAX: +46 60 57 33 29
E-MAIL: mvm.timra@mvm.se
WEB: http://www.mvm.se
CONTACT: Mr Rikard Thurdin

NYKOMB SYNERGETICS
Process Engineering,
Floragatan 10B,
SE-11431 Stockholm, Sweden
TEL: +46 8 440 4050
FAX: +46 8 440 4055
E-MAIL: bengt.olsson@nykomb.se
WEB: http://www.nykomb.se
CONTACT: Tomas Ekbom

SWEDISH GEOTECHNICAL INSTITUTE-SGI
Olaus Magnus Väg 35,
SE-58193 Linköping,
Sweden
TEL: +46 13 20 18 00
FAX: +46 13 20 19 14
E-MAIL:sgi@geotek.se
WEB:http://www.sgi.geotek.se
CONTACT:Bengt Rydell

SWEDPOWER INTERNATIONAL AB
Contract Services and
Marketing,
Warfvinges Väg 16,
PO Box 30 150,
SE-104 25 Stockholm,
Sweden
TEL : +46 8 619 60 08
FAX : +46 8 619 60 69
E-MAIL : post@swedpower.se
WEB : htpp://www.swedpower.se
CONTACT : Thomas H Mason

THEORELLS INSTALLATIONS KONSULT AB
Apeteksgränd 3,
891 Örnskölksvik,
Sweden
TEL: +46 660 17740
FAX: +46 660 82512
E-MAIL: kenneth.jonsson@sweco.se
WEB: http://www.sweco.se
CONTACT: Kjell Blomback

DESIGN & ENGINEERING

ELECTROWATT-EKONO AB
Box 1130, 18122 Lidingö, Sweden
TEL : +46 8 731 45 00
FAX : +46 8 767 63 15
E-MAIL : eleectrowatt.ekono
@poyry.se
CONTACT : Helena Fredriksson

OTHERS

ABB STA LAB
612 82 Finspong, Sweden
TEL: +44 122 81000
FAX: +44 122 18684
E-MAIL:gert.skold@
sesta.mail.abb.com
WEB: http://www.abb.se/stal
CONTACT: Gert Skold

BORAS VENTILATION AB
Box 859, 501 15 Boras, Sweden
TEL : +46 33 2570 65
FAX : +46 33 2549 85
CONTACT : Michael Barrstrand

EKSTRÖM & SON AB
Box 566, 291 25 Kristianstad,
Sweden
TEL : +46 44 20 8400
FAX : +46 44 20 8401
CONTACT : Lennart Karrberg

FAGERSTA ENERGETICS AB
Herrgordsvagen 9, Fagersta, Sweden
TEL: +46 223 45067
FAX: +46 223 16284
CONTACT : Kjell Bjorling

GOTAVERKEN MILJÖ AB
Anders Carlssons Gata 14,
40272 Göthenburg, Sweden
TEL : + 46 31 50 19 60
FAX : + 46 31 22 98 67
E-MAIL : info@gmab.se
WEB : www.gmab.se
CONTACT : Per Lindgren

GOTHERM AB
Kungsportsavenyn 14,
411 36 Goteborg, Sweden
TEL : + 46 31 18 1218
FAX : + 46 31 711 4313
E-MAIL : + gothermab@
ebox.tninet.se
CONTACT : Hans Frendin

SUPPLIERS

INSTRUMENTS

ABB POWER SYSTEMS AB
Kopparbergsvagen 6,
721 64 Vasteras, Sweden
TEL: +46 21 324953
FAX: +46 21 149260
E-MAIL: simpow-inform.sepow@se.abb.com
WEB: http:// www.abb.com/product guide/Power Transmission/ PowerSystemSimulation/SIMPOW
CONTACT: Sune Sarri

CLIMATOR AB
Skolgatan 11, 54131 Skovde, Sweden
TEL: +46 500 482350
FAX: +46 500 428499
E-MAIL: info@climator.com
WEB: http://www.climator.com
CONTACT: Rolf Ulfvengren

VATTENFALL AB
MEGA, Box 1006, 90120 Umea, Sweden
TEL: +4690151401
FAX: +4690132442
WEB: http://www.vattenfall.com

METALS

SUNSTRIP AB
Skäggebyvägen 29, 612 44 Finspang, Sweden
TEL: +46 122 866 60
FAX: +46 122 866 69
E-MAIL: sunstrip@sunstrip.se
WEB: http://www.sunstrip.se
CONTACT: Anders Lantz

GLASS

PILKINGTON FLOATGLAS AB
Box 530, S-301 80 Halmstad,
TEL: + 46 35 153 000
FAX : + 46 35 210 599
WEB : www.pilkington.com

OTHERS (S)

ENERGY OPTICONAB
Ideon, 223 70 Lund, Sweden,
TEL : + 46 46 286 2380
E-Mail : bengt.grufman@opticon.se
CONTACT : Bengt Grufmann

EKOCENTRUM
S T Jorgens Vag 20,
42240 Hisintsbacka, Sweden
TEL : +46 31 556882
FAX : +46 31 556881
E-MAIL : ekocentrum@ ekocentrum.au
WEB : http://www.ekocentrum.au
CONTACT : Lasse Gustavsson

IPS INTERPROJECT SERVICE AB
Gripensnas, S-640 33 Bettna,Sweden
TEL: +46 157 70380
FAX: +46 157 70303
E-MAIL: interproject@swipnet.se
CONTACT : Gunnar Fredrikson

MARTINSSON ELEKTRONIK AB
Sodra Gubberogatan 8,
41663 Goteborg, Sweden
TEL: +46 31 68 45 10
FAX: +46 21 68 45 30
E-MAIL: hans@martinsson.se
CONTACT: Hans Lindberg

UPPSALA ENERGI AB
PO Box 600, 75125 Uppsala, Sweden
TEL: +46 18 27 27 00
FAX: +46 18 146657
E-MAIL: uppsala.energi@ uppsalaenergi.se
WEB: http://www.uppsalaenergi.se
CONTACT: Hans Sollenberg

UPPSALA UNIVERSITY
Department of Materials Science,
PO Box 534,
S-75121 Uppsala, Sweden
TEL: +46 18 471 3067
FAX: +46 18 500 131
E-MAIL: claes-goran.granqvist@ angstrom.uu.se
CONTACT: Claes G Granqvist

We kindly request more listings in this country.

You can submit any additional listings by E-mail: unisun@vsnl.com

Fax: 91 80 22289294

We will include these in the next edition

Kindly inform us of any errors and omissions in the listings by:

E-mail: unisun@vsnl.com

Fax: 91 80 22289294

SWITZERLAND

SOLAR THERMAL

CENTRE ECOLOGIQUE ALBERT SCHWEITZER
Rue de la Cote 2, 2000 Neuchatel Switzerland
TEL : +41 32 725 08 36
FAX : +41 32 725 15 07
E-MAIL : ceas.ne@bluewin.ch
CONTACT : Daniel Schneider

CU ENOTHERM SA
10 rue de la Bergere,
1242 Satigny,
Switzerland
TEL : + 41 22 989 33 00
FAX : +41 22 989 33 01

ENERGIE SOLAIRE SA
Case Postale, CH-3960 Sierre,
Switzerland
TEL: +41 27 455 22 12
FAX: +41 27 455 22 02
E-MAIL:energie_
solaire_sa@scopus.ch
CONTACT : Jean-Pierre Rossy

HOLINGER SOLAR AG
RheinstraBe 17, 4410 Liestal,
Switzerland
TEL: +41 61 923 93 93
FAX: +41 61 921 07 69
E-MAIL: info@holinger-solar.ch
WEB: http://www.holinger-solar.ch
CONTACT: Heinrich Holinger

LENZ SOLAR & WÄRMETECHNIK
Waldbrg 4, 9244 Niederuzwill,
Switzerland
TEL: +41 71 955 70 20
FAX: +41 71 955 70 25
E-MAIL: lenz@wil.ch
CONTACT: H Lenz

MUNTWYLER ENERGIETECHNIK AG
Solarcenter Muntwyler, P O Box 512
3052, Zollikofen, Switzerland
TEL: +41 31 911 50 63
FAX: +44 31 911 51 27
EMAIL:muntwyler@solarcenter.ch
WEB:http://www.solarcenter.ch
CONTACT: Urs Muntwyler

PLANAIR
Cret 108a,2314 La Sagne,
Switzerland
TEL: + 41 32 931 88 28
FAX : + 41 32 931 88 28
E-MAIL: info@planair.ch
WEB:http://www.planair.ch
CONTACT : Pierre Renaud

SOLARMARKT GMBH
Feldackerstr 3 5040 Schaftland,
Switzerland
TEL:+41 62 721 0202
FAX:+41 62 721 02 15
E-MAIL:info@solarmarkt.ch
CONTACT:Urs Kessler

SOLARCO SA
Av Reneveyres 10, 1110Morges,
Switzerland
TEL: +41218021062
FAX: +41218030077
WEB: http://www.solarco.ch
CONTACT: Jean-Claude Enderling

SOLTOP SCHUPPISSER LTD
St Gallerstr 7, CH-8353 Elgg,
Switzerland
TEL: +41 52 364 00 77
FAX: +41 52 364 00 78
E-MAIL: energie@soltop.ch
WEB: http://www.soltop.ch
CONTACT: Fritz Schuppisser

STAR UNITY AG
8804 Au, Switzerland
TEL: +41 1 782 6161
FAX: +41 1 782 6160
WEB:http://www.starunity.ch
CONTACT:Herr Rupp

ULOG GROUP
Morgartenring 18,
CH-4054 Brasel, Switzerland
TEL : +41 61 301 66 22
FAX : +41 61 301 49 59
E-MAIL : ulobasel@swissonline.ch
WEB : http://www.ulog.ch
CONTACT : Alec Gagneaux

VAUCHER PAUL SA CENTRE ROMAND
Route du jura, 1023 Crissier,
Switzerland
TEL: +41 21 633 12 12
FAX: +41 21 633 12 13
E-MAIL:administratif@paul-
vaucher.com

VON AUW SA
Rte de Geneve 3,
1028 Preverenges, Switzerland
TEL: +41 21 801 12 22
FAX: +41 21 802 34 49
CONTACT: Alain Folly

WÄRMELADEN GIPSGRUEB
Glipsstrasse 55, 5422
Oberehrendingen, Switzerland
TEL: +41 56 221 1223
FAX: +41 56 221 1223
CONTACT: Micheal Keller

SOLAR PHOTOVOLTAIC

AMAX ENERGIE
Vy-Creuse 17, PO Box 549,
1196 Gland, Switzerland
TEL: +41 22 364 31 69
FAX: +41 22 364 43 69
E-MAIL: amax.energie@vtx.ch
WEB: http://www.amax-energie.ch
CONTACT: MJ Schleiss

ATLANTIS SOLAR SYSTEMS LTD
Lindenrain 4, 301,2, Bern,
Switzerland
TEL : +41 31 300 3280
FAX : +41 31 300 3290
E-MAIL :info@atlantisenergy.ch
WEB : http://
www.atlantisenergy.com
CONTACT : A Eckmanns

BOMIN SOLAR AG
Elisabenelnanlage
9, CH-4051, Basel
Switzerland
TEL : +41 61 271
FAX : +41 61 273 2772
E-MAIL :info@bomin.com
WEB : http://www.bomin.com
CONTACT : Hans Pleuger

BRUN (RENE) ALTERNATIVE TECHNIK AG
CH-7015 Tamins,
Switzerland
TEL : +41 8 641 2537
FAX : +41 8 641 2374
CONTACT : R Brun

CELIO ENGINEERING SA
6775 Ambri, Switzerland
TEL : +44 91 880 20 78
FAX : +44 91 880 20 80
E-MAIL : celioeng@bluewin.ch
CONTACT : Dr. T Celio

ELECTRONIC W PFEIFFER
P O Box 4009,
CH-4009, Base 9,
Switzerland
TEL : +41 61 423 14 15
FAX : +41 61 423 30 00
E-MAIL :ewp@technologist.com
CONTACT : W P Feiffer

EPFL
IPM DMT, CH-1015 Lausanne,
Switzerland
TEL: + 41 21 693 5945
FAX : +41 21 693 3891
E-Mail : julian.randall@epfl.ch
CONTACT : Mr. Jullian Randall

HCT SHAPING SYSTEMS SA
Route de Geneve 42,
1033 Cheseaux, Switzerland
TEL: +41 21 731 90 00
FAX: +41 21 731 91 01
E-MAIL: sales@hct.ch
WEB: http://www.homepage.ch/hct
CONTACT: Dr Charles Hauser

HOLINGER SOLAR AG
RheinstraBe 17, 4410 Liestal,
Switzerland
TEL: +41 61 923 93 93
FAX: +41 61 921 07 69
E-MAIL: info@holinger-solar.ch
WEB: http://www.holinger-solar.ch
CONTACT: Heinrich Holinger

INTEREL AG
Clarastrasse 2, 4005 Basel, Switzerland
TEL: +41 61 690 99 55
FAX: +41 61 681 26 06
E-MAIL: interel@datacomm.ch
CONTACT: D Massart

LENZ SOLAR & WÄRMETECHNIK
Waldbrg 4, 9244 Niederuzwill,
Switzerland
TEL: +41 71 955 70 20
FAX: +41 71 955 70 25
E-MAIL: lenz@wil.ch
CONTACT: H Lenz

MEYER + BURGER LTD
Alte Bernstrasse, CH-3613
Steffisburg, Switzerland
TEL: +41 33 439 05 05
FAX: +41 33 439 05 10
E-MAIL: schweizerk@a2000.ch

NEOGARD SOLAR AG
5728 Gontenschwil, Switzerland
TEL: +41 62 767 00 50
FAX: +41 62 767 00 67
E-MAIL: info@neogard.ch
WEB: http://www.neogard.ch
CONTACT:M Leutwiller

NOWAK ENERGY & TECHNOLOGY LTD- NET
Waldweg 8,1717 St Ursen,
Switzerland
TEL: +41 26 494 00 30
FAX: +41 26 494 00 34
E-MAIL: mail.net@bluewin.ch
CONTACT: Dr Stefan Nowak

SOLARFORCE
CP 190 1926 Fully , Switzerland
TEL:+41 27 746 33 83
FAX:+41 27 746 33 84
E-MAIL:solarforce@urbanet.ch
CONTACT:Serge Remy

SOLARMARKT GMBH
Feldackerstr 3 5040 Schaftland,
Switzerland
TEL:+41 62 721 0202
FAX:+41 62 721 02 15
E-MAIL:info@solarmarkt.ch
CONTACT:Urs Kessler

SOLENERGY
1041 Oulenss / Echallens.
Switzerland
TEL: +41 21 882 55 24
FAX: +41 21 882 55 24
CONTACT: Phillеppe Nicole

WIND

ENFLO SYSTEMS AG
Lowenstrasse 16,
CH-8280 Kreuzlingen, Switzerland
TEL: +41-71-6 70 11 44
FAX: +41-71-6 70 11 45
E-MAIL: info@enflo-systems.com
WEB: http://www.enflo-systems.com
CONTACT: Dirk Suess

INTERWIND LTD
Duchzelweg 5,
CH-8053 Zurich, Switzerland
TEL: 41 1 383 16 27
FAX: +41 1 383 04 65
E-MAIL:interwind@compuserve.com
WEB:http://www.interwind.ch
CONTACT : Mr. Mehmet

SUNWIND-ENERGY
Wind Energy Conversion Systems,
15 Chemin du Tirage,
Ch-1299 Crans-pres-Celigny,
Switzerland
TEL: +41227763037
FAX: +41227763037
CONTACT: Gerard Hollinger

BIOMASS

BERTRAMS CHEMICAL PLANTS LTD
P O Box 142, Eptingerstrabe 41,
CH-4132, Muttenz, Switzerland
TEL : +41 16 467 5353
FAX : +41 16 467 5300
WEB : www.bertrams.ch
CONTACT : H Wiist

CSD INGENIEURE UND GEOLOGEN AG
Hessstrasse 27d,
CH-3097 Liebefeld/Bern, Switzerland
TEL: +41 31 970 35 35
FAX: +41 31 970 35 36
E-MAIL: bern@csd.ch
WEB: http://www.csd.ch
CONTACT: Bernhard Matter

HOBAG BRIENZ AG FÜR AUTOMATISCHEFEUERUNGEN
Lauenenstrasse 51, 3855 Brienz,
Switzerland
TEL: +41 33 951 3272
FAX: +41 33 951 3604
E-MAIL: info@hobag.ch
WEB: http://www.hobag.ch
CONTACT: Stefan Schramli

INNOPLANA UMWELTTECHNIK AG
Hgh-Tech-Center I,
Lohstampfestrasse
11, 8274 Tagerwilen, Switzerland
TEL: +41 71 6 66 72 05
FAX: +41 71 6 66 72 70
E-MAIL: 113321.511@compuserve.com
WEB:http://www.high-tech-center.ch/innoplana.ut

TIBA AG
Hauptstrasse 147,
4416 Bubendorf, Switzerland
TEL: +41 61 935 17 10
FAX: +41 61 931 11 61
E-MAIL:tiba@tiba.ch
WEB:http://www.tiba.ch
CONTACT:H P Speringer

COGENERATION

CATERPILLAR SARL
76, Route de Frontenex 76, Case
Postale 6000, 1211 Geneve 6,
Switzerland
TEL : +41 22 849 46 86
FAX : +41 22 849 41 39
TELEX : 413 323
CONTACT : Robert A Koval

DIMAG ENERGIE AG
Bachmatten 5, 4435 NiederdorfSwitzerland
TEL: +41 61 956 24 24
FAX: +41 61 956 24 95
WEB: http://www.menag-group.com
CONTACT: Mr Jaquiery

ECOPOWER ENERGY SOLUTIONS AG
Bozingenstrasse 39,
2500 Biel Bienne 4, Switzerland
TEL: +41 3234 42009
FAX: +41 3234 16563
E-MAIL: info@ecopower.ch
WEB: http://www.ecopower.ch

TUMA TURBOMACH SA
Via Campagna 15, 6595 Riazzino,
Switzerland
TEL: +41 91 851 1511
FAX: +41 91 851 15 55
E-MAIL: sales@turbomach.com
WEB: http://www.turbomach.com
CONTACT: Mr Balinieri

SWITZERLAND

ELECTRIC VEHICLES

SUNELAGSOLAR - ELCTRIC CARS
Brandriestrasse 38,
8307 Effretikon, Switzerland
TEL: +41 52 32 80 60
FAX: +41 52 32 80 88
CONTACT:Thomas Eichenberger

SMALL HYDRO

BRUN (RENE) ALTERNATIVE TECHNIK AG
CH-7015 Tamins, Switzerland
TEL : +41 8 641 2537
FAX : +41 8 641 2374
CONTACT : R Brun

HYDRO VEYEY SA
Rue des Deux-Gares 6,
1800 Vevey, Switzerland
TEL: +41 21 925 7700
FAX: +41 21 925 7703
E-MAIL: sales@hydro.ch
CONTACT: Peter Magauer

WASTE TO ENERGY

KOMPOGAS AG
Rohrstrasse 36,
8152 Glattbrugg, Switzerland
TEL: +41 809 7100
FAX: 41 809 7110
E-MAIL: info@kompogas.ch
WEB: http://www.kompogas.ch
CONTACT : Mr. B. Sommarilla

TOSCANO-BERNARDI-FREY AG - TBF
Turnerstrasse 25, 8006 Zurich,
Switzerland
TEL: +41 1 363 2636
FAX: +41 1 363 7417
E-MAIL:tbf@tbf.ch
CONTACT:L Pelloni

VON ROLL ENVIRONMENTAL TECHNOLOGY LTD
Environmental Engineering Division,
Hardturmstrasse 133, PO Box 760,
8037 Zurich, Switzerland
TEL: +41 1 277 11 11
FAX: +41 1 277 13 13
WEB: http://www.vonroll.ch/inova
CONTACT: Ursula Schalfher-Zinski

ENERGY EFFICIENCY

ENERGIESTADT ENERGY CITY
Barenwil 195,
CH-4438 Lagenbruck, Switzerland
TEL: +41 61 922 0830
FAX: +41 61 922 0831
CONTACT : R Horbaty

GARTENMANNENGINEERING SA
zi La Veyre den- Haut,
1806 St Leger, Switzerland
TEL: + 41 21 943 65 65
FAX: + 41 21 963 65 66
CONTACT : Andri Lapport

HELBLING ENGINEERING AG
Hohlstrasse 610,
8048 Zurich, Switzerland
TEL: +41 1 438 18 11
FAX: +41 1 438 18 10
E-MAIL: hiu@helbling.ch
WEB: http://www.helbling.ch
CONTACT: Rainer Bendel

INFOENERGIE
Rue de Tivoli 16, CH - 2000
Neuchatel, Switzerland
TEL: +3 32 889 6720
FAX: +3 32 889 6060
E-MAIL: service.energie@ne.ch
WEB: http://www.ne.ch/energie
CONTACT: Jean-LucJuvet

MULTI ENERGIE AG - HEATPUMPS MANUFACTURE
Wiesentalstr, 20 8355 Aadorf,Switzerland
TEL: +41 52 365 1266
FAX: +41 52 365 3851
EMAIL:info@multienergie.ch
WEB:http://www.multienergie.ch

FINANCE / BANKING

VTZ GREEN MONEY FOR THE BLUE PLANET LTD
Bahnhofsplatz 9, 8023 Zurich,
Switzerland
TEL: +41 1 226 45 45
FAX: +41 1 226 45 46
CONTACT: Martin Brenner

ASSOCIATION

ARBEITSGEMEINSCHAFT WÄRMEPUMPEN - AWP
Konradstrasse 9, 8023 Zurich,
Switzerland
TEL : +41 1 271 90 90
FAX : +41 1 271 92 92
EMAIL : gerster@igp.ch
WEB : http://www.igp.ch
CONTACT : Kurt Egli

ASSOCIATION ROMANDEDES PROFESSIONNELS DE L'ENERGIE SOLARIE - PROMES
Case postale 6, 2013 Colombier,
Switzerland
TEL : +41 32 843 49 88
FAX : +41 32 843 49 85
CONTACT : Sabelle Opan

GLOBAL - ASSOCIATION FOR PROMOTION OF SOLAR TECHNOLOGY
Burggasse 18,
CH-4132 Muttenz,
Switzerland
TEL : + 41 61 462 24 24
FAX : + 41 61 462 24 24
E-MAIL : globosol@magiconline.ch

VSZ - VERBAND SCHWEIZ ZIEGELINDUSTRIE
Postfach,
8035 Zurich,
Switzerland
TEL: +41 1 361 96 50
FAX: +41 1361 02 05
E-MAIL: info@swissbrick.ch
WEB: http://www.swissbrick.ch
CONTACT: Dr. WP Weller

GOVERNMENT

WORLD HEALTH ORGANISATION
Via Appia,
1211 Geneve 27,
Switzerland
TEL: +41 22 791 2111
FAX: +41 22 791 4193
E-MAIL: zaffranm@who.ch
WEB: http://www.who.ch
CONTACT: Michel Zaffran

RESEARCH & DEVELOPMENT

BERNERFACHHOCHSCHULE HTA BGURGDORF
Electrical Engineering Department / Photovoltaics Laboratory, Jloweb 1
CH-3400, Burgdorf,
Switzerland
TEL : +41 34 426 6811
FAX : +41 34 426 6813
E-MAIL:heinrich.haeberlin@hta-ba.bfh.ch
WEB : www.hta-bu.bfh.ch
CONTACT : Dr. Heinrich Haberlin

BRUNNER (DR) & PARTNER AG
IndustriestraBe 5, CH-5432,
Neuenhof, Switzerland
TEL : +41 56 410 0666
FAX : +41 56 410 0669
E-MAIL : bru@twi.ch
CONTACT : Robert Brunner

BUREAU D'ETUDES KELLER BURNIER
Chemin du Renolly,
1175 Lavigny,
Switzerland
TEL : +41 21 808 64 29
FAX : +41 21 808 53 30
CONTACT : L Keller

DR EICHEIR & PAULI AG
Viktoriastrasse 69,
3000 Bern 25,
Switzerland
TEL : + 41 31 333 11 91
FAX : + 41 31 332 531
CONTACT : Mr. Berhnard Eggen

ECOLEPOLYTECHNIQUE FED DE LAUSANNE
LESO-PB, LESO-Laboratorie d'Energie Solarie, Batiment LESO Ecublens
CH-1015, Lausanne,
Switzerland
TEL : + 41 21 693 4545
FAX : + 41 21 693 2722
WEB : http://www.lescomail.epfl.ch
CONTACT : Christian Roecker

ENERCONOM AG
Hochfeldstrasse 32, 3012 Bern,
Switzerland
TEL : +41 31 306 11 11
FAX : +41 31 306 11 66
CONTACT : Jan Chuard

ENSOFOR SA
Energia Solare e Forestale,
6986, Curio,
Switzerland
TEL : +41 91 606 2424
FAX: +41 91 606 2967
CONTACT : Leon Jaccord

ENTECAG CONSULTING & ENGINEERING
Bahnhofstr 5,
90000 St. Gallen,
Switzerland
TEL : +41 71 228 1020
FAX: +41 228 1030
E-mail : main@entec.ch
WEB: http://www.entec.ch

SOLAR ENERGY AND BULDING PHYSICS LABORATORY
Swiss Federal Institute of Technology
LESO-PB/EPFL,
1015 Lausanne
Switzerland
TEL:+41 21 693 45 45
FAX:+41 21 693 27 22
E-MAIL:scartezzini@epfl.ch
WEB:http://lesowww.epfl.ch
CONTACT:Prof Jean-Louis Scartezzini

SOLARCO SA
Av du Moulins,
1110 Morges,
Switzerland
TEL:+41 21 802 1062
FAX:+41 21 803 0077
WEB:http://www.solarco.ch
CONTACT:Jean-Claude Enderlin

UNIVERSITY OF NEUCHATEL IMT
Thin-Film Silicon and Photovoltaic Group, Brequel 2, 2000 Neuchatel,
Switzerland
TEL: +41 32 718 33 38
FAX: +41 32 718 32 01
E-MAIL: steve.golay@inst-unine.ch
WEB: http://
www.micromorph.unine.ch
CONTACT: Steve Golay

NGO's

CENTRO ECOLIGOCO VOMANTURA
Strada del Lucomagno 6718
Acquacalda TI, Switzerland
TEL : +41 91 872 2610
FAX : +41 91 872 2620
E-MAIL : iferrari@tinet.ch
WEB : http://www.tinet.ch/
acquacalda
CONTACT : Luigi Ferrari

CONSULTANTS

ARCHITECTUR ENERGIE & UMWELT GMBH
Kirchstrasse 1,
CH-8304 Wallisellen,
Switzerland
TEL : +41 1 8831717
FAX : +41 1 883 1713
EMAIL : robert.hastings@freesurf.ch
CONTACT : Robert Hastings

BASLER & HOFMANN INGENIEURE UND PLANER AG
Forchstraßle 395, CH-8029,
Zurich, Switzerland
TEL : +41 1 387 11 22
FAX : +41 1 387 11 00
E-MAIL : balser-hofmann@bhz.ch
WEB : http://www.bhz.ch
CONTACT : Dr. Charles Fillenex

BONNARD & GARDEL INGENIEURS- CONSEILS SA
Avenue de Cour 61,
1001 Lausanne, Switzerland
TEL: +41 21 618 11 11
FAX: +41 21 618 11 22
WEB: http://www.bonnardgardel.ch
CONTACT: Dominique Noir

BOSCO BÜELER GMBH
Building Ecology/Building Biology.
St. Galler Strasse 28,
9230 Fawil, Switzerland
TEL : +41 71 393 22 47
FAX : +41 71 393 22 56
E-MAIL :bobueler@gibbeco.org
WEB : http://www.gibbeco.org
CONTACT : Bosco Bueler

BUCH HOFER BARBEAG
Zoilikerstr 128, 8008, Zurich
Switzerland
TEL : +41 1 422 60 40
FAX : +41 1 422 70 90

BUREAU D'ETUDES KELLER BURNIER
Chemin du Renolly, 1175 Lavigny,
Switzerland
TEL : +41 21 808 64 29
FAX : +41 21 808 53 30
CONTACT : L Keller

BURO N+I
Thunstrasse 115, Postfach 130,
3000 Bern 16, Switzerland
TEL : +41 31 350 0000
FAX : +41 31 44 77 56
E-MAIL : n+l@email.ch
CONTACT : Markers Heimlicher

E 4 TECHBAVEN & FORADINI
Ave Louis Ruchonet 57,
1003 Lausanne, Switzerland
TEL : + 41 21331 15 79
FAX : + 41 21331 15 61
E-MAIL : info@e4tech.com
Web : www.e4tect.com
CONTACT : Flavio Foradini

ELECTROWATT ENGINEERING AG
Hardturmstrasse 161, 8037
Zurich, Switzerland
TEL : +41 1 355 55 55
FAX : +41 1 355 55 56
E-MAIL :toni.kalin@ewe.ch
WEB : http://www.ewe.ch
CONTACT : Toni Kalin

ENECOLO AG
Lindhofstr 52,
8617 Mönchaltorf, Switzerland
TEL : +41 1 994 90 91
FAX : +41 1 994 90 05
E-MAIL : info@enelco.ch
WEB : http://www.solastrom.ch
CONTACT : P Toggweiler

EREP SA
Chemin du Coteau 28, 1123
Aclens, Switzerland
TEL: +41 21 869 9887
FAX: + 41 21 869 9794
E-MAIL: erep@iprolink.ch
CONTACT : George Spoehrle

ERTE INGENIEURS CONSEILS SA
Rue du Tunnel 15, 1227 Carouge
Geneve, Switzerland
TEL: + 41 22 309 08 50
FAX: + 41 22 309 08 60
E-MAIL : contact@erte.ch
WEB: http://www.ertec.ch
CONTACT : George Spoehrle

SWITZERLAND

GRAF(DR)AG UMWELTSCHUTZ UND WARMETECHINK
Privatstraße 10, 4563 Gerlafinga
Switzerland
TEL :+ 41 32 674 45 11
FAX :+ 41 32 674 45 00
E-MAIL : info@grafag.ch
WEB : grafag.ch
CONTACT : Dr. Jeilrg Liechti

HYDRELEC AG FÜR ENERGIETECHNIK
Alte Villigerstrase 184, 5318
Mandach, Switzerland
TEL: +41 56 284 22 66
FAX: +41 56 284 22 66
CONTACT: Arnold P Engel

INSTITUT BAU UND ENERGIE - IBE
Hoheweg 17, 3006 Bern,
Switzerland
TEL: +41 31 352 57 57
FAX: +41 31 352 57 30
CONTACT: Dr Andreas Wyss

LAPPERT ANDRE - ISOL CONSULT
1833 Les Avants/Montreux,
Switzerland
TEL: +41 21 964 67 43
FAX: +41 21 964 67 43

LEEE - TISO
DCT, SUPSI, 6952 Canobbio,
Switzwerland
TEL: +41 91 940 47 78
FAX: +41 91 942 88 65
E-MAIL: cereghet@dct_supsi.ch
WEB: http://leee.dct_supis.ch
CONTACT: Nerio Cereghetti

METEOTEST
Applied Meteorology,
Fabrikstrasse 14,
CH-3012 Bern, Switzerland
TEL: +41 31 307 26 26
FAX: +41 31 307 26 10
E-MAIL: office@meteotest.ch
WEB: http:.//www.meteotest.ch
CONTACT: Martin Baumgartner

MINDER ENERGY CONSULTING
Ruchweid 22,
8917 Oberlunkhofen,
Switzerland
TEL: +41 56 640 1464
FAX: +41 56 640 1462
E-MAIL: rudolf.minder@bluewin.ch
WEB: http://www.minder-energy.ch
CONTACT: Dr Rudolf Minder

NOVA ENERGIE GMBH
Schachenallee 29, CH-5000 Aarau,
Switzerland
TEL: +41 62 834 03 00
FAX: +41 62 834 03 23
E-MAIL:
office.aarau@novaenergie.ch
WEB: http://www.novaenergie.ch
CONTACT: Pius Husser

PLANAIR
Cret 108a,2314 La Sagne,
Switzerland
TEL: + 41 32 931 88 28
FAX : + 41 32 931 88 28
E-MAIL: info@planair.ch
WEB:http://www.planair.ch
CONTACT : Pierre Renaud

SOPRA SOLARPRAXIS AG
HombergstraBe 4,
4466 Ormalingen, Switzerland
TEL: +41 61 985 96 10
FAX: +41 61 985 98 11
E-MAIL: sopra@bluewin.ch
CONTACT: Vollmin

SPRING INGENIEURE A G
Langgasse 9, 3600 Thun,
Switzerland
TEL: +41 33 225 24 24
FAX: +41 33 225 24 90
E-MAIL: Siag@mus.ch
CONTACT: Ueli Spring

SYNETRUMAG
Peslalozzistrasse 10,
3280 Murten,
Switzerland
TEL: +41 26 672 90 00
FAX: +41 26 672 90 09
E-MAIL:info@synetrum.ch
WEB:http://www.synettum.ch
CONTACT:Charles Olivier

TBF + PARTNER AG
Turnerstrasse 25, 8006 Zurich,
Switzerland
TEL: +4113632636
FAX: +4113611496
E-MAIL: tbf@tbf.ch
CONTACT : L Pelloni

TNC CONSULTING AG
Seestrasse 129,
Postfach, 8810
Horgen, Switzerland
TEL: +41 1 725 3900
FAX: +41 1 7701050
E-MAIL:nordmann@tnc.ch
WEB:http://www.tnc.ch
CONTACT: Thomas Nordmann

TRACHSELSA INGENIEURSCONSEILS
Charles-Perrier 7, 2074 Marin,
Switzerland
TEL: +41 32 753 10 40
FAX: +41 32 753 10 40
CONTACT: Chirstian Trachsel

DESIGN & ENGINEERING

ASSOCIATION HUMANITEL
24 rue des Maraithers, 1211
Geneve, Switzerland
TEL : +41 22 321 00 29
CONTACT : Max Scheider

BAUMGARTNER (THOMAS) INGENIEURBURO FUR
HAUSTECHNIK Bettlistrasse 35,
8600 Dubendorf, Switzerland
TEL : +41 1 820 2757
FAX : +41 1 820 2822
CONTACT : Thomas Baumgartner

BEHREND AGHEIZUNG-LUFTUNG
Eirneldingerweg 43, 4016 Basel,
Switzerland
TEL : +41 61 692 66 88
CONTACT : Behrend

BERNARD MATTHEY INGENIEURS CONSEILS SA
CH-2205, Montezillion-NE,
Switzerland
TEL : +41 32 731 53 53
FAX : +41 32 731 44 60
E-MAIL :info@masai-conseils.com
WEB : http://www.masai-conseils.com
CONTACT : Bernard Matthey

BSI BUREAU DE SERVICE ET D'INGENIERIE
Primerose 27, 1007 Lausanne,
Switzerland
TEL : +41 21 617 17 66
FAX : +41 21 617 17 80
E-MAIL : bsi@pingnet.ch
WEB : http://
www.members.pingnet.ch/bsi
CONTACT : Bernard Saugy

CYPHELLY & CIE
P O Box 18, 2416 Les Brenets
Switzerland
TEL : +41 26 677 24 43
E-MAIL :cyphelly@ran.es

ECOLING AG ECOLOGY ENGINEERING
FreistraBe 47, 8032, Zurich Switzerland
TEL : + 41 1 251 40 46
FAX : + 41 1 251 41 57
E-MAIL : ecolog@ecoling.ch
CONTACT : Bruno Berger

ENERGY ATLAS MAX BLATTER
Gutenbergstrasse 1, 4142
Muchenstein, Switzerland
TEL: +41 61 411 58 50
FAX: +41 61 411 58 55
E-MAIL: info@energie-atlas.ch
WEB: http://www.energie-atlas.ch
CONTACT : Mrs. Renu Kreuter

EN-SOLAR
Hubel/Wangelen 153 A, CH-3615
Heimenschwand, Switzerland
TEL : +41 33 453 17 58
CONTACT : Dr. Peter Case

HALDIMANN HEINZ INGENIEURBURO FUR HEIZUNGS - UND SONNENENERGIEANLAGEN
Kuferweg 9, 8912 Obfelden.
Switzerland
TEL : + 41 1 761 44 53
FAX :+ 41 1 760 09 30
CONTACT : Heinz Haldimann

INSTITUT BAU UND ENERGIE - IBE
Hoheweg 17, 3006 Bern,
Switzerland
TEL: +41 31 352 57 57
FAX: +41 31 352 57 30
CONTACT: Dr Andreas Wyss

INTERPLAN ENERGEIETECHNIK AG
Jungfrauweg 10,
3177 Laupen, Switzerland
TEL: 41 31 740 82 82
FAX: +41 31 747 95 79
CONTACT : Peter Moser

ITECO ENGINEERING LTD
Alte Obfelderstrasse 68,
8910 Affoltern am Albis,
Switzerland
TEL: +41 762 18 18
FAX: +41 1 762 18 15
E-MAIL:iteco@itecho.ch
WEB:http://www.iteco.ch
CONTACT : Christoph Mor

MECANIX SARL
1880 Fenalet Sur Bex, Switzerland
TEL: +41 244 63 12 70
FAX: +41 244 63 16 00
E-MAIL: ppvica@infopro.spb.su
CONTACT: Pieree-Etienne

METRON ARCHITEKTURBÜRO AG
Stahlrain 2, 5200 Drugg,Switzerland
TEL: +41 56 460 9111
FAX: +41 56 460 9100
CONTACT: Heini Glawer

NEK UMWEL TTECHNIKAG
Clausiusstrase 41,
8033 Zurich, Switzerland
TEL: +41 1 261 07 07
FAX: +41 1 261 08 47
E-MAIL: info@nek.ch
WEB: http://www.nek.ch
CONTACT: Dr Christoph Kapp

SUTTER & SIEGRIST AG
Architecture, Stationsweg 3, 5702
Niederlenz, Switzerland
TEL: +41 62 891 31 50
Fax: +41 62 891 51 00
CONTACT:HU Sutter

TRITEC AG
Holeestrasse 145,
4054 Basel, Switzerland
TEL: +41 61 307 9933
FAX: +41 61 307 9939
E-MAIL: info@tritec.ch
WEB: http://www.tritec.ch
CONTACT: Georges Hefti

OTHERS

ARBI-ARBEITSGEMEINSCHAFT BIOENERGIE GMBH
Lattidistr 8, 6340 Baar, Switzerland
TEL : +41 41 7632121
FAX : +41 41 7632133
EMAIL : arbi@biogas.ch
WEB : http://www.biogas.ch/arbi
CONTACT : Werner Edelmann

BG BONNARD & GARDEL INGENIEURS-CONSEIL SA
I B Avenue De Chatlaine,
Case Postale, 1219 Chatelaine,
Switzerland
TEL : +41 22 97 92 310
FAX : +41 22 79 62 037
CONTACT : Michel Giannoni

BIARSA
1948 Lourtier, Switzerland
TEL : +41 27779 11 11
FAX : +41 27779 11 12
E-MAIL :biar@bluewin.ch
WEB : http://www.biar.com
CONTACT : Guy Marson

CALONDER ENERGY AG
UberlandstraBe 9,
Postfach 834,
8953, Dietikon,
Switzerland
TEL : +41 1 740 99 44

CRANE & CO INC (EUROPE)
Thurgauerstrasse 54, CH-8050
Zurich, Switzerland
TEL : +41 1 308 29 99
FAX : +4 1 308 29 98
E-MAIL : crane@t-online.de
WEB : http://www.crane.com
CONTACT : Balz C Miller

CSD INGENIEURE UND GEOLOGEU AG
Konasumstrasse 20,
3007 Bern,
Switzerland
TEL : +41 31 282 30 10
FAX : +41 31 383 13 43
E-MAIL : bern@csd.ch
WEB : http://www.csd.ch
CONTACT : Bernhard Matter

CSD INGENIEURS COUNSEILS SA
Chemin de Montelly 78,
CP 60, 1000 Lausanne, 20,
Switzerland
TEL : +41 21 620 70 01
FAX : +41 21 620 70 01
E-MAIL : lausanne@csd.ch
WEB : http://www.csd.ch
CONTACT : Felix Schmidt

INTEGRAL WÄRMEPUMPEN AG -IWAG
Paracelsusstrasse 1, 3072
Ostermundigen 2,
Switzerland
TEL: +41 31 931 43 55
FAX: +41 31 931 85 30
CONTACT: Dr Martin Wymann

IWS SOLAR AG IMPORT/ EXPORT
Wilen 18, 8494 Bauma,
Switzerland
TEL: +41 52 386 2882
FAX: +41 52 386 2194
E-MAIL:iwssolar@
swissonline.ch
WEB:http:/www.iwssolar.ch
CONTACT : Daniel Sommer

SOLAR KELLENBERGER
Haupstraße 67, CH_8260
Wagenhausen,
Switzerland
TEL : +41 52 741 3588
FAX : +41 52 741 35 3588
CONTACT : Karl Kellenberger

SOLARONIX SA
Rue de l'Ouriette 129 ,
1170 Aubonne,
Switzerland
TEL : +41 21 821 22 80
FAX : +41 21 821 22 89
E-MAIL : andreas@solaronix.com
CONTACT : AF Meyer

SUPPLIERS

BATTERIES/INVERTERS

SINEL SA
Via Pisone 22, CH-6616 Losone ITI, Switzerland
TEL : +41 91 859 1731
FAX : +41 91 859 1732
E-MAIL : sg@imv.ch
CONTACT : Claudio Giovannini

SPUTNIK ENGINEERING AG
HaupstraBe 135, 2560 Nidau Switzerland
TEL : + 41 32 332 20 60
FAX : + 41 32 332 20 69
E-MAIL : sputnik@solarmax.com
WEB : http://www.solarmax.com
CONTACT : Christophe von Bergen

STUDER INNOTEC
Rue des Casernes 57,
CH-1950 Sion Switzerland
TEL: +41272056080
FAX: 41272056088
E-MAIL: info@studer-inno.com
WEB: http://www.studer-inno.com

INSTRUMENTATION

ALPHA REAL LTD
Feldeggstrasse 89,8008 Zurich, Switzerland
TEL: +41 1 383 0208
FAX: +41 1 383 1895
E-MAIL: alphareal@access.ch
CONTACT: Dr Marcus Real

MARKASUBAG
Lindenhofstrasse 34,
4000 Basel 2, Switzerland
TEL: +41 61 278 96 66
FAX: +41 61 278 96 77
E-MAIL: info@markasub.ch
WEB: http://www.markasub.ch
CONTACT: Martin Kaspar

MULTI-CONTACT AG BASEL
Stockbrunnernrain 8,
4123 Alischwil 1, Switzerland
TEL: +41 61 306 55 55
FAX: +41 61 306 55 56
EMAIL:mailbox@multi-contact.com
WEB:http://www.multi-contact.com
CONTACT:Peter Springmann

PASAN/BELVAL
Sous- La- Roche, case postale 5,
2042 Valangin, Switzerland
TEL: +41 32 857 2393
FAX: +41 32 857 2295
E-MAIL: info@belval.com
WEB: http://www.belval.com/pasan
CONTACT: Pierre-R Beljean

RHYNER ENERGIE
Rue Tabac-Rhone 12, 1893 Illarsez, Switzerland
TEL: +41244663586
FAX: +41244663587
E-MAIL: renergie@bluewin.ch
CONTACT: Mr. Rhyner

UNIVERSITY CENTER FOR THE STUDY OF ENERGY PROBLEMS – CUEPE
University of Geneva,
Batelle Batimet A,
Route de Drize 7,
1227 Carouge / GE Switzerland
TEL: +41227059661
FAX: +41227059639
E-MAIL:
andre.mermoud@cuepe.unige.ch
WEB: http://www.pvsyst.com
CONTACT: Mrs. Andre Mermoud

GLASS

INTERFLOAT CORPORATION
Furst Franz Josef-Strasse, 9493 Mauren, Switzerland
TEL: +41 75 373 44 11
FAX: +41 75 373 44 13
CONTACT: Silke Wustner

CONSTRUCTION SERVICES

FORALITH AG
Bohr und Bergbautechnik, St Galler Strasse 12, CH-9201 Gossau SG, Switzerland
TEL: +41 71 388 89 29
FAX: +41 71 388 89 25
E-MAIL: foralith@foralith.ch
CONTACT : Stefan Berli

HELLER & PARTNERS
Seestraße 27, 8810 Horgen,Switzerland
TEL: +41 1 725 41 45
CONTACT: Walter Heller

ULRICH AMMANNAG
Energy Systems,Hasenmattstrasse 2, CH-4901 Lagenthal, Switzerland
TEL : +41 63 29 61 61
FAX : +41 63 22 68 13

OTHERS (S)

ABB ENERGY LEASING SARL
Zurich Branch, Thurgauerstrasse 54, PO Box 8242,8050,Zurich, Switzerland
TEL: +41 1 306 8942
FAX: +41 1 306 8966
E-MAIL: jean-louis.guiette@ch.abb.com
CONTACT: Jean-Louis Guiette-

BONNARD & GARDEL INGENIEURS CONSELS SA
Avenue de Cour 61,
& Lausanne, Switzerland
TEL : +41 21 618 1122
FAX : +41 21 618 11 22
E-MAIL : info.bgbonnardgardel.ch
WEB : http://www.bonna.garde.ch

CENTRE UNIVERSAITAIRE D'ET UDEDES PROBLEMES DE L'ENERGIE - CUEPE
University of Geneva, Batelle Batiment, A. Route de Drize 7, 1227 Carouge/GE, Switzerland
TEL : +41 22 705 9650
FAX : +41 22 705 9639
E-MAIL : andre.mermould@GAP-E-unige.ch
WEB : http://www.pvsyst.com

COMBOGLIAG HEIZUNG
MissionsstraBe I19,
Switzerland
TEL : +41 61 261 5877

DIMAG ENERGIEI AG
Bachmatten S. 4435,
Niederdorf. Switzerland
TEL : + 41 61 956 24 24
FAX : + 41 51 956 24 25
CONTACT : Mr. Jaguiery

ENERGIEBURO
Limmatstrasse 230, CH-8005 Zurich, Switzerland
TEL: +41 1 242 80 60
FAX: +41 1 242 80 86
E-MAIL: info@energleburo.ch
WEB : ww.energieburo.ch

ENUMPLANAG
Bahnhofstrasse 45,
8500 Frauenfeld, Switzerland
TEL : +41 52 720 42 40
FAX: +41 52 722 41 40
E-MAIL : enumplan@swissonline.ch
CONTACT : Johannes Forster

FMMINEGNIEURS SA
Less Vernets, CH-2035 Corcelles, Switzerland
TEL: +41 32 7324 111
FAX: +41 32 7324 459
E-MAIL: info@fmn-ing.ch

GAS AND WATER METER MANUFACTURING. GWF
Obergrundstrasse 119, CH-6002 Lucerne, Switzerland
TEL: +41 41 319 5050
FAX: + 41 41 3160 6087
CONTACT : Juan Carlos Peleteiro

INTERNATIONAL CLEAN ENERGY CONSORTIUM - ICEC AG
P O B 92B,
CH-8055 Zurich,
Switzerland
TEL: +41 1 463 9252
FAX: +41 1 463 0252
E-MAIL: info@icec.ch
WEB: http://www.icec.ch
CONTACT: G R Grob

INTERSSENVERBAND KLEINKRAFT VERK - ISKB
BP, CH-8910 Affoltern-am-aibis,
Switzerland
TEL: +41 1 776 1101
FAX: +41 1 776 1102
E-MAIL: iskb@bluewin.ch
WEB: http://www.iskb.ch
CONTACT: Hanspeter Leutwiler

We kindly request more listings in this country.

You can submit any additional listings by E-mail: unisun@vsnl.com

Fax: 91 80 22289294

We will include these in the next edition

Kindly inform us of any errors and omissions in the listings by:

E-mail: unisun@vsnl.com

Fax: 91 80 22289294

RESEARCH & DEVELOPMENT

UKRGELIOPROM SCIENTIFIC AND INNOVATION ENTERPRISE
Ap 16, Kreschatik 8,
Kiev 01001, Ukraine
TEL : +380 44 229 03 36
FAX : +380 44 2290336
E-MAIL : ukrgelio@ikr.carrier.kiev.ua
CONTACT : Dr Vyacheslav Moyseyenko

NGO's

GREEN HELP INTERNATIONAL
13-16 Malozhitomirskaya Str,
252001 Kiev, Ukraine
TEL : + 380 44 225 64 73
FAX : + 380 44 212 5968
CONTACT : Alexander V

We kindly request more listings in this country.

You can submit any additional listings by E-mail: unisun@vsnl.com

Fax: 91 80 2289294

We will include these in the next edition

Kindly inform us of any errors and omissions in the listings by:

E-mail: unisun@vsnl.com

Fax: 91 80 2289294

SOLAR THERMAL

AEROTRON
Achloa, Duneaves Road,
Aberfeldy
Perthshire PH15 2LS, UK
TEL: +44 1877 830478
FAX: +44 1887 830478
CONTACT: J Roger White

AES LTD
AES Building, Lea Road,
Forres 1V36 1AU, UK
TEL: +44 1309 676911
FAX: +44 1309 671086
E-MAIL: info@AESsolar.co.uk
WEB: http://www.gaia.org/findhorn/eco/solar.html
CONTACT: George Goudsmit

ALFA LAVAL LTD
Thermal Division,
Theta House Doman Road,
Camberley,
Surrey GU15 3DN,UK
TEL: +44 1276 63383
FAX: +44 1276 413601
E-MAIL: thermal.uk@alfalaval.com
CONTACT: Paul Kellet

AMPLIFLAIRE
Off The Square Trade Centre,
Kelso, Roxburghshire
TD5 7JH,UK
TEL: +44 1573 225 209
FAX: +44 1573 225 886
CONTACT: Dean Warwick

BARUM SOLAR HEAT
5 Burlington Grove,
Newport,
Barnstaple,
Devon EX32, 98U, UK
TEL : +44 1271 343377
FAX : +44 1271 343377

BREDONDALE SOLAR
5 Smiths Way, Pershore,
Worcestershire WR 10 IQP,
UK
TEL : +44 1386 561 133
FAX : +44 1386 556 555
CONTACT : Gary Fowles

BRITANNIA HEAT TRANSFER
Units 15-20 Coleshill Industrial
Estate, Station Road,
Coleshlll,
Birmingham B46 1JP, UK
TEL: +44 1675 466060
FAX: +44 1675 467675
E-MAIL: info@britheat.co.uk

CLAYTON THERMAL PRODUCTS LTD
5 Boleyn Court, Manor Park
Runcorn, Cheshire WA7 1SR, UK
TEL: +44 1928 579009
FAX: +44 1928 571155
E-MAIL: claytonindustries@btinternet.com
CONTACT: John S Hooson

COMBINED POWER LTD
EnerG House, Daniel AdamsonRoad,
Manchester M5 2DT, UK
TEL: +44 161 745 7450
FAX: +44 161 745 7457
E-MAIL: sales@cpsl.co.uk
WEB: http://www.cpsl.co.uk
CONTACT: Nadine Wynter

COVRAD HEAT TRANSFER LTD
Sir Henry Parkes Road,
Canley, Coventry CVS 76BN, UK
TEL : +44 24 76 675 544
FAX : +44 24 76 767 029

DAWCUL LTD
42 West Street, Marlow,
Buckinghamshire SL7 2NB, UK
TEL : + 44 1628 472737
FAX : + 44 1628 890055
CONTACT : L Cremer-Evans

ENERGY ENGINEERING
Herons Reach, Cound Moor,
Shrewsbury, Shropshire SY5 6BB, UK
TEL : + 44 1694 731648
FAX: + 44 1694 731 696
E-MAIL : energy.engineering@btinternet.com
CONTACT : G Gough

FIELDWAY LTD T/A SOLAR ECONOMY
Croft Road, Crowborough, East
Sussex TN6 IDL, UK
TEL: +44 1892 655782
FAX: +44 1892 655792
CONTACT : Noel Parkinson

FILSOL LIMITED
Unit 15, Ponthenri Industrial Estate,
Ponthenri, Camarthenshire SA 15
5RA, UK
TEL: +44 1269 860979
FAX: +44 1269 860979
E-MAIL: filsol@infotrade.co.uk
CONTACT : Roy Blower

FOUNDATION BUSINESS CENTRES
Unit 39A Park Farm Industrial Estate,
Buntingford, Herts SG9 9AZ, UK
TEL: +44 1763 271271
FAX: +44 1763 271270
E-MAIL: joe@fbc.demon.co.uk
CONTACT: Mr J Zygmunt

HEARLE AND BROWN
53 Burford Road, Evesham,
Worcs WR11 5AG, UK
TEL: +44 1386 443826
CONTACT: Paul Brown

LAFARGE BRAAS RESEARCH AND DEVELOPMENT LTD
Sussex Manor Business Park,
Gatwick Road, Crawley,
Sussex RH10 2NG, UK
TEL: +44 1293 614 545
FAX: +44 1293 614 548
CONTACT: CJ Campbell

LUMENERGY LTD
Octagon Village, Chantmarle Cattistock
Dorchester, Dorset DT2 OHD, UK
TEL: +44 870 8704650
FAX: +44 870 8704651
WEB:http://www.lumenergy.com

M LYONS SOLAR
6 Henford Gardens, March,
Cambridgeshire PE15 8NT, UK
TEL: +44 1354 52740
FAX: +44 1354 52740
CONTACT: Michael Lyons

NAPIER UNIVERSITY
Energy Center, Dept of Mechanical
Engineering, 10, Calinton Road,
Edinburgh EH10, 5DT, UK
TEL: +44 131 455 2660
FAX: +44 131 455 2264
EMAIL:k.macgregor@napier.ac.uk
CONTACT:KerrMac Gregor

NAPS UNITED KINGDOM
PO Box 83, Abingdon,
Oxon OX14 2TB, UK
TEL: +44 1993 772359
FAX:+44 1993 779338
CONTACT: Mark Godwin

NATURAL ENERGY SYSTEMS
2 Arderon Court, Adelaide Street
Norwich, Norfolk,
NR2 4ER, UK
TEL: +44 1603 661863
FAX: +44 1603 618145
E-MAIL: solar@naten.freeserver.com
CONTACT: Alan Parsons

OSPREY CORPORATION LTD
Units 82-85 John Wilson Business
Park, Thanet Way,
Whitstable,
Kent CT5 3QU, UK
TEL: +44 1227 770979
FAX: +44 1227 770949
E-MAIL: osprey@dial.pipex.com
CONTACT: AS Belcher

POWERTECH SOLAR LTD
171A New Road, West Parley,
Dorset BH22 8ED, UK
TEL: +44 8707 3001 11
FAX: +44 8707 3002 22
E-MAIL: erh@solar.org.uk
WEB: http://www.eco-shop.co.uk
CONTACT: Eric Hawkins

RAYOTEC LTD
London Road, Sunningdale,
Berkshire SL5 0DJ, UK
TEL : +44 1344 874747
FAX : +44 1344 872030
E-MAIL : sabba@btinternet.com
WEB : http://www.thermomax.com
CONTACT : S Sabba

SANDVIK STEEL
Green Lane, Walsall,
West Midlands WS2 7BW, UK
TEL: +44 1922 728800
FAX: +44 1922 728827
WEB: http://www.steel.sandvik.com

SMART ENERGY UK LTD
282 Shrub End Road, Colchester,
Essex CO3 4RL, UK
TEL: +44 1206 516677
FAX: +44 1206 516678
E-MAIL: info@smartenergyuk.com
WEB:http://www.smartenergyuk.com
CONTACT: Allan Berry

SOLAGEN
14 Heathfield Road,
WestMoors, Ferndown,
Dorset BH22 0BG, UK
TEL:+44 1202 893 801
FAX:+44 1202 893 801
E-MAIL:solagen@compuserve.com
WEB:http://
www.ourworld.compuserve.com/
homepages/solagen
CONTACT:Tony Smith

SOLAR ENERGY SYSTEMS
4 Ross Street,Dunfermline,
Fife KY12 0An,UK
TEL:+44 1383 725 499
FAX:+44 1383 725499
E-MAIL:jimnorris@solarenergysysrems.co.uk
WEB:http://www.solarenergysystems.co.uk
CONTACT:Jim Norris

SOLAR SENSE
The Energy Park Sandy Lane
Pennard,SwanseaSE3 2EN, UK
TEL : +44 1 792 371690
FAX : +44 1792 371390
E-MAIL : info@solarsence.co.uk
WEB : http//www.solarsense.com.uk
CONTACT : Keith Roberts

SOLAR SERVICES LTD
18 Ringwood Road,
Ringwood,
Hampshire BH24 2NZ, UK
TEL: +44 1425 471711
FAX: +44 1425 471712
E-MAIL: sales@solarservices.co.uk
CONTACT: I K Clark

SOLAR TWIN LTD
15 King Street,
Chester CH 1 2AH, UK
TEL: +441244403404
FAX: +441244403654
E-MAIL: hi@solartwin.com
WEB: http://www.solartwin.com

SOLAR UK PARTNERS
41 The Street,
LT Clacton,
Essex CO16 9LD, UK
TEL : +44 1255 862611
CONTACT : Simon Anselmi

SOLAR WORKS
Frogs Hall Farm Lavenham,
Sudbury Suffolk CO 10 9QH, UK
TEL : +44 1787 247359
FAX : +44 1787 248458
CONTACT : Mark Norman

SOLARSENSE UK
8 Copford Lane, Long Ashton,
Bristol BS15 INF, UK
TEL : +44 1275 540112
FAX : +44 1275 540113
E-MAIL : solarsense@
cablenet.co.uk
CONTACT : Stephen Barrett

SUN MASTER SOLAR
Unit I Charmandean Center,
Forest Road, Worthing,
WestSussex BNI4
7HS, UK
TEL: +44 1903 231110
FAX: +44 1903 823252
E-MAIL:daveackroyd@
sunmastersolar.co.uk
WEB:http://
www.sunmastersolar.co.uk
CONTACT:D Ackroyd

SUNDWEL SOLAR LIMITED
7 Tower Road,
Glover Estate, Washington,
Tyne & Wear NE37 2SH, UK
TEL : +44 191 4163001
FAX : +44 191 4163001
E-MAIL : sundwel@aol.com
WEB : http//www.sundwel.com
CONTACT : Keith Wilkinson

SUNPOWERD ENERGY SYSTEMS LTD
90 Albert Road,
Southsea PO5 2SN, UK
TEL : +44 23 92 614 925
FAX : +44 23 92 812 890
E-MAIL : sean@sunpower.free
serve.co.uk
CONTACT : Seaan Cavendish

SUNRISE ENERGY
79 Barnhall Road, Tolleshunt
Knights,
Maldon, Essex CM9 8HD, UK
TEL: +44 1621 813131
FAX: +44 1621 813131
CONTACT:Allan Reason

SUNUSER LTD
157 Buslingthorpe Lane,
Leeds LS7 2DQ, UK
TEL: +44 113 262 0261
FAX: +44 113 262 3970
E-MAIL: solar@sunuser.co.uk
CONTACT: Miss Hayton

SUSTAINABLE ENGINE SYSTEMS LTD-SES
51 Artesian Road, London W2
5DB, UK
TEL: +44 20 7 792 2241
FAX: +44 20 7 792 2543
E-MAIL:hislo@msn.com
CONTACT: Drummond Hislop

TEXSTAR INTERNATIONAL LTD
Unit 1 Chaucer House,
Biscot Road
Luton, Bedfordshire LU3 IAX, UK
TEL: +44 1582 729 937
FAX: +44 1582 450 487
E-MAIL: sales@texstar-
uk.demon.co.uk
CONTACT: Vivek Gangoli

THE FRANKLIN COMPANY CONSULTANTS
192 Franklin Road
Birmingham,
B30 2HE, UK
TEL: +44 121 459 4826
FAX: +44 121 459 8206
E-MAIL: tfc@tfc-bham.demon.co.uk
WEB: http://www.demon.co.uk/tfc
CONTACT: Dr Leslie F Jesch

THERMOMAX GB LTD
Hawtin Park, Blackwood,
Gwent NP2 2EU, UK
TEL: +44 1443 862299
FAX: +44 1443 862288
E-MAIL:thermomaxw@aol.com
CONTACT: Dr V Tabatabai

THERMOMAX LTD
Balloo Crescent Bangor
BT19 7UP, UK
TEL : +44 28 9127 0411
FAX : +44 28 9127 0572
E-MAIL : thermomax@aol.com
WEB : http://www.thermomax.com
CONTACT : Kathy Byers

TOWNSON EXPANSION JOINTS
Alexandra Street, Hyde,
Cheshire SK14 1DY, UK
TEL: +441613679278
FAX: +441613679280
E-MAIL: townson@zen.co.uk
WEB: http://www.townson.co.uk

TTL DYNAMICS LTD
PO Box 1642, Salisbury,
Wiltshire SP2 0SE, UK
TEL: +44 1722 746800
FAX: +44 1722 6801
E-MAIL: sales@ttl-dynamics.com
WEB: http://www.ttl-dynamics.com

WELLMAN ROBEY LTD
Newfield Road, Oldbury,
West Midlands B69 3ET, UK
TEL: +44 121 552 3311
FAX: +44 121 552 4571
E-MAIL: sales@wellmanrobey.com
WEB: http://www.wellmanrobey.com
CONTACT: Ken Tidd

WESSEX SOLAR SYSTEMS
6 Parham Road, Talbot Village
Bournemouth,
Dorset BH10 4BB UK
TEL: +44 1202 517526
FAX: +44 1202 517526
CONTACT: Paul Kerr

SOLAR PHOTOVOLTAIC

ADAM HARVEY ASSOCIATES
8 Southmoor Road,
Oxford OX2 6RD, UK
TEL: +44 20 7681 2670
FAX: +44 20 7681 2670
E-MAIL: damharvey@compuserve.com
CONTACT: Dr Adam Harvey

BECO BATTERIES LTD
Beco Solar, 8-10,
Speedwell Units,
Nelson Road, Dartmouth,
Devon TQ6, 9SZ,
UK
TEL : +44 1803 833 636
FAX : +44 1803 835 379
E-MAIL :info@becosolar.com
WEB : http://www.becosolar.com
CONTACT : Brian Leighton

BECOSOLAR
BecoSolar, 8-10 Speedwell Units
Nelson Road Dartmouth Devon
TQ6 9SZ, UK
TEL: +44 1803 833 636
FAX: +44 1803 835 379
E-MAIL: info@becosolar.com
WEB: http://www.becosolar.com
CONTACT: Brain Leighton

BP SOLAR
PO Box191, Chertsey Road,Sunbury-on-Thames, Middlesex TW16 7XA, UK
TEL: +44 1932 764800
FAX: +44 1932 762686
E-MAIL: hammonm@bp.com
WEB: http://www.bpsolar.com

BTU EUROPE LTD
14 Armstrong Mall, Southwood
Summit Centre, Farnborough,
Hamsphire GUI 14 0NR, UK
TEL : +44 1252 660010
FAX : +44 1252 6600111
E-MAIL : sales@btu.co.uk
WEB : http://www.btu.com

CECAD LTD
37, Chadwick Close,
NorthFleet, Kent DA11 8SB, UK
TEL : +44 1474 357963
FAX : +44 1474 333027
E-MAIL : cecad2000@cs.com
CONTACT : Gary Reading

CRYSTALOX LTD
1 Limborough Road, Wantage,
Oxon OX12 9AJ, UK
TEL : +44 1235 770044
FAX : +44 1235 770111
E-MAIL :crystalox@crystalox.btinternet.com
CONTACT : Iain Dorrity

DABBROOK LTD
Dabbrook Power Systems, Unit 23,
Bells Marsh Road, Gorleston, Great
Yarmouth, Norfolk NR31 6PT, UK
TEL : + 44 1493 441711
FAX : + 44 1493 440322
E-MAIL : dabbrookltd@btinternet.com
WEB : http://www.btinternet.com/~dabbrookltd
CONTACT : Mr Stuart Smith

DEFENCE EVALUATION AND RESEARCH AGENCY
Solar Power Laboratory, X107
Building, Farnborough, Hampshire
GU14 0LX, UK
TEL : + 44 1252 394003
FAX : + 44 1252 392664
E-MAIL : cgoodbody@dera.gov.uk
CONTACT : Chris Goodbody

DUPONT ELECTRONIC MATERIALS
Bristol Centre, Coldharbour Lane,
Frenchay, Bristol BS16 1QD, UK
TEL: +44 117 931 3294
FAX: +44 117 931 3099
E-MAIL:
peter.brenner@gbr.dupont.com
WEB: http://www.dupont.com/mcm
CONTACT: Peter Brenner

ENERGY EQUIPMENT TESTING SERVICE LTD
PV Systems, Unit 2 Glan-Y-Llyn
Industrial Estate,
Taffs Well CF15 7 JD, UK
TEL: +44 29 2082 0910
FAX: +44 29 2082 0911
WEB: http://www.eets.com
CONTACT: BM Cross

FILSOL LIMITED
Unit 15, Ponthenri Industrial Estate,
Ponthenri, Camarthenshire SA 15
5RA, UK
TEL: +44 1269 860979
FAX: +44 1269 860979
E-MAIL: filson@infotrade.co.uk
CONTACT : Roy Blower

HALCROW GROUP LIMITED
Burderop Park, Swindon,
Wiltshire SN4 0QD, UK
TEL: +44 1793 81 4756
FAX: +44 1793 81 5020
E-MAIL: halcrowgilbert@halcrow.com
WEB: http://www.halcrow.com
CONTACT: Terence Tovey

IAIN GARNER ASSOCIATES-IGA
142 Woodland Drive, Watford,
Hertfordshire WD17 3DB,UK
TEL: +44 1923 212548
FAX: +44 1923 212548
E-MAIL: Iain.garner@talk21.com
CONTACT: Iain Garner

INTERSOLAR GROUP
Magdalen Centre,
Oxford Science Park, Oxford,
Oxfordshire OX4 4GA, UK
TEL: +44 1865 784 670
FAX: +44 1865 784 681
E-MAIL: intersolar@intersolar.com
WEB: http://www.intersolar.com
CONTACT: JR Stobart

JOHNSON MATTHEY CHEMICALS
Orchard Road, Royston,
Hertfordshire SG8 5HE, UK
TEL: +44 1763 2533 85
FAX: +44 1763 2534 66
WEB: http://www.chemicals.matthey.com
CONTACT: Phil Wood

UNITED KINGDOM

LAFARGE BRAAS RESEARCH AND DEVELOPMENT LTD
Sussex Manor Business Park,
Gatwick Road,
Crawley,
Sussex RH10 2NG, UK
TEL: +44 1293 614 545
FAX: +44 1293 614 548
CONTACT: CJ Campbell

LAFARGE BRAAS ROOFING ACCESSORIES GMBH & CO KG
TEL: +49 6171 61 2590
FAX: +49 6171 61 2912
E-MAIL: roland.neuner@lafarge-braas.com

LUMEN SEAMARKS LTD
Seamarks House,
Petteridge Lane, Matifield,
Tonbridge Kent TN127LP, UK
TEL: +44 1892 722829
FAX: + 441892 722067
EMAIL: lumensea@aol.com
CONTACT: Robin Partington

MACKELLAR ENGINEERING
Strathspey Industrial Estate,
Grantown-on-Spey,
Morayshire
PH26 3NB, UK
TEL: +44 1479 872577
FAX: +44 1479 872436
E-MAIL: mackellar@aol.com
CONTACT: Dr Duncan MacKellar

MARQUES (j) & CO LTD
14 Pine Close,
Horsell, Working,
Surrey GU21, 45J, UK
TEL: +44 1483 747925
FAX: +44 1483 726745
E-MAIL: josemarques@compuserve.com
CONTACT: Jose Marques

MATTHEW JAMES & PARTNERS
The Bush Townside,
Haddenham,
Buckinghamshire HP17 8AW, UK
TEL: +44 1844 291987
FAX: +44 1844 291987
E-MAIL: dichler@dial.pipex.co.uk
CONTACT: Alan Dichler

NCL SOLAR
12 Docks Offices, Surrey Quays Road, London SE162XU, UK
TEL: +44 207 394 8667
FAX: +44 207 394 8273
E-MAIL: info@nclsolar.com
WEB: hptt://www.nclsolar.com
CONTACT: Cass Peter Biriyok

OVE ARUP & PARTNERS INTERNATIONAL LTD
New Castle Upon Tyne,
Central Square, Forth Street,
New Castle Upon Tyne NE13PL, UK
TEL: +44 191 261 6080
FAX: +44 191 261 7879
E-MAIL: david.hillcox@arup.com
WEB: http://www.arup.com
CONTACT: David Hillcox

PINNACLE LTD
Unit 15, Ponthenri Industrial Estate,
Ponthenri, Dyfed SA15 5RA, UK
TEL : + 44 1269 860229
FAX : + 44 1269 860979
CONTACT : Terry Clement

PV SYSTEMS
Unit 2 Glan-Y-Llyn Industrial Estate,
Cardiff Road, Taffs Well,
CF 15 7 JD, UK
TEL: +44 29 2082 0910
FAX: +44 29 2082 0911
E-MAIL: pvsales@pvsystems.com
WEB: http://www.pvsystems.com
CONTACT: Daniel Nuh

SCHUCO INTERNATIONAL KG
Whitehall Ave, Kingston,
Milton Keynes, Bucks Mk10 0AL,UK
TEL: +44 1908 282 111
FAX: +44 1908 282 124
CONTACT: Mr TJ Charnell

SHOREPOWER UK
PO Box 2, Wellington, Somerset
TA21 8LJ, UK
TEL: +44 1823 666177
FAX: +44 1823 666177
WEB: http://www.shorepowerUK.com
CONTACT: John W Shore

SICAME ELECTRICAL DEVELOPMENTS LTD
Riverholme Works, Huddersfield Road,
Holmfirth, West Yorkshire HD7 2TN, UK
TEL: +44 1484 681115
FAX: +44 1484 687352
E-MAIL: info@sicame.co.uk
CONTACT: Jim Henderson

SIEMENS SOLAR
Tollbridge House, Windmill Road,
Sunbury on Thames, Middlesex
TW16 7HS,UK
TEL: +44 1932 792846
FAX: +44 1932 792975
E-MAIL: solar@plcsun.siemens.co.uk
WEB: http://www.siemens.co.uk/Industrial-services
CONTACT: Matthew Douch

SOLAGEN
14 Heathfield Road,WestMoors,
Ferndown,Dorset BH22 OBG, UK
TEL:+44 1202 893 801
FAX:+44 1202 893 801
E-MAIL:solagen@compuserve.com
WEB:http://www.ourworld.compuserve.com/homepages/solagen
CONTACT:Tony Smith

SOLAPAK LTD
Cock Lane, High Wycombe,
Buckinghamshire HP13 7DE,UK
TEL:+44 1494 452945
FAX:+44 1494 437045
E-MAIL:intersolar @intersolar.com
WEB:http://www.Intersolar.com
CONTACT:Martin Bellamy

SOLAR CENTURY
91-94 LOWER MARSH,Waterloo,
London, SEI 7AB UK
TEL:+44 870 735 8100
FAX:+44 870 735 8101
E-MAIL:info@solarcentury.co.uk
WEB: http://www.solarcentury.co.uk
CONTACT: Jonathan Cockburn

SOLAR PRODUCTS INTERNATIONAL LTD
PO Box438 Watford,Hertfordshire
WDI 3GB,UK
TEL:+44 1923 212548
FAX:+44 1923 212548
E_MAIL:iain.garner@talk21.com
CONTACT:IF Garner

SOLARSENSE UK
8 Copford Lane, Long Ashton,
Bristol BS15 INF, UK
TEL : +44 1275 540112
FAX : +44 1275 540113
E-MAIL : solarsense@cablenet.co.uk
CONTACT : Stephen Barrett

SUNDWEL SOLAR LTD
1 Tower Road, Glover Estate,
Washington,
Tyne And Wear NE 37 2 SH UK
TEL: +44 191 4163001
FAX: +44 191 4154297
E-MAIL: solar@sundwel.com
WEB: http://www.sundwel.com
CONTACT: Keith Wilkinson

SUNPOWERD ENERGY SYSTEMS LTD
90 Albert Road,
Southsea PO5 2SN, UK
TEL : +44 23 92 614 925
FAX : +44 23 92 812 890
E-MAIL : sean@sunpower.freeserve.co.uk
CONTACT : Seaan Cavendish

SUNSEEKER SOLARLTD
Northern House, Moss Street East,
Ashton-u-lyne Lancashire OL6 7BU,
UK
TEL: +44 161 343 7077
FAX: +44 161 339 8669
E-MALI:sales@sunseeker-solar.co.uk
WEB:http://www.sunseeker-solar.co.uk
CONTACT:David Wright

SYNERGY POWER CORPORATION (UK) LTD
PO Box 85, Chipping Norton,
Oxfordshire OX7 6UD,UK
TEL : +44 1993 831567
FAX : +44 1993 83189
E-MAIL : spc@synergypowercorp.com
WEB : http://www.synergypower.com
CONTACT : Eric Kalkhurst

TECHNOLOGY LEADS LTD
Nightinggales, Forest Road,
East Horsley, Surrey KT24 5BT,
UK
TEL: +44 1483 28076
FAX: +44 1482 825667
E-MAIL: georgesscont_ti@compuserve.com
CONTACT: Dr George B Scott

THROPTON ENERGY SERVICES
Physic Lane,Thropton,
Morpeth, Northumberland
NE65 7HU, UK
TEL: +44 1669 621288
FAX: +44 1669 621288
E-MAIL:throptonenergy@compuserve.com
WEB:http://ourworld.compuserve.com/homepages/throptonenergy
CONTACT:Dr BA Sexon

TIDELAND SIGNAL LTD
15-19 Trowers Way,
Redhill, Surrey
RHI 2LH, UK
TEL : +44 1737 768211
FAX : +44 1737 768192
CONTACT : Tim Hall

TODAYS ENERGY SYSTEMS
19 Albany Drive,
Wolseley Gardens,
Rugeley, Staffordshire WS15 2HP,
UK
TEL: +44 1889 584667
FAX: +44 1889 584667
CONTACT:Donald J Astley

WIND

ABACHEM ENGINEERING LTD
Jessop Way,
Newark, Nottinghamshire
NG24 2ER, UK
TEL: +44 1636 676483
FAX: +44 1636 708632
CONTACT: Mr Les Barton

AERODYN-SHOREPOWER
5 Riverside, Wellington,
Somerset TA21 8LJ, UK
TEL: +44 1823 666177
FAX: +44 1823 666177
WEB: http://www.ShorepowerUK.com
CONTACT: John W Shore

AEROLAMINATES LTD
St Cross Business Park, Newport,
Isle Of Wight, UK
TEL: +44 23 80 666220
FAX: +44 23 80 666527
E-MAILS: blades@aerolaminates.co.uk

AGF PROJECTS LTD
Global House Unit 10,
Liddall Way,
West Drayton UB7 8PG,UK
TEL: +44 1895 437940
FAX: +44 1895 437945
CONTACT: Terry Bowen

AMEC BORDER WIND
Haugh Lane Industrial Estate, Hexham,
Northumberland NE46 3PU, UK
TEL: +44 1434 601 224
FAX: +44 1434 601 200
E-MAIL: info@borderwind.co.uk
WEB: http://www.borderwind.co.uk
CONTACT: Sandra Painter

AMEC WIND
Bridge End, Hexham,
Northumberland
NE6 4NU, UK
TEL: +44 1434 611300
FAX: +44 1434 601200
E-MAIL: wind@amec.com
WEB: http:// www.amec.com/wind
CONTACT: Sandra Painter

B9 ENERGY LTD
Operation & Maintenance,
Willowbank Road, Millbrook,
Industrial Estate,
Larne BT 40 2SF, UK
TEL: +44 28 2826 3900
FAX: +44 28 2826 3901
E-MAIL: k.fergie@b9energy.co.uk
WEB: http://www.b9energy.co.uk
CONTACT: Andrew Dodge

B9 ENERGY SERVICES LTD
Willow Bank Road, Millbrook
Industrial Estate, Larne BT 40 25F, UK
TEL : +44 28 2826 3899
FAX : +44 28 2826 3901
E-MAIL :
s.workman@b9energy.co.uk
WEB : http://www.b9energy.co.uk
CONTACT : Sacha Workman

BARKER SHEPLEY LTD
7 Lakeland Business Park
Cockermouth, Cumbria CA 13 0QT,
UK
TEL : +44 1900 828282
FAX : +44 1900 828281
CONTACT : J Griffiths

BAYWIND ENERGY CO-OP LTD
Unit 38 Trinity Enterprise Centre
Furness Business Park, Barrow-in-Furness, Cumbria LA14 2PN, UK
TEL: +44 1229 821028
FAX: +44 1299 821104
E-MAIL: user@windco.furness.co.uk
CONTACT: Simon Boxer

BRITISH AUTOGARD LTD
Barton Lane, Cirencester GL72EB,UK
TEL: +44 1285 640333
FAX: +44 1285 659476
CONTACT: Clive George

BROTHERHOOD MACHTECH
Peter Brotherhood Ltd,
Werringtong Parkway,
Peterborough, PE4, 5HG, UK
TEL : +44 773 292 320
FAX : +44 773 292 329
E-MAIL : sclarke@peterbrotherhood.co.uk
WEB : www.peterbrotherhood.co.uk
CONTACT: Steve Clark

CAMBRIAN ENGINEERING (CYMRU) LTD
Llandegai Industrial Estate,
Bangor,
Gwynedd LL57 4YH, UK
TEL : +44 1248 370 248
FAX : +44 1248 370 406
E-MAIL :
cambrianeng@btconnect.com
CONTACT : D J Williams

CINERGY GLOBAL POWER
Head Office, Cinergy House,
Ryon Hill Park, Warwick Road,
Stratford-Upon-Avon CV37 0UU, UK
TEL: +44 1789 200100
FAX: +44 1789 200101
CONTACT: Malcolm Harrison

CLRC RUTHERFORD APPLETON LABORATORY
Energy Research Unit,
Chilton, Didcot,
Oxfordshire OX11 0QX, UK
TEL: +44 1235 445 559
FAX: +44 1235 446 863
E-MAIL: j.a.halliday@rl.ac.uk
WEB: http://www.rl.ac.uk/departments/tech/eru.html
CONTACT: Dr Jim Halliday

COLHAM ENERGY LTD
3 Cavendish Road,
Henleaze,
Bristol BS9 4DZ, UK
TEL: +44 117 962 8772
FAX: +44 117 940 9082
CONTACT: Maureen De Pietro

CORAM ENERGY GROUP
2232 Marine Drive Suite 301,
West Vancouver,
British Columbia V7V,
UK, Canada
TEL : +1 604 921 1241
FAX : +1 604 921 1242
E-MAIL : brianosullivan@compuserve.com
CONTACT : Brian J O'Sullivan

COUPE FOUNDRY LTD
Higher Walton,
Preston PRS 4DQ, UK
TEL : +44 1772 338 151
FAX : + 44 1772 627 609
CONTACT : S R Hall

CULIGHTING LTD
Charles House,
Great Amwell, Ware
Hertfordshire SG 12 9TA, UK
TEL : +44 1920 860600
FAX : +44 1920 860635
E-MAIL : sales@cuphosco.co.uk
WEB : http://www.cuphosco.co.uk
CONTACT : William Marques

ELEMENT ENGINEERING
25 Sutherland Avenue,
Riverside,
Stirling FK8, ILU, UK
TEL : +44 1786 472259
FAX : +44 1786 472259
E-MAIL : element.eng@quissta.net
CONTACT : Charlie Robb

ENERCON (UK DIVISION)
Axiom House, Station Road,
Stroud GL5 3AP, UK
TEL : +44 1453 766 774
FAX : +44 1453 766 222
CONTACT : Dale Vince

ENRONWIND OVERSEAS DEVELOPMENT
Prince Constort House,
27-29 Albert Embankment,
London SEWI 7TJ, UK
TEL : +44 20 7 793 2800
FAX : +44 20 7 820 3401
E-MAIL : 73744.1010@compuserve.com
CONTACT : Billy N Richmond

FARM ENERGY LIMITED
2 Castle Park Road,
Whiddon Valley, Barnstaple,
Devon EX32 8PA, UK
TEL: + 44 1271 371888
FAX: + 44 1271 371333
E-MAIL: info@farmenergy.co.uk
CONTACT : Peter Crone

GAZELLE WIND TURBINES LTD
Stargate Industrial Estate,
Stargate, Ryton,
Tyne & Wear NE30 3EX, UK
TEL: + 44 191 413 0000
FAX: + 44 191 413 0047
E-Mail: gazelle @ northenergy.co.uk
WEB: http://www.mkw.co.uk
CONTACT : Dr Gary Jenkins

GREEN DRAGON ENERGY
Panteg, Cwm Llinau,
Machynlleth,
Powys SY20 9NU, UK
TEL: +44 1650 511 378
E-MAIL: dragonrg@globalnet.co.uk
CONTACT: Frank Jackson

GREEN ELECTRON LTD
800 Park Avenue,
Aztec West, Almondsbury,
Bristal Bs32 4SE, UK
TEL : + 44 1454 201101
FAX : + 44 1454 616675
CONTACT : Neil Humphreys

HEXCEL COMPOSITES
Duxford, Cambridge CB2 4QD, UK
TEL: +44 1223 838446
FAX: +44 1223 838469
E-MAIL: communications@hexcel.com
WEB: http://www.hexcelcomposites.com
CONTACT: Dr Derek Swanson

HYDRO SOIL SERVICES UK
Greenstede House,
Wood Street,
East Grinstead RH19 1UZ, UK
TEL: +44 1225 486535
FAX: +44 1225 486597
E-MAIL: cash.neil@dredging.com
WEB: http://www.hydrosoilservices.com
CONTACT: Mr Neil Cash

INAL METALS NORTH LIMITED
Unit 4, Smithfold Lane, Little Hulton
Manchesster M28 0GP, UK
TEL: +44 161 790 0118
FAX: +44 161 790 5887
CONTACT: Ian Nicklin

KEYSOLAR SYSTEMS
4 Glanmor Crescent, Newport
Gwent NP9 8AX, UK
TEL: +44 1633 280 958
FAX: +44 1633 280 958
CONTACT: Robert Keyes

LVM LTD
Aerogen House, Old Oak Close,
Arlesey, Bedforddhire SG15 6XD, UK
TEL: +44 1462 733336
FAX: +44 1462 730466
E-MAIL: lvm.ltd@dial.pipex.com
WEB: http://www.lvm-ltd.com
CONTACT: Derek Haley

M&N WIND POWER LTD
15E Cuxhaven Way, Longrock,
Penzance TR20 8HX, UK
TEL: +44 1736 330171
FAX: +44 1736 362025
E-MAIL: chris_mn@compuserve.com
CONTACT: Chris Morris

MARLEC ENGINEERING CO LTD
Rutland House, Trevithick Road,
Corby, Northamptonshire NN17 5XY, UK
TEL: +44 1536 201588
FAX: +44 1536 400211
E-MAIL: sales@marlec.co.uk
WEB: http://www.marlec.co.uk
CONTACT: Teresa Auciello

MARTINEAU COMPOSITES
Highwood Park Lane Upper
Swanmore, Hants SO32 2QQ, UK
TEL: +44 1489 893236
FAX: +44 1489 893236
CONTACT: MP Martineau

METALASTIK VIBRATION CONTROL SYSTEMS DUNLOP LTD
Evington Valley Road,
Leicester LE5 5LY, UK
TEL: +44 166 273 0281
FAX: +44 166 273 5698
CONACT: Idwal Moore

MITSUBISHI HEAVY INDUSTRIES EUROPE LTD
Bow Bells House, Bread Street,
London EC4M 9BQ,UK
TEL: +44 20 7634 5131
FAX: +44 20 7248 1329
CONTACT: A Kijima

MOTHERWELL BRIDGE SPECIAL PRODUCTS
Wellheads Road, Farburn Industrial Estate, Dyce, Aberdeen AB2 7HG, UK
TEL: +44 1224 723434
FAX: +44 1224 723545
CONTACT: Tom Burnett

NATIONAL WIND POWER LTD
Riverside House Meadowbank, Furlong Road, Bourne End, Buckinghamshire SL8 5AJ, UK
TEL : +44 1628 532 300
FAX : +44 1628 531 993
E-MAIL : mail@natwindpower.co.uk
WEB : http://www.natwindpower.co.uk
CONTACT : Dr Peter Musgrove

NATURAL POWER COMPANY
13 Lynedoch Crescent, Kelvingrove
Glasgow G3 6EQ, UK
TEL: +44 141 564 2900
FAX: +44 141 564 2901
E-MAIL: mail@naturalpower.com
WEB: http://www.naturalpower.com
CONTACT: Ted Leeming

NEG MICON UK LTD
Dolphin House, Windmill Road, Sunbury-on-Thames, Middlesex, TW 16 7HT, UK
TEL: +44 1932 732500
FAX: +44 1932 732501
E-MAIL:energy@neg-micon.co.uk
CONTACT: Bob Leicester

NOI SCOTLAND LTD
Mitchelston Drive, Mitchelston Industrial Estate, Kirkcaldy KY1 3LZ, UK
TEL: +44 1592 653753
FAX: + 44 1592 654373
E-MAIL: info@noiscotland.co.uk

NORTH ENERGY ASSOCIATES LTD
Old Queen's Head yard, 7b Old Gate Morpeth Northumberland NE61 1PY, UK
TEL: +44 1670 516949
FAX: +44 1670 510300
E-MAIL: enquiries@northenergy.co.uk
CONTACT: Dr Garry Jenkins

OLEONTEC SRL
Renewable Energy 7 Flaxman Close, Earley, Reading, Berkshire RG6 5TH, UK
TEL: +44 118 9620542
FAX: +44 118 9313327
E-MAIL: rentec@hotmail.com
CONTACT: Mr Virginillo

PROVEN WORLD FRIENDLY ENERGY
Moorfield Industrial Estate, Kilmarnock Ayrshire KA2 0BA, UK
TEL: +44 1563 543 020
FAX: +44 1563 539 119
E-MAIL: info@provenenergy.com
WEB: http://www.provenenergy.com
CONTACT: Keris Mc Leod

ROBIN MILLS
Kirby Cottage, Sundridge Road Ide Hill Sevenoaks, Kent TN14 6JR UK
TEL: +44 1732 750604
FAX: +44 1732 750717
CONTACT: Robin Mills

SCIOTECH
9 Heathwood Close, Yateley Hampshire GU46 7TP, UK
TEL: +44 1252 873564
FAX: +44 1252 873564
CONTACT: Dr Rayner Mayer

SCORAIG WIND ELECTRIC
Dundonnell, Ross-Shire IV23 2RE UK
TEL: +44 1854 633286
FAX: ı 44 1854 633233
E-MAIL: hugh.piggott@enterprise.net
WEB: http://www.scoraigwind.co.uk
CONTACT: Hugh Piggott

SCOTTISH POWER UK PLC
Cathcart Business Park, Spean Street, Glasgow G44 4BE,UK
TEL: +44 141 568 4421
FAX: +44 141 568 4499
E-MAIL:alan.mortimer@scottishpower.com
CONTACT: Alan Mortimer

SILURIAN ASSOCIATES
75 Westbourne Road, Penarth,South Glamorgan CF64 3HD, UK
TEL: +44 29 20 703221
FAX: +44 29 20 704457

SULZER (UK) LIMITED
Westmead, Farnborough, Hants, GUI4 7LP, UK
TEL: +44 1252 544311
FAX: +44 1252 518636

THE ENERGY AND ENVIRONMENTAL MANAGEMENT GROUP
Solarsaver, 22 Clay Hill Road, Sleaford, Lincolnshire NG34 7TF, UK
TEL: +44 1529 304027
FAX: +44 1529 410491
E-MAIL: action@solarsaver.co.uk
WEB: http://www.solarsaver.co.uk
CONTACT: Sharon Hutson

THE NATURAL POWER COMPANY
13 Lynedoch Crescent, Kelvingrove, Glasgow G3 6EQ, UK
TEL: +441644 430008
FAX: + 441644 430009
CONTACT: Stuart Hall

THE WIND FUND PLC
Brunel House, 11 The Promenade Clifton, Bristol BS8 3NN, UK
TEL: +44 117 973 9339
FAX: +44 117 973 9303
E-MAIL: mail@windfund.co.uk
WEB: http://www.windfund.co.uk
CONTACT: Simon Roberts

TODAYS ENERGY SYSTEMS
19 Albany Drive, Wolseley Gardens, Rugeley, Staffordshire WS15 2HP, UK
TEL: +44 1889 584667
FAX: +44 1889 584667
CONTACT:Donald J Astley

TRUSHM POWER
I Peniston Court, Melbourne, Derby DE73, IEZ, UK
TEL: +4 4 1332 862 313
CONTACT: Howard Dent

UMWELTKONTORIRELAND LTD-UKO IRELAND
55 Central Avenue, Portstewart BT55 7BT, Northern Ireland, UK
TEL : +44 28 70 835446
FAX : +44 870 1691797
E-MAIL : m.schalper@umweltkontor.com
WEB : http://www.umwelokontor.com
CONTACT : Mr Matthlas Schalper

VESTAS DANISH WIND TECHNOLOGY A/S
94-96 Wigmore Street, London WIU 3RF, UK
TEL: +44 20 7 224 1178
FAX: +44 20 7 224 1158
E-MAIL: siluk@globalnet.co.uk
WEB: http://www.vestas.dk
CONTACT: Meir M Silberman

WESTERN WINDPOWER LTD
Axiom House, Station Road, Stroud, Gloucestershire GL 5 3AP, UK
TEL: +44 1453 759408
FAX: +44 1453 759416
WEB: http://www.western-windpower.com
CONTACT: Kate Spouse

WICHITA COMPANY LTD
Ampthill Road,
Bedford MK 42 9RD, UK
TEL: +44 1234 350 311
FAX: +44 1234 350 317
E-MAIL: clutch@wichita.co.uk
WEB: http://www.wichita.co.uk
CONTACT: Peter Sharp

WIND & SUN LTD
Humber Marsh, Stoke Prior,
Leominster, Herefordshire HR6 0NE, UK
TEL: +441568760671
FAX: +441568760434
E-MAIL: steve@windandsun.co.uk
WEB: http://www.windandsun.co.uk
CONTACT: Steve Wade

WIND DIRECTIONS
Editorial Hockpitt Farm,
Nether Stowey, Bridgwater,
Somerset TA5 1EX,UK
TEL: +44 1278 732921
FAX: +44 1278 732921
E-MAIL:
crispinaubrey@compuserve.com
WEB: http://www.ewea.org
CONTACT: Mr Crispin Aubrey

WIND POWER & CO (UK) LTD
Porkellis, Helston,
Cornwall TR130LG, UK
TEL: +44 1209 860068
FAX: +44 1209 860126
CONTACT: H Beechey-Newman

WIND PROSPECT LTD
7 Berkley Square,
Clifton Bristol BS8 1HG, UK
TEL: +44 117 925 7798
FAX: +44 117 945 2493
E-MAIL:
windprospect@compuserve.com
CONTACT: Colin Palmer

WINDELECTRIC MANAGEMENT LTD
Deli, Delabole,
Cornwall PL33 9BZ, UK
TEL: +44 1840 214100
FAX: +44 1840 214102
E-MAIL: peter@windelectric.co.uk
CONTACT: Martin Edward

WIND-WAYS UK LTD
PO Box 14613, Leven,
Fife KY9 1ZB, UK
TEL: +44 1 333 33 0084
FAX: +44 1 333 33 0084
E-MAIL: cmadden160@aol.com
WEB: http://www.randall.co.uk/windways.htm
CONTACT: Charlie Madden

WINSUND
A Division of Hugh
Jennings Ltd,
Tatham Street,
Sunderland, Tyne & Wear
SRI 2AG, UK
TEL: +44 191 514 7050
FAX: +44 191 564 1096
E-MAIL: info@windsund.com
WEB: http://www.winsund.com
CONTACT: Mike Seeley

BIOMASS

ALPINE BOILERS
12 Sefton Lane, Meltham,
Huddersfield HD7 3JX, UK
TEL: +44 1484 854908
FAX: +44 1484 686553
CONTACT: Mr E Swannick

ALSTOM GAS TURBINES LTD
PO Box 1 Thorngate House,
Lincoln LN2 5DJ, UK
TEL: +44 1522 584 018
FAX: +44 1522 584 933
E-MAIL:
agtind.sales@energy.alstom.com
CONTACT: Ralph Sherwin

ALSTOM POWER
Industrial Gas Turbines,
PO Box 1, Waterside South,
Lincoln LN5 7FD, UK
TEL: +44 1522 584164
FAX: +44 1522 584915
E-MAIL: mike.welch@energy.alstom.com
WEB: http://www.abb-alstompower.com
CONTACT: Mike Welch

ARBRE ENERGY LIMITED
2, The Embankment,
Sovereign Street
Leeds LSI 4BG, UK
TEL : +44 1 113 234 3234
FAX : +44 1 113 231 2707
EMAIL : keith_pitcher@yorkshirewater.plc.uk
WEB : http:// www.arbre.co.uk
CONTACT : Keith Pitcher

ASHDOWN ENVIRONMENTAL LTD
The Oast House, Hodore,
Upper Hartfield,
East Sussex,
TN7 4AR, UK
TEL : +44 1892 770 881
FAX : +44 1892 770 885
E-MAIL : enquiries@ashdown-environmental.co.uk
CONTACT : Dr. C.J. Muskett

ASTON UNIVERSITY - BIO - ENERGY RESEARCH GROUP
CEAC, Aston Triangle,
Bermingham B4 7ET, UK
TEL : +44 121 359 3611
FAX : +44 121 359 6814
E-MAIL :
a.v.bridgwater@aston.ac.uk
CONTACT : Prof. Tony Bridgwater

B9 ENERGY BIOMASS LTD
Unit 22, Northland Road Industrial
Estate, Derry. Co
Londonderry OLD, UK
TEL : +44 28 71 27 500
FAX : +44 28 71 308090
E-MAIL :d.jenkins@b9energy.co.uk
WEB : http://www.b9energy.co.uk

BESH ENERGY LTD
34 Park Crescent Elstree,
Herts WD6, 3PU, UK
TEL : +44 20B 9539794
FAX : +44 870 0567854
E-MAIL : lar@besh.demon.co.uk
WEB : http://www.besh.co.uk
CONTACT : Lewis A Rossen

BICAL
The Old Rectory,
Thurloxton, Taunton,
Somerset TA2 8RH, UK
TEL : +44 183 413882
FAX : +44 1823 413882
E-MAIL :
david.croxton@btinternet.com
WEB : http://www.bical.net
CONTACT : David Croxton

BIOENERGY DEVICES
Unit 28 Brynmenyn
Business Centre
Saint Theodore's Way,
Brynmenyn Industrial Estate,
Bridgend CF32, 9TZ, UK
TEL : +44 1656 724300
FAX : +44 1656 724626
E-MAIL : info@bioenergy-devices.co.uk
CONTACT : Marc Howell

BIOGAS TECHNOLOGY LTD
6 Brook side Industrial Estate,
Glatton Road, Sawtry,
Cambridgeshire PE 17 5SB,UK
TEL: +44 1487 831701
FAX: +44 1487 830962
E-MAIL: info@biogas.co.uk
WEB: http://www.biogas-technology.ltd.uk
CONTACT: Lan Gadsby

BIOMASS ENGINEERING LIMITED
Junction Lane, Newton-le-Willows,
Warrington WA12, 8DN, UK
TEL : +44 1925 220338
FAX : +44 1925 220135
E-MAIL : mikew@shawton.co.uk
CONTACT : Mr. Michael Walker

BIOMASS INDUSTRIAL CROPS LTD
Kingsmill Arable Centre, Kingsmill,
Cullompton, Devon EX15 1BS, UK
TEL: +44 1884 35899
FAX: +44 1884 34457
E-MAIL: office@bical.net
WEB: http://www.bical.net
CONTACT: Rebekah Rhode

BIOMASS INDUSTRIAL CROPS LTD-BICAL
Technical and Marketing,
Easterhill Gardens, KENN, Exeter,
Devon EX6, 7UG, UK
TEL : +44 1392 877003
FAX : +44 1392 877003
E-MAIL : jon.hatkenn@aol.com
WEB : http://www.bical.net
CONTACT : Jon Harvey

BIOMASS LTD
Glasbury, Hereford HR3, 5ND, UK
TEL : +44 1497 847383
FAX : +44 1497 847675
CONTACT : Dr. J A Rees

BIOMASS PROCESSING LTD
C/o. Border Biofuels,
Newtown, St. Boswells,
Melrose TD6, OSG, UK
TEL : +44 1835 823043
FAX : +44 1835 822997
CONTACT : Dr A C Bowles

BIOMASS RECYCLING LTD
The Recycling Centre,
Yarm Road, Stockton-on-Tees
TS183RU, UK
TEL : +44 1642 654166
FAX : +44 1642 391197
E-MAIL : biomass-recycling
@yahoo.co.uk
WEB : http://www.bigwig.net/
biomass.htm
CONTACT: Dr D J Harris

BORDER BIOFUELS LTD
Tweed Horizons Centre Newtown
St Boswells,
Melrose TD6 OSG, UK
TEL: +44 1835 823043
FAX: +44 1835 822997
E-MAIL:
admin@bblnorth.demon.co.uk
CONTACT: John M Seed

BRITISH ASSOCIATION FOR BIO FUELS AND OILS
Curlew Court Guys Head Road
Sutton Bridge Spalding Lincs
PE12 9QQ, UK
TEL: +44 1406 350220
FAX: +44 1406 350252
E-MAIL: babfo@pclery.freeserve.co.uk
WEB: http://www.biodiesel.co.uk
CONTACT: Peter Clery

BRITISH BIOGEN
7th Floor 63-66 Hatton Garden,
London ECIN 8LE, UK
TEL: +44 20 7 831 7222
FAX: +44 20 7 831 7223
E-MAIL: info@britishbiogen.co.uk
WEB: http://www.britishbiogen.co.uk
CONTACT: Nikki Kerrigan

CARLSHEAD FARMS
Paddock House Farm, Sicklinghall
Wetherby LS22, 4BJ, UK
TEL : +44 1937 582421
FAX : +44 1937 585931
E-MAIL :gareth.gaunt@virgin.net
CONTACT: Gareth Gaunt

CLEAN TECHNOLOGIES LTD
42 Parkgate Road, Connor,
Ballymena, Co Antrim BT42 3LE,UK
TEL: +44 1266 898133
FAX: +44 1266 898430
E-MAIL: cleantltd@aol.com
CONTACT: Paul Ditchfield

DALES GROUP
York Street, Aberdeen
AB 11 5DP, UK
TEL: +44 1224 212778
FAX: +44 1224 212779
E-MAIL: alistair@dales-mar.co.uk
WEB: http://www.dalesgroup.co.uk
CONTACT: Alistair Gordon

DEUTZ UK LTD
2 St Martins Way,
London SW17 OUT, UK
TEL : + 44 20 8 781 7200
FAX : + 44 20 8 947 6380
E-MAIL :
mailbox@deutzbtinternet.com
WEB : http://www.deutz.com
CONTACT : Keith Marshal

DYNAMOTIVE EUROPE LTD
4th Floor, 31 Davies Street, London
WIY IFN, UK
TEL : + 44 20 7518 9380
FAX : + 44 20 7518 9381
E-MAIL : arobson@dynamotive.com
WEB : http://www.DynamotiveEurope.com
CONTACT : Antony Robson

ECONERGY LTD
35 Gwydir Street,
Cambridge CBI 2LG, UK
TEL: +44 1223 560467
FAX: +44 870 1248651
E-MAIL: robert@econergy.ltd.uk
WEB: http://www.econergy.ltd.uk
CONTACT: Dr Robert Rippengal

ENSYN INTERNATIONAL LTD
Broughton House, 6-8 Sackville
Street, London WIX IDD, UK
TEL : + 44 207 434 1821
FAX : + 44 20 7 434 1123
CONTACT : Espen Daae

ESD LTD
Overmoor, Neston, Corsham,
Wiltshire SN13 9TZ, UK
TEL: +44 1225 812102
FAX: +44 1225 812103
CONTACT: Dr Jeff Kenna

FARMATIC BIOTECH ENERGY UK LTD
5 Royal Crescent, Cheltenham,
GL50 3DA, UK
TEL: +44 1242 24 21 11
FAX: +44 1242 24 31 11
E-MAIL: uk@farmatic.com
WEB: http://www.farmatic.com
CONTACT: Mr Jorgen Fink

FIBROWATT LIMITED
Astley house,
33 Notting Hill Gate,
London WII 3JQ, UK
TEL: +44 20 7229 9252
FAX: +44 20 7221 8671
E-MAIL:fibrowatt @compuserve.com
WEB:http://www.fibrowatt.com
CONTACT : Rupert Fraser

FIRST RENEWABLES LIMITED
No.3 The Embankment,
Sovereign Street Leeds,
West,
Yorkshire LS1 4BJ, UK
TEL: +44 113 231 2562
FAX: +44 113 231 2707
E-MAIL: michelle.brown@first-
renewables.com
WEB: http://www.arbre.co.uk
CONTACT: Michelle Brown

FORBIO EUROPE LIMITED
c/o International Plant Laboratories
Ltd. Ham Street, Baltonsborough,
Glastonbury BA6 8QG, UK
TEL: +44 1458 851000
FAX: +44 1458 850999
E-MAIL: denaros@for
bioeurope.co.uk
WEB : www.forbio.com.au

FOREST ENTERPRISE
Castle Douglas Forest District,
21 King Street,
Castle Douglas,
Kirkcudbright DG7 1 AA, UK
TEL: +44 1556 503626
FAX: +44 1556 504626
CONTACT : Michael Wall

GRESHAM ENGINEERING CO LTD
104 Maybury Road, Woking
Surrey GU21 5JL, UK
TEL: +44 1483 765 538
FAX: +44 1483 765 320
CONTACT: Chris Sloane

GROUNDWORK BRIDGEND
The Environment Centre
Maesteg Road,
Tondu,
Bridgend CF32 9BT, UK
TEL: +44 1656 722315
FAX: +44 1656 72 15 57
E-MAIL: Bridgend@
groundwork.org.uk
CONTACT: Kenneth Shaw

GWM ASSOCIATES
Broughton Pumping Station,
Brake Lane,
Boughton Newark,
Notts NG22 9HQ, UK
TEL : + 44 1905 821 407
FAX : + 44 1905 821 419
CONTACT : Gerald Warcham

HESE (UK)
1 Chapel Street,
Duffield,
Derby DE56 4EQ, UK
TEL: +44 1332 842848
FAX: +44 1332 559950
CONTACT: Paul Wayman

HOLMES EB - AGRO-INDUSTRIAL CONSULTANCY
Oakwood House Oakwood Road,
Burges Hill,
Sussex RH15 0HZ, UK
TEL: +44 1444 258755
FAX: +44 1444 258766
E-MAIL: ebholmes@pavillion.co.uk
CONTACT: EB Holmes

JAMES TROOP & CO LTD
Pleasant Hill Street,
Liverpool
Merseyside L8 5SZ, UK
TEL: +44 151 709 0581
FAX: +44 151 708 5194
E-MAIL: troopj@
mail.globalnet.co.uk
CONTACT: Mr John Meakin

K & N FILTERS (EUROPE) LTD
Commercial industrial
And Marine John Street,
Warrington WA2 7UB, UK
TEL: +44 1925 636 950
FAX: +44 1925 418 948
E-MAIL: kn@kn.u-net.com
WEB: http://www.knfilters.co.uk
CONTACT: Mr D Marshall

KELBURN ENGINEERING
13 Canyon Road, Netherton
Industrial Estate, Wishaw,
Lanarkshire ML2 0DS, UK
TEL: +44 1698 355 026
FAX: +44 1698 356 321
CONTACT: Mr M Watson

LAMBDA CONTROLS INTERNATIONAL INC LTD
The Old School House,
Main Street, Blidworth,
Mansfield Notts NG21 0QH, UK
TEL: +44 1623 792999
FAX: +44 1623 796862
E-MAIL: richdee@aol.com
CONTACT: Mr Richard Butler

LANDTEC PRODUCTS
Eton Nursery,
Windsor Road, Water
Oakely, Windsor SL45US, UK
TEL : +44 1628 631033
FAX : +44 1628 631917
CONTACT : Richard McSorley

LANGWORTHY AGRICULTURAL HOLDINGS
Agri-Forestry (South West), Cwm
Twrch Farm, Ystradowen, Upper
Cwm Twrch, Swansea,
SA9 2XY, UK
TEL: +44 1639 820686
CONTACT: David Cunningham

MALTIN POLLUTION CONTROL SYSTEMS (1967) LTD
Gould's House, Horsington,
Somerset BA8 0EW, UK
TEL: +44 1963 370100
FAX: +44 1963 371300
E-MAIL:
cmamaltin@gouldshouse.com
CONTACT: Chris Maltin

NORDISTRIBUTION LTD
The Broyle, Shortgate, Lewes,
East Sussex BN8 6PH, UK
TEL: +44 1825 841222
FAX: +44 1825 841444
E-MAIL:
admin@nordist.demon.co.uk
CONTACT: A N Redman

ONYX AURORA LTD
C/O Hampshire Waste Services,
Poles Lane,
Otterbourne SO21
2EA, UK
TEL: +44 1962 764000
FAX: +44 1962 711022
E-MAIL:
clepineett@integra.hws.co.uk
CONTACT: C Lepinette

ONYX HAMPSHIRE LTD
Poles Lane, Otterbourne,
Winchester SO21 2EA,
UK
TEL: +44 1962 764000
FAX: +44 1962 715693
E-MAIL:
info.aurora@onyxgroup.co.uk
CONTACT: Jeannette Camilleri

PIPELINE SERVICES LTD
21 Princes Drive,
Kenilworth,
Warwickshire CV8 2FD, UK
TEL: +44 1926 511 316
FAX: +44 1926 512 744
CONTACT: Ian Oakley

PLC PRODUCTS
Westhall, Halesworth,
Suffolk IP 19 8Rh, UK
TEL: +44 1502 575 265
FAX:+44 1502 575 265
WEB:http://www.plcproducts.co.uk
CONTACT: Peter Clifton

PRACTICALLY GREEN ENVIRONMENTAL SERVICES
Solar House,
Magherafelt,
Northern Ireland BT45 6HW, UK
TEL: +44 28 796 32615
FAX: +44 28 796 32615
CONTACT: Dr Les Gornall

PROGRESSIVE ENERGY TECHNOLOGY
Pennington House,
Lower Woodside,
Lymington,
Hampshire SO41 8AL, UK
TEL: +44 1590 670483
FAX: +44 1590 676919
E-MAIL: jim@pentec.demon.co.uk
CONTACT: Jim Gibb

RICHARD LANDEN
29 Village Road, Cockayne Hatley,
Sandy, Beds SG19 2EE, UK
TEL: +44 1767 631535
E-MAIL: landenr@aol.com
CONTACT: Richard Landen

SEMUNDO LTD
49 North Road, Great Abington,
Cambridge CB1 6AS, UK
TEL: +44 1223 890 777
FAX: +44 1223 890 666
E-MAIL: enquiries@semundo.co.uk
WEB: http://www.semundo.co.uk
CONTACT: Christopher Green

SERVOMEX GROUP LTD
Crowborough, East Sussex TN6
3DU, UK
TEL: +44 1892 652181
FAX: +44 1892 662253
E-MAIL: info@servomex.com
WEB: http://www.servomex.com
CONTACT: Lorretta Christey

SHANKS & MCEWAN LTD
Woodside House, Church Road,
Woburn Sands, Milton Keynes
MK17 8TA, UK
TEL: +44 1908 282 727
FAX: +44 1908 282 728
CONTACT: Mr Andrews

TALBOTT'S LTD
Drummond Road, Astonfields
Industrial Estate, Stafford ST 16
3HJ, UK
TEL : +44 1785 213366
FAX : +44 1785 256418
E-MAIL : sales@talbotts.co.uk
WEB : http://www.talbotts.co.uk
CONTACT : A Talbott

TEISEN PRODUCTS LTD
Bradley Green,
Worcestershire
B96 6RP, UK
TEL: +44 1527 821 621
FAX: +44 1527 821 665
WEB: http://www.farm2000.co.uk
CONTACT: Peter Teisen

THE GREENBELT GROUP OF COMPANIES LTD
189 St Vincent Street
Glasgow G2 5QD, UK
TEL: +44 141 243 2428
FAX: +44 141 243 2429
E-MAIL: mail@greenbeltgroup.co.uk
CONTACT: Stephen Rees

TILHILL ECONOMIC FORESTRY
Kings Park House,
Laurelhill Business Park,
Stirling FK7 9NS, UK
TEL: +44 1786 435000
FAX: +44 1786 435001
E-MAIL:mailbox@tilhillforestry.co.uk
WEB:http://www.tilhillforestry.co.uk
CONTACT:Matthew Rivers

UNIVERSAL MILLING TECHNOLOGY – UMT
Stockholm Road, Hull, East
Yorkshire HU70XL, UK
TEL : +44 1482 825119
FAX : +44 1482 839806
E-MAIL : keitheyles@tateadlyle.com
CONTACT : Keith Eyles

WOODGEN LTD
Church Court,
Clewers Hill,
Hampshire SO32 2LN, UK
TEL: +44 1489 896 388
FAX: +44 1489 896 602
CONTACT: Edward Willmott

COGENERATION

BG TECHNOLOGY LTD
Gas Research and Technology
Centre, Ashby Road, Loughborough,
Leicestershire LE11, 3GR, UK
TEL : +44 1509 282-689
FAX : +44 1509 283
E-MAIL : roger.webb@bggrc.co.uk
WEB : http://www.bggrc.co.uk
CONTACT : Roger Webb

BOWMAN POWER SYSTEMS LTD
Ocean Quay, Belvidere Road,
Southampton SO 14 5QY, UK
TEL : +44 2380 236700
FAX : +44 23 80 212110
E-MAIL :dainsworth@
bowmanpower.co.uk
CONTACT : D Ainsworth

DALE GAR POWER - TT GENERGY
Electricity Buildings,
Filey, North Yorkshire
YO 14 9PJ, UK
TEL : + 44 1723 514141
FAX : + 44 1723 515723
E-MAIL : sales@ttgenergy.co.uk

MERZ ORCHARD LTD
4 Roger Street,
London WCIN 2jX, UK
TEL: +44 20 7 242 1980
FAX: +44 20 7 242 1981
E-MAIL: bowersd@pbworld.com
CONTACT: Dominic Browers

NATIONAL POWER COGEN
Cogen Court, Cranmore
Boulevard,
Solihull,
West Midlands B90 4LN, UK
TEL: +44 121 506 8000
FAX: +44 121 506 8001
CONTACT: Liz Green

SUGAR KNOWLEDGE INTERNATIONAL LIMITED
Cherry Tree House,
Mill Lane, Alwalton, Peterborough
PE7 3UZ, UK
TEL: +44 1733 232004
FAX: +44 1733 370763
E-MAIL:pbj@sucrose.com
WEB:http://www.sucrose.com
CONTACT: Peter B James

SMALL HYDRO

ALSTOM HYDROPOWER LTD
Leicester Road, Rugby,
Warwickshire CV21 1BD,UK
TEL: +44 1788 542 121
FAX: +44 1788 213 212
CONTACT: Mr Swann

AUR HYDROPOWER LIMITED
9 Beach Tree Close, Stanmore
Middlesex HA7 4UB, UK
TEL : +44 20 8 954 6464
FAX : +44 20 8 874 8827
CONTACT : R P Scott

BINNIE BLACK & VEATCH
Grosvenor House,
69 London Road,
Redhill,
Surrey RH1 ILQ, UK
TEL : +44 1737 774 155
FAX : +44 1737 772 767
E-MAIL : binnie@bv.com
CONTACT : Mr. Spolton

CALEDONIAN ENERGY MANAGEMENT LTD
Gowrie House, 52,
Tay Street,
Perth PH1 STR, UK
TEL : +44 1738 447600
FAX : +44 1738 447601
E-MAIL : mail@caleng.co.uk
WEB : http://www.caleng.co.uk
CONTACT : Simon Grey

CREWDSON & CO LTD
Beck Mills, Kendal, Cumbria,
LA9, 6NY, UK
TEL : +44 1539 730 990
FAX : +44 1539 725 316
CONTACT : D F Crewdson

DERWENT HYDROELECTRIC POWER LTD
Fern Lodge, 11/ Hazelwood Road
Duffield, Derbyshire
DE56 4AA UK
TEL : + 44 1332 840 746
FAX : + 44 1332 840 746
CONTACT : J Needle

UNITED KINGDOM

DOROTHEA RESTORATIONS LTD
Unit 6, Riverside Business Park, St. Anne's Road, Bristol BS4 4ED, UK
TEL : + 44 1179 715 337
FAX : + 44 1179 771 677
CONTACT : GJO Wallis

EVANS ENGINEERING LTD
Trecarrel Mill, Trebullet, Launceston, Cornwall, PL 15 9QE, UK
TEL: +44 1566 782 285
FAX: +44 1566 782 793
E-MAIL: evansengineering@cs.com
WEB: http://www.microhydro.com
CONTACT : Rupert Armstrong - Evans

FRANK FERGUSON AND ASSOCIATES
79 Raw Brae Road, Whitehead, Carrickfergus, Co Antrim BT38 9SZ, UK
TEL: +44 28 93 372225
FAX: +44 1690 372225

GILBERT GILKES & GORDON LTD
Canal Iron Works Kendal, Cumbria LA9 7BZ, UK
TEL: +44 1539 720028
FAX: +44 1539 732110
E-MAIL: hydro@gilkes.com
WEB: http://www.gilkes.com
CONTACT: AL Watson

GREEN & CARTER
Vulcan Works, Ashbrittle, Nr Wellington Somerset TA 21ol Q, UK
TEL : + 44 1823 672365
FAX : + 44 1749672950
CONTACT : Charles Doble

HYDRO ENERGY DEVELOPMENTS LTD
Rowanburn, Canonbie, Dumfriesshire DG14 0RG, UK
TEL: +44 1387 371 355
FAX: +44 1387 371 825
CONTACT: R Pitts

HYDRO-ACTIVE ENGINEERING
16 Luther Close, St Anns, Nottingham, NG3 3PD, UK
TEL: +44 115 958 4113
CONTACT: Arthur Williams

HYDROPLAN UK
Unit 12 Riverside Park, Station Road, Wimborne, Dorset BH21 1QU, UK
TEL: +44 1202 88 66 22
FAX: +44 1202 88 66 09
E-MAIL: info@hydroplan.co.uk
WEB: http://www.hydroplan.co.uk
CONTACT: Kieron Hanson

NEW LAND FOUNDATION
9 Cave Street, Oxford OX4 1BA,UK
TEL: +44 1865 727777
FAX: +44 1865 295063
E-MAIL: cres@technocom.com
CONTACT: James Daniels

NEW MILLS HYDRO
Mill Lane, Island Road, Ballycarry, Co Antrim BT389JW, UK
TEL: +44 28 93 378389
FAX: +44 28 93 353220
E-MAIL: newmills.hydro@onyxnet.co.uk
WEB: http://www.newmillshydro.com
CONTACT: B Brennan

SEARCH
Laurieston Hall, Castle Douglas Kirkcudbrightshire, Scotland DG7 2NB,UK
TEL: +44 164 4450 633
FAX: +44 164 4450 633
E-MAIL: richard1@lauriestonhall.demon.co.uk
CONTACT: Richard Langley

SHOREPOWER UK
PO Box 2, Wellington, Somerset TA21 8LJ, UK
TEL: +441823666177
FAX: +441823666177
WEB: http://www.ShorepowerUK.com
CONTACT: John W Shore

THE ENVIRONMENTAL TRUST
Touchwood, High Street, Stockbridge, Hampshire SO206EY,UK
TEL: +44 1264 810 516
E-MAIL: johnbarnes@hotmail.com
CONTACT: John Barnes

TOM JARDINE
4 Crew Hill Court, Alfrick Worcester WR6 5ES, UK
TEL: +44 1886 830085
FAX: +44 1886 833336
E-MAIL: tom.jardine@lineone.net
CONTACT: Dr Tom Jardine

TRUSHM POWER
I Peniston Court, Melbourne, Derby DE73, IEZ, UK
TEL: +4 4 1332 862 313
CONTACT: Howard Dent

WATER POWER ENGINEERING
Coaley Mill, Coaley, Dursley, Glos GL11 5DS,UK
TEL: +44 1453 890376
FAX: +44 1453 890958
CONTACT: OM Goring

TIDAL

MARINE CURRENT TURBINES LTD
The Warren, Bramshill Road, Eversley, Hampshire RG27 0PR, UK
TEL: +44 118 932 4416
FAX: +44 118 973 0820
E-MAIL: info@marineturbines.com
WEB: http://www.marineturbines.com
CONTACT: Peter Fraenkel

OCEAN POWER DELIVERY LTD
2 Commercial Street, Edinburgh, EH6 6JA, UK
TEL: +44 131 554 8444
FAX: +44 131 554 8544
E-MAIL: enquiries@oceanpd.com
WEB: http://www.oceanpd.com

SEACORE LTD
Marine Construction, Gweek, Helston, Cornwall TR126UD, UK
TEL: +441326221771
FAX: +441326221553
E-MAIL: drilling@seacore.co.uk
WEB: http://www.seacore.co.uk
CONTACT: Richard Reed

TRUSHM POWER
I Peniston Court, Melbourne, Derby DE73, IEZ, UK
TEL: +4 4 1332 862 313
CONTACT: Howard Dent

GEOTHERMAL

BESH ENERGY LTD
34 Park Crescent Elstree, Herts WD6, 3PU, UK
TEL : +44 20B 9539794
FAX : +44 870 0567854
E-MAIL : lar@besh.demon.co.uk
WEB : http://www.besh.co.uk
CONTACT : Lewis A Rossen

GEOSCIENCE LTD
Falmouth, Business Park, Bickland Water Road, Falmouth, Cornwall TR11 4SZ, UK
TEL: +44 1326 21 1070
FAX: +44 1326 21 2754
E-MAIL: earthenergy@geoscience.co.uk
WEB: http://www.earthenergy.co.uk
CONTACT: Robin Curtis

SMART ENERGY UK LTD
282 Shrub End Road, Colchester, Essex CO3 4RL, UK
TEL: +44 1206 516677
FAX: +44 1206 516678
E-MAIL: info@smartenergyuk.com
WEB:http://www.smartenergyuk.com
CONTACT: Allan Berry

WASTE TO ENERGY

ANSALDO VOLUND A/S
Epsilon House, Chilworth
Research Centre, Southampton,
Hampshire S016 7NS, UK
TEL: +44 23 80 767784
FAX: +44 23 80 767445
CONTACT: David Buckle

ASHDOWN ENVIRONMENTAL LTD
The Oast House, Hodore, Upper
Hartfield, East Sussex, TN7 4AR, UK
TEL : +44 1892 770 881
FAX : +44 1892 770 885
E-MAIL : enquiries@ashdown-environmental.co.uk
CONTACT : Dr. C.J. Muskett

AYLESFORD NEWSPRINT LTD
Newsprint House, Bellingham Way,
Aylesford, Kent ME20, 7DL, UK
TEL : +44 1622 796 340
FAX : +44 1622 796 351
E-MAIL
:alan.mckendrick@aylnews.com
WEB : http://www.aylesford-newsprint.co.uk
CONTACT : A S Mckendrick

BALLAST PHOENIX LTD
Victoria Stables, South Road,
Bourne, Lincs PE IO 9LZ, UK
TEL : +44 1778 423345
FAX : +44 1778 423354
CONTACT : David York

BERWICK MANLEY ASSOCIATES LTD
4 Princes Road, Bromham, Bedford
MK43 BQD, UK
TEL : +44 1234 822715
FAX : +44 1234 822715
E-MAIL : bjwrn@globalnet.co.uk
CONTACT : Berwick Manley

BESH ENERGY LTD
34 Park Crescent Elstree,
Herts WD6, 3PU, UK
TEL : +44 20B 9539794
FAX : +44 870 0567854
E-MAIL : lar@besh.demon.co.uk
WEB : http://www.besh.co.uk
CONTACT : Lewis A Rossen

BIFFA WASTE SERVICES LTD
Coronation Road, Cressex Industrial
Estate, High Wycombe,
Buckinghamshire HP 12, 3TZ, UK
TEL : +44 1494 521221
FAX : +44 1494 463308
E-MAIL : reception@biffa.co.uk
WEB : http://www.biffa.co.uk
CONTACT : Peter Davey

CAIRD GROUP
North Road, Ellesmere Port,
South Wirral L65, IAE, UK
TEL : +44 151 355 5262
FAX : +44 151 357 7550
CONTACT : David Lusher

CAPITOL WASTE MANAGEMENT LTD
Prospect House, Aykley Head
Business Centre, Aykley Heads,
Durham DH1 STS, UK
TEL : +44 191 384 4000
FAX : +44 191 375 3210
E-MAIL : cwm@capitol-waste-management.co.uk
WEB : http://www.capitol-waste-management.co.uk
CONTACT : M F Johnson

CORY ENVIRONMENTAL LTD
25 Wellington Street,
London WC2E 7DA, UK
TEL : +44 20 7 379 9090
FAX : +44 20 7 379 8053
E-MAIL : info@coryenvironmental.co.uk
WEB : http://
www.coryenvironmental.co.uk
CONTACT : John Twitchen

COVENTRY AND SOLIHULL WASTE DISPOSAL CO LTD
Bar Road, Whitley,
Coventry CV3 4AN, UK
TEL : +44 24 76507430
FAX : +44 24 76506754
E-MAIL :cswac@cswas.co.uk
CONTACT : Steve Chislett

CSMA CONSULTANTS LTD
Renewable Energy Group,
Trevenson, Pool, Redruth,
Cornwall TR15 3SE, UK
TEL: +44 1209 717724
FAX: +44 1209 710893
E-MAIL: enquiries@csmaconsultants.com
WEB: http://www.csmaconsultants.com
CONTACT: Mr Haydn Seholes

DAVIES ASSOCIATES (UK) LTD
Stoneacre, Heol Ddu, Ammanford,
Carmarthenshire SA18 2UG, UK
TEL : + 44 1269 850224
FAX : + 44 1269 851463
CONTACT : Huw Davies

DRAGON ENERGY FROM WASTE
Station Road, Sibsey, Boston PE22
OSA, UK
TEL : + 44 1205 7505 16
FAX : + 44 1205 7506 10
E-MAIL : peter@dragonheat.co.uk
WEB : http://www.dragonheat.co.uk
CONTACT : Peter Mowbray

ECOVERT GROUP
22-30 Sturt Road,
Frimley Green,
Camberley, Surrey GU16 6HZ, UK
TEL : +44 1252 834470
FAX : +44 1252 838722
E-MAIL :smartin@saur.co.uk
WEB : http://www.saur.co.uk
CONTACT : Simon Martin

ENERGY FROM WASTE LTD
The Powerhouse, Old Wharf Road,
Grantham, Lincolnshire NG31 7AA,
UK
TEL: +44 1476 566622
FAX: +44 1476 566618
CONTACT: Bill Harrison

ENVIROENERGY LTD
12 London Road,
Nottingham NG2 3AB,UK
TEL: +44 115 955 6677
FAX: +44 115 955 6688
E-MAIL: 106155.1750@compuserve.com
WEB: http://
www.ourworld.compuserve.com
CONTACT: David Bradbury

ENVIRONMENTAL BIOTECHNOLOGY LTD. EBL
PO Box 129,
Bridgwater TA5 IYR, UK
TEL : +44 1278 671 527
FAX : +44 1278 671 567
E-MAIL: info@ebl.co.uk
WEB: http://www.ebl.co.uk
CONTACT : Dr. Stephen Etheridge

FIBRE FUEL LTD
342 Edinburgh Avenue,
Slough,
Berkshire SLI 4 TU, UK
TEL: +44 1753 213 200
FAX: +44 1753 790 038
CONTACT : Dr. Andrew Ellis

FOSS-SMITH(PATRICK) TECHNICAL SERVICES
7 Longleat,
Riverfield Drive,
Bedford MK41 OSZ, UK
TEL: +44 1234 272466
FAX: +44 1234 365716
E-MAIL:fossmith@kb.co.uk
CONTACT : Patrick Foss-Smith

GALLIFORD (UK) LTD
Wolvey, Hinkey,
Leicestershire LE10
3JF, UK
TEL: +44 1455 220061
FAX: +44 1455 220749
E-MAIL:midlands@galliford.co.uk

GEMPERATIONS LTD
Unit 20 Romsey Industrial Estates,
Greatbridge Road, Romsey,
Hamshire SO51 OH, UK
TEL : + 44 1794 519022
FAX : + 44 1794 516750
E-MAIL : ebergy@gem-ltd.co.uk
WEB : www.gem-ltd.co.uk

HAMWORTHY COMBUSTION ENGIEERING LTD
Fleets Corner, Waterloo Road,
Poole, Dorset BH17 OLA, UK
TEL : + 44 1202 665566
FAX : + 44 1202 665533
WEB : hamworthygas combustion.com
CONTACT : Gerry Lane

HANSON WASTE MANAGEMENT AND RECYCLING
The Ridge,
Chipping Sodbury, Bristol, UK
TEL : + 44 1454 327999
FAX : + 44 1454 317030
WEB : www.hanson-wastemge.co.in
CONTACT : Dr. Lee Potts

HLCHENLEY BURROWES LTD
HLC House, Upper Interfield,
Malvern WR14 IUT, UK
TEL: +44 1886 830050
FAX: +44 1886 830051
E-MAIL: louise@hichb.com
CONTACT: FJ Bluck

INSTITUTE OF WASTES MANAGEMENT – IWM
9 Saxon Court
St Peter's Gardens
Northampton NNI ISX, UK
TEL: +44 1604 620426
FAX: +44 1604 621339
CONTACT: Mr P Frith

LONDON WASTE LTD
Edmonton Solid Waste
Incineration Plant,
Advent Way, Edmonton
London N18 3AG, uk
TEL: +44 20 8 394 4784
FAX: +44 20 8 345 5794
CONTACT : Brian Gallyot

NNC LTD
Booths Hall, Chelford Road,
Knutsford Cheshire WA16 8QZ, UK
TEL: +44 1565 633800
FAX: +44 1565 843835
E-MAIL: adrian.crank@nnc.co.uk
WEB: http://www.nnc.co.uk
CONTACT: Adrian Crank

ONYX UK LTD
Onyx House, 401 Mile End Road,
London E3 4PB, UK
TEL: +44 20 8 983 1000
FAX: +44 20 8 983 0100
CONTACT: Bill Prescott

OSC PROCESS ENGINEERING LTD
Europa 67, PO Box 57, Stockport,
Cheshire SK3 OTJ, UK
TEL: +44 161 428 0747
FAX: +44 161 491 1565

PLANET ADVANTAGE LTD
Planet House, Albert Place,
Lower Darwen,
Lancashire BB3 0QE, UK
TEL: +44 1254 660330
FAX: +44 1254 674316
E-MAIL: planetadvantage@msn.com
WEB: http://www.planetgroup.co.uk
CONTACT: Mr. Gary Bowater

SCIENTIFIC ANALYSIS LABORATORIES LTD
Medlock House, New Elm Road,
Manchester M3 4JW,UK
TEL: +44 161 827 1400
FAX: +44 161 827 1414
E-MAIL:
bcohen@saiman.demon.co.uk
WEB: http://www.saiman.demon.co.uk

SHANKS
Waste Services Division,
A8 Edinburgh Road,
Coatbridge ML5 4UG, UK
TEL: +44 1236 433671
FAX: +44 123 644 0801
CONTACT: Mr A Alexander

SHEFFIELD HEAT & POWER LTD
2 Sheffield Science Park,
Howard Street, Sheffield S1 2LX, UK
TEL: +441142724278
FAX: +441142720685
E-MAIL: enquiries@shpgroup.co.uk
WEB: http://www.greenenergy.co.uk
CONTACT: Lisa Marshall

SILENT VALLEY WASTE SERVICES LTD
Beechwood House, Cwm, Ebbw
Vale, Gwent NP3 6PZ, UK
TEL: +44 1495 370125
FAX: +44 1495 370125
CONTACT: Adrian Poller

SITA PACKINGTON LTD
Packington Lane, Little Packington,
Meriden, Coventry CV7 7HN, UK
TEL: +44 1675 465 880
FAX: +44 1675 465 740
CONTACT: Trevor Uncles

SITA
Turkey Mill, Ashford Road,
Maidstone, Kent ME14 5PP, UK
TEL: +44 1622 686983
FAX: +44 1622 692196
CONTACT: Tom Jeral

SITA-CLEVELAND WASTE MANAGEMENT LTD
Teesside Energy from Waste Plant,
Haverton Hill Road,
Billingham, TS23 IPY, UK
TEL: +44 1642 202 300
FAX: +44 1642 202 302
CONTACT: John Thistlewood

SOUTH EAST LONDON COMBINED HEAT AND POWER (SELCHP) LTD
Landmann Way, Surrey Canal Road,
Deptford, London SE 14 5RS, UK
TEL: +44 20 7 394 4770
FAX: +44 20 7 252 2986
CONTACT: Gerry Atkins

TYSELEY WASTE DISPOSAL LTD
James Road, Tyseley, Birmingham
B11 2BA, UK
TEL : +44 121 680 2000
FAX : +44 121 680 2051
WEB : http://www.onyxgroup.co.uk
CONTACT : Stuart Sim

UK WASTE MANAGEMENT LIMITED
Gate House castle Estate, Turnpike
Road, High Wycombe,
Buckinghmshire HP12 3NR, UK
TEL : +44 1494 449944
FAX : +44 1494 537779
CONTACT : Chris Parry

UK WASTE MANAGEMENT LIMITED
Gate House Castle Estate,
Turnpike Road, High Wycombe,
Buckinghmshire HP12 3NR, UK
TEL : +44 1494 449944
FAX : +44 1494 537779
CONTACT : Chris Parry

WARDELL ARMSTRONG
Waste Management Section,
Lancaster Building, High Street,
Newcastle-under-Lyme,
Staffordshire ST5 IPQ, UK
TEL: +44 1782 612626
FAX: +44 1782 662882
E-MAIL: wardell@walyme.demon.co.uk
WEB: http://www.wardell-armstrong.com
CONTACT: M G Staff

WASTE MANAGEMENT INFORMATION BUREAU
AEA Technology Plc, F6, Culham,
Abingdon OxfordshireOX14 3DB,UK
TEL: +44 1235 463162
FAX: +44 1235 463004
E-MAIL: wmib@aeat.co.uk
CONTACT: Heather Cholerton

WASTE TO ENERGY LIMITED
Eyston, Borley Green,
Subdury, Suffolk CO107AH, UK
TEL: +44 1787 373007
FAX: +44 1787 373535
E-MAIL: mikeling@waste-to-energy.co.uk
CONTACT: Mike Ling

WORKING BOROUGH COUNCIL
Civic Offices, Gloucester Square,
Woking, Surrey GU2 1YL, UK
TEL: +44 1483 743 490
FAX: +44 1483 768 746
E-MAIL: wokbc@woking.gov.uk
CONTACT: Allan Jones

WRI SERVICES
Donnington, Wroxeter,
Shrewsbury,
Shropshire SY5 6PU, UK
TEL: +44 1952 740414
FAX: +44 1952 740358
E-MAIL: henry@marches.county.net
CONTACT: Henry Chesshire

WYVERN WASTE SERVICES LTD
Chiltern House,
15-17 Silver Street, Taunton,
Somerset TAI 3DH,
TEL: +44 1823 324194
FAX: +44 1823 325051
E-MAIL: mailbox@wyvern waste.com.uk
CONTACT: Peter Daniel

ENERGY EFFICIENCY

BENEDICT CRITCHLEY
Sticklepark, Yarlington, Near
wincanton BA9, BDH, UK
TEL : +44 1963 440662
FAX : +44 1963 440662
E-MAIL : benedict@asheton.de mon.co.uk
CONTACT: Benedict Critchley

CPL ENERGY
Mai Lane, Winger worth
Chesterfield S42 6NG, UK
TEL : +44 1246 212244
FAX : +44 1246 212233
E-MAIL : energy@cplindustries.co.uk
CONTACT : Erik Keis

ENERGY ADVISORY ASOCIATES
I Moores Cottages, Bircher,
Leominster, Herefordshire HR60AX, UK
TEL: +44 1568 780868
FAX: +44 1568 780866
CONTACT : David Olivier

ENERGY CONSERVATION & SOLAR CENTRE – ECSC
Unit 327, 30 Great Guildford Street,
London SEI OHS, UK
TEL: +44 207 9221660
FAX: +44 207 7712344
E-MAIL: energy.ecsc@virgin.net
WEB: http://www.esc.org.uk
CONTACT : John P Thorp

ENERGY MANAGEMENT BROKERS LTD
Kingsgate House, 536 Kings Road,
Chelsea, London SW10 OTE, UK
TEL: +44 20 7 352 9616
FAX: +44 20 7 351 5731
E-MAIL:
p.carlbom@energyquote.co.uk
WEB: http://www.energyquote.co.uk
CONTACT: Paul Carlbom

FELLS ASOCIATES
29 Rectory Terrace, Newcastle-upon
Tyne NE3 IYB, UK
TEL: +44 191 285 5343
FAX: +44 191 285 5343
WEB:http://www.fellassociates.com
CONTACT : Prof. Jan Fells

FUTURE ENERGY SOLUTIONS
Harwell, Didcot Oxfordshire
OX11 0QJ, UK
TEL: +44 1235 433283
FAX: +44 1235 433434
E-MAIL: jackie.maguire@aeat.co.uk
WEB: http://www.future-energy-solutions.com
CONTACT: Jackie Maguire

GCT CONSULTANTS
PO Box 180 Bingley, West Yorkshire
BD 16 IYJ, UK
TEL: +44 1535 273499
FAX: + 44 1535 273411
E-MAIL: gct@towler99.freeserve.co.uk
WEB:http://www.community-heating.uk
CONTACT : George C Towler

HEAT-WIN LTD
Spout House, Bitterley, Ludlow,
Shropshire SY3 3HQ, UK
TEL: +44 1584 890827
FAX: +44 1584 890808
WEB: http://www.dryers-airless.mcmail.com
CONTACT: Thomas J Stubbing

INTERBATIONAL INSTITUTE FOR ENERGY CONSERVATION-EUROPE LTD
21 Tavern Quay,
Rope Street,
London SE16 7TX, UK
TEL: +44 20 7237 6523
FAX: +44 20 7237 2462
E-MAIL: iiec.europe@dial,pipex.com
WEB: http://www.iiec.org

LYNCHMOTOR CO
PO Box 919, London NI IXL, UK
TEL: +44 20 7 607 8141
FAX: +44 20 7 609 3625
E-MAIL: lynch_motor@compuserve.com
CONTACT: Richard Fletcher

MARCHES ENERGY AGENCY
The Shirehall, Abbey Foregate,
Shrewsbury SY2 6ND, UK
TEL: +44 1743 252573
FAX: +44 1743 252572
E-MAIL: marchesenergy@fsbdial.co.uk
CONTACT: Ewan Bent

NATIONAL GRID COMPANY PLC
Ntional Grid House,
Kirby Corner Road,
Coventry CV4 8JY, UK
TEL: +44 24 76 537777
FAX: +44 24 76 423768
CONTACT: A Papageorgi

NEW BERSPECTIVES
Bealings Barn,
Grundisburgh Road
Great Bealings, Woodbridge
Suffolk IP13 6PE, UK
TEL: +44 1473 735638
FAX: +44 1473 735638
E-MAIL: robin@newpersp.demon.co.uk
CONTACT: Robin Sadler

NOTTINGHAM ENERGY PARTNERSHIP
8 Regent Street,
Nottingham NG1 5BQ, UK
TEL: +44 115 9502233
FAX: +44 115 9500320
E-MAIL: nep@nde.org.uk
CONTACT: Miss Helen Weaver

RECOTHERM LTD
1437 Pershore Road,
Stirchely,
Birmingham B30 2JL, UK
TEL : +44 121 433 3622
FAX : +44 121 433 3601
E-MAIL : sales@recotherm.co.uk
WEB : http://www.recotherm.co.uk
CONTACT : Martin Killen

UNITED KINGDOM

RUTHERFORD COLLINS LTD
60 Manville Road, Tooting
London SW17 8JL, UK
TEL: +44 20 8767 7740
FAX: +44 20 8682 2457
E-MAIL: collins@btinternet.com
CONTACT: David Collins

SLP ENERGY
Hamilton House, Battery Green Lane,
Lowestoft, Suffolk NR31 1DE, UK
TEL: +441502587322
FAX: +441502585525
E-MAIL: info@slp-eng.com
WEB: http://www.slp-eng.com
CONTACT: Russell Harper

UNITED UTILITIES
Green Energy, PO Box 824,
Alexandra Gate, Rover Way,
Cardiff CF242SD, UK
TEL: +442920313600
FAX: +442920313617
E-MAIL: generation@uuplc.co.uk
WEB: http://www.unitedutilities.com

FINANCE / BANKING

ACE EUROPE
Global Power Generation,
8-11 Lime Street, London, UK
TEL: +44 20 7 5608019
FAX: +44 20 7 5608114
E-MAIL: eldred.clark@ace-ina.com
CONTACT: Eldred R W Clark

BEVAN ASHFORD
Planning and Energy, 35,
Colston Avenue, Bristol BSI 4TT, UK
TEL : +44 117 975 1600
FAX : +44 117 929 1865
E-MAIL :g.dodds@bevanashford.co.uk
WEB : http://
www.genesis.bevanashford.co.uk
CONTACT : Gerath Dodds

CLEAN ENERGY FUND
33 St James Street,
London SW1A 1HD,UK
TEL: +44 20 7930 1030
FAX: +44 20 7930 1080
E-MAIL: dunev@cleanenergyfund.org
WEB: http://
www.cleanenergyfund.org
CONTACT: Peter Dunev

DELPHI INTERNATIONAL LTD
4th Floor Broughton House, 6-8
Sackville Street, London WIW IDD, UK
TEL : + 44 20 7 734 6344
FAX : + 44 20 7 287 4775
E-MAIL : delphüntl@dial.pipex.com
CONTACT : Adrian Court

ENERGY FINANCE CONSULTANCY
41, Gorst Road, London SWII
16JB, UK
TEL : + 44 20 7 978 5073
FAX : +44 20 7 924 4491
E-MAIL : mrt@energy.u-net.com
CONTACT : Ms. Melissa Taylor

ENERGY POWER RESOURCES LTD
330 Bristol Business Park,
Coldharbour Lane, Bristol BS16 IEJ, UK
TEL : + 44 117 9650220
FAX : + 44 117 9650330
E-MAIL : lucky@eprl.co.uk
CONTACT : Lucy Cull

ERNST & YOUNG
Becket House, 1 Lambeth Palace
Road, London SEI 7EU, UK
TEL: + 44 20 7 9512000
FAX: + 44 20 7 9511345
WEB: http://www.eyuk.com

ERNST & YOUNG
Renewable Energy Unit,
Broadwalk House, Southernhay
West, Exeter EXI ILF, UK
TEL: +44 1392 284300
FAX: + 44 1392 284301
E-MAIL: jjohns@ernsty.co.uk
WEB: http://www.eyi.com/energy.nsf
CONTACT : Jonathan H Johns

FORTIS BANK SA/NV
Energy Finance Group, Camomile,
Court, 23 Camomile Street,
London EC3A 7PP, UK
TEL: +44 20 7 444 8712
FAX: +44 20 7 444 8792
WEB: http://www.fortisbank.com
CONTACT: Nick Gardiner

FORTUM
101 Wigmore Street,
London W1H 9AB, UK
TEL: +44 20 7616 1500
FAX: +44 20 7616 1515
WEB: http://www.fortum.com

FORTUM O & M (UK) LTD
3rd Floor Stuart House,
City Road Peterborough PE1 1QF,UK
TEL: +44 1733 558400
FAX: +44 1733 567449
E-MAIL: Steve.Hawes@fortum.com
CONTACT: Steve Hawes

FT ENERGY
Maple House, 149 Tottenham
Court Road, London W1T 7LB, UK
TEL: +44 20 7 896 2666
FAX: +44 20 7 896 2275
E-MAIL: emma.brady@ft.com
WEB: http://www.ftenergy.com

HYDER INDUSTRIAL LTD
PO Box 295, Alexandra Gate,
Rover Way, Cardiff CF24 5UE, UK
TEL: +44 29 20 585 800
FAX: +44 29 20 585 808
E-MAIL: generation@hyder.com
WEB: http://www.hyder.com
CONTACT: Andrew Diplock

IMPAX CAPITAL CORPORATION LTD
Broughton House,
6-8 Sackville Street,
London W1X 1DD, UK
TEL: +44 20 7 434 1122
FAX: +44 20 7 434 1123
E-MAIL: m.haggard@impax.co.uk
WEB: http://www.impax.com
CONTACT: Melville Haggard

IMPAX CAPITAL CORPORATION LTD
Broughton House, 6-8 Sackville
Street, London WIX IDD, UK
TEL: +44 20 7 434 1122
FAX: +44 20 7 434 1123
E-MAIL: mpax@impax.co.uk
WEB: http://www.impax.co.uk
CONTACT: Melville Haggard

JYA
17 Helix Gardens,
London SW2 2JJ, UK
TEL: +44 20 8 6713598
CONTACT: John Yates

NATURAL POWER LIMITED
Energy House, Daniel Adamson
Road Salford,
Manchester MS 2DT, UK
TEL: +44 161 745 7450
FAX: +44 745 3250
WEB: http://www.energ.co.uk
CONTACT: Mr David Alcock

NEW CENTURY FINANCE LIMITED
Pantiles Chamber, 85 High Street,
Tunbridge Wells,
Kent TNI IYG, UK
TEL: +44 1892 618461
FAX: +44 1892 618567
E-MAIL: rwp@newc
enturyfinance.co.uk
CONTACT: Richard W Price

NSURE RENEWABLES
Rowlands House,
48 Rowlands Road,
Worthing,
West Sussex BN11 3JT, UK
TEL: +44 1903 520200
FAX: +44 1903 520211
E-MAIL: energy@nsure.uk.com
WEB: http://www.nsure.uk.com
CONTACT: Peter Rush

RENEWABLE ENERGY SYSTEMS LTD
Beaufort House, 23 Grosvenor Road, St Albans,
Herts ALI 3AW, UK
TEL : +44 1727 797 900
FAX : +44 1727 797 929
E-MAIL : info@res-ltd.com
WEB : http://www.re-ltd.com
CONTACT : Dr Ian D Mays

SCOTIA ENERGY LTD
Suite 424, Baltic Chambers,
50 Wellington Street,
Glasgow G2 6HJ, UK
TEL: +44 141 248 6622
FAX: +44 141 248 6242
E-MAIL: scotiaenergy @mcmail.com
CONTACT: Robert Miller

SEDGWICK GLOBAL POWER AND UTILITIES
Sedgwick House,
The Sedgwick Centre,
London E1 8DX, UK
TEL: +44 20 7 377 3288
FAX: +44 20 7 481 5981
E-MAIL: mark_r._popplewell @sedgwick.com
CONTACT: Mark Popplewell

THE MILLER INSURANCE GROUP
Dawson House, 5 Jewry Street,
London EC3N 2PJ, UK
TEL: +44 207 488 2345
FAX: +44 207 410 2754
WEB: http://www.windproins.com
CONTACT: Fraser Mclachan

TRIODOS BANK NV
Brunel House,
11 The Promenade
Bristol BS8 3NN, UK
TEL: +44 117 973 9339
FAX: +44 117 973 9303
E-MAIL: simon.roberts@ triodos.co.uk
WEB: http://www.triodos.co.uk
CONTACT: Simon Roberts

TXU EUROPE POWER
PO Box 40, Whersted Park,
Apswitch,
Suffolk IP9 2AQ, UK
TEL : +44 1473 554968
FAX : +44 1473 554521
E-MAIL : gregbacon@ compuserve.com
WEB : http://www.eastern.co.uk
CONTACT : Bill Richmond

ASSOCIATION

ASSOCIATION OF CONSULTING ENGINEERS
Alliance House, 12 Caxton Street
London SWIH OQL, UK
TEL : +44 20 7 222 6557
FAX : +44 20 7 222 0750
E-MAIL : consultr@acenet.co.uk
CONTACT : John Mitchell

ASSOCIATION OF MANUFACTURERS OF POWER GENERATING SYSTEMS-AMPS
PO Box 1714, Andover SP 11, 6SL, UK
TEL : + 44 1264 365367
FAX : +44 1264 362304
E-MAIL : mail@amps.org.uk
WEB : http://www.amps.org.uk
CONTACT : Robert Wheadon

BRITISH PHOTOVOLTAIC ASSOCIATION - PVUK
The Warren, Bramshill Road,
Eversley,
Hampshire RG 27, OPR, UK
TEL : +44 118 932 4418
FAX : +44 118 973 7315
E-MAIL :pv-uk@dial.pipex.com
WEB : http://www.pv-uk.org.uk
CONTACT : Amy Francis

BRITISH WIND ENERGY ASSOCIATION
26 Spring Street,
London W2 IJA, UK
TEL : +44 20 7 402 7102
FAX : +44 20 7 402 7107
E-MAIL : info@bwea.com
WEB : http://www.bwea.com
CONTACT : Alison Hill

CADDET-UK TEAM
ETSU, Harwell, Oxfordshire,
OX11 ORA, UK
TEL : +44 1235 436806
FAX : +44 1235 432331
E-MAIL : mark.thomas@aeat.co.uk
WEB : http://www.caddet-re.org
CONTACT : Mark Thomas

COUNTRY LANDOWNERS ASSOCIATION
Agriculture and Rural Economy Department, 16 Belgrave Square,
London SWIX 8PQ, UK
TEL : +44 20 7 235 0511
FAX : +44 20 7 235 4696
E-MAIL :oliverh@cla.org.uk
WEB : http://www.cla.org.uk
CONTACT : Oliver Harwood

DOUGALL BAILLIE ASSOCIATES LTD
3 Glenfield Road, East Kilbride,
S Lanarkshire G75 ORA, UK
TEL : + 44 1355 266 480
FAX : + 44 1355 221 991
E-MAIL : dougall.baillie@ btinternet.com
CONTACT : George Baillie

ENERGY DATA ASSOCIATES EDA
Bishops Walk House,
19-23 High Street,
Pinner, Middlesex,
HA 5PJ, UK
TEL: +44 20 8866 2991
FAX: +44 20 8868 1104
E-MAIL: jatrinnaman@energyd ataassociates.co.uk
CONTACT : J Trinnaman

ENERGY FROM WASTE ASSOCIATION
26 Spring Street,
London W2 IJA, UK
TEL : +44 20 7 402 7110
FAX : + 44 20 7 402 7115
E-MAIL : ih@efw.bdx.co.uk
WEB : http//www.efw.org.uk
CONTACT : Dr. Stuart Mc Lawaghan

ENERGY TECHNOLOGY PROMOTION LTD
Box 11 Royal Stuart Workshops,
Adelaide Palace
Cardiff Bay,
Cardiff, CFI 6BR, UK
TEL : +44 29 20691393
FAX: + 44 29 20 691393
E-MAIL : 100712.1444% compuserve.com
CONTACT : Simon Burgers

ENVIRONMENTAL SERVICES ASSOCIATION
154 Buckingham Palace Road,
London SWI W9TR, UK
TEL : +44 20 7 824 8882
FAX : +44 20 7 824 8573
E-MAIL : info@esauk.org
WEB :http://www.esault.org
CONTACT : Dr K Hazell

EUROWATT
Room 8-4 Gresham House,
53 Clarendon Road,
Watford,
Hertfordshire WDI ILA, UK
TEL: +44 1923 334144
FAX: +44 1923 244180
CONTACT : J G Mordue

FORESTRY CONTRACTING ASSOCIATION LTD
Dalfling, Blairdaff, Inverurie,
Aberdeenshire AB51 5LA, UK
TEL: +44 1467 651368
CONTACT : Mr Hudson

LONDON BOROUGH OF EALING
Local Agenda 21, 3rd Floor Prceval House, 14-16 Uxbridge Road, Ealing
London WS 2HL, UK
TEL: +44 20 8758 5269
FAX: +44 208579 5453
E-MAIL: LA21@ealing.gov.uk
CONTACT : Michael Calderbank

MIDLANDS RENEWABLE ENERGY TECHNOLOGY TRANSFER – MRETT
Whittle Hill Farm Buildings,
B5330 Road, Nanpantan,
Loughborough leics LE12 9YE, UK
TEL: +44 1509 610033
FAX: +44 1509 610055
E-MAIL: jane@mrett.demon.co.uk
WEB: http://www.mrett.co.uk
CONTACT: Jane Spencer

NATIONAL FARMERS UNION
Agriculture House,
164 Shaftsbury Avenue,
London WC2H 8HL, UK
TEL: +44 20 7 331 7275
FAX: +44 20 7 331 7410
CONTACT: Rachel Barrett

NETWORK FOR ALTERNATIVE TECHNOLOGY & TECHNOLOGY ASSESSMENT-NATTA
C/o Energy and Environment Research Inst. Faculty of Technology
The Open University, Milton Keynes,
Buckinghamshire MK7 6AA, UK
TEL: +44 1908 654638
FAX: +44 1908 858407
E-MAIL: s.j.dougan@open.ac.uk
WEB:http://www.tec.open.ac.uk/eeru/natta/rol.html
CONTACT: Tam Dougan

NICHOLAS PEARSON ASSOCIATES LTD
30 Brock Street, Bath BA1 2LN, UK
TEL: +44 1225 4455 48
FAX: +44 1225 3123 87
E-MAIL: npa.bath@btinternet.com
CONTACT: Nicholas Pearson

O'MAHONEY ASSOCIATES LTD
Natson Mill, Bow Crediton,
Devon EX17 6JE,UK
TEL: +44 1363 82623
FAX: +44 1368 82623
E-MAIL: oma@oma.ws
WEB: http://www.oma.ws
CONTACT: Dr Nicholas Mahoney

OVERSEAS EXHIBITION SERVICES LTD
11 Manchester Square, London
W1 5AB, UK
TEL: +44 20 7 862 2090
FAX: +44 20 7 862 2098
E-MAIL: indo@montnet.com
WEB: http://www.montnet.com
CONTACT: Stephen Luff

RICHARD MORRIS ASSOCIATES
9 Letham Drive, Newlands,
Glasgow G43 2SL, UK
TEL: +44 141 637 3146
FAX: +44 141 586 0515
E-MAIL: richard.morris14@ntlworld.com
CONTACT: Richard Morris

SOLAR TRADE ASSOCIATION LTD
Pengillan,Lerryn,Lostwithiel,
Cornwall PL22 0QE, UK
TEL:+44 1208 873518
FAX:+44 1208 873518
CONTACT:Dr REH Swayne

TIMBER GROWERS ASSOCIATION
5 Dublin Street Lane South,
Edinburg EHI 3PX, UK
TEL: +44 131 538 7111
FAX: +44 131 538 7222
CONTACT:Mr John Gunn

WORLD RENEWABLE ENERGY NETWORK WREN
147 Hilmanton, Lower Earley,
Rading RG6 4HN, UK
TEL: +44 118 961 1364
FAX: +44 118 961 1365
E-MAIL: asayigh@netcomuk.co.uk
WEB: http://www.wrenuk.co.uk
CONTACT: Prof A A M Sayigh

WORLD RESOURCE FOUNDATION
Warmer Bulletin, Heath House,
133 High Stret, Tonbridge,
Kent TN9 IDH, UK
TEL: +44 1732 368333
FAX: +44 1732 368337
E-MAIL: wrf@wrf.org.uk
WEB: http://www.wrf.org.uk
CONTACT: Kit Strange

RESEARCH & DEVELOPMENT

AIR INFILTRATION AND VENTILATION CENTRE- AIVC
Unit 3a, Sovereign Court,
Sir William Lyons Road,
Coventry CV4 7EZ, UK
TEL: +44 24 7669 2050
FAX: +44 24 76 416 306
E-MAIL: airvent@aivc.org
WEB: http://www.aivc.org

AMRITE LTD
PO Box 421, High Wycombe,
Bucks HP10 8QP,
UK
TEL: +44 1494 813205
FAX: +44 1494 813206
E-MAIL:
aduncan@investorsinenergy.com
WEB: http://
www.investorsinenergy.com
CONTACT: Andrew Duncan

AMSET CENTRE
Horninghold,
Leicestershire
LE16 8DH, UK
FAX: +44 1858 555 504
E-MAIL: amset@compuserve.com
CONTACT: Prof John Twidell

BRISTOWS
3 Lincoln's Inn Fields,
London WC2A 3AA,
UK
TEL: +44 20 7 400 8000
FAX: +44 20 7 400 8050
E-MAIL: info@bristows.com
WEB: http://www.bristows.com
CONTACT: Elizabeth Loughran

BRITISH ANTARCTIC SURVEY
Technical Services,
Madingley Road,
Cambridge CB3 0ET,
UK
TEL: +44 1223 221477
FAX: +44 1223 3541730
E-MAIL: d.blake@bas.ac.uk
WEB: http://www.antarctica.ac.uk
CONTACT: David M Blake

BSRIA LTD
Old Bracknell Lane
West Bracknell,
Berks RG12 7AH,
UK
TEL: +44 1344 426511
FAX: +44 1344 487575
E-MAIL: reginald.brown@bsria.co.uk
WEB: http://www.bsria.co.uk
CONTACT: Mr Reginald Brown

CENTRE FOR ECOLOGY AND HYDROLOGY
CEH Wallingford,
Wallingford,
Oxfordshire, UK
TEL: +44 1491 838 800
FAX: +44 1491 692424
E-MAIL: grees@ceh.ac.uk
WEB: http://www.ceh.ac.uk
CONTACT: Mr Gwyn Rees

CENTRE FOR RENEWABLE ENERGY SYSTEMS TECHNOLOGY – CREST
Angela Marmont Renmewable Energy Laboratory,
Loughborough University,
Loughborough,
Leicestershire, LE11 ITU, UK
TEL : +44 1509 223466
FAX : +44 1509 610031
E-MAIL : A.J.Whitel@lboro.ac.uk
WEB : http://www.lboro.ac.uk/departments/el/research/crest
CONTACT : Allison White

CENTRE FOR SUSTAINABLE ENERGY
The Create Centre,
B-Bond Warehouse,
Smeaton Road,
Bristol BSI 6XN, UK
TEL : +44 117 929 9950
FAX : +44 117 929 91114
E-MAIL :info@cse.org.uk
WEB : http://www.cse.org.uk
CONTACT : Gareth Jones

COMBINED LANDFILL PROJECTS LIMITED-CLP
20-22 Queen Street, Mayfair,
London W1X 7PJ, UK
TEL: +44 20 7 629 2668
FAX: +44 20 7 408 1216
WEB: http://www.clp-energy.com
CONTACT: David Fitzherbert/
Christopher Eden

CRANFIELD UNIVERSITY
Applied Energy Group,
Bedfordshire,
MK43 OAL, UK
TEL : +44 1234 750111
FAX : +44 1234 750728
E-MAIL : c.anderson@cranfield.ac.uk
CONTACT : Prof. Doug Probert

DAVID LANGHAM
Stone End, 6 Ratten Row,
Seamer,
Scarborough YO12 4BQ, UK
TEL: +44 1723 864 813
FAX: +44 1723 864 813
CONTACT: David Langham

DJ CONSTRUCTION LIMITED
Plas Eirias, Abergele Road,
Colwyn Bay,
Clwyd LL29 8BF, UK
TEL: +44 1492 517 534
FAX: +44 1492 514 886
E-MAIL: admin@djc.co.uk
CONTACT: Huw Smallwood

DM ENERGY
23 The Gallops, Lewes,
East Sussex BN7 ILR, UK
TEL : + 44 1273 474 446
FAX : + 44 1273 474 446
E-MAIL : dmilborrow@compuserve.com
CONTACT : David Milborrow

DYFI ECO VALLEY PARTNERSHIP
Unit I Dyfi Eco Parc,
Machynlleth,
Powys SY20 8AX, UK
TEL: +44 1654 705018
FAX: +44 1654 703000
E-MAIL: ecodyfi@gn.apc.org
CONTACT: Andy Rowland

EA TECHNOLOGY LTD
Power Systems,
Capenhurst, Chester,
CHI 6ES, UK
TEL: +44 151 339 4181
FAX: +44 151 347 2226
E-MAIL: hb@eatl.co.uk
WEB: http://www.eatl.co.uk
CONTACT: Eleanor Brown

ECOGEN LTD
PO Box 7, Machynlleth,
Powys, SY20 8WE, UK
TEL: +44 1654 703141
FAX: +44 1654 703105
E-MAIL: timkirby@ecogen.co.uk
WEB: http://www.ecogen.co.uk
CONTACT: Tim Kirby

EDINBURGH SUSTAINABLE ARCHITECTURE UNIT
University of Edinburgh, 20
Chalmers Street,
Edinburgh EH1 IJZ, UK
TEL : +44 131 650 2300
FAX : +44 131 650 8019
CONTACT : Dr Roger Talbot

ELECTRECOL ENGINEERING
Bishops Offley,
Stafford ST21 6ET, UK
TEL : +44 1785 280 447
FAX : +44 1785 280 678
E-MAIL : electrecol@webfactory.co.uk
Contact : Patrick Horton

ENERGY POWER RESOURCES LTD
330 Bristol Business Park,
Coldharbour Lane, Bristol BS16 1EJ,
UK
TEL: +44 117 9650220
FAX: +44 117 9650330
E-MAIL: lucy@eprl.co.uk
CONTACT: Lucy Cull

FOREST RESEARCH STATION
Silviculture & Seeds Research
Branch, Forestry Commission,
Alice Holt Lodge, Farnham, Surrey
GU10 4LH, UK
TEL: +44 1420 22255
FAX: +44 1420 23653
E-MAIL: a.armstrong@forestry.gov.uk
CONTACT: Alan Armstrong

H MELL & SON
Old Trent Road, Beckingham,
Doncaster, Yorkshire DN10 4PY, UK
TEL: +44 1427 848210
FAX: +44 1427 848069
CONTACT: Chris Mell

HEAT-WIN LTD
Spout House, Bitterley, Ludlow,
Shropshire SY8 3HQ, UK
TEL: +44 1584 890827
FAX: +44 1584 890808
WEB: http://www.dryersairless.mcmail.com
CONTACT: Thomas J Stubbing

HEBE
Tamarisk, Bishops Walk,
Whiteshill, Stroud Gloucestershire
GL6 6BW, UK
TEL: +44 1453 756571
FAX: +44 1453 756571
CONTACT: Jackie Carpenter

HERIOT-WATT UNIVERSITY
International Centre for Island
Technology, Old Academy,
Back Road,
Stomness, Orkney
KW16 3AW, UK
TEL: +44 1856 850 605
FAX: +44 1856 851 349
E-MAIL: library@icit.civ.hw.ac.uk
WEB: http://www.icit.demon.co.uk
CONTACT: Colin Bullen

IEA GREENHOUSE GAS PROG
CRE Group Stroke Orchard
Cheltenham GL52 4RZ, UK
TEL: +44 1242 680753
FAX: +44 1242 680758
E-MAIL: paul@ieagreen.demon.co.uk
WEB: http://www.ieagreen.org.uk
CONTACT: Dr Paul Freund

IMAGINE MEDIA LTD
Kennel House, Hammersley Lane
Penn, Bucks HP10 8HE, UK
TEL: +44 1494 812890
FAX: +44 1494 813151
E-MAIL: help@imaginemedia.co.uk
WEB: http://www.imaginemedia.co.uk
CONTACT: Mr Jake Brumby

UNITED KINGDOM

IMPERIAL COLLEGE OF SCIENCE TECHNOLOGY & MEDICINE
Electrical & Electronic Engineering Department, Prince Consort Road, London, SW7 2BT, UK
TEL: +44 20 7 589 5111 ext 5205
FAX: +44 20 7 823 8125

INNOGY PLC
Corporate Communications
Windmill Hill Business Park
Whitehill Way, Swindon SN5 6PB, UK
TEL: +44 1793 892616
FAX: +44 1793 893741
E-MAIL: robert.lewis@natpower.com
CONTACT: Robert Lewis

INSTITUTE OF HYDROLOGY
Maclean Building,
Crowmarsh Gifford,
Wallingford,
Oxon OX10 8BB, UK
TEL: +44 1491 838800
FAX: +44 1491 692424
E-MAIL: n.runnalls@ioh.ac.uk
WEB: http://www.nwl.ac.uk/in
CONTACT: Neil Runnalls

LAFARGE BRAAS ROOFING ACCESSORIES GMBH & CO KG
TEL: +49 6171 61 2590
FAX: +49 6171 61 2912
E-MAIL: roland.neuner@lafarge-braas.com

LONDON RESEARCH CNETER
Environment and Transport,
81 Black Prince Road,
London SEI 75Z, UK
TEL: +44 207 787 5648
FAX: +44 20 7 983 4706
EMAIL:david.hutchinson@london-research.gov.uk

NATIONAL ENGINEERING LABORATORY
East Kilbride Glasgow,
G75, 0QU, UK
TEL: +44 1355 220222
FAX: +44 1355 272333
EMAIL:rhunter@net.uk
CONTACT:Ray Hunter

NICERT
University Of Ulster, Cromore Road,
Coleraine, Co Londonderry
BT52 1SA, UK
TEL: +44 28703 24477
FAX: +44 28703 24900
E-MAIL: info@nicert.org
WEB: http://www.nicert.org
CONTACT: Dr David McIlveen-Wright

OFFSHORE TECHNOLOGY MANAGEMENT LTD
44 Quarry Street,
Guildford,
Surrey GU1 3XQ, UK
TEL: +44 1483 598000
FAX: +44 1483 598010
E-MAIL:
chris.dudgeon@otment.co.uk
CONTACT: Christopher Dudgeon

OXFORD BROOKES UNIVERSITY
School Of Engineering,
Gipsy Lane Campus,
Headington,
Oxford OX3 0PB, UK
TEL: +44 1865 483604
FAX: +44 1865 484263
E-MAIL: mhutchins@brookes.ac.uk
CONTACT: Prof MG Hutchins

REACH POWER LTD
Lamorna House, Alstone,
Tewkesbury GL20 8JD, UK
TEL: +44 1242 620 193
FAX: +44 870 137 2725
E-MAIL: reach@reach.co.uk
WEB: http://www.reach.co.uk
CONTACT: Mr. Iain Johnston

SCIENCE POLICY RESEARCH UNIT -SPRU
Mantell Building,
University Of Sussex, Brighton,
East Sussex BN1 9RF, UK
TEL: +44 1273 686758
FAX: +44 1273 685865
E-MAIL: m.e.winder@sussex.ac.uk
WEB: http://www.sussex.ac.uk/spru
CONTACT: Maureen Winder

SCOTTISH SOLAR ENERGY GROUP-SSEG
C/O School Of Engineering,
Napier University,
10 Colinton Road,
Edinburgh EH10 5DT,
UK
TEL: +44 131 455 2660
FAX: +44 131 455 2264
E-MAIL: k.macgregor@napier.ac.uk
WEB: http://www.sseg.org.uk
CONTACT: Kerr MacGregor

SOUTH BANK UNIVERSITY
School Of Electrical Engineering,
103 Borough Road,
London SE10AA, UK
TEL: +44 20 7 815 7513
FAX: +44 20 7 815 7599
E-MAIL: reehalhs@sbu.ac.uk
CONTACT: Dr HS Reehal

TUV ENERGY SERVICE
12 Marshall Road, Hillmead,
Swindon, Wiltshire SN5 9FZ, UK
TEL: +44 1793 882422
FAX: +44 1793 882433
E-MAIL: wgoetz@sw.tuvps.co.uk
WEB: http://www.tuv-energy.co.uk
CONTACT: Dr. Werner Goetz

UNIVERSITY OF BIRMINGHAM
Department of Civil Engineering,
PO Box 363, Birmingham
B15 2TT, UK
TEL: +44 121 414 5069
FAX: +44 121 414 3675
E-MAIL: c.f.forster@bham.ac.uk
CONTACT: Dr. C Forster

UNIVERSITY OF EAST ANGLIA
School of Environmental Sciences
Norwich NR4 7TU, UK
TEL: +44 1603 592994
FAX: +44 1603 507719
E-MAIL: darch@uea.ac.uk/env
CONTACT: Dr. JP Darch

UNIVERSITY OF GLASGOW
CERPD, 72 Oakfield Avenue,
Glasgow G12 8LT, UK
TEL: +44 141 330 5242
FAX: +44 141 330 6004
E-MAIL : v.agelidis@elec.gla.ac.uk
CONTACT: Dr. Vassilios G Agelidis

UNIVERSITY OF LEICESTER
Electrical And Electronic Power Engineering Group, University Road,
Leicester LE1 7RH, U
TEL: +44 116 252 2553
FAX: +44 116 252 2619
E-MAIL: j.bleijs@le.ac.uk
WEB: http://www.le.ac.uk/engineering/bleijs.htm
CONTACT: Dr JAM Bleijs

UNIVERSITY OF NORTH LONDON
Low energy Architecture Research unit faculty of environmental and social studies, 166-220 Holloway Road, London n78db, UK
TEL+44 20 7753
FAX :+442077536166
E-MAIL : a.vijoen@unl.ac.uk/learn
CONTACT : Andre Vijoen

UNIVERSITY OF NORTHUMBRIA
Northumbria Photo Voltaics Applications Centre-NPAC Ellison Place Newcastle Upon Tyne Neistuk
TEL : +441912274595
FAX : +441912273650
E-MAIL : nicola.pearsall@unn.ac.uk
CONTACT : Dr Nicola Pearsall

UNIVERSITY OF NOTTINGHAM
Division of Mechanical Engineering
University Park, Nottingham
NG72RD, UK
TEL : +44115951 3785
FAX :+44 1159513800
E-MAIL : stephenpickering@
nottingham.ac.uk
WEB : http://www.nottingham.ac.uk
CONTACT : Dr Stephen Pickering

UNIVERSITY OF READING
Centre for Agricultural Strategy,
Po Box 236, Earley Gate,
Reading RG6 2AT, UK
TEL: +44 1189 318150
FAX: +44 1189 353 423

UNIVERSITY OF READING
Department of cybernetics
Whiteknights PO Box 225,
Reading Berkshire RG6'6ay, UK
TEL : +44 1189 318223
FAX : +44 1189 318220
E-MAIL : cybgrw@cyber.
readingac.uk
WEB : http://www.cyber.rdg.ac.uk
CONTACT : Dr George Whitfield

UNIVERSITY OF READING
Energy group
Department of Engineering,
Whitknights Reading,
Berkshire G6 6ay, UK
TEL : +44118931 8756
FAX : +44118 931 3327
E-MAIL : energy.group@
reading.ac.uk
WEB :http://www.reading.
ac.uk.energy
CONTACT : Dr Annie Ewheldon

UNIVERSITY OF SOUTHAMPTON
Department of engineering
Materials, Highfield,Southampton
Hampshire SO17 IBJ, UK
TEL : 44 2380 593783
FAX : 44 2380 593016
E-MAIL : t.markvart@soton.ac.uk
WEB : http://www.unisa.edu.ac.uk
CONTACT : Dr Thomas Markvart

UNIVERSITY OF SOUTHAMPTON
Sustainable Energy Research Group
Civil and Environmental Engineering
Department, Southampton
SO17 IBJ, UK
TEL : 442380592051
FAX : 442380677519
E-MAIL : bahaj@soton.ac.uk
WEB : www.soton.ac.uk
CONTACT : Dr A S Bahaj

UNIVERSITY OF SUNDERLAND
Renewable Energy Centre,
School Of Sciences, Ryhope Road,
Sunderland SR2 7EE, UK
TEL: +44 191 515 2845
FAX: +44 191 515 2741
E-MAIL:
bob.harrison@sunderland.ac.uk
CONTACT: R Harrison

UNIVERSITY OF ULSTER
School of the Built Environment
Faculty of Engineering,
Newtownabbey,
BT370QB, UK
TEL: +44 28 90 366907
FAX: +44 28 90 368239
E-MAIL: sng.lo@ulst.ac.uk
CONTACT: Dr. Stevelo

WASTE GAS TECHNOLOGY UK LTD
Unit 2 Vicarage Farm
Business Park,
Winchester Road,
Fair Oak Near Eastleigh,
Hampshire SO50 7HD, UK
TEL: +44 1703 695422
FAX: +44 1703 695433
CONTACT: Tony Grimshaw

WRC PLC
Soil Waste and Groundwater Group,
Henley Road, Medmenham, Marlow,
Buckinghamshire SL7 2HD,
TEL: +44 1491 636629
FAX: +44 1491 579 094
E-MAIL: solutions@wrcplc.co.uk
WEB: http://www.wrcplc.co.uk
CONTACT: Drusilla Riddell Black

UNIVERSITIES

BARTLETT SCHOOL OF ARCHITECTURE
University College London,
Gower Street,
London WC IE 68T, UK
TEL : +44 20 7 380 7890
FAX : +44 20 7 916 1987
E-MAIL : b.croxford@ucl.ac.uk
WEB : http://www.barlett.ucl.ac.uk/
web/ben
CONTACT : Dr. Ben Croxford

CITY UNIVERSITY
School Of Engineering,
Northampton Square,
London EC1V OHB, UK
TEL: +44 20 7 477 8112
FAX: +44 20 7 477 8570
WEB: http://www.city.ac.uk/
engineering/ete
CONTACT: Linda Brooks

DEMONTFORT UNIVERSITY
Institute of Energy and Sustainable
Development, Netherleys Building,
Scraptoft Campus, Scraptoft,
Leicester LE7 9SU UK
TEL : + 44 116 2577961
FAX : + 44 116 2577977
E-MAIL : klomas@dmu.ac.uk
CONTACT : Prof Kevin Lomas

LIVERPOOL JOHN MOORES UNIVERSITY
Environmental Solutions Unit,
Clarence Street,Liverpool L3 5UG, UK
TEL : +44 151 231 3182
FAX : +44 151 231 3182
E-MAIL :m.e.sweeney@livjm.ac.uk
CONTACT : Mary Sweeney

OPEN UNIVERSITY
Energy And Environment Research
Unit – EERU, Walton Hall, Milton
Keynes MK7 6AA, UK
TEL: +44 1908 653 335
FAX: +44 1908 858 407
E-MAIL: g.a.boyle@open.ac.uk
WEB: http://www.tec.open.ac.uk/eeru
CONTACT: Christopher Pym

SUSSEX UNIVERSITY -SCHOOL OF CHEMISTRY PHYSICS AND ENVIRONMENTAL SCIENCE
Brighton BNI 9QJ, UK
TEL: +44 1273 678 389
FAX: +441273 677 196
E-MAIL:m.a.tribe@sussex.ac.uk
CONTACT:Dr Michael Tribe

UNIVERSITY OF ABERDEEN
Land Economy Department,
St. Marys, Aberdeen, UK
TEL: +44 1224 272357
FAX: +44 1224 273487
E-MAIL: landecon@abdn.ac.uk
WEB: http://www.abdn.ac.uk/landecon
CONTACT: Mrs. Maureen Wattie

UNIVERSITY OF BIRMINGHAM
Department of Civil Engineering,
PO Box 363, Birmingham
B15 2TT, UK
TEL: +44 121 414 5069
FAX: +44 121 414 3675
E-MAIL: c.f.forster@bham.ac.uk
CONTACT: Dr. C Forster

UNIVERSITY OF EAST ANGLIA
School of Environmental Sciences
Norwich NR4 7TU, UK
TEL: +44 1603 592994
FAX: +44 1603 507719
E-MAIL: darch@uea.ac.uk/env
CONTACT: Dr. JP Darch

NGO's

CENTRE FOR ENVIRONMENTAL INITIATIVES – CEI
The Old school House,
Mill Lane
Carshalton, SMS 2JY, UK
TEL : +44 20 8 770 6611
FAX : +44 20 8 647b 0719
E-MAIL : cei@oxford.com
WEB : http://www.a4u.com/cei
CONTACT : Lisa Loughlin

ENERGY21
PO Box 154, Stroud,
Gloucester GL5 4YS,
UK
TEL: +44 1453 752277
FAX: +44 1459 752244
E-MAIL: info@energy21.org.uk
WEB: http://www.energy21org.uk
CONTACT : Jackie Carpenter

GREEN PEACE UK
Canonbury Villas,
London NI 2PN, UK
TEL : + 44 207865 8100
FAX : + 44 20 7 865 8200
WEB : www.greenpeace.org.uk

WASTE WATCH
Ground Floor,
Europa House,
13-17 Ironmonger Row,
London ECIV 3QG, UK
TEL: +44 20 7 253 6266
FAX: +44 20 7 253 5962
E-MAIL: info@wastewatch.org.uk
WEB: http://
www.wastewatch.org.uk
CONTACT: Ray Georgeson

WORLD ENERGY COUNCIL
5th Floor Regency House, 1-4
Warwick Street,
London W1B SLT, UK
TEL: +44 20 7734 5996
FAX: +44 20 7734 5926
E-MAIL: info@worldenergy.org
WEB: http://www.worldenergy.ord
CONTACT: Mr Gerald Doucet

WWF-UK
Panda House,
Weyside Park,
Godalming,
Surrey GU7 IXR, UK
TEL: +44 1483 412545
FAX: +44 1483 426409
E-MAIL: rmarsh@wwfnet.org
WEB: http://www.wwf-uk.org
CONTACT: Russell Marsh

CONSULTANTS

A FERRAND STOBART & ASSOCIATES
Bower Orchard, Church Lane,
Orleton, Near Ludlow SY8 4HU, UK
TEL: +44 1568 780837
FAX: +44 1568 780837
CONTACT: AF Stobart

ABB OFFSHORESYSTEMS LTD
Rosemanowes, Herniss, Penryn,
Cornwall TR109DU, UK
TEL: +44 1209 860141
FAX: +44 1209 861013
CONTACT: John Cowles

ACOUSTIC DESIGN LTD
Unit 41A Lady Lane Estate,Hadleign
Ipswich, Suffolk IP7 6BQ, UK
TEL: +44 1473 824452
FAX: +44 1473 824408
E-MAIL: adl@acoustic.co.uk
WEB: http://www.acoustic.co.uk
CONTACT: PW Eade

ADAC (ENGINEERING SERVICES) LTD
10 Nellfield Road,
Crieff PH7 3DU, UK
TEL: +44 1764 656 097
FAX: +44 1764 656 097
CONTACT: Mr AO Armstrong

ADAMS ENVIRONMENTAL LTD
The Business Centre, 103-109
Lavender Hill, London SW11 5QL,
UK
TEL: +44 20 7 350 0140
FAX: +44 20 7 350 1450
E-MAIL:
robertk@adamsenviro.demon.co.uk

ADAS ENVIORNMENT
Gleadthorpe Grange, Meden Vale,
Mansfield, Nottinghamshire
NG20 9PD, UK
TEL: +44 1623 846 742
FAX: +44 1623 847 424
E-MAIL: chris.stansfield@adas.co.uk
WEB: http://www.adasenviornment.com
CONTACT: Chris Stansfield

ADVANTICA TECHNOLOGIES LTD
Gas Research And Technology
Centre, Ashby Road, Loughborough,
Leicestershire LE11 3GR, UK
TEL: +44 1509 282 000
FAX: +44 1509 283 064
E-MAIL:
nigel.clark@advanticatech.com
WEB: http://www.advanticatech.com
CONTACT: Nigel Clark

AEOLUS PARTNERSHIP
I The Weald, Ashford,
Kent TN24 8RA, UK
TEL: +44 1233 621341
FAX: +44 1233 621341
E-MAIL:
dteal@aeolus.worldonline.co.uk
WEB: http://www.aeolus-partnership.co.uk
CONTACT: DLE Teal

ALBRO PLANNING & ENVIRONMENTAL
Albro Castle, St Dogmaels,
Cardigan, Ceredigion SA43 3LH, UK
TEL: +44 1239 615730
FAX: +44 1239 615730
E-MAIL: PeteAlbro@aol.com
CONTACT: Peter Newland

ALLEN & OVERY
One New Change,
London EC4M 9QQ, UK
TEL: +44 20 7 330 3000
FAX: +44 20 7 330 9999
WEB: http://www.allenovery.com
CONTACT: John Scriven

ALLOT & LOMAX
Fairbairn House, Ashton Lane,
Sale, Manchester M33 1WP, UK
TEL: +44 161 962 1214
FAX: +44 161 905 5855
E-MAIL: allot@allot.co.uk
CONTACT: David Compston

AML CONSULTANTS
Westbury House,
44 Dome Hill,
Caterham, Surrey CR3 6EB, UK
TEL: +44 1883 330123
FAX: +44 1883 330123
CONTACT: Martin Walters

ARUP
Arup Energy, 13 Fitzroy Street,
London W1T 4BQ, UK
TEL: +44 20 77554054
FAX: +44 20 77552270
E-MAIL: rupert.blackstone@arup.com
WEB: http://www.arup.com
CONTACT: Mr Rupert Blackstone

ASPINWALL & COMPANY
Walford Manor,
Baschurch,
Shrewsbury SY4, 2HH, UK
TEL : +44 1939 262 312
FAX : +44 1939 238 312
E-MAIL:
howard.robinson@aspinwall.co.uk
CONTACT : B. Latham

BABTIE GROUP LIMITED
Environmental Technology 95
Bothwell Street, Glasgow G2 7HX, UK
TEL: +44 141 204 2511
FAX: +44 141 226 3109
E-MAIL:
100634.1540@compuserve.com
WEB: http://www.babtie.com
CONTACT: Bruce Durning

BARTON WILLMORE PARTNERSHIP
2nd floor, Elizabeth House,
1 High Street, Chesterton,
Cambridge CB4 IWB, UK
TEL : +44 1223 345555
FAX : +44 1223 345550
E-MAIL : planning@anglia.barton willmore.co.uk
WEB : http://
www.bartonwillmore.co.uk
CONTACT : Adrian James

BEACON ENERGY LTD
Whittle Hill Farm Buildings, B5330
Road Nanpantan, Loughborough
Leicestershire LE12 9YE, UK
TEL : +44 1509 610033
FAX : +44 1509 610055
E-MAIL : wendy@mrett.co.uk
CONTACT : Prof. Antony Marmont

BENEDICT CRITCHLEY
Sticklepark, Yarlington,
Near Wincanton BA9 8DH, UK
TEL: +44 1963 440662
FAX: +44 1963 440662
E-MAIL:
benedict@asheton.demon.co.uk
CONTACT: Benedict Critchley

BERWICK MANLEY ASSOCIATES LTD
4 Princes Road, Bromham,
Bedford MK 43 8QD, UK
TEL: +44 1234 822 715
FAX: +44 1234 822 715
E-MAIL: bjwm@globalnet.co.uk
CONTACT: Berwick Manley

BETZDEARBORN LTD
Foundery Lane, Widnes, Cheshire,
WAB 8ud, UK
TEL : +44 151 424 5351
FAX : +44 151 423 2722
CONTACT : Gill Evans

BIRSE PROCESS ENGINEERING
Alexander House 4,
Station Road, Cheadle Hulme,
Cheshire SK8, 5AE, UK
TEL : +44 161 486 9191
FAX : +44 161 488 4686
CONTACT : Andrew Horsefield

BLACK & VEATCH
Grosvenor House, 69 London Road,
Redhill, Surrey RHI ILQ, UK
TEL : +44 1737 77 41 55
FAX : +44 1737 85 64 41
E-MAIL : unsworth@bv.com
CONTACT : Ian D Unsworth

BRAID CONSULTING
13 Great Stuart Street,
Edignburgh EH3 7TP, UK
TEL : +44 131 466 5544
FAX : +44 131 466 7755
E-MAIL : mvbrown@compuserve.com
CONTACT : Michael Brown

BRITISH ENERGY
10 Lochside Place, Edinburgh
EH12 9DF, UK
TEL: +44 131 527 20 00
FAX: +44 131 527 20 99
CONTACT: David Hollick

BUSINESS AND THE ENVIRONMENT
Woodlands Wheatsheaf Close, Horsell,
Woking, Surrey GU21, 4BL, UK
TEL : +44 1483 770458
FAX : +44 1483 764203
E-MAIL : alan.turnerl@
btinternet.com
CONTACT : Dr Alan Turner

CAA BARNES & PARTNERS
Loyton Farm, Morebath,
Tiverton, Devon, EX 16 9AS, UK
TEL : +44 1398 331051
FAX : +44 1398 331052
E-MAIL :
alickbarnes.swic@farmline.com
WEB : http://www.swic.uk
CONTACT : Alick Barnes

CADOGAN CONSULTANTS
Corruna House, 39, Cadogan Street
Glasgow G2 7AB, UK
TEL : +44 141 270 7060
FAX : +44 141 270 7061
E-MAIL : r.loudon@cadoganco nsultants.co.uk
WEB : http://www.cadogan consultants.co.uk
CONTACT : Mr Robert Loudon

CAMBRIDGE ARCHITECTURAL RESEARCH LTD
The Eden Centre, 47 City Road,
Cambridge CDI IDP, UK
TEL : +44 1223 460475
FAX : +44 1223 464142
E-MAIL : k.steemers@carltd.com
WEB : http://www.carltd.com
CONTACT : Dr. Koen Steemers

CARTER (M) ASSOCIATES
Station House, Long Street,
Atherstone, Warwickshire CV9, IBH,
UK
TEL : +44 1827 717891
FAX : +44 1827 718507
CONTACT : Leslie Heasman

CHRIS BLANDFORD ASSOCIATES
The Old Crown High Street,
Blackboys, Near Uckfield,
East Sussex TN22 5JR, UK
TEL: +44 1435 866488
FAX: +44 1435 864381
CONTACT: Chris Blandford

CINAR LTD
11 Elvaston Place,
London SW7 5QG, UK
TEL: +44 20 7 581 2245
FAX: +44 20 7 581 2265
E-MAIL: tahir@cinar.co.uk
WEB: http://www.cinar.demon.co.uk
CONTACT: Frances Scott

COMMUNITY POWER LTD
The Cottage, Llanwern, Newport,
Gwent NP18 2DS, UK
TEL: +44 1633 411856
FAX: +44 1633 411856
E-MAIL:
100045.3040@compuserve.com
CONTACT: Alan Lloyd

CONSULTANTS IN ENVIRONMENTAL SCIENCES LTD
Maunsell House, 160 Croydon Road,
Beckenham, Kent BR3 4DE, UK
TEL: +44 20 8 663 6730
FAX: +44 20 8 663 6731
E-MAIL: post@beckces.demon.co.uk
WEB: http://www.ces-environmental.co.uk
CONTACT: Dr RM Sterritt

CONSULTANTS ON PROCESS ENGINEERING LTD-COPE
29 Starbold Crescent, Knowle,
Solihull B93 9LA, UK
TEL: +44 1564 777995
FAX: +44 1564 774134
CONTACT: Prof AV Bridgwater

CONVERSION AND RESOURCE EVALUATION LTD
9 Myrtle House, 5 Cassowary Road,
Birmingham 820, INE, UK
TEL : +44 121 551 0344
FAX : +44 870 0542981
E-MAIL :
cpeacocke@care.demon.co.uk
WEB : http://www.care.demon.co.uk
CONTACT : Dr Cordner Peacocke

CORDAH ENVIRONMENTAL MANAGEMENT CONSULTANTS
Kettock Lodge, Aberdeen Science and Technology, Park, Bridge of Don, Aberdreen AB22 8GU, UK
TEL : +44 1244 414200
FAX : +44 1244 414250
E-MAIL : main@cordah.co.uk
WEB : http://www.cordah.co.uk
CONTACT : Tim Curtis

CPL SCIENTIFIC LTD
43 Kingfisher Court, Newbury
Berkshire RG 14 5SJ, UK
TEL : +44 1635 524064
FAX : +44 1635 529322
E-MAIL : info@cpsci.demon.co.uk
CONTACT : Dr Jim Coombs

CRE GROUP LTD
Stoke Orchard, Cheltenham, Gloucestershire, GL52, 4RZ, UK
TEL : +44 1242 673 361
FAX : +44 1242 677010
E-MAIL : enquiry@cregroup.co.uk
CONTACT : John Gale

CT LUKEHURST
52 Broadstairs Road, St Peters, Broadstairs, Kent CT10 2RJ, UK
TEL: +44 1843 861690
FAX: +44 1843 861960
CONTACT: Dr CT Lukehurst

DAVID WOLFENDEN & COMPANY LIMITED
Be Havillands Crux Easton, Newbury, Berkshire PG20 9QF, UK
TEL : + 44 1635 255230
FAX : + 44 1635 254707
E-MAIL : DWCLMati@aol.com
WEB : http://members.aol.com/dwolfendenco
CONTACT : Phil Stevens

DPM INTERNATIONAL LTD
Management Division,
Suite 539,
Baltic Chambers,
50 Wellington Street,
Glasgow G2 6HJ, UK
TEL: +44 141 226 4915
FAX: +44 141 248 6242
E-MAIL: scotiaenergy@mcmail.com
CONTACT: Robert Miller

DRYAD FFWRNAIS
Plas Einion, Ffwrnais, Machynlleth
Powsys SY20 8PG, UK
TEL : + 44 1674 781375
FAX : + 44 1654 781417
E-MAIL : dyfitrees@enterprise.net
CONTACT : Philip Potter

DULAS LTD
Unit1 Dyfi Eco Park,
Machynlleth,
Powys SY20 8AX, UK
TEL: +44 1654 705000
FAX: +44 1654 703000
E-MAIL: dulas@dulas.org.uk
WEB: http://www.dulas.org.uk
CONTACT: Ian Draisey

ECD ENERGY AND ENVIRONMENT LTD
11-15 Emerald Street,
London WC 1N 3QL, UK
TEL: +44 20 7 405 3121
FAX: +44 20 7 405 1670
E-MAIL: ecde@ecde.demon.co.uk
WEB: http://www.ecde.demon.co.uk
CONTACT: Hannah Routh

ECLIPSE RESEARCH CONSULTANTS
The Eden Centre,
47 City Road,
Cambridge CBI IDP, UK
TEL: +44 1223 351485
FAX: +44 1223 351487
CONTACT: Sebastian Macmillan

ECOGEN CONSULTANTS LTD
PO Box 7,
Machynlleth, Powys,
SY20 8WE, UK
TEL: +44 1654 703 141
FAX: +44 1654 703 105
E-MAIL: timkirby@ecogen.co.uk
WEB: http://www.ecogen.co.uk
CONTACT: Tim Kirby

ECOTEC RESEARCH & CONSULTING LTD
28-34 Albert Street,
Birmingham B4 7UD, UK
TEL: +44 121 616 3600
FAX: +44 121 616 3699
E-MAIL:
richard_haines@ecotec.co.uk
WEB: http://www.ecotec.com
CONTACT: John Butson

EDWARD STENHOUSE LTD
The Farm Office,
Newbridge,
Coleman's Hatch, Hartfield East Sossex TN7 4ES, UK
TEL : +44 1342 826661
FAX : +44 132 826466
E-MAIL : esl@stenhse.demon.co.uk
WEB : http://www.stenhse.demon.co.uk/homepages
CONTACT : Edward Stenhouse

ELECTROWATT-EKONO (UK) LTD
Electrowatt House, North Street
Horsham RH12, 1RF, UK
TEL : +44 1403 224200
FAX : +44 1403 210 758
E-MAIL :pnorth@hrh.ewe.ch
WEB : http://www.energy.pofey.com
CONTACT : Peter North

ENERGY FOR SUSTAINABLE DEVELOPMENT LTD
Overmoor, Neston, Corsham, Wiltshire SNI3 9TZ. UK
TEL : +44 1225 812102
FAX : +44 1225 812103
E-MAIL : esd@.co.uk
WEB : www.esd.co.uk
CONTACT : Dr. Jeff Kenna

ENERGY UNLIMITED
5 Leighton Avenue, Dunbalane, Stirling, FK 15 OEB, UK
TEL: + 44 1786 825839
FAX : + 44 1786 821133
E-MAIL : eunlim@aol.com
CONTACT : Robert Forrest

ENGINEERED SOLUTIONS
15 Newtown, Easton-On-The-Hill, Stamford, Lincs PE9 3NR, UK
TEL : + 44 1780 754327
E-MAIL : Ian.Arbon@ukgateway.net
CONTACT : Ian M Arbon

ENTECUK LTD
Windsor House, Gadbrook Business Centre, Northwich,
Cheshire CW9 7TN, UK
TEL : +44 1606 49077
FAX: +44 1606 49194
E-MAIL : righbk@entecuk.co.uk
WEB: http://www.entecuk.com
CONTACT : David Lyth

ENVIRONMENTAL RESOURCES MANAGEMENT – ERM
8 Cavendish Square, London WIM OER, UK
TEL : +44 20 7 456 7251
FAX: +44 20 7 465 7350
E-MAIL : dcw@ermuk.com
WEB: http://www.ermuk.com
CONTACT : G H Eduljee

ENVIRONMENTAL TECHNOLOGY CONSULTANTS MOTHERWELL BRIDGE GROUP
Boston House, 5th Avenue Business Park, Team Valley, Gateshead NEII OHF, UK
TEL : +44 191 421 0042
FAX: + 44 191 421 0043
E-MAIL: wpescod@mb-nuclear.co.uk
CONTACT : Prof M B Pescod

EPD CONSULTANTANTS LIMITED
Burrator House, Peninsula Park,
Rydon Lane, Exeter EX2 7NT, UK
TEL : +44 1392 444345
FAX : + 44 1392 44880
E-MAIL: epdco@pellfrischmann.com
WEB: http://
www.pellfrischmann.com
CONTACT : John Russell

ESCOVALE CONSULTANCY SERVICES
Nutley Dean Business Park,
Norwood Hill, Horley, Surrey,
RH6 OHR, UK
TEL: +44 1293 86 20 86
FAX: + 44 1293 86 30 02
E-MAIL: info@escovale.com
WEB: http:/www.escovale.com
CONTACT : Frank Escombe

ETPLTD
Box 11 Royal Stuart Workshops,
Adelaide Place, Cardiff Bay, Cardiff
CF4 1BA, UK.
TEL: +44 29 20 464141
FAX: +44 29 20 464500
E-MAIL: etp_ltd@compuserve.com
CONTACT : Simon Burgess

FICHTNER CONSULTING ENGINEERS LTD
8 The Acorn Business Park, Heaton
Lane, Stockport SK4 1AS UK,
TEL: +44 161 476 0032
FAX: +44 161 474 0618
CONTACT: Nick Gamble

FRED TREBLE CONSULTING
43 Pierrefondes Avenue, Farnborough,
Hampshire GU14 8PA, UK
TEL: +44 1252 542037
CONTACT : Fred Treble

FUGRO LTD
18 Frogmore Road, Hemel
Hempstead, Hertfordshire HP3
9RT, UK
TEL: +44 1442 240781
FAX: +44 1422 258961
E-MAIL: info@fugro.co.uk
WEB: http://www.fugro.co.uk
CONTACT: Ms Henrietta Flynn

FULCRUM CONSULTING
62-68 Roseberry Avenue,
London EC1R 4RR, UK
TEL: +44 20 8520 1300
FAX: +44 20 8520 1350
E-MAIL: andrew.ford@fulcrum-
consulting.co.uk
WEB: http://www.fulcrumfirst.com
CONTACT: Andrew Ford

FUTURE SOLUTIONS LTD
2 Paulet Road, Camberwell,
London SE5 9HZ, UK
TEL: +44 20 7 733 2019
E-MAIL: eddie@fdsos.com
CONTACT: Eddie Drayton

GARBHAIG HYDRO POWER COMPANY LTD
Unit 1, James Keiller Buildings, 32-34
Mains Loan, Dundee DD4 7BT, UK
TEL: +44 1382 455 565
FAX: +44 1382 455 518
E-MAIL :d.j.t.mckenzie@btinternet.com
CONTACT : Mr Mc Kenzie

GARRAD HASSAN AND PARTNERS LTD
2064 Maryhill Road,
Glasgow G20 0AB, UK
TEL: +44 141 945 4774
FAX: +44 141 945 5076
E-MAIL: fellows@garradhassan.co.uk
WEB: http://www.garradhassan.com
CONTACT: Dr Andrew Fellows

GARRAD HASSAN AND PARTNERS LTD
St Vincent's Works, Silverthorne
Lane Bristol BS2 0QD, UK
TEL: +44 117 972 9900
FAX: +44 117 972 9901
E-MAIL: garrad@garradhassan.co.uk
WEB: http://www.garradhassan.com
CONTACT: Dr Andrew Garrad

GIBBE LTD
Environmental, Gibb House,
London Road, Reading,
Berkshire RG6 I BL, UK
TEL :+ 44 118963 5000
FAX : + 44 118 966 9554
E-MAIL : hbeverid@gibb.co.uk
WEB : www.gibblfd.com
CONTACT : David Wood

GLOBAL IMPRTESSIONS LTD
68 Albert Road, Chaddesden, Derby
DE21 6SH, UK
TEL : + 44 1332 739721
FAX : + 44 1332 200061
E-MAIL : globaly@aol.com
CONTACT : Chris Day

GOCHST LIMITED
I Akerman Road, Surbiton, Surrey
KT6 5NS, UK
TEL : + 44 20 8 399 90 10
FAX : + 44 208 399 90 10
E-MAIL : gordon@
gord.demon.co.uk
WEB : www.gord.demon.co.uk
CONTACT : Gordon Johnson

GREEN LAND RECLAMATION LTD
I Furze Platt Road, Maidenhead,
Berkshire SI6 7nd UK
TEL : + 44 1628 778077
FAX : + 44 1628 634340
E-MAIL : greenland2glr@
dial.pipe.com
CONTACT : A J Limbrick

HALCROW GROUP LTD
Burderop Park, Swindon,
Wiltshire SN4 0QD, UK
TEL: +44 1793 814756
FAX: +44 1793 815020
E-MAIL: hackerrj@halcrow.com
CONTACT: Rod Hacker

HASTINGS OPEN TECHNOLOGY
23 Marline Avenue,
St Leonards- On-Sea TN38 9HS, UK
TEL: +44 7980 275633
FAX: +44 1424 851235
E-MAIL: kevyoung@hot1066.co.uk
WEB: http://
www.hastingsopentechnology.co.uk
CONTACT: Kevin Young

HERITAGE ENGINEERING
22 Carmyle Avenue,
Glasgow G32 8HJ, UK
TEL: +44 141 763 0007
FAX: +44 141 763 0583
WEB: http://
zwww.heritageengineering.com
CONTACT: JS Mitchell

HIGHLAND LIGHT & POWER LTD
James Keiller Building, 32-34
Mains Loan, Dundee DD4 7BT, UK
TEL: +44 1382 455565
FAX: +44 1382 455518
E-MAIL:
d.j.t.mckenzie@btinternet.com
CONTACT: David JT Mckenzie

HOARE WOOTON
Environment House,
Lexden,
Lodge Crowborough,
East Sussex, TN6 2NQ, UK
TEL: +44 1892 668313
FAX: +44 1892 668302
CONTACT : Ron Wootton

HOLMES EB - AGRO-INDUSTRIAL CONSULTANCY
Oakwood House Oakwood Road,
Burges Hill,
Sussex RH15 0HZ, UK
TEL: +44 1444 258755
FAX: +44 1444 258766
E-MAIL: ebholmes@pavillion.co.uk
CONTACT: EB Holmes

HUNTER ENERGY
3 Peel Terrace, Edinburgh EH9 2AY, UK
TEL: +44 131 468 2616
FAX: +44 131 468 2617
E-MAIL: agmh@hunter.bizexplore.co.uk
CONTACT: Alastair Hunter

HYDER CONSULTING LTD
2-3 Cornwall Terrace, Regents Park
london NW1 4QP, UK
TEL: +44 20 7 544 6600
FAX: +44 20 7 470 0019
E-MAIL: info.centre@hyder-con.co.uk
WEB: http://www.hyder-consulting.com
CONTACT: Maxine Watson

IAN GRANT
High House, Upper Ladyes Hills
Kenilworth, Warwickshire CV8 2FB, UK
TEL: +44 1926 851741
FAX: +44 1926 851741
CONTACT: Ian Grant

ILEX
King Charles House Park End Street, Oxford, UK
TEL: +44 805 722 660
FAX: +44 805 722 988
E-MAIL: energy.consult@ilex.co.uk
WEB: http://www.iles.co.uk
CONTACT: Hugh Babington Smith

INDEPENDENT ENERGY SERVICES
2 Curlew Walk, Deeping St. James
Peterborough PE6 8RY, UK
TEL: +44 973 505 213
FAX: +44 1778 347928
E-MAIL: ies2000@aol.com
CONTACT: Allan Wright

INGENCO
45-47 Hawbank Road,
College Milton North, East Kilbridge,
Glasgow G74 5EG, UK
TEL: +44 1355 814000
FAX: +44 1355 814055
E-MAIL: ian.irvine@ingenco.co.uk
WEB: http://www.ingenco.co.uk
CONTACT: Ian Irvine

INTERMEDIATE TECHNOLOGY DEVELOPMENT GROUP- ITDG
Schumacher Centre For Technology
And Development, Bourton Hall,
Bourton-on-Dunsmore,
Warwickshire CV23 9SD, UK
TEL: +44 1926 634400
FAX: +44 1926 634400
E-MAIL: alisond@itdg.org.uk
WEB: http://www.oneworld.org/itdg
CONTACT: Dr Alison Doig

INTERMEDIATE TECHNOLOGY CONSULTANTS – ITC
Bourton Hall, Bourton-on-Dunsmore,
Warwickshire CV23 9QZ, UK
TEL: +44 1788 661103
FAX: +44 1788 661105
E-MAIL: itc@itdg.org.uk
WEB: http://www.itcltd.com
CONTACT: Dr Rona Wilkinson

ISECO
Environmental Consultancy,
Steanbow Farm, Pilton, Shepton
Mallet, Somerset BA4 4EH, UK
TEL: +44 1479 830377
FAX: +44 1479 890008
E-MAIL: marksen5@hotmail.com
WEB: http://www.materialresource.co.uk
CONTACT: Mark Christensen

IT POWER LTD
The Manor House, Lutyens Close,
Chineham, Hampshire RG24 8AG, UK
TEL: +44 1256 392700
FAX: +44 1256 392701
E-MAIL: naomi.davidge@itpower.co.uk
WEB: http://www.itpower.co.uk
CONTACT: Naomi Davidge

IT POWER LTD
The Warren,
Bramshill Road, Eversley,
Hampshire RG27 0PR, UK
TEL: +44 118 973 0073
FAX: +44 118 973 0820
E-MAIL: itpower@itpower.co.uk
WEB: http://www.itpower.co.uk
CONTACT: Bernard McNelis

JR STAMMERS
19 Priory Park,
Blackheath,
London SE3 9UY, UK
TEL: +44 20 8 852 5148
FAX: +44 20 8 297 0301
E-MAIL: J.R.Stammers@btinternet.com
CONTACT: Judith Stammers

JUNIPER CONSULTANCY SERVICES LTD
Sheppards Mill, Uley,
Gloucestershire
GL11 5SP, UK
TEL: +44 1453 860750
FAX: +44 1453 860882
E-MAIL: info@juniper.co.uk
WEB: http://www.juniper.co.uk
CONTACT: J Schwager

KNIGHT PIESOLD LTD
Kanthack House,
Station Road Ashford,
Kent TN23 1PP, UK
TEL: +44 1233 658200
FAX: +44 1233 658299
E-MAIL: busdev@knightpiesold.co.uk
WEB: http://www.knightpiesold.co.uk
CONTACT: Chris Head

KS CONSULTING LTD
73 Leigh Park Road,
Bradford
On Avon BA15 1TG, UK
TEL: +44 1225 867011
FAX: +44 1225 867011
E-MAIL: info@ksconsulting.co.uk
WEB: http://www.ksconsulting.co.uk
CONTACT: Kevin Sharpe

LFT-FICHTNER COUSULTING ENGINEERS LTD
Allen House, Boltro Road,
Haywards Heath,
West Sussex RH16 IBP, UK
TEL: +44 1444 4015
FAX: +44 1444 441 630
WEB:http://www..lft-fichtner.demon.co.uk
CONTACT: Deborah Weller

LINDLEY AND ASSOCIATES
Woodfield House,
Farm Lane, Jordans,
Beaconsfield Bucks
HP9 2UP, UK
TEL: +44 1494 67 65 70
FAX: +44 1494 67 89 17
E-MAIL:energy@lindley.demon.co.uk
CONTACT:Dr David Lindley

LLOYD'S REGISTER INDUSTRIAL SERVICES
22, Clyde Road,
Croydon CRO 6SU, UK
TEL: +44 2 8 681 4040
FAX: +44 20 8 681 4745
CONTACT: T Karelis

LLOYD'S REGISTER INTERNATIONAL POWER GROUP
Delta 200,
Delta Business Park,
Great Western Way Swindon,
Wiltshire SN5 7XN, UK
TEL: +44 1793 427 821
FAX: +44 1793 427 830
EMAIL: mike.eyre@lr.org
WEB:http://www.lr.org
CONTACT: Mike Eyre

MANX WIND ENERGY SERVICES LTD
1 Church Road, Port Erin,
Isle of Man 1M9 6AH, UK
TEL: +44 1624 832021
FAX: +44 1624 832176
E-MAIL: geoff@manxwind.com
WEB: http://www.enterprise.net/manxwind
CONTACT: Dr Geoff Watson

MATTHEW JAMES & PARTNERS
The Bush, Townside, Haddenham,
Buckinghamshire,
HP17 8AW, UK
TEL: +44 1844 291987
FAX: +44 1844 291987
E-MAIL: dichler@dial.pipex.co.uk
CONTACT: Alan Dichler

MCKINNON & CLARKE
Claymore House,
Enterprise Way,
Edinburgh KY11 8PY, UK
TEL: +44 131 220 5665
FAX: +44 131 220 5775
E-MAIL: s.w.long@mckinnon-clarke.co.uk
WEB: http://www.mckinnon-clarke.co.uk
CONTACT: Philip Wilkinson

MCLELLAN & PARTNERS LTD
Sheer House,
Station Approach,
West Byfleet,
Surrey KT14 6NL, UK
TEL: +44 1932 343271
FAX: +44 1932 348037
E-MAIL: mclellan_uk@compuserve.com
WEB: http://www.mclellan.co.uk
CONTACT: David Linisell

MOTTMACDONALD LIMITED
Power Generation Division,
Victory House, Trafalgar Place,
Brighten, BN 4FY, UK
TEL: + 44 1273 509000
FAX: +44 1273 509100
E-MAIL : jbl@mm-brig.mottmac.com
WEB : http://www.mottmac.com
CONTACT : John Bacon

MOTTMACDONALD
Power Civil & Hydro,
Victory House Trafalgar Place,
Brighton BNI 4FY, UK
TEL: +44 1273 365000
FAX: + 44 1273 365100
E-MAIL:lja@mm-brig.mottmac.com
WEB:http://www.mottmac.com
CONTACT:James Arthur

MOTTMACDONALD
St.Anne House, Wellesley Road
Croydon CR92UL,UK
TEL: + 4420 8 774 2000
FAX: +44 20 8 681 5706
E-MAIL: marketing@mottmac.com
CONTACT: Mr.AGG Powlesland

NATURAL POWER CONSULTANTS LTD
The Green House, Forrest Estate,
Dalry Castle Douglas DG3 4EJ, UK
TEL: +441644 430614
FAX: + 441644 430405
E-MAIL: mail@naturalpower.com
WEB: http://www.naturalpower.com
CONTACT: Jeremy Sainsbury

NB WOOD CONSULTANCY
Beifield, Farm Lane,
Ashtead, Surrey KT21 ILR, UK
TEL: +44 1372 272 905
FAX: +44 1372 813637
E-MAIL: n.b.wood@city.ac.uk
CONTACT: Nigel Wood

NEW ENERGY TRUST
24 Park Road Abingdon,
Oxon OX14 1DS, UK
TEL: +44 1235 528873
FAX: +44 1235 528874
E-MAIL: alana.dixon@which.net
CONTACT: Alana Dixon

NIFES CONSULTING GROUP
8 Woodside Terrace,
Glasgow G3 7UY, UK
TEL: +44 141 332 2453
FAX: +44 141 333 0402
E-MAIL: glasgow@nifes.co.uk
WEB: http://www.nifes.co.uk
CONTACT: Maurice N Miller

NOTTINGHAM CONSULTANTS LTD
Nottingham Trent University
Department Of Electrical
Engineering,
Burton Street,
Nottingham NG1 4BU, UK
TEL: +44 115 848 2313
FAX: +44 115 848 6567
E-MAIL: arthur.williams@ntu.ac.uk
WEB: http://www.eee.ntu.ac.uk/research/microhydro
CONTACT: Arthur Williams

ORKNEY SUSTAINABLE ENERGY LTD
Njordhuis, North End Road,
Stromness, Orkney KW16 3AG UK
TEL: +44 1856 850054
FAX: +44 1856 851239
E-MAIL: orkneywind@compuserve.com
CONTACT: Richard Gauld

OSCAR FABER CONSULTING ENGINEERINGS LTD
Marlborough House,
Upper Marlborough Road,
St Albans, Hertfordshire AL1 3UT, UK
TEL: +44 20 8 784 5784
FAX: +44 20 8 784 5700
E-MAIL: enquiries@fabere.oscarfaber.co.uk
CONTACT: Anthony Wilson

OWEN WILLIAMS CONSULTING ENGINEER
Environmental And Geotechnical
Division, Edgbaston House, 3
Duchess Place, Hagley Road
Birmingham B16 8NH, UK
TEL: +44 121 456 1568
FAX: +44 121 456 1757
E-MAIL: owen.williams@dial.pipex.com
CONTACT: Ed Bullivant

OXERA ENVIRONMENTAL LTD
Blue Boar Court, Alfred Street,
Oxford OX1 4EH, UK
TEL: +44 1865 253000
FAX: +44 1865 251172
E-MAIL: enquiries@oxera.co.uk
WEB: http://www.oxera.co.uk
CONTACT: Clare O'Brien

PATRICK WATERFIELD
24 Galwally Avenue, Belfast BT8 7AJ, UK
TEL: +44 28 9059 8199
FAX: +44 28 9022 3545
E-MAIL: patrick.waterfield@net.ntl.com
WEB: http://www.websites.ntl.com/-patrick.waterfield
CONTACT: Patrick Waterfield

PB POWER LTD
Amber Court, William Armstrong
Drive New Castle Business Park,
New Castle Upon Tyne NE4 7YQ, UK
TEL: +44 191 226 1899
FAX: +44 191 226 1104
E-MAIL: pbpower@pbworld.com
WEB: http://www.pbpower.com/power
CONTACT: Ian P Burdon

PMSS PARTNERSHIP
2 Hulles Way, Norht Baddesley,
Southampton, Hants SO52 9NS, UK
TEL: +44 23 80 411058
FAX:+44 23 80 731436
E-MAIL : pmss@compuserve.com
CONTACT: Alan Chivers

POWERGEN RENEWABLES LTD
Westwood Way,
Westwood Business Park, Coventry
CV4 8LG, UK
TEL: +44 24 76 424 000
FAX: +44 24 76 425 443
CONTACT: Chris Morris

PROMAN ASSOCIATES
Proman House, Station Approach,
Filey, North Yorkshire YO14 9PF, UK
TEL: +44 1723 516454
FAX: +44 1723 516451
E-MAIL: info@promanenergy.co.uk
WEB: http://
www.promanenergy.co.uk
CONTACT: Theo Labuschagne

PROMAN ENERGY
Unit 3, Park Farm Courtyard,
Malton, North Yorkshire YO17 6QX,
UK
TEL: +44 1653 6998 88
FAX: +44 1653 6997 29
E-MAIL: info@promanenergy.co.uk
WEB: http://
www.promanenergy.co.uk
CONTACT: Stephen Parker

R PAXTON AND ASSOCIATES LTD
Cathedral House, Beacon Street,
Lichfield, Staffordshire WS13 7AA,
UK
TEL: +44 1543 250939
FAX: +44 1543 250940
E-MAIL: rpa@on-edie.net
CONTACT: Dr RG Paxton

REGEN
6 Shaftoe Crescent, Hexham,
Northumberland NE46 3DS, UK
TEL : +44 1434 600177
FAX : +44 1434 600176
CONTACT : Norman Rogers

RENEWABLE HEAT AND POWER LTD
New Mills Farm, Snapper,
Barnstaple, Devon EX32 7JZ, UK
TEL : +44 1271 850859
FAX : +44 1271 850245
E-MAIL : rhp@sosi.net
CONTACT : Adam Giffard

ROBERT WEBB ASSOCIATES-RWA
1-3 Leonard Street, London EC2A
4AQ, UK
TEL: +44 207 689 6345
FAX: +44 207 689 6346
E-MAIL: info@rw-a.co.uk
WEB: http://www.rw-a.co.uk
CONTACT: Robert Webb

ROGER BOOTH CONSULTANCY
Firtree Cottage, Newnham Road,
Newnham, Hook RG27 9AE, UK
TEL: +44 1256 762 456
FAX: + 44 1256 761 523
E-MAIL: roger@booths.demon.co.uk
CONTACT: Roger Booth

RUBICON APPLIED RESEARCH
11 Rambling Way, Potten End,
Berkhamsted HP4 2SF, UK
TEL: +44 1442 875433
FAX: +44 1442 875433
E-MAIL:
emmckay@compuserve.com.uk
CONTACT: DR EM McKay

SCOTT WILSON RESOURCE CONSULTANTS
Avalon House, Marcham Road,
Abingdon, Oxfordshire OX14
1UG, UK
TEL: +44 1235 555535
FAX: +44 1235 553203
WEB: http://swkeurope.com
CONTACT: Russel Matthews

SEVERN TRENT SYSTEMS LTD
2800 The Crescent,
Birmingham B37 7YL,UK
TEL: +44 121 717 7755
FAX: +44 121 717 3030
E-MAIL: sales@sts.co.uk
WEB: http://www.sts.co.uk
CONTACT: Stella Medlicott

SOLANNE
Woodgate Farm, Church Lane,
Beckley, Nr Rye East Sussex TN31
6UH, UK
TEL:+44 1797 260 278
FAX:+44 1797 260 278
CONTACT:R Setter

SOLAR CENTURY
91-94 Lower Marsh, Waterloo,
London SE1 7AB, UK
TEL: +442078030116
FAX: +442078030101
E-MAIL:
clive.weatherby@solarcentury.co.uk
WEB: http://www.solarcentury.co.uk
CONTACT: Dr. Tracey Mills

SOLAR ENERGEY ALLIANCE
8A Battery Green Road,
Lowerstoft
NR32 IDE, UK
TEL:+44 1502 515532
FAX:+44 1502 561399
E-MAIL:energy@gosolar,u-net.com
WEB:http://www.gosolar.u-net.com

SOLAR HOUSING DESIGN & BUILD
Tir Gaia Solar Village,
Rhayader, Mid Wales
LD6 5DY, UK
TEL:+44 1597 810929
FAX:+44 1597 810929
E-MAIL:david@sustain.force9.co.uk
WEB:http://
www.sustain.force9.co.uk
CONTACT:David Sstephens

SOLAR WHEEL
Fforest Brechfa,
Carmarthenshire SA32 7BL, UK
TEL:+44 1267 202388
FAX:+44 1267 202388
E-MAIL:bobbybaz@aol.com
CONTACT:Bob Bazalgette

SOUTHWARK ENERGY AGENCY LTD-SEA
42 Braganza Street,
London SE17 3RJ, UK
TEL: +44 20 7 582 9191
FAX: +44 20 7 582 4888
E-MAIL: sowthwark-ea@lineone.net
WEB: http://www.southwark-
energy.co.uk
CONTACT: Chris Dunham

SUGAR KNOWLEDGE INTERNATIONAL LIMITED
Cherry Tree House,
Mill Lane,
Alwalton,
Peterborough PE7 3UZ, UK
TEL: +44 1733 232004
FAX: +44 1733 370763
E-MAIL:pbj@sucrose.com
WEB:http://www.sucrose.com
CONTACT: Peter B James

SUSTAINABLE ENERGY CONCEPTS LTD
I Paddocks Green,
Mossley, Congleton,
Cheshire CW 12 3UB, UK
TEL: +44 1260 278134
FAX: +44 1260 281369
E-MAIL:graham@
sustainable.demon.co.uk
CONTACT:Graham Hurd

SUSTAINABLE ENERGY LTD
Cambrian Buildings, Mount Stuart
Square,Cardiff CFI 0 5FL, UK
TEL : +44 2920 408990
FAX : +442920 408999
E-MAIL: david.thomas@sustainable-
energy.co.uk
CONTACT : David Thomas

SUSTAINABLE ENERGY MARKETING LTD
PO Box 33,Hilton,Huntingdon
Cambs PEI 8 9HN, UK
TEL: +44 1480 830 388
FAX: +441480 831 098
E-MAIL:susten@dial.pipex.com
CONTACT:John Buckley

SWIFT-HOOK ASSOCIATES
Coxhill Manor,
Chobham, Surrey,
GU24 8AU, UK
TEL: +44 1483760-678
FAX: +44 1483776 710
CONTACT:Prof Donald T Swift-Hook

SYMONDS GROUP LTD
Power &Energy Division, 65
Northgate, Newark, Notts NG24
1HD, UK
TEL: +44 1636 614500
FAX: +44 1636 703456
CONTACT:David Aldred

TASK CENTRE LTD
Dovercourt, 22 Forde Park, Newton
Abbot, Devon TQ12 IDD, UK
TEL : +44 162 663 339
FAX : +44 162 663 339
E-MAIL : mail@taskcentre.co.uk
CONTACT : J Rushmer

THE CENTRE FOR ALTERNATIVE TECHNOLOGY
Machynlleth,
Powys SY20 9AZ, UK
TEL: +44 1654 702400
FAX: +44 1654 702782
E-MAIL: consultancy@cat.org.uk
WEB: http://www.cat.org.uk
CONTACT: Phil Horton

THE DYER WARNER PARTNERSHIP
Cliffe House,
Church Hill, Birstall,
Leicester LE4 4DN, UK
TEL : + 44 116 267 7017
FAX : + 44 116 267 3819
E-MAIL : dyerwarner@aol.com
CONTACT : David Dyer

THE ENERGY WORKSHOP
Denby House, Minskip,
York YO51 9JF, UK
TEL: +44 1423 325222
FAX: +44 1423 325222
E-MAIL:
philip@theenergyworkshop.co.uk
WEB: http://
www.theenergyworkshop.co.uk
CONTACT: Dr Philip Surman

TM ENVIRONMENTAL POWER
17 Hazel End, Wootton Bassett,
Wilshire SN4 7ET, UK
TEL: +44 1793 840048
FAX: +44 1793 840048
E-MAIL:tristan@tm-
enviropower.demon.co.uk
CONTACT:Tristan Mackie

TORPY ENERGY
Merchants House,
26-28 Regent
Street,Bristol BS8 4HG, UK
TEL: +44 117 938 9300
FAX: +44 117 938 9315
E-MAIL:roger.hawes@torpy.co.uk
WEB:http://www.torpy.co.uk/energy
CONTACT:Roger Hawes

TRINITY HOUSE LIGHT HOUSE SERVICE
Engineering Directorate,
East Cowes, Isle of Wight ,
PO32 6RE, UK
TEL: +44 1983 292651
FAX: +44 1983 294317
CONTACT: Malcolm Wannell

UNIVERSITY OF THE WEST OF ENGLAND
Faculty of the Built Environment
Coldharbour Lane, Frenchay,
Bristol BST6 IQY, UK
TEL: +44 117 9656261
FAX: +44 117 3443002
E-MAIL: fbe.entry@uwe.ac.uk
WEB: http://www.uwe.ac.uk

WA FAIHURST & PARTNERS
Environment Division,
11 Woodside Terrace,
Glasgow G37XQ, UK
TEL: +44 141 332 8754
FAX: +44 141 3325083
E-MAIL: info@fairhurst.co.uk
WEB: http://www.fairhurst.co.uk
CONTACT: Alan Simpson

WARM PETER
Boxhedge, Horsley, Stroud,
Glos GL6 OPP, UK
TEL: +44 1453 835060
FAX: +44 1453 834060

WATER MANAGEMENT CONSULTANTS
2/3 Wyle Cop, Shrewsbury,
Shropshire SY1 1UT, UK
TEL: +44 1743 231793
FAX: +44 1743 232894
E-MAIL:
watman_uk@compuserve.com
CONTACT: Mark Anderson

WAVEGEN
50 Seafield Road,
Longman Industrial Estate,
Inverness IV1 1LZ, UK
TEL: +44 1463 238094
FAX: +44 1463 238096
E-MAIL: enquiries@wavegen.com
WEB: http://www.wavegen.com
CONTACT: David Langston

WHITBY BIRD & PARTNERS
60 Newman Street,
London W1P 4DA, UK
TEL: +44 20 7631 5291
FAX: +44 20 7323 4645
E-MAIL: dpric@whitby-bird.co.uk
WEB: http://www.whitbybird.com
CONTACT: Duncan Price

DESIGN & ENGINEERING

ACWA SERVICES LTD
Water And Sewage Equipment
Division, ACWA House,
Keighley Road, Skipton,
North Yorkshire BD23 2UE, UK
TEL: +44 1756 794794
FAX: +44 1756 790898
E-MAIL: acwa@compuserve.com

AERPAC UK LTD
Mitchelston Industrial Estate,
Kirkcaldy, Fife KY1 3LZ, UK
TEL: +44 1592 653753
FAX: +44 1592 654373
E-MAIL:
101723.525@compuserve.com
CONTACT: Dr Colin Anderson

AHRENDS BURTON AND KORALEK
Architects 7 Chalcot Road
London NW1 8LH, UK
TEL: +44 20 7 586 3311
FAX: +44 20 7 722 5445
CONTACT: Richard Burton

AIRCOGEN LIMITED
Werrington Parkway,
Peterborough PE4 5HG, UK
TEL: +44 1733 292 450
FAX: +44 1733 292 460
E-MAIL: info@aircogen.co.uk
WEB: http://www.aircogen.co.uk
CONTACT: Roy Carter

ALSTOM POWER
Flowsystems, Burnden Works,
Burnden Road, Bolton BL3 2RB, UK
TEL: +44 1204 554 540
FAX: +44 1204 554 544
E-MAIL: tim.ward@flowsystems.co.uk
WEB: http://www.flowsystems.co.uk
CONTACT: Tim Ward

AMEC BIRWELCO LIMITED
Mucklow House,
Mucklow Hill,
Halesowen,
West Midlands B62 8DG, UK
TEL: +44 121 550 4777
FAX: +44 121 550 7946
E-MAIL:
efw@halesowen.birwelco.ltd.uk
WEB: http://www.amec.com
CONTACT: Brain Harding

ATLANTIC ENERGY LTD
Riverside House, Heron Way,
Newham,
Truro Cornwall TR 1 2XN, UK
TEL : +44 1872 260423
FAX : +44 1872 222424
E-MAIL :atlanticen@aol.com
CONTACT : Chairman Larke

B & M PIPELINE SERVICES LTD
Dock Road, South,
Bromborough,
Wirral L62 4SQ, UK
TEL : +44 151 334 0122
FAX : +44 151 334 5067
E-MAIL : blmpipe@aol.com
CONTACT : Roger Dixon

BAESEMA
1 Atlantic Quay,
Broomielaw,
Glasgow, G2 8JE, UK
TEL : +44 141 204 2737
FAX : +44 141 221 6435
CONTACT : Eileen Fehily

BALCKE DUERR LTE
Holy Farm Business Park,
Honiley,
Kenilworth CVB INP, UK
TEL : +44 1926 484 101
FAX : +44 1926 484 082
CONTACT : Steve Fairgrieve

BARRETT ENERGY LTD
5 Cuckoo Holt Gateford,
Worksop,
Nottingham S8I 8TN, UK
TEL: +44 1909 479208
FAX: +44 1909 479208
CONTACT: B Barrett

BAYLISS PRECISION COMPONENTS LTD
Lysander Works,
Blenheim Road,
Airfield Industrial Estate
Ashbourne Derbyshire DE6 1HA, UK
TEL: +44 1335 342981
FAX: +44 1335 343860
CONTACT: Kenneth L Bayliss

BDA
Hope House, Molember Road, East
Molesey, Surrey KT8 9NH, UK
TEL : +44 181 339 1242
FAX : +44 181 339 0429
E-MAIL :bill.dunster@btinternet.com
WEB : http://www.zedfactory.com
CONTACT : Bill Dunster

BDS
95 Summerleys Road, Princes
Risborough, Bucks HP27 9QA, UK
TEL: +44 1844 274654
FAX: +44 1844 342715
E-MAIL: tony@bds-uk.com
CONTACT: T Brooks

BILL DUNSTER ARCHITECTS
Hope House, Molember Road,
East Moseley, Surrey KT8, 9NH, UK
TEL : +44 181 339 1242
FAX : +44 181 339 0429
E-MAIL : bill.dunster@btinternet.com
WEB : http://www.zedfactory.com
CONTACT: Bill Dunster

BLYTH & BLYTH GROUP
The Blyth Building, 6 Redheughs
Rigg, South Gyle,
Edinburgh EH12, 9HL, UK
TEL : +44 131 317 7337
FAX : +44 131 339 7077
CONTACT : T D Neville

BURO HAPPOLD
17, Newman Street, London
WIP 3HD, UK
TEL : +44 20 79279700
FAX : +44 20 79279701
E-MAIL : bill.addis@buro
happold.com
WEB : http://www.burohappold.com
CONTACT : Bill Addis

CASELLA SCIENCE AND ENVIRONMENT LTD
Yorkshire House,
Chapel Street,
Liverpool L3 9AG, UK
TEL : +44 151 255 1115
FAX : +44 151 258 1511
E-MAIL : stewartlowther@casella.co.uk
WEB : http://www.casella.co.uk
CONTACT : Stewart Cowther

CHARLES ANDREWS & SONS
Andrews House, 58,
Talbot Road, Old Tafford,
Manchester M16 0PN, UK
TEL : +44 161 973 6782
FAX : +44 161 962 0167
E-MAIL : candrewson@aol.com
CONTACT : B Benson

CHRIS JACKSON ACOUSTICS
45 Bures Road, Great Cornard,
Sudbury CO10 0EJ, UK
TEL: +44 1787 315628
FAX: +44 1787 315627
E-MAIL:
chrisjackson.acoustics@virgin.net
CONTACT: Mr Jackson

CONSTRUCTION RESOURCES
16 Great Guildford Street,
London SEI 0HS, UK
TEL: +44 20 7 450 2205
FAX: +44 20 7 450 2206
E-MAIL: casimiri@ecoconstruct.com
WEB: http://www.ecoconstruct.com
CONTACT: Casimir Iwaszkiewicz

COOPER RESEARCH
Bayard House, Church Lane,
Middleton, Scaffordshire,
B78 2AL,UK
TEL : +44 121 308 7521
FAX : +44 121 308 6444
E-MAIL : coores@compuserve.com
WEB : http://
ourworld.compuserve.com/
homepages/cooper
CONTACT : Chris Cooper

COSTAIN LTD
Anchor Bay Wharf,
Manor Road,
Erith, Kent DAB 2AW, UK
TEL : +44 1322 397616
FAX : +44 1322 397743
E-MAIL : john.douglas@
costain.com
CONTACT : John Douglas

D. SQUARED DESIGN
Studio H Eden Mews,
5th Eden Garden,
London N7 8ES
TEL : + 41 1717 60931
FAX : + 44 171 609 0931
E-MAIL : dsquared@globalnet.co.uk

DALKIA PLC
Energy & Technical Services,
Buchanan House,
24-30 Holborn,
London ECIN 2LX, UK
TEL : + 44 20 7 421 2300
FAX : + 44 20 7 421 2320

DALKIA UTILITY SERVICES PLC
Elizabeth House,
56-60 London Road, Staines,
Middlesex TW 18 4 BQ, UK
TEL : + 44 1784 496200
FAX : + 44 1784 496332
CONTACT : Mike Rundle

DAVID CLARKE ASSOCIATES
Toll House Studio, Cambridge
Cottages, Kew Green, Richmond
TW93AY, UK
TEL : + 44 20 8 332 9696
FAX : + 44 20 8 332 2626
E-MAIL : dca@compuserve.com
WEB : http://www.dcalondon.com
CONTACT : David Clarke

ECLECTRIC ENERGY LIMITED
High Street, Edwinstowe,
N Notts NG21 9PR, UK
TEL: +44 1623 821535
FAX: +44 1623 821540
E-MAIL: sales@duogen.co.uk
WEB: http://www.duogen.co.uk
CONTACT: Peter J Anderson

ENERGY DEVELOPMENT CO-OP LTD
Solar And Wind Energy Systems
The Old Brewery, Oulton Broad
Industrial Estate, Harbour Road
Oulton Broad, Suffolk NR32 3LZ, UK
TEL: +44 870 745 1119
FAX: +44 870 745 112
E-MAIL: info@unlimited-power.co.uk
WEB: http://www.unlimited-power.co.uk
CONTACT: Ms S Lacey

ENVIRONMENTALLY SUSTAINABLE SYSTEMS
130 St Stephen Street,
Edinburgh EH3 5AD, UK
TEL: +44 131 226 7773
FAX: +44 131 226 7773
E-MAIL: paul.ess@dial.pipex.com
WEB: http://
dspacepauless.dial.pipese
CONTACT : Gill Paul

EPCAD CONSULTANTS
Woolstone Centre,
6 Mill Lane,
Woolstone,
Milton Keynes, UK
TEL: + 44 1908 231125
FAX : +44 1908 672611
CONTACT : Jeffrey Stevenson

FEILDEN CLEGG BRADLEY ARCHITECTS
Bath Brewery,
Toll Bridge Road, Bath
BAI 7 DE, UK
TEL: +44 1225 852545
FAX: +44 1225 852528
E-MAIL:bath@feildenclegg.com
WEB:http://www.feildenclegg.com
CONTACT : Magali Marcouire

FRANCIS & LEWIS INTERNATIONAL LTD
Drive Waterwells Business Park,
Gloucester GL2 4AA, UK
TEL: +44 1452 616500
FAX: +44 1452 616900
WEB : www.sli.co.uk
CONTACT : David Perry

GENCOR BEVERLEY
Billinghurst, West Sussex
RH14 9SA, UK
TEL: +44 1403 782091
FAX: +44 1403 782087
WEB: http://ww.gencorbeverley.co.uk
CONTACT: Brain Riley

GEOTECHNICAL INSTRUMENTS (UK) LTD
Sovereign House Queensway,
Leamington Spa,
Warwickshire CV31 3JR, UK
TEL: +44 1926 338111
FAX: +44 1926 338110
E-MAIL: sales@geotech.co.uk
WEB: http://www.geotech.co.uk
CONTACT: Paul Rhodes

GREENFINCH LTD
Burford Houses, Tenbury Wells,
Worcester WR15 8HQ, UK
TEL : + 44 1584 810 777
FAX : + 44 1584 810 673
E-MAIL : greenfinch@burford.co.uk
CONTACT : M. Chesshire

HEAP & DIGBY LTD
17 High Street Carshalton,
Surrey SMS 3AP, UK
TEL: +44 20 8 669 5971
FAX: +44 20 8 669 3754
E-MAIL: 10137.1155@
compuserve.com
CONTACT: James Davies

HEBE
Tamarisk, Bishops Walk, Whiteshill,
Stroud Gloucestershire GL6 6BW,UK
TEL: +44 1453 756571
FAX: +44 1453 766974
E-MAIL: hebe@care4free.net
CONTACT: Jackie Carpenter

HERIOT–WATT UNIVERSITY
International Centre For Island
Technology, Old Academy,
Black Road, Stomness,
Orkney KW16 3AW, UK
TEL: +44 1856 850 605
FAX: +44 1856 851 349
E-MAIL: library@icit.civ.hw.ac.uk
WEB: http://www.icit.demon.co.uk
CONTACT: Colin Bullen

HLC HENLEY BURROWES LTD
HLC House,
Upper Interfield,
Malvern WR14 1UT, UK
TEL: +44 1886 830050
FAX: +44 1886 830051
E-MAIL: louise@hlchb.com
CONTACT: FJ Bluck

HOPKINS (MICHAEL) & PARTNERS
27 Broadley Terrace,
London NWI 6LG, UK
TEL: +44 20 7 724 1751
FAX: +44 20 7 723 0932
E-MAIL: hopkins@dial.pipex.com
CONTACT: Annette Main

HR WALLINGFORD LTD
Howbery Park,
Wallingford Oxon
OX10 8BA, UK
TEL: +44 1491 822320
FAX: +44 1491 832233
E-MAIL: hrinfo@hrwallingford.co.uk
WEB: http://www.hrwallingford-group.co.uk
CONTACT: Dr Jane Lawson

HYDRO SOIL SERVICES NV
Offshore Wind Energy Department,
2nd Floor Greenstede House,
Wood Street,
East Grinstead
RH19 1UZ, UK
TEL: +44 1225 486535
FAX: +44 1225 486597
E-MAIL: cash.neil@dredging.com
WEB: http://www.hydrosoilservices.com
CONTACT: Mr Neil Cash

HYDRO-ACTIVE ENGINEERING
16 Luther Close, St Anns,
Nottingham NG3 3PD, UK
TEL: +44 115 958 4113
CONTACT: Arthur Williams

INVENTERPRISE LTD
PO Box 13897,
London N6 4WA, UK
TEL: +44 20 8 348 1063
FAX: +44 20 8 348 1063
E-MAIL: inventerprise@london.com
CONTACT: David Stern

ISODAQ LTD
Unit 115,
Stirling Enterprise Park,
Stirling FK7 7RT, UK
TEL: +44 1786 449577
FAX: +44 1786 449588
CONTACT: Tim Campbell

J TURTON ENGINEERING LTD
Woodpeckers, Cold Harbour Road,
Hailsham, East Sussex
BN27 3PZ, UK
TEL: +44 1323 843819
FAX: +44 1323 843819
CONTACT: Dr John Turton

KENNEDY & DONKIN LTD
A Parsons Brinckerhoff Company,
Westbrook Mills, Godalming
Surrey GU7 2AZ, UK
TEL: +44 1483 425900
FAX: +44 1483 425136
CONTACT: Kirsten Nye

LANDSCAPE DESIGN ASSOCIATES
17 Minister Premcincts,
Peterborough PE1 1XX, UK
TEL : +44 1733 310471
FAX : +44 1733 5536611
E-MAIL : landscape_design
@compuserve.com
CONTACT : Colin Go odrum

LIVESTOCK WASTE MANAGEMENT LTD
The Long Barn,
Clevedon Road,
Tickenham, Bristol BS21 6RY, UK
TEL : +44 1275 857 799
FAX : +44 1275 853 123
E-MAIL : sales@milbury.u-net.com
CONTACT : Brain Mees

LOGLOGIC
Unit T9, Elm Park, Blundells Road
Tiverton, Devon EX16 4BZ, UK
TEL : +44 1884 243699
FAX : +44 1884 243300
E-MAIL : loglogic@aol.com
CONTACT : marcus Frankpitt

LUCAS ENERGY PROJECTS LTD
The Derwent Business Center,
Unit 3 Clarke Street,
Derby DEI 2BU UK
TEL +44 1332 297 362
FAX: +44 1332 331 178
E-MAIL:info@lucasenergy.com
WEB:http://www.lu
casenergy.com/furnaces
CONTACT : Mr. A W Harvey

MAN B&W DIESEL LTD
Mirrlees Blackstone,
Bramhall Moor Lane,
Hazel Grove,
Stockport,
Cheshire SK7 5AH, UK
TEL: +44 161 483 1000
FAX: +44 161 487 1465
CONTACT: DWJ Copeland

MAX FORDHAM & PARTNERS
42/43 Gloucester Crescent,
London NW1 7PE, UK
TEL: +44 20 7 2675161
FAX: +44 20 7 4820329
E-MAIL: post@mfp.co.uk
WEB: http://www.mfp.co.uk
CONTACT: Henry Luker

MELLER PROCESS EQUIPMENT LTD
Process Machinery Division,
Orion Park, Northfield Avenue,
Ealing London W13 9SJ, UK
TEL: +44 20 8 579 2111
FAX: +44 20 8 567 0576
E-MAIL: info@mellerprocess.co.uk
WEB: http://www.mellerprocess.co.uk
CONTACT: Martin Hearmon

MILBURY SYSTEMS LTD
The Long Barn, Clevedon Road,
Tickenham, Bristol BS21 6RY, UK
TEL: +44 1275 857799
FAX: +44 1275 853123
E-MAIL: sales@milbury-u-net.com
CONTACT: Brian Mees

MINIMUM SYSTEMS
Ty'n Y Nant,
Lianfihangel GM,
Corwen LL21 9UW, UK
TEL: +44 7980 158661
CONTACT: Frank Bowman

MOWLEM ENGINEERING PROJECTS
Energy and Environmental,
Port Causeway, Bromborough,
Wirral Merseyside L624TP, UK
TEL:+44 151 334 4990
FAX: + 44151 343 0381
EMAIL:ndavies@mowlern.co.uk
CONTACT:Mark C Lewis

P A HILTON LTD
Heat Technology Division
Horsebridge Mill,
Kings Somborne, Stockbridge,
Hampshire S020 6PX, UK
TEL: +44 1794 388 382
FAX: +44 1794 388 129
E-MAIL: heatt@p-a-hilton.co.uk
CONTACT: Mark Pontin

PENNMARITME INTERNATIONAL LIMITED
Photovoltaic Engineering, PO Box
35, Virginia Water, GU25 4XG,
TEL:+44 1344 843528
Fax : +44 1344 843528
E-MAIL:pennmartiti
me99@yahoo.co.uk
CONTACT : MD Penney

PETER BROTHERHOOD LTD
Werrington Parkway,
Peterborough PE4 5HG, UK
TEL: +44 1733 292200
FAX: +44 1733 292300
TELEX:32154
E-MAIL:sales@peter
brotherhood.co.uk
WEB:http://www.peterbro
therhood.co.uk
CONTACT : Stephen M Canham

POWER MANAGEMENT ASSOCIATES
Henshaw Farm, Todmorden,
Lancashire OL14 6QR, UK
TEL: +44 1706 814911
FAX: +44 1706 814911
Contact: Bernard Wilkins

POWER STEMS UK LTD
Badminton Road Trading Estate,
Badminton Road, Yate,
Bristol BS37 5GG, UK
TEL: +44 1454 318000
FAX: +44 1454 318111
E-MAIL: sales@power
systemsuk.co.uk
WEB: http://
www.powersystemsuk.co.uk
CONTACT: Larry Fedrick

RENEWABLE ENERGY SYSTEMS LTD
Beaufort House,
23 Grosvenor Road,
St Albans,
Herts ALI 3AW, UK
TEL : +44 1727 797 900
FAX : +44 1727 797 929
E-MAIL : info@res-ltd.com
WEB : http://www.re-ltd.com
CONTACT : Dr Ian D Mays

ROY FLEETWOOD LTD
1Cowley Road,
Cambridge CB4 4WS, UK
TEL: +44 1223 240074
FAX: +44 1223 240069
E-MAIL:
roy.fleetwood@fleetwoodinc.com
WEB: http://www.fleetwoodinc.com
CONTACT: Roy Fleetwood

RS LANE & ASSOCIATES
Crix Cottage, Forest Road,
Binfield,
Berkshire RG42 4DU, UK
TEL: +44 1344 423627
FAX: +44 1344 454006
E-MAIL: rslane@iee.org
CONTACT: Robert Lane

SAGE ENGINEERING LTD
26-45 Cheltenham Street,
Bath BA2 3EX,
UK
TEL: +44 1225 486500
FAX: +44 125 486597
E-MAIL: jcarey@sage-uk.com
CONTACT: John Carey

SHAW GROUP UK LTD
Stores Road, Derby,
Derbyshire DE21 4BG, UK
TEL: +44 1332 291122
FAX: +44 1322 291123
E-MAIL: info@shawuk.co.uk
CONTACT: Mr Neil Clark

SLP ENGINEERING LTD
Hamilton House,
Battery Green Lane,
Lowestoft NR31 IDE, UK
TEL: +44 1502 587322
FAX: +44 1502 585525
E-MAIL: info@slp-eng.com
WEB: http://www.slp-eng.com
CONTACT: Russell Harper

SMS CONSULTANTS
School Of Materials Science,
University Of Bath,
Bath BA2 7AY,
UK
TEL: +44 1225 826 447
FAX: +44 1225 826 098
E-MAIL: sms@bath.ac.uk
WEB: http://www.bath.ac.uk/departments/MatSci/SMS
CONTACT: Nick Gathercoll

SOLAR ENERGY ALLIANCE LTD-SEA
8A Battery Green Road,
Lowestoft,
Suffolk NR 32 1DE,
UK
TEL: +44 1502 515532
FAX: +44 1502 589159
E-MAIL: energy@gosolar.u-net.com
WEB: http://www.gosolar.u-net.com
CONTACT: Mr Chris Goodings

SPACE-ON-EARTH LTD
Greendale House,
The Green Northleach,
Gloucestershire
GL54 3EX,
UK
TEL: +44 1451 860345
FAX: +44 8451 861199
E-MAIL: molecule@earth-sheltered.com
WEB: http:www.earth-sheltered.com
CONTACT: Stuart Bexon

STAFFS SILENT GEAR CO LTD
Sales, Gear Works Salem Street,
Etruria, Stoke-On-Trent,
Staffordshire ST1 5PR, UK
TEL: +44 1782 280136
FAX: +44 1782 269913
E-MAIL:
graham.moore@staffsgears.co.uk
WEB: http://www.staffsgears.co.uk
CONTACT: Graham Moore

SUMMERLEAZE RE-GENERATION LTD
7 Summerleaze Road,
Maidenhead, Berks SL6 8SP, UK
TEL: +44 1628 762350
FAX: +44 1628 773160
E-MAIL: regen@summerleaze.co.uk
WEB: http://www.summerleaze.com/regen
CONTACT: BG Prior

SUNDOG
Fell Cottage,Matterdale End,
Penrith, Cumbria
CA11 OLF, UK
TEL:+44 17684 82282
FAX:+44 17684 82600
E-MAIL:info@sundog-energy.co.uk
CONTACT:Martin Cotterell

T P BENNETT
1 America Street,
London SE1 ONE, UK
TEL: +44 20 7 208 2000
FAX: +44 20 7 208 2020
E-MAIL: tpbennett@tpbennett.co.uk
WEBB: http://www.tpbennett.co.uk
CONTACT: Lisa Thomas

TANARIS ENERGY LTD
Tanaris House, The Common,
Stokenchurch, Buckinghamshire HP 14 3TZ, UK
TEL : +44 1494 485 550
FAX : +44 1494 485 556
E-MAIL : tanaris@tanaris.com
WEB : http://www.tanaris.com
CONTACT : M Candlish

TERENCE O'ROURKE PLC
Everdene House, Wessex Fields,
Deansleigh Road,
Bournemouth BH7 7DK, UK
TEL: +44 1202 42114
FAX: +44 1202 430055
E-MAIL: maildesk@torplc.com
CONTACT: Tim Hancock

THE CERAMIC STOVE COMPANY
4 Earl Street, Oxford OX2 0JA, UK
TEL: +44 1865 245077
FAX: +44 1865 245077
CONTACT: Nick Hills

THE ENGINEERING BUSINESS LTD
Broomhaugh House,
Riding Mill,
Northumberland NE44 6EG, UK
TEL: +44 1434 682 800
FAX: +44 1434 682 801
E-MAIL: mike.watchorn@engb.com
WEB: http://www.engb.com
CONTACT: Mike Watchorn

UNIVERSITY COLLEGE LONDON
The Bartlett School of Graduate Studies, Phillips House,
University College London,
Gower Street,
London WCIE 6BT, UK
TEL: +44 20 7 504 5906
FAX: +44 20 7 916 3892
E-MAIL: t.oreszczyn@ucl.ac.uk

WALTHAM FOREST ENERGY SERVICES LTD
Energy Centre,
31 Church Hill,
Walthamstow,
London E17 3RU, UK
TEL: +44 20 8 520 9880
FAX: +44 20 8 520 9882
E-MAIL: wfes.ltd@aol.com
CONTACT: M Turpin

WARDELL ARMSTRONG
Head Office,
Lancaster Building, High Street, Newcastle Under Lyme,
Staffordshire STS IPQ, UK
TEL: +44 1782 612626
FAX: +44 1782 662882
E-MAIL: jbailey@wardell-armstrong.com
WEB: http://www.wardell-armstrong.com
CONTACT: J Bailey

WILBRAHAM & CO-SOLICITORS
Minerva House,
East Parade,
Leeds LS1 5PS, UK
TEL: +44 113 243 2200
FAX: +44 113 244 9777
E-MAIL: pw.co.@dial.pipex.com
CONTACT: Carolyn Stephenson

WS ATKINS CONSULTANTS LTD
Head Office, Woodcote Grove,
Ashley Road Epsom,
Surrey KT 18 5BW,UK
TEL: +44 1372 726 140
FAX: +44 1372 740 055
E-MAIL: info@wsaktins.com
WEB: http://www.wsaktins.com
CONTACT: Mike Woolgar

HYBRID SYSTEMS

CHRIS VERNEY
t/a Barum Road Solarheat,
5 Burlington Grove, Newport,
Barnstaple Devon EX32 9BU, UK
TEL: +44 1271 343377
FAX: +44 1271 343211
CONTACT: Chris Verney

OTHERS

ARBRE ENERGY LIMITED
First Renewables, Selby Road,
Eggborough DN14 OFG, UK
TEL : +44 1977 660000
FAX : +44 1977 663024
E-MAIL : vicky-penrose@first-renewable.com
CONTACT : Vicky Penrose

AUTOMATED POWER EXCHANGE
European Headquarters,
26-28 Mount Row, London, UK
TEL : +44 20 7647 9793
FAX : +44 20 7647 9781
WEB : http://www.apx.com
CONTACT : David Selzer

B G PLC
100 Thames Valley Park Drive,
Reading, Berkshire RG6, IPT, UK
TEL : +44 1189 292 830
FAX : +44 1189 293397
E-MAIL : will.davies@bg-group.com
CONTACT : William Davies

BEAVER POWER LTD
Mayphil Industrial Estate, Goat Mill Road, Dowlais, Methyr, UK
TEL : +44 1543 491066
FAX : +44 1543 493500
E-MAIL : sales@beaverpower.co.uk
WEB : http://www.beaverpower.co.uk
CONTACT : Melvyn Fern

BG TECHNOLOGY
MiniGen, Ashby Road,
Loughborough, LE11 3GR, UK
TEL : +44 1509 283096
FAX : +44 1509 283144
E-MAIL :minigen@bgtechnology.com
WEB : http://www.bgtechnology.co.uk
CONTACT : Tim Foster

BLACKWATER ELECTRONICS
Marine Drive, Torpoint, Cornwall, UK
TEL : +44 1752 812500
FAX : +44 1752 812280
E-MAIL : tonyweldon@blackwaterelectronics.com
CONTACT : Tony Weldon

BOND PEARCE SOLICITORS
Ballard House,
West Hoe Road,
Plymouth PL1 3AE, UK
TEL : +44 1752 266633
FAX : +44 1752 22350
E-MAIL : xgmt@bondpearce.com
WEB : http://www.bondpearce.com
CONTACT : Marcus Trinick

BP ENERGY LTD
BP House Langley Quay,
Waterside Drive, Langley, Slough
Berkshire SL 3 6EY, UK
TEL : +44 1753 585585
FAX : +44 1753 580366
CONTACT : Ian Smith

BRE
Bucknalls Lane, Garston,
Watford Hertfordshire WD2 7JR, UK
TEL : +44 1923 664000
FAX : +44 1923 664010
E-MAIL : enquiries@bre.co.uk
WEB : http://www.bre.co.uk
CONTACT : Simon Guy

BRIAN MAGGS AGRICULTURAL LTD
Knowle Farm,
Compton Dando,
Bristtol BS18, 4LN, UK
TEL : +44 1761 490 351
CONTACT : Brian Maggs

BRIDGESTONE INDUSTRIAL LTD
5th Floor, Clifton House,
83-89, Uxbridge Road,
Ealing, London W5 5TA, UK
TEL : +44 20 8 567 8080
FAX : +44 20 8 567 2066
E-MAIL : info@bsil.co.uk
CONTACT : Andres Thompson

BRIGHT WELLS
Energy Crops, 38,
South Street
Leominster HR6, 8JG, UK
TEL : +44 1568 611166
FAX : +44 1568 611802
E-MAIL : renewables@rbbm.co.uk
WEB : http://www.rbbm.co.uk
CONTACT : Ross Ivy

BROADCROWN LTD
Alliance Works,
Airfield Industrial
Estate, Hwen Stafford,
Staffordshire
ST18, OFF, UK
TEL : +44 1889 272200
FAX : +44 1889 272 220
CONTACT : Barry Wilshaw

BROOK HALL ESTATE
65 Culmore Road,
Londonderry
Northern Ireland BT 48 8JE, UK
TEL : +44 28 71 354635
FAX : +44 28 71 350970
CONTACT : John Gilliland

BROOK HANSEN
St. Thomas Road,
Huddersfield,
W York HDI, UK
TEL : +44 488 422150
FAX : +44 488 559 856
CONTACT : Rick Robbins

BSS (UK)
Pumps & Controls,
Fleet House, Lee Circle,
Leicester LE1 3QQ, UK
TEL : +44 116 262 3232
FAX : +44 116 256 7493
E-MAIL : a.rowland@bssgroup.com
CONTACT: Andrew Rowland

BUSINESS COSTS ADVISORY SERVICE-BCAS
97 Beechwood Road,
Sanderstead,
South Croydon,
Surrey CR2 OAF, UK
TEL : +44 20 8 668 2287
CONTACT : A K Pawlowski

BUYINFO LIMITED
Edgefield Hall Farm,
Melton Constable
Norfolk NR 24 2RS, UK
TEL : +44 1263 712437
CONTACT : Gerald Gent

CALOREX HEAT PUMPS LTD
The Causeway, Maldon,
Essex CM9,
5PU, UK
TEL : +44 1621 856611
FAX : +44 1621 850871
E-MAIL : sales@calorex.com
WEB : www.calorex.com
CONTACT : Tony Bowen

CANTOR (JOHN) HEAT PUMPS
The Workshop,
Denis Street, Lancaster,
LA1, IQX, UK
TEL : +44 1524 844 996
FAX : +44 1524 844 996
E-MAIL : john.cantor@heatpumps.co.uk
WEB : http://www.heatpumps.co.uk
CONTACT : John Cantor

CENTRAX LTD
Gas Turbine Division,
Shaldon Road,
Newton Abbot,
Devon TQ12, 4SQ, UK
TEL : +44 1626 352251
FAX : +44 1626 352250
E-MAIL : sales@gtd.centrax.co.uk
WEB : http://www.centrax.co.uk
CONTACT : Guy M West

CERAM RESEARCH LTD
Queens Road, Penkhull,
Stoke-on-Trent,
Staffordshire,
ST4, 7LQ, UK
TEL : +44 1782 845 431
FAX : +44 1782 412 331
CONTACT : David Poole

CRESSALL RESISTORS
Evington Valley Road,
Leicester LES, SLZ, UK
TEL : +44 116 273 3633
FAX : +44 116 273 7911
E-MAIL : sales@cresall.com
WEB : http://www.cressall.com
CONTACT : Peter Duncan

CUMMINS POWER GENERATION LTD
Manston Park, Columbus Avenue,
Manston Ramsgate,
Kent CT12 5BF, UK
TEL : +44 1843 255 000
FAX : +44 1843 255 902
E-MAIL : cpg.uk@cummins.com
WEB : http://
www.cumminspower.com
CONTACT : Thomas Mathen

DEUTZ ENERGY
Tower House,
Fishergate,
York YO10 4UA, UK
TEL : + 44 1904 624 888
FAX : + 44 1904 678 644
E-MAIL : energy.uk@deutz.de
WEB : http://www.deutzuk.com
CONTACT : Mark Burnett

DUPONT (UK) LT HIGH PERFORMANCE FILMS
Maylands Avenue,
Hemel Hemel Hempstead,
Hertfordshire
HP2 7DP, UK
TEL : + 44 1442 218637
FAX : + 44 1442 218639
E-MAIL : robin.j.thorn@
gbr.dupont.com
CONTACT : Robin J Thorn

DYNAMOTIVE TECHNOLOGIES (UK) LTD
33 Waterloo Road,
Bedford MK 40 3PQ, UK
TEL : + 44 1234 356 889
FAX : + 44 1234 356 889
CONTACT : HDT Moss

EDGE ELLISON SOLICITORS
18 Southampton Place, London
WCIA 2AJ, UK
TEL : +44 20 7 404 4701
FAX : +44 20 7 400 7976
WEB : http://www.edge.co.uk

EDINBURGH DESIGNS LTD
27 Ratcliffe Terrace, Edinburgh Ettg
1SX, UK
TEL : + 44 131 662 4748
FAX : +44 131 662 9150
WEB : http://www.edesign.co.uk
CONTACT : J M Haslam

ELM ENERGY & RECYCLING (UK) LTD
Em Energy House, Ettingshall Road,
Wolverhampton WV2, 2LA, UK
TEL : +44 1902 408608
FAX : +44 1902 408517
E-MAIL : elmenergy@aol.com
CONTACT : Peter Fisher

ELSEVIER SCIENCE
The Boulevard, Langford Lane,
Kidlington, Oxford OX5, IGB, UK
TEL : +44 1865 843800
FAX : +44 1865 843986
E-MAIL : a.verkoeven@elsevier.co.uk
WEB : http://www.elsevier.com
CONTACT : Alex Verhoeven

EM TECHNOLOGY LTD
Leyes House, Kinthall Lane,
Broadheath Tenbury Wells,
Worcestershire WR 15 8QR, UK
TEL : +44 1886 853448
FAX : +44 1886 853448
CONTACT : Dr Roy JS Thurston

ENERGY ADVANTAGE LTD
Green Lane, Tewkesbury,
Gloucester, GL20 8HD, UK
TEL: +44 1684 850 123
FAX: +44 1684 291 919
E-MAIL: eal@softnet.co.uk
CONTACT : William Smith

ENERGY MANAGEMENT BROKERS LTD.
Kingasgate House, 536 Kings Road,
Chelsea, London SW10 OTE, UK
TEL : +44 20 7 352 9616
FAX : + 44 20 7 31 5731
E-MAIL : p.carlbom@energyquote.co.uk
WEB:http://www.energyquote.co.uk
CONTACT : Paul Carlbom

ESD LTD
Overmoor,
Neston, Corsham,
Wiltshire SN 13 9TZ UK
TEL: + 44 12325 812122
FAX: + 44 1225 812103
E-MAIL : e.esd@esd.co.uk
WEB : www.esd.co.uk

ETA PROCESS PLANT LTD
The Levels Brereton,
Rugeley, Staffordshire
WSI5 IRD, UK
TEL: +44 1889 576501
FAX: +44 1889 579856
CONTACT : Janet Armshaw

ETSU
B156 Harwell Laboratory,
Oxfordshire OXII ORA, UK.
TEL: +44 1235 433517
FAX: +44 1235 432948
E-MAIL: etsu.business@aeat.co.uk
WEB: http://www.etsu.com
CONTACT : Debbie Warren

EUROPEAN RENEWABLE ENERGY EXCHANGE – EUROREX
Overmoor Farm,
Neston, Corsham,
Wiltshire SN 13 9TZ, UK
TEL: +44 1225 816805
FAX: +44 1225 812103
E-MAIL: eurorex@esd.co.uk
WEB: http://www.eurorex.com

F WALTER AND SONS LTD
Sutton Grange,
Sutton-cum Lound,
Retford, Notts DN22 8SB, UK
TEL: +44 1777 818264
FAX: +44 1777 816560
CONTACT : Fred Walter

FAWLEY AQUATIC RESEARCH LABORATORIES LTD
Marine and Freshwater
Biology Unit Fawley,
Southampton
SO45 ITN, UK
TEL: +44 23 80 893 513
FAX: +44 23 80 243 274
E-MAIL: ajonas@fawley,arl.co.uk
CONTACT : Andy Jonas

FG WILSON (ENGINEERING) LTD
Old Glenarm Road,
Larne, Cuonty
Antrim BT40 1EJ.UK
TEL: +44 28 28 261000
FAX: +44 28 28 261111
WEB: http://www.fgwilson.com
CONTACT : Patrick Malcomson

FINNING (UK) LTD
Power Systems Division, Watling Street, Cannock,
Staffordshire WS11 3LL, UK
TEL: +44 1543 461 461
FAX: +44 1543 461 700
CONTACT : John Dalgarno

FINNING POWER SYSTEMS LTD
Stirling Road, Slough,
Berkshire SLI 4ST, UK
TEL: +44 1753 845 221
FAX: +44 1753 845 232
CONTACT : G Cannon

GENCOR BEVERLEY
Billinghurst, West Sussex RHI 4 9SA, UK
TEL : + 44 1403 782091
FAX : + 44 1403 782987
WEB : www.gencor-beverley.co.uk
CONTACT : Brian Riley

GRANUTECH-SATURN SYSTEMS LTD
Bolton Business Centre,
44-46 Lower Bridgeman Street,
Bolton, Lancs BL 2 IDG, UK
TEL : + 44 1204 388 400
FAX : + 44 1204 688 410
E-MAIL : + tcr@mcmail.com
WEB : www.granutech.com

GREENWOOD AIR MANAGEMENT
PO Bos 3, Brookside Induistrial Estate, Rustington, West Sussex
BN 16 3LH, UK
TEL :+ 44 1903 771021
FAX : + 44 1903 782398
CONTACT : A Fairbourn

GROUND WORKBRIDGEND
The Environment Centre,
Maestef Road Tondu, Brigend
CF 32 9BT UK
TEL : + 44 1656 722315
FAX : + 44 1656 72 15 57
E-MAIL : brigend@groundwork.org.uk
CONTACT : Kenneth Stano

HADENDRYSYS INTERNATIONAL LTD
Haden Drysys Environment,
Swan Office Centre 1506-15-8
Coventry Road,
Yardley Birrmingham
B25 BAD, UK
TEL : + 44 121 765 4040
FAX : +44 121 706 6865
E-MAIL : environmental@hadenmac.com
CONTACT : Gerald Warchem

HAMMOND SUDDARDS
2 Park Lane, Leeds LS3 IES, UK
TEL : + 44 113 284 7000
FAX : + 44 113 284 7001
E-MAIL :enquires@hammondsuddards.co.uk
WEB :www.hammondsuddards.co.uk
CONTACT : Terence Torey

HAMPSHIRE WASTE SERVICES LTD
Poles Lane, Otterbourne SQ21 2EA, UK
TEL :+ 44 1962 714000
FAX : + 44 1962 71102
E-MAIL :enquire@integra.hws.co.uk
CONTACT : Keitn Riley

HOME GROWN ENERGY
The Barton Laneast, Launceston
PL15 8PN, UK
TEL: +44 1556 86001
FAX: +44 1556 86013
E-MAIL: gmacpherson@farmline.com
WEB: http://www.farmline.com
CONTACT: George Macpherson

HOWDEN SIROCCO LTD
Old Govan Road, Renfrew,
Strathclyde, PA4 8XJ, UK
TEL: +44 141 885 2590
FAX: +44 141 885 2887
CONTACT: K D Ramsay

HYDER INFRASTRUCTURE MANAGEMENT LTD
Hyder Infrastructure Services,
Willow House Pascal Close,
St Mellons, Cardiff, UK
TEL: +44 29 20 775294
FAX: +44 29 20 775240
E-MAIL: infrastructure-management@hyder.com
WEB: http://www.hyder.com
CONTACT: Tony Taylor

INDEPENDENT ENERGY UK LIMITED
Radcliffe House, Blenheim Court,
Solihull West Midlands B91 2AA, UK
TEL: +44 121 705 1111
FAX: +44 121 705 7226
E-MAIL: sales@independentenergy.co.uk
WEB: http://www.independentenergy.co.uk
CONTACT: Bob Hatton

INNOGY PLC
Corporate Communications,
Windmill Hill Business Park, White Hill Way Swindon 5N5 6PB, UK
TEL: +44 1793 892616
FAX: +44 1793 893741
E-MAIL: robert.lewis@natpower.com
CONTACT: Robert Lewis

INNOVATION MANAGEMENT
Station Yard, Wilbraham Road
Fulbourn, Cambridge CBI 5ET, UK
TEL: +44 1223 881887
FAX: +44 1223 881553
E-MAIL: enquire@innovation.u-net.com
CONTACT: Bruce Knight

INSTEM COMPUTER SYSTEMS
Walton Industrial Estate, Stone
Staffordshire ST15 0LT, UK
TEL: +44 1785 812131
FAX: +44 1785 815615
E-MAIL: sales@instem-computersystems.co.uk
CONTACT: Julie Jones

LIGHT WORKS LIMITED
2a Greenwood Road, London E8 IAB, UK
TEL: +44 20 7 259 3627
FAX: +44 20 7 254 0306
CONTACT: Charies Paton

LILLEY GRANT RUSH LIMITED
Rowlands House, 48 Rowlands Road, Worthing, West
Sussex BN11 3JT, UK
TEL : +44 1903 520200
FAX : +44 1903 520211
CONTACT : Peter Rush

LODGE STURTEVANT LTD
George Street Parade,
Birmingham B3 1QQ, UK
TEL: + 44 121 214 1300
FAX: +44 121 200 2555
CONTACT: Ian Fantom

LONDON ELECTRICITY PLC
34-38 Aybrook Street,
London WIM 3JL, UK
TEL: +44 20 7 747 9594
FAX: +44 20 7 839 0390
E-MAIL: john_shearer@londoneiec.co.uk
CONTACT: John Shearer

LURGI(UK) LTD
Dukes Court, Duke Street,
Woking, Surrey GU21 5BH, UK
TEL: +44 1483 730 044
FAX: +44 1483 729 595
CONTACT: David Porter

MAGNAV INTERNATIONAL LTD
91 Chester Drive, Harrow, Middlesex
HA2 7PX, UK
TEL: +44 20 8 840 4190
FAX: +44 20 8 566 1962
CONTACT: N M Patel

MALCOLM LYNCH SOLICITORS
19 High Court Lane, The Calls,
Leeds LS2 7EU, UK
TEL: +44 113 242 9600
FAX: +44 113 234 2080
E-MAIL: law@malcolmlynch.com
WEB: http://www.malcolmlynch.com
CONTACT: Malcolm Lynch

MALTIN POLLUTION
CONTROL SYSTEMS(1967) LTD
Gould's House, Horsington,
Somerset BA8 0EW,UK
TEL: +44 1963 370100
FAX: +44 1963 371300
E-MAIL: cmamltin@gouldshouse.com
CONTACT: Chris Maltin

MARCHES ENERGY AGENCY
The Shirehall, Abbey Foregate,
Shrewsbury SY2 6ND, UK
TEL: +44 1743 252573
FAX: +44 1743 252572
E-MAIL: marchesenergy
@fsbdial.co.uk
CONTACT: Ewan Bent

MARICK GASIFICATION INTERNATIONAL
3 Farndale Close, Whittle Hall, Great
Sankey, Warrington Cheshire WA5
3FX, UK
TEL: +44 1925 711155
FAX: +44 1925 711155
CONTACT: Dr Donald C Patrick

MARTON GEOTECHNICAL SERVICES LTD
Geotechnical Centre,
Rougham Industrial Estate,
Bury St Edmunds,
Suffolk IP30 9ND,
UK
TEL: +44 1359 271167
FAX: +44 1359 271168
E-MAIL: geomart@mgs.co.uk
CONTACT: Martin Clegg

MATRIX INTERNATIONAL LTD
East Mill Road,
Brechin, Angus,
DD9 7EP, UK
TEL: +44 1356 622212
FAX: +44 1356 624 799
CONTACT: John S Pettifer

MATTHEW HALL MECHANICAL & ELECTRICAL ENGINEERS LTD
7-14 Great Dover Street,
London, SEI 4YR, UK
TEL: +44 20 7 407 7272
FAX: +44 20 403 7553
CONTACT: Adrienne Baker

MAYR TRANSMISSIONS LTD
10-11 Valley Road
Business Park,
Keighley, West Yorkshire
BD21 14Lz, UK
TEL: +44 1535 663900
FAX: +44 1535 663261
CONTACT: GA Harrison

MCL ENERGY LTD
Everton Road,
Mattersey,
Doncaster
DN10 SDS, UK
TEL: +44 1777 817536
FAX: +44 1777 816045
CONTACT: Jasson Perry

MDC TECHNOLOGY LTD
Startforth Road,
Riverside Park,
Middlesbrough,
Cleveland TS2 IPT, UK
TEL: +44 1642 773000
FAX: +44 1642 773077
E-MAIL: sales@mdctech.com
WEB: http://www.mdctech.com
CONTACT: Ross Smith

MEL COURT INDUSTRIES LTD
Eight Bells House,
Tetbury,
Gloucestershire GL8 8jg,
UK
TEL: +44 1666 503919
FAX: +44 1666 504398
E-MAIL: mail@melcourt.co.uk
WEB: http://www.melcourt.co.uk
CONTACT: jLatter

MITSUI BABCOCK ENERGY LTD
Technology Centre,
High Street,
Renfrew,
Renfrewshire PA48UW, UK
TEL: +44 141 886 2201
FAX: +44 141 885 3370
E-MAIL: technology@
mitsuibabcock.co.uk
WEB: http://www.mitsuibabcock.com
CONTACT: Mr Douglas J Spaiding

MONITAN INFORMATION CONSULTANTS
Sandyford,
Healey,
Riding Mill
Northumberland NE44 6BA,
UK
TEL:+44 1434 682496
FAX: +44 1434 682019
CONTACT: Monica Anderton

MONODRAUGHT LTD
Halifax House, Cressex Business
Park High Wycombe,
Buckinghamshire HP12 35E, UK
TEL: +44 1494 897700
FAX:+44 1494 532465
E-MAIL:info@monodraught.com
WEB:http://www.monodraught.com
CONTACT: Terry M Payne

NABARRO NATHANSON
Lacon House, 84 Theobald Road
London WCHIX 8RW, UK
TEL: +44 20 7 524 6000
FAX: +44 20 7 524 6524
WEB:http://www.nabarro.com
CONTACT:Robert Tudway

NATIONAL HOME ENERGY RATING SCHEME
The National Energy Centre,
Davy Avenue, Knowlhill,
Milton Keynes MKS 8NA, UK
TEL: +44 1908 672787
FAX: +44 1908 662296
E-MAIL: neil@nesltd.demon.co.uk
CONTACT; Neil Cutland

NAVCARE LTD
Cornerways House,
12 Kensington Road, Lowestoft,
Suffolk NR33 0HY, UK
TEL: +44 1502 518086
FAX: +44 1502 519628
CONTACT: Martin Brooks

NEATWORLD LTD
Alington Road Industrial
Estate.St Neots.
Cambridge
PE19 2UX, UK
TEL: +44 1480 470700
FAX: +44 1480 470701
E-MAIL:infoline@networld.com
WEB: http://www.networld.com
CONTACT: Colin Ashton

NEDALO (UK) LTD
Fraser House,
14A The Carfax, Horsham,
West Sussex RH12 1ER, UK
TEL: +44 1403 320200
FAX: +44 1403 320201
CONTACT: Steve Guttridge

PEOPLE PAPER OIL AND CANS PPOC
30 Whitehead Close,
Earlsfield
London SWI8, 3BT, UK
TEL : +44 20 8 265 1092
FAX : +44 20 8 265 1092
CONTACT : SteveParry

PERKINS ENGINES (SHREWSBURY) LTD
Sentienl Works, LancasterRoad
Shrewsburry SYI3NX, UK
TEL:+44 1743 212000
FAX:+44 1743 212701
CONTACT:D Smithson

PERKINS ENGINES COMPANY LTD
Tixall Road,Stafford ST16 3UB, UK
TEL:+44 1785 223141
FAX:+44 1785 215110

PERKINS ENGINES COMPANY LTD
Frank Perkins Way,
Peterborough,
Cambridgeshire PEI 5NA, UK
TEL:+44 1733 583000
FAX:+44 1733 582240
WEB:http://www.perkins.com

PIPELINE SERVICES LTD
21 Princes Drive, Kenilworth,
Warwickshire CV8 2FD, UK
TEL : + 44 1926 511 316
FAX : + 44 1926 512 744
CONTACT : Ian Oakley

POWER PLANT SERVICES LIMITED
Langthwaite Grange Industrial
Estate, South Kirkby,
West Yorkshire WF9 3AP, UK
TEL: +44 1977 641 144
FAX: +44 1977 648 180
E-MAIL: sales@power-plant-servies.co.uk
CONTACT: Mr Paul Clark

POWERGEN CHP LTD
Westwood Way, Westwood
Business Park, Coventry CV4 8LG, UK
TEL: +44 24 76 424359
FAX: +44 24 76 425425
WEB: http://www.pgen.com
CONTACT: Nader Bahri

POWERGEN ENERGY MANAGEMENT
17 Pebble Close, Amington,
Tamworth, Staffs B77 4RD, UK
TEL: +44 1827 312 136
FAX: +44 1827 312 137
CONTACT: Gary Cottrell

POWERGEN PLC
Power Technology, Power
Technology
Centre, Ratcliffe on Soar,
Nottingham
NG11 OEE, UK
TEL: +44 115 936 2000
FAX: +44 115 936 2649
CONTACT: Dr Tim Hill

REDLAND AGGREGATES LTD
Great North Road, Little Paxton, St
Neots, Cambridgeshire PE19 4BG, UK
TEL : +44 1530 242151
FAX : +44 1530 243515
CONTACT : Mr C Mulholland

REED EXHIBITION COMPANIES LTD
Oriel House 26 The Quadrant,
Richmond, Surrey TW9 IDL, UK
TEL : +44 20 8 910 7976
FAX : +44 20 8 910 7829
E-MAIL :
rob.schulp@reedexpo.co.uk
CONTACT : Rob Schulp

RENEWABLE POWER SYSTEMS LTD
Unit 11 Bedford Business Centre,
Mile Road, Bedford MK42 9TW, UK
TEL : +44 1234 271700
FAX : +44 1234 271709
E-MAIL :
rps@renewablepower.co.uk
CONTACT : Andrew Leach

RESOFT LTD
7 Church Lane, Flitton, Bedford,
Bedfortshire MK45 5el, UK
TEL : +44 1525 862616
FAX : +44 1525 862616
E-MAIL : alan@resoft.co.uk
WEB : http://www.resoft.co.uk
CONTACT : Alan Harris

SHERWOOD ENERGY VILLAGE
Unit 1 Boughton Pumping Station,
Brake Lane, Boughton,
Nottinghamshire NG22 9HQ, UK
TEL: +44 1623 860222
FAX: +44 1623 863373
E-MAIL: sev@netcomuk.co.uk
WEB: http://
www.sherwoodenergyvillage.co.uk
CONTACT: Carla Jamison

SHURFLO LIMITED
Unit 5 Sterling Park, Gatwick Road,
Crawley, West Sussex RH102QT, UK
TEL: +44 1293 424000
FAX: +44 1293 421880
E-MAIL: sales@shurflo.co.uk
WEB: http://www.shurflo.com
CONTACT: Scott Pearce

SIEMENS ENVIRONMENTAL SYSTEMS LTD
Sopers Lane, Poole,
Dorset BH17 7ER, UK
TEL: +44 1202 782779
FAX: +44 1202 782335
WEB: http://www.siemens.co.uk/
env.sys
CONTACT: Ian Bywaters

SIMS SYSTEMS LTD
259 Whapload Road,
Lowerstoft, Suffolk NR32 IUL, UK
TEL: +44 1502 567890
FAX: +44 1502 586291
CONTACT: Nicholas Sims

SLOUGH HEAT AND POWER LTD
342 Edinburgh Avenue,
Slough,
Berkshire SLI4TU, UK
TEL: +44 1753 213200
FAX: +44 1753 213213
CONTACT: Steve Garrett

SOILTEC LTD
Ledian Farm Industrial Estate,
Upper Street, Leeds,
Maidstone Kent ME17 IRZ, UK
TEL: +44 1622 861350
FAX: +44 1622 862752
E-MAIL: info@soiltec.co.uk
CONTACT: Chris Epps

SOLARMATT LTD
82 The Ryde, Hat field,
Hertfordshire
AL9 5DL, UK
TEL : +44 1707 266197
FAX : +44 1707 881782
E-MAIL : solarmatt@aol.com
WEB : http://www.solarmatt.com
CONTACT : David Johnson

SOLARTECH (UK) LTD
Sales,Tudorleaf Business Centre,2-8
Fountayne Road,
London N15 4QI, UK
TEL:+44 208 801 2198
FAX:+44 208 808 5605
E-MAIL:solect638@aol.com
WEB:http://www.solartech-uk.co.uk
CONTACT:David Lindenberg

SONDEX (UK) LTD
Unit 10, 106A Beford Road,
Wootton,
Bedford MK43 9JB, UK
TEL: +44 1234 768255
FAX: +44 1234 768361
E-MAIL: sales@sondexuk.com
CONTACT: Peter F Collins

SOUTH INDUSTRIAL CROPS LTD
Mamhead Castle,
Mamhead, Exeter,
Devon EX6 8HD, UK
TEL: +44 1626 892600
FAX: +44 1626 892634
E-MAIL: jonathan.whiteley@adas.co.uk
WEB: http://www.adas.co.uk
CONTACT: JAC Whiteley

SOUTH WESTERN ELECTRICITY PLC
Green Electron, 800 Park Avenue,
Attec West, Almondsbury, Bristol
BS35 3UA, UK
TEL: +44 1454 452 180
FAX: +44 1454 616 675
E-MAIL: green_electron@sweb.co.uk
WEB: http://www.greenelectron.com
CONTACT: Nicky Bishop

SP SYSTEMS LTD
St Cross Businesss Park, Newport,
Isle Of Wight PO30 5WU, UK
TEL: +44 1983 828000
FAX: +44 1983 828100
E-MAIL: info@spsystems.com
WEB:http://www.spsystems.com
CONTACT: Andy Day

STARK SOFTWARE INTERNATIONAL LTD
Claremont Buildings, Salbrook Road,
Salfrods, Redhill Surrey RHI 5DY, UK
TEL: +44 1293 776747
FAX: +44 1293 820361
E-MAIL:office@stark.co.uk
WEB:http://www.stark.co.uk
CONTACT: HP Stark

SUMMERLEAZE REGENERATION
Keer Bridge House,
Warton, Carnforth,
Lancashire LA5 9HA, UK
TEL: +44 1524 734744
FAX: +44 1524 734711
CONTACT: S H Ashton

SURECAST (DEVIZES) LTD
Roundway Mill,
London Road,
Devizes, SN10 2EA, UK
TEL: + 44 1380 723402
FAX: + 44 1380 729063
E-MAIL:sales@surecast.co.uk
CONTACT:C Franklin

SVM PLC
Telford House, Cornerhall,
Hemel Hempstead,
Hertfordshire HP3 9HN, UK
TEL: +44 1442 231999
FAX: +44 1442 230449
E-MAIL:solutions@sum.co.uk

SWITCHROADRUNNER LTD
Unit B6, Plough Road Center,
Great Bentley,
Colchester Essex CO7 8LQ, UK
TEL: +44 1206 251 620
FAX: +44 1260 251 755
E-MAIL:sales@abtrans.com
WEB:http://www.abtrans.com
CONTACT:Peter Hurne

TARMAC WATER ENGINEERING
Westlink House, 981, Great West Road,
Brentford, Middlesex TW8 9DN, UK
TEL : +44 20 8 380 5000
FAX : +44 20 8 380 5308
CONTACT : Phil Cowley

THERMAL ENGINEERING INTERNATIONAL LTD
PO Box 80, Calder Vale Road,
Wakefild, West Yorkshire WF1 5YS, UK
TEL: +44 1924 780000
FAX: +44 1924 201910
E-MAIL: sales@tel.co.uk
WEB: http://www.tei.co.uk
CONTACT: John Sewell

THERMAL TECHNOLOGY (SALES) LTD
Bridge House, Station Road,
Westbury, Wiltshire BA13 4HS UK
TEL: +44 1373 865454
FAX: +44 1373 864425
E-MAIL: thermaltech@compuserve.com
WEB: http://www.thermaltechnology.co.uk
CONTACT: David Applegate

THORNE INTERNATIONAL BOILER SERVICES LTD
Broad Lanes,
Bilston WV14 0RQ,UK
TEL: +44 1902 404223
FAX: +44 1902 404224
E-MAIL:tibs.boilers@btinternet.com
CONTACT:Jack Broughton

TILSLEY & LOVATT LTD
Newstead Trading Estate,
Trentham, Stoke on Trent
ST4 8HT, UK
TEL: +44 1782 657 331
FAX: +44 1782 644 600
CONTACT:Mr J Caldwell

TORAY EUROPE LTD
Carbon Fibre Department, Third
Floor, 7 Old Park Lane,
London WIY 4AD, UK
TEL: +44 20 7 663 7774
FAX: +44 20 7 663 7777
E-MAIL:okumura@toray-tel.co.uk
CONTACT:Yigo Okumura

TORFTECH LTD
Ferndale Court, West End Road,
Mortimer, Reading Berkshire RG7
3SY, UK
TEL: +44 1189 333009
FAX: +44 1189 331376
E-MAIL: 100434.107@
compuserve.com
WEB:http://www.torftech.co.uk
CONTACT: Martin Groszek

TOWNSON EXPANSION JOINTS
Alexandra Street,
Hyde, Cheshire
SKI4 IDY, UK
TEL: +44 161 367 9278
FAX: +44 161 367 9280
E-MAIL:townson@zen.co.uk

TURBINE CONTROLS LTD
41 Kenilworth Drive Oadby,
Leicester LE2 5LT, UK
TEL: +44 116 271 7248
FAX: +44 116 271 7250
E-MAIL: graham@turbine
controlsltd.com
WEB: http://
www.turbinecontrolsltd.com

TURBOMECA LTD
Land and Marine Division,
4 Grosvenor Place,
London SWIX 7HH, UK
TEL: +44 20 7 235 1177
FAX: +44 20 7 245 6385
E-MAIL: christophe.poulain@
rrtm-tml.co.uk
CONTACT: Christophe Poulain

TWIFLEX LIMITED
104 The Green,
Twickenham,
Middlesex, TW2 5AQ, UK
TEL: +44 20 8 894 1161
FAX: +44 20 8 894 6056
CONTACT: Peter Wood

VERDER LTD
Whitehouse Street,
Hunslet,
Leeds LS10 IAD, UK
TEL: +44 113 222 0250
FAX: +44 113 246 5649
E-MAIL: verder@legend.co.uk
WEB: htttp://www.verder.com
CONTACT: M C Heap

VILLAVENT LTD
Avenue 2, Station Lane
Industrial Estate, Witney,
Oxfordshire OX8 6YD, UK
TEL: +44 1993 778481
FAX: +44 1993 779962
CONTACT: Gary Clarkson

VOLVO AERO TURBINES (UK) LIMITED
PO Box 422,
Coventry CV3, 4YX, UK
TEL: +44 24 76 308 900
FAX: +44 24 76 308 910
E-MAIL: vat.iagr@memo.volvo.se
CONTACT: David Hague

WABAG WATER ENGINEERING LTD
Aynho Road, Adderbury, Banbury,
Oxfordshine OX17 3NL, UK
TEL: +44 1295 810581
FAX: +44 1295 811997
CONTACT: M Andrews

WASTE MANAGEMENT INFORMATION BUREAU
AEA Technology Plc, F6,
Culham Abingdon
Oxfordshire OX14 3DB, UK
TEL: +44 1235 463162
FAX: +44 1235 463004
E-MAIL: wmib@aeat.co.uk
CONTACT: Heather Cholerton

WINDPOWER DEVELOPMENTS (UK) LIMITED
94/96 Wigmore Streer,
London WIU 3RF
TEL: +44 20 7 224 1178
FAX: +44 20 7 224 1158
E-MAIL: siluk@globalnet.co.uk
CONTACT: Jerry Silberman

WRITE-ON
5 Christchurch Drive,
Blackwater, Camberley BUI7 0HA,UK
TEL: +44 1252 874489
E-MAIL: mgascoigne@gn.apc.org
WEB: http://ourworld.compuserve.com/homepages/mgascoigne
CONTACT: Michael Gascoigne

BATTERIES/INVERTERS

ALSTOM POWER CONVERSION LTD
Boughton Road, Rugby,
Warwickshire CV21 1BU, UK
TEL: +44 1788 563625
FAX: +44 1788 563780
E-MAIL:genral.drives@powerconv.alstom.com
WEB: http://www.alstom.com
CONTACT: Dave Sowerby

ALSTOM POWER FLOWSYSTEMS
Flowsystems, Burnden Works,
Burnden Road,Bolton, BL3 2RB, UK
TEL: +44 1204 554 540
FAX: +441204 554544
E-MAIL: tim.ward@flowsystems.co.uk
WEB: http://www.flowsystems.co.uk
CONTACT: Tim Ward

BATTERY TECHNOLOGY SERVICES
7 Field Place, Liphook, Hampshire,
GU30 7DZ, UK
TEL : +44 1428 725600
FAX : +44 8701 336655
E-MAIL :info@battery-technology.com
WEB : http://www.battery-technology.com
CONTACT : Douglas Lambert

CHLORIDE INDUSTRIAL BATTERIES LTD
Rake Lane, Clifton Junction,
Swinton, Manchester M27 8LR, UK
TEL: +44 161 794 4611
FAX: +44 161 793 6606
E-MAIL: sales.cibl@btrinc.com
CONTACT: Dave Cowgill

CMP BATTERIES STANDBY DIVISION
14 Gunnels Wood Park, Stevenage,
Hertfordshire SGI 2BH, UK
TEL: +44 1438 359090
FAX: +44 1438 727684
E-MAIL: alleng@cmpstandby.co.uk
WEB: http://www.cmpstandby.co.uk
CONTACT: Peter Meeds

FUTRONICS POWER DESIGNS LTD
Unit 74 The Maltings, Stanstead
Abbotts, Herts SG12 8HG, UK
TEL: +44 1920 872668
FAX: +44 1920 872669
E-MAIL: fpd@futronics.co.uk
WEB: http://www.futronics.co.uk
CONTACT: Karen Brewster

HAWKER ENERGY PRODUCTS LTD
Stephenson Street, Newport
Gwent NP9 OXJ, UK
TEL: +44 1633 277673
FAX: +44 1633 281787
E-MAIL: dave.rice@btrinc.com
CONTACT: Dave Rice

HAWKER
Rake Lane, Clifton Junction,
Swinon,
Manchester M27 8LR, UK
TEL : + 44 161 727 3960
FAX : + 44 161 727 3812
E-MAIL : tony.smith@hawker.invensys.com
WEB : hawker.invensys.com

IIR GRAPHEX
29 Bressenden Place,
London SW1E 5RD, UK
TEL: +44 207 9155533
FAX: +44 207 9155001
E-MAIL: ahunter@iirltd.co.uk
CONTACT: Alison Hunter

INNOGY LIMITED
Harwell International Business
Centre, Didcot,
Oxon OX11 0QA, UK
TEL: +44 1235 862601
FAX: +44 1235 44 4909
E-MAIL: kate.Avenelu@innogy.com
WEB: http://www.innogy.com
CONTACT: Kate Aveneil

INVERTEC LTD
Whelford Road, Fairford,
Gloucestershire GL7 4DW, UK
TEL: +44 1285 713 550
FAX: +44 1235 713 548
E-MAIL: sales@invertec.co.uk
WEB: http://www.invertec.co.uk
CONTACT: J Valentine

JEFF CAPPER DESIGNS
PO Box 956, Finchley,
London N3 1YY, UK
TEL: +44 20 8 346 6958
FAX: +44 20 8 445 9862
CONTACT: Jeff Capper

LABCRAFT LTD
Church Road, Harold Wood,
Romford, Essex RM3 0HT, UK
TEL: +44 7002 522272
FAX: +44 7002 522273
E-MAIL: sales@labcraft.co.uk
WEB: http://www.labcraft.co.uk
CONTACT: Nick Luscombe

LUMIC LTD
First Floor The Doughty Building,
Crow Arch Lane, Ringwood,
Hampshire BH24 1NZ, UK
TEL: +44 1425 480 780
FAX: +44 1425 479 497
E-MAIL: ampair@ampair.com
WEB: http://www.ampair.com
CONTACT: George Durrant

MASTERVOLT UK LTD
Unit DS The Premier Centre,
Abbey Park Industrial Estate,
Romsey, Hampshire SO51 9AQ, UK
TEL: +44 1794 516 443
FAX: +44 1794 516 453
E-MAIL: info@mastervolt.com
WEB: http://www.mastervolt.com
CONTACT: Paul Kinsman

MITSUI BABCOCK ENERGY LTD
New Ventures Division,
11 The Boulevard,
Crawley,
West Sussex, RH10 1UX, UK
TEL: +44 1293 612888
FAX: +44 1293 584981

MONODRAUGHT LTD
Halifax House,
Cressex Business Park,
High Wycombe,
Buckinghamshire HP12 3SE, UK
TEL: +44 1494 897700
FAX: +44 1494 532465
E-MAIL: info@monodraught.com
WEB: http://www.monodraught.com
CONTACT: Terry M Payne

NADA ELECTRONICS LTD
Unit 2 Nest Road, Felling Shore Industrial Estate, Gateshead, Tyne & Wear NE10 0ES, UK
TEL: + 44 191 477 5623
FAX: + 44 191 477 6679
WEB:http://www.nada.co.uk
CONTACT: Robin Dyas

POWER PROTECTION SCOTLAND
39 Woodside Avenue, Lenzie, Glasgow G66 4NG, UK
TEL: +44 141 776 3559
FAX: +44 141 776 3559
CONTACT: Douglas Fraser

POWER PROTECTION SCOTLAND
39 Woodside Avenue, Lenzie, Glasgow G66 4NG, UK
TEL: +44 141 776 3559
FAX: +44 141 776 3559
CONTACT: Douglas Fraser

POWER-SONIC EUROPE LTD
3-4 Buckingham Square, Hurricane Way, Wickford, Essex SS11 8YQ, UK
TEL: +44 1268 560686
FAX: +44 1268 560902
E-MAIL: sales@power-sonic.co.uk
WEB: http://www.power-sonic.co.uk
CONTACT: Ms SK Jefferys-Emrys

SEC INDUSTRIAL BATTERY CO LTD
Thorney Weir House, Iver, Buckinghamshire SL09AQ, UK
TEL: +441895431543
FAX: +441895431880
E-MAIL: sales@secbattery.com
WEB: http://www.secbattery.com
CONTACT: Gerry Taylor

SHURFLO LIMITED
Unit 5 Sterling Park, Gatwick Road, Crawley, West Sussex RH 10 2QT, UK
TEL: +441293424000
FAX: +441293421880
E-MAIL: sales@shurflo.co.uk
WEB: http://www.shurflo.com
CONTACT: Scott Pearce

SOLLATEK (UK) LTD
Unit 4/5 Trident Industrial Estate, Blackthorne Road, Poyle, Slough SL3 Oax, UK
TEL: +44 1753 688 300
FAX: +44 1753 685 306
E-MAIL: sales@sollatek.com
WEB: http://www.sollatek.com
CONTACT: Sarah Hill

THE MET OFFICE
Services & Business, Sutton House, London Road, Bracknell, Berkshire RG12 2SY, UK
TEL: +44 1344 420242
FAX: +44 800 252356
E-MAIL: snwass@meto.gov.uk
WEB: http://www.meto.gov.uk
CONTACT: Stewart Wass

TORNADO POWER SYSTEMS
Yew Tree House, Main Street, Tingewick, Buckinghamshire MK I8 4NL, UK
TEL: +44 1280 848361
FAX: +44 1280 847877
E-MAIL:tornpower@aol.com
WEB:http://www.nettrader.co.uk/custom/tornado.html
CONTACT:Peter Hanbury

INSTRUMENTATION

AB BUTT LTD
Frog Island, Leicester LE3 5AZ, UK
TEL: +44 1162 513 344
FAX: +44 1162 536 377
E-MAIL: simon.butt@btinternet.com
WEB: http://www.abbutt.co.uk
CONTACT: Kenneth G Muddimer

AB PHAROS MARINE LTD
Steyning Way, Hounslow, Middlesex TW4 6DL, UK
TEL: +44 208 538 1100
FAX: +44 208 577 4170
E-MAIL: sales@pharosmarine.com
WEB: http://www.pharosmarine.com
CONTACT: Mr Alan Tassell

AEA TECHNOLOGY ENVIORNMENT
B154, Harvell, Oxfordshire OX110QJ, UK
TEL: +44 1235 433513
FAX: +441235 432948
WEB: http://www.aeat-env.co.uk
CONTACT: Tony Duffin

AEA TECHNOLOGY ENVIORNMENT
Culham, abingdon, Oxfordshire OX14 3ED, UK
TEL: +44 1235 433513
FAX: +441235 432948
WEB: http://www.aeat-env.com
CONTACT: Tony Duffin

AEA TECHNOLOGY ENVIORNMENT
ETSU, Harvell, Oxfordshire OX110RA, UK
TEL: +44 1235 433154
FAX: +441235 433434
WEB: http://www.etsu.com
CONTACT: Caroline Livingstone

AF HILL & SON
Dunstall Court, Feckenham, Nr Redditch, Worcester B96 6QH, UK
TEL: +44 1527 892 472
FAX: +44 1527 893 401
CONTACT: Lionel Hill

ALLEN GEARS LIMITED
Atlas Works, Pershore, Worcestershire WR10 2BZ, UK
TEL: +44 1386 552211
FAX: +44 1386 554491
E-MAIL: sales@allengears.com
WEB: http://www.allengears.com
CONTACT: Geoff Horton

ALSTOM POWER UK LTD
Industrial Gas Turbines, PO Box 1, Waterside South, Lincoln LN5 7FD, UK
TEL: +44 1522 584000
FAX: +441522 584900
E-MAIL: mike.welch@energy.alstom.com
WEB: http://www.power.alstom.com
CONTACT: Mike Welch

AMEC FACILITIES
200 Great Dover Street, London SEI, UK
TEL: +44 20 7 574 3999
WEB: http://www.amec.co.uk
CONTACT: Miss Kingsbury

AMPAIR NATURAL ENERGY
Doughty Building, Crow Arch Lane, Ringwood BH24 1NZ,UK
TEL: +44 1425 480780
FAX: +441425 479497
E-MAIL: sales@ampair.com
WEB: http://www.ampair.com
CONTACT: HG Durrant

AVIONICS SYSTEMS CONSULTING LIMITED-ASCL
17, Mapledene Avenue, Hultbridge, Hockley, Essex SS5, 6JB, UK
TEL : +44 1268 742472
E-MAIL : wmitchell@iee.org
CONTACT : W H Mitchell

BRISTOL INDUSTRIAL &RESEARCH ASSOCIATES LTD-BIRAL
PO Box 2 Portishead, Bristol BS20 9JB, UK
TEL: +44 1275 847787
FAX: +44 1275 847303
E-MAIL: info@biral.com
WEB: http://www.biral.com
CONTACT: James Squires

CAMPBELL SCIENTIFIC LTD
Campbell Park, 80 Hathern Road,
Shepshed, Leicestershire LE 12 9RP, UK
TEL : +44 1509 601141
FAX : +44 1509 601091
E-MAIL : sales@campbellsci.co.uk
WEB : http://www.campbellsci.co.uk
CONTACT : Tim Clarke

CASELLA LTD
Regent House, Wolseley Road,
Kempston, Bedford MK42 7JY, UK
TEL : +44 1234 841441
FAX : +44 1234 841490
E-MAIL :sales@casella.co.uk
WEB : http://www.cassela.co.uk
CONTACT : Victoria Bryan

CASELLA STANGER
Blakelands House, 400 Aldridge
Road, Birmingham, B44 8BH, UK
TEL: +44 121 344 6100
FAX: +44 121 344 6111
E-MAIL:
mitchwainwright@casellagroup.co.uk
WEB: http://www.casellagroup.co.uk
CONTACT: Stewart Lowther

CNS SUBSEA LTD
7 Rubislaw Terrace,
Aberdeen AB10 1XE UK
TEL: +44 1224 649753
FAX: +44 1224 644211
E-MAIL: cns@cns-ltd.com
WEB: http://www.cns-ltd.com

COGEN AN INNOGY BUSINESS
Cogen Court, Cranmore
Boulevard, Solihull,
West Midlands B90 4LN, UK
TEL: +44 121 506 8000
FAX: +44 121 506 8001
WEB: http://www.cogenuk.com
CONTACT: Chris Townsend

COGEN ENERGY UK LTD
1st Floor Unit 2 Merlin Business
Park, fairoak Close, Clyst Honiton,
Exeter EX5 2UL,UK
TEL: +44 1392 671567
FAX: +44 1392 671569
E-MAIL: claire@cogenenergy.co.uk
WEB: http://www.cogenenergy.co.uk
CONTACT: Claire Symons

COLT INTERNATIONAL LTD
New Lane, Havant,
Hampshire P09 2LY, UK
TEL: +44 23 92 451111
FAX: +44 23 92 454220
E-MAIL: info@coltgroup.com
WEB: http://www.coltinternational.co.uk
CONTACT: Robert Buck

CONNECT SOUTH WEST LIMITED
5 Abbey Court, Eagle Way,
Exeter EX2 7HY, UK
TEL: +44 1392 209740
FAX: +44 1392 444743
CONTACT: Tim Pope

CONNIK TREE CARE
New Pond Farm,
Woodhatch Road,
Reigate, Surrey RH2 7QH, UK
TEL: +44 1737 779191
FAX: +44 1737 765775
E-MAIL: mike@connick-tree.co.uk
WEB: http://www.connick-tree.co.uk
CONTACT: Mike Connick

CPL ENERGY
Mill Lane,
Wingerworth,
Chesterfield S42 6NG, UK
TEL: +44 1246 212244
FAX: +44 1246 212233
E-MAIL: energy@cplindustries.co.uk
WEB: http://www.cplenergy.co.uk
CONTACT: Graham Lucas

DELTA-T DEVICES LTD
128 Low Road,
Burwell,
Cambridge CB50EJ, UK
TEL : + 44 1638 742922
FAX : + 44 1638 743155
E-MAIL : sales@delta.co.uk
CONTACT : Dick Jenkins

DEUTZ UK LTD
2 St Martins Way,
London SW17 0UT, UK
TEL: +44 20 8 781 7200
FAX: +44 20 8 947 6380
E-MAIL:
mailbox@deutzbtinternet.com
WEB: http://www.deutz.com
CONTACT: Stuart F Asbury

DOUGLAS -WESTWOOD LTD
Whitebeams,
Pett Bottom,
Canterbury CT4 6EH, UK
TEL: +44 1227 831879
FAX: +44 1227 832092
E-MAIL: renewables@dw-1.com
WEB: http://www.dw-1.com
CONTACT: John D Westwood

DYNAMOTIVE TECHNOLOGIES (UK) LTD
33 Waterloo Road,
Bedford MK40 3PQ, UK
TEL: +44 1234 356 889
FAX: +44 1234 356 889
CONTACT: HDT Moss

ECOBALANCE UK
Old Bank House, I High Street,
Arundel, West Sussex
BN18 9AD,UK
TEL: +44 1903 884 663
FAX: +44 1903 882 045
WEB: http://www.ecobalance.com

ECONNECT LTD
Energy House,
19 Haugh Lane
Industrial Estate,
Hexham,
Northumberland
NE46 3PU, UK
TEL: +44 1434 613600
FAX: +44 1434 609080
E-MAIL: info@econnect.co.uk
WEB: http://www.econnect.co.uk
CONTACT: Rachel Taylor

ECOSECURITIES
The Delawarr House,
45 Raleigh Park Road,
Oxford OX2 9AZ,
UK
TEL: +44 1865 202 635
FAX: +44 1865 251 438
E-MAIL: uk@ecosecurities.com
WEB: http://www.ecosecurities.com
CONTACT: Paul Soffe

ECOTRICITY
Axiom House, Station Road,
Stroud, Gloucestershire
GL5 3AP, UK
TEL: +44 1453 756111
FAX: +44 1453 756222
E-MAIL: info@ecotricity.co.uk
WEB: http://www.ecotricity.co.uk
CONTACT: Dale Vince

ELE INTERNATIONAL LTD
Eastman Way, Hemel Hempstead
Hertfordshire HP2,
7HB, UK
TEL : +44 1442 218355
FAX : +44 1442 252474
E-MAIL :ele@eleint.co.uk
WEB : http://www.eleint.co.uk
CONTACT : Graham Meller

ENER-G COMBINED POWER LTD
ENER-G House,
Daniel Adamson Road,
Manchester
M50 1DT, UK
TEL: +44 161 745 7450
FAX: +44 161 745 7547
E-MAIL: info@energ.co.uk
WEB: http://www.energ.co.uk
CONTACT: David Alcock

ENERGY EQUIPMENT TESTING SERVICE LTD
PV Systems,
104 Portmanmoor Road
Industrial Estate,
Cardiff CG 24 5HB, UK
TEL : +44 29 2049 0871
FAX : +44 29 2045 4887
E-MAIL : sales@ects.com
WEB : www.eets.com
CONTACT : B M Cross

ENERGY FOR SUSTAINABLE DEVELOPMENT LTD- ESD
Overmoor, Neston,
Corsham,
Wiltshire SN 13 9TZ, UK
TEL: +44 1225 812102
FAX: +44 1225 812103
E-MAIL: esd@esd.co.uk
WEB: http://www.esd.co.uk
CONTACT: David Alcock

ESS
130 St Stephen Street,
Edinburgh EH3 5AD, UK
TEL: +44 131 226 7773
FAX: +44 131 226 7773
E-MAIL: paul.ess@dial.pipex.com
WEB: http://
www.dspace.dial.pipex.com/paul.ess
CONTACT: J Paul Gill

ETA PROCESS PLANT LTD
The Levels, Brereton,
Rugeley,
Staffordshire WS15 1RD, UK
TEL: +44 1889 576501
FAX: +44 1889 579856
CONTACT: Janet Armshaw

ETSU
Harwell, Didcot,
Oxfordshire
OX11 0QJ, UK
TEL: +44 1235 433513
FAX: +44 1235 432948
E-MAIL: tony.duffin@aeat.co.uk
WEB: http://www.etsu.com
CONTACT: Tony Duffin

ETSU-NEW & RENEWABLE ENERGY ENQUIRIES BUREAU
Harwell, Didcot,
Oxfordshire
OX11 0QJ, UK
TEL: +44 1235 432450
FAX: +44 1235 433066
E-MAIL: nre-enquiry@aeat.co.uk
WEB: http://www.dti.gov.uk/
renewable/index.html
CONTACT: Diana Chapman

FISH GUIDANCE SYSTEMS LTD
Marine and Freshwater Biology
Unit,
Fawley, Southampton,
Hampshire SO45 1TW, UK
TEL: +44 2380 890 850
FAX: +44 2380 891 471
E-MAIL: fgs@fish-guide.com
WEB: http://www.fish-guide.com
CONTACT: David Lambert

FUSION GROUP PLC
Smeckley Wood Close,
Chesterfield Trading Estate,
Chesterfield S41 9PZ, UK
TEL: +44 1246 260111
FAX: +44 1246 450472
CONTACT: David William

GAS MEASUREMENT INSTRUMENTS LTD. GMI
Inchinnan Estate, Renfrew PA4
9RG, UK
TEL: + 44 141 812 3211
FAX: +44 141 812 7820
E-MAIL: sales@gmiluk.com
CONTACT : Jane Mc Leod

GILL INSTRUMENTS LTD
Saltmarsh Park,
67 Gosport Street,
Lymington,
Hampshire SO41 9EG,UK
TEL : + 44 1590 613500
FAX : + 44 1590 613501
E-MAIL : gill@gill.co.co.uk
CONTACT : Christophen Stock

GP ELECTRONICS
Pottery Road Tracey, Devon
TQ 13 9DS, UK
TEL : + 44 1626 832 670
FAX : + 44 1626 832 670
CONTACT : G Pope

HITECH INSTRUMENTS
20 Titan Court, Laporte way Luton
Bedfordshire LU4 8EF, UK
TEL: +44 1582 456 900
FAX: +44 1582 400 901
E-MAIL: enq@hitech-ins.co.uk
WEB : http://www.mtl-
inshitech.com
CONTACT : Mr A Trucian

IECS LTD
Unit I Abbey Busines Park, Monks
Walk, Farnham, Surrey GU9 8HT, UK
TEL: +44 1252 719799
FAX: +44 1252 719799
E-MAIL: contact@iecsltd.co.uk
WEB: http://www.iecsltd.co.uk
CONTACT: Simon Pini

IVO ENERGY LTD
101 Wigmore Street,
London W1H 9QF, UK
TEL: +44 20 7 616 1500
FAX: +44 20 7 616 1515
WEB: http://www.fortum.com
CONTACT: Dr Valerie Kohler

LAND COMBUSTION
Division Of Land Instruments
International, Stubley Lane,
Dronfield, Sheffield S18 1DJ, UK
TEL: +44 1246 417691
FAX: +44 1246 290274
E-MAIL: combustion.info@landinst.com
WEB: http://www.landinst.com/comb
CONTACT: A Todd

NORTHERN DESIGN (ELECTRONICS) LTD
228 Bolton Road, Bradford,
West Yorkshire BD3 0QW, UK
TEL: +44 1274 729533
FAX: +44 1274 721074

NORTHERN IRELAND ELECTRICITY PLC
PO Box 2, Danesfort,
120 Malone Road,
Belfast BT9 5HT, UK
TEL: +44 28 90 661 100
FAX: +44 28 90 689 244
CONTACT: Brain Dolaghan

NORTHERN IRELAND ELECTRICITY
Environmental Services, Supply
Business, Woodchester House,
Newforge Lane, Belfast BT9
5NW,UK
TEL: +44 28 90 685061
FAX: +44 28 90 685035
E-MAIL: david.guiney@nie.co.uk
CONTACT: David Guiney

ORGANICS LIMITED
Sales, The Barclay Centre,
University of Warwick Science Park,
Coventry CV4 7EZ, UK
TEL: +44 24 7669 2141
FAX: +44 24 7669 2238
E-MAIL: comms@organics.com
WEB: http://www.organics.com
CONTACT: Terry Scott

PACSCOM
Unit 6 Majestic Road,
Nursling Industrial Estate,
Southampton SO16 0YT, UK
TEL: +44 23 8073 7557
FAX: +44 23 8073 1600
E-MAIL: sales@pacs.co.uk
WEB: http://www.pacscom.com
CONTACT: Mrs. Lynne Chattaway

PENNWELL CORPORATION
Penn Well House, Horseshoe Hill,
Upshire, Essex EN9 3SR, UK
TEL: +44 1992 656 600
FAX: +44 1992 656 702
WEB: http://www.pennwell.com

PROCEDAIR LTD
Midland House, Ounsdale Road,
Wombourne,
Wolverhampton WV5 8BY, UK
TEL: +44 1902 891330
FAX: +44 1902 891317
E-MAIL: procedair@aol.com
WEB: http://www.procedair.co.uk
CONTACT: Mr. BN Heap

PUMA POWER PLANT
Sales, 37 Sandwich Road, Ash,
Canterbury CT3 2AJ, UK
TEL: +44 130 481 2818
FAX: +44 130 481 3331
E-MAIL: sales@puma.uk.co
WEB: http://www.pumauk.com
CONTACT: A Inglis

QINETIQ
KI Systems, Space Test Facilty,
Y60 Building, Farnborough,
Hampshire GU14 OLX, UK
TEL: +44 1252 394003
FAX: +44 1252 395647
E-MAIL: cgoodbody@qinetiq.com
WEB: http://www.qinetiq.com
CONTACT: Chris Goodbody

QUALITY MONITORING INSTRUMENTS LTD
5 Hampstead West,
224 Iverson Road,
London NW6 2HL, UK
TEL: +44 20 7 328 3121
FAX: +44 20 7 328 5888
E-MAIL: qmi@oilmist.com
E-MAIL: http://www.oilmist.com
CONTACT: Mr. BJ Smith

R GOODWIN & SON
Ashmans Farm, Kelvedon,
Colchester, Essex CO5 9BT, UK
TEL: +44 1376 573236
FAX: +44 1376 473236
E-MAIL: rwg27198@aol.com
CONTACT: Robert W Goodwin

RECUPERATOR LTD
1437 Pershore Road, Stirchley
Birmingham B30 2JL, UK
TEL: +44 121 433 3677
FAX: +44 121 433 3601
E-MAIL: sales@recuperator.co.uk
WEB: http://ww.recuperator.co.uk
CONTACT: R W Griffiths

RJB MINING PLC
Harworth Park, Blyth Road,
Harworth, Doncaster DN11 8DB, UK
TEL: +44 1302 751751
FAX: +44 1302 751707
COPNTACT: Ken Le Geyt

SCOTTISH & SOUTHERN ENERGY PLC
Inveralmond House,
200 Dunkeld Road,
Perth PH1 3AQ, UK
TEL: +44 1738 457724
FAX: +44 1738 454003
WEB: http://
www.scottish.southern.co.uk
CONTACT: Sandy Honeyman

SCOTTISH ENTERPRISE
Energy Group,
120 Bothwell Street,
Glasgow G2 7JP, UK
TEL: +44 141 228 2252
FAX: +44 141 228 2637
E-MAIL:
blair.armstrong@scotent.co.uk
CONTACT: Blair Armstrong

SELTEK INSTRUMENTS LTD
Leeside Works, Lawrence Avenue,
Stanstead Abbotts,
Hertfordshire SG12 8DL, UK
TEL: +44 1920 871094
FAX: +44 1920 871853
E-MAIL: seltek@compuserve.com
CONTACT: TJ Hooper

SEMIKRON LTD
Martin House, 7 Fountain Drive
Hertford Herts SG13 7UB, UK
TEL: +44 1992 584677
FAX: +44 1992 554942

SIEMENS POWER GENERATION LTD
Siemens House, Oldbury,
Bracknell,
Berkshire RG12 8FZ, UK
TEL: +44 1344 784480
FAX: +44 1344 784152
E-MAIL:
southworrtp@plcbrk.siemens.co.uk
CONTACT: Mr Peter Southworth

SKYE INSTRUMENTS LTD
32 Ddole Industrial Estate,
Liandrindod Wells,
Pwys LDI 6DF, UK
TEL: +44 1597 824811
FAX: +44 1597 824812
E-MAIL: skyemai@
skyeinstruments.com
CONTACT: Melina Fry

SUSTAINABLE CONTROL SYSTEMS LTD
4 Charleston House,
Peel Street,
Nottingham NGI, UK
TEL: +44 115 941 8941
FAX: +44 115 948 3694
E-MAIL:info@scs.www.com
WEB:http://www.scs.www.com
CONTACT:Dr Nigel Smith

SYSTEMS TO SILENCE – STS
Unit 10 Waldegraves Business Park,
West Mersea,
Essex CO5 8SE, UK
TEL: +44700745362
FAX: +44700745368
CONTACT: Kevin Cranfield

THE UTILE ENGINEERING COMPANY LTD
New Street, Irthlingborough
Northamptonshire,
NN9 5UG, UK
TEL: +441933650216
FAX: +441993652738
E-MAIL: sales@utileengineering.com
WEB: http://www.utileengineering.com
CONTACT: Nick Peck

TOR TECHNOLOGIES LTD
I Tor Drive, Earl Shilton,
Leicestershire LE97LY,UK
TEL: +44 1455 844114
FAX: +44 1455 844116
E-MAIL: 100446.1156@
compuserve.com
CONTACT: Emma Cooke

TORQUE METERS LTD
Ravenssthorpe Northampton
NW6 BET, UK
TEL: +44 1604 77 02 32
FAX: +44 1604 77 07 78
CONTACT:Chris Flavell

UNIDATA EUROPE LIMITED
Enterprise House, Lloyd Street
North, Manchester M15 6SE, UK
TEL : +44 161 227 9685
FAX : +44 161 227 9498
E-MAIL : sales@unidata.eng.net
WEB : http://www.unidata.com.au
CONTACT : John Steephenson

VECTOR INSTRUMENTS
115 Marsh Road, Rhyl,
N Wales LL18 2AB, UK
TEL: +44 1745 350700
FAX: +44 1745 344206
E-MAIL: sales@windspeed.co.uk
WEB:http://www.windspeed.co.uk
CONTACT: John Penlington

WATSON NORIE LTD
Head Office, Wincomblee Road,
Walker, Newcastle upon Tyne
NE6 3PL, UK
TEL: +44 191 262 7411
FAX: +44 191 263 0496
E-MAIL:
headoffice@watsonnorie.co.uk
WEB: http://www.watsonnorie.co.uk
CONTACT: JW Hall

WEST COAST ENERGY LTD
The Long Barn, Waen Farm,
Nercwys Road,
Mold Flintshire
CH7 4ED, UK
TEL: +44 1352 757 604
FAX: +44 1352 700 291
E-MAIL: wce.gkj@tinternet.com
CONTACT: Gerry Jewson

WILO SALMSON PUMPS LTD
Centrum 100, Burton on Trent,
Staffs DE14 2WJ, UK
TEL: +44 1283 523000
FAX: +44 1283 523099
E-MAIL: sales@wilco.co.uk
WEB: http://www.wilco.co.uk
CONTACT: Mark Sowden

WIMTEC ENVIRONMENTAL LTD
Energy And Building Technology,
Head Office St Peters House, 6-8
High Street, Iver Bucks SL0 9NG,UK
TEL: +44 1753 737 744
FAX: +44 1753 792 321
E-MAIL:
wimtecenivronmental@compuserve.com
CONTACT: R H Clough

INSULATIONS

ARMSTRONG INSULATION PRODUCTS
A Business Division of Armstrong
World Industries,
Mars Street,
Off Prospect Road,
Oldham, Lancashire
OL9 6LY, UK
TEL : +44 161 287 7000
FAX : +44 161 287 7099
E-MAIL : insulationuk@armstrong.com
CONTACT : Mrs. Etchells

DAYLIGHT INSULATION LTD
Brandelside,
Dunlop, Kilmarnock,
Ayrshire KA3 4BJ,
UK
TEL: +44 141 952 4956
FAX: +44 141 951 1211
CONTACT: Alastair Price

LAND COMBUSTION
Division of Land Instruments
International, Dornfield,
Sheffield S181DJ, UK
TEL : +44 1246 417691
FAX : +44 1246 290274
E-MAIL : combustionlandi
nstinfo@landist.com
WEB : http://www.landinst.com/
comb
CONTACT : N Bettles

POWER PLASTICS LTD
Station Road, Thirsk,
North Yorkshire YO7 1PZ,
UK
TEL: +44 1845 525503
FAX: +44 1845 525485
E-MAIL: info@powerplastics.co.uk
WEB: http://
www.powerplastics.co.uk
CONTACT: John R Spencer

SYSTEMS TO SLIENCE-STS
Unit 10 Waldegraves Business Park,
West Mersea, Essex COS 8SE, UK
TEL: +44 700 745362
FAX: +44 700 745368
E-MAIL:systems2sil
ence@dial.pipex.com
CONTACT:Klevin Crainfield

METALS

FAIRFIELD MABEY LIMITED
Chepstow,Monmouthshire
NP 16 5YL, UK
TEL: +44 1291 623801
FAX: +44 1291 625453
E-MAIL: mail@
fairfieldmabey.com
WEB:http://
www.fairfield@mabey.com
CONTACT : Alex Cole

INCO ALLOYS
Holmer Road,
Hereford HR4 9SL, UK
TEL: +44 1432 382200
FAX: +44 1432 264030
WEB: http://www.incoalloys.com
CONTACT: DR Munasinghe

STAINTON METAL CO LTD
Dukes Way,
Teesside Industrial Estate,
Thornaby,
Cleveland TS17 9LT,
UK
TEL: +44 1642 766242
FAX: +44 1642 765509
CONTACT:Philip J Plackett

CONSTRUCTION SERVICES

A+J FABRICATION (BATLEY) LTD
Walkey Works, Walkey Lane,
Heckmondwike,
West Yorkshire
WF16 0PH, UK
TEL: +44 1924 402151
FAX: +44 1924 410227
E-MAIL: aj.john@btinternet.com
CONTACT: Mr Alan Wright

BALFOUR BEATTY INTERNATIONAL LTD
Marlowe House,
Station Road, Sidcup
Kent DA 15 7AU, UK
TEL : +44 20 8 308 7000
FAX : +44 20 8 308 5308
E-MAIL :lewisj@bbi.bicc.co.uk
CONTACT : Mr. Lewis

BRONZE OAK LIMITED
Bronzeoak House,
Stafford Road,
Caterham,
Surrey, CR3 6JG, UK
TEL : +44 1883 341055
FAX : +44 1883 347523
E-MAIL : mail@bronzeoak.com
WEB : http://www.bronzeoak.com
CONTACT : Graham R Stowell

CARL BRO GROUP
Civil & Transportation, 7-15,
Dean Bank Lane,
Edinburgh, EH3, 5BS, UK
TEL : +44 131 343 2601
FAX : +44 131 332 0455
E-MAIL : dcttrn@carlbro.dk
WEB : http://www.carlbro.dk
CONTACT : D C Taylor

DJ CONSTRUCTIONS LIMITED
Plas Eirias,
Abergele Road, Colwyn Bay, Clwyd
LL29 8BF, UK
TEL : + 44 1492 517 534
FAX : + 44 1492 514 886
E-MAIL : admin@djc.co.uk
CONTACT : Huw Smallwood

ENVIRONMENTAL CONSTRUCTION LTD
Stirling House,
Danebury Court,
Old Sarum Park, Salisbury Wiltshire
SP4, 6EB, UK
TEL: +44 1722 41339
FAX: +44 1722 413306
CONTACT : R C A Cherry

FOUNDATION & EXPLORATION SERVICES LTD
Brunel House, Stephenson Road,
Houndsmill Estate, Basingstoke
Hampshire RG21 RXR, UK
TEL: +44 1256 340000
FAX: +44 1256 841 798
E-MAIL: basingstoke@fes.co.uk
WEB : www.fes.co.uk
CONTACT : Mr Shinner

GE ENERGY SERVICES (UK) LTD
John Brown Engineering Works.
Clydebank,
Dunbarthonshire G81, IYL, UK
TEL: + 44 141 952 2030
FAX: + 44 141 952 5327
E-MAIL: http://www.kvaerner.com
CONTACT : Stephen Rodgers

MARTINEAU JOHNSON
St Philips House, St. Philips Place,
Birmingham B3 2PP, UK
TEL: +44 121 678 1527
FAX: +44 121 233 3911
WEB: http://www.martineau-johnson.co.uk
CONTACT: Mr Paul Brennan

MEARSDON MANOR TECHNOLOGIES
Mearsdon Manor, Cross Street,
Moretonhampstead, Devon TQ 13 8NL, UK
TEL: +44 1647 440483
FAX: +44 1647 440483
CONTACT: John Dodds

MEDLOCK LTD
Unit 7A, Callendar Business Park,
Falkirk, FK IXR, UK
TEL: +44 1324 617617
FAX: +44 1324 638259
E-MAIL: niall@medlock.co.uk
CONTACT: Niall baird

SCHOOLS & HOMES ENERGY EDUCATION PROJECT
41 Oak Hill Road, Sheffield S7 1SJ, UK
TEL: +44 114 249 9459
FAX: +44 114 249 9459
E-MAIL: davidgarlovsky@sheep.solis.co.uk
WEB: http://www.solis.co.uk/sheep
CONTACT: David Garlovsky

UNITED HOUSE LTD
United House Goldel Road,
Swanley Kent BRB EX, UK
TEL: +44 1322 665522
FAX: +44 1322 662313
CONTACT: Robert Perkins

WSATKINS CONSULTANTS LTD
Head Office, Woodcote Grove,
Ashley Raod, Epson,
Surry KT18 5BW, UK
TEL: +44 1372 726140
FAX: +44 1372 740055
E-MAIL: gtg@wsatkins.co.uk
WEB: http://www.wsatkins.co.uk
CONTACT: John Brindley

GLASS

PILKINGTON PLC
Head Office, Prescott, St Helens,
Merseyside WA103TT, UK
TEL : + 44 1744 28882
FAX : + 44 1744 692660
WEB :http://www.pilkington.com
CONTACT: Paolo Scoroni

PILKINGTON SPECIAL GLASS DIVISION
Fourth Avenue,
Deeside Industrial Estate Park,
Deeside, Clwyd CH5 2NR, UK
TEL :+ 44 1244 833 265
FAX : + 44 1244 288 473

PILKINGTONSPACE TECHNOLOGY
Unit 2 Kimmel Park,Bodelwyddan,
Rhyl,Clwyd LL18 5TY, UK
TEL : + 44 1745 584584
FAX : + 44 1745 584208
WEB : http://www.pilkington.com
CONTACT : David Jones

SOLAGLASS SAINT-GOBAIN
Glass Facts Service
Herald Way Binley,
Coventry CV3 2ND,UK
TEL:+44 24 76 458844
FAX:+44 24 76 636473
WEB:http://www.solarglas.co.uk
CONTACT:Donna Munro

FORESTS

FORESTRY COMMISSION
Technical Development Branch,
Ae Village, Dumfries DG IQB, UK
TEL: +44 1387 860 264
FAX: +44 1387 860 386
E-MAIL: tdbae@forestry.gov.uk
CONTACT : Bill M Jones

OXFORD FORESTRY INSTITUTE
Department Of Plant Sciences,
University Of Oxford,
South Parks Road,
Oxford OX1 3RB, UK
TEL: +44 1865 275000
FAX: +44 1865 275074
E-MAIL: j.burley@plants.ox.ac.uk
WEB: http://www.plants.ox.ac.uk/ofi

OTHERS (S)

AARDVARK EM LIMITED
Staplecross, Staple Cross,
Wellington, Somerset TA21 0NH,UK
TEL: +44 1398 361579
FAX: +44 1398 361429
E-MAIL: aem@mjic.demon.co.uk
WEB: http://www.mjic.demon.co.uk
CONTACT: Mark Clayton

ABB POWER
Power House, Silverlink Business
Park, Wallsend, Tyne and Wear
NE289nd, UK
TEL: +44 191 295 2000
FAX: +44 191 295 2011
CONTACT: Iain R Robertson

AD WASTE LTD
3 Hilliards Court,
Chester Business Park, Wrexham
Road, Chester CH4 9QX, UK
TEL: +44 1244 301 887
FAX: +44 1244 301 970
CONTACT: PM Mulhall

AUTOMATED POWER EXCHANGE
European Headquarters, 26-28
Mount Row, Mayfair,
London W1K 3SQ, UK
TEL: +44 20 7647 9793
FAX: +44 20 7647 9781
WEB: http://www.apx.com
CONTACT: David Selzer

BALDWINS INDUSTRIAL SERVICES LTD
Churchill House,
20-2B, Mill Street,
Slough, Berkshire SL2 5DH, UK
TEL : +44 1753 512100
FAX : +44 1753 512402

BARTIE GROUP LIMITED
Environmental Technology 95
Bothwell Street,
Glasgow G2 7HX, UK
TEL : +44 141 204 2511
FAX : +44 141 226 3109
E-MAIL : 10634.1540@compuserve.com
WEB : http://www.babde.com

BEEL INDUSTRIAL BOILERS PLC
Becor House,
Green Lane, Lincoln
LN6, 7DN, UK
TEL : +44 1522 510510
FAX : +44 1522 525900
E-MAIL : mail@bib-group.plc.uk
CONTACT : R Allsop

BRE
Bucknalss Lane, Garston, Watford,
Hertfordshire WD25 9XX, UK
TEL: +44 1923 664000
FAX: +44 1923 664010
E-MAIL: enquiries@bre.co.uk
WEB: http://www.bre.co.uk
CONTACT: Simon Guy

BROWN MCFARLANE LTD
Ladywell Works,
New Century Street,
Off Etruria Road,
Hanley
Stoke-on-Trent ST1 5QH, UK
TEL: +44 1782 289909
FAX: +44 1782 289804
CONTACT: Bob Crawford

BSRIA LTD
Old Bracknell Lane West,
Bracknell, Berks RG 12,
7AH, UK
TEL : +44 1344 426511
FAX : +44 1344 487575
E-MAIL :reginald.brown@bsria.co.uk
WEB : http://www.bsria.co.uk
CONTACT : Mr Reginald Brown

CLARK MASTS TEKSAM LTD
Binstead, Ryde,
Isle Of Wight PO33 3PA, UK
TEL: +44 1983 563691
FAX: +44 1983 566643
CONTACT: Colin G Thornton

CLARKE ENERGY LIMITED
Power House Senator Point,
South Boundary Road,
Knowsley Industrial Park,
Liverpool L33 7RR, UK
TEL: +44 151 546 4446
FAX: +44 151 546 4447
E-MAIL: info@clarke-energy.com
WEB: http://www.clarke-energy.com
CONTACT: John Munnery

CT LUKEHURST
52, Broadstairs Road,St.Peters
Broadsatairs,
Kent CT 10 2RJ, UK
TEL: +44 1843 861690
FAX: +44 1843 861690
CONTACT:Dr. ct Lukehurst

DALKIA PLC
Energy & Technical Services,
Bachanan House,
24-30 Hoborn,
London ECI 21X, UK
TEL : + 44 20 7 421 2300
FAX : + 44 20 7 421 2300

DAVID LANGHAM
Stone End, 6 Ratten Row,
Seamer, Scarborough
YO12 4BQ, UK
TEL: +44 1723 864 813
FAX: +44 1723 864 812
CONTACT: David Langham

DELPHINTERNATIONAL LTD
4th Floor,
Broughton House,
6-8, Sackville Street,
London, WIW IDD, U.K.
TEL : + 44 20 7 734 6344
FAX : + 44 20 7 287 4775
E-MAIL : dephintl@dd.pipex.com

DEMCO
Units 11-12 Star Industrial Park,
Bodmin Road,
Coventry CV2 5DB, UK
TEL : + 44 24 76 602323
FAX : + 44 24 76 602116
E-MAIL : sales@demco.co.uk
WEB : http://www.demco.co.uk
CONTACT : Mr Paul Flude

D-SQUARED DESIGN
Studio H. Eden Mews,
5th Eden Garden
London N7 8ES, UK
TEL : + +41 171 609 0931
FAX : +44 171 609 0931
E-MAIL : dsquared@globalnet.co.uk

DYNAMOTIVE EUROPE LTD
4th Floor,
31 Davies Street,
London, WIY IPN UK
TEL : + 44 20 7518 9380
FAX : + 44 20 7518 9381
E-MAIL : arobson@dynamotive.com
WEB : http://www.dynamotive europe.com

ECO ENERGY AND ENVIRONMENT LTD
11-15 Emerlad Street,
London, WCIN IQL, UK
TEL : + 44 20 7 405 3121
FAX : + 44 20 7 405 1670
E-MAIL :ecde@ecde.demon.co.uk
WEB : http://www. Demon.co.uk

EDECO PETROLEUM SERVICES LTD
Trent Lane, Castle Donington,
Derbyshire DE74 2NP, UK
TEL: +44 1332 850060
FAX: +44 1332 850553
E-MAIL: sales@edeco.co.uk
WEB: http://www.edeco.co.uk
CONTACT: A J Beswick

EDS LTD
Overmoor, Neston. Corsham,
Wiltshire SN 13 912, UK
TEL: +44 1255 812 102
FAX: + 44 1225 812 103
E-MAIL: esd@esd.co.uk
WEB: http://www.esd.co.uk

ELYO UK
The Broadway,
Great Central Road,
Mansfield,
Notts NG 182RL, UK
TEL : +44 1623 650 202
FAX : +44 1623 420 188
E-MAIL : david.wragg@elyo.co.uk
CONTACT : David Wragg

ENERGY & POWER CONSULTANTS LTD
30 Grear, Guildford Street,
London SEI OHS UK
TEL: +44 20 76203394
FAX: +44 870 1695811
E-MAIL:
pms@energyandpower.co.uk
WEB: http://
www.energyandpower.co.uk

FOCSA SERVICES (UK) LTD
Brook House, Oldham Road,
Middleton, Manchester
M24 IAY, UK
TEL: +44 161 643 8822
FAX: +44 161 643 8827
CONTACT : Stephen Denaro

GARDLINE SURVEYS LTD
Endeavour House,
Admiralty Road Great Yarmouth,
Norfolk NR30 3NG,UK
TEL: +44 1493 845600
FAX: +44 1493 852106
CONTACT: Ian Wilson

GARRAD HASSAN AND PARTNERS LIMITED
2064 Maryhill Road, Glasgow G20
OAB UK
TEL: + 44 141 945 4774
FAX: + 44 141 945 5076
E-Mail: fellows@garradhassan.co.uk
WEB: http://www.garadhassan.com
CONTACT : Andrew Fellows

GILL INSTRUMENTS LTD
Saltmarsh Park, 67 Gosport Street
Lymington, Hampshire SO419EG,UK
TEL: +44 1590 61 3500
FAX: +44 1590 61 3555
E-MAIL: anem@gill.co.uk
WEB: http://
www.gillinstruments.com
CONTACT: Christopher Stock

GREEN TECHNICAL RESOURCING LTD- GTR
Riverside Business Centre,
River Lawn Rd, Tonbridge,
TN9 1EP, UK
TEL: +44 1732 783 567
FAX: +44 1732 783 568
E-MAIL: sales@gtr.uk.com
WEB: http://www.gtr.uk.com
CONTACT: Grant Beveridge

GREENWOOD AIR MANAGEMENT
PO Box 3, Brookside Industrial
Estate, Rustington,
West Sussex BN16 3LH, UK
TEL: +44 1903 771021
FAX: +44 1903 782398
CONTACT: Angela Fairbourn

HIGHLAND LIGHT & POWER LTD
Unit 1, James Keiller Buildings,
32-34 Mains Loan,
Dundee DD4 7BT, UK
TEL: +44 1382 455565
FAX: +44 1382 455518
E-MAIL: d.j.t.mckenzie@btinternet.com
CONTACT: David JT McKenzie

IAN GRANT
High House, Upper Ladyes Hills,
Kenilworth, Warwickshire
CVB 2FB, UK
TEL :+ 44 1926 851741
FAX : + 44 1926 851741

INTERNATIONAL INSTITUTE FOR ENERGY CONSERVATION -EUROPE LTD
21 Tavern Quay, Rope Street,
London SE16 7TX, UK
TEL: +44 20 7237 6523
FAX: +44 20 7237 2462
E-MAIL: iiec.europe@dial.pipex.com
WEB: http://www.cerf.org/ieec
CONTACT: Lea Swanson

INTERSOLAR GROUP
Unit 2, Cock Lane, High Wycombe,
Buckinghamshire HP13 7DE, UK
TEL: +44 1494 452945
FAX: +44 1494 437045
E-MAIL: intersolar@intersolar.com
WEB: http://www.intersolar.com
CONTACT: JR Stobart

IS CONSULTANTS
hool of Materials Science,
University Bath, Bath BA2 7AY, UK
TEL: +44 1225 826 447
FAX: +44 1225 826 098
E-MAIL: sms@bath.ac.uk
WEB:http://www.bath.ac.uk/
departments/MatSci/SMS
CONTACT:Nick Gathercoll

ITH (EC) & SONS LTD
ts H&J, Kingsway Industrial Estate,
gsway Luton Bedfordshire LUI, UK
TEL:+44 1582 729721
FAX:+44 1582 458893
CONTACT:ECSmith

JAMES & JAMES (SCIENCE PUBLISHERS) LTD
35-37 William Road,
London NW1 3ER, UK
TEL: +44 20 7 387 8558
FAX: +44 20 7 387 8998
E-MAIL: james@jxj.com
WEB: http://www.jxj.com
CONTACT: Robin George

KIELDER FOREST PRODUCTS LTD
Molesden House, Mitford,
Morpeth,
Northumberland, UK
TEL: +44 1670 775 346
FAX: +44 1670 775 404
E-MAIL: kfwaugh@dircon.co.uk
CONTACT: Simon Waugh

MICRO TECH LTD
Nada House,
Hawks Road,Gateshead Tyne and
Wear NE8 3BL, UK
TEL: +44 191 477 4755
FAX: +44 191 477 8733
CONTACT: Rod Lakin

NJ ASH
Little Brock,
Pasture Lane, Hose
Melton Mowbray, UK
TEL : +44 1664 444395
FAX : +44 1664 444425
E-MAIL : n.j.ash@btinternet.com

POWER ECONOMICS
Wilmington Publishing Ltd,
Wilmington House Church Hill
Wilmington,
Dartford Kent DA2 7EF, UK
TEL: +44 1322 394759
FAX: +44 1322 287038
E-MAIL: dappleyard@wilmington.co.uk
WEB: http://www.connectingpower.com
CONTACT: David Appleyard

RECOTHERM LTD
1437 Pershore Road,
Stirchley,
Birmingham B30 2JL, UK
TEL: +44 121 433 3622
FAX: +44 121 433 3601
E-MAIL: sales@recotherm.co.uk
WEB: http://www.recotherm.co.uk
CONTACT: Martin Killen

REDLER LTD
Redler House, Dudbridge, Stroud,
Gloucestershire GL5 3EY, UK
TEL: +441453763611
FAX: +441453763582
E-MAIL: sales@redler.com
WEB: http://redler.com

REGENESYS TECHNOLOGIES LIMITED
Harwell International Business
Centre, Didcot, Oxon OX11 0QA, UK
TEL: +44123544499
FAX: +441235444909
E-MAIL: info@regenesys.com
WEB: http://regenesys.com
CONTACT: Gavin Print

RICHARD LADEN
29 Village Road, Cockayne Hatley,
Sandy, Beds SG19 2EE, UK
TEL : +44 1767 631535
CONTACT : Richard Laden

RN WILLMER FARMS LTD
Friars Court, Clanfield, Bampton
Oxon OX18 2SU, UK
TEL: +44 1367 810206
FAX: +44 1367 810207
CONTACT: John H Willmer

ROVES FARM
Roves Farm, Severnhampton
Highworth, Wiltshire SN6 7QG, UK
TEL: +44 1793 763939
FAX: +44 1793 763939
CONTACT: Rupert Burr

SALANS HERZFELD & HEILBRONN HRK
Clements House 14-18 Gresham
Street, London EC2V 7NN, UK
TEL: +44 20 7509 6036
FAX: +44 20 7726 6191
E-MAIL: rtait@salans.com
WEB: http://www.salans.com
CONTACT: Rory Tait

SEVERN TRENT LABORATORIES LTD
STL Business Centre,
Torrington Avenue,
Coventry CV4 9GU, UK
TEL: +44 24 76 421213
FAX: +44 24 76 856575
E-MAIL: sales@stl-analytical.co.uk
WEB: http://www.stl-analytical.co.uk
CONTACT: Duncan Smith

SMITH (EC) & SONS LTD
Units H & J,
Kingsway Industrial Estate,
Kingsway, Luton
Bedfordshire LU1 1LP, UK
TEL: +44 1582 729721
FAX: +44 1582 458893
CONTACT: EC Smith

SOLAGLASS SAINT-GOBAIN
Glass Facts Service, Herald Way,
Binley, Coventry CV3 2ND, UK
TEL: +44 24 76 458844
FAX: +44 24 76 636473
WEB: http://www.solaglas.co.uk
CONTACT: Donna Munro

SOLAR ENERGY LIMITED
90A Notting Hill Gate,
London W11 3HP, UK
TEL: +33494411059
FAX: +33494362138
E-MAIL: dominic.michaelis@wanadoo.fr
CONTACT: Dominic Michaelis

SP SYSTEMS LTD
St Cross Business Park, Newport,
Isle of Wight PO30 5WU, UK
TEL: +441983828000
FAX: +441983828100
E-MAIL: ubfi@spsystems.com
WEB: http://www.spsystems.com
CONTACT: Andy Day

THE RENEWABLE ENERGY COMPANY LTD
Axiom House, Station Road, Stroud,
Gloucestershire GL5 3AP,
TEL : +44 1453 756111
FAX : +44 1453 756222
E-MAIL : info@ecoticity.co.uk
WEB : http://www.ecotricity.co.uk
CONTACT : Karen Lane

THE BOOTS COMPANY PLC
Central Engineering,
D19 Building Thane Road
Nottingham NG2 3AA, UK
TEL: +44 115 959 4715
FAX: +44 115 959 4555
CONTACT: Andrew Jones

THE CENTRE FOR ALTERNATIVE TECHNOLOGY
Machyntleth,Powys SY20 9AZ, UK
TEL : +44 1654 702400
FAX : +44 1654 702782
E-MAIL : consultancy@cat.org.uk
WEB : http://www.cat.org.uk

THE CERAMIC STOVE COMPANY
4 Earl Street, Oxford OX2,OJA, UK
TEL : +44 1865 245077
FAX : +44 1865 245077

THE DYER WARNER PARTNERSHIP
Cliffe House, Church Birasll,
Leicesser L34 4 DN UK
TEL : + 44 116 267 7017
FAX : + 44 116 267 3819
E-MAIL : dyerwarner@sol.com

THE ENGINEERING BUSINESS LTD
Broomhaugh House, Riding Mill,
Northumberland NE44, 6EG, UK
TEL : + 44 1434 682 800
FAX : + 44 1434 682 801
E-MAIL : mike.watchorn@engb.com
WEB: http://www.engb.com

THE FRANKLIN COMPANY CONSULTANTS LTD
192 Franklin Road,
Birmingham, B30 2HE, UK
TEL: +44 121 459 4826
FAX: +44 121 459 8206
E-MAIL: tfc@tfc-bham.demon.co.uk

THE GREEN CERTIFICATE COMPANY
3rd Floor, 12 The Broadway,
Amersham, UK
TEL: +44 1494 43 23 23
FAX: +44 1494 43 48 88
E-MAIL: ed_everson@campbellcarr.co.uk
WEB: http://www.greencertificates.co.uk
CONTACT: Mr Edmund Everson

THE GREENBELT GROUP OF COMPANIES LIMITED
189, St Vincent Street,
Glosgow G2 5QD, UK
TEL : + 44 141 243 2428
FAX : + 44 141 243 2429
E-MAIL : made@greeng
eltgroup.co.uk

THE MARTIN CENTRE FOR ARCHITECTURAL AND URBAN STUDIES
University of Cambridge,
6 Chaucer Road,
Cambridge CB2 2EB, UK
TEL: +44 1223 332981
FAX: +44 1223 332983
CONTACT: Nick Baker

THE MERLIN GROUP
Unit Hithercroft Court,
Lupton Road, Wallingford,
Oxfordshire OX10 9BT, UK
TEL: +44 1491 824333
FAX: +44 1491 824466
E-MAIL: 101756.3500@compuserve.com
CONTACT: David Small

THE MET OFFICE
Services & Business,
Sutton House, London Road,
Bracknell, Berkshire
RG 12 2SY, UK
TEL: +44 1344 420242
FAX: +44 800 252356
E-MAIL: snwass@meto.gov.uk
WEB: http://www.meto.gov.uk
CONTACT: Stewart Wass

THE MOROCCO STORE
1 Leathermarket Street,
London SEI 3HN, UK
TEL : +44 20 7 403 2889
FAX : +44 20 7 407 5283
E-MAIL : dan_sh@architype.co.uk
CONTACT : DanStainer-Hutchins

THE NATIONAL CENTER FOR BUSINESS SUSTAINBILITY
Peel Building,
Unviersity of Saiford,
Greater Manchester
M5 4WT, UK
TEL : +44 161 295 5276
FAX : +44 161 5041
E-MAIL : c.visco@thencbs.co.uk
WEB : http://www.thencbs.co.uk
CONTACT : Mary Parkinson

THE NATIONAL ENERGY FOUNDATION
nef Renewables,
Davy Avenue
Knowhill, Milton Keynes
MKS BNG, UK
TEL: +44 1908 665555
FAX: +44 1908 665577
E-MAIL:renewables@
natenerg.demon.co.uk
WEB:http://www.naternergy.org.uk
CONTACT:Gareth Ellis

THE SOLAR COMPANY
Solary House,
112 Victoria Drive
Eastbourne, East Sussex
BN20 BLG, UK
TEL:+44 1323 646979
FAX:+44 1323 411224
E-MAIL:thesolarco@aol.com
WEB:http://www.the-solar-co.com
CONTACT:Jenny Holly

THE SOLAR DESIGN COMPANY
57 Wood Lane Greasby,
Wirral CH49 2 PU, UK
TEL:+44 151 606 0207
FAX:+44 8700 526 977
E-MAIL:enquiries@solardesign.co.uk
WEB:http://www.solardesignm.co.uk
CONTACT:Chris Laughton

THE SOLAR SHOP
7 Highgield Chase,
Basingstoke
Rg21 7SA,UK
TEL:+44 1256 350567
FAX:+44 1252 851820
WEB:http://www.solarshop.co.uk
CONTACT:Mark Strangroom

THE TAYLOR GROUP
Muirhall Road, Larbert, Central Region FK5 4ES, UK
TEL : +44 1324 558567
FAX : +44 1324 552888
CONTACT : Stuart Campbell

THE UK SOLAR ENERGY SOCIETY-UK-ISES
Co School of Engineering, Oxford Brookes University, Gipsy Lane, Campus, Headington OX3 0BP, UK
TEL : +44 4865 484367
FAX : +44 4865 484263
E-MAIL : uk-isess@brookes.ac.uk
WEB : http://www.brookes.ac.ul/uk-isess
CONTACT : Christiane Buckle

THE UTILE ENGINEERING COMPANY LTD
New Street, Irthlingborough, Northamptonshire NN9 5UG, UK
TEL: +44 4933 650 216
FAX: +44 1933 652 738
E-MAIL: utile@dial.pipex.com
WEB: http://www.utileengineering.com
CONTACT: Nick Peck

UNITED ENERGY LTD
16 Avon Reach, Mornkton Hill, Chippenham, Wiltshire Sn15 IEE UK
TEL: +44 1249 705550
FAX: +44 1249 445374
E-MAIL: admin@unit-energy.co.uk
WEB: http://www.unit-energy.co.uk
CONTACT: Brian J Swindells

VARIDOR WASTE MANAGEMENT LTD
Malling House, Townhill, West Malling, Kent ME19 6QL, UK
TEL: +44 1732 220 044
FAX: +44 1732 220 055
WEB: http://www.viridor-waste.co.uk
CONTACT: R Turner

WILLET T AND SON LTD
51 Queen Square, Bristol BS1 4LJ, UK
TEL: +44 1179 262231
FAX: +44 1179 262835
E-MAIL: jrw@willetts.co.uk
CONTACT: JR Wright

WRITE-ON
5 Christchurch Drive, Blackwater, Camberley GU17 0HA, UK
TEL: +44 1252 874489
E-MAIL: mike@write-on.co.uk
WEB: http://www.write-on.co.uk
CONTACT: Michael Gascoigne

We kindly request more listings in this country.

You can submit any additional listings by E-mail: unisun@vsnl.com

Fax: 91 80 22289294

We will include these in the next edition

Kindly inform us of any errors and omissions in the listings by:

E-mail: unisun@vsnl.com

Fax: 91 80 22289294

NORTH AMERICA

SOLAR THERMAL

ASTRAVAN DISTRIBUTORS LTD
123 Charles Street, North Vancouver, BC V7H, ISI, Canada
TEL : +1 604 929 5488
FAX : +1 604 929 4883
E-MAIL : infoj@stravan.com
WEB : http://www.astravan.com
CONTACT : Donna Lewis

GENERATION SOLAR RENEWABLE ENERGY SYSTEMS INC
Suite 405, 340 George Street North, Peterborough, Onatario K9H 7E8, Canada
TEL : + 1 705 741 1700
FAX : + 1 705 741 1700
E-MAIL : gensolar@nexicom.net
CONTACT : R Heslett

MATRIX ENERGY INC
16807 Hymus, Kirkland, Quebec H9H 3L4, Canada
TEL: +1 514 630 5630
FAX: +1 514 426 9123
E-MAIL: matrixenergy@sympatico.ca
CONTACT: B Wilkinson

RENEWABLE ENERGY OF PLUM HOLLOW INC
93 Counter Street, Kingston, Ontario K7K 6C7
TEL : +1 613 544 5575
FAX : +1 613 544 7050
WEB : http://www.renewable energy.on.ca
CONTACT : Charles Gobeil

SOLARJOULES
115 Ingleton Boulevard, Toronto Ontario MIV 2Y3, Canada
TEL:+1 416 737 5839
FAX:+1 416 737 2958
E-MAIL:solarjoules@yahoo.com
WEB:http://www.eieihome.com/pages/110/solrjoules
CONTACT : Patrick Lai

SOLARWALL INTERNATIONAL LTD
200 Wildcat Road, Toronto, Ontario M3j 2N5, Canada
TEL:+416 661 7057
FAX:+416 661 7146
CONTACT : John Hollick

SOLCAN LTD
126 Wychwood Park, London, Ontario N6GIR7 Canada
TEL:+519 473 0501
FAX:+519 473 0501
E-MAIL : solcan@ican.net
CONTACT : Bob Swartman

TAYLOR MUNRO ENERGY SYSTEMS INC
11-7157 Honeyman Street, Delta, British Columbia V4G IE2, Canada
TEL: +1 604 946 4433
FAX: +1 604 946 3804
E-MAIL:thwaites@taylormunro.com
WEB:http://www.taylormunro.com
CONTACT : Joe Thwaites

THERMOMAX INDUSTRIES LTD
3181 Kingsley Street Victoria. British Columbia, V8P 4j5 Canada
TEL: +1 250 721 4360
FAX: +1 250 721 4329
E-MAIL : patrick@solarthermal.com
WEB : http://www.solarthermal.com
CONTACT : Patrick Spearing

SOLAR PHOTOVOLTAIC

ATLAS POLYTECHNIC
400 Marie Victoria, Boucherville, Quebec J4B, IW2, Canada
TEL : +1 450 449 4041
FAX : +1 450 449 7454
E-MAIL : scholler@videotran.ca
CONTACT : Martin Scholler

CANROM PHOTOVOLTAICS INC
108 Aikman Avenue, Hamilton Ontario, L8M, IP9, Canada
TEL : +1 905 526 7634
FAX : +1 905 526 9341
E-MAIL : ndalacu@fox.nstn.ca
WEB : http://www.canrom.com
CONTACT : N Dalaiu

ICP GLOBAL TECHNOLOGIES
6995 Jeanne-Mance, Montreal, QC H3N IW5, Canada
TEL: +41 514 270 5770
FAX: +1 514 270 3677
E-MAIL: customers@icoglobal.com
WEB: http://www.icpglobal.com
CONTACT: Michael Willems

INTELCAN TECHNOSYSTEMS INC
69 Auriga Drive Nepean, Ontario
K2E 7Z2, Canada
TEL: +1 613 228 1150
FAX: +1 613 228 1149

INUVIK RESEARCH CENTRE
Box 1430, Inuvik, NT XOE OTO, Canada
TEL: +1 867 777 3838
FAX: +1 862 777 4264
E-MAIL:research_ari@gov.nt.ca
WEB:http://www.nwtresearch.com
CONTACT: L Kutny

KYOCERA SOLAR INC
Global Distribution Canada, 122 Queen Street, Trenton, Ontario K8V 4Y4, Canada
TEL: +1 613 392 6776
FAX: +1 613 392 2263
E-MAIL: mpaddison@kyocera.com
WEB: http://www.kyocerasolar.com
CONTACT: Mr M Paddison

MATRIX ENERGY INC
16807 Hymus, Kirkland, Quebec H9H 3L4, Canada
TEL : +1 514 630 5630
FAX : +1 514 426 9123
E-MAIL :matrixenergy@sympatico.ca
CONTACT: B Wilkinson

NEWSUN TECHNOLOGIES LTD
138-880 Wellington Street, Ottawa Ontario K1R 6K7, Canada
TEL: +1 613 723 5750
FAX: +1 613 723 5980
E-MAIL: sales@newsun.ca
WEB: http://www.newsun.ca
CONTACT: Dr RE Thomas

PHANTOM ELECTRON CORPORATION
110 Ash Street, 2nd Floor, Whitby Ontario LIN 4A9, Canada
TEL: +1 905 430 6512
FAX: +1 905 666 1188
E-MAIL:solar@phantomelectron.com
WEB:http://www.phantomelectron.com
CONTACT:Leonard Allen

POWERSOURCE ENERGY SYSTEMS INC
5 2928-18 Street NE, Calgary, Alberta, Canada
TEL: +1 403 291 9039
FAX: +1 403 291 9049
E-MAIL: info@powersourceenergy.com
WEB: http://www.powersourceenergy.com
CONTACT: Ken Newel

RENEWABLE ENERGY OF PLUM HOLLOW INC
93 Counter Street, Kingston, Ontario K7K 6C7
TEL : +1 613 544 5575
FAX : +1 613 544 7050
WEB : http://www.renewableenergy.on.ca
CONTACT : Charles Gobeil

CANADA

SOLAR CANADA
PO Box 84591 2336 Floor
Street West Toronto,
Ontario M6S ITO. Canada
TEL : +1 416 503 9741
E-MAIL : jsteel@hotmail.com
WEB:http://www.bcity.com/
solar_canada/index.html
CONTACT:Jonathan Steel

SUN DIRECT ENERGY INC
PO Box 136, Colinton,
Alberta TOG ORO, Canada
TEL: +1 403 675 2586
FAX: +1 403 675 2634
CONTACT:Ron La Place

SUN MOTOR INTERNATIONAL INC
5037 50TH Street,Suite 104,Olds,
Alberta T4H IR8, Canada
TEL: +1 403 556 8775
FAX: +1 403556 7799
E-MAIL:sunmotro@telusplannet.net
WEB:http://www.sunpump.com
CONTACT : Mr Jensen

SUNERGY SYSTEMS LTD
Box 70 Cremona,
AB TOM ORO, Canada
TEL: +1 403 637 3973
FAX: +1 403 637 3973
E-MAIL : sunergy@telusplanet.net
WEB:http://
www.compostingtoilet.com
CONTACT: Michael Kerfoot

SUNHENGE SOLAR INC
328 Varsity Estates Place
NW,Calgary, Alberta T3B 3B8, Canada
TEL: +1 403 286 5009
FAX: +1 403 286 5003
E-MAIL:johnpope@sunhenge.com
WEB:http://www.sunhenge.com
CONTACT : John A Pope

Thermo Dynamics Ltd
44 Borden Avenue,
Burnside Industrial Park, Dartmouth,
Novia Scotia B3B 1C8, Canada
TEL: +19024681001
FAX: +19024681002
E-MAIL:solarinfo@thermo-dynamics.com
WEB: http://www.thermo-dynamics.com

THOMSON & HOWE ENERGY SYSTEMS INC
Site 17. Box 2, SSI Kimberly,
British Columbia VIA 2Y3, Canada
TEL: +1 250 4274326
FAX: +1 250 4273577
E-MAIL:thes@cyberlink.bc.ca
WEB:http://www.small
hydropower.com
CONTACT: Fred Howe

WIND

CORAM ENERGY GROUP
2232 Marine Drive Suite 301,
West Vancouver, British Columbia
V7V 1K4, Canada
TEL: +1 604 921 1241
FAX: +1 604 921 1242
E-MAIL: briano@emailonly.com
CONTACT: Brian J O'Sullivan

HELIMAX ENERGY INC
5215 rue Berri Bureau 3000,
Montreal, Quebec H2J 254, Canada
TEL: +1 514 272 2175
FAX: +1 514 272 0410
E-MAIL: legaultr@helimax.com
WEB: http://www.helimax.com
CONTACT: Ms Louise Lauzon

ISLAND TECHNOLOGIES INCORPORATED
P O Box 832, 49 Pownal Street,
Charhlottetown,
Prince Edward Island
CIA 7L9, Canada
TEL: +1 902 368 7171
FAX: +1 902 368 7139
E-MAIL:iti@isn.net
CONTACT : M A Lodge

PH COMPOSITES INC
Huron Industrial Park, Building 3,
Huron Park, Ontario NOM IYO,
Canada
TEL: +1 519 228 6598
FAX: +1 519 228 6460
E-MAIL:phc@composites.on.ca
WEB : http://www.composites.on.ca
CONTACT : Helge Wittholz

PHOENIX ENGINEERING INC
161 Lakeside Greens Drive,
Chestermere,
Alberta TI X I B9,
Canada
TEL: + 1 403 248 9463
FAX : + 1 403 272 1071
E-MAIL:bakerdr@phoenixengg.com
CONTACT: David R Baker

POLYMARIN-BOLWELL COMPOSITES INC
Wind Energy Department, Huron,
Industrial Park,
Building 3, Huron Park,
Ontario NOM 1YO,
Canada
TEL: +1 519 2286598
FAX: +1 519 2286460
E-MAIL: pch@composites.on.ca
WEB: http://www.composites.on.ca
CONTACT: Helge Wittholz

SUSTAINABLE ENERGY TECHNOLOGIES
422 11 Ave SE, Suite 200,
Calgary, AB T2G 0Y4, Canada
TEL: +1 403 508 7177
FAX: + 403 205 2509
E-MAIL:harris@su
stainableenergy.com
WEB:http://
www.sustainableenergy.com
CONTACT : Mr Brent Harris

TRILLIUM WINDMILLS INC
250 Angus Point Road,
RR # 1, South River,
Ontario P0A 1X0, Canada
TEL: +1 705 386 1717
FAX: +1 705 386 2121
E-MAIL:
go4wind@trilliumwindmills.com
WEB: http://
www.trilliumwindmills.com
CONTACT: Peter Sanguinetti

VISION QUEST WINDELECTRIC INC
100, 3553 - 31st Street NW,
Calgary, Alberta T2L 2K7, Canada
TEL: +1 403 289 4553
FAX: +1 403 282 1238
E-MAIL: visionq@greenergy.com
WEB: http://www.greenergy.com
CONTACT: Jason Edworthy

WIND POWER INC
PO Box609, Pincher Creek,
Alberta TOK 1W0, Canada
TEL: +14036272923
FAX: +14036273239
E-MAIL: wpi@windpower.ca
WEB: http://www.windpower.ca
CONTACT: Dale Johnson

BIOMASS

BIOTHERMICA INTERNATIONAL INC
3333 Cavendish Boulevard,
Room 440, Montreal,
Quebec H4B,
2MS Canada
TEL : +1 514 488 3881
FAX : +1 514 488 3125
E-MAIL : biotherm@total.net
WEB : http://www.biothermica.com
CONTACT : G Drouin

ENSYN GROUP INC
380 Hunt Club Road,
Suite 201, Ottawa,
Ontario KIV ICI, Canada,
TEL : +1 613 248 2257
FAX: + 1 613 248 2260
WEB: http:/www.ensyn.com
CONTACT : G Gorsky

GROUPE PYROVAC INC
333 rue Franquet, Sainte-Foy,
Quebec G1P 4C7, Canada
TEL: +1 418 652 2298
FAX: +1 418 652 2275
E-MAIL: groupe@pyrovac.com
WEB: http://www.pyrovac.com
CONTACT: Michele Dubois

IOGEN CORP
400 Hunt Club Road, Ottawa,
Ontario K1V 1C1, Canada
TEL: +1 613 733 9830
FAX: +1 613 733 5127
WEB: http://www.iogen.ca

PYROVAC TECHNOLOGIES INC
333 rue Franquet,
Quebec G1P 4C7, Canada
TEL: +1 418 652 2298
FAX: +1 418 652 2275
E-MAIL: groupe@pyrovac.com
WEB: http://www.pyrovac.com
CONTACT: Michele Dubois

SMALL HYDRO

ASIAN PHOENIX RESOURCES LTD
2-416 Dallas Road, Victoria,
BC V8V 1A9, Canada
TEL: +1 250 361 4348
FAX: +1 250 360 9012
E-MAIL: info@powerpal.com
WEB: http://www.powerpal.com
CONTACT: Glenn Whalan

BC HYDRO
Green And Alternative Energy Division
1000- 401 West Georgia Street,
Vancouver, BC V6B 5A1, Canada
TEL: +1 604 663 3600
FAX: +1 604 663 3608
E-MAIL:
brenda.goehring@bchydro.com
WEB: http://www.bchydro.com
CONTACT: Brenda Goehring

DEPNEDABLE TURBINESS LTD
7, 3005, Murray Street, Port Moody,
British Columbia V3H IX3, Canada
TEL : + 1 604 461 3121
FAX : + 1 604 461 3086
E-MAIL : dthydro@towncore.com
CONTACT : R Prior

ENERGY SYSTEMS & DESIGN
PO Box 4557, Susse, NB E4E 5L7,
Canada
TEL : + 1 506 433 3151
FAX: + 1 506 433 6151
E-MAIL : hydropow@nbnet.nb.ca
WEB: http://
www.microhydropower.com

ENERTECSOLAR
2470, O Reilly Road,
Kelowna, BC,
VIW 2V4, Canada
TEL : + 1 250 763 3465
FAX: + 1 250 763 3426
E-MAIL :fletcher@cnx.net
CONTACT : P Fletcher

GE HYDRO
795 Georges V,
Lachine, Quebec,
Canada H8S 4K8
TEL: +1 514 485 4037
FAX: +1 514 485 4231
WEB: www.gepower.com
CONTACT: Joseph Disalvo

PO SJOMAN HYDROTECH CONSULTING
9035 Altair Place,
Burnaby, British Columbai, V3J I
A8, Canada
TEL: +1 604 421 0293
FAX:+1 604 420 9540
E-MAIL : penttis@dowco.com
CONTACT: Pentti O Sjoman

TIDAL / OCEAN

BLUE ENERGY CANADA INC
Organization Development, 1111
Melville Street, Suite 820,
Vancouver,
British Columbia,
V6E, 3V6, Canada
TEL : +1 6904 682 2583
FAX : +1 604 682 8683
E-MAIL : mjburger@blueenergy.com
WEB : http://www.blueenergy.com
CONTACT : M Burger

ENERGY EFFICIENCY

INPOL CONSULTING
23 Peary Way, Kanata,
Ontario K2L IZ9, Canada
TEL: +1 613 592 4967
FAX: +1 613 592 5582
E-MAIL: kujawski@intranet.ca
WEB: http://www.greenbuilding.ca
CONTACT: Woytek Kujawski

NATURAL RESOURCES CANADA
Canmet Energy Diversification
Research Laboratory,
1615 Lionel-Boulet Boulevard,
Varennes,
Quebec J3X 1S6, Canada
TEL: +1 514 652 4621
FAX: +1 514 652 5994
E-MAIL: jeclouti@nrcan.gc.ca
WEB: http://cedrl.mets.nrcan.gc.ca
CONTACT: Jean-Claude Cloutier

FINANCE / BANKING

STS ENERGY
10364 Francis, Montreal,
QC H2C 3A2,
Canada
TEL: +1 514 389 5950
E-MAIL:pbelley@crosswinds.net
CONTACT:Philippe Belley

ASSOCIATION

CANADIAN SOLAR INDUSTRIES ASSOCIATION — CANSIA
250-2415,
Holly Lane,
OTTawa,
Ontario KIV, 7P2,
Canada
TEL : +1 613 736 9077
FAX : +1 613 736 8938
E-MAIL : info@cansia.ca
WEB : http://www.cansia.ca
CONTACT : A Pritchard

PLANETARY ASSOCIATION FOR CLEAN ENERGY INC.
100 Bronson Avenue,
Suite 1001 Ottawa,
Ontario KIR 6G8,
Canada
TEL: +613 236 6265
FAX:+613 235 5876
CONTACT: A Michrowski

TORONTO RENEWABLE ENERGY CO-OPERATIVE - TREC
401 Richmond Street West
Box 80, Toronto,
Ontario MSV 3A8,
Canada
TEL: +1 416 977 5093
FAX: +1 416 977 7411
E-MAIL:info@trec.on.ca
WEB:http://www.trec.on.ca
CONTACT:Bryan Young

GOVERNMENT

DEPARTMENT OF NATURAL RESOURCES CANADA
Energy Technology Branch,
CADDET Energy Efficiency,
580 Booth Street,
13th Floor, Ottawa,
Ontario KIA OE-4,
Canada
TEL : + 1 613 947 3812
FAX : + 1 613947 1016
E-MAIL : mlamanqu@nrcan.gc.ca
WEB : http://www.caddet-ee.org
CONTACT : M Lamanque

RESOURCES WILDLIFE AND ECONOMIC DEVELOPMENT GOVERNMENT OF THE NWT
Energy Program Branch
Environmental Protection Service,
600 5102 - 50th Avenue, Canada
Yellowknife NT X1A 3S8
TEL : +1 867 873 7654
FAX : +1 867 873 0221
E-MAIL : lloyd.henderson@gov.nt.ca
WEB : http://www.gov.nt.ca/RWED/eps
CONTACT : Lloyd Henderson

RESEARCH & DEVELOPMENT

ARISE TECHNOLOGIES CORPORATION
Marketing And Communication, 321 Shoemaker Street, Kitchener, Ontario N2E 3B3, Canada
TEL: +1 5 19 725 2244
FAX: +1 5 19 725 8907
E-MAIL:ryan.kennedy@arisetech.com
WEB: http://www.aristech.com
CONTACT: Ryan Kennedy

BRACE RESEARCH INSTITUTE
P O Box 900, Mac Donald campus,
Ste Anne de Believue,
Quebec H9X, 3V9 Canada
TEL : +1 514 398 7835
FAX : +1 514 398 7767
E-MAIL : ael2000@musica.mcgill.ca
CONTACT : T Lawand

ENERGY DIVERSIFICATION RESEARCH LABORATORY CEDRAL
1615 Lionel - Boulet Boulevard,
Varennes, Quebec J3X,IS6, Canada
TEL: +1 514 652 4261
FAX: +1 514 652 0999
E-MAIL: rmajumda@cedrl.mets.nrcan.gc.ca
CONTACT : M Poireer

MEMORIAL UNIVERSITY
Ocean Engineering Research Centre,
Faculty of Engineeing & Applied Science, St John's,
Newfoundland AIB 3XS, Canada
TEL: +1 709 737 8805
FAX: +1 709 737 2116
CONTACT : Dr Neil Bose

PHOTOVOLTAIC ENERGY APPLIED RESEARCH LABORATORY - PEARL
3700 Willingdon Avenue, BCIT,
Burnaby, BV V5G 3H2, Canada
TEL:+1 604 451 6934
FAX : +1 604 436 0286
E-MAIL : lstameni@bcit.bc.ca
WEB:http://www.bcit.ca/-tc/html/photovoltaics.html
CONTACT: L Stamenic

REGIONAL MUNICIPALITY OF SUDBURY
PO Box 3700,
Station A, Sudbury, Canada
Ontarion P3A 5W5
TEL : +1 705 673 2171
FAX : +1 705 673 5171
E-MAIL: david.caverson@region.sudbury.on.ca
CONTACT : Mr David Caverson

UNIVERSITIES

DALHOUSIE UNIVERSITY
Daitech, PO Box 1000, Halifax,
Nova Scotia B3J 24, Canada
TEL : + 1 903 494 3299
FAX : + 1 902 421 6711
E-MAIL : peter.allen@dal.ca

UNIVERSITY OF OTTOWA
International Water Engineering Centre - IWEC,
Civil Engineering Department,
155 Marlborough Ottaowa,
Ontario KIN 8GI, Canada
TEL : +16135650408
FAX : +161-5625173
E-MAIL : schiller@gemie.uottawa.ca
CONTACT : E J Schiller

UNIVERSITY OF QUEBEC IN MONTREAL
1190 Elizabeth Street,
St-Laurent. Province of Quebec
H4L 4LI. Canada
TEL: +514 747 9565
FAX: +514 747 9565
E-MAIL: esq@clic.net
CONTACT: Benoit Perron

CONSULTANTS

ATLANTIC WIND TEST SITE
RR 4 Tignish,
North Cape,
PEI COB 280, Canada
TEL : +1 902 882 2746
FAX : +1 902 882 3823
E-MAIL : info@awts.pe.ca
CONTACT : Carl Brothers

ENERGY ALTERNATIVES LTD
B-6782 Veyaness Road,
Victoria,
British Colombia,
VBM 2C2, Canada
TEL: +1 250 544 0488
FAX: +1 250 544 0478
E-MAIL: sales @energyalts.com
WEB: http://www.energyalts.com
CONTACT : K Pegg

ENERNAT
406-4055 St Jean Boulevard,
Dollard Des Ormeaux,
Quebec H9G 1X9, Canada
TEL : +1 514 624 2918
CONTACT : R Sulica

ENERMODAL ENGINEERING LTD
650 Riverbend Drive, Kitchener,
Ontario N2K 3S2, Canada
TEL: +1 519 7438777
FAX: +1 519 7438778
E-MAIL: scarpenter@enermodal.com
WEB: www.enermodal.com

EOLETECH
Les Consutalnts Eoletech S Q Inc.
P O Box 307, Beaconsfield,
Quebec H9W 5T8, Canada
TEL: +1 514 697 6313
FAX: +1 514 697 9389
E-MAIL : eoletech@luckson.com
CONTACT : S. Qureshi

GPCO INC
2516 St Jacques Street,
Montreal, Quebec H3j 2T4,
Canada
TEL : + 1 514 939 1511
FAX : + 1 514 8793415
E-MAIL : gpco@videotron.ca
WEB: http://www.pages.inginit.net/gpco

HOWELL-MAYHEW ENGINEERING INC
15006-103 Avenue, Edmonton
Alberta T5P 0N8, Canada
TEL: +1 780 484 0476
FAX: +1 780 484 3956
E-MAIL: ghowell@compusmart.ab.ca
CONTACT: Gordon Howell

MACLELLAN MANAGEMENT LTD
151 John Street West,
Waterloo, Ontario N2L IC4,
Canada
TEL: +1 519 745 2100
FAX: +1 519 745 9232
E-MAIL: imaclein@interram.com
CONTACT: Ian MacLennan

PEMBINA INSTITUTE
Eco- Efficient Technologies Program, 2050 Pine Place,
Courtenay, BC V9N 3CI,
Canada
TEL : +1 250 334 8514
FAX : + 1 250 334 8454
E-MAIL :andrewp@pembina.org
WEB: http://www.pembina.org
CONTACT : Andrew Pape

SHEPHERD MONDROW
5710 Timberlea Boulevard,
Suite 103, Mississauga,
Ontario L4B 3NS, Canada
TEL: +1 905 629 9035
FAX: +1 905 629 4035
E-MAIL: imondrow@sgwmiss.com
WEB: http://www.sgwmiss.com
CONTACT: Ian Mondrow

SOLAR PLUS CANADA
P O Box76 Shawnigan Lake,British
Columbia VOR 2Wo,Canada
TEL:+1 250 743 9796
FAX:+1 250 743 9744
E-MAIL:solar@pinc.com
WEB:http://www.vvv.com/~solar
CONTACT:Gary Giles

SOLAR SYSTEMS
RR 4, Highway 41, Pembroke,
Ontario, KBA 6WS, Canada
TEL:+1 613 73 1659
E-MAIL:emilraym@ontario.enorio.on.ca
CONTACT : Emile Raymond

SOLENER INC
50 Cote Dinan Suite 202, Quebec,
QC G1K 8N6, Canada
TEL: +14186407444
FAX: +14186407445
E-MAIL: jroyer@solener.ca
CONTACT: Mr. Jimmy Royer

THE HUMAN DIMENSION
283 Victoria Street, Kingston,
Ontario K7L3Z2, Canada
TEL: +1 613 549 4290
FAX: +1 613 5476089
E-MAIL: 5d4@qsilver.queensu.ca
CONTACT: Dorothy Leie

DESIGN & ENGINEERING

A B C POWER AND BOILER INCORPORATED
2500 Ave P Dupuy,
Suite 603, Montreal,
Quebec J3H 4LI, Canada
TEL: +1 514 441 5717
FAX: +1 514 441 5711
CONTACT: Jan Wrzesien

JONES GROUP ENGINEERING LIMITED
3, 100-10 Avenue,
NE Calgary,
Alberta T2o OWY,
Canada
TEL: +1 403 276 5406
FAX: +1 403 276 4692
E-MAIL: jonesm@cadvision.com
CONTACT : M E Jones

KMW SYSTEMS INC
3330 White Oak Road,
London, Ontario N6E 1L8,
Canada,
TEL: +1 519 686 1771
FAX: +1 519 686 1132
E-MAIL:kmwinfo@kmwgroup.com
CONTACT : B. Rosen

MCCALLUM SATHER ARCHITECTS INC
41 King Williams Street,
Suite 300 Hamilton,
Ontario L8R IA2, Canada
TEL: +1 905 526 6700
FAX: +1 905 526 0906
E-MAIL: msarch@bestnet.org
CONTACT: Joanne McCallum

REDI
28 Yonge Street, Tara,
Ontario NOH 2NO, Canada
TEL : +1 519 934 0940
FAX : +1 519 934 2005
E-MAIL : solarlady@bmts.com
CONTACT : Judy Kitto

SOLAR NORTH SYSTEMS
241-15 St West,
Prince Albert, SK,
s6v 3p9, Canada
TEL:+1 306 953 0053
FAX:+1 306 953 0053
E-MAIL:solarn@sk.sympatico.ca
CONTACT:Brian R Clavier

SOLTEK SOLAR ENERGY LTD
#2 - 745 Vanalman Avenue,
Victoria BC V8Z 386 Canada
TEL: +1 250 727 7720
FAX: +1 250 727 2135
E-MAIL: soltek@soltek.ca
WEB: http://www.soltek.ca
CONTACT: Chris Hanson

SUNCURRENT INC
PO Box 6044, Station A, Calgary,
Alberta, Canada
TEL: +1 403 264 2880
FAX: +1 403 264 2881
E-MAIL : admin@suncurrent.ab.ca
WEB : http://www.suncurrent.ab.ca
CONTACT : Mr Paul Liddy

HYDROGEN

STUART ENERGY SYSTEMS
5101 Orbitor Drive, Mississauga,
Ontario, Canada
TEL: +19052827700
FAX: +19052827706
E-MAIL: lshen@stuartenergy.com
CONTACT: Lyn Shen

OTHERS

ARCAND SPARK ELECTRICAL CONTRACTORS LTD
1780 7th Avenue, Prince George,
BCV2L, 3P8, Canada
TEL : +1 250 564 2316
FAX : +1 250 565 6886
E-MAIL : gb_willis@hotmail.com

BODYCOTE MATERIALS TESTING CANADA INC
National Solar Test Facility, Canada,
2395 Speakman Drive, Mississauga,
Ontario L5K 183, Canada
TEL : +1 905 822 4111
FAX : +1 905 823 1446
E-MAIL : brunger.@bodycote-mt-com
CONTACT : Dr. A Brunger

CAMPBELL SCIENTIFIC (CANADA) CORP
192 St. Clair Street, Chatham,
Ontario N7L, 3J6, Canada
TEL : +1 519 354 7356
FAX : +1 519 354 1558
CONTACT : R Herfst

MARITIME ELECTRIC COMPANY LIMITED
180 Kent Street, Box 1328,
Charlotte Town, PEI CIA 7N2,
Canada
TEL: +1 902 566 1599
FAX: +1 902 566 2692
CONTACT: Mr James Lea

SOLARGETICS LTD
20385 Lakeshore Road, Baie d'Urfe.
Quebec H9X IR2, Canada
TEL: +1 514 457 6968
CONTACT : Claudette Marsolais

UNITED POWER LTD
198 Perberton Avenue, North
Vancouver, BC V7P 2RS, Canada
TEL: +1 604 983 2819
FAX: +1 604 983 2869
E-MAIL: unitedpower@
mindlink.bc.ca
WEB:http://www.hwired.com/
unitedpower
CONTACT: Mr George W Ingham

VORTEK INDUSTRIES LTD
605 West Kent Ave, Vancouver,
British Columbia V6P 6TZ, Canada
TEL: +1 604 251 2451
FAX: +1 604 251 3356
E-MAIL: mailbox@vortek.com
WEB: http://www.vortek.com
CONTACT: David C Fox

SUPPLIERS

BATTERIES/INVERTERS

ARISE TECHNOLOGIES CORPORATION
156 Colombia Street West,
Waterloo,Ontario, N2L 3L3, Canada
TEL : +1 519 725 2244
FAX : +1 519 725 8907
E-MAIL : ian.maclellan@arisetech.com
WEB : http://www.arisetech.com
CONTACT : Ian Maclellan

POWERSOURCE ENERGY SYSTEMS INC
1-6809 Kirkpatrick Crescent, Victoria
British Columbia V8M 1Z8, Canada
TEL: +1 250 544 2115
FAX: +1 250 544 1773
E-MAIL: info@powersourceenergy.com
WEB: http://www.powerso urceenergy.com
CONTACT: Mrs Dianne S Goodfellow

STATPOWER TECHNOLOGIES CORPORATION
7725 Lougheed Highway, Burnaby,
British Columbia V5A 4V8, Canada
TEL: +1 604 420 1585
FAX: +1 604 420 1591
E-MAIL:support@statpower.com
WEB:http://www.statpower.com
CONTACT:Lindsay Hardie

SURRETTE BATTERY COMPANY LIMITED
1 Station Road, PO Box 2020,
Springhill,
Nova Scotia BOM 1XO, Canada
TEL: +19025974027
FAX: +19025978447
E-MAIL: batsales@surrette.com
WEB: http://www.surrette.com
CONTACT: James Surrette

INSTRUMENTATION

CANADIAN SUNFLOWER SOLAR CONTROLLERS LTD
General Delivery, Rosseau,Ontario
POC, IJO, Canada
TEL : +1 705 732 4363
FAX : +1 705 732 4363
CONTACT : S J Gammage

SOLAR CONVERTERS INCORPORATED
490 York Road, Unit A104 Guelph.
Ontario NIE 6VI, Canada
TEL:+1 519 824 5272
FAX:+1 519 823 0325
CONTACT:dan Pringle

ZEPHYR NORTH
4034 Mainway, Burlington,
Ontario, L7M 4B9, Canada
TEL: +1 905 335 9670
FAX: +1 905 335 0119
E-MAIL:
Jim.Salmon@ZephyrNorth.com
WEB: http://www.zephyrnorth.com
CONTACT: Dr Jim Salmon

OTHERS(S)

DYNAMOTIVE EUROPE LTD
1700 West 75th Avenue, Suite 105,
Vancouver, British Colombia V6P 6G2, Canada
TEL: +1 604 267 6000
FAX: +1 604 267 6005
E-MAIL: investor@dynamotive.com
WEB: http://www.dynamotive.com
CONTACT: Antony Robson

DYNAGE SYSTEMS INC
PO Box 5300, Sydney,
Nova Scotia BIP 6L2, Canada
TEL : + 1 902 562 0133
FAX : + 1 8902 567 0633
E-MAIL : chisholm@dynagensystems.com
WEB : http://www.dynagesystem.com
CONTACT : K L Chisholm

ENERGIE SOLAIRE QUEBEC
460 rue Ste-Catherine O Bureau 701
Montreal QC, H3B 1A7, Canada
TEL: +1 514 392 0095
FAX: +1 514 392 0952
E-MAIL: info@esq.qc.ca
WEB: http://www.esq.qc.ca
CONTACT: Benoit Perron

HELIOSYS
10364 Francis, Montreal,
QC H2C 3A2, Canada
TEL: +1 514 389 5950
E-MAIL: pbelley@softhome.net
CONTACT: Philippe Belley

HELIOTECH INC
1050 Ottawa Street, Montreal,
Quebec H3E 5X6, Canada
TEL: +1 514 398 9292
FAX: +1 514 398 9022
E-MAIL: heliotech@qc.aira.com
CONTACT: Andrew Evan Doorn

INDUSTRIAL ELECTRICAL CONTROL
663 Birch Street, Campbell River,
British Columbia V9W 2T2, Canada
TEL: +1 250 286 6129
CONTACT: Alex Nicholl

ORENDA AEROSPACE CORPORATION
3160 Derry Road East, Mississauga,
Ontario L4T 1A9, Canada
TEL: +1 905 673 3250
FAX: +1 905 678 1538
E-MAIL: fbutton@orenda.com
WEB: http://www.orenda.com
CONTACT: Frank Button

THERMO DYNAMICS LTD
44 Borden Avenue,
Burnside Industrial Park, Dartmouth,
Novia Scotia B3B IC8, Canada
TEL: +1 902 468 1001
FAX: +1 902 468 1002
E-MAIL:solarinfo@thermo-dynamics.com
WEB: http://www.thermo-dynamics.com

UNIFIN INTERNATIONAL INC
1030 Clarke Road, London,
Ontario N6A 4P4, Canada
TEL : +1 519 451 0310
FAX : +1 519 451 1732
E-MAIL : YuT@kochind.com
WEB : http:// www.unifin.com
CONTACT : Stephen R Carr

SASKATCHEWAN POWER CORPORATION – SASKPOWER
2025 Victoria Avenue, Regina
Saskatchewan S4POS1, Canada
TEL: +13065662993
FAX: +13065662916

SOLSOURCE ENGINEERING
66 Lewis Drive, Newmarket,
Ontario L3Y IR7, Canada
TEL: +1 905 898 0098
FAX: +1 905 898 1661
E-MAIL: perdreews@home.com
CONTACT: Per Drewes

YUKON ENERGY CORPORATION-YEC
PO Box5970, Whitehorse,
Yukon Y1A 5L6, Canada
TEL: +1 867 393 5347
FAX: +1 867 393 5323
E-MAIL: john.maissan@yec.yk.ca
CONTACT: John Maissan

Kindly inform us of any errors and omissions in the listings by:

E-mail: unisun@vsnl.com

Fax:91 80 22289294

SOLAR THERMAL

BUFETE DE TECHNOLOGIA SOLAR SA BUTESCA
Rosal 180, Col. San Pedro Martir
Tlalpan 14650 Mexico, DF, Mexico
TEL : +42 55 134297
FAX : +52 55 134297
E-MAIL : strevel@data.net.mx
CONTACT : R M Strevel

SUNWAY DE MEXICO SA DE CV
Ejercito Nacional 1162-PB,
Col Polanco, DF 11570, Mexico
TEL: +52 5 395 0041
FAX: +52 5 395 5771
E-MAIL: sunway@mpsnet.com.mx
CONTACT: Jorge Davila

RESEARCH & DEVELOPMENT

CENTRO DE INVESTIGACION EN ENERGIA UNAM
Priv Xochicalco S/N Col,
Ruben Jaramilo, 62580,
Temixco, Morales, Mexico
TEL : +52 56 229744
FAX : +52 73 250018
E-MAIL : aov@mazatl.cie.unam.mx
WEB : http://www.cie.unam.mx
CONTACT : Y M Kuwabara

ENERGY RESEARCH CENTER UNAM
Laboratorio de Energia Solar,
Privada Xochicalo s/n,
Col Centro, Temixco,
Morelos 62580, Mexico
TEL : + 52 73 14 1838
FAX : + 52 73 14 1662
E-MAIL : gace@infosel.net.mx
CONTACT : Claudio Estrada

GRUPO DE ACCION INTER-DISCIPLINARIA AMBIENTALAC
Priv San Dieguito # 16,
Acapantzingo, Cuernavaca Morelos,
CP 62440, Mexico
TEL : + 52 73 18 90 16
FAX : + 52 73 18 9016
E-MAIL : ecaldera@infosel.net.mx
CONTACT : A Caldera

NATIONAL UNIVERSITY OF MEXICO
Energy Research Centre, PO Box 34,
62580 Temixco, Mexico
TEL: +52 73 250052
FAX: +52 73 25 0018
E-MAIL: dir@mazatl.unam.mx
WEB: http://www.ie.unam.mx
CONTACT: M Martinez

NATIONAL UNIVERSITY OF MEXICO
Institute de Ingenieria Apdo Postal
70-472, Ciudad Universitaria, 04510
Mexico DF, Mexico
TEL: +52 5 6228138
FAX: +52 5 6228137
E-MAIL: raz@pumas.lingen.unam.mx
WEB: http://www.lingen.unam.mx
CONTACT: Prof raftel Almanza

UNIVERSITIES

UAM-IZTAPALAPA
IPH CBI, Area de Ingenieria en
Energia, AP 55-534 Deptc IPH,
DF 09340, Mexico
TEL : +52 5724 4900
FAX : +52 5724 4900
E-MAIL : ebc@xanuim.uam.mx
CONTACT : E Calva

UNIVERSIDAD AUTONOMA METROPOLITANA-IZTAPALAPA
Processes and Hydraulics
Engineering Department, Av
Michoacan y La
Purisima, Iztapalapa 09340, Mexico
TEL: +52 5804 4644
FAX: +52 5804 4900
E-MAIL: hrp@xanum.uam.mx
WEB: http://www.uam.mx
CONTACT: Dr Hernando Romero

DESIGN & ENGINEERING

TECNOLOGIA INTERCONTINENTAL SA DE CV
Rio Lerma 171,4th Floor, Col Cuauhtemoc,
06500 Mexico DF, Mexico
TEL: +52 5 514 03 21
FAX: +52 5 207 24 78
CONTACT: Jose A Primelles

WORT ARCHITECTS
Environmental Design, Pestalozzi
1204-201, Col del Valle,
Mexico DF 03100, Mexico
TEL: +52 5 6043018
FAX: +52 5 6042370
E-MAIL: wort@mati.net.mx
WEB: http://www.wort.com.mx
CONTACT: Jorge Wolpert

COGENERATION

PEGI SA DE CV
Operation, Gral Miguel Barragan
702 Pte, Col Industrial, Monterrey,
Nuevo Leon CP64440, Mexico
TEL: +52 8 352 0006
FAX: +52 8 351 2886
E-MAIL: ehgarcia@att.net.mx
CONTACT: Edgar H Garcia Guerra

SUPPLIERS

OTHERS (S)

ASHMOR
Privada de Chaipas #5,
62030 Cuernavaca,
Morelos, Mexico
TEL : +52 73 14 3042
FAX : +52 73 14 3042
E-MAIL : ashmor@infosol.net.mx
CONTACT : A Saldana

SOLARTRONIC SA DE CV
Morelos Sur No 90,
Col Chipitlan, 62070
Cuernavaca, Morelos, Mexico
TEL: +527773189714
FAX: +527773188609
E-MAIL: mexico@solartronic.com

ECO TURISMO Y NUEVAS TECHNOLOGIAS SA
Paseo de las Palomas 168, Las
Alamedas, Atizapan de Zaragoza,
Estado de Mexico 52970, Mexico
TEL : +52 5 824 1358
FAX : +52 5 8251734
E-MAIL:aromerop@mail.internet.com.mx
CONTACT : A R Paredes

Kindly inform us of any errors and omissions in the listings by:

E-mail: unisun@vsnl.com

Fax: 91 80 2289294

SOLAR THERMAL

AY MCDONALD MFG CO
4800 Chavenelle Road,
Dubuque, Iowa 52002, USA
TEL: + 1 319 583 7311
FAX: + 1 319 588 0720
E-MAIL: sales@aymcdonaldmfg.com
CONTACT: John Bennier

ABSOLUTE COMFORT
3230 N Cascade, Suite A,
Colorado Springs,
Colorado 80907, USA
TEL: +1 719 471 2347

ACR SOLAR INTERNATIONAL INC
5840 Gibbons Drive,
Suite G, Carmichael,
California 95608, USA
TEL: +1 916 481 7200
FAX: +41 916 481 7203
E-MAIL: acrich@solarroofs.com
WEB: http://www.solarroofs.com

ACTIVE SOLAR COMPANY
24241 Craig Drive, Moreno Valley,
California 92388, USA
TEL: + 1 909 247 1835
FAX: + 1 909 247 1835
CONTACT: Robert Danielson

ADVANCED ENERGY CONSTRUCTION
20505 US Highway 19, Suite 12,
Clearwater, Florda 34624, USA
TEL: + 1 727 441 2808
CONTACT: David Oldack

ADVANCED SOLAR TECHNOLOGIES
6193 Wooded Run Drive,
Columbia, Maryland 21044, USA
TEL: + 1 410 381 9776
FAX: + 1 410 997 0779
E-MAIL: info@thermomax.com
CONTACT: Dr. Fariborz Mahjouri

ALLIANCE INTERNATIONAL
143 Oakhurst Road,
Cape Elizabeth
ME 04107, USA
TEL: + 1 207 767 3800
FAX: + 1 207 767 3800
CONTACT: HT Hawkes

ALLSOLAR SERVICE CO INC
PO Box 1263, Maitland,
Florida 32751, USA
TEL: + 1 407 644 4159
FAX: + 1 407 774 4751
E-MAIL: bessettedn@aol.com
WEB: http://www.allsolarservice.com
CONTACT: David E Bessette

ALTAS CORPORATION
1401 Laurent Street,
Santa Cruz, California 95060, USA
TEL: + 1 408 425 1211
FAX: + 1 408 425 8533
E-MAIL: fdw@ecotopia.com
WEB: http://www.ecotopia.com
CONTACT : Francis de Winter

ALTERNATIVE ENERGY CONCEPT INC
PO Box 564, Palm Springs,
California 92263-0564, USA
TEL: + 1 619 324 5880
CONTACT : David Ames

ALTERNATE ENVIRONMENT
7017 Helmsdale Road, West Hills,
California 91307, USA
TEL: + 1 818 348 4436
FAX: + 1 818 598 1692
CONTACT: Oded Vogel

AMERICAN ENERGY TECHNOLOGIES INC
1057 N Ellis Road Unit 4,
Jacksonville, Florida 32254, USA
TEL: + 1 904 781 7000
FAX: + 1 904 781 1911
E-MAIL: sales@aetsolar.com
WEB: http://www.aetsolar.com
CONTACT : Dell Jones

AMERICAN SOLAR ENERGY SOCIETY INC
2400 Central Avenue G-1,
Boulder, Colorado 80301, USA
TEL: + 1 303 443 3130
FAX: + 1 303 443 3212
E-MAIL: ases@igc.apc.org
CONTACT : Larry Sherwood

ANDRESUN SOLAR
6307 Kapalapala Place,
Honolulu, Hawaii 96825-1212, USA
TEL: + 1 808 396 9288
FAX: + 1 808 396 0861
E-MAIL: asunbug@lava.net
WEB: http://www.andersunsolar.com
CONTACT : Bill Anderson

AQUA THERM INDUSTRIES INC
1940 Rutgers University Boulevard,
Lakewood, New Jersey 08701, USA
TEL: + 1 732 905 0440
FAX: + 1 732 905 9899
WEB: http://www.warmwater.com
CONTACT : Dave Sizelove

ASPEN SOLAR SYSTEMS
PO Box 2391, Aspen, CO 81612, USA
TEL : +1 970 925 3659
FAX : +1 970 925 3659
E-MAIL : mike@aspensolar.com
WEB : http://www.aspensolar.com
CONTACT : M Jierney

AWS SCIENTIFIC INC
251 Fuller Road, Albany,
New York 12203-3640, USA
TEL : +1 518 437 8660
FAX : +1 518 437 8659
E-MAIL :awwssci@mindspring.com
WEB : http://www.awsscientific.com
CONTACT : B H Bdiley

AZTEC SOLAR
5045 College Oak Drive #E
Sacramento, California 95838, USA
TEL : +1 916 929 3916
FAX : +1 916 929 8652
CONTACT : Ed. Murray

BSAR SOLAR
980, Santa Estella, Solano Beach
California, 92075, USA
TEL : +1 619 259 8864
FAX : +1 619 259 8864
CONTACT : J Butler

BURNS-MILWAUKEE INC
4010 West Douglas Avenue,
Milwaukee, Wisconsin 53209, USA
TEL : +1 414 438 1000
FAX : +1 414 438 0841
WEB : http://www.sunoven.com
CONTACT :J Burns

CALIFORNIA SOLAR
675 Greenwich Drive, Thousand
Oaks California 91360, USA
TEL : +1 805 379 3113
FAX : +1 805 379 3027
E-MAIL : casolar@aol.com
WEB : http://www.californiasolar.com
CONTACT : R White

CAPITAL SUN GROUP LTD
6503 81st Street, Cabin John
Maryland 20818, USA
TEL : +1 301 229 0671
FAX : +1 202 229 0434
CONTACT : C L Ports

CHALEFF & ROGERS ARCHITECTS
1514 Montauk Highway,
PO Box 990, Water Mill,
NY 11976, USA
TEL : +1 516 726 4477
FAX : + 1 516 726 4478
E-MAIL : billarchtx@aol.com
CONTACT : Bill Chaleff

CLIMATIC-SOLAR CORPORATION
356 Eugenia Road, Vero Beach,
Florida 32963-1526, USA
TEL : + 1 407 567 3104
CONTACT : John Drudak

CONSERVAL SYSTEMS INC
4254 Ridge Lea Road,
Suite 101 Buffalo,
New York 14226, USA
TEL : + 1 716 835 4903
FAX : + 1 716 835 4904
E-MAIL : conserval@aol.com
WEB : http://www.solarwall.com

CROSSTONE SOLAR COMPANY
2202 Bermondsey Drive,
Mitchelville, Maryland, 20721, USA
TEL : +1 301 249 7943
CONTACT : B Besman

CUMMINS ENGINE COMPANY INC
500 Jackson Street, Columbus,
Indian 47202-3005, USA
TEL : +1 812 377 3192
FAX : +1 812 377 3272

CURRIN CORPORATION
PO Box 2006, Midland,
Michigan 48641, USA
TEL : +1 517 835 7387
FAX : +1 517 835 7395
E-MAIL : currcorp@tm.net
CONTACT : C G Currin

DANKOFF SOLAR PRODUCTS INC
2810 Industrial Road,
Santa Fe, NM 87505-3120, USA
TEL: + 1 505 473 3800
FAX: + 1 505 473 3830
E-MAIL: pumps@dankoffsolar.com
WEB: http://www.dankoffsolar.com
CONTACT : P Benson

DONALD ROBERT SMITH CONSULTING
468 49th Street, Oakland,
California 94609, USA
TEL: + 1 510 658 3461
FAX: + 1 510 658 3461
E-MAIL: dr_smith@ix.netcom.com
CONTACT : Don Smith

SOLAR RESEARCH INTERNATIONAL
850 W Morgan Street,
Raleigh, NC 27603-1614, USA
TEL: + 1 919 832 3404
FAX: + 1 919 832 3339
E-MAIL: johnmyles@srisolar.com
CONTACT : Mr. John Myles

SOLAR RESEARCH INTERNATIONAL
400 S Tryon Street, PO Box 1004,
Charlotte, North Carolina 28201, USA
TEL: +1 704 382 8795
FAX: +1 704 382 3105
E-MAIL: johnmyles@srisolar.com
WEB: http://www.dukesolar.com
CONTACT: Mr. John Myles

ECLECTIC ELECTRIC
PO Box 310, Sandia Park,
New Mexico 87047-0310, USA
TEL: + 1 505 281 9538
CONTACT: Robert Thacter

ECO MALL
PO Box 20553 Cherokee Station
New York 10021, USA
TEL: + 1 212 535 1876
FAX: + 1 212 535 4394
WEB: http://www.ecomail.com

ELECTRO SOLAR PRODUCTS INC
502 Ives Place, Pensacola,
Florida, 32514, USA
TEL : +1 850 479 2191
FAX : +1 850 857 0070
E-MAIL :espsolar@pcola.gulf.net
WEB : http://members.xoom.com/
espsolar
CONTACT : A E Mackinney

ENERGY CONCEPTS COMPANY
627 Ridgely Avenue, Annapolis,
Mary land 21401, USA
TEL: +1 410 266 6521
FAX: +1 410 266 6539
E-MAIL: enerconcep@aol.com

ENERGY CONVERSION DEVICES INC
Manufacturing Technology, 1675,
West Maple Road,
Troy, Michigan 48084, USA
TEL: +1 313 280 1900
FAX: +1 313 280 1456
E-MAIL: ovonic@aol.com
WEB: http://www.ovonic.com
CONTACT : M Ixu

ENERGY SERVICE COMPANY
399 E 10th Avenue, Eugene,
Oregon 97401 USA
TEL : + 1 541 302 6808
FAX : + 1 541 302 6810
E-MAIL : info@escosolar.com
WEB: http://www.escosolar.com
CONTACT : J Scott

ENERTIA BUILDING SYSTEMS INC
Solar/Geothermal Homes, 13312
Garffe Sherron Road, Wake Forest,
North Carloina 27587, USA
TEL : + 1 919 556 0177
FAX: + 1 919 556 1135
E-MAIL: enertia@mindspring.com
WEB: http://www.enertia.com
CONTACT : M Sykes

ETM SOLAR WORKS INC
PO Box 67, Endicott,
New York 13761, USA
TEL: +1 607 785 6499
FAX: +1 607 785 6499
E-MAIL: etm@tier.net
WEB: http://www.tier.net/etm
CONTACT : Dr G E Conough

FAFCO INC
2690 Middlefield Road
Redwood City
California 94063, USA
TEL : +1 650 363 2690
FAX : +1 650 363 2890
CONTACT : F A Ford

FAFCO SOLAR
901 SE 13th Place, Cape Coral,
Florida 33990, USA
TEL: + 1 941 574 1500
FAX: + 1 941 574 6198
E-MAIL: dan@fafcosolar.com
WEB: http://www.fafcosolar.com
CONTACT : D Morrissey

GLOBAL RESOURCE OPTIONS LLP
4 Kibling Hill Road, PO Box 51,
Strafford, VT 05072, USA
TEL : + 1 800 374 4494
FAX : + 1 802 765 9983
E-MAIL : global@sover.net
WEB: http://www.globalresource
options.com
CONTACT : J Wolfe

GRAHAM MANUFACTURING CO INC
20 Florence Avenue, Batavia,
New York 14020, USA
TEL : + 1 716 343 2216
FAX : + 1 716 343 1097
E-MAIL : equipment@graham-mfg.com
WEB: http://www.graham.mfg.com
CONTACT : J P Gorman

GRAND SOLAR
4882-4 Kilauea Avenue, Honolulu,
Hawai 96816, USA
TEL : + 1 808 737 3536
FAX : + 1 808 737 3536
E-MAIL : info@safewatersystems.com
WEB: http://www.safewater
systems.com
CONTACT : J Grandineth

GULL INDUSTRIES
2127 South 1st Street, San Jose
California 95112, USA
TEL : + 1 408 293 3523
FAX : +1 408 289 1605
CONTACT : M Kennedy

HARRIMANS INCORPORATED
109-A, James Street, Venice,
Florida 34292, USA
TEL : +1 813 488 4453
FAX : + 1 813 366 6680
CONTACT : J Harriman

HARTER INDUSTRIES INCORPORATED
PO Box 502,
Holmdel New Jersey 07733, USA
TEL : + 1 732 566 7055
FAX : + 1 732 566 6977
E-MAIL : harter101@aol.com
WEB: http://www.harterindustries.com
CONTACT : D G Harter

HEALEY & ASSOCIATES
120 Venetian Way, Suite#16,
Merritt Island, Florida 32953, USA
TEL: +1 407 452 2173
FAX: +1 407 459 3682
E-MAIL: healey@flaenergy.com
WEB: http://www.flaenergy.com
CONTACT : Hesley

HELIODYNE INC
4910 Seaport Avenue Richmond
California 94804, USA
TEL: + 1 510 237 9614
FAX: + 1 510 237 7018
E-MAIL: info@heliodyne.com
WEB: http://www.heliodyne.com
CONTACT : C D Bieri

HELIOCOL USA INC
927 Fern Street #200, Altamonte
Springs, FL 32701, USA
TEL: +1 407 831 1941
FAX: +1 407 831 1208
E-MAIL: heliocol@iag.net
CONTACT : V Eyal

HELIOTROPE GENERAL
3733 Kenora Drive, Spring Valley,
California 91977, USA
TEL: +1 619 460 3930
FAX: +1 619 460 9211
E-MAIL: heliotrope@hgl.com
WEB: http://www.hgl.com
CONTACT : S Dowson

HI TEC SOLAR
PO Box 926, Coarsegold,
California 93614, USA
TEL: +1 209 683 3712
CONTACT : G Rollens

HORIZON INDUSTRIES
2120 Mission Road,
Suite L, Escondido,
California 92029-0403,
USA
TEL: +1 760 480 0403
FAX: +1 760 480 8322
E-MAIL: horizonsolar@abac.com
WEB: http://www.horizonsolar.com
CONTACT : M Landry

HUTTON COMMUNICATIONS
775 Tipton Industrial Drive Suite F,
Lawrenceville, GA30043, USA
TEL: +1 877 896 2806
FAX: +1 770 963 7796
WEB: http://www.huttonsolar.com

INDUSTRIAL SOLAR TECHNOLOGY CORPORATION
4420 McIntyre Street,
Golden Colorado 80403, USA
TEL: +1 303 279 8108
FAX: +1 303 279 8107
E-MAIL: industrialsolar@uswest.net
WEB: http://www.industrial
solartech.com
CONTACT : K May

INTEGRAL DESIGN
4708 Raley Boulevard,
Sacramento,
California 95838, USA
TEL: +1 916 920 2356
FAX: +1 916 920 2356
CONTACT : J Burton

INTER-ISLAND SOLAR SUPPLY
761 Ahua Street, Honolulu,
Hawaii 96819, USA
TEL: +1 808 523 0711
FAX: +1 808 536 5586
E-MAIL: rreed@solarsupply.com
WEB: http://www.solarsupply.com
CONTACT : R Reed

JOHN G MEEKER BS TECHNICAL MANAGEMENT
160 S Allison Street,
Lakewood Colorado 80226, USA
TEL: + 1 303 237 1952
CONTACT : J Mecker

JVP ELECTRO SOLAR PRODUCTS
Manufacturing, 502 Ives Place
Pensacola, Florida 32514, USA
TEL: + 1 850 479 2191
FAX: + 1 850 857 0070
E-MAIL: espsolar@pcola.gulf.net
WEB: http://members.zoom.com/espsolar
CONTACT : A E Mckinney

KELELO ENGINEERING
3404 Angela St, Cocoa,
Florida 32926, USA
TEL: + 1 321 632 7964
FAX: + 1 321 638 1010
E-MAIL: Thornbloom@fsec.ucf.edu
CONTACT : M D Jhornbloom

LIGHT ENERGY SYSTEMS
965 D Detroit Avenue,
Concord, CA 94518, USA
TEL: +1 925 681 4343
FAX: +1 925 680 6588
E-MAIL: solar@lighenergysystems.com
WEB: http://www.lighten
ergtsystems.com
CONTACT : B O'Nesl

MATERIALS TECHNOLOGY INC
220 Churchill Avenue, Somerset,
New Jersey 08873, USA
TEL: +1 732 246 1000
FAX: +1 732 246 3568
E-MAIL: mtisolar@aol.com
CONTACT : M Stanleo

MIAMI WATER HEATER
1324 NW 29th Street,
Maimi, Florida 33142, USA
TEL: +1 305 633 2656
FAX: +1 305 633 0374
E-MAIL: miawh@bellsouth.net
WEB: http://
www.miamiwaterheater.com
CONTACT : C Sanchez

MILLHOLEN MECHANICAL
Box 1483, Truckee,
California 96160, USA
TEL: +1 916 587 2318
CONTACT : W L Millholen

MR SUN SOLAR
0326 SW Pendleton Street,
Portland, Oregon 97201, USA
TEL:+1 503 222 2468
FAX: +1 503 245 4387
E-MAIL: 70663.2146@compuserve.com
CONTACT : J Panerson

NEKOLUX
1433 W Chicago Ave,
Chicago, IL 60622, USA
TEL: +1 312 738 3776
FAX: +1 312 738 3776
E-MAIL: vladimir@nekolux.com
WEB: http://www.nekolux.com
CONTACT : V Nekots

NORTH CANYON SOLAR
23643 North 40th Avenue,
Glendale, Arizona 85310, USA
TEL: + 1 623 582 2708
FAX: + 1 623 582 6667
E-MAIL: northcanyon@uswest.net
WEB: http://www.solardish.com
CONTACT : J Gilchrist

NORTH STAR COMPANY INC
14912 South Broadway, Gardena,
California 90248, USA
TEL: + 1 310 515 2200
FAX: + 1 310 715 8090
CONTACT : R W Lichtsinn

OCCIDENTAL POWER
3629 Taraval Street, San Francisco,
California 94116, USA
TEL: + 1 415 681 8861
FAX: + 1 415 681 9911
E-MAIL: solar@oxypower.com
WEB: http://www.oxypower.com
CONTACT: Greg Kennedy

PARADISE POWER COMPANY
Box 7484, Taos, NM 87571, USA
TEL: + 1 505 737 5896
FAX: + 1 505 737 5896
E-MAIL: paradise@taosnet.com
WEB: http://www.paradisepower.net
CONTACT: Daniel Weinman

PERRY ENERGY SERVICE
1904 Madison Avenue, Baltimore,
Maryland 21217, USA
TEL:+1 410 669 5211
FAX:+1 410 669 4640
E-MAIL:perryenergy@erols.com
CONTACT:Roger Perry

POLAR POWER INC
22520 Avalon Boulevard, Carson,
California 90745-4113, USA
TEL: +1 310 320 3514
FAX:+1 310 320 3135
CONTACT : A Sams

POWERWORKS INC
5356 North Cattail, Way Bolse,
Idaho 83703, USA
TEL: +1 208 853 4602
FAX: +1 208 853 4628
E-MAIL: rskoebbe@powerworksinc.com
CONTACT: Rick S Koebbe

RPI INDUSTRIES INC
2897 Industrial Parkway,
Santa Maria, California 93455, USA
TEL: + 1 805 928 5577
FAX: + 1 805 346 2119
CONTACT : R Wane

SAFE WATER SYSTEMS
2800 Woodlawn Drive, Suite 131,
Honolulu, Hawaii 96822-1864, USA
TEL: + 1 808 539 3937
FAX: + 1 808 539 3937
E-MAIL: info@safewatersystems.com
WEB: http://
www.safewatersystems.com
CONTACT : W Hartzell

SANDIA NATIONAL LABORATORIES
MS 0752, Albuquerque,
New Mexico 87185, USA
Tel : +1 505 844 0317
CONTACT : P Kumas

SCHOLFIELD SOLAR ENERGY AND RADIANT HEATING COMPANY
2450 Channel Drive, Suite A,
Ventura California 93003, USA
TEL: + 1 805 653 0797
FAX: + 1 805 648 6203
E-MAIL: scholfield@ucnet.com
WEB: http://www.vcnet.com/scholfield
CONTACT : A Carrozza

SCIENCE APPLICATIONS INTERNATIONAL CORPORATION
15874 West 6th Avenue,
Golden, Colorado 80401, USA
TEL: + 1 303 279 3030
FAX: + 1 303 384 0320
CONTACT : R Davenport

SEALED AIR CORPORATION
Solar Division, 3433 Arden Road,
Hayward, California 94545, USA
TEL: + 1 510 887 8090
FAX : + 1 510 785 1742
CONTACT : W Groechel

SKS INC
8 Sherman Avenue, Takoma Park
Maryland 20912, USA
TEL: +1 301 270 8959
FAX: +1 301 565 2228
CONTACT : A Nunez

SOL-AIR CO
129 Miller Street, Belfast,
Maine 04915, USA
TEL:+1 207 338 9513
FAX:+1 603 853 9339
E-MAIL:Kreamer@mint.net

SOLAMERICA CORPORATION
1046 Harper Boulevard SW,
Palm Bay, Florida 32908, USA
TEL:+1 407 723 2725
FAX:+1 407 728 9150
E-MAIL:solarbill @aol.com
CONTACT : W Winters

SOLAQUA INC
PO Box 4976, EL Paso,
TX 79914, USA
TEL:+1 915 726 2893
CONTACT : M Corrmier

SOLAR INTERNATIONAL TECHNOLOGIES INC
PO Box 1619, Orange Park,
Florida 32067, USA
TEL:+1 904 284 1135
FAX:+1 904 284 1135

SOLAR CITY INC
4305 West Alva Street, Tampa,
Floridia 33614, USA
TEL:+1 813 875 5300
FAX:+1 813 877 4862
CONTACT : R W Schabes

SOLAR CONSULTANTS
601 Old Halifax Road,
Louisburg,
NC 27549, USA
TEL:+1 919 831 5304
FAX:+1 919 496 6031
E-MAIL:Wills@mail.schsr.unc.edu
CONTACT : F Stewart

SOLAR ELECTRIC LIGHT COMPANY SELCO
35 Wiscosin Circle, Suite 510,
Chevy Chase, MD 20815, USA
TEL:+1 301 657 1161
FAX:+1 301657 1165
E-MAIL:hqtrs@selco-intl.com
WEB:http://www.selco-intl.com
CONTACT : N Williams

SOLAR ENERGY SYSTEMS
1244 Bell Avenue,
Fort Pierce,
Florida 34982, USA
TEL:+1 561 464 2663
FAX:+1 561 466 7937
E-MAIL:rzrallack@msn.com
CONTACT : B Zrallock

SOLAR HEATED SWIMMING POOLS AND DOMESTIC HOT WATER SYSTEMS
42 Ladd Street,
East Greenwich,
RI 02818, USA
TEL:+1 401 884 6990
FAX:+1 401 885 1500
WEB:http://www.goldlinecontrols.com
CONTACT : D Pickard

SOLAR SOURCE
13620 49th Street North,
Clearwater, Florida 33762, USA
TEL:+1 813 572 4247
FAX:+1 813 572 8793
E-MAIL:solarsource@webtv.net
WEB:http://www.heliosol.com
CONTACT : W D Wallace

SOLAR WATER HEATERS OF HUDSON INC
18845 Sakera Road,
Hudson, Florida 34667, USA
TEL:+1 813 868 3262
FAX:+1 813 869 2332
CONTACT : E Elwinger

SOLARTROPE SUPPLY CORPORATION
739 West Taft Avenue, Orange
California 92865, USA
TEL:+1 714 637 6226
FAX:+1 714 637 1149
E-MAIL:solartrope@aol.com
CONTACT : D Mowlsv

SPRINGHOUSE ENERGY SYSTEMS INC
Room 412, Washington Trust
Building, Washington,
Pensylvania 15301, USA
TEL: +1 724 225 8685
CONTACT : L Olslewski

STIRLING TECHNOLOGY COMPANY-STC
4208B West Clearwater Avenue,
Kennewick, Washington 99336, USA
TEL: +1 509 735 4700
FAX: +1 509 736 3660
CONTACT : M A White

STM POWER INC
275 Metty Drive, Ann Arbor,
Michigan 48103, USA
TEL: +1 734 995 1755
FAX: +1 734 995 0610
WEB:http://www.stmpower.com
CONTACT : S Johansson

SUN KING INC
PO Box 330879,
Kahului, HI 96733-0879, USA
TEL: +1 808 871 9721
FAX: +1 808 877 9088
E-MAIL:sunking@shaka.com
CONTACT : P Spenckr

SUN TRAPPER SOLAR SYSTEMS INC
12118 Radium, San Antonio,
Texas 78216, USA
TEL: +1 210 341 2001
FAX: +1 210 341 2652

SUN WIND AND FIRE
7637 SW 33rd Avenue, Portland,
OR 97219-1860, USA
TEL: +1 503 245 2661
FAX: +1 503 245 0414
CONTACT : B Guderson

U.S.A.

SUNDANCE POWER SYSTEMS INCORPORATED
Route 3, Box 121A, Mars Hill,
North Carolina 28754, USA
TEL: +1 828 689 2080
E-MAIL: earthfaith@aol.com
CONTACT : K J Kalorney

SUNWATER SOLAR
PO Box 1220, Woodruff,
Arizona 85942-1220, USA
TEL: +1 520 524 2855
FAX: +1 520 524 1703
Solar stills for purifying water
CONTACT : H Mc Cracken

SUPERIOR SOLAR SYSTEMS INC
1302 Bennett Drive,
Longwood,
Florida 32750, USA
TEL: +1 407 331 9077
FAX: +1 407 331 0305
E-MAIL:sssolar@aol.com
CONTACT : D Haddsway

TALLAHASSEE ENERGY EQUIPMENT
POB 2437, Tallahassee,
Florida 32316, USA
TEL : +1 904 575 0021
CONTACT : D Marsh

TECHNO-SOLIS INCORPORATED
12929 44th Street N, Clearwater,
Florida 33762, USA
TEL : +1 727 573 2881
FAX : +1 727 573 3746A
CONTACT : S Bourgeois

THE ALTERNATIVE POWER SOURCE
4962 Old Winter
Garden Road
Orlando, Florida, USA
TEL: + 1 407 532 2899
FAX: + 1 407 292 7647
E-MAIL: tapsource@aol.com
CONTACT: Sam Martinez

THE MOST FROM CALIFORNIA
1075 Clle Ciruelo,
Thousand Oaks,
California 91360, USA
TEL: +1 805 496 0560
FAX: +1 805 495 7814
E-MAIL:mfctnx@juno.com
WEB:http://www.solargarden.com

THE SOLAR ENERGY COMPANY
1216 State Street,
Suite 606,
Santa Barbara,
California 93101, USA
TEL:+1 805 962 8898

THE SOLAR UTILITY NETWORK (SUN)
1001 S Ed Carey Drive,
Box#181 Harlingen,
Texas 78552, USA
TEL:+1 956 440 0800
FAX:+1 956 440 0800
E-MAIL:richardson@alnet.net

THERMAL CONVERSION TECHNOLOGY
PO Box 3887, Sarasota
Florida 34230, USA
TEL: +1 941 953 2177
FAX: +1 941 957 0106
CONTACT : G Carrison

TMI
10621 Campbell, Chicago,
Illinois 60655, USA
TEL: +1 773 238 1842
E-MAIL:tmi99@aol.com
CONTACT : Mr J Malloy

UNITED SOLAR ENERGY INC
2850 West State Road 520, Cocoa,
Florida, 32926, USA
TEL: +1 407 631 8898
CONTACT : A Cadorin

WHOLESALE SOLAR SUPPLY INC
2213 Andrea Ln, Fort Myers,
Flordia 33912, USA
TEL: + 1 941 482 5756
FAX: + 1 941 481 9750
E-MAIL: rwilson577@aol.com
CONTACT: R Reed Wilson

ZOMEWORKS CORPORATION
1011A Sawmill Road NW,
PO Box 25085, Albuquerque,
New Mexico 87125, USA
TEL: + 1 505 242 5534
FAX: + 1 505 243 5187
WEB: http://www.zomeworks.com
CONTACT : D Hughes

ZON SOLAR AND SPAS INC
696 South Yonge Street (US #1)
Ormond Beach, Florida 32174, USA
TEL: + 1 904 673 4343
CONTACT : B Ballash

SOLAR PHOTOVOLTAIC

ABRAHAM SOLAR EQUIPMENT
124 Creekside Place, Pagosa
Springs, Colorado 81147, USA
TEL: +1 970 731 4675
FAX: +1 970 731 4675

ADVANCED ENERGY CONSTRUCTION
20505 US Highway 19, Suite 12,
Clearwater, Florda 34624, USA
TEL: + 1 727 441 2808
CONTACT: David Oldack

ADVANCED SOLAR TECHNOLOGIES
6193 Wooded Run Drive,
Columbia, Maryland 21044,
USA
TEL: + 1 410 381 9776
FAX: + 1 410 997 0779
E-MAIL: info@thermomax.com
CONTACT: Dr. Fariborz Mahjouri

ALLSOLAR SERVICE CO INC
PO Box 1263,
Maitland, Florida 32751, USA
TEL: + 1 407 644 4159
FAX: + 1 407 774 4751
E-MAIL: bessettedn@aol.com
WEB: http://www.allsolarservice.com
CONTACT: David E Bessette

ALTERNATIVE ENERGY ENGINEERING INC
1155 Redway Drive, PO Box 339
Redway, California 95560, USA
TEL: + 1 707 923 7216
WEB: http://www.asis.com/aee

ALTERNATE ENVIRONMENT
7017 Helmsdale Road,
West Hills,
California 91307, USA
TEL: + 1 818 348 4436
FAX: + 1 818 598 1692
CONTACT: Oded Vogel

AMERICAN PHOTOVOLTAICS & HOMES LTD
Photovoltaics Solar Water Pumping,
Solar Systems & Energy Savers
Box 1199, Riverdale,
New York 10471, USA
TEL: + 1 718 548 0428
E-MAIL: sunsenergy@aol.com
WEB: http://members.aol.com/
sunsenergy
Contact: Charles A Cerussi

AMERICAN SOLAR ENERGY SOCIETY INC
2400 Central Avenue G-1,
Boulder, Colorado 80301, USA
TEL: + 1 303 443 3130
FAX: + 1 303 443 3212
E-MAIL: ases@igc.apc.org
CONTACT: Larry Sherwood

APPLIED POWER CORPORATION
1210 Homann Drive South East,
Lacey, Washington 98503,
USA
TEL: + 1 360 438 2110
FAX: + 1 360 438 2115
E-MAIL: sales@appliedpower.com
CONTACT : T Jensen

ARIZONA STATE UNVERSITY EAST
Electronics and Computer
Engineering Technology
Photovoltaic Testing Laboratory,
7349 E Unity Ave,
Williams Campus,
Mesa, AZ 85212, USA
TEL: + 1 480 727 1220
FAX: + 1 480 727 1223
E-MAIL : manit@asu.edu
WEB: http://www.asu.edu/east/ptl
CONTACT : G Tamizh Mani

ASE AMERICAS INC
4 Suburban Park Drive,
Billerica,
Massachusetts 01821,
USA
TEL : +1 508 667 5900
FAX : +1 508 663 2868
E-MAIL : pwormser@ase-americas.com
WEB : http://www.asepv.com
CONTACT : M Azzam

ASTROPOWER INC
One Solar Park,
Newark,
Delaware 19716-2000,
USA
TEL : +1 302 366 0400
FAX : +1 302 368 6474
E-MAIL : sales@astrapower.com
WEB : http://www.astropower.com
CONTACT : P Ashenbreme

ATLANTIC SOLAR PRODUCTS
PO Box 70060,
Baltimore, Maryland, USA
TEL : +1 410 686 2500
FAX : +1 410 686 6221
E-MAIL : mail@atlantic.solar.com
WEB : http://atlantic.solar.com
CONTACT : A Eckmanns

ATLANTIS ENERGY INC
North American Operation,
4610 Northgate Blvd,
Suite 150, Sacramento,
CA 95834, USA
TEL : +1 916 920 9500
FAX : +1 916 927 1697
E-MAIL :atlantis@gv.net
WEB: http://www.atlantisenergy.com
CONTACT : J Morrissey

BACKWOODS SOLAR ELECTRIC SYSTEMS
1395 Rolling Thunder Ridge,
Sandpoint, Idaho 83864, USA
TEL : +1 208 263 4290
FAX : +1 208 265 4788
CONTACT : E Fehily

BEKART ECD SOLAR SYSTEMS LLC
(Formerly United Solar Systems Corp)
Corporate and Sales Office,
1100 West Maple Road,
Troy, Michigan 48084, USA
TEL : +1 248 362 4170
FAX : +1 248 362 4442
E-MAIL :unisolarinfo@ovonic.com
WEB : http://www.uni-solar.com
CONTACT : A P Burton

BIG FROG MOUNTAIN CORPORATION
100 Cherokee Boulevard,
Suite 2109, Chattanooga,
Tennessee 37405, USA
TEL : +1 423 265 0307
FAX : +1 423 265 9030
E-MAIL : sales@bigfrogmountain.com
WEB : http://www.bigfrog
mountain.com
CONTACT : J Jripp

BLUE MOUNTAIN ENERGY
70177 Ponderosa Lane, Cove,
Oregon, 97824, USA
TEL : +1 541 568 4473
FAX : +1 541 568 4882
CONTACT : Mr Martin Burger

BP SOLAR INC
2300 North Watney Way,
Fairfield
CA 94533, USA
TEL : +1 707 428 7800
FAX : +1 707 428 7078
E-MAIL : mcdonasv@bp.com
WEB:http://www.bp.com/bpsolarindex.html

BP SOLAR
International Corporate Headquarters,
989 Corporate Boulevard,
Baltimore,
Maryland 21090-2227, USA
TEL: +1 410 981 0240
FAX: +1 410 981 0278
WEB: http://www.bpsolar.com

BRADLEY BUILDERS AND DEVELOPERS INCORPORATED
PO Box 214, Temple,
Pennsylvana 19560, USA
TEL : +1 215 464 4780
FAX : +1 215 464 4780
CONTACT : D Bradley

CAPITAL SUN GROUP LTD
6503 81st Street,
Cabin John
Maryland 20818, USA
TEL : +1 301 229 0671
FAX : +1 202 229 0434
CONTACT : C L Ports

CONNECTIV / DELMARVA POWER
800 King Street, PO Box 231,
Wilmington,
Delaware 19899, USA
TEL : + 1 302 429 3055
FAX : + 1 302 429 3801
E-MAIL : ferguson@delmarva.com
CONTACT : William D Ferguson

CURRIN CORPORATION
PO Box 2006,
Midland,
Michigan 48641, USA
TEL : +1 517 835 7387
FAX : +1 517 835 7395
E-MAIL : currcorp@tm.net
CONTACT : C G Currin

DELIVERED SOLUTIONS
PO Box 891240,
Temecula,
California 92589, USA
TEL: + 1 909 698 1700
FAX: + 1 909 698 5758
E-MAIL: sales@deliveredsolutions.com
WEB: http://www.delivered
solutions.com

DIGITAL SOLAR TECHNOLOGIES
5775 Arapahoe Avenue,
Boulder
Colorado 80303, USA
TEL: + 1 303 442 6553
FAX: + 1 303 442 6555
WEB: http://www.digitalsolar.com

DIRECT GLOBAL POWER INC
1482 Erie Boulevard,
Schenectady,
New York 12301, USA
TEL: + 1 518 395 2696
FAX: + 1 518 395 2607
E-MAIL: rlewand@worldnet.att.net

DONALD ROBERT SMITH CONSULTING
468 49th Street,
Oakland,
California 94609, USA
TEL: + 1 510 658 3461
FAX: + 1 510 658 3461
E-MAIL: dr_smith@ix.netcom.com
CONTACT: Don Smith

SOLAR RESEARCH INTERNATIONAL
850 W Morgan Street,
Raleigh,
NC 27603-1614, USA
TEL: + 1 919 832 3404
FAX: + 1 919 832 3339
E-MAIL: johnmyles@srisolar.com
CONTACT : Mr. John Myles

SOLAR RESEARCH INTERNATIONAL
400 S Tryon Street,
PO Box 1004,
Charlotte,
North Carolina 28201, USA
E-MAIL: johnmyles@srisolar.com
WEB: http://www.dukesolar.com
CONTACT: Mr John Myles III

EBARA SOLAR INC
13 Airport Road, Belle Vernon,
Pennsylvania 15012, USA
TEL: +1 724 379 2001
FAX: +1 724 379 4028
CONTACT: Richard Rosey

ECLECTIC ELECTRIC
PO Box 310, Sandia Park,
New Mexico 87047-0310, USA
TEL: + 1 505 281 9538
CONTACT: Robert Thacter

ECO MALL
PO Box 20553 Cherokee Station
New York 10021,
USA
TEL: + 1 212 535 1876
FAX: + 1 212 535 4394
WEB: http://www.ecomail.com

ELECTRISOL LTD
1215 East Harmont Drive,
Phoenix Arizona 85020, USA
TEL : +1 602 997 6855
FAX : +1 602 943 5842

ELECTRO SOLAR PRODUCTS INC
502 Ives Place, Pensacola,
Florida, 32514, USA
TEL : +1 850 479 2191
FAX : +1 850 857 0070
E-MAIL :espsolar@pcola.gulf.net
WEB : http://members.xoom.com/espsolar
CONTACT : A E Mckinney

ENERGY CONVERSION DEVICES INC
Manufacturing Technology,
1675, West Maple Road, Troy,
Michigan 48084, USA
TEL: +1 313 280 1900
FAX: +1 313 280 1456
E-MAIL: ovonic@aol.com
WEB: http://www.ovonic.com

ENERGY PHOTOVOLTAICS INC EPV
PO BOX 7456, Princeton,
NJ 08543, USA
TEL : + 1 609 587 3000
FAX : + 1 609 587 5355
E-MAIL : info@epv.net
WEB: http://www.epv.net

ENERGY SERVICE COMPANY
399 E 10th Avenue, Eugene,
Oregon 97401 USA
TEL : + 1 541 302 6808
FAX : + 1 541 302 6810
E-MAIL : info@escosolar.com
WEB: http://www.escosolar.com
CONTACT : J Scott

ENHANCEMENT ELECTRONICS INC
10 Camino del Senador,
Tijeras, New Mexico
87059 - 7420, USA
TEL : +1 505 281 0399
FAX : +1 505 281 4248
E-MAIL: tmleonard@aol.com
WEB: http://members.aol.com/eeiboards
CONTACT : J M Leonard

ENTECH INC
1077, Chisolm Trail, Keller,
Texas 76248, USA
TEL : +1 817 379 0100
FAX: + 1 817 379 0300
E-MAIL : marketing@entechsolar.com
WEB: http://www.entechsolar.com
CONTACT : W Hessle

ETA ENGINEERING INC
2010 E University, Drive # 11,
Tempe, Arizona 85281, USA
TEL: +1 480 966 1380
FAX: +1 480 966 1516
E-MAIL: sales@etaengineering.com
WEB: http://www.etaengineering.com
CONTACT : J Armshan

ETM SOLAR WORKS INC
PO Box 67, Endicott,
New York 13761, USA
TEL: +1 607 785 6499
FAX: +1 607 785 6499
E-MAIL: etm@tier.net
WEB: http://www.tier.net/etm
CONTACT : Dr G S Canough

EVERGREEN SOLAR INC
259 Cedar Hill St,
Marlboro,
Massachusetts 01752, USA
TEL: +1 508 357 2221
FAX: +1 508 357 2279
E-MAIL: sales@evergreensolar.com
WEB: http://www.evergreensolar.com
CONTACT: Rex D'Agostino

FIRST SOLAR LLC
28101 Cedar Park
Boulevard,
Perrysburg, Ohio 43551, USA
TEL: + 1 419 662 8500
FAX: + 1 419 662 8525
E-MAIL:rbaumgartner@firstsolar.com
WEB: http://www.firstsolar.com
CONTACT : Mr V Banmgarther

GEN-SUN ELECTRICSOLAR SYSTEMS
32112 Highway 18, Lucerne Valley,
CA 92356 USA
TEL : + 1 760 248 2689
FAX : + 1 760 248 2424
E-MAIL : solars@gensun.com
WEB : http://www.gensun.com
CONTACT : T Jenzen

GLOBAL RESOURCE OPTIONS LLP
4 Kibling Hill Road, PO Box 51,
Strafford, VT 05072, USA
TEL : + 1 800 374 4494
FAX : + 1 802 765 9983
E-MAIL : global@sover.net
WEB: http://www.globalresourceoptions.com
CONTACT : J Wolfe

GLOBAL SOLAR ENERGY
B130 Shaffer Parkway, Littleton,
Colorado 80127-4207, USA
TEL : + 1 303 420 1141
FAX : + 1 303 420 1551
E-MAIL : info@globalsolar.com
WEB: http://www.globalsolar.com
CONTACT : S Ksminky

GREAT NORTHERN SOLAR
Route I, Box 71, Port Wing,
Wisconsin 54865, USA
TEL :+1 715 774 3374
E-MAIL : gosolar@win.bright.net

GT SOLAR TECHNOLOGIES INC
472 Amherst Street,
Nashua,
New Hamshire 03063, USA
TEL : + 1 603 883 5200
FAX : + 1 603 595 6993
E-MAIL : matthei@gtsolar.com
WEB : http://www.gtsolar.com
CONTACT : K Maner

HARRIMANS INCORPORATED
109-A, James Street, Venice,
Florida 34292, USA
TEL : +1 813 488 4453
FAX : + 1 813 366 6680
CONTACT : J Harrimon

HEALEY & ASSOCIATES
120 Venetian Way, Suite#16,
Merritt Island,
Florida 32953, USA
TEL: +1 407 452 2173
FAX: +1 407 459 3682
E-MAIL: healey@flaenergy.com
WEB: http://www.flaenergy.com
CONTACT : H Hesley

HELIOKINETICS CORPORATION
PO Box 040, Agoura Hills,
California 91376-1040, USA
TEL: + 1 818 991 5235
FAX: + 1 818 919 5235

HELIOS INTERNATIONAL INC
Eco Corp,21315 Lighthill Drive
Topanga CA 90290, USA
TEL: +1 818 884 8782
FAX: +1 818 884 7668
E-MAIL: jgingersoll@ecocorp.com
WEB: http://www.ecocorp.com
CONTACT : Dr J G Ingersoll

HELIOTROPE GENERAL
3733 Kenora Drive, Spring Valley,
California 91977, USA
TEL: +1 619 460 3930
FAX: +1 619 460 9211
E-MAIL: heliotrope@hgl.com
WEB: http://www.hgl.com
CONTACT : S Danson

INDEPENDENT POWER SYSTEMSINC
1320 Freeport # 101, Sparks,
Nevada 89431, USA
TEL: +1 775 331 0228
FAX: +1 775 331 8474
E-MAIL: ipssolar@aol.com
CONTACT : J Pizar

INTEGRATED SOLAR LTD
1331 Conant Street, Suite 107
Maumee, Ohio 43537, USA
TEL: +1 419 893 8565
FAX: +1 419 893 0006
E-MAIL: isolar@juno.com
CONTACT : J Witte

INTERNATIONAL SOLAR ELECTRIC TECHNOLOGY INC-ISET
8635 Aviation Boulevard,Inglewood,
California 90301, USA
TEL: +1 310 216 1423
FAX: +1 310 216 2908

IOWA THIN FILM TECHNOLOGIES INC
2337 230th Street, Boone,
Iowa 50036, USA
TEL: + 1 515 292 7606
FAX : + 1 515 292 1922
CONTACT : Dr L Brookes

JVP ELECTRO SOLAR PRODUCTS
Manufacturing, 502 Ives Place
Pensacola, Florida 32514, USA
TEL: + 1 850 479 2191
FAX: + 1 850 857 0070
E-MAIL: espsolar@pcola.gulf.net
WEB: http://members.zoom.com/espsolar
CONTACT : A E Mckinney

JX CRYSTALS INC
1105 12th Avenue NW, Suite A2
Issaquah, WA 98027-8994, USA
TEL: + 1 425 392 5237
FAX: + 1 425 392 7303
E-MAIL: sales@jxcrystals.com
WEB: http://www.jxcrystals.com
CONTACT : J B Keyes

KELELO ENGINEERING
3404 Angela St, Cocoa,
Florida 32926, USA
TEL: + 1 321 632 7964
FAX: + 1 321 638 1010
E-MAIL: Thornbloom@fsec.ucf.edu
CONTACT : Mr M D Thornbloom

KYOCERA SOLAR INC
7812 East Acoma Drive, Scottsdale,
Arizona 85260, USA
TEL: +1 480 948 8003
FAX: +1 480 483 6431
E-MAIL: info@kyocerasolar.com
WEB: http://www.kyocerasolar.com

KYOCERA SOLAR INC
Latin America/ Caribbean Sales,
4331 Pine Island Road,
Matlacha, Florida 33993, USA
TEL : +1 941 283 0060
FAX : +1 941 283 4788
E-MAIL: smccarney@kyocerasolar.com
Web : http://www.kyocera.com
Contact : S McCarney

LIGHT CORPORATION
14800 172nd Avenue,
Grand Haven, MI 49417, USA
TEL: +1 616 842 5100
FAX: +1 616 846 2144
WEB: http://www.lightcorp.com

LIGHT ENERGY SYSTEMS
965 D Detroit Avenue, Concord,
CA 94518, USA
TEL: +1 925 681 4343
FAX: +1 925 680 6588
E-MAIL: solar@lighenergysystems.com
WEB: http://www.lighten
ergtsystems.com
CONTACT : B Onesl

LIGHTPATH TECHNOLOGIES INC
6820 Academy Parkway E NE,
Albuquerque,
New Mezico 87109, USA
TEL: +1 505 342 1100
FAX: +1 505 342 1111
E-MAIL: pdempewolf@light.net
CONTACT : P Dempewolf

LIVE OAK SOLAR
232 Anacapa Street, Suite I-B,
Santa Barbara, California 93101, USA
TEL: +1 805 966 9034
FAX: +1 805 730 7357
E-MAIL : info@liveoaksolar.com
WEB : http://www.liveoaksolar.com
CONTACT : S Glidden

MECS SOLAR SYSTEMS
11707 Fairford Avenue, Norwalk,
California 90650, USA
TEL: +1 562 864 5299
FAX: +1 562 868 4250
E-MAIL: j.deboer@worldnet.att.net
CONTACT : J D Boer

MORNINGSTAR CORPORATION
1098 Washington Crossing Road
Washington Crossing, PA 18977, USA
TEL: + 1 215 321 4457
FAX: +1 215 321 4458
E-MAIL:info@morningstarcorp.com
WEB:http://www.morningstarcorp.com
CONTACT : L Gordon

MOTION DYNAMICS GROUP INC
Aerospace Tech, Box 97,
Freeland, PA, 18224, USA
TEL: +1 717 443 7892
FAX: +1 717 443 7892
E-MAIL:hanging@ptd.net
CONTACT : S Schwiks

MR SUN SOLAR
0326 SW Pendleton Street,
Portland, Oregon 97201, USA
TEL:+1 503 222 2468
FAX: +1 503 245 4387
EMAIL: 70663.2146@compuserve.com
CONTACT : J Patterson

MVSYSTEMS INC
17301 W Colfax, Avenue, Suite 305
Golden, Colorado 80401, USA
TEL: +1 305 271 9907
FAX: +1 303 271 9771
E-MAIL:MVSystems@mho.net
CONTACT : Dr A Msdon

NEKOLUX
1433 W Chicago Ave,
Chicago, IL 60622, USA
TEL: +1 312 738 3776
FAX: +1 312 738 3776
E-MAIL: vladimir@nekolux.com
WEB: http://www.nekolux.com
CONTACT : V Nekold

NORTH CANYON SOLAR
23643 North 40th Avenue,
Glendale, Arizona 85310, USA
TEL: + 1 623 582 2708
FAX: + 1 623 582 6667
E-MAIL: northcanyon@uswest.net
WEB: http://www.solardish.com
CONTACT : J Gilchrist

NOVA ELECTRIC
100 School Street, Bergenfield,
New Jersey 07621, USA
TEL: + 1 201 385 0500 x 128
FAX: + 1 201 385 0702
E-MAIL: novasales@theallpower.com
WEB: http://wwwnovaelectric.com
CONTACT: Howard Schrier

OASIS MONTANA INC
436 Red Fox Lane,
Stevensville, MT 59870, USA
TEL: + 1 406 777 4321
FAX: + 1 406 777 2632
E-MAIL: info@oasismontana.com
CONTACT : C Doum

OCCIDENTAL POWER
3629 Taraval Street,
San Francisco,
California 94116, USA
TEL: + 1 415 681 8861
FAX: + 1 415 681 9911
E-MAIL: solar@oxypower.com
WEB: http://www.oxypower.com
WEB: http://www.oasismontana.com
CONTACT: Greg Kennedy

OFFLINE INDEPENDENT ENERGY SYSTEMS
Po Box 231, North Fork,
California 93643, USA
TEL: + 1 559 887 7080
FAX: + 1 559 887 2980
E-MAIL: ofln@aol.com
WEB: http://www.psnw.com/`ofln
CONTACT: Cynthia Loweburg

PACIFIC SOLAR COMPANY
1725 E Bayshore Road # 103
Redwood City,
California 95063, USA
TEL: + 1 650 556 9450
FAX: + 1 650 556 9451
E-MAIL: mwalpert@pacificsolar.com
WEB: http://www.pacificsolar.com
CONTACT: Marianne Walpert

PARADISE POWER COMPANY
Box 7484, Taos,
NM 87571, USA
TEL: + 1 505 737 5896
FAX: + 1 505 737 5896
E-MAIL: paradise@taosnet.com
WEB: http://www.paradisepower.net
CONTACT: Daniel Weinman

PHASOR ENERGY COMPANY INC
4202 East Evans Drive,
Phoenix,
Arizona 85032-5469, USA
TEL: +1 480 556 6902
FAX: +1 602 404 1765
E-MAIL:tlepley@aol.com
WEB:http://www.phasorenergy.com
CONTACT : J Lepley

PHOTOVOLTAIC RESOURCES INTERNATIONAL
PVCAD Division,
1440 West Meseto Avenue,
Mesa, Arizona 85202,
TEL: +1 480 345 1686
FAX : +1 480 345 6698
E-MAIL:pvcad@primenet.com
CONTACT : W J Kaszets

PISTACCHIO PUMP COMPANY
PO Box 459, Sanger,
California 93657, USA
TEL : + 1 559 875 4528
FAX : + 1 559 875 2688
CONTACT : Larry Pistacchio

POWERLIGHT CORPORATION
2954 San Pablo Avenue,
Berkeley,
California 94710, USA
TEL: +1 510 540 0550
FAX: +1 510 540 0552
E-MAIL: shugar@powerlight.com
WEB: http://www.powerlight.com
CONTACT : D Shugar

POWERWORKS INC
5356 North Cattail,
Way Bolse, Idaho 83703, USA
TEL: +1 208 853 4602
FAX: +1 208 853 4628
E-MAIL: rskoebbe@powerworksinc.com
Contact: Rick S Koebbe

PULSE ENERGY SYSTEMS INC
PO Box 1783,
Nevada City,
NV 95959, USA
TEL: + 1 530 265 9771
FAX: + 1 530 265 9756
E-MAIL: info@pulseenergy.com
WEB: http://www.pulseenergy.com

PV CELLS & MATERIALS
Corporate International Operations,
2841 Marietta Circle,
Thousand Oaks,
California 91360, USA
TEL: + 1 805 493 4532
FAX: + 1 805 493 5969
E-MAIL: ygal@pvcell.com
WEB: http://www.pvcell.com
CONTACT : Mr Y Giramberk

REAL GOODS TRADING CORP
200 Clara Street,
Ukiah, CA 95482, USA
TEL: + 1 707 468 9292
FAX: + 1 707 468 9394
E-MAIL: realgood@realgood.com
CONTACT : J Odham

REMOTE POWER INTERNATIONAL
18 Whedbee Street,
Fort Collins,
Colorado 80524, USA
TEL : +1 970 498 8947

RENEWABLE ENERGY SERVICES INC
PO Box 278,
Paauilo,
Hawaii 96776, USA
TEL : +1 808 775 0852
FAX : +1 808 7775 0852

SANDIA NATIONAL LABORATORIES
Department 6201, PO Box 5800
Albuquerque,
New Mexico 87185, USA
TEL : +1 505 844 5159
FAX : +1 505 845 9500
CONTACT : Paul Klimas

SANDIA NATIONAL LABORATORIES
PV System Assistance Center,
PO Box 5800, MS-0752,
Albuquerque, New Mexico 87185, USA
TEL: + 1 505 844 0558
FAX: + 1 505 844 6541
E-MAIL: pvdac@sandia.gov
WEB: http://www.sandia.gov/pv

SCHOTT APPLIED POWER CORPORATION
PO Box 339, Redway,
CA 95560, USA
TEL: +17079232277
FAX: +17079233039
E-MAIL:
david.rippner@us.schott.com

SCHOTT APPLIER POWER
4051 Alvis Ct #1, Rocklin,
CA 95677, USA
TEL: +13604382110
FAX: +13604382115
E-MAIL: sales@appliedpower.com
WEB: http://www.appliedpower.com
CONTACT: Jennifer Sponseller

SEADS SOLAR
PO Box 192, Harrington,
Maine 04643, USA
TEL: + 1 207 483 9763
E-MAIL: seadssolar@hotmail.com
WEB: http://seads@nemaine.com/
seads
CONTACT : C Ewing

SEPCO-SOLAR ELECTRIC POWER COMPANY LTD
7984 SW Jack James Drive,
Stuart, Florida 34997, USA
TEL: + 1 561 220 6615
FAX: + 1 561 220 8616
E-MAIL: sepco@tcol.net
WEB: http://sepco-solarlighting.com
CONTACT : S Robbins

SIEMENS SOLAR INDUSTRIES
4650 Adohr Lane, Camarillo
California 93012-6032, USA
TEL: + 1 805 388 6289
FAX: + 1 805 388 6395
E-MAIL: sunpower@solarpv.com
WEB: http://www.solarpv.com
CONTACT : A Rodin

SIEMENS SOLAR INDUSTRIES
Sales and Marketing, 6909 SW 18th
Street, Suite 301-B, Boca Raton,
Florida 33433, USA
TEL: +1 561 416 7205
FAX: +1 561 362 5513
WEB: http://www.siemenssolar.com
CONTACT : Mr P Dr Napoli

SIERRA SOLAR SYSTEMS
109 Argall Way, Nevada City
California 95959, USA
TEL: +1 530 265 8441
FAX: +1 530 265 6151
E-MAIL: solarjon@sierrasolar.com
WEB: http://www.sierrasolar.com
CONTACT : J Will

SKS INC
8 Sherman Avenue, Takoma Park
Maryland 20912, USA
TEL: +1 301 270 8959
FAX: +1 301 565 2228
CONTACT : A Nunez

SOLAMERICA CORPORATION
1046 Harper Boulevard SW,
Palm Bay, Florida 32908, USA
TEL:+1 407 723 2725
FAX:+1 407 728 9150
E-MAIL:solarbill @aol.com
CONTACT : W Winters

SOLAR INTERNATIONAL TECHNOLOGIES INC
PO Box 1619, Orange Park,
Florida 32067, USA
TEL:+1 904 284 1135
FAX:+1 904 284 1135

SOLAR DEPOT INC
61 Paul Drive, San Rafael,
California 94903, USA
TEL:+1 415 499 1333
FAX:+1 415 499 0316
E-MAIL:stafi@solardepot.com
WEB: http://www.solardepot.com
CONTACT : K Mizany

SOLAR ELECTRIC LIGHT FUND
1775 K Street NW,
Suite 595, Washington,
District of Columbia 20006, USA
TEL:+1 202 234 7265
FAX:+1 202 328 9512
E-MAIL:solarlight@self.org
WEB: http://www.self.org
CONTACT : R A Freling

SOLAR ELECTRIC LIGHT COMPANY SELCO
35 Wiscosin Circle, Suite 510,
Chevy Chase, MD 20815, USA
TEL:+1 301 657 1161
FAX:+1 301657 1165
E-MAIL:hqtrs@selco-intl.com
WEB:http://www.selco-intl.com
CONTACT : N Williams

SOLAR ELECTRIC SYSTEMS OF KANSAS CITY INC
13700 W, 108th Street Lenexa,
Kansas 66215, USA
TEL:+1 913 338 1939
FAX:+1 913 469 5522
E-MAIL : solarbeacon@email.msn.com
CONTACT : B Roush

SOLAR ELECTRIC INC
5555 Santa Fe Street
#D, San Diego,
California, 92109-1602, USA
TEL:+1 619 581 0051
FAX:+1 619 581 6440
E-MAIL:solar@cts.com
WEB:http://www.solarelectricinc.com

SOLAR ENERGY SYSTEMS
1244 Bell Avenue, Fort Pierce,
Florida 34982, USA
TEL:+1 561 464 2663
FAX:+1 561 466 7937
E-MAIL:rzrallack@msn.com
CONTACT : Bzrauask

SOLAR ENGINEERING AND CONTRACTING
P O Box 690, Lawai,
Hawaii 96765, USA
TEL:+1 808 322 8890
FAX:+1 808 322 8629
E-MAIL:solarenc@has-kaugi.net
CONTACT : P Lucos

SOLAR OUTDOORLIGHTING
3131 SE Waaler Street, Stuart,
Floorida 34997, USA
TEL:+1 561 286 9461
FAX:+1 561 286 9616
E-MAIL:lightsolar@aol.com
WEB: http://www.solarlighting.com

SOLAR VILLAGE INSTITUTE INC
5840 Jewell Road, Graham,
North Carolina 27253, USA
TEL:+1 910 376 9530

SOLAR WATER TECHNOLOGIES INC
426-B Elm Avenue, Portsmouth,
VA 23704, USA
TEL:+1 757 398 0098
FAX:+1 603 925 1964
E-MAIL:swt@solarwater.com
WEB:http://www.solarwater.com

SOLARJACK
325 East Main Street,
Safford, Arizona 85546, USA
TEL:+1 602 428 1092
FAX:+1 602 428 1291
CONTACT : J Allen

SOLAR TEK INTERNATIONAL
508 Wilmington Island Road,
Savannah, Georgia 31410, USA
TEL:+1 954 209 2606
E-MAIL:solartek@ruonline.net
WEB:http://www.solartek.com

SOLARTROPE SUPPLY CORPORATION
730 West Taft Avenue, Orange
California 92865, USA
TEL:+1 714 637 6226
FAX:+1 714 637 1149
E-MAIL:solartrope@aol.com
CONTACT : D Mowlvi

SOLEC INTERNATIONAL INC
970 East 236th Street Carson,
CA 90745, USA
TEL:+1 310 834 5800
FAX:+1 310 834 0728
CONTACT : J Shahryar

SOLUTIONS IN SOLAR ELECTICITY
PO Box 5089, Culver City,
CA 90231, USA
TEL: +1 310 202 7882
FAX: +1 310 202 1399
CONTACT : J Davidson

SOUND POWER INC
801 27th Avenue, Seattle,
Washington 98122, USA
TEL; +1 206 324 7340
E-MAIL: dtrione@netscape.net
CONTACT : Mr D Jrione

SOUTHWEST PHOTOVOLTAIC (PV) SYSTEMS INC
212 East Main Street, Tomball,
Texas 77375, USA
TEL: +1 281 351 0031
FAX: +1 281 351 8356
E-MAIL: southwestpv.com
CONTACT : M Bcslock

SPECTROLAB INC
12500 Gladstone Avenue,
Sylmar, California, 91342, USA
TEL: +1 818 365 4611
FAX: +1 818 361 5102

SPIRE CORPORATION
One Patriots Park, Bedford,
Massachusetts 01730-2396, USA
TEL: +1 781 275 6000
FAX: +1 781 275 7470
E-MAIL: pvsales@spirecorp.com
WEB: http://www.spirecorp.com
CONTACT : Mr D Mellecker

SPRINGHOUSE ENERGY SYSTEMS INC
Room 412, Washington Trust
Building, Washington,
Pensylvania 15301, USA
TEL: +1 724 225 8685
CONTACT : D Olszewski

STEEL HEDDLE
Flat Wire Products Division,
692 Plant Road,
Post Office Box 610, Westminster,
SC 29693, USA
TEL: +1 864 647 6087
FAX: +1 864 647 1549
E-MAIL:bud.frick@steelheddle.com
WEB:http://steelheddle.com

SUNDANCE SOLAR DESIGNS
PO Box 321, Placervaille,
Colorado 81430, USA
TEL: +1 970 252 1978
FAX: +1 970 252 1978
E-MAIL:solar@rmi.net
WEB:http://www.powerpod.com
CONTACT : K T Kilerney

SUN ELECTRIC
PO Box 92221, Austin,
Texas 78709, USA
TEL: +1 512 288-4813
FAX: +1 512 301 8573
CONTACT : D Petri

SUN FROST
PO Box 1101, 824 T Ste #7, Arcata,
California 95518, USA
TEL: +1 707 822 9095
FAX: +1 707 822 6213
E-MAIL:info@sunfrost.com
CONTACT : L Schlusslez

SUN WIND AND FIRE
7637 SW 33rd Avenue, Portland,
OR 97219-1860, USA
TEL: +1 503 245 2661
FAX: +1 503 245 0414
CONTACT : B Gunderson

SUNDANCE POWER SYSTEMS INCORPORATED
Route 3, Box 121A, Mars Hill,
North Carolina 28754, USA
TEL: +1 828 689 2080
E-MAIL: earthfaith@aol.com

SUNELCO
PO Box 787, Hamilton, MT 59840, USA
TEL: +1 406 363 6924
FAX: +1 406 363 6046
E-MAIL:info@sunelco.com
WEB:http://www.sunelco.com
CONTACT : K T Kalarney

SUNLIGHT POWER INTERNATIONAL
1800 M Street NW, Suite 300,
Washington, DC 20036-5802, USA
TEL: +1 202 293 6238
FAX: +1 202 223 5537
E-MAIL:sunlight@ttcorp.com
WEB:http://www.hcorp.com/sunlight
CONTACT : W Rodenhiser

SUNNYSIDE SOLAR INC
1014 Green River Road, Guilford,
Vermont 05301-8117, USA
TEL: +1 802 257 1482
FAX: +1 802 254 4670
E-MAIL : sunnysde@sover.net
WEB: http://www.sunny
sidesolar.com
CONTACT : R Gottlieb

SUNPOWER CORPORATION
435 Indio Way, Sunnyvale,
California 94086, USA
TEL: +1 408 991 0908
FAX: +1 408 739 7713
E-MAIL:rswanson@sunpowercorp.com
CONTACT : R Swanson

SUNWIZE TECHNOLOGIES INC
I Sun Street, Stelle,
Illinois 60919, USA
TEL: +1 815 256 2222
FAX: +1 815 256 2221
E-MAIL: mwwpv@stelle.net
WEB: http://www.sunwize.com
Unsurpassed expertise in system integration and custom module manufacturing
CONTACT : M W Wilkerson

SUNWIZE TECHNOLOGIES INC
1155 Flatbush Road, Kingston,
New York 12401, USA
TEL: +1 845 336 0146
FAX: +1 845 336 0457
E-Mail: sunwize@besicorp.com
WEB: http://www.sunwize.com
Designs, manufacturers integrated photovoltaic power systems and custom-engineered solar modules
CONTACT : B Gould

SUPERIOR SOLAR SYSTEMS INC
1302 Bennett Drive, Longwood,
Florida 32750, USA
TEL: +1 407 331 9077
FAX: +1 407 331 0305
E-MAIL:sssolar@aol.com
International manufacturing, sales, service and installation of renewable energy products
CONTACT : D Haddsway

SUSTAINABLE ENERGY SYSTEMS INC
7 Hilltop Road, Troy,
New York 12180, USA
TEL: +1 518 272 7863
FAX: +1 518 270 5204
E-MAIL:bortond@rpi.edu
CONTACT : D Barton

TALLAHASSEE ENERGY EQUIPMENT
POB 2437, Tallahassee,
Florida 32316, USA
TEL : +1 904 575 0021
CONTACT : D Marsh

TECSTAR INC
15251 Don Julian Road, City of
Industry, California 91749-1002, USA
TEL: +1 626 968 3000
FAX: +1 626 961 1897
E-MAIL: busmqmt@appliedsolar.com
WEB: http://www.appliedsolar.com

TEMPO PLASTIC CO INC
1227 North Miller Park Court,
Visalia, CA 93291, USA
TEL: +15596517711
WEB: http://www.tempo-foam.com
CONTACT: Doug Rogers

TEXAS SOLAR POWER COMPANY
1703 West Koenig Lane, Austin,
Texas 78756, USA
TEL: +1 512 459 9494
FAX: +1 512 451 5934
E-MAIL: solar@onramp.net
WEB http://
www.txsolarpowercompanycom
CONTACT : C Overmiller

THE ALTERNATIVE POWER SOURCE
4962 Old Winter Garden Road
Orlando, Florida, USA
TEL: + 1 407 532 2899
FAX: + 1 407 292 7647
E-MAIL: tapsource@aol.com
CONTACT: Sam Martinez

THE SOLAR CONNECTION
PO Box 1138, Morro Bay
California 93443, USA
TEL:+1 805 772 8601
FAX:+1 805 772 8722
E-MAIL:solar.connection@thegrid.net

THE SOLAR ENERGY COMPANY
1216 State Street, Suite 606,
Santa Barbara,
California 93101, USA
TEL:+1 805 962 8898

THE SOLAR UTILITY NETWORK (SUN)
1001 S Ed Carey Drive,
Box#181 Harlingen,
Texas 78552, USA
TEL:+1 956 440 0800
FAX:+1 956 440 0800
E-MAIL:richardson@alnet.net

THOMAS SOLAR WORKS
106 South Water Street,
Wilmington,
Illinois 60481, USA
TEL: +1 815 476 9208
FAX: +1 815 476 2689
E-MAIL:solarworks@surfree.com
CONTACT : D Thomas

TMI
10621 Campbell, Chicago,
Illinois 60655, USA
TEL: +1 773 238 1842
E-MAIL:tmi99@aol.com
CONTACT : J Malloy

TRACE ENGINEERING
5916 195th Northeast, Arlington, Washington 98223, USA
TEL: +1 360 435 8826
FAX: +1 360 435 2229
E-MAIL:tracesales@seanet.com
WEB:http://www.traceengineering.com
CONTACT : S Vandershoof

UNIRAC INC
2300 Buena Vista SE, Suite 134
Albuquerque, NM 87106, USA
TEL: +1 505 242 6411
FAX: +1 505 254 6412
E-MAIL: info@unirac.com
WEB: http://www.unirac.com
CONTACT : H Newnsn

UNISUN
587-F North Ventu Park Road, PMB #124, Newbury Park, Callifornia 91320, USA
TEL: +1 805 987 7258
FAX: +1 805 987 7268
E-MAIL: unisun@aol.com
WEB:http://members.aol.com.unisun
CONTACT : Dr C Eperspacher

UTILITY POWER GROUP
21250 Califa Street Suite 111, Woodland Hills, California 91367-5029, USA
TEL: +1 818 700 1995
FAX: +1 818 700 2518
E-MAIL: upgpv@aol.com
CONTACT : G Duran

WHOLE BUILDERS COOPERATIVE
2928 Fifth Avenue, South Minneapolis, Minnesota 55408-2412, USA
TEL: + 1 612 824 6567
FAX: + 1 612 824 9387

YUCO ELECTRICAL
PO Box 210281, San Francisco, California 94121-0281, USA
TEL: + 1 925 932 3793
FAX: + 1 925 932 3793
E-MAIL: yucol@earthlink.net
CONTACT : V Yusupov

ZOMEWORKS CORPORATION
1011A Sawmill Road NW, PO Box 25085, Albuquerque, New Mexico 87125, USA
TEL: + 1 505 242 5534
FAX: + 1 505 243 5187
WEB: http://www.zomeworks.com
CONTACT : D Hughes

WIND

AERMOTOR WINDMILL CORPORATION
PO Box 5110, 4277 Dan Hanks Lane, San Angelo,Texas 76902, USA
TEL: + 1 915 651 4951
FAX: + 1 915 651 4948
CONTACT: Mike Hardegree

AIRFOILS IN CORPORATED
122 Rose Drive, Port Matilda, Pennsylvania 16870-9483, USA
TEL: + 1 814 357 0500
FAX: + 1 814 357 0357
E-MAIL: dan@airfoils.com
CONTACT : D M Somers

ALLIANCE INTERNATIONAL
143 Oakhurst Road, Cape Elizabeth ME 04107, USA
TEL: + 1 207 767 3800
FAX: + 1 207 767 3800
CONTACT: HT Hawkes

AMERICAN WIND ENERGY ASSOCIATION - AWEA
122 C Street NW, Fourth Floor, Washington, District of Colombia 20001, USA
TEL: + 1 202 383 2500
FAX: + 1 202 383 2505
E-MAIL: windmail@awea.org
WEB: http://www.igc.apc.org/awea
CONTACT: Randall Swisher

ANCONA INTERNATIONAL
6557 Wolftree Lane, Annandale, VA 22003, USA
TEL: + 1 703 256 0299
FAX: + 1 703 256 7929
E-MAIL: ancona @prodigy.net
CONTACT: Daniel Ancona

ARIZONA STATE UNIVERSITY ASU
Photovoltaic Testing Laboratory, 7349 East Unity Avenue, Mesa, Arizona 85212, USA
TEL : +1 480 727 1220
E-MAIL : ptl@asu.edu
WEB : http:///www.asu.edu/east/ptl
CONTACT : Dr Mani

ATLANTIC ORIENT CORPORATION
Farrell Farm Road, Route 5N,PO Box 1097-D, Norwich Vermont 05055, USA
TEL : +1 802 649 5446
FAX : +1 802 649 5404
E-MAIL :aoc@vermontel.com
WEB : http://www.aocwind.com
CONTACT : R W Sherwin

ATLANTICA INTERNATIONAL GROUP INC
1690 Edgemere Drive, Rochester, NY 14612, USA
TEL : +17 16 766 4832
FAX : +17 16 368 9883
E-MAIL :atlantica_ig@hotmail.com
CONTACT : J Buberis

AWS SCIENTIFIC INC
251 Fuller Road, Albany, New York 12203-3640, USA
TEL : +1 518 437 8660
FAX : +1 518 437 8659
E-MAIL :awwssci@mindspring.com
WEB : http://www.awsscientific.com
CONTACT : B Bsiley

BAYWINDS
1533 Kimball Street, Green Bay, WI 54302, USA
TEL: + 1 920 468 5500
FAX: + 1 414 468 5500
E-MAIL: sales@baywinds.com
CONTACT: Douglas Johnson

BERGEY WINDPOWER COMPANY INC
2001 Priestley Avenue, Norman, Oklahoma 73069, USA
TEL : +1 405 364 4212
FAX : +1 405 364 2078
E-MAIL : sales@bergey.com
WEB : http://www.bergey.com
CONTACT : L Sever

BERTOIA STUDIO LIMITED
644, Main Street, Bally, PENNSYLIVANIA 19503, USA
TEL : +1 610 845 7096
FAX : +1 610 845 7096
CONTACT : D Plum

BIG FROG MOUNTAIN CORPORATION
100 Cherokee Boulevard, Suite 2109, Chattanooga, Tennessee 37405, USA
TEL : +1 423 265 0307
FAX : +1 423 265 9030
E-MAIL : sales@bigfrogmountain.com
WEB : http://www.bigfrog mountain.com
CONTACT : T. Tripp

BROWER AND COMPANY
154 Main Street, Andover, Massachusetts 01810, USA
TEL : +1 978 749 9591
FAX : +1 978 749 9713
E-MAIL : mbrower@mediaone.net
WEB : http://www.browerco.com
CONTACT : M Brower

CRONIN STONE SOLAR AND WIND POWERED DEVICES USA
616 Hyde Park Avenue, Boston, MA 02131, USA
TEL : +1 617 469 9463
FAX : +1 617 327 7240
E-MAIL :dewind-usa@aol.com
CONTACT : J Stone

DONALD ROBERT SMITH CONSULTING
468 49th Street, Oakland,
California 94609, USA
TEL: + 1 510 658 3461
FAX: + 1 510 658 3461
E-MAIL: dr_smith@ix.netcom.com
CONTACT: Don Smith

EDO FIBER SCIENCE
PO Box 22540, Salt Lake City,
Utah 84122, USA
TEL : +1 801 537 1800
FAX : +1 801 363 9554

ENDLESS ENERGY CORPORATION
9 Casstle Road,New Glocester,
Maine 04260, USA
TEL : +1 207 926 4698
FAX : +1 207 926 3016
E-MAIL : eec@ime.net
CONTACT : H Lee

ENERPRO INC
5780 Thornwood Drive,
Goleta, California 93117, USA
TEL : + 1 805 683 2114
FAX: + 1 805 964 0798
E-mail: enerpro@aol.com
WEB: http://
www.enerpro.thomasregister.com
CONTACT : J Turney

ENRON WIND CORP
13861 Chantico Road, Tehachapi,
CA 93561, USA
TEL : +1 661 823 6700
FAX: + 1 661 823 1829
E-MAIL: wind@enron.com
WEB: http://www.wind.enron.com
CONTACT : M Mc Lann

ENRON WIND CORP
PO Box 1910, 13000 Jameson Road,
Tehachapi, California 93581, USA
TEL : + 1 805 823 6700
FAX: 1 805 822 7880
E-MAIL : wind@enron.com
WEB: http://www.wind.enron.com

ENXCO INC
PO Box 581043,
North Palm Springs,CA 92258, USA
TEL: +1 760 329 1437
FAX: +1 760 329 1503
E-MAIL: stevey@enXco.com
WEB: http://www.enxco.com
CONTACT: Stephen A Yatsko

FIRETRACE INTERNATIONAL
7898 E Acoma Drive, Suite 106,
Scottsdale, AZ 85260, USA
TEL: +1 480 607 1218
FAX: +1 480 315 1316
E-MAIL: firetrace@firetrace.com
WEB: http://www.firetrace.com/info.html
CONTACT: William Eckholm

GLOBAL ENERGY CONCEPTS LLC
5729 Lakeview Drive NE Suite 100,
Kirkland, WA 98033, USA
TEL : + 1 425 822 9008
FAX : + 1 425 822 9022
E-MAIL : gec@aa.net
WEB: http://www.globalenergy
concepts.com
CONTACT : J Wolfe

INDEPENDENT POWER SYSTEMS INC
1320 Freeport # 101,
Sparks, Nevada 89431, USA
TEL: +1 775 331 0228
FAX: +1 775 331 8474
E-MAIL: ipssolar@aol.com
CONTACT : J Pizur

KELELO ENGINEERING
3404 Angela St, Cocoa,
Florida 32926, USA
TEL: + 1 321 632 7964
FAX: + 1 321 638 1010
E-MAIL: Thornbloom@fsec.ucf.edu
CONTACT : K Bowker

LAKE MICHIGAN WIND & SUN LTD
1015 County U, Sturgeon Bay,
Wisconsin 54235-8253, USA
TEL: +1 920 743 0456
FAX: +1 920 734 0466
E-MAIL: lmwands@itol.com
CONTACT : M D Zuteck

MDZ CONSULTING
601 Clear Lake Road,
Clear Lake Shores,
Texas 77565, USA
TEL: +1 713 334 5681
FAX: +1 713 334 5681
CONTACT : M d Zuteck

MECS SOLAR SYSTEMS
11707 Fairford Avenue, Norwalk,
California 90650, USA
TEL: +1 562 864 5299
FAX: +1 562 868 4250
E-MAIL: j.deboer@worldnet.att.net
CONTACT : John De Boer

NASSAUX-HEMSLEY INC
56 North Second Street
Chambersurg, Pennsylvania 17201, USA
TEL: +1 717 263 4109
FAX: +1 717 263 4117
CONTACT : W Hemsley

NEG MICON INC
2850 West Golf Road,
Suite 405 Rolling Meadows,
Illinois 60008, USA
TEL: +1 847 981 6800
FAX: +1 847 981 6801
E-MAIL:salesinfo@negmicon-
usa.com
WEB: http://www.neg-micon.com
CONTACT: Jesper J Michaelsen

NEKOLUX
1433 W Chicago Ave,
Chicago, IL 60622, USA
TEL: +1 312 738 3776
FAX: +1 312 738 3776
E-MAIL: vladimir@nekolux.com
WEB: http://www.nekolux.com
CONTACT : V Nekola

NOVA GREENING
Marketing and Sales,
4961 N Del Mar Avenue,
Fresno, CA 93704, USA
TEL: + 1 559 225 9495
E-MAIL: kaufher@lightspeed.net
CONTACT: Mike Kaufher

NRG SYSTEMS INC
110 Commerce Street,
Hinesburg,
Vermont 05461, USA
TEL: + 1 802 482 2255
FAX: + 1 802 482 2272
E-MAIL: sales@nrgsystems.com
WEB: http://www.nrgsysystems.com
CONTACT: Julia Austin

OILAIR HYDRAULICS INC
219 P Berlin Road,
Suite 251, Cherry Hill,
NJ 08034, USA
TEL: + 1 609 854 2991
FAX: + 1 609 854 3395
CONTACT: Ron Gordon

ORION ENERGY LLC
405 14th Street, Suite 712,
Oakland,
California 94612, USA
TEL: +1 510 267 9323
FAX: +1 510 267 0325
E-MAIL: Rbuckley@orion-energy.com

PANAERO CORPORATION
12345 West Alameda Parkway
Suite 113, Lakewood,
Colorado 80228-2827,
USA
TEL: + 1 303 989 9060
FAX: + 1 303 989 9066
E-MAIL: panaerp@compuserve.com
WEB:http://
ourworld.compuserve.com/
homepage/panaero
CONTACT: Donald M Hardy

PARADISE POWER COMPANY
Box 7484, Taos,
NM 87571, USA
TEL: + 1 505 737 5896
FAX: + 1 505 737 5896
E-MAIL: paradise@taosnet.com
WEB: http://www.paradisepower.net
CONTACT: Daniel Weinman

POWER ENGINEERS
Box 1066,
3940 Glenbrook Drive
Hailey, Idaho 83333, USA
TEL: +1 208 788 3456
FAX:+1 208 788 2082
E-MAIL : mralph@powereng.com
WEB: http://www.powereng.com
CONTACT : M Ralph

POWERWORKS INC
5356 North Cattail,
Way Bolse,
Idaho 83703, USA
TEL: +1 208 853 4602
FAX: +1 208 853 4628
E-MAIL: rskoebbe@powerworksinc.com
CONTACT: Rick S Koebbe

PRIME ENERGY CORPORATION
1331 SW Broadway, Portland,
OR97201, USA
TEL: +1 503 228 3225
FAX: +1 503 222 1313
E-MAIL: rjbefa@aol.com

REAL GOODS TRADING CORP
200 Clara Street,
Ukiah, CA 95482, USA
TEL: + 1 707 468 9292
FAX: + 1 707 468 9394
E-MAIL: realgood@realgood.com
CONTACT : S Rogers

SEAWEST WINDPOWER INC
1455 Frazee Road,
9th Floor, San Diego,
California 92108-4310, USA
TEL: +16192933340
FAX: +16192933347
E-MAIL: info@seawestwindpower.com
WEB: http://
www.seawestwindpower.com
CONTACT: Dave Roberts

SECOND WIND INCORPORATED
366 Summer Street,
Sommerville,
Massachusetts 02144, USA
TEL: +16177768520
FAX: +16177760391
WEB: http://www.secondwind.com
CONTACT: Mike Jacobs

SIERRA SOLAR SYSTEMS
109 Argall Way,
Nevada City
California 95959, USA
TEL: +1 530 265 8441
FAX: +1 530 265 6151
E-MAIL: solarjon@sierrasolar.com
WEB: http://www.sierrasolar.com
CONTACT : J Hill

SINDAL MARKET ANALYST
Wind Energy, 1251 Cabrillo Park
Drive, Santa Ana, CA 92701, USA
TEL: +1 714 836 5384
FAX: +1 617 687 7937
E-MAIL: info@sindal-lundsberg.com
WEB: http://www.sindal-lundsberg.com
CONTACT : A M Lundsberg

SOLAR WATER TECHNOLOGIES INC
426-B Elm Avenue, Portsmouth,
VA 23704, USA
TEL:+1 757 398 0098
FAX:+1 603 925 1964
E-MAIL:swt@solarwater.com
WEB:http://www.solarwater.com

SOUND POWER INC
801 27th Avenue, Seattle,
Washington 98122, USA
TEL : +1 206 324 7340
E-MAIL: dtrione@netscape.net
CONTACT : Mr D Trione

SOUTHWEST WINDPOWER
2131 North First Street, Flagstaff,
Arizona 86004, USA
TEL: +1 520 779 9463
FAX: +1 520 779 1485
E-MAIL: info@windenergy.com
WEB: http://www.windenergy.com
CONTACT : C Molello

SPRINGHOUSE ENERGY SYSTEMS INC
Room 412,
Washington Trust Building,
Washington,
Pensylvania 15301, USA
TEL: +1 724 225 8685
CONTACT : L Olszewski

SUNDANCE POWER SYSTEMS INCORPORATED
Route 3, Box 121A,
Mars Hill,
North Carolina 28754, USA
TEL: +1 828 689 2080
E-MAIL: earthfaith@aol.com
CONTACT : K T Kalarney

SUNELCO
PO Box 787, Hamilton,
MT 59840, USA
TEL: +1 406 363 6924
FAX: +1 406 363 6046
E-MAIL:info@sunelco.com
WEB:http://www.sunelco.com
CONTACT : T Bishop

SUPPORT RESOURCES INCORPORATED
220 Loma Metisse, Malibu,
California 90265, USA
TEL: +1 310 456 1374
FAX: +1 310 456 3174
CONTACT : P Banner

THE ALTERNATIVE POWER SOURCE
4962 Old Winter Garden Road
Orlando, Florida, USA
TEL: + 1 407 532 2899
FAX: + 1 407 292 7647
E-MAIL: tapsource@aol.com
CONTACT: Sam Martinez

THE CINCINNATI GEAR COMPANY
5657 Wooster Pike,
Cincinnati, Ohio 45227, USA
TEL : + 1 513 271 7700
FAX : + 1 513 271 0049
E-MAIL : cintigear@worldnet.att.net
CONTACT : Steve Crowell

TIM OLSEN CONSULTING
1428 South Humboldt, Street,
Denver, Colorado 80210, USA
TEL: +1 303 777 3341
FAX: +1 303 777 3383
E-MAIL:tolsen@aol.com
WEB:http://www.windtechnology.com
CONTACT : T L Olsen

VESTAS AMERICAN WIND TECHNOLOGY INC
19020 North Indian Avenue,
Suite 4-C, North Palm Springs,
California 92258, USA
TEL: +1 760 329 5400
FAX: +1 760 329 5558
E-MAIL: pandres@swbi.net

W A VACHON & ASSOCIATES INC
149, 25 Tappan Street,Manchester,
Massachusetts 01944, USA
TEL: +1 978 526 4315
FAX: +1 978 526 8180
CONTACT : W Vachon

WECS ELECTRIC SUPPLY INC
PO Box 580276, 19465 –3A North
Indian Avenue, North Palm Springs,
California 92258-0276, USA
TEL: +1 760 251 0040
FAX: +1 760 251 0771
E-MAIL: wecsman@aol.com
WEB: http://www.WECSelectric.com
CONTACT: Bruce Hammett

WIND EAGLE CORPORATION
4767 Willow Bend Drive, Wichita
Falls, Texas 76310-1024, USA
TEL: + 1 817 567 3338
CONTACT: Jay W Carter

WIND ECONOMICS & TECHNOLOGY INC
511 Frumenti Court,
Martinez, CA 94553, USA
TEL: + 1 925 229 0648
FAX: + 1 925 229 0685
E-MAIL: wectecfm@aol.com
WEB: http://www.wectec.com
CONTACT: Edward F McCarthy

WIND TURBINE INDUSTRIES
16801 Industrial Circle South East,
Prior Lake, Minnesota 55372, USA
TEL: +19524476064
FAX: +19524476050
E-MAIL: wtic@windturbine.net
WEB: http://www.windturbine.net
CONTACT: Steve Turek

WINDLAND INC
10480 Garverdale Court, Suite 804A,
Boise, ID83704, USA
TEL: +1208377777
FAX : +12083752894
E-MAIL : wind@windland.com

WINDRIDGE INC
PO Box 1587, Tehachapi,
California 93581, USA
TEL: +1 661 822 6789
CONTACT : J Brust

WINDSTREAM POWER SYSTEMS INCORPORATED
PO Box 1604-E, Burlington,
Vermont 05402-1604, USA
TEL: +1 802 658 0075
FAX: +1 802 658 1098
E-MAIL: mail@windstreampower.com
WEB: http://
www.windstreampower.com
CONTACT : C Kerr

WINDTECH INTERNATIONAL LLC
125 Maple Ave,
Katonah,
New York 10536, USA
TEL: +1 914 232 2354
FAX: +1 914 232 2356
E-MAIL: info@windmillpower.com
WEB: http://
www.windmillpower.com
CONTACT : D Michcelis

WINDWARD ENGINEERING LC
4661 Holly Lane,
Salt Lake City,
UT 84117, USA
TEL: +1 801 278 7852
FAX: +1 801 272 4132
E-MAIL: chansen@windward
engineering.com
WEB: http://www.windward
engineering.com
CONTACT : C Hansen

WINTEC ENERGY LTD
125 E Taaquitz Canyon #201,
Palm Springs,
CA 92267, USA
TEL: +1 760 323 9490
FAX: +1 760 323 0688
E-MAIL: fwnoble@wintecenergy.com
WEB: http://www.wintecenergy.com
CONTACT : F W Noble

WORLD POWER TECHNOLOGIES INC
19 N Lake Avenue, Rew, Duluth,
Minnesota 55802, USA
TEL: +1 218 722 1492
FAX: +1 218 722 0791
E-MAIL: sales@worldpowertech.com
WEB: http://
www.worldpowertech.com
CONTACT : P Dewont

BIOMASS

ABCO INDUSTRIES INCORPORATED
2675 ER Highway 80,
Abilene, Texas 79604, USA
TEL: +1 915 677 2011
FAX: +1 915 677 1420

AEROSPACE RESEARCH CORPORATION
5454 Aerospace Road,
Roanoke,
Virginia 24014, USA
TEL: + 1 540 427 3014
FAX: + 1 540 427 3015
CONTACT: Joseph Hamrick

AMERICAN BIOMASS CORPORATION
251 W Dekalb Piko C-211,
King of Prussia,
Pennsylvania 19406, USA
TEL: + 1 540 427 3014
FAX: + 1 540 427 3015

CLEAVER-BROOK
221 Law Street, Thomasville,
Georgia 31799-2258, USA
TEL : + 1 912 226 3024
FAX : + 1 912 226 3027
CONTACT : Walter Horton

COEN COMPANY INC
1510 Rollins Road, Burlingame,
California 94010, USA
TEL : + 1 650 697 0440
FAX : + 1 650 686 5655
E-MAIL : marketing@coen.com
WEB : http://www.coen.com
CONTACT : James H White

CONTINENTAL BIOMASS INDUSTRIES INC
22 Whittier Street,
Newton, New Hamsphire
NH 03858, USA
TEL : +1 603 383 0556
FAX : +1 603 382 0557
E-MAIL : info@cbi-inc.com
WEB : http://www.cbi-inc.com
CONTACT : A Ragnarsson

COUNCIL OF GREAT LAKES GOVERNORS
Bromass Program,
35 E Wacker Drive Suite 1850,
Chicago IL 60601, USA
TEL : +1 312 407 0177
FAX : +1 312 407 0038
E-MAIL : fkuzel@cglg.org
WEB : http://www.cglg.org/projects/
biomass
CONTACT : F Kuzel

DECKER ENERGY INTERNATIONAL INCORPORATED
PO Box 2397, Winter Park,
Florida 32790, USA
TEL: + 1 407 628 8900
FAX: + 1 407 628 8535
CONTACT: Macauley Whiting

ELLICOTTVILLE ENERGY INC
Route 219, PO Box 749,
Ellicottville,
New York 14731, USA
TEL : +1 716 699 2425
FAX : +1 716 699 4139
E-MAIL: sddent@unm.edu
CONTACT: Stephen Dent

GE DISTRIBUTED POWER
1 River Road, Building 59E-1,
Schenectady, NY 12345, USA
TEL: +1 518 385 8393
FAX: +1 518 782 8701
E-MAIL: kate.brass@ps.ge.com
WEB: http://
www.gedistributedpower.com
CONTACT: Katharine Richter Brass

GENERAL BIOENERGY INC
3115 Northington Court, PO Box
26, Floence, AL 35630, USA
TEL : + 1 256 740 5634
FAX : + 1 256 740 5535
E-MAIL : pbadger@bioenergyupdate.com
WEB : http://www.bioenergyupdate.com
CONTACT :P C Badger

LAIDIG INDUSTRIAL SYSTEMS
14535 Dragon Trail, Mishawaka,
Indiana 46544, USA
TEL: +1 219 562 0204
FAX: +1 219 356 5575
CONTACT: R. Laidig

LIGNETICS INC
PO Box 489, Glenville,
West Virginia 26351, USA
TEL: + 1 304 462 4848
FAX: + 1 304 462 4852
E-MAIL : bwilson@lignetics.com
WEB: http://www.lignetics.com
CONTACT: WH Pickering

LIGNETICS INC
787 West Woodbury,
Suite 9, Altadena,
CA 91001, USA
TEL : +1 626 797 7510
FAX : +1 626 797 1209
WEB: http://www.lignetics.com
CONTACT : W H Pickering

MCBURNEY CORPORATION
PO Box 1827, Norcross,
Georgia 30091, USA
TEL: +1 770 925 7100
FAX: +1 770 925 7400
E-MAIL: askmcburney@mcburney.com
WEB: http://www.mcburney.com
CONTACT : B McBurney

MESSERSMITH MANUFACTURING INCORPORATED
2612 F Road, Bark River,
MI 49807, USA
TEL: +1 906 466 9010
FAX: +1 906 466 2843
E-MAIL: messersmith@uplogon.com
WEB: http://www.burnchips.com
CONTACT : G Messersmith

MORBARK SALES INC
International Sales,
8507 S Winn Road
Michigan 48896, USA
TEL:+1 517 866 2381
FAX: +1 517 866 2280
E-MAIL:morbark@worldnet.att.net
WEB:http://www.morbark.com
CONTACT : J Foote

NEO CORPORATION
1221 Nicollet Mall, Suite 700,
Minneapolis 55403-2445, USA
TEL: +1 612 373 5310
FAX: +1 612 373 5465
E-MAIL: pete.jones@nrgenergy.com
CONTACT : P D Jones

NOVA GREENING
Marketing and Sales,
4961 N Del Mar Avenue,
Fresno, CA 93704, USA
TEL: + 1 559 225 9495
E-MAIL: kaufher@lightspeed.net
CONTACT: Mike Kaufher

NOVUS SYSTEMS INC
Corporate Headquarters,
12621 Featherwood, #380, Houston,
Texas 77034, USA
TEL: + 1 281 484 0052
FAX: + 1 281 922 1471
E-MAIL: info@woodfuel.com
WEB: http://www.woodfuel.com

NRH ASSOCIATES INCORPORATED
PO Box 178, Swanton,
Vermont 05488, USA
TEL: + 1 802 868 5015
FAX: + 1 802 868 5015
CONTACT : Nancy Holmes

PHILIP SERVICES CORPORATION
31 Waldron Way, Portland,
Maine 04103, USA
TEL: +1 207 797 0006
FAX: +1 207 797 0013
CONTACT : J Fogagey

PLANETEC / MICROGY
1767A Denver West Boulevard
Suite # 19, Golden,
Colorado 80401, USA
TEL: + 1 303 674 1147
FAX:+ 1 303 674 0889
E-MAIL: bbrant@microgy.com
WEB : http://www.microgy.com
CONTACT: Benjamin Brant

SAM DANIELS COMPANY INCORPORATED
PO Box 868,
US Route 2,
Montpelier,
Vermont 05601, USA
TEL : +1 802 223 2801
CONTACT : J E Daniels

STANLEY CONSULTANTS INCORPORATED
225 Iowa Avenue,
Stanley Building, Muscatine,
Iowa 52761, USA
TEL: +1 319 264 6600
FAX: +1 319 264 6658
CONTACT : R Rusch

STONE & WEBSTER ENGINEERING CORPORATION
245 Summer Street,
Boston Massachusetts
02210-2325, USA
TEL: +1 617 589 2010
FAX: +1 617 589 1887
WEB:http://www.stoneweb.com
CONTACT : W F Griffith

TIC - THE INDUSTRIAL COMPANY
2211 Elk River Road,
PO Box 774848,
Colorado 80477, USA
TEL: +1 303 879 2561
FAX: + 303 879 6078
E-MAIL:compton@tic-inc.com
WEB:http://www.tic-inc.com
CONTACT : D Scott

WEBSTER INDUSTRIES INC
325 Hall Street,
Tiffin, Ohio 44883, USA
TEL: + 1 419 447 8232
FAX: + 1 419 448 1618
E-MAIL : websteri@bright.net
Web : http://www.webster.thomasregister.com
CONTACT: James Riedel

WELLONS INCORPORATED
PO Box 1030, Sherwood,
Oregon 97140-1030, USA
TEL: + 1 503 625 6131
CONTACT: Kenneth Kinsley

WEST SALEM MACHINERY CO
PO Box 5288,
Salem Oregon 97304, USA
TEL: + 1 503 364 2213
FAX: + 1 503 364 1398
E-MAIL: sales@westsalem.com
WEB: http://westsalem.com
CONTACT: Bob De Souza

WINROCK INTERNATIONAL
Renewable Energy and the
Environment Program,
1611 N Kent Street,
Suite 600, Arlington,
Virginia 22209-2143, USA
TEL: +1 703 525 9430
FAX: +1 703 243 1175

WOODFUEL.COM LP
Corporate Headquarters, 5900
Haynesworth, Houston,
Texas 77034, USA
TEL: +12814840052
FAX: +12819221471
E-MAIL : info@woodfuel.com
WEB: http://www.woodfuel.com
CONTACT: Billy Holt

COGENERATION

ADVANCED ENERGY CONSTRUCTION
20505 US Highway 19,
Suite 12, Clearwater,
Florda 34624, USA
TEL: + 1 727 441 2808
CONTACT: David Oldack

ELLICOTTVILLE ENERGY INC
Route 219,
PO Box 749,
Ellicottville,
New York 14731, USA
TEL : +1 716 699 2425
FAX : +1 716 699 4139
E-MAIL: sddent@unm.edu
CONTACT: Stephen Dent

ENVIRONMENTAL RISK LIMITED
1132 Hemingway Lane,
Rosewell,
Georgia 30075, USA
TEL : +1 860 242 9933
FAX: +1 860 243 9055

ESI INC OF TENNESSEE
1250 Roberts Boulevard,
Kennesaw,
Georgia 30144, USA
TEL: + 1 770 427 6200
FAX: +1 770 425 3660
E-MAIL: info@esitenn.com
WEB: http:/www.esitenn.com
CONTACT : R Davis

HOUGH ASSOCIATES
105 Town Center Road,
King of Prussia,
Pennsylvania 19406, USA
TEL: +1 215 992 9990
FAX: +1 215 992 9992
CONTACT : T Hough

INDEPENDENT ENERGY PARTNERS INC
12150 East Briarwood Avenue,
145, Englewood,
Colorado 80122, USA
TEL: +1 303 792 0055
FAX: +1 303 799 8828
CONTACT : A Forbes

POLSKY ENERGY CORPORATION
650 Dundee Road,
Suite 150
Northbrook,
Illinois 60062, USA
TEL: +1 847 559 9800
FAX:+1 847 559 1805
E-MAIL : mleaman@polskyenergy.com
CONTACT : M R Hesman

TRIDENT ENGINEERING ASSOCIATES INCORPORATED
2010 Industrial Drive, Annapolis,
Maryland 21401-2942, USA
TEL: +1 410 224 3550
FAX: +1 410 224 8630
CONTACT : W D Henderson

WHEELABRATOR ENVIRONMENTAL SYSTEMS INC
4 Liberty Lane West, Hampton,
New Hampshire 03842, USA
TEL : +1 603 929 3000
FAX : +1 603 929 3365
E-MAIL : William-carison@wastemanagement.com
WEB : http://www.wheelaboratoretechnologies.com
CONTACT : William H Carlson

HYDROGEN

AMERICAN HYDRO CORPORATION
135 Stonewood Road, PO Box 3628
York, Pennsylvania 17402-0136, USA
TEL: + 1 717 755 5300
FAX: + 1 717 755 5522
E-MAIL: http://www.ahydro.com
CONTACT: Doug Miller

WALTER JUDA ASSOCIATES INC
4 Colby Street, Tufts Science and
Technology Center, Medford,
MA 02155, USA
TEL: +1 617 627 2786
FAX: +1 617 627 3991
E-MAIL: dbholmes@aol.com

FUEL CELL

FUEL CELL ENERGY INC
1800 M Street NW, Suite 300,
Washington DC 20036, USA
TEL: +1 202 296 8790
FAX: +1 202 296 8681
E-MAIL: ercc@erols.com
WEB: http://www.fuelcellenergy.co
CONTACT: Eric L Simpkins

GE MICROGEN INC
968 Albany-Shaker Road, Building,
Latham, NY 12110, USA
TEL: +1 518 782 8700
FAX: +1 518 782 8701
E-MAIL: kate.brass@ps.ge.com

ONSI CORPORATION
195 Governor's Highway,
Po Box 1148, South Windsor,
Connecticut 06074, USA
TEL: +1 203 727 2388
FAX: +1 203 727 2366
E-MAIL: troccio@ifc.utc.com
WEB: http://www.InternationalFuelCells.com
CONTACT: John Trocciola

WALTER JUDA ASSOCIATES INC
4 Colby Street,
Tufts Science and
Technology Center, Medford,
MA 02155, USA
TEL: +1 617 627 2786
FAX: +1 617 627 3991
E-MAIL: dbholmes@aol.com

ELECTRIC VEHICLES

MOONLIGHT SOLAR
3451 Cameo Lane, Blacksburg,
Virgina 24060, USA
TEL: +1 540 381 4971
FAX: + 1 540 381 4971

RA PATTERSON & ASSOCIATES
10205 Holme Lacey Lane,
Austin, Texas 78750-4023, USA
TEL: + 1 808 262 5651
FAX: + 1 808 254 0522
E-MAIL: RAPatterson@compuserve.com

SMALL HYDRO

BIG FROG MOUNTAIN CORPORATION
100 Cherokee Boulevard,
Suite 2109, Chattanooga,
Tennessee 37405, USA
TEL : +1 423 265 0307
FAX : +1 423 265 9030
E-MAIL : sales@bigfrogmountain.com
WEB : http://www.bigfrogmountain.com
CONTACT : T Tripp

CANYON INDUSTRIES INC
5500 Blue Heron Lane,
Deming, Washington 98244-9309, USA
TEL : +1 360 592 5552
FAX : +1 360 592 2235
E-MAIL : citurbines@aol.com
WEB : http://www.canyonindustriesinc.com
CONTACT : D A New

ENERGY SERVICE COMPANY
399 E 10th Avenue, Eugene,
Oregon 97401 USA
TEL : + 1 541 302 6808
FAX : + 1 541 302 6810
E-MAIL : info@escosolar.com
WEB: http://www.escosolar.com
CONTACT : T Scott

HARZA ENGINEERING COMPANY
Sears Tower, 233 SouthWacker Drive
Chicago, Illinois 60606-6392, USA
Tel :+ 1 312 831 3000
FAX: + 1 312 831 3999
E-MAIL : info@harza.com
WEB: http://www.harza.com
CONTACT : S W Douglas

INDEPENDENT POWER SYSTEMSINC
1320 Freeport # 101,
Sparks, Nevada 89431, USA
TEL: +1 775 331 0228
FAX: +1 775 331 8474
E-MAIL: ipssolar@aol.com
CONTACT : J Pizor

KELELO ENGINEERING
3404 Angela St, Cocoa,
Florida 32926, USA
TEL: + 1 321 632 7964
FAX: + 1 321 638 1010
E-MAIL: Thornbloom@fsec.ucf.edu
CONTACT : M D Thornbloom

LAKE MICHIGAN WIND & SUN LTD
1015 County U, Sturgeon Bay,
Wisconsin 54235-8253, USA
TEL: +1 920 743 0456
FAX: +1 920 734 0466
E-MAIL: lmwands@itol.com
CONTACT : Kim Bowker

NEKOLUX
1433 W Chicago Ave,
Chicago, IL 60622, USA
TEL: +1 312 738 3776
FAX: +1 312 738 3776
E-MAIL: vladimir@nekolux.com
WEB: http://www.nekolux.com
CONTACT : V Nekols

NEO CORPORATION
1221 Nicollet Mall, Suite 700,
Minneapolis 55403-2445, USA
TEL: +1 612 373 5310
FAX: +1 612 373 5465
E-MAIL: pete.jones@nrgenergy.com
CONTACT : P D Tones

OASIS MONTANA INC
436 Red Fox Lane, Stevensville,
MT 59870, USA
TEL: + 1 406 777 4321
FAX: + 1 406 777 2632
E-MAIL: info@oasismontana.com
WEB: http://www.oasismontana.com
CONTACT: Chris Daum

REAL GOODS TRADING CORP
200 Clara Street,
Ukiah, CA 95482, USA
TEL: + 1 707 468 9292
FAX: + 1 707 468 9394
E-MAIL: realgood@realgood.com
CONTACT : S Rogers

SIERRA SOLAR SYSTEMS
109 Argall Way, Nevada City
California 95959, USA
TEL: +1 530 265 8441
FAX: +1 530 265 6151
E-MAIL: solarjon@sierrasolar.com
WEB: http://www.sierrasolar.com
CONTACT : J Hill

SOUND POWER INC
801 27th Avenue, Seattle,
Washington 98122, USA
TEL; +1 206 324 7340
E-MAIL: dtrione@netscape.net
CONTACT : Mr D Trione

SOUTHWEST WINDPOWER
2131 North First Street, Flagstaff,
Arizona 86004, USA
TEL: +1 520 779 9463
FAX: +1 520 779 1485
E-MAIL: info@windenergy.com
WEB: http://www.windenergy.com
CONTACT : C Molello

SUNDANCE POWER SYSTEMS
INCORPORATED
Route 3, Box 121A, Mars Hill,
North Carolina 28754, USA
TEL: +1 828 689 2080
E-MAIL: earthfaith@aol.com
CONTACT : K Decroot

SUNELCO
PO Box 787, Hamilton,
MT 59840, USA
TEL: +1 406 363 6924
FAX: +1 406 363 6046
E-MAIL:info@sunelco.com
WEB:http://www.sunelco.com
CONTACT : J Bishop

UEK CORPORATION
PO Box 3124, Annapolis, MD 21403, USA
TEL : +1 410 267 6507
FAX : +1 410 280 3717
E-MAIL : uekus@juno.com
WEB : http://www.uekus.com
CONTACT : D Vanthur

TIDAL / OCEAN

RA PATTERSON & ASSOCIATES
10205 Holme Lacey Lane, Austin,
Texas 78750-4023, USA
TEL: + 1 808 262 5651
FAX: + 1 808 254 0522
E-MAIL: RAPatterson@compuserve.com
CONTACT : R Patterson

GEOTHERMAL

ALLIANCE INTERNATIONAL
143 Oakhurst Road, Cape Elizabeth
ME 04107, USA
TEL: + 1 207 767 3800
FAX: + 1 207 767 3800
CONTACT: HT Hawkes

BAKERSFIELD PIPE AND SUPPLY
2903 Patton Way, Bakersfield,
California 93302-0639, USA
TEL : +1 805 589 9141
FAX : +1 805 589 3739
CONTACT : J Trohan

BEN HOLT COMPANY
201, South Lake Avenue,
Suite 300 Pasadena,
California 91101, USA
TEL : +1 626 795 6866
FAX : +1 626 584 9210
E-MAIL :phmesser@bibb.com
WEB : http://www.bibb.com
CONTACT : P H Messer

CAITHNESS CORPORATION
305 Indiana Street,
Suite 601,
Golden Colorado 80401, USA
TEL : +1 303 279 5701
FAX : +1 303 279 3486
CONTACT : P Stein

CALENERGY COMPANY INC
2101 I Street, NW,
Washington DC 20037, USA
TEL : +1 202 828 1378
FAX : +1 202 828 1380
CONTACT : J W Weisgall

CALPINE CORPORATION
50 West San Fernando Street,
San Jose, California, 95113, USA
TEL : +1 408 995 5115
FAX : +1 408 995 0505
CONTACT : R Woller

CASCADIA EXPLORATION CORPORATION
3358 Apostol Road, Escondido
California, 92025, USA
TEL : +1 760 489 0969
FAX : +1 760 489 0426
E-MAIL : ciancanell@aol.com
CONTACT : E Cianconelli

CHEMCO CONSULTING Inc
8 May Street, Marblehead
Massachussets 01945, USA
TEL : +1 781 631 3537
CONTACT : Dr M Cohen

COENERGY INC
5065 Westheimer, Suite 815 East,
Houston, Texas 77056, USA
TEL : + 1 713 622 6114
FAX : + 1 713 622 9182
CONTACT : John Dickinson

CONSTELLATION ENERGY INC
250 West Pratt Street,
20th Floor,
Baltimore,
Maryland 21201-2423,
USA
TEL : + 1 410 783 3264
FAX : + 1 410 783 3610
CONTACT : Steve Morris

DANIEL VALVE COMPANY
PO Box 40421, Houston,
Texas 77240, USA
TEL: + 1 281 469 0550
FAX: + 1 281 894 1332
E-MAIL: lbabbidg@danielind.com
CONTACT: Lew Babbidge

DOUGLAS ENERGY COMPANY INC
181 West Orangethorpe Avenue,
Suite D Placentia,
California 92670,
USA
TEL: + 1 714 524 3338
FAX: + 1 714 524 3341
E-MAIL: deco@interserv.com
WEB: http://home.sprynet.com/interserv/deco
CONTACT : W Studhalter

EARTH POWER RESOURCES INC
3203 S Owasso,
Tulsa, Oklahoma 74105, USA
TEL: + 1 918 743 5593
FAX: + 1 918 743 5594
CONTACT: Ronald Barr

ENERTIA BUILDING SYSTEMS INC
Solar/Geothermal Homes,
13312 Garffe Sherron Road,
Wake Forest,
North Carloina 27587, USA
TEL : + 1 919 556 0177
FAX: + 1 919 556 1135
E-MAIL: enertia@mindspring.com
WEB: http://www.enertia.com
CONTACT : M Sykes

ERSKINE MC PHD - CONSULTING GEOLOGIST
5413 Silva Avenue, El Cerrito,
California 94530, USA
TEL : +1 510 234 6214
FAX: + 1 510 234 5371
E-MAIL: merskine@ix.netcom.com
CONTACT : M C Erskine

EXERGY INC
22320 Foothill Boulevard,
Suite 540 Hayward,
California 94541, USA
TEL: +1 510 537 5881
FAX: +1 510 537 8621
CONTACT : H Leibowitz

FPL ENERGY
PO Box 1286,
Fullerton,
California 92836, USA
TEL: +1 714 738 8224
FAX: +1 714 525 2852
E-MAIL: mesqgroup@aol.com

GABELMANJOHN W AND ASSOCIATES INCORPORATED
23, Portland Court, Danville,
California 94526, USA
TEL: + 1 925 837 5989
FAX: +1 925 837 5989
CONTACT : J W Gabelman

GEO-HEAT CENTER
Oregon Institute of Technology,
3201 Campus Drive,
Klamath Falls,
Oregon 97601, USA
TEL : + 1 541 885 1750
FAX : + 1 541 885 1754
E-MAIL : geoheat@oit.edu
CONTACT : J W Lund

GEOLOGIST EXTRAORDINAIRE
36700 Oak Point Road,
Oregon 97478, USA
TEL : + 1 503 741 7198
FAX : + 1 503 741 7198
E-MAIL : lafleur113@aol.com
CONTACT : J Lafleur

GEOTHERMAL DEVELOPMENT ASSOCIATES
770 Smithridge Drive Suite 550,
Reno, Nevada 89503, USA
TEL : + 1 775 825 5800
FAX : + 1 775 825 4880
E-MAIL : mbooth@gda.reno.nv.us
WEB : http://www.greatbasin.net/gda
CONTACT : G M Booth III

GEOTHERMAL EDUCATION OFFICE - GEO
664 Hilary Drive, Tiburon,
CA 94920 USA
TEL : + 1 415 435 4574
E-MAIL : geo@marin.org
CONTACT : M Namzer

GEOTHERMAL HEAT PUMP CONSORT
701 Pennsylvania Avenue NW
Washington DC 20004-2696, USA
TEL : + 1 202 508 5500
FAX : +1 202 508 5222
E-MAIL : info@ghpc.org
WEB : http://www.geoexchange.org
CONTACT : C Abuce

GEOTHERMAL POWER COMPANY INC
1460 West Water Street,
Elmira, New York 14905, USA
TEL : + 1 607 733 1027
FAX : + 1 607 734 2709
CONTACT : G Shulman

GEOTHERMEX INC
5221 Central Avenue, Suite 201,
Richmond, California 94804, USA
TEL : + 1 510 527 9876
FAX : + 1 510 527 8164
E-MAIL : mw@geothermex.com
WEB: http://www.geothermex.com
CONTACT : Dr S Sanyal

HAMEL GEOTECHNICALCONSUTANTS
1992 Butler Drive, Monroeville,
Pennsylvania 15146-3918, USA
TEL : + 1 412 824 5943

J&M INDUSTRIAL SUPPLY COMPANY
301 Ohio Avenue, Richmond
California 94804, USA
TEL: + 1 510 232 2600
FAX: + 1 510 232 5228
E-MAIL: pneumapress@earthlink.net
WEB: http://home.earthlink.net/~pneumapress
CONTACT : J Hamel

MAXWELL TECHNOLOGIES SYSTEMS DIVISION INC
9210 Sky Park Court, San Diego,
California 92123-1506, USA
TEL: +1 858 576 7752
FAX: +1 858 637 7411
E-MAIL: garg@maxwell.com
WEB: http://www.maxwell.com/products/Reservoir.html
CONTACT : Dr S K Garg

MILLHOLEN MECHANICAL
Box 1483, Truckee,
California 96160, USA
TEL: +1 916 587 2318
CONTACT : W L Millholen

NITECH INC
64 Horsehill Road, Cedar Knolls,
New Jersey 07927, USA
TEL: + 1 201 538 1940
FAX: + 1 201 538 3511
WEB: http://www.nitech-vac.com
CONTACT: Tony Newton

OC KARKALITS ENGINEERING INCORPORATED
1161 Bayeauwood Drive,
Lake Charles,
Louisiania 70605, USA
TEL: + 1 318 478 4517
CONTACT: O C Karkalits

ORMAT INTERNATIONAL INC
980 Greg Street, Sparks
Nevada 89431-6039,USA
TEL: + 1 702 356 9029
FAX: + 1 702 356 9039
E-MAIL: ormat@ormat.com
WEB: http://www.ormat.com
CONTACT: Daniel Schochet

OXBOW POWER CORPORATION
1601 Forum Place,
West Palm Beach
Florida 33401, USA
TEL: + 1 561 697 4300
FAX: + 1 561 640 8847
CONTACT: Ken Kerr

OXBOW POWER SERVICES INC
9790 Gateway Drive,
Suite 220, Reno,
Nevada 89511, USA
TEL: + 1 702 851 1199
FAX: + 1 702 850 2211
CONTACT: Vince Zodiaco

POWER ENGINEERS
Box 1066,
3940 Glenbrook Drive
Hailey, Idaho 83333, USA
TEL: +1 208 788 3456
FAX:+1 208 788 2082
E-MAIL : mralph@powereng.com
WEB: http://www.powereng.com
CONTACT : M Ralph

RA PATTERSON & ASSOCIATES
10205 Holme Lacey Lane,
Austin,
Texas 78750-4023, USA
TEL: + 1 808 262 5651
FAX: + 1 808 254 0522
E-MAIL: RAPatterson@compuserve.com
CONTACT : R Patterson

SANTAE GEOTHERMAL INC
Two Lincoln Center, 5420 LBJ Freeway, Suite 110,
Dallas Texas 75240-2648, USA
TEL: + 1 214 701 7542
FAX: + 1 214 701 7339
E-MAIL: jpeters@mcimail.com
CONTACT : J Peters

TRANS-PACIFIC GEOTHERMAL CORPORATION
111 Broadway, Suite 102,
Okland, CA 94607, USA
TEL: +1 510 763 7812
FAX: +1 510 763 2504
E-MAIL: tgcorp@earthlink.net
CONTACT : Dr T Meidar

TWO-PHASE ENGINEERING & RESEARCH
3209 Franz Valley Road, Santa Rosa, California 95404, USA
TEL : +1 707 523 4585
FAX : +1 707 528 2071
E-MAIL : two-phase@juno.com
CONTACT : D Jung

VEIZADES & ASSOCIATES INCORPORATED
90 New Montgomery Street,
Suite 207, San Francisco,
California 94105, USA
TEL: +1 415 495 8519
FAX: +1 415 495 4874
CONTACT : H Veizades

WILLIAMS TOOL COMPANY INC
PO Box 6155, Fort Smith,
Arkansas 72906, USA
TEL: + 1 501 646 8866
FAX: + 1 501 646 3502
WEB: http://williamstool.com
CONTACT: Don Hannegan

WASTE TO ENERGY

BASIC ENVIRONTECHNIC
21, West 181 Hill Avenue,
Glen Ellyn, Illinois 60137, USA
TEL : +1 630 790 9404
FAX : +1 630 790 9453
E-MAIL :
102600.1321@compuserve.com
CONTACT : John Lieslak

DYNECOLOGY INC
611 Harrison Avenue,
Harrison,
New York 10528, USA
TEL: + 1 914 967 8674
FAX: + 1 914 967 8530
E-MAIL: hwschulz@msn.com
CONTACT: Dr. Helmut W Schulz

ENERWASTE INTERNATIONAL CORP
PO Box 1194, Bellingham,
Washington 98227, USA
TEL: + 1 360 738 1254
FAX: + 1 360 738 1376
E-MAIL: enerwaste@aol.com
WEB: http://www.enerwaste.com
CONTACT : T Dutcher

FUTURE ENERGY RESOURCES CORP-FERCO
3500 Parkway Lane, Suite 440
Norcross, GA 30092, USA
TEL : + 1 770 662 7800
FAX : + 1 770 662 7807
E-MAIL : markpaisley@future-energy.com
CONTACT : M A Paisley

HOUGH ASSOCIATES
105 Town Center Road,
King of Prussia,
Pennsylvania 19406, USA
TEL: +1 215 992 9990
FAX: +1 215 992 9992
CONTACT : T Hough

JEFFREY
398 Willis Road, Woodruff,
South Carolina 29388, USA
TEL: + 1 864 476 7523
FAX: + 1 864 476 7510
WEB: http://www.jeffrey company.com
CONTACT : J C Eiliot

LB INTERNATIONAL INC
1294 S Hwy 87, Winslow,
Arizona 86047, USA
TEL: +1 520 289 5634
FAX: +1 520 289 5630
E-MAIL:
ecoflame@flagstaffcentral.com
WEB: http://www.PureFlame.com
CONTACT : J F Lehman

MONTGOMERY INDUSTRIES INTERNATIONAL INCORPORATED
PO Box 3687, Jacksonville,
Florida, 32206, USA
TEL:+1 904 355 5671
FAX: +1 904 355 0401
CONTACT: Angela Nachman

RESOURCES AUTHORITY IN SUMMER COUNTY TENNESSEE
625 Rappahannock
Wire Road, Gallatin,
Tennessee 37066, USA
TEL : +1 615 452 1114
FAX : +1 615 452 0039
CONTACT : R E Brown

STANLEY CONSULTANTS INCORPORATED
225 Iowa Avenue,
Stanley Building Muscatine,
Iowa 52761, USA
TEL: +1 319 264 6600
FAX: +1 319 264 6658
CONTACT : R Rusch

TRIGEN-BIOPOWER INC
9140 Arrow Point Boulevard,
Suite 370, Charlotte,
North Carolina 28273, USA
TEL: +1 704 525 5819
FAX: +1 704 527 1245
CONTACT : P Sanguinetti

UNITED AMERICAN ENERGY CORP
2420 Camino Ramon, Suite 101,
San Ramon, California 94583, USA
TEL: +1 510 244 1100
FAX: +1 510 244 1101
WEB: http://www.uaecorp.com
CONTACT : E W Tomeo

ENERGY EFFICIENCY

ENERGY SERVICES INTERNATIONAL
P.O. Box 4430, Boulder,
CO 80306-4430, USA
TEL : + 1 303 530 9768
FAX : + 1 509 227 1828
WEB: htpp://www.energetica.com
CONTACT : J Roberts

SOUTHPORT PARTNERSHIP LLC
PO Box 1167, Southport,
Connecticut 06490-2167, USA
TEL: +1 203 256 8849
CONTACT : K Butteke

FINANCE / BANKING

ABELES & ASSOCIATES
3704 11th Avenue Street,
Minneapolis,
Minnesota 55407-2628, USA
TEL: +1 612 823 3154
FAX: +1 612 825 6865

ABN AMRO BANK NV
135 LaSalle Street,
Chicago, Illmois
60603, USA
TEL: +1 312 443 2641
FAX: +1 312 750 6387

ACCRUED EQUITIES INC
150 Bradhollow Road,
Suite 306, Melville,
NY 11747, USA
TEL: +1 631 423 7373

BROAD STREET RESOURCES INC
286 State Route 65, River Falls
Wisconsin 54022-2369, USA
TEL : +1 715 425 9798
FAX : +1 715 425 9596
E-MAIL : bsrinc@ibm.net
CONTACT : C Murphy

CATAMOUNT ENERGY CORPORATION
71 Allen St. Suite 101 Rutland
Vermont 05701-4570, USA
TEL : +1 802 747 5530
FAX : +1 802 747 5478
E-MAIL : dbarba@catenergy.com
WEB : http://www.catenergy.com
CONTACT : L D Barbo

CONNECTICUT CLEAN ENERGY FUND
999 West Street, Rocky Hill,
CT 06067-3019, USA
TEL : + 1 860 563 0015
FAX : + 1 860 563 6978
WEB : http://
www.ctcleanenergy.com
CONTACT : John V Anderson

CONVERGENCE LLC
1183 Parkway, Suite 200A,
Howell, MI 48443, USA
TEL : +1 517 505 0257
FAX : +1 517 545 5988
E-MAIL :
convergence@metroshores.net
CONTACT : S R Rebarn

DELUCIA AND ASSOCIATES INCORPORATED
The Carriage House,
5 Hastings Square, Cambridge
Massachusetts 02139-4724, USA
TEL: + 1 617 576 0646
FAX: + 1 617 547 4286
E-MAIL: dla@world.std.com
CONTACT: Michael Lesser

E & CO
383 Franklin Street,
Bloomfield, NJ 07003, USA
TEL: + 1 973 680 9100
FAX: + 1 973 680 8066
E-MAIL: eco@energyhouse.com
WEB:http://www.energyhouse.com
Contact: Dr. Michael Allen

ELECTROCHEM INC
400 West cummings Park,
Woburn, MA 01801, USA
TEL : +1 781 938 5300
FAX : +1 781 935 6966
E-MAIL :fuelcell@ma.ultranet.com
WEB : http://www.fuelcell.com

ENERGY & ENIVORNMENTAL VENTURES LLC
23 Cardinal Road,
Weston, CT 06883, USA
TEL: +1 203 227 4111
FAX: +1 203 227 4103
E-MAIL: info@eeventures.com
WEB: http://www.eeventurates.com

ENERGY CENTER
Department of Natural Resources,
PO Box 176, Jefferson City, MO
65102-0176, USA
TEL: +1 573 751 40000
FAX: +1 573 751 6860
E-MAIL: webmanager@
mail.dnr.state.mo.us
WEB:http://www.dnr.state.mo.us/energy.htm
CONTACT : S G Orr

ENERGY INSURANCE BROKERS
1525, Mel Avenue, Palm Springs,
California 92262, USA
TEL : + 1 760 325 6205
FAX : + 1 760 325 9545
E-MAIL : energyins@worldnet.att.net
WEB:http://www.energyinsurancebrokers.com
CONTACT : B Fox

ENERGY RESEARCH CORPORATION
1800 M Street NW, Suite 300,
Washington, DC 20036, USA
TEL : + 1 202 296 8790
FAX : + 1 202 296 8681
E-MAIL : ercc@erols.com
WEB: http://www.ercc.com
CONTACT : E Simpkins

ENERGY SERVICES & MANAGEMENT CORPORATION
QED, 116 Norfolk Street,
Cambridge, Mass 02139, USA
TEL : + 1 617 491 4578
FAX : + 1 617 491 4578
CONTACT : John Cooke

ENERGY SOLUTIONS
PO Box 261, WALDOBORO,
Maine 04572, USA
TEL : + 207 759 7085
E-MAIL : energysolutions@gmx.net
CONTACT : D Kaufman

ENVIRONMENTAL MARKET SOLUTIONS INC-EMS
6856 Eastern Avenue NW, Suite
206, Washington, DC 20012, USA
TEL: +1 202 291 3102
FAX: 1 202 291 3107
E-MAIL: klanger@e-m-sol.com
WEB:http://www.Environmental-
market-solutions.com
CONTACT : Dr Cheryl Woerne

FAC EQUITIES
A Division of First Albany
Corporation,
53 State Street,
29th Floor, Boston,
MA 02109-2811, USA
TEL: +1 617 228 3515
FAX: +1 617 228 3515
E-MAIL: eric_prouty@fac.com
CONTACT : E A Prouty

GE CAPITAL CORPORATION
1600 Summer Street,
5th Floor, Stamford,
Connecticut 06927, USA
TEL: +1 203 357 3872
FAX: +1 203 357 4386
CONTACT : C Reynolds

HELLER FINANCIAL INCORPORATED
500 West Monroe Street,
Chicago,
Lllinois 60661, USA
TEL: +1 312 441 7624
FAX: +1 312 441 7827
E-MAIL: mhammond@hellerfin.com
WEB: http://www.hellerfinancial.com
CONTACT: Gar Seifullin

LAWRENCE I THORPE & CO
41 Woodstock Road,
Roswell,
Georgia 30075, USA
TEL: +1 770 993 1463
FAX: +1 770 993 1484
E-MAIL: lit@mindspring.com
CONTACT : P Shipkovs

NEW ALTERNATIVES FUND INC
150 Broad Hollow Road,
Melville,
New York 11747, USA
TEL: +1 631 423 7373
FAX: +1 631 423 7393
E-MAIL: newalternatives_fund@
compuserve.com
WEB: http://
www.newalternativesfund.com
CONTACT: Maurice Schoenwald

ONSI CORPORATION
195 Governor's Highway,
PO Box 1148,
South Windsor,
Connecticut 06074, USA
TEL: + 1 203 727 2388
FAX: + 1 203 727 2366
E-MAIL: troccio@ifc.utc.com
WEB: http://www.Internaitonal
FuelCells.com
CONTACT: John Trocciola

PHOTOVOLTAIC ENERGY SYSTEMS INC
4539 Old Auburn Road,
Warrenton,
Virginia 20187, USA
TEL: + 1 540 349 4497
FAX: + 1 540 349 4497
E-MAIL:pvenergy@crosslink.net
WEB:http://www.pvenergy.com
CONTACT : P D Maycook

RENEWABLE RESOURCES GROUP LLC
66 Cedar Street,
Suite 104,
Newington,
CT 06111, USA
TEL : +1 860 594 0915
FAX : +1 860 594 7184
E-MAIL : dmrode@
renewresourcesgroup.com
WEB : http://
www.renewresoursesgroup.com
CONTACT : A Lesch

RODE & ASSOCIATES LLC
66 Cedar Street, Suite 301
Newington, CT 06111, USA
TEL: + 1 860 594 7183
FAX: + 1 860 594 7184
E-MAIL: rode@rode-llc.com
WEB: http://www.rode-llc.com
CONTACT : D M Rode

SOLAR DEVELOPMENT GROUP
1655N Ft Myer Drive, Suite 520,
Arlington, VA 22209, USA
TEL: +1 703 522 592
FAX: +1 703 522 6450
E-MAIL: eeaf@igc.org
WEB: http://
www.solardevelopment.org
CONTACT: Candace Smith

SOLAR ELECTRIC LIGHT FUND
1775 K Street NW,
Suite 595,
Washington,
District of Columbia 20006, USA
TEL:+1 202 234 7265
FAX:+1 202 328 9512
E-MAIL:solarlight@self.org
WEB: http://www.self.org
CONTACT : Robert A Freling

SOLAR INTERNATIONAL MANAGEMENT INC
1825 I Street NW, Suite 400,
Washington
DC 20006, USA
TEL:+1 202 429 2030
FAX:+1 202 429 9574
E-MAIL:info@solarbank.com
WEB:http://www.solarbank.com

TRADEWIND INSURANCE BROKERAGE
Risk Mitigation Services,
PO Box 2334,
Glendora, California 9174, USA
TEL: +1 625 914 2903
FAX: +1 626 924 3903
E-MAIL: energy.solutions@gte.net
WEB: http://www.tradewind-ins.com
CONTACT : M Cook

TRADEWIND INSURANCE BROKERS
1242 Concord, Glendora,
CA 91740, USA
TEL: +16269142903
FAX: +16269143903
WEB: http://www.tradewind-ins.com

WINROCK INTERNATIONAL
Renewable Energy and the
Environment Program,
1611 N Kent Street, Suite 600,
Arlington, Virginia 22209-2143, USA
TEL: +17035259430
FAX: +17032431175
CONTACT: Robert Bell

WINROCK INTERNATIONAL
Renewable Energy and the
Environment Program,
1611 N Kent Street,
Suite 600, Arlington,
Virginia 22209-2143, USA
TEL: +1 703 525 9430
FAX: +1 703 243 1175

WORLD BANK
F2K-146, 1818 H Street NW,
Washingon, DC 20433, USA
TEL: +1 202 458 2872
CONTACT : K Jechoutek

ASSOCIATION

AMERICAN SOLAR ENERGY SOCIETY INC
2400 Central Avenue G-1,
Boulder, Colorado 80301, USA
TEL: + 1 303 443 3130
FAX: + 1 303 443 3212
E-MAIL: ases@igc.apc.org
CONTACT: Larry Sherwood

AMERICAN WIND ENERGY ASSOCIATION - AWEA
122 C Street NW, Fourth Floor,
Washington, District of
Colombia 20001, USA
TEL: + 1 202 383 2500
FAX: + 1 202 383 2505
E-MAIL: windmail@awea.org
WEB: http://www.igc.apc.org/awea
CONTACT: Randall Swisher

EDISON ELECTRIC INSTITUTE
701 Pennysylvania Avenue NW,
Washington DC 20004-2696,
USA
TEL : +1 202 508 5652
FAX : +1 202 508 5225
E-MAIL : chucklee@eei.org
CONTACT : C Linderman

GEOTHERMAL ENERGY ASSOCIATION
1025 Thomas Jefferson
St NW #109 Washington,
DC 20007-5201, USA
TEL : + 1 202 383 2676
FAX : + 1 202 383 2678
E-MAIL : gea@geotherm.org
CONTACT : D N Anderson

HAWAII SOLAR ENERGY ASSOCIATION
C/o R&R Services
1916 Democrat Street,
Honolulu, Hawaii, USA
TEL : + 1 808 521 9085
FAX : + 1 808 847 4938
E-MAIL : rolf@r7.net
CONTACT : B Harmer

INTERNATIONAL DISTRICT ENERGY ASSOCIATION – IDEA
1200 19th Street NW, Suite 300
Washington DC 20036-2412, USA
TEL: +1 202 429 5111
FAX: +1 202 429 5113
E-MAIL: idea@dc.sba.com
WEB: http://www.districtenergy.org
CONTACT : J Fiegd

NORTHEAST SUSTAINABLE ENERGY ASSOCIATION-NESEA
50 Miles Street, Greenfield
Massachusetts 01301, USA
TEL: + 1 413 774 6051
FAX: + 1 413 774 6053
E-MAIL: nesea@nesea.org
CONTACT : D Minor

SOLAR ENERGY INDUSTRIES ASSOC
1111 North 19th Street, Suite 260
Arlington, VA 22209, USA
TEL:+1 703 248 0704
FAX:+1 703 248 0713
E-MAIL:solarsklar@aol.com
WEB:http://www.seia.org
CONTACT : S Sklar

SOLID WASTE ASSOCIATION OF NORTH AMERICAN-SWANA (R)
PO Box 7219, Silver Spring,
Maryland 20907, USA
TEL: +1 301 585 2898
FAX: +1 301 589 7068
E-MAIL: info@swana.org
WEB: http://www.swana.org
CONTACT : H Rylander

TEXAS RENEWABLE ENERGY INDUSTRIES ASSOCIATION
PO Box 16469, Austin,
Texas 78761-6469, USA
TEL: +1 512 345 5446
FAX: +1 512 345 6831
E-MAIL: r1346@aol.com
WEB: http://treia.org
CONTACT : R E Smith

UINTED BIOENERGY COMMERCIALIZATION ASSOCIATION-UBECA
7164 Gateway Drive, Columbia,
Maryland 21046, USA
TEL: +1 301 621 3002
FAX: +1 301 621 3725
E-MAIL: jbadin@energetics.com
WEB: http://www.ubeca.org
CONTACT : J Kirschner

USGIC
PO Box 2425, Frisco,
Colorado 80443, USA
TEL: +1 303 668 3465
FAX: +1 303 668 3074
CONTACT : G Huttrer

GOVERNMENT

IDAHO DEPARTMENT OF WATER RESOURCES
Energy Division, 1301 N Orchard
Boise, Idaho 83706, USA
TEL: +1 208 327 7962
FAX: +1 208 327 7866
E-MAIL: jbcrocke@idwr.state.id.us
WEB: http://www.idwr.state.id.us
CONTACT : J B Crockett

NATIONAL RENEWABLE ENERGY LABORATORY
409 12th Street South West,
Suite 710 Washington
DC 20024-2188, USA
TEL: +1 202 651 7542
FAX: +1 202 651 7502
CONTACT : G Thompson

NATIONAL RENEWABLE ENERGY LABORATORY
1617 Cole Boulevard,
MS-1613, Golden CO80401, USA
TEL: +1 321 638 1527
FAX: +1 303 275 2905
WEB: http://www.nrel.gov/bioam
CONTACT: Dee Scheaffer

NATIONAL RENEWABLE ENERGY LABORATORY
US Department of Energy,
1617 Cole Blvd, Golden,
Colorado 80401, USA
TEL: +1 303 275 3000
FAX: +1 303 275 3097
E-MAIL: public_affairs@nrel.gov
WEB: http://www.nrel.gov
CONTACT: Bob Noun

SACRAMENTO MUNICIPAL UTILITY DISTRICT
6201 S Street, Mail Stop 75 A-401,
Sacramento, California 95817-1830, USA
TEL: + 1 916 732 6679
FAX: + 1 916 732 5695
CONTACT : D Osborn

STATE OF HAWAII
Department of Business Economic
Development and Tourism,
Energy Resources and
Technology Division
PO Box 2359, Honolulu,
Hawaii 96804, USA
TEL: +1 808 587 3812
FAX: +1 808 586 2536
E-MAIL:mkaya@dbedt.hawaii.gov
WEB:http://www.state.hi.us/dbedt/ert

UNITED NATIONS STATISTICS DIVISION
Energy Statistics Unit, Room DC2-1648, Two United Nations Plaza,
New York 10017, USA
TEL: +1 212 963 8491
FAX: +1 212 963 0623
E-MAIL: shih@un.org
CONTACT : D Shih

US DEPARTMENT OF ENERGY
Energy Information Administration,
1000 Independence Avenue SW,
Washington, DC 20585, USA
TEL: +1 202 586 6582
FAX: +1 202 586 1876
E-MAIL: tpetersi@eia.doe.gov

US DEPARTMENT OF ENERGY
Golden Field Office, 1617 Cole
Boulevard, Golden, Colorado 80401, USA
TEL: +1 303 275 4771
FAX: +1 303 275 4753
E-MAIL: jim_spaeth@nrel.gov
WEB: http://www.eren.doe.gov/golden
CONTACT : James Spdeth

US TRADE AND DEVELOPMENT AGENCY
1621, North Kent Street,
Suite 200,
Arlington, VA 22209, USA
TEL: +1 703 875 4357
FAX: +1 703 875 4009
E-MAIL: info@tda.gov
WEB: http://www.tda.gov
CONTACT : J Greene Stenner

USDA-AGRICULTURAL RESEARCH SERVICE
Conservation and Production
Research Laboratory, PO Drawer 10,
Bushland, Texas 79012, USA
TEL: +1 806 356 5734
FAX: +1 806 356 5750
E-MAIL: rnclark@ag.gov
WEB: http://www.net.usda.gov/cprl
CONTACT : R N Clark

USGIC
PO Box 2425, Frisco, Colorado
80443, USA
TEL: +1 303 668 3465
FAX: +1 303 668 3074
CONTACT : G Huther

RESEARCH & DEVELOPMENT

ABT ASSOCIATES INC
55 Wheeler Street, Cambridge,
Massachussets, USA
TEL: +1 617 492 7100
FAX: +1 617 520 2990
E-MAIL: clarkabt@aol.com

ALFA LAVAL
955 Mearns Road, Warminster,
PA 18974, USA
TEL: + 1 215 443 4000
FAX: + 1 215 957 4859
WEB: http://www.alfalval.com

ANTARES GROUP INCORPORATED
4351 Garden City Drive,
Suite 301, Landover,
Maryland 20785, USA
TEL: + 1 301 731 1900
FAX: + 1 301 731 1904
E-MAIL:mailroom@antares.org
CONTACT : E E Gray

BRADLEY UNIVERSITY
1501 West Bradley Avenue,
Peorial, Illinois 61625, USA
TEL : +1 309 677 2708
FAX : +1 309 677 3670
CONTACT : Dr Vehya B Safdan

CENTER FOR BUILDING AND THERMAL SYSTEMS-NATIONAL RENEWABLE ENERGY LABORATORY
1617 Cole Boulevard, Golden
Colorado 80401, USA
TEL : +1 303 384 7538
FAX : +1 303 384 7540
E-MAIL: exemplary_buildings@nrel.gov
CONTACT : D A Paiz

CHI ENERGY INC
680 Washington Boulevard,
Suite 500 Stamford, CT 06901, USA
TEL: +1 203 425 8850
FAX: +1 203 425 8880
WEB: http://www.chienergy.com
CONTACT: James F Groelinger

CLEANGEN
Los Angeles, CA90017, USA
TEL: +1 877 630 8800
FAX: +1 213 622 9285
E-MAIL: ivoronyak@cleangen.com
WEB: http://www.cleangen.com
CONTACT: Larry Voronyak

CMS VIRON ENERGY SERVICES
216 North West Platte Valley Drive
Kansas City, Missouri,
64150 9703, USA
TEL: +1 816 741 3500
FAX: +1 816 746 0260
WEB: http://www.viron.com
CONTACT: Steven Spurgeon

COLD FUSION TECHNOLOGY INC
PO Box 2816, Concord NH, USA
TEL : + 1 603 228 4516
FAX : + 1 603 224 5975
E-MAIL : editor@infinite-energy.com
WEB : http://www.infinite-energy.com
CONTACT : Dr Eugene F Mallone

ELECTRIC POWER RESEARCH INSTITUTE – EPRI
3412 Hillview Avenue, Palo Alto
California 94304-1395, USA
TEL : +1 415 855 2000
FAX : +1 415 856 6621
CONTACT : E Davis

ENTECH INTERNATIONAL INC
25543 West Scott Road, Barrington,
Illionis 60010 - 2422, USA
TEL : +1 847 382 5595
FAX : +1 847 382 5595
E-MAIL :
entechinternational@excite.com
CONTACT : Dr D Klass

ENVIRONMENTAL ENGINEERING CORPORATION INC-EEC
294 9th Avenue, San Francisco,
California 94118, USA
TEL: +1 415 386 6424
FAX: + 1 415 386 6484
E-MAIL: eeco@eeco.net
WEB: http://www.eeco.net
CONTACT : J Rondio

FLORIDA SOLAR ENERGY CENTER –FSEC
1679 Clearlake Road, Cocoa,
Florida 32922-5703, USA
TEL: + 1 321 638 1000
FAX: + 1 321 638 1010
E-MAIL:block@fsec.ucf.edu
WEB:http://www.fsec.ucf.edu
CONTACT : Dr D Block

GEO-HEAT CENTER
Oregon Institute of Technology,
3201 Campus Drive, Klamath Falls,
Oregon 97601, USA
TEL : + 1 541 885 1750
FAX : + 1 541 885 1754
E-MAIL : geoheat@oit.edu
CONTACT : J W Lund

HEALEY & ASSOCIATES
120 Venetian Way, Suite#16,
Merritt Island, Florida 32953, USA
TEL: +1 407 452 2173
FAX: +1 407 459 3682
E-MAIL: healey@flaenergy.com
WEB: http://www.flaenergy.com
CONTACT : J Hesley

MIDWEST RESEARCH INSTITUTE
425 Volker Boulevard, Kansas City,
Missouri 64110-2299, USA
TEL: +1 816 753 7600
FAX: +1 816 753 8420

NATIONAL RENEWABLE ENERGY LABORATORY
409 12th Street South West,
Suite 710 Washington
DC 20024-2188, USA
TEL: +1 202 651 7542
FAX: +1 202 651 7502
CONTACT : G Thompson

NATIONAL RENEWABLE ENERGY LABORATORY
Science & Technology,
1617 Cole Blvd,
Golden, CO 80401, USA
TEL: +1 303 275 3030
FAX: +1 303 275 3097
E-MAIL: stanley_bull@nrel.gov
CONTACT : Stan Bull

NATIONAL RENEWABLE ENERGY LABORATORY
US Department of Energy,
1617 Cole Blvd, Golden,
Colorado 80401, USA
TEL: +1 303 275 3000
FAX: +1 303 275 3097
E-MAIL: public_affairs@nrel.gov
WEB: http://www.nrel.gov
CONTACT: Bob Noun

NORTH CAROLINA SOLAR CENTER
Box 7401, North Carolina
State University, Raleigh,
North Carolina 27695-7401, USA
TEL: + 1 919 515 3480
FAX: + 1 919 515 5778
E-MAIL: larry-shirley@ncsu.edu
WEB: http://www.ncsc.ncsu.educ
CONTACT : H Rogers

PHD RESEARCH GROUP INC
PO Box 24833, Coral Gables
Florida 33124, USA
TEL: +1 305 665 7415
FAX: +1 305 665 8749
E-MAIL : sroy@phdresearch.com
CONTACT : T Lepley

POWERCOM ENERGY & COMMUNICATIONS ACCESS INC
1055 West 7th Street, Suite 100,
Los Angeles, CA 90017, USA
TEL: +1 213 622 9226
FAX: +1 213 622 9332
E-MAIL:
cawetherby@powercomenergy.com
WEB: http://
www.powercomenergy.com
CONTACT: Chris Wetherby

SANDIA NATIONAL LABORATORIES
MS 0752, Albuquerque,
New Mexico 87185, USA
TEL : +1 505 844 0317

SANDIA NATIONAL LABORATORIES
PV System Assistance Center,
PO Box 5800, MS-0752,
Albuquerque, New Mexico 87185,
USA
TEL: + 1 505 844 0558
FAX: + 1 505 844 6541
E-MAIL: pvdac@sandia.gov
WEB: http://www.sandia.gov/pv

SOLAR ENERGY AND ENERGY CONVERSION LABORATORY-UNIVERSITY OF FLORIDA
Department of Mechanical
Engineering, PO Box 116300,
220 Mechanical Engineering
Bulding Gainesville,
Florida 32611-6300, USA
TEL:+1 352 392 0812
FAX:+1 352 392 1071
E-MAIL:solar@cimar.me.ufl.edu
WEB:http://www.me.ufl.edu/solar
CONTACT : Dr Y Goswani

STRATEGIC RESEARCH INSTITUTE
333 Seventh Avenue, 9th Floor,
New Your 1001-5004, USA
TEL: +12129670095
FAX: +12129677973
WEB: http://www.srinstitute.com
CONTACT: Nadine Harris

SUN WIND CONCEPTS
889 Sands View Road, Camano
Island, Washington 98282-7557, USA
TEL: +1 360 387 5806
FAX: +1 360 387 2868
E-MAIL:econergy@whidbey.net
WEB:http://home.switchboard.com/sunwind

SUNSUHBHISHI OF ARIZONA
PO Box 43896, Tuscon,
Arizona 85733, USA
TEL: +1 520 571 4631
FAX: +1 520 290 6030

U.S.A.

UNIVERSITY OF HAWAII
Hawaii Natural Energy Institute,
2540 Dole Street, Holmes 246,
Honolulu, Hawaii 96822, USA
TEL: +1 808 956 8366
FAX: +1 808 956 2336
WEB: http://www.soest.hawaii.edu/HNEI/hnei.html
CONTACT : P K Takahashi

UNIVERSITIES

ARIZONA STATE UNVERSITY EAST
Electronics and Computer Engineering Technology Photovoltaic Testing Laboratory,
7349 E Unity Ave,
Williams Campus,
Mesa, AZ 85212, USA
TEL: + 1 480 727 1220
FAX: + 1 480 727 1223
E-MAIl: manit@asu.edu
WEB: http://www.asu.edu/east/ptl
CONTACT : G Tamizh Mani

ARIZONA STATE UNIVERSITY ASU
Photovoltaic Testing Laboratory,
7349 East Unity Avenue,
Mesa, Arizona 85212, USA
TEL : +1 480 727 1220
E-MAIL : ptl@asu.edu
WEB : http:///www.asu.edu/east/ptl
CONTACT : Dr Mani

BRADLEY UNIVERSITY
1501 West Bradley Avenue,
Peorial,
Illinois 61625, USA
TEL : +1 309 677 2708
FAX : +1 309 677 3670
CONTACT : Dr Y B Safalari

ELECTRIC POWER RESEARCH INSTITUTE-EPRI
34 12 Hillview Avenue,
Palo Alto,
California 94304-1395,
USA
TEL: +1 415 855 2000
E-MAIL: ttanton@epri.com
WEB: http://www.epri.com
CONTACT: Tom Tanton

FLORIDA SOLAR ENERGY CENTER –FSEC
1679 Clearlake Road, Cocoa,
Florida 32922-5703, USA
TEL: + 1 321 638 1000
FAX: + 1 321 638 1010
E-MAIL:block@fsec.ucf.edu
WEB:http://www.fsec.ucf.edu

HOWARD UNIVERSITY
School of Architecture and Design,
Architecture Department,
2366 6th Street NW,Washington,
DC 20059, USA
TEL: +1 202 806 7424
FAX: +1 202 462 2158
E-MAIL: kprigmore@eypae.com
WEB: http://www.howard.edu
CONTACT : Mrs K T Prigmore

NAUGATUCK VALLEY COLLEGE
Tamarack Arboretum,
750 Chase Parkway,
Waterbury, CT 06708, USA
TEL: +1 203 596 8635
FAX: +1 203 596 2164
E-MAIL: nv_faryniarz@apollo.cmmnetedu
CONTACT: Joseph V Faryniarz

NEW MEXICO STATE UNIVERSITY
Southwest Technology Development Institute - SWTDI,
PO Box 30001 College of Engineering MSC 3 Solar,
Las Cruces,
New Mexico 88003-8001, USA
TEL: + 1 505 646 1049
FAX: + 1 505 646 3841
E-MAIL: http://www.nmsu.edu/~tdi
CONTACT: Mr. Robert Foster

PIMA COMMUNITY COLLEGE
Arizona State Environmental Technology Training Centre-ASETT,
8181 E Irvington Road, Tucson,
Arizona 85709-4000, USA
TEL : + 1 520 206 7888
FAX : + 1 520 206 7825
E-MAIL:rflood@pimacc.pima.edu
WEB :http://pimacc.pima.edu/~asett/asett.htm

UNIVERSITY OF HAWAII
Hawaii Natural Energy Institute,
2540 Dole Street, Holmes 246,
Honolulu, Hawaii 96822, USA
TEL: +1 808 956 8366
FAX: +1 808 956 2336
WEB: http://www.soest.hawaii.edu/HNEI/hnei.html
CONTACT : C Lee

UNIVERSITY OF NEW MEXICO
School of Architecture and Planning, Albuquerque,
New Mexico 87131-1226, USA
TEL: +1 505 277 2903
FAX: +1 505 277 0076
E-MAIL: sddent@unm.edu
CONTACT : S Dent

UNIVERSITY OF NORTH DAKOTA
Energy and Environmental Research Centre -EERC,
PO BOX 9018, Grand Forks,
ND 58202, USA
TEL: +1 701 777 5268
FAX: +1 701 777 5181
E-MAIL: jpavlish@undeerc.org
WEB :http://www.undeerc.org
CONTACT : J Parlish

UNIVERSITY OF TEXAS / AUSTIN
Mechanical Engineering Departments
ETC 5.160, Austin, Texas 78712,
USA
TEL: +1 512 471 3120
FAX: +1 512 471 1045
E-MAIL:gvliet@mail.utexas.edu
WEB:http://www.me.utexas.edu~solarlab
CONTACT : Mr G Vilet

UNIVERSITY OF UTAH
Departnment of Mechanical Engineering, Salt Lake City,
Utah 84112, USA
TEL: +1 801 581 4145
FAX: +1 801 585 9826
E-MAIL: cahansen@eng.utah.edu
CONTACT : C Hasasen

UNIVERSITY OF UTAH
Energy and Geoscience Institute,
423 Wakara Way, Salt Lake City,
Utah 84108, USA
TEL: +1 801 585 7783
FAX: +1 801 585 3540
E-MAIL: pwright@egi.utah.edu
CONTACT : D Neilson

UNIVERSITY OF WISCONSIN-MADISON SOLAR ENERGY LABORATORY
1500 Johnson Drive,
Madison,
Wisconsin 53706, USA
TEL: +1 608 263 1586
FAX: +1 608 262 8464
E-MAIL: trnsys@sel.me.wisc.edu
WEB: http://sel.me.wisc.edu/trnsys
CONTACT : W Beckman

WASHINGTON STATE UNIVERSITY - WSU
Energy Program, 925 Plum Street,
Olympia, Washington 98504,
USA
TEL: +1 360 956 2016
FAX: +1 360 956 2030
E-MAIL: bloomquistr@energy.wsu.edu
CONTACT : Dr R D Bloomquist

WEST TEXAS A & M UNIVERSITY
Alternate Energy Institute,
PO Box 60248 WT, Canyon,
Texas 79016, USA
TEL: + 1 806 651 2295
FAX: + 1 806 651 2733
E-MAIL: aeimail@mail.wtamu.edu
WEB: http://www.windenergy.org
CONTACT: Dr Vaughn Nelson

NGO's

ROCKY MOUNTAIN INSTITUTE
1739 Snowmass, Creck Road,
Snowmass, CO 81654, USA
TEL: + 1 970 927 3851
FAX: + 1 970 927 3420
E-MAIL: outreach@rmi.org
WEB: http://www.rmi.org
CONTACT : R Heede

SOLAR ENERGY INTERNATIONAL
PO Box 715, Carbondale,
Colorado 81623, USA
TEL:+1 970 963 8855
FAX:+1 303 970 8866
E-MAIL:sei@solarenergy.org
WEB:http://solstice.crest.org/renewables/sci
CONTACT : L Stone

TEXAS SOLAR ENERGY SOCIETY-TXSES
PO Box1447, Austin,
Texas 78767-1447. USA
TEL: +1 512 326 3391
FAX: +1 512 326 3391
E-MAIL: info@txses.org
WEB: http://www.txses.org
CONTACT : K Hower

CONSULTANTS

ADVANCED CRYOGENICS LIMITED
PO Box 419,
Tavernier, Flordia 33070,
USA
TEL: + 1 305 852 2597
FAX: + 1 305 852 2598
E-MAIL: rushing@terranova.net
CONTACT : San A Rushing

ADVANCED ENERGY
28 Riverview Mill,
Box 262, Wilton,
New Hampshire 03086,
USA
TEL: +1 603 654 9322
FAX: +1 603 654 9324
E-MAIL: info@advancedenergy.com
WEB: http://www.advancedenergy.com
CONTACT: Daniel Two Eagles

ARCHITECTURAL ENERGY CORPORATION
2540, Frontier Avenue,
Suite 201, Boulder,
Colorado 80301, US
ATEL : +1 303 444 4149
FAX : +1 303 444 4304
EMAIL : aecinfo@archenergy.com
WEB : http://www.archenergy.com
CONTACT : M J Holtz

ALLIED BUSINESS INTELLIGENCE INC
202 Townsend Square,
Oyster Bay, NY 11771, USA
TEL: + 1 516 624 3113
FAX: + 1 516 624 3115
E-MAIL: info@alliedworld.com
WEB: http://www.alliedworld.com

ZANE ANDERSON
44 Church Street, Bristol,
Rhode Island 02809, USA
TEL: + 1 401 254 0338
E-MAIL: andersonzane@aol.com
CONTACT: Zane Anderson

APPLIED ENERGY GROUP INC
46 Winding Hill Drive,
Hockessin, Delaware 19707, USA
TEL: + 1 302 239 8325
FAX: + 1 302 239 8325
E-MAIL: ralph.nigro@dol.net
WEB: http://www.appliedenergygroup.com
CONTACT: Mr Ralph M Nigro

BIBB & ASSOCIATES
Process Division,
201 South Lake Avenue,
Suite 300, Pasadena,
CA 91101, USA
TEL : +1 626 795 6866
FAX : +1 626 584 9210
E-MAIL : phmesser@bibb.com
WEB : http://www.bibb.com
CONTACT : P H Messer

BIBB & ASSOCIATES INC
A Kiewit company,
6750 Antioch Road,
Shawnee Mission,
Kansas 66204, USA
TEL : + 1 913 236 7200
FAX : + 1 913 236 7200
CONTACT: Robert A Bibb

BOSSCHIETER CONSULTING
15901 East Kings, Canyon #3,
Sanger California,
93657, USA
TEL : +1 209 787 3448
FAX : +1 209 787 3448
CONTACT : A Bossohieter

BPA / NSRI
25 North Bradley Road,
Tacoma WA 98406, USA
TEL : +1 253 7569661
E-MAIL : rdjones@bpa.gov
CONTACT : R Jones

BRADLEY BUILDERS AND DEVELOPERS INCORPORATED
PO Box 214, Temple,
Pennsylvana 19560, USA
TEL : +1 215 464 4780
FAX : +1 215 464 4780
CONTACT : D Bridley

BROWER AND COMPANY
154 Main Street, Andover,
Massachusetts 01810, USA
TEL : +1 978 749 9591
FAX : +1 978 749 9713
E-MAIL : mbrower@mediaone.net
WEB : http://www.browerco.com
CONTACT : M Brower

BUILDING ENVIRONMENT SCIENCE TECHNOLOGY BEST
PO Box 1107, Edgewater,
MD 21037, USA
TEL : +1 410 867 8000
FAX : +1 301 889 0889
E-MAIL : info@energybuilder.com
WEB: http://www.energybuilder.com
CONTACT : B D Howard

CAPITAL SUN GROUP LTD
6503 81st Street, Cabin John
Maryland 20818, USA
TEL : +1 301 229 0671
FAX : +1 202 229 0434
CONTACT : C L Potra

CHEMCO CONSULTING Inc
8 May Street, Marblehead
Massachussets 01945, USA
TEL : +1 781 631 3537
CONTACT : D M Cohen

CLEAN TECHNOLOGIES CONSULTING
PO Box 10631, Arlington,
VA 22210, USA
TEL : + 1 202 298 7601
FAX : + 1 202 298 7602
E-MAIL : steve.kalland@starpower.net
WEB : http://www.cleantech.org
CONTACT : Stephen S Kalland

CMG INTERNATIONAL ENERGY CONSULTANCY
9619 W Bexhill Drive,
Kensington MD 20895,USA
TEL : + 1 301 942 8826
FAX : + 1 707 897 8311
E-MAIL : cmgm@erols.com

CT DONOVAN ASSOCIATES INC
150 Adwood Lane,
PO Box 402, Stowe,
Vermont 05672, USA
TEL : +1 802 658 9385
FAX : +1 802 862 1514
E-MAIL:donovan@vbimail.champlain.edu

DAYSTAR CONSULTING LLC
PO Box 761, Clarkdale,
Arizona 86324, USA
TEL: + 1 520 634 5595
FAX: + 1 520 634 5595
E-MAIL: mrandall@daystar-consulting.com
CONTACT : M Randall

DCAM DESIGN
150 Private Drive, Union Mills,
North Carolina 28167-8837, USA
TEL: + 1 828 287 7931
E-MAIL: dcam@blueridge.net
CONTACT: Mr. David B Cameron

DELUCIA AND ASSOCIATES INCORPORATED
The Carriage House,
5 Hastings Square, Cambridge
Massachusetts 02139-4724, USA
TEL: + 1 617 576 0646
FAX: + 1 617 547 4286
E-MAIL: dla@world.std.com
CONTACT: Michael Lesser

DIRECT GLOBAL POWER INC
1462 Erie, Boulevard, Schenectady,
New York 12305, USA
TEL: +1 845 687 2406
FAX: +1 845 687 2408
E-MAIL: rlewand@worldnet.att.net
CONTACT: Richard Lewandowski

DISTRIBUTED UTILITY ASSOCIATES
1062 Concannon Boulevard
Livermore, CA 94550, USA
TEL: + 1 925 447 0624
FAX: + 1 925 447 0601
E-MAIL: dua@ix.netcom.com
CONTACT: Joseph Iannucci

DIVERSIFIED HEATING WHOLESALERS INC
3305 Vasser NE, Albuquerque,
New Mexico 87107, USA
TEL: + 1 505 884 1980
CONTACT: Chris Fairchild

DONALD ROBERT SMITH CONSULTING
468 49th Street, Oakland,
California 94609, USA
TEL: + 1 510 658 3461
FAX: + 1 510 658 3461
E-MAIL: dr_smith@ix.netcom.com
CONTACT: Don Smith

DYNCORP I & ET
6101 Stevenson Avenue, Alexandria,
Virginia 23304, USA
TEL: + 1 703 461 2055
FAX: + 1 703 461 2020
E-MAIL: ted@usva3.dyncorp.com
WEB: http://www.dyncorp.com
CONTACT: Ted Kennedy

ECOLOGY & ENVIRONMENT INC
368 Pleasant View Drive, Lancaster,
New York 14086-1397, USA
TEL: + 1 716 684 8060
FAX: + 1 716 684 0844
CONTACT: Gerhard J Nuemaier

EGS INC
PO Box 2914, Santa Rosa,
California 95405, USA
TEL : +1 707 544 0958
FAX : +1 707 544 4602
E-MAIL : pabroph@aol.com
CONTACT : P Brophy

ENDECON ENGINEERING
347 Norris Ct., San Ramon,
California 94583, USA
TEL : +1 925 552 1330
E-MAIL : info@endecon.com
WEB : http://www.endecon.com

ENECO
3 Lenora Drive, West Simsbury
CT 06092, USA
TEL : +1 860 651 0061
FAX : +1 860 651 0061
E-MAIL : enecowind@aol.com
CONTACT : A L Weisbrich

ENERGETICS INC
7164 Columbia Gateway Drive,
Columbia, MD 21046, USA
TEL : +1 410 953 6252
FAX : +1 410 423 2195
WEB : http://www.energetics.com

ENERGY SERVICE COMPANY
399 E 10th Avenue, Eugene,
Oregon 97401 USA
TEL : + 1 541 302 6808
FAX : + 1 541 302 6810
E-MAIL : info@escosolar.com
WEB: http://www.escosolar.com
CONTACT : J Scott

ENERGY SERVICES INTERNATIONAL
P.O. Box 4430, Boulder,
CO 80306-4430, USA
TEL : + 1 303 530 9768
FAX : + 1 509 227 1828
WEB: htpp://www.energetica.com
CONTACT : J Koberts

ENERTRON CONSULTANTS
418, Benvenue Avenue, Los Altos,
California 94024-4006, USA
TEL : + 1 650 949 5719
FAX : + 1 650 948 3442
E-MAIL : mail@enertroncons.com
CONTACT : J C Pepper

ENTECH INTERNATIONAL INC
25543 West Scott Road, Barrington,
Illionis 60010 - 2422, USA
TEL : +1 847 382 5595
FAX : +1 847 382 5595
E-MAIL : entechinternational@excite.com
CONTACT : Dr D Klass

ENVIRONMENTAL ENGINEERING CORPORATION INC-EEC
294 9th Avenue, San Francisco,
California 94118, USA
TEL: +1 415 386 6424
FAX: + 1 415 386 6484
E-MAIL: eeco@eeco.net
WEB: http://www.eeco.net

ENVIRONMENTAL RISK LIMITED
1132 Hemingway Lane,
Rosewell, Georgia 30075, USA
TEL : +1 860 242 9933
FAX: +1 860 243 9055
CONTACT : R Atkins

ERSKINE MC PHD - CONSULTING GEOLOGIST
5413 Silva Avenue, El Cerrito,
California 94530, USA
TEL : +1 510 234 6214
FAX: + 1 510 234 5371
E-MAIL: merskine@ix.netcom.com
CONTACT : M C Erskine

EXERGY INC
22320 Foothill Boulevard, Suite 540
Hayward, California 94541, USA
TEL: +1 510 537 5881
FAX: +1 510 537 8621
CONTACT : H Leibowz

FBT ENGINEERING
One Northgate Park,
Suite 903, Chattanooga,
Tennessee 37415, US
TEL: +1 615 877 0871
FAX: +1 615 877 0296
CONTACT : J W Bass

FPL ENERGY
PO Box 1286, Fullerton,
California 92836, USA
TEL: +1 714 738 8224
FAX: +1 714 525 2852
E-MAIL: mesqgroup@aol.com
CONTACT : D Campbell

GABELMANJOHN W AND ASSOCIATES INCORPORATED
23, Portland Court,
Danville, California 94526, USA
TEL: + 1 925 837 5989
FAX: +1 925 837 5989
CONTACT : J W Gabelman

GEOTHERMAL DEVELOPMENT ASSOCIATES
770 Smithridge Drive Suite 550,
Reno, Nevada 89503, USA
TEL : + 1 775 825 5800
FAX : + 1 775 825 4880
E-MAIL : mbooth@gda.reno.nv.us
WEB : http://www.greatbasin.net/gda
CONTACT : G Martin Booth III

GEOTHERMAL HEAT PUMP CONSORT
701 Pennsylvania Avenue NW
Washington DC 20004-2696, USA
TEL : + 1 202 508 5500
FAX : +1 202 508 5222
E-MAIL : info@ghpc.org
WEB : http://www.geoexchange.org
CONTACT : Conn Anbee

GLOBAL ENERGY CONCEPTS LLC
5729 Lakeview Drive NE Suite 100,
Kirkland, WA 98033, USA
TEL : + 1 425 822 9008
FAX : + 1 425 822 9022
E-MAIL : gec@aa.net
WEB: http://www.globalenergy concepts.com
CONTACT : R Roore

GREEN MOUNTAIN CONSULTANTS
19 Candlewood Acres Road
Brookfield, Connecticut 06804, USA
TEL: + 1 203 740 0100
FAX: + 1 203 740 0064
E-MAIL : dwarner149@aol.com
CONTACT : Dr Warner

GRIDWISE ENGINEERING COMPANY
121, Starlight, Place, Danville,
CA 94526, USA
TEL : + 1 925 838 2448
FAX : + 1 925 838 2622
E-MAIL : bnorris@gridwise.com
WEB: http://www.gridwise.com
CONTACT : B J Norris

HAMEL GEOTECHNICAL CONSUTANTS
1992 Butler Drive, Monroeville,
Pennsylvania 15146-3918, USA
TEL : + 1 412 824 5943
CONTACT : Dr J Hamel

HARZA ENGINEERING COMPANY
Sears Tower, 233 SouthWacker
Drive Chicago,
Illinosis 60606-6392, USA
TEL :+ 1 312 831 3000
FAX: + 1 312 831 3999
E-MAIL : info@harza.com
WEB: http://www.harza.com
CONTACT : S W Douglas

HEALEY & ASSOCIATES
120 Venetian Way, Suite#16,
Merritt Island,
Florida 32953, USA
TEL: +1 407 452 2173
FAX: +1 407 459 3682
E-MAIL: healey@flaenergy.com
WEB: http://www.flaenergy.com
CONTACT : H Hesley

HELIOKINETICS CORPORATION
PO Box 040, Agoura Hills,
California 91376-1040, USA
TEL: + 1 818 991 5235
FAX: + 1 818 919 5235

HELIOS INTERNATIONAL INC
Eco Corp, 21315 Lighthill Drive
Topanga CA 90290, USA
TEL: +1 818 884 8782
FAX: +1 818 884 7668
E-MAIL: jgingersoll@ecocorp.com
WEB: http://www.ecocorp.com
CONTACT : Dr J G Ingersoll

HH BURKITT PROJECT MANAGEMENT INC
PO Box 8549, Portland,
Oregon 97207-8549, USA
TEL: +1 503 297 4520
FAX: +1 503 297 4519
CONTACT : H H Burkitt

HOLLANDER ASSOCIATES
1605 Sherwood Road,
Reading Wyomissing,
Pennsylvania
19610-1127, USA
TEL: +1 215 678 9756
FAX: +1 610 678 2877
CONTACT : H Hollander

HOMESTEAD ENTERPRISES
Renewable Energy,
30151 Navarro Ridge Road,
Albion,
California 95410, USA
TEL: +1 707 937 0338
FAX: +1 707 937 0338
E-MAIL: steve@renewables.com
WEB: http://www.renewables.com
CONTACT : S Heckeroth

HOUGH ASSOCIATES
105 Town Center Road,
King of Prussia,
Pennsylvania 19406, USA
TEL: +1 215 992 9990
FAX: +1 215 992 9992
CONTACT : T Hough

KATZEN INTERNATIONAL INC
2300 Wall Street, Suite K,
Cincinnati, Ohio 45212, USA
TEL: +1 513 351 7500
FAX: +1 513 351 0810
E-MAIL: projects@katzen.com
CONTACT: Philip W Madson

KELELO ENGINEERING
3404 Angela St,
Cocoa,
Florida 32926, USA
TEL: + 1 321 632 7964
FAX: + 1 321 638 1010
E-MAIL: Thornbloom@fsec.ucf.edu
CONTACT : M A Thornbloona

LEETZOW LIGHTING CONSULANT
PO Box 990-C,
Brandenton,
Florida 34206, USA
TEL: +1 941 756-5666
FAX: +1 941 751 5483

LFR
5 Johnson Drive, Raritan,
New Jersey
08869-0137, USA
TEL: +1 732 526 1000
FAX: +1 732 526 7886
CONTACT : A Donaldson

MACDONALD FAIA
45-090 Namoku Street #709
Kaneohe,
HI 96744, USA
TEL: +1 808 247 3051
FAX: +1 808 236 4249
E-MAIL: macapple@lava.net
CONTACT: V. Macdonald

MANAGEMENT SYSTEMS INC
PO Box 516,
Winchester,
Massachusetts 01890, USA
TEL: +1 781 729 3707
CONTACT : G P Taggart

MARK CHALOM ARCHITECT
21 Calimo Circle,
Santa FE,
New Mexico 87505,
USA
TEL: +1 505 983 1885
CONTACT : Mr M Chalon

MASON BRUCE & GIRARD INCORPORATED
PO Box 9902 18, Redding,
California 96099-0218, USA
TEL: +1 530 246 2455
FAX: +1 530 246 7008
E-MAIL: gzane@masonbruce.com
WEB: http://www.masonbruce.com
CONTACT : G Lane

MAXWELL TECHNOLOGIES SYSTEMS DIVISION INC
9210 Sky Park Court, San Diego,
California 92123-1506, USA
TEL: +1 858 576 7752
FAX: +1 858 637 7411
E-MAIL: garg@maxwell.com
WEB: http://www.maxwell.com/products/Resevoir.html
CONTACT : Dr Saboth K Garg

MCNEIL TECHNOLOGIES INC
6564 Loisdale Court Suite 800,
Springfield, Virgina 22150, USA
TEL: +1 703 921 1600
FAX: +1 703 921 1610
E-MAIL: kdegroat@mcneiltech.com
WEB: http://www.mcneiltech.com
CONTACT : K Debrost

MDZ CONSULTING
601 Clear Lake Road, Clear Lake
Shores, Texas 77565, USA
TEL: +1 713 334 5681
FAX: +1 713 334 5681
CONTACT : M D Zuleck

MILLER/DAVIES ASSOCIATES INC
60 East 42nd St., Suite #1440,
New York, New York 10165-1440,
USA
TEL: +1 212 662 7032
FAX: +1 212 682 8218
E-MAIL: millerdavis@msn.com
CONTACT: R J Miller

MORSE ASSOCIATES INC
1808 Corcoran Street NW,
Washington DC 20009, USA
TEL: +1 202 483 2393
FAX: +1 202 265 2248
EMAIL:fredmorse@morseassociatesInc.com
CONTACT : Dr F Morse

NATIVE SOL DESIGN GROUP
PO Box 5024,
Laguna Beach,
California 92652, USA
TEL: +1 714 494 8333
FAX: +1 714 494 8333
E-MAIL: nativesol@aol.com
CONTACT : C Prehitz

NEXT WAVE ENERGY INC
1600 Broadway, Suite 2400,
Denver , CO 80202, USA
TEL: + 1 303 352 0377
FAX: + 1 303 573 1830
E-MAIL:info@nextwave-energy.com
WEB: http://www.nextwave-energy.com
CONTACT: Richard T Stuebi

RON NIERENBERG
Consulting Meterologist,
153 Sacramento Avenue,
San Anselmo, California 94960, USA
TEL: + 1 415 457 4206
FAX: + 1 415 457 4212
CONTACT: Ron Nierenberg

NORTH CAROLINA SOLAR CENTER
Box 7401, North Carolina
State University, Raleigh,
North Carolina 27695-7401, USA
TEL: + 1 919 515 3480
FAX: + 1 919 515 5778
E-MAIL: larry-shirley@ncsu.edu
WEB: http://www.ncsc.ncsu.educ
CONTACT : H Rogers

NORTHERN RENEWABLES LLC
5142 Shorecrest Drive, Anchorage,
Alaska 99515, USA
TEL: + 1 907 243 9963
FAX: + 1 907 243 9962
CONTACT: Nicholas Goodman

NRH ASSOCIATES INCORPORATED
PO Box 178, Swanton,
Vermont 05488, USA
TEL: + 1 802 868 5015
FAX: + 1 802 868 5015
CONTACT: Nancy Holmes

ONGRID SOLAR ENERGY SYSTEMS
107 South Mary Avenue,
Suite 130 Sunnyvale,
CA 94086, USA
TEL: + 1 408 746 0327
E-MAIL: ongrid@aol.com
WEB: http://hometown.aol.com/ongrid
CONTACT: Andy Black

PADIA CONSULTING INC
201 Commonwealth Court,
Suite 260, Cary,
NC 27511, USA
TEL: + 1 919 481 1777
FAX: + 1 919 460 8999
E-MAIL: harshad@padiaconsulting.com
WEB: http://www.padiaconsulting.com
CONTACT: Harshad Padia

PANAERO CORPORATION
12345 West Alameda Parkway
Suite 113, Lakewood, Colorado
80228-2827, USA
TEL: + 1 303 989 9060
FAX: + 1 303 989 9066
E-MAIL: panaerp@compuserve.com
WEB:http://ourworld.compuserve.com/homepage/panaero
CONTACT: Donald M Hardy

PHOTOVOLTAIC ENERGY SYSTEMS INC
4539 Old Auburn Road,
Warrenton, Virginia 20187, USA
TEL: + 1 540 349 4497
FAX: + 1 540 349 4497
E-MAIL:pvenergy@crosslink.net
WEB:http://www.pvenergy.com
CONTACT : P D Maycock

POWER ENGINEERS
Box 1066, 3940 Glenbrook Drive
Hailey, Idaho 83333, USA
TEL: +1 208 788 3456
FAX:+1 208 788 2082
E-MAIL : mralph@powereng.com
WEB: http://www.powereng.com
CONTACT : M Ralph

POWER TECHNOLOGIES INC
PO Box 1058, 1482 Erie Boulevard,
Schenectady,New York 12301-1058, USA
TEL: +1 518 395 5078
FAX: +1 518 395 2777
E-MAIL: pp.barker@pit-us.com
WEB: http://www.pti-us.com
CONTACT : P Baker

PV ENTERPRISES INC
4620 N Park Avenue, Suite 1606 W
Chevy Chase, Maryland 20815, USA
TEL: + 1 301 657 9110
FAX: + 1 301 657 9110
E-MAIL: pvaradi@aol.com
CONTACT : P V Varadi

PV MEASUREMENTS
780 38th Street, Boulder,
Colorado 80303, USA
TEL: + 1 303 786 7345
E-MAIL: info@pvmeas.com
WEB: http://www.pvmeas.com
CONTACT : Mr H Field

RW BECK INC
1125 Seventeenth Street,Suite 1900,
Denver, Colorado 80202-2615, USA
TEL: + 1 303 299 5315
FAX: + 1 303 297 2811
E-MAIL: tmams@rwbeck.com
WEB: http://www.rwbeck.com

RESEARCH TRIANGLE INSITUTE
PO Box 12194, Research Triangle Park, North Carolina 27709-2194, USA
TEL : +1 919 541 6000
FAX : +1 919 541 5985
E-MAIL : listen @rti.org
WEB : http://www.rti.org

RMS ELECTRIC INC
1844, 55th Street, Boulder, Colorado 80301, USA
TEL: + 1 303 444 5909
FAX: + 1 303 444 1615
E-MAIL: info@rmse.com
WEB: http://www.rmse.com
CONTACT : Dr M McCray

ROBERT H OWEN JR PE
1311 Middleton Street, Middleton Wisconsin 53562 0858, USA
TEL: + 1 608 831 6150
FAX: + 1 608 831 1504
E-MAIL: robreeze@compuserve.com
CONTACT : R Owen

RUSSELL ASSOCIATES
2555 Park Boulevard, Suite 32, Palo Alto, California 94306, USA
TEL: + 1 650 321 9545
FAX: + 1 650 321 9550
E-MAIL: stuart_russel@msn.com
CONTACT : Stuart Russel

JOHN SCHAEFER
43 South G Street, Arcata, CA 95521, USA
TEL: + 1 847 713 2446
E-MAIL: jcschaef@igc.org
WEB: http://www.cleanpowerworks.com

SIMON RICHARDL L CONSULTING METEOROLOGIST
80 Alta Vista Avenue, Mill Valley, California 94941, USA
TEL: +1 415 381 2245
FAX: +1 415 381 2248
E-MAIL: risimon@firstworld.net
CONTACT : R L Simon

SOLAR CITY INC
4305 West Alva Street, Tampa, Floridia 33614, USA
TEL:+1 813 875 5300
FAX:+1 813 877 4862
CONTACT : R W Schabes

SOLECTRICA CONSULTING CO
7006 1st Avenue NW, Seattle, WA 98117, USA
TEL:+1 206 706 2575
FAX:+1 206 706 2579
E-MAIL:roberto@solectrica.com
WEB:http://www.solectrica.com
CONTACT : R Serralus

SOLUTIONS IN SOLAR ELECTICITY
PO Box 5089, Culver City, CA 90231, USA
TEL: +1 310 202 7882
FAX: +1 310 202 1399
CONTACT : J Davidson

SOUTHPORT PARTNERSHIP LLC
PO Box 1167, Southport, Connecticut 06490-2167, USA
TEL: +1 203 256 8849
CONTACT : K Buttke

SPECIALIZED TURBINE SERVICES
785 Tucker Road
Suit G #422, Tehachapi, California 93561-2502, USA
TEL: +1 805 822 0514
FAX: +1 805 822 8675
CONTACT : S Aagaard

SPRINGHOUSE ENERGY SYSTEMS INC
Room 412, Washington Trust Building, Washington, Pensylvania 15301, USA
TEL: +1 724 225 8685
CONTACT : L Oiszewski

STANLEY CONSULTANTS INCORPORATED
225 Iowa Avenue, Stanley Building, Muscatine, Iowa 52761, USA
TEL: +1 319 264 6600
FAX: +1 319 264 6658
CONTACT : R Rusch

STATE OF WISCONSIN ENERGY BUREAU
PO Box 7868, Madison, Wisconsin 53711, USA
TEL: +18007627077
FAX: +16082676931
WEB: http://www.wifocusonenergy.com
CONTACT: Mr. Don Wichert

STERLING ENERGY OPERATIONS INCORPORATED
26893 Calle Hermosa, Capistrano Beach, California 92624, USA
TEL: +1 714 248 2917
FAX: +1 714 248 2539
CONTACT : T Burns

STONE & WEBSTER ENGINEERING CORPORATION
245 Summer Street, Boston Massachusetts 02210-2325, USA
TEL: +1 617 589 2010
FAX: +1 617 589 1887
WEB:http://www.stoneweb.com
CONTACT : Dr R J Kulzkowski

STRATEGIES UNLIMITED
201 San Antonio Circle, Suite 205, Mountain View, California 94040, USA
TEL: +1 650 941 3438
FAX: +1 650 941 5120
E-MAIL:info@strategies-u.com
CONTACT : R O Johnson

SUNNYSIDE SOLAR INC
1014 Green River Road, Guilford, Vermont 05301-8117,USA
TEL: +1 802 257 1482
FAX: +1 802 254 4670
E-MAIL : sunnysde@sover.net
WEB: http://www.sunnysidesolar.com
CONTACT : R Gottlieb

SUPPORT RESOURECES INCORPORATED
220 Loma Metisse, Malibu, California 90265, USA
TEL: +1 310 456 1374
FAX: +1 310 456 3174
CONTACT : P Baner

TAIT SOLAR CO INC
51 W 13th Street, Tempe, Arizona 85281, USA
TEL : +1 480 829 8422
FAX : +1 480 829 8619
E-MAIL : David@Taitsolar.com
WEB : http://www.taitsolar.com
CONTACT : D Tait

TECHNICON ENTERPRISES INCORPORATED
2675 Morgantown Road, Suite Number 4100, Reading, Pennsylvania 19607, USA
TEL: +1 610 855 5000
FAX: +1 610 855 5030
E-MAIL: technicon@tei-inc.com
WEB: http://www.tei-inc.com
CONTACT : D Ranft

VIRTUS ENERGY RESEARCH ASSOCIATES
9061/2 Congress Avenue, Austin, Texas 78701, USA
TEL: +1 512 476 9899
FAX: +1 512 476 9896
E-MAIL: sloan@vera.com
WEB: http://www.vera.com
CONTACT : M Sclon

WINROCK INTERNATIONAL
Clean Energy Group, 1611 N Kent Street, Suite 600, Arlington, Virginia 22209-2134, USA
TEL: +1 703 525 9430
E-MAIL: fellis@winrock.org
WEB: http://www.winrock.org

XENERGY INC
Three Burlington Woods,
Burlington, MA 01803, USA
TEL: +1 781 273 5700
E-MAIL: lronsivalli@xenergy.com
WEB: http://www.xenergy.com
CONTACT : L Ronsivalli

DESIGN & ENGINEERING

AGILIS GROUP INC
3910 RCA Boulevard,
Suite 1008
Palm Beach Gardens,
FL 33410-4213, USA
TEL: + 1 561 626 8900
FAX: + 1 561 626 2929

AGRA INC
One West Court Square,
Decatur,
GA 30030, USA
TEL: + 1 404 370 3200
FAX: + 1 404 370 3646

AIRFOILS IN CORPORATED
122 Rose Drive, Port Matilda,
Pennsylvania
16870-9483,
USA
TEL: + 1 814 357 0500
FAX: + 1 814 357 0357
E-MAIL: dan@airfoils.com
CONTACT : D M Somers

ALSTOM POWER
2000 Dayhill Road,
Windsor Connecticut
06095-0500, USA
TEL: + 1 203 285 5895
FAX: + 1 203 285 4250
CONTACT: Paula A Mc Gill

ALTERNATIVE POWER INC
160 Fifth Avenue Suite 711
New York 10010-7003, USA
TEL: + 1 212 206 0022
FAX: + 1 212 206 0893
E-MAIL: info@altpower.com
WEB: http://www.altpower.com
CONTACT: Anthony P Pereira

BALCKE-DURR INC
405 North Reo Street,
Suite 300,
Tampa,
Florida 33609, USA
TEL : +1 813 342 4985
FAX : +1 813 342 7985
E-MAIL : info@balckedurr.com
WEB: http://
www.bdtengineering.com
CONTACT : C Madson

BARBER NICHOLS INC
6325, West 55th Avenue, Arvada,
Colorado 80005, USA
TEL : +1 303 421 8111
FAX : +1 33 420 4679
E-MAIL : cbni@aol.com
CONTACT : K E Nichols

BARR ENGINEERING CO
8300 Norman Center Drive,
Minneapolis MN 55437, USA
TEL : +1 612 832 2600
FAX : +1 612 832 2601
E-MAIL : tkramer@barr.com
WEB : http://www.barr.com
CONTACT : T E Karmer

BLACK & VEATCH
11401 Lamar Avenue,
Overland Park
Kansas 66211, USA
TEL : +1 913 339 3114
FAX : +1 913 339 3511
CONTACT : L Stoddard

BOEING COMPANY
Rocketdyne, 6633 Canoga Avenue,
PO Box 7922,
Canoga Park,
California 91309-7922, USA
TEL: +1 818 586 3829
FAX: +1 818 586 6155
E-MAIL:
stan.pinkowski@boeing.com
WEB: http://www.boeingenergy.com
CONTACT: Stan Pinkowski

BOGART ENGINEERING
19020 Two Bar Road,
Boulder Creek,
California 95006, USA
TEL: +1 831 338 0616
WEB: http://
www.bogartengineering.com

CEM DESIGN
520 Anderson Avenue,
Rockville
Maryland 20850, USA
TEL : +1 301 294 0682
FAX : +1 301 762 3128
WEB : http://www.cemdesign.com
CONTACT : C Maboney

CHESAPEAKE WIND & SOLAR LLC
9486 Cameldriver Court,
Columbia,
Maryland 21045, USA
TEL : +1 301 879 9600
FAX : +1 410 992 4352
E-MAIL : info@cwsenergy.com
WEB : http://www.cwsenergy.com
CONTACT : Mr R Deutschman

COENERGY INC
5065 Westheimer, Suite 815 East,
Houston, Texas 77056, USA
TEL : + 1 713 622 6114
FAX : + 1 713 622 9182
CONTACT : John Dickinson

CONSERVAL SYSTEMS INC
4254 Ridge Lea Road, Suite 101
Buffalo, New York 14226, USA
TEL : + 1 716 835 4903
FAX : + 1 716 835 4904
E-MAIL : conserval@aol.com
WEB : http://www.solarwall.com

CONTECHS ENGINEERING DESIGN INCORPORATED-CTX
8 Arlington Street, Essex Junction,
VT 05452, USA
TEL : + 1 802 872 7827
FAX : + 1 802 872 7829
E-MAIL : tmp@contechs.com
WEB : http://www.contechs.com
CONTACT : Tim Peery

ELEMENTAL RESOURCES
PO Box 21, Haysville KS 67060,
USA
TEL : +1 316 788 3678
FAX : +1 316 788 1793
E-MAIL :dowenerchi@earthlink.net
WEB : http://www.home.earth
link.net/ndowernerchi
CONTACT : C J Dow

ENERGY OUTFITTERS LTD
136 S Redwood Highway,
P.O.Box 1888, Cave Junction,
Oregon 97523, USA
TEL : + 1 541 592 6903
FAX : 1 541 592 6747
WEB: http://
www.energyoutfitters.com
CONTACT : B Maynard

ESI INC OF TENNESSEE
1250 Roberts Boulevard,
Kennesaw,
Georgia 30144, USA
TEL: + 1 770 427 6200
FAX: +1 770 425 3660
E-MAIL: info@esitenn.com
WEB: http:/www.esitenn.com
CONTACT : R Davis

EXERGY INC
22320 Foothill Boulevard,
Suite 540 Hayward,
California 94541, USA
TEL: +1 510 537 5881
FAX: +1 510 537 8621
CONTACT : H L Orbowitz

FBT ENGINEERING
One Northgate Park,
Suite 903, Chattanooga,
Tennessee 37415, USA
TEL: +1 615 877 0871
FAX: +1 615 877 0296
CONTACT : J W Bass

FOSTER WHEELER POWER SYSTEMS INC
Perryville Corporate Park, Clinton,
New Jersey 08809, USA
TEL:+1 908 713 2766
FAX: +1 908 713 2770
E-MAIL: fw-power-systems@fwc.com
WEB: http://www.fwc.com
CONTACT : B Sinclair

FOSTER WHEELER CORPORATION
Perryville Corporate Park,
Clinton, New Jersey 08809-4000,
USA
TEL: +1 908 730 4439
FAX: +1 908 730 5292
WEB: http://www.fwc.com
CONTACT : R Cumy

FUTURE ELECTRIC ENERGY COMPANY
PO Box 1024, San Luis,
Obispo, California 93406, USA
TEL : + 1 805 542 0250
FAX : + 1 805 542 0222
E-MAIL : future@slonet.org
WEB : http://www.futureelectricenergy.com
CONTACT : N Stchle

GLOBAL RESOURCE OPTIONS LLP
4 Kibling Hill Road, PO Box 51,
Strafford, VT 05072, USA
TEL : + 1 800 374 4494
FAX : + 1 802 765 9983
E-MAIL : global@sover.net
WEB: http://www.globalresource
options.com
CONTACT : J Wolfe

GREAT NORTHERN SOLAR
Route I, Box 71, Port Wing,
Wisconsin 54865, USA
TEL :+1 715 774 3374
E-MAIL : gosolar@win.bright.net

HOMESTEAD ENTERPRISES
Renewable Energy,
30151 Navarro Ridge Road,
Albion, California 95410, USA
TEL. +1 707 937 0338
FAX: +1 707 937 0338
E-MAIL: steve@renewables.com
WEB: http://www.renewables.com
CONTACT : S Heckeroth

HOWARD ALAN ARCHITECTS
849 Arnitage Avenue,
Chicago,
IL 60614-4328, USA
TEL: +1 773 929 2121
FAX: +1 773 929 2122
E-MAIL: halan@speedsite.com
WEB: http://www.howar
dalanarchitects.com
CONTACT : K Shiokawa

KULJIAN CORPORATION
3700 Science Center,
Philadelphia
Pennsylvania 19104, USA
TEL: + 1 215 243 1900
FAX: + 1 215 243 1942
E-MAIL: kulcorp@ix.netcom.com
CONTACT : W J Kleponis

MAZRIA ASSOCIATES INC
607 Cerrillos Road,
Santa Fe, New
Mexico 87501, USA
TEL: +1 505 988 5309
FAX: +1 505 983 9526
CONTACT : E Mazria

MCBURNEY CORPORATION
PO Box 1827, Norcross,
Georgia 30091, USA
TEL: +1 770 925 7100
FAX: +1 770 925 7400
E-MAIL: askmcburney@
mcburney.com
WEB: http://www.mcburney.com
CONTACT : B McBurney

MOONLIGHT SOLAR
3451 Cameo Lane, Blacksburg,
Virgina 24060, USA
TEL: +1 540 381 4971
FAX: + 1 540 381 4971

NEW ENGLAND SOLAR ELECTRIC INC
PO Box 435, Worthington,
Maine 01098, USA
TEL: + 1 800 914 4131
FAX: + 413 238 0203
E-MAIL:
nesolar@newenglandsolar.com

NORTHERN POWER SYSTEMS
PO Box 999,
One North Wind Road
Waitsfield, VT 05673, USA
TEL: + 1 802 496 2955
FAX: + 1 802 496 2953
E-MAIL: jmcnamara@
northernpower.com
CONTACT : J Coleman

NORTHERN POWER SYSTEMS
182 Mad River Park,
PO Box 999, Waitsfield,
Vermont 05673, USA
TEL: + 1 802 496 2955
FAX: + 1 802 496 2953
E-MAIL:
dscannell@northernpower.com
CONTACT : Dennis Scannell

NORTHERN RESEARCH & ENGINEERING CORPORATION-NREC
39 Olympia Ave, Woburn,
MA 01801, USA
TEL: + 1 617 935 9050
FAX: + 1 617 935 9052
E-MAIL: sales@nrec.com
WEB: http://www.nrec.com
CONTACT: Peter Baldwin

NU-TECH ENERGY
1407 Kinross Court,
Walnut Creek, CA 94598, USA
TEL: + 1 925 933 7691
FAX: + 1 925 933 7691
E-MAIL: y2kenergy@aol.com
CONTACT: Jack M Hagler

PERFECTPOWER.NET
9436 N Arroya Vista Drive
Phoenix, Arizona 85028, USA
TEL: + 1 602 971 2588
E-MAIL: john@perfectpower.net
WEB: http://www.perfectpower.net
CONTACT: Bruno Legendre

PHASOR ENERGY COMPANY INC
4202 East Evans Drive,
Phoenix, Arizona 85032-5469, USA
TEL: +1 480 556 6902
FAX: +1 602 404 1765
E-MAIL:tlepley@aol.com
WEB:http://www.phasorenergy.com
CONTACT : T Lepely

PHOTOVOLTAIC RESOURCES INTERNATIONAL
PVCAD Division,
1440 West Meseto Avenue,
Mesa, Arizona 85202,
TEL: +1 480 345 1686
FAX : +1 480 345 6698
E-MAIL:pvcad@primenet.com
CONTACT : P D Maycock

REAL GOODS TRADING
200 Clara Street, Ukiah,
CA 95482, USA
TEL : +1 707 468 9292
FAX : +1 707 468 0399
E-MAIL : stever@realgoods.com
WEB : http://www.realgoods.com/renew
CONTACT : Steve Rogers

U.S.A.

RENEWABLE TECHNOLOGIES INC
PO Box 1569, Sutter Creek,
CA 95685, USA
TEL: +12092671303
FAX: +12092671264
E-MAIL: info@renewable.com
WEB: http://www.renewable.com
CONTACT: Darryl J Conklin

SIBOS ASCOR INC
120 North Street, York,
PA 17403, USA
TEL: +17174280994
FAX: +17174289725
E-MAIL: info@sibosascorinc.com
WEB: http://www.sibosascorinc.com
CONTACT: Timothy L Wallace

SOUND POWER INC
801 27th Avenue, Seattle,
Washington 98122, USA
TEL; +1 206 324 7340
E-MAIL: dtrione@netscape.net
CONTACT : D Trione

STONE & WEBSTER ENGINEERING CORPORATION
245 Summer Street, Boston
Massachusetts 02210-2325, USA
TEL: +1 617 589 2010
FAX: +1 617 589 1887
WEB:http://www.stoneweb.com
CONTACT :Dr R J Kulzkowski

SUNNYSIDE SOLAR INC
1014 Green River Road,
Guilford,
Vermont 05301-8117, USA
TEL: +1 802 257 1482
FAX: +1 802 254 4670
E-MAIL : sunnysde@sover.net
WEB: http://www.sunny sidesolar.com
CONTACT : R Gottlieb

TIM OLSEN CONSULTING
1428 South Humboldt,
Street, Denver,
Colorado 80210, USA
TEL: +1 303 777 3341
FAX: +1 303 777 3383
E-MAIL:tolsen@aol.com
WEB:http://
www.windtechnology.com
CONTACT : T L Olsen

TRIPLE PONT ENGINEERING
3475 West Justin Street,
Appleton, Wisconsin 54914-4165,
USA
TEL: +1 414 734 7775
CONTACT : P Kronberg

UEK CORPORATION
PO Box 3124, Annapolis, MD
21403, USA
TEL : +1 410 267 6507
FAX : +1 410 280 3717
E-MAIL : uekus@juno.com
WEB : http://www.uekus.com
CONTACT : D Vanthier

WINDWARD ENGINEERING LC
4661 Holly Lane,
Salt Lake City, UT 84117, USA
TEL: +1 801 278 7852
FAX: +1 801 272 4132
E-MAIL: chansen@windward engineering.com
WEB: http://www.windward engineering.com
CONTACT : C Hansen

HYBRID SYSTEMS

CRYSTAL PINES ALTERNATIVE ENERGY
61 Zonalea Lane,
Cherokee,
CA 95965, USA
TEL : +1 530 532 1972
FAX : +1 530 532 1359
E-MAIL : cpael@aol.com
WEB : http://www.solaerenergy-alt.com
CONTACT : F Fowler

ELEMENTAL RESOURCES
PO Box 21,
Haysville KS 67060, USA
TEL : +1 316 788 3678
FAX : +1 316 788 1793
E-MAIL :dowenerchi@earthlink.net
WEB : http://www.home.earth link.net/ndowernerchi
CONTACT : C Rob

FUTURE ELECTRIC ENERGY COMPANY
PO Box 1024, San Luis,
Obispo, California 93406, USA
TEL : +1 805 542 0250
FAX : +1 805 542 0222
E-MAIL : future@slonet.org
WEB : http://
www.futureelectricenergy.com
CONTACT : W Staple

PEERLESS WINSMITH INC
172 Eaton Street,
Springville,
New York 14141, USA
TEL: + 1 716 592 9311
FAX: + 1 716 592 9546
CONTACT: Joe Peters

SEADS SOLAR
PO Box 192, Harrington,
Maine 04643, USA
TEL: + 1 207 483 9763
E-MAIL: seadssolar@hotmail.com
WEB: http://seads@nemaine.com/ seads
CONTACT : D Edwing

STM POWER INC
275 Metty Drive, Ann Arbor,
Michigan 48103, USA
TEL: +1 734 995 1755
FAX: +1 734 995 0610
WEB:http://www.stmpower.com
CONTACT : S Johansson

TIM OLSEN CONSULTING
1428 South Humboldt
Street, Denver,
Colorado 80210, USA
TEL: +1 303 777 3341
FAX: +1 303 777 3383
E-MAIL:tolsen@aol.com
WEB:http://
www.windtechnology.com

OTHERS

1ST CENTURY ENERGY
2021 Zearing North West,
Albuquerque,
New Mexico 87104,
USA
TEL: + 1 505 243 4900
FAX: + 1 505 243 0885
CONTACT : Jeff Schmitt

AAF INTERNATIONAL
215 Central Avenue, Louisville
Kentucky 21202, USA
TEL: + 1 502 637 0690
FAX: + 1 502 637 0351

AALBORG INDUSTERIES INC
5300 Knowledge Parkway,
Erie, PA 16503, USA
TEL: + 1 814 879 7300
FAX: + 1 814 870 7188
WEB: http://www.aalborg industries.com

AARON EQUIPMENT COMPANIES
Areco,
735 East Green
Street Bensenville,
Illinois 60106, USA
TEL: + 1 630 350 2200
FAX: + 1 630 350 9047
E-MAIL: areco@aaronequip.com
WEB: http://www.aronequip.com
CONTACT: Jerrold Cohen

ADVANCED ENERGY SYSTEMS INC
28 Riverview Mill, Wilton,
New Hampshire 03086, USA
TEL: + 1 603 654 9322
FAX: + 1 603 654 9324
E-MAIL: mhensley@ad vancedenergy.com
WEB: http:// www.advancedenergy.com
CONTACT: Mark Hensley

AEROFIN CORPORATION
4621 Murray Place,
Lynchburg, VA 24502, USA
TEL: + 1 804 528 6300
FAX: + 1 804 528 6242
E-MAIL: sales@aerofin.com
WEB:http://www.aerofin.com
CONTACT: Geff Hagwood

ALLIED ENVIRONMENTAL TECHNOLOGIES INC
15182 Bolsa Chica Road,
Suite D, Huntingdon Beach,
California 92649, USA
TEL: + 1 714 799 9895
FAX: + 1 714 799 9795
E-MAIL: alentec@alentecinc.com
WEB: http://www.alentecnic.com
CONTACT: Dr. Henry V Krigmont

ALLIED SIGNAL POWER SYSTEMS INC
8725 Pan American Freeway Ne,
Albuquerque, NM 87113, USA
TEL: + 1 505 798 6000
FAX: + 1 505 798 6050
E-MAIL: parallon@alliedsignal.com
WEB: http://www.alliedsignal.com
CONTACT: Peter A Broussard

ALM SYSTEMS INC
1920 N St NW, Suite 750,
Washington, DC 20036, USA
TEL: + 1 202 778 8538
FAX: + 1 202 822 6410
E-MAIL: katya@eifer.com

ALTURDYNE
8050 Armour, San Diego,
California 92111, USA
TEL: + 1 858 565 2131
FAX: + 1 858 279 4296
E-MAIL: alturdyne@att.net
CONTACT: Frank Verbeke

AMERICAN HOFMANN CORPORATION
3700 Cohen Pl, PO Box 10369
Lynchburg, VA 24506, USA
TEL: + 1 804 522 0300
FAX: + 1 804 845 9229
E-MAIL: ken@hofmann.mhs.compuserve.com

AMERICAN LINE BUILDERS INC
246 Tucannon Rd.,
Dayton, WA 99328, USA
TEL: + 1 509 382 4766
FAX: + 1 509 382 2443
E-MAIL: jan@albinc.com
WEB: http://www.albinc.com
CONTACT: Jan B Willis

AMERICAN PULVERIZER-HUSTLER CONVEYOR
5540 West Park Avenue, St. Louis,
Missouri 63110, USA
TEL: + 1 314 781 6100
FAX: + 1 314 781 9209
E-MAIL: american@anet-stl.com
WEB: http://www.ampulverizer.com
CONTACT: Ed Kramer

ARLAND TOOOL & MANUFACTURING
421 Main Street, Sturbridge,
MA 01566, USA
TEL : +1 508 347 3368
FAX : +1 508 347 2986
E-MAIL : keith@arland.com

ARRAY TECHNOLOGIES
3312, Stanford NE, Alburqurque,
New Mexico 87107, USA
TEL : +1 505 881 7567
FAX : +1 505 881 7572
E-MAIL : sales@wattsun.com
WEB : http://www.wattsun.com
CONTACT : M Reed

ASCOR INC
100 Leader Heights Road,
York PA 17403, USA
TEL : +1 717 741 9436
FAX : +1 717 741 5941
E-MAIL : info@ascorinc.com
WEB : http://www.ascorinc.com
CONTACT : B Mecciche

AUTOMATED POWER EXCHANGE
5201, Great America Parkway,
Suite 522, Santa Clara, CA 95054, USA
TEL : +1 408 517 2100
FAX : +1 408 517 2985
E-MAIL :pepper@apx.com
WEB : http://www.apx.com
CONTACT : J C Pepper

AVIDA AMERICAS LLC
39, Broadway, Suite 1440,
New York, NY 10006, USA
TEL : +1 212 425 0400
FAX : +1 212 425 0455
E-MAIL : avidamericas@aol.com
WEB: http:// www.avidaamericas.com
CONTACT : J Lanccer

BABCOCK & WILCOX
Power Generation Group,
20 South van Buren Avenue,
Barberton, Ohio 44203, USA
TEL : +1 330 860 1186
FAX : +1 330 860 6362
E-MAIL: jsgittinger@pgg.mcdermott.com
WEB : http://www.babcock.com
CONTACT : J Gittinger

BAYLOR COMPANY
500 Industrial Boulevard, Sugarland,
Texas 77478, USA
TEL: + 1 281 240 6111
FAX: + 1 281 240 5074
E-MAIL: tpurtill@baylor.com
CONTACT: Tom Purtill

BELYEA COMPANY INC
2200 Northwood Avenue,
Easton, PA 18045-2239, USA
TEL : +1 610 515 8775
FAX : +1 610 515 1263
E-MAIL : sales@belyeapower.com
WEB : http://www.belyeapower.com
CONTACT : M Edwards

BESICORP DEVELOPMENT INC
1151 Flatbush Road, Kingston, NY
12401, USA
TEL : +1 845 336 7700
FAX : +1 845 336 7172
E-MAIL :wseils/besicorp.com
WEB : http://www.besicorp.com
CONTACT : W J Seils

BIOTECHNICAL PROCESSES INC
GPO Box 363549, San Juan,
00936 Puerto Rico, USA
TEL : +1 787 788 1500
FAX : +1 787 788 5075
E-MAIL : mszendrey@bacardi.com
CONTACT : Dr L M Szendrey

BOUNDLESS CORPORATION
PO Box 20510, Boulder,
CO 80308-3510, USA
TEL : +1 303 664 9962
FAX : +1 303 664 9960
E-MAIL : tfeaver@uswest.net
CONTACT : T Fesver

CES/WAY INTERNATIONAL INCORPORATED
2500 City West Boulevard, Suite
1800, Houston, Texas 77041, USA
TEL : +1 713 666 3541
FAX : +1 713 666 8455
E-MAIL : lat@cesway.com
WEB : http://www.cesway.com
CONTACT : M D Leach

CHEMCO WATER TECHNOLOGY INC
6014 North East,
124th Court, Vancouver,
Washington 98682, USA
TEL : +1 206 892 2418
FAX : +1 206 892 3518
E-MAIL : jwr@pacifier.com
CONTACT : Jon Robson

CITIZENS POWER
530 Atlantic Avenue, Boston,
Massachusetts 02210, USA
TEL : 1 617 912 6000
CONTACT : Matt Most

COGENEX CORPORATION
Boott Mills South, 100 Foot of
John Street, Lowell,
Massachusetts 01852, USA
TEL : + 1 978 441 0090
FAX : + 1 978 441 9299
E-MAIL : pryan@cogenex.com
WEB : http://www.cogenex.com
CONTACT : Paula Ryan

COLD FUSION TECHNOLOGY INC
PO Box 2816,
Concord NH, USA
TEL : + 1 603 228 4516
FAX : + 1 603 224 5975
E-MAIL : editor@infinite-energy.com
WEB : http://www.infinite-energy.com
CONTACT : Dr Eugene F Mallone

COLORADO COALITION FOR NEW ENERGY TECHNOLOGIES
7725 Malamute Trail, Evergreen,
Colorado 80439, USA
TEL : + 1 303 679 9331
FAX : + 1 815 328 1304
E-MAIL : coxcraig@att.net
CONTACT : Craig Cox

COMMUNITY POWER CORPORATION
306 McChain Road, Finleyville,
Pennsylvania 15332, USA
TEL : + 1 724 348 6386
FAX : + 1 724 348 8923
E-MAIL : artsolar@gocpc.com
WEB : http://www.gocpc.com
CONTACT : Mr Art Lilley

CONNECTIV / DELMARVA POWER
800 King Street,
PO Box 231, Wilmington,
Delaware 19899, USA
TEL : + 1 302 429 3055
FAX : + 1 302 429 3801
E-MAIL : ferguson@delmarva.com
CONTACT : William D Ferguson

CONTINENTAL FIELD MACHINING COMPANY INCORPORATED
1475 Rodenburg Road,
Schaumburg, Illinois 60193, USA
TEL : +1 708 893 1393
FAX : +1 708 893 7593
CONTACT : M Conway

CONVERGENCE LLC
1183 Parkway, Suite 200A,
Howell, MI 48443, USA
TEL : +1 517 505 0257
FAX : +1 517 545 5988
E-MAIL :
convergence@metroshores.net
CONTACT : S R Rebain

COSTICH COMPANY
15509 NE 129 Street,
Brush Prairie WA 98606, USA
TEL : +1 360 254 5416
E-MAIL : costich@pacifier.com

CREST
1200 18th Street NW, Suite 900,
Washington, DC 20036, USA
TEL : +1 202 530 2202
FAX : +1 202 887 0497
E-MAIL : info@crest.org

CRYSTAL SYSTEMS INC
27 Congress Street Salem,
Massachussets, 01970, USA
TEL : +1 978 745 0088
FAX : +1 978 744 5059
E-MAIL :crystalsystems.com
CONTACT : F Fowler

CURTIS THAXTER STEVENS BRODER AND MICOLEAU
1 Canal Plaza, Portland,
Maine 04112 USA
TEL : +1 207 775 2361
FAX : +1 207 775 0612
E-MAIL : jwb@curthax.com
CONTACT : J Bernotavich

DANIEL VALVE COMPANY
PO Box 40421,
Houston,
Texas 77240, USA
TEL: + 1 281 469 0550
FAX: + 1 281 894 1332
E-MAIL: lbabbidg@danielind.com
CONTACT: Lew Babbidge

DAY BERRY & HOWARD
CityPlace I, Hartford,
Connecticut 06103-3499, USA
TEL: + 1 860 275 0100
FAX: + 1 860 275 0343
E-MAIL: ggarfield@dbh.com
CONTACT: Gerald Garfield

DAYSTAR INC
3240 Majestic Ridge, Las Cruces,
New Mexico 88011, USA
TEL: + 1 505 522 4943
FAX: + 1 505 522 4943
E-MAIL: pvvern@zianet.com
WEB: http://www.zianet.com/daystar
CONTACT : Vern Risser

DELTAK A UNIT OF JASON INCORPORATED
2905 Northwest Boulevard, Suite
150 Plymouth, Minnesota 55441, USA
TEL: + 1 612 557 7440
FAX : + 1 612 557 4700
CONTACT : Dr. Wendell Hung

DIGITAL SOLAR TECHNOLOGIES
5775 Arapahoe Avenue, Boulder
Colorado 80303, USA
TEL: + 1 303 442 6553
FAX: + 1 303 442 6555
WEB: http://www.digitalsolar.com

DOMESTIC TECHNOLOGIES INC
Box 44, Evergreen,
Colorado 80439, USA
TEL: + 1 303 674 7700
FAX: + 1 303 674 7772

DRILL COOL SYSTEMS INC
627 William Street,
Bakersfield, California 93305, USA
TEL: + 1 661 633 2665
FAX: + 1 661 327 5890
E-MAIL: seymour@kernsteel.com
CONTACT: Philip Potter

DSV SAMSON TRANSPORT INC
200 Route 22 East, Hillside,
NJ 07205, USA
TEL: + 1 310 726 0444
FAX: + 1 310 726 0455
E-MAIL: projects@dsvsamson.com
WEB: http://www.dsvsamson.com
CONTACT: Frank Harzold

ECO ENERGIES
171 Commercial Street, Sunnyvale,
California 94086, USA
TEL: + 1 408 746 3062
FAX: + 1 408 746 3890
E-MAIL: Watts@ecoenergies.com
WEB: http://www.ecoenergies.com
CONTACT: Julie Forbes

ECO-ARCH DESIGN WORKS
PO Box 86, Woodstock,
NY 12498-0086, USA
TEL: + 1 914 247 4620
FAX: + 1 914 247 4620
E-MAIL: ecoarch_des@earthling.net
WEB: http://home.earthling.net/~ecoarch-des
CONTACT : Janue Welton

ENERGY PRODUCTS OF IDAHO EPI
4006, Industrial Avenue,
Coeur d'Alene, Idaho 83815, USA
TEL : + 1 208 765 1611
FAX : + 1 208 765 0503
E-MAIL : epi@energyproducts.com
WEB:http://
www.energyproducts.com
CONTACT : C Estrada

ENVIRONMENTAL BUILDING NEWS
122 Birge Street Suite 30,
Brattleboro, VT 05301, USA
TEL: +1 802 257 7300
FAX: +1 802 257 7304
E-MAIL: ebn@buildingreen.com
WEB: http://www.buildingreen.com

EXEL TECH
2225 East Loop 820 North,
Fort Worth, Texas 76118-7101, USA
TEL: +1 817 595 4969
FAX: +1 817 595 1290
E-MAIL: info@exeltech.com
WEB: http://www.exeltech.com
CONTACT : K Parsons

F-CHART SOFTWARE
4406 Fox Bluff Road, Middleton,
Wisconsin 53562, USA
TEL: + 1 608 836 8531
FAX: + 1 608 836 8536
E-MAIL: becman@engr.wisc.edu
WEB: http://bestware.net/tess/
fchart.html
CONTACT: William Beckman

FAIRFIELD ENGINEERING COMPANY
240 North Boone Avenue,
Marion, Ohio 43302, USA
TEL: +1 740 387 3327
FAX: + 1 740 387 4869
CONTACT : M McFann

FORAS SERVICE CORPORATION
63-66 S 19th Avenue,
PO Box 1043, N Palm Springs,
California 92258, USA
TEL: +1 619 329 1437
FAX: +1 619 329 1503
CONTACT : J Larsen

GATEWAY ASSOCIATES
524, San Anselmo Ave Ste 238,
San Anselmo, California 94960,
USA
TEL: + 1 415 461 3064
FAX: +1 415 461 2038
E-Mail: gateway@earthlink.net
WEB: http://homeearthlink.net/
~gatewaydes
CONTACT : A Stelman

GODDARD & GODDARD ENGINEERING-ENVIRONMENTAL STUDIES
6870 Frontage Road, Lucerne,
California 95458, USA
TEL : + 1 707 274 2171
FAX : + 1 707 274 2172
E-MAIL : goddardw@jps.net
CONTACT : Dr W Gooddard

GRAHAM MANUFACTURING CO INC
20 Florence Avenue, Batavia,
New York 14020, USA
TEL : + 1 716 343 2216
FAX : + 1 716 343 1097
E-MAIL : equipment@
graham-mfg.com
WEB: http://www.graham.mfg.com

GREEN PCS OF FLORIDA
2603 NE 17th Terrace, Gainesville,
FL 32609-3241, USA
TEL: + 1 352 376 1755
FAX: + 1 352 373 3399
E-MAIL: solardan@greenpcs.com
WEB: http://www.greenpcs.com
CONTACT : J P Gorman

HCI PUBLICATIONS
410 Archibald Street, Kansas City,
Missouri 64111-3001, USA
TEL: +1 816 931 1311
FAX: +1 816 931 2015
E-MAIL: info@hcipub.com
WEB: http://www.hcipub.com
CONTACT : C Vansant

HEC INCORPORATED
24 Prime Parkway,
Natick, Massachusetts 01760, USA
TEL: +1 508 653 0456
E-MAIL: jguertin@hecenergy.com
WEB: http://www.hcenergy.com
CONTACT : J Guertin

HOME BUILDERS INSTITUTE
1325 Iris Avenue,
Imperial Beach,
California 92032, USA
TEL: +1 619 429 8500
FAX: +1 619 424 9145
CONTACT: Karl Hansen

HOME POWER MAGAZINE
PO Box 520, Ashland,
OR 97520, USA
TEL: +1 541 512 0201
FAX: +1 541 512 0343
E-MAIL: hp@homepower.com
WEB: http://www.homepower.com
CONTACT : R Perez

HURST BOILER & WELDING COMPANY INC
Post Office Drawer 529,
21971 US Highway 319 South,
Coolidge, Georgia 31738, USA
TEL: +1 912 346 3545
FAX: +1 912 346 3874
E-MAIL: hboiler@rose.net
WEB: http://www.thomas
register.com/hurstboiler
CONTACT : G Zebley

HUTTON COMMUNICATIONS INC
Power Systems Group,
2520 Marsh Lane, Dallas,
Texas 75006, USA
TEL: +1 972 417 0508
FAX: +1 972 417 0260
WEB: http://www.huttoncom.com
CONTACT : P McClusky

IDAHO DEPARTMENT OF WATER RESOURCES
Energy Division, 1301 N Orchard
Boise, Idaho 83706, USA
TEL: +1 208 327 7962
FAX: +1 208 327 7866
E-MAIL: jbcrocke@idwr.state.id.us
WEB: http://www.idwr.state.id.us
CONTACT : J B Crockett

IDA-WEST ENERGY COMPANY
PO Box 7867, Boise,
Idaho 83702, USA
TEL: +1 208 395 8930
FAX: +1 208 395 8931
E-MAIL: mail@da-west.com
WEB: http://www.ida-west.com
CONTACT : R Hill

IDEAL ELECTRIC COMPANY
330 East First Street, Mansfield,
Ohio 44902, USA
TEL: +1 419 522 3611
FAX: +1 419 522 9386
CONTACT : J Adams

INTERMOUNTAIN SOLAR TECHNOLOGIES
10288 South Jordan Gateway #D,
South Jordan, Utah 84095, USA
TEL: +1 801 501 9353
FAX: +1 801 501 9352
WEB: http://www.intermountain
wholesale.com

INTERNATIONAL CHIMNEY CORPORATION
PO Box 260, Buffalo,
New York 14231-0260, USA
TEL: +1 800 828 1446
FAX: +1 716 634 3983
CONTACT : G Brand

INTERNATIONAL POWER MACHINERY CORPORATION
834 Terminal Tower, Cleveland,
Ohio 44113, USA
TEL: +1 216 621 9514
FAX: +1 216 621 9515
E-MAIL: kernX06@ibm.net
CONTACT : A H Kern

J&M INDUSTRIAL SUPPLY COMPANY
301 Ohio Avenue, Richmond
California 94804, USA
TEL: + 1 510 232 2600
FAX: + 1 510 232 5228
E-MAIL: pneumapress@earthlink.net
WEB: http://home.earthlink.net/~pneumapress
CONTACT : S Benesi

JADE MOUNTAIN INC
717 Poplar Avenue, Boulder,
CO 80304, USA
TEL: + 1 303 222 3500
FAX: + 1 303 222 3599
E-MAIL:steve.trog@jademountain.com
WEB: http://www.jademountain.com
CONTACT : Steve Trog

JB SYSTEMS INCORPORATED
21800 Oxnard Street, Woodland
Hills, California 91367, USA
TEL: + 1 818 340 9430
FAX: + 1 818 716 4168
CONTACT : D Pulleasse

JERICO ASSOCIATES
632 Plank Road Centre, Suite 108
Clifton Park, NY 12065, USA
TEL: + 1 518 383 1692
FAX: + 1 518 383 1658
CONTACT : J Coury

KEITH MANUFACTURING COMPANY
PO Box 1, 401 North West Adler,
Madras, Oregon 97741, USA
TEL: + 1 541 475 3802
FAX: + 1 541 475 2169
E-MAIL: sales@keithwalkingfloor.com
WEB: http://www.keithwalkingfloor.com
CONTACT : D Jackson

KELLY DRYE & WARREN LLP
101 Park Avenue, New York,
New York 10178, USA
TEL: + 1 212 808 7800
FAX: + 1 212 808 7897
WEB: http://www.kelleydrye.com
CONTACT : L E Carpenito

K JC OPERATING COMPANY
41100 Highway 395,
Boron,
California 93516, USA
TEL: + 1 760 762 5562
FAX: + 1 760 762 5546
WEB: http://www.kjcsolar.com
CONTACT : S Frier

KVAERNER
2600 Reach Road,
Williamsport
Pennsylvania 17701-0308, USA
TEL: + 1 570 326 3361
FAX: + 1 570 327 3121
CONTACT : D Williams

LAWRENCE I THORPE & CO
41 Woodstock Road,
Roswell,
Georgia 30075, USA
TEL: +1 770 993 1463
FAX: +1 770 993 1484
E-MAIL: lit@mindspring.com
CONTACT : L I Thrope

LEETZOW LIGHTING CONSULANT
PO Box 990-C,
Brandenton,
Florida 34206, USA
TEL: +1 941 756-5666
FAX: +1 941 751 5483

LOF ENERGY SYSTEMS INC
PO Box 9133 Denver,
Colorado 80209, USA
TEL: +1 303 777 2865
FAX:+1 303 777 2864
E-MAIL:lesipool@aol.com
WEB: http://www.energysavingpoolCovers.com
CONTACT : L OD Loff

M-E-C COMPANY
PO Box 330,
Neodesha,
Kansas 66757, USA
TEL: +1 316 325 2673
FAX: +1 316 325 2678
E-MAIL: mec@m-e-c.com
WEB: http://www.m-e-c.com

MIAMI WATER HEATER
1324 NW 29th Street,
Maimi,
Florida 33142, USA
TEL: +1 305 633 2656
FAX: +1 305 633 0374
E-MAIL: miawh@bellsouth.net
WEB: http://www.miamiwaterheater.com
CONTACT : C Sanchez

MOLDED FIBER GLASS COMPANIES/WEST
9400 Holly Road,
Adelanto,
California 92301, USA
TEL: + 1 760 246 4042
FAX: + 1 760 246 5500
EMAIL:denglemfg@aol.com
WEB: http://www.moldedfiberglass.com
CONTACT : D Engle

MONTGOMERY INDUSTRIES INTERNATIONAL INCORPORATED
PO Box 3687,
Jacksonville,
Florida, 32206, USA
TEL:+1 904 355 5671
FAX: +1 904 355 0401
CONTACT: Angela Nachman

MUNGER OIL INFORMATION SERVICE INCORPORATED
9800 S Sepulvada Boulevard,
Los Angeles, California 90045-0738, USA
TEL: +1 213 776 3990
FAX: +1 310 645 9147
CONTACT : W Gilbert

NAHB RESEARCH CENTER INC
400 Prince George's Boulevard,
Upper Marlboro,
Maryland 20774, USA
TEL: +1 301 249 4000
FAX: +1 303 231 1448
CONTACT : L Bowles

NASH US
700 McKeesport Road, Elizanbeth
Pennsylvania 15037, USA
TEL:+1 412 384 3610
FAX: +1 412 384 2929
CONTACT : P Fieldman

NEPCCO ENVIRONMENTAL SYSTEM
2140-100 NE 36th Avenue
Ocala Florida 34470, USA
TEL: +1 352 867 7482
FAX: +1 352 867 1320
E-MAIL: jsreese@nepcco.com
WEB: http://www.nepcco.com/enviro

NIAGARA MOHAWK POWER CORPORATION
300 Erie Boulevard West,
Syracuse, New York 13201, USA
TEL: + 1 315 428 6654
CONTACT: Art Peterson

NIXON PEABODY
1 Thomas Circle, Suite 800,
Washington,
District of Columbia 20005, USA
TEL: + 1 202 457 5300
FAX: + 1 202 457 5355
CONTACT: William Andrews

NOGEE & WARTEL
900 Ellison Avenue, Suite 211,
Westbury, New York 11590, USA
TEL: + 1 516 222 6575
FAX: + 1 516 222 6577
E-MAIL: jnogee00@counsel.com
CONTACT : J L Nogee

O'MELVENY & MYERS LLP
400 South Hope Street,Los Angeles,
California 90071-2899, USA
TEL: + 1 213 430 6000
FAX: + 1 213 430 6407
E-MAIL: omminfo@omm.com
WEB: http://www.omm.com
CONTACT: A C Schaffhauser

OGDEN ENERGY GROUP INC
40 Lane Road, Fairfield,
New Jersey 07007, USA
TEL: + 1 973 882 9000
FAX: + 1 973 882 7220
WEB: http://www.ogdencorp.com
CONTACT: Gloria A Mills

PAJARITO ENTERPRISES CONSULTING SERVICES INC
3 Jemez Lane,
Los Alamos,
New Mexico 87544, USA
TEL: + 1 505 672 9770
FAX: + 1 505 672 0358
E-MAIL:
75033.2375@compuserve.com
CONTACT: Dr. John G Rowley

PAUL GIPE & ASSOCIATES
208 S Green Street,
5, Tehachapi,
California 93561-1741, USA
TEL: + 1 661 822 9150
FAX: + 1 661 822 8452
E-MAIL: pgipe@igc.org
CONTACT: Mr Paul Gipe

PAWLING CORPORATION
Extrusion Division,
157 Charles Colman Boulevard,
Pawling,
New York 12564, USA
TEL: + 1 914 855 1000
FAX: + 1 914 855 1937
E-MAIL: s.smith@pawlingcorp.com
WEB: http://www.pawling.com
CONTACT: Stephen J Smith

PEARLESS CORPORATION
PO Box 760, Paragould,
Arizona 72450, USA
TEL: + 1 501 236 7753
FAX: + 1 501 239 2230
CONTACT: Phil Williams

PERFECTPOWER.NET
9436 N Arroya Vista Drive
Phoenix, Arizona 85028, USA
TEL: + 1 602 971 2588
E-MAIL: john@perfectpower.net
WEB: http://www.perfectpower.net
CONTACT: Bruno Legendre

PGI EXHIBITIONS
8989 Rio San Diego Drive,
Suite 160, San Diego,
CA 92108-1647, USA
TEL: +1 619 294 2999
FAX: +1 619 294 6699
E-MAIL:kmoon@pgi.com
CONTACT : K Moon

PHILIP SERVICES CORPORATION
31 Waldron Way, Portland,
Maine 04103, USA
TEL: +1 207 797 0006
FAX: +1 207 797 0013
CONTACT : Jo Fogagey

PHOTOVOLTAIC RESOURCES INTERNATIONAL
PVCAD Division,
1440 West Meseto Avenue,
Mesa, Arizona 85202, USA
TEL: +1 480 345 1686
FAX : +1 480 345 6698
E-MAIL:pvcad@primenet.com
CONTACT : W J Kaszeta

PHOTRON INC
PO Box 578, Willits,
California 95490- 0578, USA
TEL: + 1 707 459 3211
FAX : + 1 707 459 2165
CONTACT : Clindy Kammer

PLANERGY INC
901 South MoPac Expressway,
Barton Oaks Plaza Suite 495,
Austin, Texas 78746, USA
TEL: +1 512 327 6830
FAX: + 1 512 327 2553
WEB:http://www.planergy.com
CONTACT : S M Wiese

PLUMLEY ASSOCIATES
341 Abbe Road Ext,
South Windsor CT 06074, USA
TEL: +1 860 644 8364
FAX:+1 860 644 7386
E-MAIL : alplumley@snet.net
CONTACT : A Plumley

POINT EIGHT POWER INCORPORATED
1510 Engineers Road,
Belle Chasse,
Lousiana 700 37, USA
TEL: + 1 504 394 6100
FAX: + 1 504 394 6686
CONTACT: Carl Boudreaux

POSITIVE ENERGY INC
3900 Paseo Delsel #210,
Santa Fe,
New Mexico 87505, USA
TEL: +1 505 424 1112
FAX:+1 505 424 1113
E-MAIL : info@positivenergy.com
WEB:http://www.positivenergy.com
CONTACT : A Sindelar

POWER QUEST INC
3400 Corporate Way Suite C,
Duluth, GA 30096, USA
TEL: +1 770 418 1850
FAX: +1 770 418 0258
E-MAIL: niklas@powerquest.com
WEB: http://www.powerquest.com
CONTACT : N Gerborg

PPC INDUSTRIES INCORPORATED
3000 East Marshall,
Langview, Texas 75601, USA
TEL: +1 903 758 3395
FAX: +1 903 758 6487
E-MAIL: gerry@ppcesp.com
CONTACT: Gerry Graham

PV NETWORK NEWS
2303 Cedros Circle,
Sante Fe,
NM 87505-5252, USA
TEL: + 1 505 473 1067
FAX: + 1 505 473 1067
E-MAIL: pvpaulset@aol.com
CONTACT : P Wilkins

RADIANT TECHNOLOGY CORPORATION
1335 S Arcadia Avenue,
Fullerton,
California 92831-5315,
USA
TEL: + 1 714 991 0200
FAX: + 1 714 991 0600
CONTACT : L R McNamee

RANSOME ENGINE
2975 Galloway Road,
Bensalem,
Pennsylvania 19020, USA
TEL: + 1 215 244 0600
FAX: + 1 215 245 2779
CONTACT : J Sherman

RANSOME MANUFACTURING
3495 South Maple Avenue,
Fresno,
California 93725, USA
TEL: + 1 559 485 0979
FAX: + 1 559 485 8869
CONTACT : K Hanchett

REDUCTION TECHNOLOGY INC
PO Box 297, Leeds,
Alabama 35094-0297, USA
TEL : +1 205 699 6022
FAX : +1 205 699 6025
E-MAIL : reductiontechnology
@bham.net
WEB : http://www.reduction
technology.com
CONTACT : Don Farnham

REMOTE POWER INTERNATIONAL
18 Whedbee Street,
Fort Collins,
Colorado 80524, USA
TEL : +1 970 498 8947

RESOURCE ENERGY CORP
PO Box 10985, Fort Smith,
Arkansas 72917-0985, USA
TEL : +1 501 452 2127
FAX : +1 501 452 2128
E-MAIL : pslbg@ipa.net
CONTACT : R Gillson

RODE & ASSOCIATES LLC
66 Cedar Street, Suite 301
Newington, CT 06111, USA
TEL: + 1 860 594 7183
FAX: + 1 860 594 7184
E-MAIL: rode@rode-llc.com
WEB: http://www.rode-llc.com
CONTACT : D M Rode

RUSSELECTRIC
South Shore Park, Hingham,
Massachusetts 02043-4387, USA
TEL: + 1 617 749 6000
FAX: + 1 617 749 8077
E-MAIL: marketing@russelectric.com
WEB: http://www.russelectric.com
CONTACT : J Meuleman

RV POWER PRODUCTS
1058 Monterey Vista Way,
Encinitas CA 92024, USA
TEL: + 1 760 944 8882
E-MAIL: info@rvpowerproducts.com
WEB: http://
www.rvpowerproducts.com

SBT DESIGNS
8924 Saddle Trail, San Antonio,
Texas 78255, USA
TEL: + 1 210 698 7109
FAX: + 1 210 698 7147
E-MAIL: sbtdesigns@bigplanet.com
WEB: http://www.sbtdesigns.com
CONTACT : S Sheperd

SEA SOLAR POWER INC
2422 South Queen Street, York
Pennsylvania 17402, USA
TEL: + 1 717 741 0884
FAX: + 1 717 741 0886
CONTACT: Robert Nicholson

SEACO TECHNOLOGIES INC
PO Box 80205,
Bakersfield,
California 93380, USA
TEL: + 1 661 326 1522
FAX: + 1 661 871 6757
E-MAIL: chowell@seacotech.com
WEB: http://www.seacotech.com
CONTACT : C Howell

SENTRY EQUIPMENT CORP
856 East Armour Road,
PO Box 127, Oconomowoc,
Wisconsin 53066-0127, USA
TEL: + 1 262 567 7256
FAX: + 1 262 567 4523
E-MAIL: sales@sentry-equip.com
WEB: http://www.sentry-equip.com
CONTACT : W Mebly

SHERMAN FEHER
5350 South Fulton Court,
Englewood,
Colorado 80111-3666, USA
TEL: + 1 303 843 9607

SHURFLO PUMP MFG CO
12650 Westminister Avenue,
Santa Ana,
California 92706-2100, USA
TEL: +1 714 554 7709
FAX: +1 714 554 4721
WEB: http://www.shurflo.com
CONTACT : T Barber

SIGARCA INC
3658 NW 41st Place Gainesville
Florida 32605-1469, USA
TEL: +1 352 373 2973
FAX: +1 352 373 2491
E-MAIL: sebac@juno.com
WEB: http://www.agen.ufl.edu/
~sifontes
CONTACT : Dr J R Sifontes

SKINNER ENGINE CO
Power Division,
337 West 12th Street,
PO Box 1149, Erie,
Pennsylvania 16403, USA
TEL: +1 814 459 0570
FAX: +1 814 452 6259
E-MAIL: skinnereng@aol.com
CONTACT : J Feuell

SOCIAL ARCHITECT ASSOCIATES
45, High Bluff Road,
Cape Elizabeth ME 04107, USA
TEL:+1 207 799 0072
E-MAIL:joannegus@msn.com
CONTACT : A T Jaccaci

SOLAQUA INC
PO Box 4976, EL Paso, TX 79914, USA
TEL:+1 915 726 2893

SOLAR WATER TECHNOLOGIES INC
426-B Elm Avenue, Portsmouth,
VA 23704, USA
TEL:+1 757 398 0098
FAX:+1 603 925 1964
E-MAIL:swt@solarwater.com
WEB:http://www.solarwater.com

SOLUZ INC
55 Middlesex Street Unit 221,
North Chelmsford,
Massachusetts 01863, USA
TEL: +1 978 251 5290
FAX: +1 978 251 5291
E-MAIL: soluz@igc.org
WEB: http://www.soluz.net

SOUTHPORT EQUIPMENT CORPORATION
6914 Canby Avenue #102,
Reseda, CA 91335, USA
TEL: +1 818 705 8300
FAX: +1 818 705 8762
CONTACT : K Buttke

STELLAR SUN
2121 Watt Street, Little Rock,
Arkansas 72227-4000, USA
TEL: +1 501 225 0700
FAX: +1 501 225 2920
E-MAIL:stellarsun@aristole.net
WEB:http://www.stellarsun.com
CONTACT : W Ball

STONE & WEBSTER MANA GEMENT CONSULTANTS INC
250 West 34th Street, New York,
New York 10119, USA
TEL: +1 212 290 7190
FAX: +1 212 290 7033
CONTACT : W F Griffifth

SUNWATT CORP
RR2 Box 7751, Jonesport,
ME 04649, USA
TEL: +1 207 497 2204
FAX: +1 505 204 5626
E-MAIL: sunwatt@juno.com
WEB: http://www.ecomall/biz/sunwatt.htm
CONTACT : R J Komp

TEMTEX TEMPERATURE SYSTEMS & COMPONENTS CO.,
PO Box 1420, 715 West Sears
Street Denison, TX 75020-3239, USA
TEL: +1 903 463 7000
FAX: +1 903 465 5037
E-MAIL: temtex@texoma.net
WEB: http://www.temtex.net
CONTACT : W M Wright

THE BLUEMENAUER CORPORATION
2708 Rew Circle, Ocoee,
Florida 34761-2997, USA
TEL : +1 407 656 7575
FAX : +1 407 656 8589

THE CINCINNATI GEAR COMPANY
5657 Wooster Pike,
Cincinnati, Ohio 45227, USA
TEL : + 1 513 271 7700
FAX : + 1 513 271 0049
E-MAIL :
cintigear@worldnet.att.net
CONTACT : Steve Crowell

THE TRADE FAIR GROUP INC
1220 Blalock Rd., Suite 310,
Houston, TX 77055, USA
TEL: +1 713 463 9595
FAX: +1 713 463 9595
WEB: http://
www.electricpowerexpo.com

THELEN REID & PRIEST LLP
701 Pennsylvania Avenue
NW, Suite 800, Washington
DC 20004, USA
TEL: +1 202 508 4000
FAX: +1 202 508 4321
E-MAIL: mzimmer@thelenreid.com
CONTACT : M J Zimmer

THIN-LITE CORPORATION
530 Constitution Avenue,Camarillo,
California 93012, USA
TEL: +1 805 987 5021
FAX: +1 805 388 0921
E-MAIL:thinlite@thinlite.com
WEB:http://www.thinlite.com
CONTACT : L Fleming

THOMASON MECHANCIAL CORPORATION
Corporate Office,
19002 South Santa
Fe Avenue, Rancho Dominquez,
California 90221, USA
TEL: +1 310 639 3523
FAX: +1 310 639 8217
E-MAIL:bperry@thomasonmech.com
WEB:http://
www.thomasonmech.com
CONTACT : B Perry

TIDELAND SIGNAL CORPORATION
PO Box 52430, Houston,
Texas 77052, USA
TEL: +1 713 681 6101
FAX: +1 713 681 6233
E-MAIL:hq@tidelandsignal.com
WEB:http://www.tidelandsignal.com

TRACE TECHNOLOGIES CORPORATION
161G South Vasco Road, Livermore,
California 94550, USA
TEL: +1 925 245 5400
FAX: +1 925 245 1022
WEB:http://www/tracetec.com

TRANS MOUNTAIN CONSULTING CO
123 South Paradise Road,
Golden, Colorado 80401, USA
TEL: +1 303 526 9296
FAX: +1 303 526 7841
E-MAIL: tmcco@msn.com
WEB: http://www.waterconflicts.com
CONTACT : H C Young

TRANTER PHE INC
PO Boz 2289, Wichita Falls,
TX 76307, USA
TEL: +1 940 723 7125
FAX: +1 940 723 5131
E-MAIL: sales@tranter.com
WEB: http://www.tranter.com
CONTACT : R Hill

TUV ENERGY SERVICE
C/o Strategic Power Systems,
11301 Carmel Commons
Boulevard Suite 308,
Charlotte, NC 28226, USA
TEL: +1 704 544 5501
FAX: +1 704 554 5505
E-MAIL: Kevin.licata@spcinc.com
CONTACT : K Licata

TVIG INC
100 Cherokee Boulevard, Suite 100,
Chattanooga, TN 37405, USA
TEL: +1 423 266 0502
FAX: +1 703 995 0328
E-MAIL: rhe_tvig@compuserve.com
WEB: http://www.tvigroup.com
CONTACT : R Blenker

TWIN CITY CLARAGE FANS
245 Center St. North, Birmingham,
Albama 35204, USA
TEL: +1 205 581 3267
FAX: +1 205 251 6258
E-MAIL: sales@clarage.com
WEB: http://www.clarage.com
CONTACT : M Carroll

UTILITY DATA INSTITUTE
1200 G Street NW, Suite 250,
Washington DC 20005, USA
TEL: +1 202 942 8788
FAX: +1 202 942 8789
E-MAIL: info@udidata.com
WEB: http://www.udidata.inter.net
CONTACT : L Hannon

VANNER INC
Vanner Power Group, 4282
Reynolds Drive, Hilliard, Ohio
43026, USA
TEL: +1 614 771 2718
FAX: +1 614 771 4904
E-MAIL: pwrsales@vanner.com
WEB: http://www.vanner.com
CONTACT : M Taylor

VIRON ENERGY SERVICES
216 North West Platte
Valley Drive, Kansas City,
Missouri 64150-9703, USA
TEL: +1 816 741 3500
FAX: +1 816 746 0260
E-MAIL: marketing@viron.com
CONTACT : J Mahoney

WEATHERFORD INTERNATIONAL INC
1000 Church Road,
Rio Vista California 94571, USA
TEL: + 1 707 374 6493
FAX: + 1 707 374 6192
E-MAIL:
rickbenton@weatherford.com
WEB: http://www.weatherford.com
CONTACT: Rick Benton

WESTERN RESOURCES
818 South Kansas Avenue
PO Box 889, Topeka,
Kansas 66601, USA
TEL: + 1 785 575 1664
FAX: + 1 785 575 1774

WILLIAMS FORM ENGINEERING CORPORATION
280 Ann Street, PO Box 7389,
Grand Rapids, MI 49510, USA
TEL: + 1 616 365 9220
FAX: + 1 616 365 2668
E-MAIL: wfec@iserv.net
WEB : http://www.williamform.com
CONTACT: Kevin Heinert

WILLIAMS PATENT CRUSHER & PULVERISER COMPANY
2701 North Broadway, St. Louis,
Missouri 63102, USA
TEL: + 1 314 621 3348
FAX: + 1 314 436 2639
E-MAIL:crusher@inlink.com
WEB : http://www.willcrush.com
CONTACT : C Rehmer

WISCONSIN ENERGY BUREAU
PO Box 7868, Madison,
Wisconsin 53707-7868, USA
TEL: +1 800 762 7077
WEB: http://
www.wifocusonenergy.com
CONTACT : Mr D Wichert

U.S.A.

WOLF AND ASSOCIATES INC
13911 Unity Street NW, Ramsey,
Minnesota 55303, USA
TEL: +1 612 576 9040
FAX: +1 612 576 9070
E-MAIL: wolf@bitstream.net
CONTACT : K Surma

WORLDWATCH INSTITUTE
1776 Massachusetts Avenue,
Washington DC 20036-1904, USA
TEL: +1 202 452 1999
FAX: +1 202 296 7365
E-MAIL: worldwatch@worldwatch.org
WEB: http://www.worldwatch.org
CONTACT : R Bell

YOUNG SOMMER LLC
5 Palisades Drive, Albany,
New York 12205, USA
TEL: + 1 518 438 9907
AX: + 1 518 438 9914
E-MAIL: dwooley@igc.org
CONTACT : D Wooley

SUPPLIERS

BATTERIES/INVERTERS

ATLANTIC SOLAR
9351-J Philadelphia Road,
PO Box 70060, Baltimore,
MD 21237,
USA
TEL: +1 410 686 3120
FAX: +1 410 686 4271
E-MAIL: partners@atlanticsolar.com
CONTACT: Dough Keller

CELL ENERGY
3190 B Orange Grove Avenue,
North Highlands,
California 95660,
USA
TEL : +1 916 484 7974
FAX : +1 916 484 1415
CONTACT : Mac Maclure

CONCORDE BATTERY CORPORATION
2009 San Bernadino Road,
West Covina,
California 91790, USA
TEL : + 1 626 813 1234
FAX : + 1 626 813 1235
E-MAIL : skipkoss@aol.com
WEB : http://
www.concordebattery.com
CONTACT : Skip Koss

CONE CONSTRUCTION / SOLAR TECHNOLOGIES
PO Box 52,
Salida,
Colorado 81201, USA
TEL : + 1 719 530 0718
E-MAIL : coneco@rmii.com

CRUISING EQUIPMENT COMPANY
5245 Shilsole avenue,
NW, Seattle WA 98107-4833,
USA
TEL : +1 206 782 8100
FAX : +1 206 782 4336
E-MAIL :ceco@nwlink.com
WEB : http://
www.cruisingequip.com
CONTACT : G A Ure

ENERSYS INC
Corporate Headquarters,
2366 Bernville Road,
PO Box14145,
Reading,
Pennsylvania 19612-4145, USA
TEL: +1 610 208 1991
E-MAIL:
special.batteries@uk.enersysinc.com
WEB: http://www.enersysinc.com

ENERGY APPLICATIONS INC
384 Rutherford Avenue,
Franklin, New Jersey 07416, USA
TEL: +1 973 827 1010
FAX: +1 973 209 4666
CONTACT : G Mckenna

GNB TECHNOLOGIES
Telecommunications and Power
Control, 829 Parkview Boulevard,
Lombard Illinois 60148-3249,
USA
TEL : + 1 630 932 3750
FAX : + 1 630 629 2635
WEB : http://www.gnb.com
CONTACT : Sean Blaylock

HELIOTROPE GENERAL
3733 Kenora Drive,
Spring Valley,
California 91977, USA
TEL: +1 619 460 3930
FAX: +1 619 460 9211
WEB: http://www.hg1.com
CONTACT: Sam Dawson

HYDROCAP CORP
975 NW 95th Street Miani,
Florida 33150, USA
TEL: +1 305 696 2504
CONTACT : G Peroni

INDUSTRIAL BATTERY ENGINEERING INC
9121 DeGarmo Avenue,
Sun Valley California 91352,
USA
TEL: +1 818 767 7067
FAX: +1 818 767 7173
WEB: http:.//www.ibe-inc.com

JOHNSON CONTROLS INCORPORATED
Specialty Battery Division,
900 East Keefe Avenue, Milwaukee,
Wisconsin 53212, USA
TEL: + 1 414 961 6502
FAX: + 1 414 961 6506
CONTACT : B Crowe

KURZ INSTRUMENTS INC
2411 Garden Road, Monterey,
California 93940, USA
TEL: +1 831 646 5911
FAX: +1 831 646 8901
E-MAIL: sales@kurz-instruments.com
WEB: http://www.kurz-instruments.com
CONTACT: Tom Setliff

NIAGARA MOHAWK POWER CORPORATION
300 Erie Boulevard West,
Syracuse, New York 13201, USA
TEL: + 1 315 428 6654
CONTACT: Art Peterson

PHOTO EMISSION TECH INC
3255 Grande Vista Drive,
Newbury Park CA 91320, USA
TEL: +1 805 499 7667
FAX: +1 805 499 6854
E-MAIL: sales@photoemission.com
WEB: http://
www.photoemission.com

POWERCELL CORPORATION
Powerblock Division,
9202 South Darlington,
Tulsa,
OK 74137, USA
TEL: +1 918 645 3973
FAX: +1 918 496 7853
E-MAIL: slatteryje@aol.com
WEB: http://www.powercell.com
CONTACT : J E Slattery

RAESTORAGE BATTERY COMPANY
51 Deming Road, PO Box 8005
Berlin, Connecticut 06037, USA
TEL: + 1 860 828 6007
FAX: + 1 860 828 4540
CONTACT : R A Earley

S&C ELECTRC COMPANY
2010 Energy Drive,
PO Box 879, East Troy,
WI53120, USA
TEL: +12626427200
FAX: +12626427760
E-MAIL: thuber@sandc.com
WEB: http://www.sandc.com
CONTACT: Tom Huber

SAFT AMERICA INC
3 Powdered Metals Drive,
North Haven, CT 06473, USA
TEL: + 1 203 239 4718
FAX: + 1 203 234 7598
WEB: http://www.saft.alcatel.com

SEMIKRON INC
11 Executive Drive, Hudson,
NH 03051, USA
TEL: +16038838102
FAX: +16038838021
E-MAIL: sales.skusa@semikron.com
WEB: http://www.semikron.com

SOLAR ELECTRIC INC
5555 Santa Fe Street #D, San
Diego, California, 92109-1602, USA
TEL:+1 619 581 0051
FAX:+1 619 581 6440
E-MAIL:solar@cts.com
WEB:http://www.solarelectricinc.com
CONTACT : Michael Collins

TROJAN BATTERY COMPANY
12380 Clark Street,
Santa Fe Springs,
California 90670, USA
TEL: +1 562 946 8381
FAX: +1 562 906 4033
WEB: http://www.trojanbattery.com

STORAGE TANK

AO SMITH HARVESTORE PRODUCTS INCORPORATED
345 Harvestore Drive,
Dekalb, Illinois 60115, USA
TEL: + 1 815 756 1551
FAX: + 1 815 756 7821
CONTACT: Francis Grillot

PIPING

LABARGE PIPE & STEELS COMPANY
901 North Tenth Street,
St Louis
Missouri 63101, USA
TEL: + 1 314 231 3400
FAX: + 1 314 982 9395
CONTACT : T R Engles

NORTH WEST PIPE & STEEL COMPANY
3030 North Washington Street
Denver, Colorado 80216, USA
TEL: + 1 303 289 4080
FAX: + 1 303 288 1068

INSTRUMENTATION

ABUNDANCE TECHNOLOGIES
Product Development,
776 NW 8th Court, Suite B,
Hillsboro, Oregon 97124-2202, USA
TEL : + 1 503 648 6750
FAX : + 1 503 648 5662
E-MAIL : westlake@aracnet.com
CONTACT : Richard T Westlake

ALTERNATIVE ENERGY DEVELOPMENT INC-AED
8455 Colesville Road, Suite 1225,
Silver Spring, MD 20910, USA
TEL: +1 301 608 3666
FAX: +1 301 608 3667
CONTACT: Mathew S Mendis

AIXTRON INC
1670 Barclay Blvd, Buffalo Grove,
Lllinos 60089, USA
TEL: +1 847 215 7335
FAX: +1 847 215 7341
CONTACT: Mr Andreas Melas

AMETEK POWER & INDUSTRIAL PRODUCTS
Station Square Two, Paoli,
PA 19301, USA
TEL: + 1 610 647 2121
FAX: + 1 610 296 3412
E-MAIL: bill.mullan@ametek.com

AUGUSTYN + COMPANY
PO Box 7075, Berkeley,
California 94707, USA
TEL: +1 510 525 2505
E-MAIL: jaugustyn@dgms.com
WEB: http://www.dqms.com
CONTACT: James Augustyn

BALMAC INC
4010 Main Street, Hilliard,
Ohio 43026-1423, USA
TEL : +1 614 876 1295
FAX : +1 614 771 5608
E-MAIL : balmacinc@aol.com
CONTACT : M Slebodnik

BTU INTERNATIONAL INC
23 Esquire Road, North Billerica
Massachussetts 01862, USA
TEL : +1 508 667 4111
FAX : +11 508 667 9068
E-MAIL : sales@btu.com
WEB : http://www.btu.com
CONTACT : N Kivlehan

BZ PRODUCTS
7614 Manon Court, St. Louis
Missouri, 63143, USA
TEL : +1 314 644 2490
FAX : +1 314 644 6121

EXEL TECH
7317 Jack Newell Blvd North,
Fort Worth Texas 76118-7101, USA
TEL: +1 817 595 4969
FAX: +1 817 595 1290
E-MAIL: info@exeltech.com
WEB: http://www.exeltech.com
CONTACT: Kevin Parsons

GENERAL KINEMATICS CORP
Sales, 777 Lake Zurich Road,
Barrington, Lllinols 60010, USA
TEL: +1 847 381 2240
FAX: +1 847 381 1376
E-MAIL: mail@generalkinematics.com
WEB: http://www.generalkinematics.com
CONTACT: Bill Guptail

GRANUTECH- SATURN SYSTEMS
201 East Shady Grove Road, Grand
Prairie, Texas 75050, USA
TEL: +1 972 790 7800
FAX: +1 972 790 8733
WEB: http://www.granutech.com

HONEYWELL
21111 North 19th Avenue, Phoenix,
AZ 85027-2708, USA
TEL: +1 602 436 2021
FAX: +1 602 436 6661
E-MAIL: greg.miller@honeywell.com
WEB: http://www.honeywell.com
CONTACT: Gregory Miller

INDEPENDENT ENERGY INC
42 Ladd Street,East Greenwich,
Rhode Island 02818, USA
TEL: +1 401 884 6990
FAX: +1 401 885 1500
WEB: http://www.goldline
controls.com
CONTACT : J Pizeir

MORNINGSTAR CORPORATION
1098 Washington Crossing Road
Washington Crossing,
PA 18977, USA
TEL: + 1 215 321 4457
FAX: +1 215 321 4458
E-MAIL:info@morningstarcorp.com
WEB:http://www.morningstarcorp.com
CONTACT : L Gordon

MOTION DYNAMICS GROUP INC
Aerospace Tech, Box 97,
Freeland, PA, 18224, USA
TEL: +1 717 443 7892
FAX: +1 717 443 7892
E-MAIL:hanging@ptd.net
CONTACT : S Schwiks

SMA AMERICA INC
20830 Red Dog Road,
Grass Valley,
CA 95945, USA
TEL: +15302734895
FAX: +15302747271
E-MAIL: berdner@sma-america.com
WEB: http://www.sma-america.com
CONTACT: John Berdner

SOLAR HEATED SWIMMING POOLS AND DOMESTIC HOT WATER SYSTEMS
42 Ladd Street,
East Greenwich,
RI 02818, USA
TEL:+1 401 884 6990
FAX:+1 401 885 1500
WEB:http://
www.goldlinecontrols.com
CONTACT : D Pickard

SOUTHWEST TECHNOLOGY DEVELOPMENT INSTITUTE
1505 Payne Street, NMSU, Las Cruces, New Mexico 88003, USA
TEL: +1 505 646 1049
FAX: +1 505 646 3841
E-MAIL: swtdi@nmsu.edu
CONTACT : A Kosenthal

SPECIALITY CONCEPTS INC
8954 Mason Avenue,
Chatsworth,
California 91311, USA
TEL: +1 818 998 5238
FAX: +1 818 998 5253
E-MAIL: speccon@earthlink.net
WEB: http://www.specialityconcepts.com
CONTACT : L Gonzalez

TEXAS ELECTRONICS INC
5529 Redfield Street,
Dallas, TX 75235, USA
TEL: +1 214 631 2490
FAX: +1 214 631 4218
E-MAIL: info@texaselectronics.com
WEB:http://www.texas
electronics.com
CONTACT : J Young

THE EPPLEY LABORATORY INC
12 Sheffield Avenue,
PO Box 419, New Port,
Rhode Island 02 840, USA
TEL: +1 401 847 1020
FAX: +1 401 847 1031
E-MAIL: eplab@mail.bbsnet.com
WEB: http://www.eppleylab.com
CONTACT: Thomas D Kirk

THE FOXBORO COMPANY
33 Commercial Street, Foxboro,
Massachusetts 02035, USA
TEL: +1 508 543 8750
FAX: +1 508 549 6750
WEB: http://www.foxboro.com

XANTREX TECHNOLOGY INC
5916 195th Northeast, Arlington,
WA 98223, USA
TEL: +1 360 435 8826
FAX: +1 360 435 2229
WEB: http://www.xantrex.com
CONTACT: Kevin Hagen

COATINGS & PAINTS

SOLAR ENERGY CORPORATION
PO Box 3065, Princeton,
New Jersey 08543-3065, USA
TEL:+1 609 883 7700
FAX:+1 609 497 0182
E-MAIL:71263.413@compuserve.com
WEB:http://www.solec.org

SOLEC-SOLAR ENERGY CORPORATION
129 Walters Avenue Ewing Township,
New Jersey 08638 -1829, USA
TEL:+1 609 883 7700
FAX:+1 609 497 0182
E-MAIL:71263.413@compuserve.com
WEB:http://www.solec.org
CONTACT : R J Aresty

INSULATIONS

API CONSTRUCTION COMPANY
2366 Rose Place,
St. Paul,
Minnesota 55113-2588,
USA
TEL:+ 1 651 636 4320
FAX: + 1 651 636 0312
E-MAIL: ryan.miner@apigroupinc.com
WEB: http://www.apigroupinc.com
CONTACT: Ryan Miner

SOLAR ENERGY CORPORATION
PO Box 3065,
Princeton,
New Jersey 08543-3065,
USA
TEL:+1 609 883 7700
FAX:+1 609 497 0182
E-MAIL:71263.413@compuserve.com
WEB:http://www.solec.org

SOLEC-SOLAR ENERGY CORPORATION
129 Walters Avenue,
Ewing Township,
New Jersey 08638 -1829,
USA
TEL:+1 609 883 7700
FAX:+1 609 497 0182
E-MAIL:71263.413@compuserve.com
WEB:http://www.solec.org
CONTACT : R J Aresty

METALS

CRUCIBLE COMPACTION METALS
1001 Robb Hill Road, Oakdale,
Pennsylvania 15071,USA
TEL : +1 412 923 2670
FAX : +1 412 788 4240
E-MAIL : sperber@crucibl
ecompaction.com
WEB : http://www.crucible
compaction.com
CONTACT : M S Sperber

FERRO CORPORATION
1395 Aspen Way, Vista,
CA 9208, USA
TEL: + 1 760 305 1043
FAX: + 1 760 305 1100
EMAIL: akhtarm @ferro.com
WEB : http://www.ferro.com
CONTACT : Dr M Akthar

ROLLED ALLOYS INCORPORATED
125 West Sterns Road, Temperance,
Michigan 48182, USA
TEL: + 1 734 847 0561
FAX: + 1 734 847 3227
CONTACT : J Skarda

STR
Extruded Products Division,
10 Water Street, Enfield,
Connecticut 06082-4899, USA
TEL: +1 860 749 8371
FAX: +1 860 749 8234
E-MAIL :
robert.yorgensen@strus.com
WEB : http://www.strlab.com
CONTACT : Robert S Yorgensen

GLASS

AFG INDUSTRIES INC
1400 Lincoln Street, PO Box 929
Kingsport, Tennesse 37662, USA
TEL: + 1 423 229 7200
FAX: + 1 423 229 7319
WEB: http://www.afg.com
CONTACT: Mark Montgomery

CONSTRUCTION SERVICES

ABACUS CONTROLS INC
80 Readington Road,
Somerville
New Jersey 08876,
USA
TEL: + 1 908 526 6010
FAX: + 1 908 526 6866
E-MAIL: abacuson@worldnet.att.net
WEB: http://
www.abacuscontrols.com
CONTACT: George a O' Sullivan

ADVANCED ENERGY CONSTRUCTION
20505 US Highway 19, Suite 12,
Clearwater, Florda 34624, USA
TEL: + 1 727 441 2808
CONTACT : David Oldack

BUILDING ENVIRONMENT SCIENCE TECHNOLOGY BEST
PO Box 1107,
Edgewater,
MD 21037, USA
TEL : +1 410 867 8000
FAX : +1 301 889 0889
E-MAIL : info@energybuilder.com
WEB: http://www.energybuilder.com
CONTACT : B D Howard

CRUISING EQUIPMENT COMPANY
5245 Shilsole avenue,
NW, Seattle WA 98107-4833, USA
TEL : +1 206 782 8100
FAX : +1 206 782 4336
E-MAIL :ceco@nwlink.com
WEB : http://
www.cruisingequip.com
CONTACT : M S Sperber

DH BLATTER & SONS INC
Heavy Civil, 400 County Road 50
Avon MN 56310, USA
TEL: + 1 320 356 7351
FAX: + 1 320 356 2373
E-MAIL: dougf@dhblattner.com
WEB:http://www.dhblattner.com
CONTACT: Randy Ronning

DIRECT POWER & WATER CORPORATION
4000 Vassar NE, Albuquerque,
New Mexico 87107, USA
TEL: + 1 505 889 3538
FAX: + 1 505 889 3548
E-MAIL: dirpowdd@directpower.com
CONTACT: Kevin M Goodreau

ENERGY CONVERSION DEVICES INC
Manufacturing Technology,
1675, West Maple Road,
Troy, Michigan 48084, USA
TEL: +1 313 280 1900
FAX: +1 313 280 1456
E-MAIL: ovonic@aol.com
WEB: http://www.ovonic.com
CONTACT : M Izu

ENERGY SERVICES & MANAGEMENT CORPORATION
QED, 116 Norfolk Street,
Cambridge, Mass 02139, USA
TEL : + 1 617 491 4578
FAX : + 1 617 491 4578
CONTACT : J J Cooke

ENERTIA BUILDING SYSTEMS INC
Solar/Geothermal Homes, 13312
Garffe Sherron Road, Wake Forest,
North Carloina 27587, USA
TEL : + 1 919 556 0177
FAX: + 1 919 556 1135
E-MAIL: enertia@mindspring.com
WEB: http://www.enertia.com
CONTACT : M Sykes

FINEGOLD ALEXANDER & ASSOC INC
2 Rouse Rd, Gloucester,
Massachusetts 01930-441B, USA
TEL: +1 617 227 9272
FAX: + 1 617 227 5582

FOSTER WHEELER POWER SYSTEMS INC
Perryville Corporate Park, Clinton,
New Jersey 08809, USA
TEL:+1 908 713 2766
FAX: +1 908 713 2770
E-MAIL: fw-power-
systems@fwc.com
WEB: http://www.fwc.com
CONTACT : B Sinclair

HOWARD ALAN ARCHITECTS
849 Arnitage Avenue,
Chicago, IL 60614-4328, USA
TEL: +1 773 929 2121
FAX: +1 773 929 2122
E-MAIL: halan@speedsite.com
WEB: http://www.howar
dalanarchitects.com
CONTACT : K Shiokawa

INNOVATIVE DESIGN INC
850 West Morgan Street,
Raleigh,
North Carolina 27603, USA
TEL: +1 919 832 6303
FAX: +1 919 832 3339
E-MAIL: 74147.3412@
compuserve.com
CONTACT : M Nicklas

KISS AND CATHCART ARCHITECTS
150 Nassau Street,
23rd Floor,
New York 10038, USA
TEL: + 1 212 513 1711
FAX: + 1 212 513 7267
CONTACT : G Kiss

MARK CHALOM ARCHITECT
21 Calimo Circle, Santa FE,
New Mexico 87505, USA
TEL: +1 505 983 1885
CONTACT : M Chalom

MAZRIA ASSOCIATES INC
607 Cerrillos Road, Santa Fe,
New Mexico 87501, USA
TEL: +1 505 988 5309
FAX: +1 505 983 9526
CONTACT : E Mazria

MODERN ALLOYS INC
11172 Western Avenue, Stanton,
California 90680, USA
TEL: +1 714 893 0551
FAX: +1 714 895 9924
E-MAIL: modalloys@aol.com
WEB: http://www.modernalloys.com
CONTACT : Grey

MULTITRADE GROUP INCORPORATED
PO Box 717,
Ridgeway, Virginia 24148, USA
TEL: +1 703 632 4071
FAX: + 1 703 632 5150
CONTACT : B E Brammer

NATIONAL ENERGY PRODUCTION COMPANY NEPCO
11831 N Creek Pkwy N,
Bothell, WA 98011 USA
TEL:+1 425 869 3000
FAX: +1 425 869 3095
E-MAIL:steved@nepco.com
WEB:http://www.nepco.com
CONTACT : S Daniels

PAUL WEISSMAN ARCHITECTS INC
PP Box 726, Kilauea,
Hawaii 96754, USA
TEL: + 1 808 826 9245
FAX: + 1 808 826 9245
E-MAIL: pauljw@aloha.net
CONTACT: Mr Paul Weissman

POWERLIGHT CORPORATION
2954 San Pablo Avenue, Berkeley,
California 94710, USA
TEL: +1 510 540 0550
FAX: +1 510 540 0552
E-MAIL: shugar@powerlight.com
WEB: http://www.powerlight.com
CONTACT : D Shugar

SOLAR DESIGN ASSOCIATES INC
252 Old Littleton Road,
PO Box 242, Harvard,
Massachusetts
01451-0242, USA
TEL:+1 978 456 6855
FAX:+1 978 456 3030
E-MAIL:sda@solardesign.com
WEB: http://www.solardesign.com/
~sda
CONTACT : Steve Strong

STEVEN WINTER ASSOCIATES INC
1331 H Street North West,
Suite 1000, Washington
DC 20005-4706, USA
TEL: +1 202 628 6100
FAX: +1 202 393 5043
E-MAIL:swinter@swinter.com
WEB:http://www.swinter.com
CONTACT : H English

STOPPIELLO ARCHITECTS
PO Box 72, Ilwaco,
Washington 98624, USA
TEL: +1 360 642 4256

SUNPOWER BUILDERS
80 Pechins Mill Road, Collegeville,
Pennsylvania 19426, USA
TEL: +1 610 489 1105
FAX: +1 610 489 8300

TERRA NOVA PLANNING & RESEARCH INC
400 South Farrell Drive,
Suite B-205, Palm Springs,
California 92262, USA
TEL: +1 760 320 9040
FAX: +1 760 322 2760
E-MAIL: tnprps@aol.com

TIERRA CONCRETE HOMES INC
PO Box 1924, Pueblo, Colorado
81002-1924, USA
TEL: +1 719 947 3040
FAX: +1 719 947 3050
E-MAIL:tierrach@ria.net
WEB: http://www.tierraconcretehomes.com
CONTACT : Ms T Niemeyer

TOWER STRUCTURES
2562 Silver State Parkway A3,
Mirder, NV 89423, USA
TEL: +1 619 421 1181
FAX: +1 619 421 0533
WEB: http://www.towerstructures.com
CONTACT : J Mitchell

TWO SEAS METAL WORKS
291 Shell Lane, Willits,
CA 95490, USA
TEL: +1 707 59 9523
FAX: +1 707 459 1833
E-MAIL: sales@2seas.com
WEB: http://www.2seas.com
CONTACT : David Hughes

VAN DER RYN ARCHITECTS
245 Gate Five Road, Sausalito,
California 94965, USA
TEL: +1 415 332 5806
FAX: +1 415 332 5808
E-MAIL: rpena@ecodesign.org
WEB: http://www.vanderryn.com
CONTACT : Ekops

CABLES/WIRES

STEEL HEDDLE
Flat Wire Products Division,
692 Plant Road,
Post Office Box 619,
Westminster, SC 29693, USA
TEL: +1 864 647 6087
FAX: +1 864 647 1549
E-MAIL:bud.frick@steelheddle.com
WEB:http://steelheddle.com

ULBRICH PRECISION FLAT WIRE LLC
692 Plant Road, Post Office Box
619 Westminster, SC 29693, USA
TEL: +18646476087
FAX: +18646471549
E-MAIL: Bfrick@ulbrich.com
WEB: http://www.ulbrich.com
CONTACT: Bud Frick

CARBON EXCHANGE

INTERNATIONAL CARBON BANK AND EXCHANGE INC
6651 NW 23rd Avenue, Gainesville
Florida 32606-8400, USA
TEL: +1 352 367 1144
FAX: +1 352 335 9140
WEB: http://www.icbe.com
CONTACT : M V Soesbergen

NATSOURCE
140 Broadway, 30th Floor,
New York 10005, USA
TEL: +1 212 232 5305
FAX: +1 212 232 5353
E-MAIL: ghginfo@natsource.com
WEB: http://www.natsource.com
CONTACT : N Cohn

THE INTERNATIONAL CARBON BANK AND EXCHANGE
6651 NW 23rd Avenue Gainesville,
Florida, 32606-8400, USA
TEL: +1 352 367 1144
FAX: +1 352 335 9149
WEB: http://www.icbe.com

5/FIVE COUNTRY WHOLESALE DISTRIBUTORS
2431 Crystal Drive, Fort Myers,
Florida 33907, USA
TEL: + 1 941 939 2470
FAX: + 1 941 939 2946
CONTACT: James Fields

ADVANCE SOLAR SYSTEMS INCORPORATED
2431 Crystal Drive, Fort Myers,
Florida 33907, USA
TEL: + 1 813 939 7446
FAX: + 1 813 939 2946
CONTACT: Brian Goldberg

ADVANCED COMBUSTION TECHNOLOGY INC
8837 W Monroe, Houston,
TX 77061,USA
TEL: + 1 713 910 8800
FAX: + 1 713 910 8889
E-MAIL: act@iwl.net

AGGREKO INC
3732 Magnolia Street, Pearland,
TX 77584, USA
TEL: + 1 713 512 6782
FAX: + 1 713 512 6788
E-MAIL: lanisefi@aggreko.com

AIXTRON INC
1670 Barclay Blvd,
Buffalo Grove,
Illinois 60089, USA
TEL: + 1 847 215 7335
FAX: + 1 847 215 7341
CONTACT: Mr Andreas Melas

BAKER HUGHES INTEQ
2050 W Steele Lane, Suite C,
Santa Rosa, CA 95403, USA
TEL : +1 707 523 1751
FAX : +1 707 523 1398
CONTACT : N Nickels

BOGART ENGINEERING
19020 Two Bar Road, Boulder
Creek, California 95006, USA
TEL : +1 836 338 061
WEB : http://
www.bogardengineering.com

THE BLUMENAUER CORPORATION
2708 Rew Circle, Ocoee,
Florida 34761 2997, USA
TEL : 1 407 656 7575
FAX : 1 407 656 8589
CONTACT: Wes Blumlenauer

BTU INTERNATIONAL INC
23 Esquire Road, North Billerica
Massachussetts 01862, USA
TEL : +1 508 667 4111
FAX : +11 508 667 9068
E-MAIL : sales@btu.com
WEB : http://www.btu.com

BZ PRODUCTS
7614 Manon Court, St. Louis
Missouri, 63143, USA
TEL : +1 314 644 2490
FAX : +1 314 644 6121

EMCORE CORPORATION
394, Elizabeth Avenue,
Somertset, New Jersey 08873, USA
TEL : +1 732 271 9090
FAX : +1 732 271 9686
E-MAIL : info@emcore.com
WEB : http://www.emcore.com
CONTACT : P Broskie

EXCEL FOUNDRY AND MACHINE INC
Power Components Division,
Box 400 Pekin, IL 6155-50400,
USA
TEL: +1 309 347 3031
FAX: +1 309 347 1931
E-MAIL: jerry@excelfoundry.com
WEB: http://www.excelfoundry.com
CONTACT : N Palacios

FECON INCORPORATED
10350 Evendale Drive,
Cincinnati, Ohio,
45241, USA
TEL: + 1 513 860 3113
FAX: + 1 513 874 2914
E-MAIL: fecon@fuse.net
WEB:http://www.fecon.com

FILPRO CORPORATION
P.O.Box 374, West Point,
Pennsylvania
19486-0374, USA
TEL: + 1 215 256 4121
FAX: + 1 215 256 6571
CONTACT : M Lowe

FIRE WIND AND RAIN TECHNOLOGIES INC
3920 East Huntingdon Drive.
Flagstaff, AZ 86004, USA
TEL:+1 520 526 1133
FAX: + 1 520 527 4664
WEB: http://
www.firewindandrain.com

FITTON/FOX SYSTEMS LTD
260 West Exchange Street 305,
Providence, RI 02903, USA
TEL: + 1 401 331 5461
FAX: + 1 401 331 2203

FLENDER SERVICE
4234 Foster Avenue,
Bakersfield,
California 93308-4559, USA
TEL: + 1 805 325 4478
FAX: + 1 805 325 4470
E-MAIL:flender@lightspeed.net
WEB:http://www.flenderusa.com/
service-c.htm
CONTACT : H Schreiber

GENERAL KINEMATICS CORP
777 Lake Zurich Road,
Barrington,
Illinois 60010, USA
TEL : + 1 847 381 2240
FAX : + 1 847 381 1376
E-MAIL : genkinco@ig.netcom.com
CONTACT : B Guptail

GRANUTECH-SATURN SYSTEMS
201 East Shady Grove Road,
Grand Prairie, Texas 75050, USA
TEL: + 972 790 7800
FAX: + 1 972 8733
E-MAIL: sizesreduction@
granutech.com
WEB: http://www.granutech.com

GT SOLAR TECHNOLOGIES INC
472 Amherst Street, Nashua,
New Hamshire 03063, USA
TEL : + 1 603 883 5200
FAX : + 1 603 595 6993
E-MAIL : matthei@gtsolar.com
WEB : http://www.gtsolar.com
CONTACT : K Matthei

HEART INTERFACE CORPORATION
21440 68th Avenue South, Kent.
Washington 98032, USA
TEL: +1 253 872 7225
FAX: +1 253 872 3412
E-MAIL: sales@heartinterface.com
WEB: http://www.heartinterface.com
CONTACT : C Tindall

HELIOTRONICS INC
1083 Main Street,
Hingham MA 02043, USA
TEL: +1 781 749 9593
FAX: +1 781 749 3406
E-MAIL: enoch1680@mediaone.net
WEB: http://www.Heliotronics.com
CONTACT : C Handleman

IMPSA INTERNATIONAL INC
Manor Oak II Suite 605,
1910 Cochran Road,Pittsburgh,
Pennsylvania 15220, USA
TEL: +1 412 344 7003
FAX: +1 412 344 7009

INNOVATIVE SPUTTERING TECHNOLOGY - 1ST
12 TW Alexander Drive,
P O Box 12056,
Research Triangle Park,
North Carolina 27709-2056,
USA
TEL: +1 919 485 8900
FAX: +1 919 485 8905
WEB: http://www.bekaert.com/ist
CONTACT : A Taylor

INVERTRIX INC
2259 Portola Road,
Ventura,
CA 93003, USA
TEL: + 1 805 642 7184
E-MAIL: info@invertrix.com
WEB: http://www.invertrix.com

POLAR POWER INC
22520 Avalon Boulevard, Carson,
California 90745-4113, USA
TEL: +1 310 320 3514
FAX:+1 310 320 3135
CONTACT : A Sams

SPIRE CORPORATION
One Patriots Park, Bedford,
Massachusetts 01730-2396, USA
TEL: +1 781 275 6000
FAX: +1 781 275 7470
E-MAIL: pvsales@spirecorp.com
WEB: http://www.spirecorp.com
CONTACT : Mr Dans Mcllecker

TERRA VAC CORPORATION
1555 Williams Drive,
Suite 102, Marietta,
Georgia 30066-6282, USA
TEL: +1 770 421 8008
FAX: +1 770 421 8188
CONTACT : C D Pineo

OTHERS (S)

ACUREX ENERGY
Business Unit, 555 Clyde Avenue,
Mountain View, CA 94043, USA
TEL : +1 650 254 2470
FAX : +1 650 254 2497
E-MAIL : hmason@acurex.com
WEB : http://www.cofire.com
CONTACT : H. Mason

CATAMOUNT ENERGY CORPORATION
71 Allen St Suite 101,
Rutland Vermont 05 701-4570,
USA
TEL: +1 802 7736684
FAX: +1 802 7475478
E-MAIL: dlittle@catenergy.com
WEB: http://www.catenergy.com
CONTACT: L Douglas Barba

DAYSTAR TECHNOLOGIES INC
303 S Broadway,
PMB-415, Denver
Colorado 80209, USA
TEL : +1 303 279 9505
FAX : +1 303 742 1899
E-MAIL : info@daystartech.com
WEB : http://www.daystartech.com
CONTACT : J R Tuttle

DESERT SUN SOLAR INC
2034 North 13th Street Phoenix,
Arizona 85006,
USA
TEL : +1 602 258 3422
FAX : +1 602 258 3422
CONTACT : M. Neary

DIAB INC
315 Seahawk Drive, DeSoto,
TX 75115, USA
TEL: +1 972 228 7600
FAX: +1 972 228 2667
CONTACT: Alex Gutierrez

DIRECT GAIN LLC
23 Coxing Road, Cottekill,
New York 12419, USA
TEL : +1 914 687 2406
FAX : +1 914 687 2408

ERA-TECH INTERNATIONAL
PO Box 475, Dolan Springs,
Arizona 86441, USA
TEL: +1 520 767 4945
FAX: +1 520 767 4350
E-MAIL: eratech@ctaz.com
CONTACT: Rodney D Jones

FULGHUM FIBREFUELS LTD
PO Box 15022, Savannah,
Georgia 31406, USA
TEL: +1 912 691 0607
FAX: +1 912 352 7463
E-MAIL: john@fulghumfibrefuels.com
WEB: http://
www.fulghumfibrefuels.com

GE POWER SYSTEMS
1 Riverside Road,
Building 37 Room517,
Schenectady, NY 12345, USA
TEL: +1 518 385 9318
FAX: +1 515 385 3821

LINDQUIST MACHINE CORPORATION
610 Baeten Road, PO Box 2327,
Green Bay, WI 54306,USA
TEL: +1 920 713 4133
FAX: +1 920 499 8482
E-MAIL: jdenis@lmc-corp.com

OAK RIDGENATIONAL LABORATORY
Energy Efficiency and Renewable
Energy Program, PO Box 2008
Oak Ridge, Tennessee 37831-6186
USA
TEL : +1 423 574 5204
FAX : +1 423 576 7572
E-MAIL : acs@ornl.gov
WEB : http://www.ornl.gov/energy-eff
CONTACT : AC Schaffhauser

OCEAN POWER TECHNOLOGIES INC
1590 Reed Road,
West Trenton,
New Jersey 08628, USA
TEL: + 1 609 730 0400
FAX: + 1 609 730 0404
E-MAIL: oceanpwr@aol.com
CONTACT: Mr. Dunleavy

OREGON OFFICE OF ENERGY
625 Marion Street, Salem,
Oregon 97301-3742, USA
TEL: + 1 503 378 8325
FAX: + 1 503 373 7806
WEB: http://www.energy.state.or.us
CONTACT : Mr. Christopher Dymond

SOL INC
3210 SW 42nd Ave, Palm City,
Florida 34990, USA
TEL: +17722869461
FAX: +17722869616
E-MAIL: lightsolar@aol.com
WEB: http://www.solarlighting.com
CONTACT: A Hurst

SOLUZ INC
55 Middlesex Street Unit 221, North
Chelmsford, Massachusetts 01863,
USA
TEL: +19782515290
FAX: +19782515291
E-MAIL: soluz@igc.org
WEB: http://www.soluz.net

STATE OF WISCONSIN ENERGY BUREAU
PO Box 7868, Madison,
Wisconsin 53711, USA
TEL: +18007627077
FAX: +16082676931
WEB: http://
www.wifocusonenergy.com
CONTACT: Mr. Don Wichert

TUV ENERGY SERVICE
5 Cherry Hill Drive, Danvers,
MA 01923 USA
TEL: +19787397047
FAX: +19787778441
E-MAIL : onothdurft@tuvam.com
CONTACT: Mrs. Ortrud Nothdurft

THE FRANKLIN COMPANY CONSULTANTS LTD
192 Franklin Road, Birmingham,
B30 2HE, UK
TEL : +44 121 459 4826
FAX : +44 121 459 8206
E-MAIL : tfc@tfc-bham.demon.co.uk
WEB : http://www.demon.co.uk/tfc
CONTACT : Dr L F Jesch

ZYVAX INC
PO Box825, Boca Raton,
Florida 33429 USA
TEL: +1 706 698 4405
FAX: +1 706 635 8103
E-MAIL: scottlayman@zyvax.com
WEB: http://www.zyvax.com
CONTACT: Scott Layman

SOUTH AMERICA

SOLAR PHOTOVOLTAIC

ELECTRICDAD ALTERNATIVA
CC 1575, 8400 bariloche,
Rio Negro, Argentina
TEL : +54 2944 42328
FAX : +54 2944 42328
E-MAIL : mackinlay@bariloch.com.ar
CONTACT : A Mackinlay

SMALL HYDRO

ELECTRICDAD ALTERNATIVA
CC 1575, 8400 bariloche,
Rio Negro, Argentina
TEL : +54 2944 42328
FAX : +54 2944 42328
E-MAIL : mackinlay@bariloch.com.ar
CONTACT : A Mackinlay

RESEARCH & DEVELOPMENT

NATIONAL TECHNOLOGICAL UNIVERSITY
Seceretariat of Science and Technology, Sarmiento 440,
1347 Buenos Aires, Argentina
TEL: +54 1 394 00 95
FAX: +54 1 394 00 95
E-MAIL: gareb@deltanet.com.ar
WEB: http://www.utn.edu.ar
CONTACT: Garciaebbens C A

DESIGN & ENGINEERING

INSTITUTO SOLAR ARQUITECTURA BUENOS AIRES
Acoyte 217 1405,
Buenos Aires, Argentina
TEL: +54 11 4902 3001
E-MAIL: yarke@abaconet.com.ar
CONTACT: Eduardo Yarke

ASSOCIATION

CONGRESOS INTERNACIONALES SA
General Secretariat, Moreno 584,
Piso 9, 1091 Buenos Aires, Argentina
TEL: +54 11 4342 3216
FAX: +54 11 4331 7482
WEB: http://www.18th-wec.com.ar

We kindly request more listings in this country.

You can submit any additional listings by E-mail: unisun@vsnl.com

Fax: 91 80 2289294

We will include these in the next edition

Kindly inform us of any errors and omissions in the listings by:

E-mail: unisun@vsnl.com

Fax: 91 80 2289294

SOLAR THERMAL

TERMOQUIP ENERGIA ALTERNATIVA LTD
Rua Flavio Telles, 260 Sta Genebra,
13080-290 Campinas SP, Brazil
TEL: +551932080371
FAX: +551932080371
E-MAIL: termoquip@uol.com.br
WEB: http://www.termoquip.com
CONTACT: Themistocles Rocha Neto

SOLAR PHOTOVOLTAIC

GRUPO FA E - UFPE
Departmentode Energia Nuclear,
Av Prof Luiz Freire,
1000 Cidade Universitaria,
Recife,Pernambuca, Brazil
TEL : +55 81 271 8252
FAX : + 55 81 271 8250
E-MAIL : tiba@npd.ufpe.br
WEB : www.ufpe.br/grupofae

HELIODINAMICA SA
President, Rodovia Raposo Tavares,
KM 41, Vargem Grande Paulista,
CEP 06730-970, Brazil
TEL: +55 11 4158 3511
FAX: +55 11 4158 3755
E-MAIL: heliodin@terra.com.br
WEB: www.heliodinamica.com.br
CONTACT: Bruno Topel

RESEARCH & DEVELOPMENT

UNIVERSIDADE DE CAMPINAS - UNICAMP
Caiza Postal 6165, 13081-000
Campinas, Sao Paulo, Brazil
TEL : +55 192 39 1232
FAX : +55 192 39 3127
CONTACT : Ivan Emilio

UNIVERSIDADE DE SAO PAULO
Instituto de Electrotecni & Energia -IEE
USP, Av Prof Luciano Gualberto 1289,
Cidade Universitaria,
05508-900 Sao Paulo, Brazil
TEL : +55 11 815 7216
FAX : +55 112 210 7750
CONTACT : Prof Melges de Andrade

NGO's

SUNPOWER ENGENHARIA
Travessa R 400,Cidade Universitaria.
Sao Paulo 05508-900, Brazil
TEL: +55 11 212 8466
FAX: +55 11 212 7093
E-MAIL : sunpower@cietec.ipen.br
WEB : http://www.sunpower.com.br
CONTACT : Augustin Woelz

DESIGN & ENGINEERING

POWER TECH DO BRASIL ENERGIA E SISTEMAS LTD
Av Rio Branco 45 Suite 605,
Rio de Janeiro 20090-003, Brazil
TEL: +55 21 2631845
FAX: +55 21 2631845
E-MAIL: powertc@attglobal.net
CONTACT: Guilherme Jose Binelli

UNIVERSIDADE FEDERALDE ALAGOAS
Centro de Technologia, Campus AC
Simoes, CEP 57072-979 Maccio,
Brazil
TEL : +55 82 2141283
FAX : +55 82 2141625
E-MAIL : isb@ctec.ufal.br
WEB : http://www.ctec.ufal.br
CONTACT : G Barbristo

OTHERS

GOLDEN GENESIS DO BRASIL
Rua Pres Carlos de Campos 332,
22231-080 Rio de Janeiro, Brazil
TEL : + 55 21 553 4894
FAX : + 55 21 552 9476
CONTACT : A F Granadeiro

SUPPLIERS

OTHERS (S)

SOLFLEX ENERGIA SOLAR & EOLICA LTD
Av Cel Jose Dias Bicalho 250,
31275-050 Belo Horizonte MG,
Brazil
TEL: +55 31 441 5408
FAX: +55 31 441 5408
E-MAIL: wisc@inetminas.es
taminas.com.br
WEB: http://www.netpage.em.
com.br/wisc
CONTACT: Dietrich Wischhoff

ECOLOGY CONSULTANTS ASSOCIATES
Rue Jose Peroba 349,
15th Floor STIEP, Salvdor,
BA 41760-320, Brazil
TEL : + 55 71 341 0407
E-MAIL : paulolima@ecoluz.com.br

We kindly request more listings in this country.

You can submit any additional listings by E-mail: unisun@vsnl.com

Fax: 91 80 2289294

We will include these in the next edition

Kindly inform us of any errors and omissions in the listings by:

E-mail: unisun@vsnl.com

Fax: 91 80 2289294

SOLAR PHOTOVOLTAIC

SISTEMASSOLARESDE HONDURAS
Col Palmira, Ave Republic de Chile
No. 218, Teguicigalpa MDC,
Honduras, Chile
TEL: +504 32 8213
CONTACT: Lic Ricardo Membrenot

WIND

WIRELESS ENERGY CHILE LTDA
Marketing, PO Box Casilla 287,
Puerto Montt, Chile
TEL: +5665292100
FAX: +5665292102
E-MAIL: sales@wireless-energy.cl
WEB: http://www.wireless-energy.cl
CONTACT: Rene Contreras

We kindly request more listings in this country.

You can submit any additional listings by E-mail: unisun@vsnl.com

Fax: 91 80 2289294

We will include these in the next edition

Kindly inform us of any errors and omissions in the listings by:

E-mail: unisun@vsnl.com

Fax: 91 80 2289294

SOLAR THERMAL

SOLARCO
Carrera 68N 147 49, Santafe de Bogata, Colombia
TEL:+57 1 6830552
FAX:+57 1 6830552
E-MAIL:solarco@col-online-com
WEB:http://www.col-online.com
CONTACT:Geoffrey Halliday

RESEARCH & DEVELOPMENT

UNIVERSIDAD AD DE LOS ANDES
Departamento de Ingenieria Mecanica,
Carrera I Este #18A-10, Bogota, Colombia
TEL : +57 1 3324322
FAX : +57 1 3324323
E-MAIL : apinilla@uniandes.edu.co
WEB : http://www.uniandes.edu.co
CONTACT : Alvaro Pinilla

UNIVERSIDAD DE LOS ANDES
Depto de Ing Mecanica, Cra IA Este No 18A-70, Bogota, Colombia
TEL : +57 1 3324322
FAX : +57 1 3324323
E-MAIL : jlobogue@uni andes.edu.co
WEB : http:// mecanica.uniandes.edu.co
CONTACT : Jaime Lobo Guerrero

WASTE TO ENERGY

ENERCONSULT
AA 100102, Bogota 10, Columbia
TEL : +47 1 6148488
FAX : +47 1 6148488
E-MAIL : hrodig@colciencias.gov.co
CONTACT : Humberto Rodrigues

CONSULTANTS

EMPRESAS PUBLICAS MEDELLIN
Carrera 58, No. 42-125,
Piso 8, Colombia
TEL : +57 380 2900
FAX : +57 380 6740
E-MAIL : hrelex@eepp.com
CONTACT : Ines Helena Velez P

SUPPLIERS

OTHERS (S)

APROTEC TECNOLOGIA APROPIADA
Carrera 7 Norte # 52 N- 167 Cali Colombia
TEL: +57 2 4478 162
FAX: 57 2 4470 082
E-MAIL: aprotec@bigfoot.com
WEB: http://aprotec.tripod.com
CONTACT: Jesus Eduardo Gomez

We kindly request more listings in this country.

You can submit any additional listings by E-mail: unisun@vsnl.com

Fax: 91 80 22289294

We will include these in the next edition

Kindly inform us of any errors and omissions in the listings by:

E-mail: unisun@vsnl.com

Fax: 91 80 22289294

RESEARCH & DEVELOPMENT

UNIVERSIDAD DE CIENFUEGOS
Center for Energy and Environmental Studies, Cuatro Caminos,
Cienfuegos 58430, Cuba
TEL: +53 432 22962
FAX: +53 432 22762
E-MAIL: aborroto@ucf.edu.cu
CONTACT: Anibal E Borroto

UNIVERSITIES

CENTER OF STUDIES OF RENEWABLE ENERGY TECHNOLOGIES - CETER
Renewable Energy, Calle 127 s/n
Cujae CP 19390 Marianao 15,
de la Habana Apdo 6028, Cuba
TEL : +53 7 20 50 60
FAX : +53 7 27 29 64
E-MAIL : ceter@mecanica.ispjae.edu.cu
WEB : http://www.ispjae.edu.cu/centros/ceter/ceter.htm
CONTACT : Dr A Sera

GOVERNMENT

MINISTERIO DE ENERGIA Y MINAS
Direccion de Energias Alternativas, Paez N24-06 y Mercadillo, Edificio Interandiana Ier Piso Of 4, Quito, Ecuador
TEL: +593 2 565980
FAX: +593 2 565474
E-MAIL: mbalseca@uio.satnet.net
CONTACT: G Milton Balseca

HYBRID SYSTEMS

ELECTROCOM INGENIERS
Renewable Energy Systems,
Jose Rivadenier 658, Catalina,
Lima 13, Peru
TEL : + 51 14 716263
FAX : + 51 14 7250690
E-MAIL : elecing@ibm.net

SUPPLIERS

OTHERS (S)

ACEROS AREQUIPA SA
Logistics, PO Box 1595,
Lima 100, Peru
TEL: +51 1 5171800
FAX: +51 1 4525310
E-MAIL: jbaertl@aasa.com.pe
WEB: http://www.acerosarequipa.com.pe
CONTACT: Jose Baertl

We kindly request more listings in this country.

You can submit any additional listings by E-mail: unisun@vsnl.com

Fax: 91 80 22289294

We will include these in the next edition

Kindly inform us of any errors and omissions in the listings by:

E-mail: unisun@vsnl.com

Fax: 91 80 22289294

SOLAR THERMAL

INDUSTRIA SOLAR CA-INSOL
Caracas 1020A,
Apdo 20 459, Venezuela
TEL : + 58 2 471 16 81
FAX : + 58 2 471 37 13
E-MAIL : kjahne@cantv.net
CONTACT : Karljahne

SOLAR PHOTOVOLTAIC

INDUESA CA
Av Fco de Miranda,
Esq 2a Av Campo Alegre,
Edif LAINO, Piso 3 Ofic 31 Caracas,
Venezuela
TEL : + 58 2 32 8096
FAX : + 58 2 32 2362
CONTACT : Jesus Esparza

SMALL HYDRO

EDELCA-HIDROELECTRIC POWER
Electrification del Caroni, CA,
Avenida La Estancia, Chuso,
Torre Las Mercedes Pent House,
Venezuela
TEL : + 58 2 950 11 11
FAX : + 58 2 950 27 29
CONTACT : E C Saud

OTHERS

TECNO CONTROLES CA
Ave Republica Dominicana.
Edif Feltre Oficiana 5-B Piso 5,
Boleita Sur
Caracas 1070, Venezuela
TEL : + 58 2 239 2434
FAX : + 58 2 239 7328

OCTONSOLAR CA
Alternate Energy, Bulevar Sabana
Grande, Edificio Mimi Piso 1 of 5,
Caracas 1050, Venezuela
TEL: +58 2 7636264
FAX: +58 2 7632683
E-MAIL: opitz@cantv.net
CONTACT: Francisco Opitz

We kindly request more listings in this country.

You can submit any additional listings by E-mail: unisun@vsnl.com

Fax: 91 80 22289294

We will include these in the next edition

Kindly inform us of any errors and omissions in the listings by:

E-mail: unisun@vsnl.com

Fax: 91 80 22289294